SUNIL KEWALRAMANI'S
"2014: A Roadmap for Investors"

SUNIL KEWALRAMANI'S
"2014: A Roadmap for Investors"

Sunil Kewalramani

Notion Press

5 Muthu Kalathy Street, Triplicane,

Chennai - 600 005

First Published by Notion Press 2014

Copyright © Sunil Kewalramani 2014

All Rights Reserved.

ISBN: 978-93-84381-14-1

To **Jeremy Siegel**, Russell E Palmer Professor of Finance at the Wharton School of the University of Pennsylvania

-- my teacher, mentor, philosopher and guide

CONTENTS

MY PREDICTIONS FOR 2014

The Bull and the Bear outside the Frankfurt Stock Exchange

The road ahead for 2014

Nothing depicts the outlook for the rest of 2014 better than the **Bull and the Bear outside the Frankfurt Stock Exchange** (notice the Bear comes first, then the Bull and this is how I visualize the rest of 2014):

Most global stock indices should see good correction of **10-15% from July 12, 2014 and lasting until August 26, 2014.**

Also, from November 7, 2014 to November 18, 2014; **expect another correction of 5-8% in most global stock indices due to fresh geopolitical tensions.**

The following weeks shall see tremendous downside in global stocks, so investors should be careful:

a) From 12th July 2014 to 8th August 2014

b) 13th August 2014 to 16th August 2014

c) 22nd September 2014 to 16th October 2014

d) 7th November 2014 to 18th November 2014.

e) 1st December 2014 to 12th December 2014.

The markets like India which have risen on favorable poll outcomes could get a 10%-15% correction during the 12th July 2014 to 26th August 2014 period.

Oil prices could rise substantially from 11th August to 26th August 2014.

Markets in India are already rejoicing the poll results of a month-long election; however, this will only be short-lived as I expect global factors such as slowing China, asset deflation in Europe and Japan and tensions in Iraq/Ukraine take centre stage once again. Global stocks will witness selling pressure from 12th July thru 26th August 2014; most global stock indices could correct 10-15% in this period.

In particular, I see China slowing down dramatically in this period followed by further bad news from the Euopean contingent.

Further downside could also be there until 26th August 2014 and this could present excellent entry points for patient investors who are willing to ride out this period of intense downside.

Why summer 2014 correction?

The risk-reward ratio is currently not in favor in the world stock markets.

In Indian stock markets, which have been flying of late, there has been very heavy retail participation. Even if retail were to double their holdings and take them back to their record highs for the last 10 years, something like 55-60% of that buying has already been done.

The RSIs are now extremely elevated; the RSI on the MSCI Index is also very high.

'At the peak of FIFA World Cup, I am expecting volumes to be down between 25 and 33% in Asia and up to 90% in Latin America'.

After the ECB decision, the market is short-term overbought. We are aware that ECB is driving liquidity and India is a market that is going to be a beneficiary of that liquidity. It is just that the liquidity is not going to be coming until at least September.

There is also concern about US bond yields. Above 260 bps, we could start getting pressure on emerging market currencies that could start melting down again. Below 240 bps, we could get concerns about global growth.

If there is a growth scare that happens in July that will probably be coinciding with the period after the FICA world cup, you could potentially get a risk-off environment. At a time when there isn't actually any central bank support in the market—the US Fed will be tapering, the Bank of Japan has already frozen its fianancing schedule, and ECB money is not expected until September. This is the period from mid-June thru mid-August that is most susceptible to a global stock market correction.

The new ECB money that comes in September will cause resumption of the global stock market rally and India for one will be a very important beneficiary of this stock market revival.

Banks and infrastructure stocks in India will correct the most in the summer and they will also benefit the most in the subsequent stock market revival. Investment could also be considered in the small to mid-cap sectors, which are still something like 40-50% off its highs.

Roadmap for Investors 2014

I am giving what I believe could be a roadmap for investors in 2014. I do not profess to have a monopoly over wisdom. But I have seen so many investors burn their fingers with wrong and biased investment advice, that I believed a roadmap and vision for the future would be helpful to them than simply listen to haphazard investment advice and make incorrect decisions.

During the period from 12th July 2014 to 26th August 2014, we could see good correction in most global indices. July (from 12th onwards), August and first half of December 2014 could be especially very difficult for world stock markets and we could see good correction till 26th August 2014 after which markets could resume their northward journey.

In the month of June 2014, it may appear as though global growth is beginning to stall and it may appear that most countries, developed and emerging are re-entering a recession. The Iraq /Ukraine crisis could also, return to haunt with a vengeance.

Beginning 27th August 2014, you will see a great revival in global stock markets. This could propel the Dow Jones to 19,000 levels by the end of 2014. The Indian SENSEX could scale 33,000 levels by the end of 2014.

First three weeks of September 2014 and December 2014 (12th December onwards) should be the best for stock markets. Most global stock indices should boom and zoom during these months. In the month of December 2014, a very powerful stock market rally which could take most global stock indices higher by 8 to 10% in just three weeks is on the cards.

From 22nd September 2014 to 16th October 2014, global stocks could recede substantially.

From 7th November 2014 upto 18th November 2014, fresh geopolitical conerns could cause global stocks to recede substantially.

December 2014 (after 12th December) should be extremely constructive for investors and they should be able to recover lot of their losses incurred earlier in the year 2014.

Long-term investors should wait until 26th August 2014 to time their entry into stocks. Fed taper, US shutdown and emerging market elections should all be out of the way by then and should pave the way for a tremendous upside in stocks thereon until end-March 2015 where fresh downside could reappear in global stocks.

Can you identify periods during which stock market will rally at its best?

There is a school of thought in the world of investing that says that there are brief periods in a year when swift and sharp rallies in market indices takes place. So, you should stay invested throughout the year because you do not really know when these swift and short rallies will occur. I disagree. If I give you idea of when the short and swift rallies can occur, you can stay invested in these periods only, stay out of the market for the remaining part of the year and you will be able to clearly outperform the market. Here is my prediction of when the short and swift rallies are expected to occur in the remaining of 2014:

Short and swift rallies: For short-term traders and fund managers, expect short and swift rallies between

Between 21st April 2014 and 24th April 2014

Between 2nd July 2014 and 9th July 2014

Between 27th August 2014 and 21st September 2014

Between 13th December 2014 and 1st January 2015 (Very strong rally)

For **very short-term traders,** you can see good upside in global stock markets on 4th April, 1st May, 28th May, 29th May, 22nd July, 18th August, 15th September, 12th October and 5th December 2014. Investment even with a days' perspective on these dates can yield good returns.

Slowdown in growth in 2014:

You can also expect downside on 19th May, 20th May, 16th June, 3rd October, 31st October, 27th November and 24th December 2014.

Markets will start factoring in this negative trend along with the Iraq/Ukraine crisis which should rear its ugly head once again– so I expect a good summer correction in global stocks.

'Most global stock market indices could fall between 10 and 15% during the period from 12th July 2014 to 26th August 2014'.

Other than the problems which have now persisted for quite some time—Iraq/Ukraine crisis and asset deflation in Europe, activity has not been so effervescent in China's manufacturing sector. HSBC's preliminary purchasing managers' index signalled contraction for a fourth month in April. The gauge in the "flash survey" hit 48.3, below the level of 50 that signifies expansion.

Downside risks to growth are still evident as both new export orders and employment has contracted.

Although facing real estate bubble, China is no mood to enhance liquidity. Yet, seeing the steadily declining GDP, Beijing could after few months of watching, be forced to unveil further stimulus measures say around mid-July to keep sufficient liquidity in the system.

However, I continue to hold the view that investment in markets should be viewed as investment in businesses and should be for the long term.

Gold could be the comeback kid for 2014

Gold, I believe, could be the comeback kid and increase dramatically from May to October 2014. In particular, gold price could spurt between June and October 2014. From the current $ 1300/ oz. levels, one could expect to see 25% appreciation within a six moths period and gold could reach $ 1750/oz. levels by the November 2014; thus, presenting an excellent investment opportunity.

Emerging-market bashing has become fashionable notwithstanding the fact that almost half of the revenues of multinationals are derived from this suddenly much-hated class. Although we have seen some inflows in emerging market stocks of late, they seem to be a reversal of extreme oversold positions rather than renewed interest in emerging markets as an asset class.

Besides, we are seeing a rotation from the high-valued growth (Internet stocks) into the value stocks over the last one month and this trend is expected to gather momentum as stock markets begin to reward earnings more than just eyeballs.

Besides, you see the currencies of many emerging markets gain unusual strength as they near elections. Although the financial world prefers to call it foreign flows, one needs to evaluate whether undisclosed money of natives which had gone abroad is returning to fight the country's elections.

The Indian rupee appreciated around 12.5% in March alone. This on surely justified expectations that a new pro-growth government (viz. the BJP) was about to assume centre-stage. But what is forgotten is that this phenomenon is repeated every time before the elections. In order for dollar-rupee to stabilize or sustainably break below 56, there needs to be a decisive improvement in the country's growth and inflation dynamics amid the backdrop of a solid global recovery. While there has been a let-up in price pressures recently, because of unseasonal rain, many agricultural crops have been destroyed. Inflation is going to pick its ugly head again. Besides, lot of exporters seem to be losing out and the new pro-growth government (the BJP) is expected to take steps to rein in the rupee to keep the country export-competitive.

In May of 2009, the Bombay Stock Exchange, on announcement of favorable victory for a strengthened Congress opened circuit up. Normally, stock markets discount news in advance. This was a rare instance where stock markets moved much ahead of what the policy actions and fundamentals would dictate over the years to come.

Although the SENSEX and other global indices have scaled new highs; they are still lagging behind, if adjusted for inflation.

Can you tailor-make a stock market portfolio? There is a widely held view that a strong general election outcome is a necessary condition for India to cure its macro ills. A strong general election outcome is a necessary condition for India to cure its macro ills.

Analysts had **tailor-made** two sets of investment portfolio to play the Indian poll results. **Strong election result basket Strong flavours:** Basket of high-beta, high-leverage, cyclical, strong short momentum stocks likely to outperform as the market gains conviction in a strong poll result. Picks: Axis Bank Bank of India BPCL DLF Hindalco JP Associates JSPL JSW Steel L&T Power Finance Tata Motors Tata Steel Yes Bank.

Fragmented election result basket Strong flavours: Good quality GARP basket,low PEG, high ROE, low beta and strong long-term momentum Picks Bajaj Auto HDFC Bank HUL Infosys ITC Lupin M&M Finance Sun Pharma TCS Tata Motors Tech Mahindra Zee Entertainment.

So, which basket which you as an investor should have chosen: *Strong election result basket OR the Fragmented election result basket?* Or would you rather have waited until the results are announced to choose your basket—by which time, your basket would already have been full of investors clinging to it.

Notwithstanding what I have mentioned above, Elections are usually a good time for the Indian market, which is evident from the fact that nearly 80 percent of the Mumbai Sensex returns in the last 30 years have come in during the two years of a new government. Typically, post elections, cheaper stocks tend to rally.

Typically, new government tends to bring new economic vigour in the country that leads to a stock market rally. We seem to be in the midst of one such rally although I believe this Indian stock market rally has been far extended.

PREFACE

MY PAST PREDICTIONS:
THE "GREAT FINANCIAL CRISIS" AND HOW
I COULD PREDICT THE TIMING OF THE END

"Things will never be the same. Risk taking has been destroyed." "Another leg down." "Banking Institutions are Insolvent. S&P will drop to 600 or lower." "It's a bear-market rally because we have not yet turned the economy around."

Follow any of the links in the quotes I've provided above and you'll find they were tall made by pundits in a two-month span beginning 12 calendar days before and a month and a half after the March 9th, 2009 global bear market low. Perversely, this was your best buying opportunity—at the precise point when the prevailing sentiment was, "It's different this time (for the worse, that is)."

At the peak of the **Great Financial Crisis**, I was interviewed by CNBC on November 5, 2008. The crux of the interview was how far would **the Great Financial Crisis** last. Most commentators at that time were looking at parallels with the Great Depression.

However, I had pointed out that I saw markets stabilize by Jan-March 2009.

I am enclosing various instances of how I could predict the market in advance and how you can benefit and what to look forward to in the remainder of 2014 and beyond.

Many thanks to CNBC TV 18 for interviewing me on November 12, 2008. During the interview, I was able to identify and correctly predict the timing of the end of the 'Great Financial Crisis'.

This interview was at the heat of the financial crisis and I had clearly predicted that world stock markets will start stabilizing post Jan-March 2009 and they indeed started stabilizing from March 9, 2009.

The transcript of the above interview is as under:

Nov 12, 2008, 10.09 AM IST See markets stabilizing post Jan-March '09: Global Cap Adv Sunil Kewalramani, CEO, Global Capital Advisors, believes India will not decouple from the developed world. He feels stability will return in India post January-March 2009.

Share . Email . Print . A+ Sunil Kewalramani, Global Capital Advisors Sunil Kewalramani, CEO, Global Capital Advisors, believes India will not decouple from the developed world. He feels stability will return in India post January-March 2009. "FDI should be opened up since portfolio flows alone add volatility and irregularity in the market." According to him, lagged credit card lending norms could create problems for India. Here is a verbatim transcript of the exclusive interview with Sunil Kewalramani on CNBC-TV18. Also watch the accompanying video. Q: What is your own sense of what the market is trying to do at this point? A: According to chaos theory, if a butterfly flaps its wings in Tokyo we can see the impact in other parts of the worlds like in Texas. Basically, what we are seeing is the impact of the Yen Carry Trade getting wound up. Quite sometime we have seen the Japanese investors represented by Mrs. Watanabe as a symbolic example, who had invested in high yielding assets in emerging markets in various parts of the world. Now the turning point I believe came on July 15, when the Securities and Exchange Commission (SEC) banned the short sale of financials and hedge funds for mainly- they were shorting financials and they were buying oil. That disturbed the entire rally and the momentum in various parts of the world, and the hedge funds had to flee because the credit lines were choked, they had to go and sell their assets even at distressed levels in various parts of the world. So, what I believe is happening is that this selling is still continuing and at some point of time sanity is bound to return, when these things get lost. The important thing that we have to remember is that we are really not decoupled from the rest of the world and Joe the

Plumber was a great symbolic example of aspirations of millions of Americans, who was brought out during the election campaign and was in fact was referred to 24 times during the third televised debate between Barack Obama and Senator John McCain. Whether it is Joe the Plumber in America or it is Kalavati in India, who was used to represent the aspirations of millions of Indians. The terminologies may change, the semantics may change but the ways that we do things are the same. The financial practices, which have been adopted in the emerging economies and various other parts of the world have been absolutely similar. We had the subprime mortgage problem in America, but even in India and various other countries we have the subprime credit cards being given, loans being given to people who did not deserve it. Faith is indeed all about relationships and relationships are all about trust and I have all respect for trust but you cannot just go out and give a credit card to every single person, who steps out of a super market and who has bought Rs 2,000 of goods- and that is all he may have bought all in that year. So all these lack practices, the financial practices, which have been adopted in various parts of the world are contributing to this problem. It is sad that this is all happening at one point of time.

Disclosure: It is safe to assume that my clients & I may have an investment interest in the stocks/sectors discussed. Read more at: http://www.moneycontrol.com/news/fii-view/see-mkts-stabilizing-post-jan-march-09-global-cap-adv_365609.html?utm_source=ref_article

"Many thanks to the 'Outlook Money' magazine for publishing my article 'FIRST THE DIP THEN THE SPIKE' in their July 2014 issue.

Stock Market

By Sunil kewalramani

FIRST THE DIP THEN THE SPIKE

The current market rally is due for a pause in the next two months before resuming in September

Now that the elections are over, all eyes are on the Union Budget. The government, too, realises that big reforms will boost investor sentiment. So, it will unleash policies on investments in infrastructure and creation of smart cities, which the BJP had outlined in its pre-poll manifesto. Yes, the poll victory has all the underpinnings of a structural bull market that should continue for many years, but investors need to be cautious. **Indian stock markets currently look over-stretched.** India looks overvalued in comparison to other emerging markets. The valuations, after a shart rally on the BJP's election win, appear 'very stretched' against lower GDP growth. Since 13 September 2013, when the BJP declared Modi as its prime ministerial candidate, the Nifty has risen 24.4 per cent. Overseas funds pumped in excess of $14 billion in the case shares over that period.

True, a long-term bull story in India has started, but there is still a need for greater clarity. Both Mexico and China witnessed sell-off in the past as reform euphoria waned. Also to be noted is the fact that Modi's comparison with former UK PM Margaret Thatcher raises short-to medium-term risks. As such, non-emerging market investors should wait for a better buying opportunity—around mid-August 2014.

Also the Indian stock market is discounting FY 16 earnings. Besides, earnings upgrades look difficult in the short term. So, reforms that can drive economic and earnings growth in the medium term will be critical.

Why the summer 2014 correction?

The risk-reward ratio is currently not in favour in the bourses across the world. The RSI (relative strength index) is also extremely elevated. The RSI on the Morgan Stanley Capital International (MSCI) Index is also very high. In the backdrop of the FIFA World Cup, stock trading volumes are expected to be down by 25-33 per cent and 90 per cent in Asia and Latin America, respectively. Another fact to note is that the European Central Bank (ECB) is driving liquidity and, though India will benefit from that liquidity, it won't come at least until September.

There is also concern about US bond yields. Above 260 basis points (bps), pressure could start mounting on emerging markets and below 240 bps, there could be concerns about global growth. The mid-June to mid August period is most susceptible to a global stock market correction.

Also, at present, there is no central bank support in the market—the US Federal Reserve will be tapering while the Bank of Japan has already frozen its financing schedule and ECB money is not expected soon.

The new ECB money that will come in September will boost the global stock market rally and Indian will be a very important beneficiary of that revival. Banks and infrastructure stocks here will correct the most this summer and they will also benefit the most in the subsequent stock market revival. Investment could be likely in the small- to mid-cap sectors, which are 40-50 per cent off its highs.

THE BIG PICTURE

In 2008, oil traded at US$ 140 per barrel

*Currently, oil is trading at US$ 110 per barrel. Flattening of oil prices would help in controlling CAD, fuel led inflation, stability of currency

2008-13 Policy logjam

2014 onwards Several policies cleared & key bills passed in recent times. PM's Project Monitoring Group has cleared 147 projects, entailing a total investment of around ₹5 lakh crore

At present, investors would be better off taking some money off sectors such as banking, capital goods, cement and, metals and mining and here's the reason why:

Banking. The government seems hesitant on further capital infusion in public sector banks, which means they have been left to fend for themselves. Also, the steep increase in stock prices of banks suggests that the market is no longer worried about the non-performing loan (NPL) problem in the sector. But, this is a serious issue and banks, particularly PSU banks, continue to report high slippages. Even assuming that the NPL problem is contained and book values of banks reflect the true value of the book (adjusted basis), many PSU banks now trade close to or above book value despite low return on equity (RoE).

Cement. Valuations of cement stocks are expensive even after factoring in a strong recovery in their volumes and profitability over the next two years. Even assuming near-peak profitability for cement companies in FY16, cement stocks trade at 7-11 times FY16 estimated earnings before interest, tax, depreciation and ammortisation (EBITDA) and 15-21 times FY16 estimated earnings per share (EPS).

"Banks and infra stocks will correct the most this summer and they will also benefit the most in the subsequent stock market revival"

S. KEWALRAMANI
CHIEF INVESTMENT OFFICER,
GLOBAL MONEY INVESTOR

Capital goods. The order booking of companies over the past few quarters signals improvement. Still, valuations are stiff for capital goods companies after factoring a significant recovery in their earnings.

Metals & Mining. It is difficult to fathom whether the new government can award coal blocks or mineral ore mines in a discretionary fashion, given allegations of corruption in previous such allocations. Even assuming the government is able to kickstart the process of allocation quickly, it will take a few years to develop the new mines. Also, the market is ignoring the risk of market- related pricing of resources through price discovery in auctions. Actually, the government could increase the royalty on coal and mineral ores, which is quite low compared to the royalty on other resources, such as oil and gas.

We are today celebrating the 5-year anniversary of the revival in the above bull market in stocks.

In June 2008, oil was on the boil. It had crossed $ 135 a barrel and there was talk of oil going as far as $ 250 a barrel.

Using advanced models, I had predicted oil was due for a correction, a prophesy which turned out to be true.

Many thanks to the *Business Line* for publishing my article predicting the crash in oil prices. Article was titled 'Oil Prices: Correction on cards' and published on June 15, 2008

Oil prices: Correction on cards

Physical markets do not seem to be displaying distress in demand.

An evaluation of the oil and gas futures and options markets indicates that supply is sufficient to meet current demand and the oil price increase seems to be overdone with speculative interests in abundance.

Sunil Kewalramani

After oil hit its recent record of $135 a barrel, consumers and politicians have started venting their anger in various ways. This seems to indicate $135 was a 'Tipping Point', at least temporarily. Veteran Hedge fund manager George Soros, while finding the increase in oil prices analogous to a bubble, feels a crash in oil markets in not imminent.

On June 4, 2008, India and Malaysia became the latest Asian countries to increase the price of subsidised fuel. Consumers in India will now pay an average Rs 50 a litre for gasoline, or about $4.45 a gallon, well above the average $3.79 a gallon that US drivers are paying.

In Malaysia, petrol prices have risen by 78 sen (24 Cents), a 41 per cent jump from RM 1.92 per litre. Indonesia has hiked fuel prices by an average 29 per cent.

Dotcom analogy?

There are indeed parallels between the late stages of the dotcom mania and the current oil boom. Both mega trends were rooted in a powerful economic shift; the dotcom boom was associated with several technological breakthroughs and new killer applications that change the way we live and do things, the oil-led commodity boom is attributed to the emergence of China and India as economic powerhouses, and the decoupling of the emerging economies from the developed world.

From January 2006 to mid-April 2008, more than $90 billion of incremental investor flows went into assets managed by commodity indexes. For every $100 million in new inflows; the price of West Texas intermediate, the US benchmark, increased by 1.6 per cent.

An evaluation of the oil and gas futures and options markets seems to be indicating that supply is sufficient to meet current demand and the oil price increase seems to be overdone with speculative interests in abundance. I believe we are nearing a steep correction in oil prices. Let's see why:

Spot vs futures

Physical markets do not seem to be displaying any signs of distress in demand. Whereas crude-oil futures prices have repeatedly hit record highs in recent months (Brent crude at the time of this writing is trading at $132 a barrel on the Intercontinental Exchange in London, up over 80 per cent since last year).

Yet today, traders dealing with physical cargos of crude oil see the spot market so awash with oil that some producers such as Iran are starting to hoard it in hopes that greater demand for crude will lift spot prices as well.

They cite seasonal closure of refineries for maintenance and a poor return on refining operations for the lack of interest in buying spot cargoes. According to the OPEC's departing governor, Hossein Kazempour Ardebili, around 25 million barrels of his country's heavy, sour crude oil are being stored in offshore vessels in the Persian Gulf.

According to him, there are no buyers because the world market has more than enough oil to meet its requirements.

The lag

Since prices for gasoline and other refining products have not risen as much as prices for crude oil, refiners have had little incentive to hurry their maintenance processes, and those able to operate at normal levels are opting to reduce production. Global cracking margins — the profit refiners earn from processing crude into high-quality end products —have fallen to less than $7.50 a barrel this month, approximately half the level at this time last year.

To lend credence to this view, some of Europe's biggest refineries have been taken offline in recent months, including the region's largest — Royal Dutch Shell PLC's giant 4,20,000 barrel-a-day Pernis refinery. The Netherlands plant underwent partial maintenance for more than a month starting end of March 2008.

The widely traded Forties is now selling at a discount of 75 cents a barrel to a benchmark North Sea mixture, swinging from a premium of about 15 cents a barrel a year ago.

The "Peak Oil Theory" (the theory that global oil output has already peaked and can only decline from here) is behind much of the oil price increase. On one side of the fence are billionaire oilman T. Boone Pickens, oil banker Matthew Simmons, and many others suggesting that the world is reaching Peak Oil now. On the other side of the fence, as indicated in this figure, are Cambridge Energy Research Associates (CERA) headed by Pulitzer prize writer Daniel Yergin, and others such as Exxon Mobil, who are not predicting a Peak in global oil production until circa 2040 followed by a gradual decline.

Back to Fundamentals

Over the past 10 years, global oil reserves have increased by 140 billion barrels to 1,200 billion barrels. If you add Canadian oil sands to the total, the increase was 300 billion barrels.

Over the same time span, the increase in world oil demand has been a benign 45 billion barrels. If supply and demand aren't entirely behind the recent price increases, speculation has played a key role. Over-the-counter commodity derivatives held globally grew sevenfold, to $7,000 billion in the three years to June 2007. If we assume that about 50 per cent of the open positions on commodities are accounted for by oil, the exposure as of the last data point equated to 48.5 billion barrels of oil, or about 20 times the size of the New York Mercantile Exchange.

Some light, sweet crude-oil grades — typically prized by refiners for their easy conversion into high-quality diesel and gasoline — have also come under pressure. While light, sweet crude futures prices have shown little signs of slowing, their price structure is starting to hint at an easier short-term supply outlook.

Slipping Into 'contango'

To the greatest extent in the history of oil futures trading, oil prices are now in continuous contango — that is, oil futures get progressively more expensive each year into the future. (Contango is when the futures are trading above the expected spot price at a future date. Because the futures price must converge on the expected future spot price, contango implies that futures prices are falling over time as new information brings them in line with the expected future spot price). A contango structure usually indicates that oil-market players expect crude-oil supplies to be less scarce in the short term than they will be in the future. Evidence seems to be suggesting that supply is sufficient to meet current demand.

The above contango structure and dramatic shift from backwardation to contango in the oil futures market, in the space of just six weeks, are also an indication that a correction in oil prices could be on the cards in the near future.

The author is CEO, Sunil Kewalramani Global Capital Advisors. Feedback can be sent to globalequity@sunilkewalramani.com

(This article was published in the Business Line print edition dated June 15, 2008)

I believe an investor can gain an added advantage if he does his homework and is able to see things and events before others do.

Many thanks to the *Financial Express* for publishing this article of mine, warning of the upcoming downtrend in gold prices and published on June 1 2012

Is gold losing its safe haven status?

Written by Sunil Kewalramani | June 01, 2012 03:03

Summary

Not only has its price fallen, but also it has fallen most when fears about growth and the Eurozone crisis have picked up, confusing investors who bought it as a security from financial turmoil.

Related

FSDC to be the 'war room' during crisis: FM

'India's Q3 gold demand down 32%'

World Gold Council: Gold Q4 demand to be lower than same period last year

Gold has traditionally been known for its 'safe haven' status, which holds up and increases in value in dire economic and political circumstances. Today, if we look at the world all around us, we notice gloom and doom. The asset class of choice that should traditionally hold value under these circumstances is gold.

When Lehman Brothers declared bankruptcy in September 2008,investors rushed to buy gold. When the Eurozone crisis erupted in 2010,they bought more. When the US lost its AAA debt rating last summer, they bought even more. However, for some reason, gold has lost its safe haven status of late and is just being traded like any other asset. Stocks fall, and gold falls with it. Oil falls and gold falls with it. Stocks go upland gold goes up.

The widespread apathy towards the precious metal has taken its toll on prices. Last week, gold slid to a four-month low of $1,527 a troy ounce, down 20.5% from its record high of $1,920 last September. Not only has gold fallen in price, but also it has fallen most when fears about growth and the Eurozone crisis have picked up, confusing investors who bought it as a haven from financial turmoil. Some asset managers have also been selling a portion of their gold holdings, according to the

World Gold Council. Investor positioning in gold futures and options is the least bullish since December 2008.

Hedge funds have reduced their exposure to commodities overall by 15% in the latest reporting period, with exposure to gold taking the biggest hit and resulting in what Bloomberg News calls a "flight from gold" by investors. Particularly in the US, but also in Europe and Asia, interest in gold and silver has waned. Western importers say that sales in the past two months are down 50% or more years on year. The shift is most clearly seen at the level of coin demand—often seen as a leading indicator for sentiment.

Sales of gold American Eagles, the popular investment coin, are down 63% year on year since February, according to the US Mint. Sales of Vienna Philharmonics, more popular in Europe, fell 19 % for gold and 31% for silver in the first quarter, according to the Austrian Mint. With even retail investors appearing to lose interest in gold, the overwhelmingly bullish consensus among traders is being questioned. Part of the reason for the fall in demand is the better economic data emanating out of the US that has dimmed hopes of further quantitative easing, or emergency Federal Reserve bond-buying.

Let's have a look at the fundamentals that drove the gold price down about 20% from the record peak of $1,920 per ounce registered in September 2011.

First and foremost, it rose too high, too fast. In the nine-week period between July 1 and September 6,2011,gold prices shot up by 30%, from $1,478/oz. on July 1 to $1,920 on September 6,2011. That's not the hallmark of a sustainable, 'safe haven' investment—and it was proved so when prices slumped more than $360/ oz. to $1,528/oz. within a short period before regaining some ground. Second, gold prospects were dampened when India, the world's largest gold consumer, decided to add an import tax on gold and a new tax on jeweler earlier this year in a bid to reduce gold imports and contain the country's ballooning current account deficit. That, combined with a weakening rupee, meant that gold became "very expensive" for Indian consumers. Latest World Gold Council data shows that Indian consumption dropped 29% to 207.6 million tones in the first quarter of 2012 compared with the same period in 2011.

In India, giving gold as small gifts have totally stopped, and people now buy 25-30% less weight than usual for weddings. Unless there is a clearer message emanating from the US Federal Reserve on the continuation of its quantitative easing programme,gold will at best remain volatile. The traditional link between gold and inflation-adjusted interest rates—as interest rates fall,so does the opportunity cost of holding gold—has also broken down. I am not hearing the intensity in people's voices now in terms of being driven by fear to buy precious metals. Apart from frenzied buying during Akshaya Tritiya 2012,the past two months have been quieter than any time since 2007.

The traditional prop of the Asian physical markets has been absent. Despite the recovery that pulled gold prices back from bear market conditions and lows under the critical $1,527 pivot point,the latest set of CFTC positioning reports does not offer much in the way of encouragement for the bulls. The net speculative length in gold is currently hovering near a one-year low of just over 330 tonnes. If Greece were to leave the eurozone,gold could initially fall on euro weakness and a flight to cash. The extent and length of any drop in gold ultimately could be influenced by how central bankers and other authorities view any Greek exit. If they decide to build a very strong wall to prevent the contagion spreading,that could again be bullish for gold. The yellow metal might then bounce due to a policy response from central banks. At least there will be an end to the horror-thriller. As a German proverb puts it,"Better an end with horror,than a horror without end." The European Central Bank may seek to backstop the financial system and the Federal Reserve might implement quantitative-easing measures to help the US economy stave off the spillover weakness from Europe. That would potentially mean concerns that inflation is here to stay once things stabilise on the euro front.

Furthermore, gold may also rise simply because the long-running Greek debt saga would no longer be an anchor for the US greenback.

The author is CEO,Global Money Investor

Many thanks to the *Economic Times* for publishing this article of mine on 19 May 2011 predicting the upcoming end of the 'commodities supercycle'

Oil, commodities set to plunge between 25% and 40%

By Sunil Kewalramani, | 19 May, 2011, 10.23AM IST

7 comments |Post a Comment

Commodity prices have a major bearing on inflation, global monetary policy and GDP growth; hence, it is essential to understand important turning points and trend reversals. Some blame the current correction in commodities on algorithmic trading and others on Chinese monetary tightening. A narrow focus on every tweak in China's monetary policy risks missing the bigger picture. Demand has indeed weakened in China to the point where its imports of key commodities are dwindling. It is further evidence of demand destruction globally resulting from an earlier surge in commodity prices, led by commodity-in-chief, oil.

As the chart shows, there is a relationship between the change in commodity prices and indicators of global economic activity, such as the OECD global leading indicator (GLI). However, the recent rise in commodity prices has been much more than it 'should' have been, based on the strength of the GLI, suggesting that easy money could have influenced prices. There was a notion that commodities were a one-way bet. This tied substances which had little to do with one another - industrial commodities like oil and copper, renewable ones such as wheat and corn, and those with largely intrinsic value such as silver and gold - to the same fate.

Some commodities were in blatant speculative bubbles. Silver's price relative to gold doubled during first three months of 2011 to reach a 30-year high and then fell 30% in two weeks. But silver is still as expensive as on March 18. Gold remains above its 50-day moving average, a short-term trend measure. Brent crude, in spite of its sharp selloff, has dropped below its 50-day moving average, for the first time since last September, an abnormally long upward streak. The run-up in oil went further last time, but the end looked similar to first week of May - right down to the weekly fall of 13.8%, against May first week's 13.3%. Demand is slowing down from the torrid pace of a year ago.

The International Energy Agency forecasts a growth of just 1.3 million barrels per day (mb/d) in 2011, down from a near record 2.8 mb/d last year, showing a fall in demand driven by high prices. Eurozone debt problems and the arrest of IMF's chief have amplified concerns. The flash crash in oil prices still leaves Brent crude well above the first quarter average. It will need to come down much further before global growth comes to above-trend levels. "Dr Copper" lived up to its reputation as the only metal with an economics PhD in 2008, as its daily close peaked three months before the wider commodity crash. This year, it peaked in February. From high to low in the two weeks after oil plunged in July 2008, copper fell 9.62 %.

In the past two weeks, 9.68 %. Copper is considered the industrial metals bellwether. It peaked more than two months before the wider CRB basket of commodities. This is pertinent because, unlike oil, which faces supply worries but still enjoys ample production and silver, which departed from fundamentals long ago, copper output is being hobbled as mines are denuded. This means it is most likely to be falling demand that is putting pressure on copper prices.

Tighter monetary policy from Beijing is discouraging Chinese consumers from holding copper. While silver did not move so fast in 2008, it managed a 33% drop in four weeks after oil topped. In the past two weeks, it has fallen 30%. Gold is an even better match, with almost identical 12-month gain before its fall.

Harvard economists Larry Summers and Robert Barsky, in a paper titled 'Gibson's Paradox and the Gold Standard' found strong correlation between the inverse relative price of gold (and other metals) on one hand, and real interest rates on the other. When real returns are high, the fiatcurrency price of gold will stagnate or decline. When real returns are low, as they have been during past decade, gold price has been strong. During the past three years, as one rescue operation or monetary stimulus has followed another, the S&P 500 cumulative total return has been less than 0.5% while the dollar gold price has jumped more than 78 %. Thanks to the profligacy of central banks, real interest rates are negative.

The most recent run in gold coincided with the Fed's QE2 monetary expansion after the Jackson Hole summit in August 2010. Its recent weakness has followed Bernanke's confirmation that QE2 will end in June. Cheap money, expensive gold; expensive money, cheap gold. In the first week of May 2011, one of the biggest bubbles of the past century seemed to have burst. Silver tumbled 31% from its peak near $50 an ounce to $35. But in the second week, silver bounced nearly 20%. In September 1979, silver crashed 23% in three days, very much like May first week. The silver crash of 1980 was often interrupted as greed triumphed, briefly, over fear - in four days in February 1980 silver recovered almost 20 % to $40.25.

In the long term, the real price of commodities is determined by the costs of extraction, both in existing commodities like oil and substitutes like shale gas. But over shorter horizons, these factors can't explain commodity fluctuations. Market herd behaviour can drive prices far above or below those levels for long periods. Given these, I expect that oil and other commodities could plunge between 25% and 40% through October 2011.

Many thanks to the *Financial Express* for publishing this article of mine on December 22, 2009 predicting the upcoming Greek crisis or 'Greek tragedy' as popularly began to be known:

After Dubai, will Greece be next?

Summary

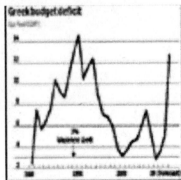

Greece's bond and stock markets have fallen sharply in the past few weeks amid fears for its banks and economy, as the European Central Bank prepares to wind down emergency funding for the Eurozone financial system.

Greece's bond and stock markets have fallen sharply in the past few weeks amid fears for its banks and economy, as the European Central Bank (ECB) prepares to wind down emergency funding for the Eurozone financial system.

The volatility in financial markets in Greece, one of the weakest Eurozone economies, is an early warning of potential problems for other Eurozone banks and economies after the ECB ends its unlimited offer of loans to financial institutions. When ECB's Jean-Claude Trichet said that certain sinners on the edges of the Eurozone were "very close to losing their credibility", everybody knew he meant Greece.

Greece's budget deficit is expected to reach 12.7% of GDP this year, more than four times the EU deficit limit of 3% of GDP, while the country's gross government debt is forecast to rise to 125% of GDP next year.

The desirability of slashing the Greek budget deficit from over 12% of GDP to less than 3% is clear. Since 1981, the Greek budget deficit has only been that low once, in 2006. True, over the previous decade the deficit did shrink from a ruinous 15% of GDP to within a whisker of 3%. But that took more than 9 years. Now, PM George Papandreou proposes tightening almost as much, in half the time. Increasing public sector pay and taxing bankers' bonuses will not get him there.

The interest spread between 10-year Greek bonds and German bunds has jumped to 178 basis points (bp). Greek debt has decoupled from Italian debt. Athens can no longer hide behind others in EMU's soft South.

It is also worth noting the growing divergence between the PIIGS CDS spreads and those of Germany. Greece's five-year CDS spreads have risen from a recent low of 100 bp reached in August to 208bp on November 26 and 171bp at present, while the CDS spread on German bunds was virtually flat over the same period at 22bp. With Greece's public debt higher than 100% of GDP, investors have suddenly woken up to the scary prospect that the budget deficit is also forecast to hit 12% of GDP in 2010 and 2011.

On the eve of the Dubai crisis unfolding, Greek stocks plunged (on Thanksgiving day), posting their biggest loss in more than a year and dragging the country's benchmark index into a so-called bear market, as shares in the nation's lenders slumped.

The ASE Index fell 6.2% to 2,225.32 at the close in Athens, the worst performer among 18 western European benchmarks. The gauge extended its fall from last month's high to 23%. A bear market is generally defined as a drop of more than 20%. The FTSE/ASE 20 Index of the country's biggest companies slipped 7.3% to 1,153.29. The Cypriot General Index plummeted 11.4% to 1,432.3.

Greece has long been skating on thin ice. The current account deficit hit 14.5% of GDP in 2008. External debt has reached 144%. Eurozone creditors—German banks—hold euro 200bn of Greek debt.

A warning from the Bank of Greece that lenders must wean off the ECB's emergency funding has brought matters to a head. Greek banks have borrowed euro 40bn from the ECB at 1%, playing the 'yield curve' by purchasing state bonds. This EU subsidy has made up for losses on property, shipping, and Balkan woes.

Greek banks are more dependent than others in the Eurozone on ECB loans, with those outstanding from the central bank of $57bn, 7.9% of their total assets. The fall in the Greek markets is a warning to financial institutions not to become too addicted to the support of the central bank.

The ECB has $995bn in outstanding loans to commercial banks. It is expected to announce that its unlimited offer of one-year loans in December will be the last of its kind. In the past two one-year liquidity operations, banks have borrowed at 1%, significantly lower than rates offered in the private markets, which means they will face higher costs for their funding in future.

In essence, the Greeks have issued a warning to the rest of the Eurozone. Other Eurozone financial institutions will have taken note as the time has come to prepare for life outside. The days of unlimited cheap funding from the ECB are coming to an end. It's not imminent, but the writing is definitely on the wall.

Credit default swaps

Recession has come late to Greece, but will bite deep in 2010. It takes three years for defaults to peak once the cycle turns. In 2007, Greek CDS was nearer 15bp, because it was a member of the European Monetary Union, and its euro-denominated bonds were considered quasi-protected by other euro states. But in the past year the fiscal positions of many emerging market nations, such as Turkey, have become more favourable relative to the western world. Meanwhile, Greece has plunged into a profound budgetary mess, notwithstanding its use of the euro.

As markets reeled from the Dubai shock and investors fled from risk, the bid-offer spread on five year Greek CDSs was 201bp-208bp, according to Markit. All this is a bitter blow to Greek pride. However, there is a much bigger moral here, which cuts to the heart of the Dubai saga as well.

Two years ago, global investors generally did not spend much time worrying about so-called 'tail risk' (a banking term for the chance that seemingly remote, nasty events might occur). After all, before 2007, when the world was supposedly enjoying the era of the Great Moderation, the world seemed so stable and predictable that it was hard to imagine truly unpleasant events occurring. But in the past two years, a seemingly safe financial system has crumbled. And while the financial markets have stabilised in the past six months, that lesson about tail risk cannot be easily unlearnt. The sheer psychological shock of 2007 and 2008, in other words, has left investors looking like veterans from a brutal war.

The Greek economy is flirting with deflation and, unlike the wider Eurozone, could go on shrinking for some time. Its real exchange rate has appreciated, almost at par with Spain, which for its part finds a fifth of its workforce unemployed. Since labour costs have risen as well.

Prior to the global slowdown, the country was growing at annual rates of 4% or more, with consumption boosted by the low interest rates it enjoyed as a Eurozone member. But Europe's recession has exposed a massive loss of competitiveness. Unit labour costs have soared more than 40% since Greece joined the Eurozone in 2001 (in Germany, they remained almost constant before edging up this year). Even currency devaluation will not help regain competitiveness.

In February of this year, Peer Steinbrück, the former German FM, abruptly ended speculation by saying the Eurozone would act if someone got into trouble. There was no concrete action plan. No work had been done to amend European treaties. There was no budgetary appropriation. Just a sentence. Investors believed him and all was well—for a while.

The speculation is now back, but there is one difference. The Eurozone will not come to the rescue this time unless Greece meets a number of conditions the European Union is likely to impose in the coming months. This is how a Greek default could differ from the Dubai debt bailout by Abu Dhabi.

This year, Greece's budget deficit will rise to 12.7% of GDP. The country's public debt-to-GDP ratio is headed for 135%. Gross external debt—private and public sector debt owed to foreign creditors—was 149.2% at the end of last year. The real exchange rate has gone up by 17% since 2006, which means the country is losing competitiveness at an incredibly fast rate. Had Greece not been in the Eurozone, it would be heading straight for default.

The government's 2010 draft budget foresees deficit reduction, to about 9.1% of GDP. But, lion's share of the total deficit reduction effort is earmarked to come from tax measures, and most of those from the fight against tax evasion. Tax evasion is always the first item on the list of desperate governments.

The European Commission and Europe's FMs are rightly asking for genuine deficit reduction. So is George Provopoulos, the Greek central bank governor, who demanded that two-thirds of the entire deficit reduction effort should come from spending cuts. Athens has been shortening debt maturities to trim costs, storing up a roll-over crisis next year. Some euro 18bn comes due in the second quarter of 2010.

Modern economies have reached such debt levels before, and survived, but never in the circumstances facing Greece. They can't devalue: they can't print money.

The tourist trade is withering, down 20% last season by revenue. It is hard to pin down how much is a currency effect, but clearly Greece has priced itself out of the Club Med market. Wages rose a staggering 12% in the 2008-09 pay-round alone, suicidal in a Teutonic currency union. Greece has slipped to 71st in the competitiveness index of the World Economic Forum, behind Egypt and Botswana.

Greece's most pressing financial problem is the possibility of a buyers' strike by nervous foreign investors. The ruling Pasok party has pledged to shrink the deficit by 3 percentage points. That will be a painful adjustment, with little track record to support it, although perhaps credible this time given Pasok's parliamentary majority. And while Brussels has censured Greece for its Maastricht-busting budget, France, Spain, Italy, Belgium and Portugal are close behind. Raising funds is likely to become increasingly hard for all profligate countries.

So what happens if Greece cannot meet a payment on its bonds, or fails to roll over existing debt? About two-thirds of Greece's public debt is held by foreigners. Greece is looking to raise some euro 31bn ($46bn) in new borrowing and euro 16bn to roll over existing debt next year. In the absence of help from the Eurozone, the Greek government would have to resort to the International Monetary Fund if it were to encounter difficulties refinancing the debt.

It can be estimated that in Greece, the real effective exchange rate would need to decline by more than 30% to secure a return to balance. Since devaluation is not an option, the adjustment has to take place through inflexible labour markets. The unpalatable question is the level of unemployment at which competitiveness is restored. While some adjustment is now taking place, the German consumer will have to do more to support the deficit countries. That cannot be taken for granted.

What, then, is the risk of a regional version of the break-up of the Bretton Woods semi-fixed exchange rate system in the early 1970s? Suggestions that Italy or Greece might choose to leave the club seem implausible, because the prospect of devaluation would cause money to drain from the banking system, while the value of debt and the cost of debt service would soar.

All this does not mean that it is correct to expect the world to melt down imminently. The fact that the CDS spread for Greek bonds has swung from 5bp to 200bp, in other words, should not be interpreted as a sign of an imminent Greek default, or a likely break-up of the euro. The CDS market is pretty illiquid and prices can swing on low volumes.

But what the CDS market does capture is the perception of tail risk, or low-probability outcomes. Or, to put it another way, the market projects what could occur if the current fiscal and political situations were taken to logical extremes.

Much of the time investors are tempted to ignore those logical extremes. After all, investors have known for months that Dubai World was dangerously over-leveraged. They assumed that this would not be too dangerous, because they thought that foreign investors would always be protected.

Now, however, that assumption has been challenged. Tail risk has resurfaced with a vengeance.

Little wonder that CDS spreads of some other debt-laden emerging markets, such as Hungary, have swung adversely on the coattails of Dubai and Greece.

The downgrade of Greek sovereign debt by Fitch to triple B-plus has come as a shock. S&P has placed Greece's sovereign's A- rating on negative CreditWatch. The agency expressed doubts that the government's fiscal policies will deliver a sustained reduction in the budget deficit and national debt burden. Of course, this view has been shared by the CDS market for some time, with spreads widening significantly in recent months. But the threat of a downgrade to BBB+ added to negative sentiment on Greece. If the downgrade is implemented, Greece will be the first member of the Eurozone to have a rating below single A.

If other rating agencies followed Fitch's and Standard & Poor's lead, then Greek government debt could no longer be used as collateral. Greek banks would be left high and dry. In extremis, Athens would also have lost an important source of funding given that government bonds account for about 10% of Greek bank assets.

Still, this remains a drama rather than a tragedy, for now.

Default remains a long way off. Further, if rising bond yields and the downgrade shock force the government to slash spending, then markets will have done what neither local politicians nor Euro-entry managed to do.

—*The author is a Wharton Business School MBA and CEO, Global Money Investor*

Many thanks to *The Hindu Business Line* for publishing my article predicting steep fall in the Indian rupee published on June 19, 2013:

Slip slidin' away

The rupee could cross Rs 60/$ shortly.

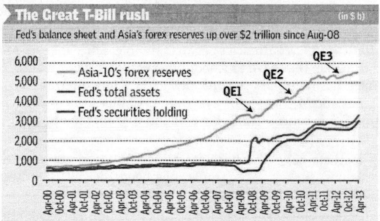

The Great T-Bill rush		(in $ b)

Fed's balance sheet and Asia's forex reserves up over $2 trillion since Aug-08

Asia's dollar chest		(in $ b)

Growth of Asia-10's forex reserves

	Aug-08	Mar-12	Growth
Asia-10	3,344	5,509	2,165
China	1,884	3,443	1,558
Hong Kong	158	304	146
Taiwan	282	402	120
Singapore	170	258	88
Korea	243	327	84
Thailand	99	168	69
The Philippines	37	84	47
Indonesia	58	105	46
Malaysia	117	127	10
India	295	292	-3

The dollar exodus from emerging markets is likely to accelerate.

The Indian rupee plummeted to a record low of Rs 58.98/$ on June 11, deepening worries about the country's current account deficit and complicating the task of the RBI as it tries to loosen monetary conditions in a bid to spur economic recovery.

The latest slide is also significant as it has come in the backdrop of RBI foreign currency reserves depleting by $3 billion during the last week of May alone.

Foreign investors have been heavy sellers in recent weeks of Indian debt (over $7.5 billion with another $2 billion in the waiting), a key risk for a country that has come to depend on capital inflows to finance its current account deficit and support its markets.

Sell in May and go away? This old adage certainly came to the forefront in emerging markets. The only difference — selling is likely to continue in June, July and August if investment returns in the once-hot sector keep getting slammed by moves in US bond yields and the dollar.

The genesis of the recent fall in emerging markets may be traced to yields on 10-year benchmark US Treasuries rising above 2 per cent on May 22, after the Federal Reserve's latest policy minutes sparking fears the central bank could start tapering off its bond purchasing programme as soon as this month.

Shortly afterwards, EM currencies began to tumble. Since then, the South African rand and the Brazilian real have touched four-year lows against the US dollar, and the Indian rupee has fallen to a record low. Even relatively robust countries such as the Philippines and Mexico — long favourites of investors — have been hit by a spate of selling. Some central banks have begun to intervene to stem the currency slides.

Emerging markets have also been hit by weakness in commodity prices and local political issues. Turkey, for example, has been rocked by protests that have sent the nation's markets into a tailspin.

The Fed's balance sheet has expanded by $2.29 trillion since Quantitative Easing (QE) began in August 2008 (see graph). In the same period, forex reserves at the Asia-10 expanded by $2.17 trillion (see Table).

The growing forex reserves act like an increase in the money supply that fuels deposits and loans. If the Fed scales back, the process "should inevitably go into reverse." It could be akin to "a margin call on Asia."

One would expect the Fed to keep its exit as orderly as possible. My concern is that, as expectations start to build, no one will want to be the last to exit. This could prompt markets to scramble to cover dollar-short and build dollar-long positions, exacerbated by multiplier effects, which could still lead to disorderly consequences.

Table 2 shows the risk is greatest in China, where forex reserves have soared by $1.56 trillion.

US gain, our pain

The weakness that you see in EM [emerging markets] is a trend weakness because emerging markets have lost their growth model. Exports aren't doing very well, current accounts surpluses are coming under strain, deficits are rising.

Memories of 1994 have been stirred by recent talk that signs of a US economic recovery could induce the Federal Reserve to scale back its money-printing, risking a repeat of the EM (emerging market) bloodbath that followed Alan Greenspan's decision to start tightening policy almost 20 years ago.

As years of rock-bottom US yields draw to a close, emerging markets may be victims of the Fed's success in pulling the US economy out of its stalemate.

During these years they have enjoyed an investment bonanza. Over $46 billion has flowed to emerging stock and bond funds since January, after almost $90 billion last year.

But 10-year US Treasury yields, considered the risk-free benchmark for most assets, rose 40 bps in May while the greenback surged. And while some weak US economic data has dampened expectations the Fed will end, or taper, money-printing early, the emerging markets sell-off shows no sign of abating.

The big picture is: the US economy is recovering and the Fed has signalled that tapering will happen.

Put simply, an investor comparing 10-year US yields at 2.2 per cent with the 5.2 per cent offered by, say, Chile, might well, given the skew of currency risk, opt for the former.

That is partly because real interest rates — taking into account inflation — in most emerging markets are negative and have fallen below US real rates. This round of US recovery, possibly fuelled by re-industrialisation rather than relying on emerging market imports, may not be bullish for the developing world.

The boom in recent years has meanwhile slashed yields on emerging debt. JPMorgan's GBI-EM index yielded a record low 5.2 per cent in early May, 120 bps less than a year earlier.

What FIIs Sold in May

The panic over US rates blew emerging dollar bond spreads almost 20 bps wider over Treasuries in May to bring 2013 returns to (-) 3 per cent. Local debt yields meanwhile rose 50 bps, with returns tipping into the red in the past week.

Emerging equities slumped more than 3 per cent, their biggest monthly loss in a year, while currencies, which typically make up a significant portion of investors' annual return, have also slipped.

According to UBS, an equally weighted basket of 20 emerging market currencies that it tracks has lost 3.7 per cent to the dollar this year.

Foreign investors are estimated to hold a third of emerging local debt and more in countries such as Peru and Hungary.

The money flowing out of China funds was the largest amount since February 2011. The Shanghai Composite, Asia's laggard index, has struggled to gain traction in recent months, weighed down by the uncertain growth outlook for the world's second largest economy. It is down 2.6 per cent year to date.

However, fellow BRIC markets have fared much worse than China. Brazil's benchmark Bovespa Index has lost 13 per cent since the start of the year, while Russia's RTS Index is down 15 per cent over the same period.

The MSCI Emerging Markets Index is down 7 per cent year to date, far underperforming the MSCI All Country World Index which is up almost 7 per cent.

The Fed's bond buying programme has led to ample liquidity in emerging markets in search of higher returns, but a paring back of stimulus is expected to heavily dampen appetite for risky assets.

While all currencies are depreciating against the dollar, the ones that have declined the most are from countries with large current account deficits, viz. South Africa, Turkey and India. South Africa's rand is at four-year lows while bond yields have jumped a whole percentage point in May.

REFORM IN INDIA

India is, unfortunately, a leader in this category. Despite all the public hand-wringing about the size of the current account deficit, very little has actually been done to rein it in. While domestic fuel prices are gradually being corrected, consumers are yet to pay the full rupee price of diesel and liquefied petroleum gas for domestic use.

Measures to dampen demand for gold are widely perceived to be misdirected and unlikely to have material impact.

On the mineral front, little has been done to revive the once substantial iron ore exports, while the country's power sector remains dependent on imported coal.

The Food Security Bill sought to be introduced by the UPA government will only add to the already bourgeoning deficit.

Indian government needs to simplify tax, reducing the necessity to file so many tax returns, even if electronically. A single window clearance for all Greenfield projects is the need of the hour. All this does not require the approval of the Opposition.

Auctioning is still the best way to allocate scarce natural resources. A strict hand is required to deal with all corruption cases. I am surprised IPL6 was even allowed to conclude.

Due diligence needs to be exercised while and after appointing people to positions of power as there is rampant misuse of power for personal gain.

The EM sell-off has been much more fixed income-focused than equity-focused... correlations between EM bonds and foreign exchange have shifted to high levels; a sign of indiscriminate position liquidation.

I believe the fall in emerging markets as an asset class is expected to accelerate over the next few months. Rupee could cross the psychologically important level of Rs 60/$ shortly and bring with it further pressure on the Indian stock indices and severely curtail the ability of the RBI to cut interest rates, thus resulting in a vicious circle of low growth and negative real interest rates.

(The author is CEO, Global Money Investor)

(This article was published on June 14, 2013)

Keywords: Indian rupee plummets, record low of Rs 58.98/$, current account deficit, RBI, loosen monetary conditions, spur economic recovery

Many thanks to the *Economic Times* for publishing my article, a sell call on silver, on 4th May 2011:

Time to sell silver this Akshaya Tritiya, buy around Diwali

In 1980, it was the Hunt brothers. In 1998, it was Warren Buffett. And in 2011?

For those unversed in the history of silver market, those dates refer to market squeezes that caused massive surges in the metal's price.

Silver prices shot up 24% in April 2011 alone, as retail investors rode on the coattails and pros moved en masse into silver futures and options pits.

During the last 12 months, the price of silver has risen 154%, outpacing gold (32%), wheat (65%), oil (45%) and, indeed, any investment class.

Healthy markets don't go up in a straight line. The move in silver has been parabolic and any panic could trigger a steep and swift correction.

In Quantum Mechanics in physics, the Heisenberg Uncertainty Principle states that an act of locating a particle in space tends to change its momentum and an act of measuring the momentum of the particle tends to change its location.

Silver has rallied moving exponentially while gold is moving linear. The metric of $1,600 gold and $50 silver may signal profit-taking opportunity. It is hard to see the same real-world factors driving silver's rise as we have seen with oil and grain. The silver market remains in substantial physical surplus.

One table-pounding silver bull was heard touting silver's use in solar energy panels. Is this time different once again?

Silver appears to be in classic mania. While prices of silver have soared, large silver-mining stocks have gone down lately, indicating buyer exhaustion.

Silver's rally needs to be put into perspective. At almost 150% over seven months, it is stunning, but far short of the spectacular 400% in five months managed during the Hunt brothers episode. Put against gold, silver does look distinctly racy. The ratio of gold to silver prices is at its lowest since 1980, and has plunged from 46 in January this year to 33.

The last time the ratio fell even close to this level was in 1998, when Warren Buffett's Berkshire Hathaway quietly accumulated a huge position in silver, driving prices up 90% in a few months to what was then a 10-year high of $7.90.

As silver is thinly traded, exchanges need to raise margin requirements or run the risk of a record-setting crash in silver. Correction in silver prices will not occur in a vacuum, especially since commodities have been trending up as a group, i.e., same hedge funds and banks are trading all the risk-on commodities as well such as gold, copper, crude oil, wheat, etc.

The reason for contagion risk is that while gold is going up 0.5-1 %, silver is logging in 3.5% days routinely. Such buying panic invariably leads to mean reversion. In other words, if silver gets a 10% down day, rest of commodities pack will be forced to overshoot on the downside in sympathy.

Does the 8% fall in silver on April 26 and May 2 indicate market 'sticker shock' — the jittery trading that surrounds big round numbers ($50)? Or is it indicative of end of a frothy, speculative rally?

When the market fell through the 20- and 10-day moving averages on April 26, a 'lot of weak longs in silver' were forced to cut gross longs by 3,131 contracts (they added 2,282 gross shorts), thus lowering their net longs to 25,791 — lowest since February 1.

On May 2, silver's sell-off occurred before official announcement of Osama bin Laden's death. It wasn't the cause of the sell-off, but added fuel to the fire. It took very little time to decline from $48 to $42.50. Socalled 'weak' positions chose to exit quickly than put up additional money to meet margin calls.

Undoubtedly, there is genuine end-user interest: Indian consumers, priced out by the rally in gold, are increasingly turning to silver.

In the US, sales of silver coins have rocketed since the financial crisis. Some of this is linked to fear of damage to dollar from Fed's ultraloose monetary policy. Ongoing political tensions across the Arab world and eurozone sovereign risk will continue to keep investors on edge.

Yet, the huge silver sell-off on April 26 was accompanied with massive volumes, confirming a bearish 'buying exhaustion tail' had occurred on the daily bar chart.

When adjusted for inflation, gold and silver prices still have a long way to go. Gold rose to $825.50 per ounce on January 21, 1980, which is $2,238.74 in today's dollars. Meanwhile, silver's inflation-adjusted price peaks at $136.55 per ounce in today's dollars. Along the way, 15-25 % short-term pullbacks are not unlikely.

As the US dollar approaches its 2008 nominal low, a temporary technical bounce is possible as volatility looks unsustainably low and real interest rates in US cannot fall lower.

The most likely cause of a serious dollar rally, though, is investor panic and flight to supposed safety of US bonds. This could cause the 'buy gold and silver, sell US dollar' trade to reverse.

Again, history may be informative. After the Hunt brothers' squeeze in 1980, the silver price collapsed 80% in four months; the Hunts were sanctioned for market manipulation and went bankrupt. And following Warren Buffett's silver play in 1998, the metal's price dropped 40% and Berkshire Hathaway recorded its worst annual results on record, relative to S&P 500, in 1999.

An easing in global inflationary pressures and a return to positive real interest rates in US could see investors lose their appetite for silver. Both gold and silver trades are currently overcrowded.

At elevated levels, if new production emerges and silver remains industrial-driven, we could see silver fallback to around 32/troy oz. Gold could similarly retrace to around $1,300/troy oz.

Diwali 2011, rather than Akshaya Tritiya, would be better time to make fresh and incremental investments in gold and silver.

Enclosed is a youtube presentation predicting the US Fed would announce sketch of tapering of its bond purchase program on June 19, 2013

FED WILL ANNOUNCE TAPERING OF QE TODAY JUNE 19 2013

...Although the Committee left the pace of purchases unchanged at today's meeting, it has stated that it may vary the pace of purchases as economic conditions evolve. Any such change will reflect the incoming data and their implications for the outlook, as well as the cumulative progress made toward the Committee's objectives since the program began in September. Going forward, the economic outcomes that the Committee sees as most likely involve continuing gains in labor markets, supported by moderate growth that picks up over the next several quarters as the near-term restraint from fiscal policy and other headwinds diminishes. We also see inflation moving back toward our 2 percent objective over time. **If the incoming data are broadly consistent with this forecast, the Committee currently anticipates that it would be appropriate to moderate the monthly pace of purchases later this year; and if the subsequent data remain broadly aligned with our current expectations for the economy, we would continue to reduce the pace of purchases in measured steps through the first half of next year, ending purchases around midyear.** In this scenario, when asset purchases ultimately come to an end, the unemployment rate would likely be in the vicinity of 7 percent, with solid economic growth supporting further job gains, a substantial improvement from the 8.1 percent unemployment rate that prevailed when the Committee announced this program.

I would like to emphasize once more the point that our policy is in no way predetermined and will depend on the incoming data and the evolution of the outlook, as well as on the cumulative progress toward our objectives. If conditions improve faster than expected, the pace of asset purchases could be reduced somewhat more quickly. If the outlook becomes less favorable, on the other hand, or if financial conditions are judged to be inconsistent with further progress in the labor markets, reductions in the pace of purchases could be delayed; indeed, should it be needed, the Committee would be prepared to employ all of its tools, including an increase in the pace of purchases for a time, to promote a return to maximum employment in a context of price stability.

It's also worth noting here that, even if a modest reduction in the pace of asset purchases occurs, we would not be shrinking the Federal Reserve's portfolio of securities but only slowing the pace at which we are adding to the portfolio, while continuing to reinvest principal payments and proceeds from maturing holdings as well. These large and growing holdings will continue to put downward pressure on longer-term interest rates. To use the analogy of driving an automobile, any slowing in the pace of purchases will be a kin to letting up a bit on the gas pedal as the car picks up speed, not to beginning to apply the brakes.

I will close by drawing again the important distinction between the Committee's decisions about adjusting the pace of asset purchases and its forward guidance regarding the target for the federal funds rate. As I mentioned, the current level of the federal funds rate target is likely to remain appropriate for a considerable period after asset purchases are concluded. To return to the driving analogy, if the incoming data support the view that the economy is able to sustain a reasonable cruising speed, we will ease the pressure on the accelerator by gradually reducing the pace of purchases. However, any need to consider applying the brakes by raising short-term rates is still far in the future. In any case, no matter how conditions may evolve, the Federal Reserve remains committed to fostering substantial improvement in the outlook for the labor market in a context of price stability.

'In this youtube presentation of April 18, 2014; I had predicted a summer 2014 correction in global stock markets':

Stage set for correction in global stock market indices Chinese slowdown, uncertain election results in India and Indonesia, asset deflation in Europe and faster rise in interest rates in the USA set the stage for a correction in global stock market ind...

AUTHOR'S NOTE

This book is not another treatise on finance. It would be very easy to dwell on the theory of finance and dwell on risk-profiling of investors and how they should go forward.

It would be very easy to write a book on developed markets, emerging market, frontier markets and how some are in flavor and some not.

The truth is that all these markets have their day under the sun. The key is to find out what markets will do well, when and when should a long-term investor enter.

BRICs were in favor sometime back and now there is a lot of commentary against them. They had their day under the sun and will return to take investors' attention sometime in the future.

My book is meant to be useful to any investor who wants to invest money; it is not meant to be for arm-chair reading of economics.

What is the **Baltic Dry Index (BDI)** currently indicating?

The **Baltic Dry Index** (BDI) is a number (in USD) issued daily by the London-based Baltic Exchange. Not restricted to Baltic Sea countries, the index provides "an assessment of the price of moving the major raw materials by sea.

Most directly, the index measures the demand for shipping capacity versus the supply of dry bulk carriers. The demand for shipping varies with the amount of cargo that is being traded or moved in various markets (supply and demand).

The index indirectly measures global supply and demand for the commodities shipped aboard dry bulk carriers, such as building materials, coal, metallic ores, and grains.

Because dry bulk primarily consists of materials that function as raw material inputs to the production of intermediate or finished goods, such as concrete, electricity, steel, and food; the index is also seen as an efficient economic indicator of future economic growth and production. The **BDI** is termed a leading economic indicator because it predicts future economic activity.

The **Baltic Dry Index (BDI)** is breaking down to new lows. The BDI suggests demand in the global economy remains a worrying factor. Since the beginning of 2014, the BDI is down 65%.

Yet, one must not forget that the supply of cargo ships is generally both tight and inelastic—it takes two years to build a new ship, and a ship's fixed costs are too expensive to take out of circulation the way airlines park unneeded jets in deserts. So, marginal increases in demand can push the index higher quickly, and marginal demand decreases can cause the index to fall rapidly.

An economic slowdown in the global economy affects the corporate earnings of companies in the key stock indices because they earn a massive amount of their earnings from overseas.

Consider **Caterpillar Inc. (NYSE/CAT).** In the second quarter of this year, the company earned more than 55% of its revenue from outside North America. It experienced a three-percent decline in overall revenue in its second quarter because of weak sales in the global economy.

Almost 50% of the revenues for the S&P 500 companies come from outside of the U.S. economy.

Are Stocks ignoring geopolitics?

Geopolitical tensions are heating up globally, but it isn't clear whether investors need to react, with stock markets not paying the conflicts much attention so far.

You can be forgiven for thinking that the world is a pretty terrible place right now-- everything from Russia-Ukraine tensions, the Gaza conflict, civil wars in Syria, Afghanistan, Iraq and Somalia, insurgencies in Nigeria and Mali, and even the long-running North Korea rumblings.

Strange as it might seem, such conflicts are not affecting the world's largest equity markets very much and that's "nothing new."

Currently, war zone countries have a small global footprint, representing just 0.7 percent of global *equity market* capitalization, 0.4 percent of portfolio investment flows and 0.8 percent of corporate profits, offset only by their 9.0 percent share of global oil production.

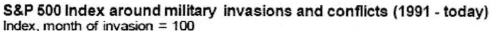

S&P 500 Index around military invasions and conflicts (1991 - today)
Index, month of invasion = 100

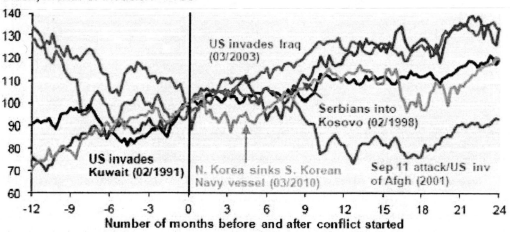

Number of months before and after conflict started

Note: 1) Equity index represents price returns.

2) It is not possible to invest directly in an index.

Since 1950, with the exception of the Israeli-Arab war of 1973 (which led to a Saudi oil embargo against the U.S. and a quadrupling of oil prices), military confrontations did not have a lasting medium-term impact on **equity markets.** The business cycle has been an overwhelmingly more important factor for investors to follow than war.

Emerging market assets would have run up much more without the increased geopolitical tensions and investors haven't accounted for discounting the risks.

Political and Economic Significance of 2014:

2014 is the year that marks the 100th anniversary of the start of the First World War, the 70th anniversary of D-Day and the 25th anniversary of the collapse of the Soviet empire and the savage crackdown around China's Tiananmen Square.

Brics bank

2014 is also a momentous year for the world because it is the year of the formation of the much awaited Brics bank.

Thirteen years ago, Brics was a marketing ploy conceptualized by Jim O'Neill, then chief economist at Goldman Sachs. Now it is a bank.

Recently, in Fortaleza, the five Brics nations – Brazil, Russia, India, China and South Africa – agreed to establish a development bank. They also set up a $100bn swap line, known formally as a contingent reserve arrangement, a deal which gives each country's central bank access to emergency supplies of foreign currency.

There are two ways to look at the BRICS bank. One is to scoff at the very idea of five such disparate nations organising anything coherent or staying the course. The other is to worry that the world order reflected in the two US-led institutions set up at the Bretton Woods conference of 1944 is about to crumble.

It is indeed a minor miracle that five countries whose initials happen to form a catchy acronym have so quickly gone from Brics to a bricks-and-mortar bank. This is a reprimand to western-led institutions that have failed to adapt.

The new Brics bank, which will fund infrastructure projects, will have initial capital of $50bn and maximum allowable capital of $100bn. Each country will pay in $10bn, giving them a theoretically equal say. The bank will be based in Shanghai, a sop to Beijing, which clearly intends to wield influence. Yet the presidency will be rotated, starting with India. China will not have a turn until 2021.

By contrast, the five countries will contribute to the CRA swap line according to size, with China pitching in $41bn to South Africa's $5bn. The contingent reserve is a safety net for times of financial stress, for example if one country's currency comes under speculative attack. The BRICS bank is modelled on the Chiang Mai Initiative, a $240bn Asian currency swap arrangement concluded after the 1997 Asian crisis when the region's proposal to launch its own IMF equivalent was squashed by Washington.

The Brics bank, too, was born of frustration. The IMF in particular is disliked in much of the developing world. In the 1990s, its rigid adherence to market reforms led many to see it as an instrument to keep poor countries down, not to lift them out of poverty. In 1997, IMF insisted on ruinous austerity in countries such as Indonesia. Following the 2008 financial crisis it has happily embraced monetary and fiscal laxity in the west.

Shares of global GDP and IMF voting rights 2014 (%)

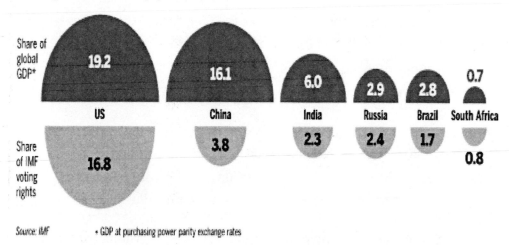

Source: IMF   + GDP at purchasing power parity exchange rates

If the IMF has changed its spots it has not changed its structure. Its quota system, which determines what each country pays in and how many votes they are given, fails to reflect the reality of a changing world. The Brics nations, which account for more than a fifth of global output, have just 10.3 per cent of quota. European countries, by contrast, are allocated 27.5 per cent for just 18 per cent of output.

Besides, the IMF presidency is reserved for a European, while that of the World Bank routinely goes to an American. Reforms were agreed in 2010 that would have doubled the IMF's capital to $720bn and transferred 6 percentage points of quota to poorer countries. That this did not go far enough is a moot point. The reforms were never ratified by the US Congress.

From the Brics' perspective, the global financial system is stacked against them. The fact that the US Federal Reserve, without warning, announced plans to "taper" its bond purchases showed it was willing to turn the monetary spigots on and off even at the expense of turmoil in the emerging world. Last year, this had ensured a run on emerging market currencies.

One reason to welcome the new bank is that it will bring competition. China's lending in Africa has drawn valid criticism that it is not tied to good governance or environmental standards. Yet the presence of alternative Chinese funding in Africa has been a net positive. The same should be true of the new Brics bank, given the huge number of roads, power plants and sewerage systems that need funding.

The new bank is no panacea. As critics point out, it is relatively small. Ben Steil and Dinah Walker of the US-based Council on Foreign Relations note that, between them, China, India and Brazil have borrowed $66bn from the World Bank alone, more than the entire subscribed capital of the Brics bank. While the idea of conditionality can be overdone, it would not be a good thing if the new bank lent willy-nilly to dictators intent on ransacking their countries' natural resources. Nor is the Brics bank necessarily as democratic as it makes out. Its articles ensure the founders will never see their voting rights drop below 55 per cent, no matter how many countries join.

Still, the Bretton Woods institutions reflect the realities of a receding age. The world has changed, mostly for the better, as the emerging world closes the gap on the developed world. The Brics bank encapsulates this.

Thrust of my book--drawing meaningful correlations

My book draws correlations between various variables macro-economic and micro-economic.

Correlations are of various kinds. Is this a good correlation?

On May 22, 2014 three new items appeared simultaneoulsy:

(A) A survey by the Country Financial Security Index found:

    a) 25% of Americans across all age groups admit they are not saving at all for retirement, or are unsure

    b) 38% of those 40 and older said they regret decisions they have made with their retirement savings

    c) 47% dis not start to save early enough

(B) A US government forecast said that California's Monterey Shale deposit will yield only 4% of what was originally hoped. California's shale deposit has been considered the U.S.'s most prolific energy reserve: the agency's prior estimate of 13.7 billion barrels comprised about two-thirds of America's shale bounty.

(C) Road rage cases are on the rise in the U.S. According to AAA (American Automobile Association) road rage is defined as aggressive driving that arises from disagreements between motorists that can lead to physical assault. Now, it is found that road rage is reflecting in 'aggressive texting' by motorists.

So, from (A), (B) and (C), can we derive the conclusion that America's savings are on the decline and that lesser gas is being discovered and this is leading to frustration and road rage aong motorists who are resorting to greater texting as an outlet to their emotions?

The lighter side apart, are there questions to America's increasing energy independence?

Has Monterey downgrade dented America's shale boom?

Gas is flared as waste from the Monterey Shale formation where gas and oil is extracted using hydraulic fracturing or fracking. Near Buttonwillow in California, USA

Because the Bakken and Eagel Ford shale plays currently generate nearly 70% of U.S. unconventional oil and gas, the downgrade to Monterey does little to alter the near-term trajectory of America's energy renaissance.

However, it does bring into focus two major red flags: A well depletion factor that ramps up the urgency of finding new shale plays, and the need to upgrade new technology for that same purpose. Shale wells are prone to rapid depletion rates—spots in North Dakota's Bakke lose 85% of their capacity within a few years.

If the U.S. boom is to be sutained beyond 202, new shale plays will need to be discovered withing the next few years.

Early in the U.S. boom, most estimates were fairly conservative, which changed as rapid advances in hydraulic fracturing technology made it easier to pull oil and gas from the ground. Forecasts need to be contually refined, so I think this is not a death knell for the shale gas boom.

The good news is that supply grows short-term but the bad news is that we may have a very serious supply issue 10-15 years out.

Fracking has fed a renaissance in domestic manufacturing, helping the U.S. drill and export the most oil it has in at least three decades. Investment and technological innovation could go a long way towards turning recoverable reserves into actual barrels of black gold.

10 or 15 years ago, nobody would have projected Bakken or Eagle Ford to produce 1 million barrels a day. These technoloiges weren't in place 10 years ago. Now they clearly are.

No two investors or investments are the same:

Every investment made has to be uniquely fitted to suit the needs of the individual investor. There are no two institutions or two retail investors which would have the same risk profile and the same investment horizons.

Palm Jumeirah   in Dubai, United Arab Emirates (completed at a cost of $12.3 billion) is a man-made cluster of islands (artificial archipelago). They are created by reclaiming land. The project was carried out by Dubai government's company Nakheel. It is one of three planned islands called the Palm Islands (Palm Jumeirah, Palm Jebel Ali and Palm Deira) which would have extended into the Persian Gulf, increasing Dubai's shoreline by a total of 520 kilometres.

The Palm Jumeirah is one of its kinds—the world's largest man-made island.

Let's look at the world ahead.

The growth momentum is slowing down in China and is threatening to take down the rest of the world with it.

I have mentioned broadly the various periods during which global stock markets could see correction/upside; if you need to analyze more closely, please email us at **globalmoneyinvestor@gmail.com.** We would he happy to provide further analysis or insights and a more closer look at markets during 2014 and beyond.

Janet Yellen's intervention in biotech and internet stocks

It is a very good thing that the Fed is prepared to take action to cool excessive risk taking on a macro level. Up to now, Chair Yellen has appeared somewhat complacent about the risks inherent in "artificially high" asset prices. But they need to be careful that they do not interfere too much in the market's role in the allocation of capital among growth sectors in the economy.

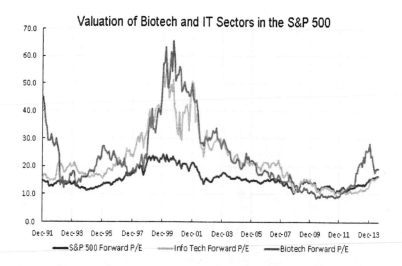

Valuation of Biotech and IT Sectors in the S&P 500

It is not clear that they need to have any view at all about the valuations of the biotech and internet sectors of the stockmarket. Together, these sectors account for under 6 % of US market capitalisation, so there is a school of thought which believes it is difficult to fathom how they can be affecting the macro-economy or financial stability.

As of July 2 2014	Biotech Sector	Internet Sector	S&P 500
S&P 500 Weight (%)	2.9	2.3	100
Earnings Growth 2014 %	62.7	21.9	8.4
Earnings Growth Long Term (%)	24.0	21.0	11.0
P/E multiple, next 12 months	17.9	23.9	16.1
Ratio of P/E to Long Term Growth	0.8	1.1	1.4

Furthermore, earnings growth has been very strong in these sectors, and their price-to-forward-earnings valuations are not obviously out of line with past norms. Compared to long term growth in earnings, their valuations are below the average for the S&P 500. Nor do they seem to be dragging up the valuation of the IT sector, still less the entire stockmarket, as they did in the late 1990s.

Yet; I, for one believe that one needs to be careful—sentiment change in one section of the market is contagious and could lead to collateral damage in other areas of the market quite easily.

HOW DOES THE WORLD OF
INVESTMENTS STACK UP TODAY

There is a great talk that most global indices are at all-time highs and that patient investors have eventually benefitted. Oh really?

Let's look at how the major global indices have performed over short and longer periods of time:

Here is a look at 2014 so far:

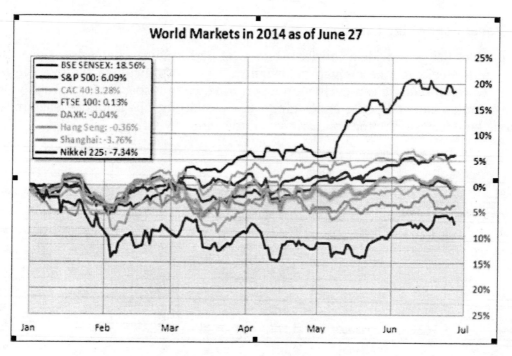

Here is a table highlighting the year-to-date index performance, sorted from high to low, along with the 2014 interim highs for the eight indexes. At this point, four of the eight indexes are in the green, unchanged from last week.

Index	2014 Peak	YTD
BSE SENSEX	20.84%	18.56%
S&P 500	6.20%	6.09%
CAC 40	6.96%	3.28%
FTSE 100	1.92%	0.13%
DAXK	2.13%	-0.04%
Hang Seng	0.14%	-0.36%
Shanghai	1.26%	-3.76%
Nikkei 225	0.00%	-7.34%

As of June 27, 2014

A Closer Look at the Last Four Weeks

The tables below provide a concise overview of performance comparisons over the past four weeks for these eight major indexes. I've also included the average for each week so that we can evaluate the performance of a specific index relative to the overall mean and better understand weekly volatility. The colors for each index name help us visualize the comparative performance over time.

June 6		June 13		June 20		June 27	
BSE SENSEX	4.87%	Shanghai	2.01%	Nikkei 225	1.67%	Shanghai	0.49%
Nikkei 225	3.04%	Hang Seng	1.60%	S&P 500	1.38%	Hang Seng	0.12%
CAC 40	1.36%	Nikkei 225	0.14%	DAXK	0.75%	BSE SENSEX	-0.02%
S&P 500	1.34%	BSE SENSEX	-0.66%	FTSE 100	0.70%	S&P 500	-0.10%
DAXK	0.44%	S&P 500	-0.68%	CAC 40	-0.04%	FTSE 100	-0.99%
FTSE 100	0.20%	DAXK	-0.74%	BSE SENSEX	-0.49%	Nikkei 225	-1.66%
Shanghai	-0.45%	CAC 40	-0.83%	Hang Seng	-0.54%	DAXK	-1.72%
Hang Seng	-0.57%	FTSE 100	-1.17%	Shanghai	-2.13%	CAC 40	-2.30%
Average	1.28%	Average	-0.04%	Average	0.16%	Average	-0.77%

The chart below illustrates the comparative performance of World Markets since March 9, 2009. The start date is arbitrary: The S&P 500, CAC 40 and BSE SENSEX hit their lows on March 9th, the Nikkei 225 on March 10th, the DAX on March 6th, the FTSE on March 3rd, the Shanghai Composite on November 4, 2008, and the Hang Seng even earlier on October 27, 2008. However, by aligning on the same day and measuring the percent change, we get a better sense of the relative performance than if we align the lows.

The chart below illustrates the comparative performance of World Markets since March 9, 2009. The start date is arbitrary: The S&P 500, CAC 40 and BSE SENSEX hit their lows on March 9th, the Nikkei 225 on March 10th, the DAX on March 6th, the FTSE on March 3rd, the Shanghai Composite on November 4, 2008, and the Hang Seng even earlier on October 27, 2008. However, by aligning on the same day and measuring the percent change, we get a better sense of the relative performance than if we align the lows.

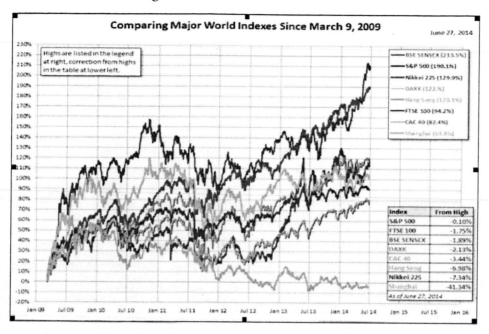

A Longer Look Back

Here is the same chart starting from the turn of 21st century. The relative over-performance of the emerging markets (Shanghai, Mumbai SENSEX and Hang Seng) up to their 2007 peaks is evident, and the SENSEX remains by far the top performer. The Shanghai, in contrast, formed a perfect Eiffel Tower from late 2006 to late 2009.

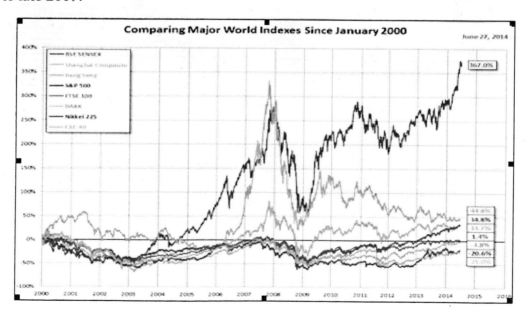

Deadbeats do best even as stocks stall

Investors tend to pigeonhole themselves to one investing style; hence, tend to lose out easily.

Fundamentally cheap stocks are often held in low regard by market participants. Something may be tainting their perception in investors' minds. If a stock's results begin to demonstrate that its woes are overstated, its price/earnings multiple will expand. If a stock's multiple goes from, say, eight to ten, and its EPS rises by 12%, it can move a stock 40%.

Generally variations in earnings aren't nearly as impactful on glamour growth stocks as are changes in image and, well, sexiness. I often think of glamour stocks as though they are attractive women dressing to the nines. You need to figure out whether your hot prospect is real or just a tease, because it's a lot harder to expand a P/E of 30 even with a 25% EPS boost. When a growth stock's sex appeal is real and its earnings jump, a multiple boost can produce big price gains.

Financial markets rarely stick to the script, and this year is no different.

Investments traditionally considered safe bets such as utilities, gold and government bonds were supposed to flop in 2014 as investors started to pour money into higher-risk, higher-growth stocks that would benefit from a pickup in the economy.

Instead, these safe investments are among the year's best performers. Utilities, for example, are up more than twice as much as the next-best sector in the **Standard & Poor's 500 index.**

The surprisingly strong returns from these so-called havens are happening for several reasons. In the U.S., a severe winter slowed the economy, and a slump in trendy technology stocks has undermined prices. From overseas, worries about China's economy are growing and chaos in Ukraine has increased global political tensions. Safe and steady assets have fared much better.

Utilities:

Power companies in the S&P 500 are up 11.4 percent this year, making them the best performers in the index by far. The next-best performer is up 5.2 percent, and that's energy stocks.

Investors buy utilities when they are worried about stock market volatility or the outlook for economic growth. Typically, utility stocks rise less than others when the overall market is climbing, but they fall less when prices are down. These stocks also pay big dividends, which are attractive to investors, particularly when bond yields are historically low, like they are now.

The dividend yield, a measure of a company's dividend compared with its stock price, is 3.6 percent for utility companies in the S&P 500. That compares with a dividend yield of 1.5 percent for technology companies and a yield of 2.71 percent for **10-year Treasury notes**.

The dividends will provide you with some support-those names will go down less than the names that don't pay dividends.

Exelon, a Chicago-based utility is up 31 percent this year and PSgEG, a utility based in New Jersey, has gained 23 percent.

Gold:

Gold has been one of the year's best performing financial assets, climbing 10.32% to $ 1326 an ounce. The price of the metal is rebounding after a 2013 slump of 28 percent, its biggest decline in more than 30 years.

Investors have also been buying gold as a hedge against a weakening dollar. The U.S. currency has dropped against the euro and the Japanese yen this year as the **Federal Reserve** has reiterated its message that it will continue its efforts to support the economy with low interest rates.

I still view gold as one of the best alternatives I view of the looming geopolitical uncertainties, at least from a six months perspective (till end October 2014).

Demand for gold as a safe asset has also risen as tensions between Russia and the West have escalated over Ukraine. Russia annexed the Crimea region on March 21.

Another explanation for gold's gains is that investors' psychology on the metal has shifted this year, after being unrelentingly negative for most of 2013. The metal fell as low as $1,187 an ounce in December, having climbed as high as $1,900 an ounce in August 2011.

The richest temple in the world--Padmanabhaswamy temple

is located in the centre of Thiruvananthapuram, the capital of Kerala, India.

As per the evaluation of the value of treasures found from the underground cellars of the Sree Padmanabhaswamy Temple there is around 1,00,000 crore rupees (1 Lakh Crore Rupees)There are 6 cellars in the Sree Padmanabhaswamy Temple that were marked from A to B. Among them the cellars A and B are not opened for past 150 years. Other cellars were containing precious items for festivals, daily poojas .etc.

Srikrishna idol 8 kg gold Padmanabhaswamy temple

Swarna Gold Dhanuss

Old gold coins india

Indian old gold coin collection

Indian old gold coins

Padmanabhaswamy temple Gold Chains 18 ft

Gold KashuMala Necklaces

Padmanabhaswamy temple Treasure box

Padmanabhaswamy temple Treasure   Padmanabhaswamy temple golden biscuits

Sri Padmanabhaswamy Temple Mahavishnu Idol 32 KG gold

Sri Padmanabhaswamy Temple Mahavishnu Idol - 32 KG gold. aside siva lingam and naabi kamala brahmmah Unearthed a rich and glorious past in Padmanabha Temple, Thiruvananthapuram, India

Treasurys:

Many analysts expected Treasury prices to slump after the Fed announced in December that it would start winding down its massive monthly bond purchases. That program is aimed at stimulating the economy by holding down long-term borrowing rates for consumers and businesses.

But bond prices climbed even as the Fed's buying has slowed. Barclays index of U.S. Treasurys that mature within seven to 10 years has climbed 2.8 percent since the start of 2014, and long-maturity Treasury bonds have risen even more. The bank's index of Treasurys with maturities of 20 years or more has surged 9.2 percent.

Prices got a lift when big investors like pension funds and insurance companies rebalanced their portfolios at the start of this year, booking some of their gains after stock prices had risen and buying bonds, says Kathy Jones, fixed income strategist at Charles Schwab.

While stocks had surged in 2013, bonds had declined, pushing up their yields. The 10-year Treasury yield stood at 1.76 percent at the start of 2013. It climbed to 2.97 percent by this January.

If you think back to the beginning of the year, bond yields were up and stocks had just had a good year--that 3 percent level, or close to it, was pretty attractive.

Another reason for the strong performance of Treasurys is that inflation has remained tame. The latest reading of consumer prices showed that prices in March climbed just 1.5 percent from a year earlier, well below the 2 percent level that the Fed considers acceptable. Low **inflation** is good for bonds because it helps preserve the value of a bond's fixed payments to investors.

Of late, global bond yields have been falling in the backdrop of falling world economic growth which has led to rally in the global bond markets.

In this backdrop, I have used various analytical tools to give a roadmap for investors for the rest of 2014. Please bear in mind that I have written various trend-changing events in my book, each of which has a bearing on how I believe the global stocks markets will perform for the remainder of 2014 and beyond.

Tracking the market with social media

The *Twitter Sentiment algorithm* looks for actions, events, fundamental analysis, technical analysis, observations, and opinions from market participants who use many different investment and trading techniques. When market participants tweet positive messages from their own analysis of the stock market or *individual stocks* the momentum indicator moves up. As *more* people tweet constructive information an uptrend in momentum created. Conversely, as negative analysis builds it turns the momentum of the herd lower.

We use the trend of seven day momentum to create short term signals for the stock market and individual stocks. Currently, momentum from the Twitter stream for the S&P 500 Index is signaling a *consolidation* warning. This warning came after an uptrend in momentum that lasted over two months. The recent rise in price has brought momentum back to a down trend line. As long as the down trend in momentum stay intact the consolidation warning will remain open.

Momentum from the StockTwits stream has broken its downtrend line which shows more optimism from the StockTwits community and clears its consolidation warning. So we currently see a divergence from traders on Twitter and those on StockTwits.

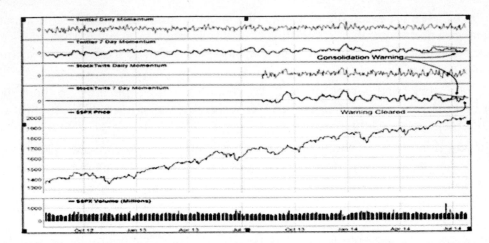

Support and resistance levels generated from the Twitter stream for the S&P 500 index (SPX) have compressed to a 50 point range. There are many calls for SPX to climb to 2000, but very few above that level. This makes 2000 on SPX a resistance level. Below the market the recent low at 1955 is getting almost all of the attention which makes it support.

Sector relative strength is confirming the StockTwits community with leading sectors showing support from market participants and defensive sectors lacking support.

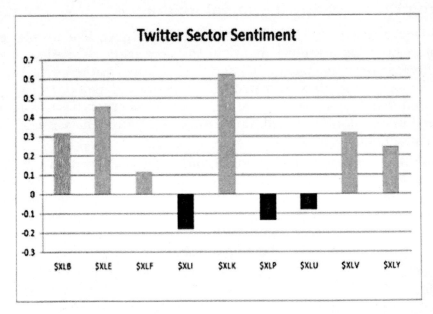

The overall picture from social media is mostly positive. Although Twitter Momentum is still on a consolidation warning, it is above zero and close to breaking a down trend line (which will clear the warning). Traders are mostly tweeting about the 2000 level on SPX so it should act as a magnet and then serve as short term resistance.

Stocks: The Four Totally Bad 'Bear Market Recoveries'

This chart series features an overlay of the Four Bad Bears in U.S. history since the market peak in 1929. They are:

1. The **Crash of 1929**, which eventually ushered in the Great Depression,
2. The **Oil Embargo of 1973**, which was followed by a vicious bout of stagflation,
3. The 2000 **Tech Bubble** bust and,
4. The **Financial Crisis** following the nominal all-time high in 2007.

The series includes four versions of the overlay: nominal, real (inflation-adjusted), total-return with dividends reinvested and real total-return.

The first chart shows the price, excluding dividends for these four historic declines and their aftermath. As of writing this book, we are now 1708 market days from the 2007 peak in the S&P 500.

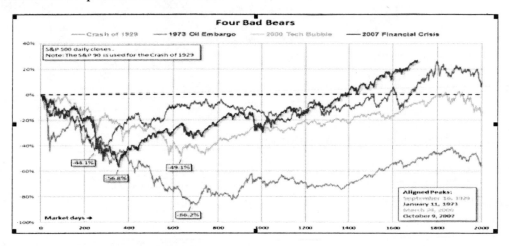

Inflation-Adjusted Performance

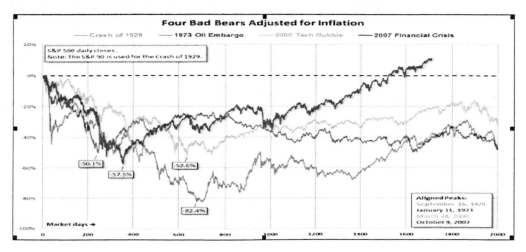

Nominal Total Returns

Now let's look at a total return comparison with dividends reinvested. The recovery following the 1973 Oil Embargo Bear is the top performer, up 48.3% from the 2007 peak, with the current post-Financial Crisis recovery in close second.

Real (Inflation-Adjusted) Total Returns

When we adjust total returns for inflation, the picture significantly changes. The spread between three of the four markets narrows and the current real total return has pulled far ahead of the others. Second place, by this metric, goes to the recovery following the Crash of 1929.

Here is a table showing the relative performance of these four cycles at the equivalent point in time.

After 1708 Market Days	Index Price		Total Return	
Peak	Nominal	Real	Nominal	Real
Crash of 1929	-50.3%	-38.2%	-26.7%	-8.8%
1973 Oil Embargo	9.0%	-39.9%	48.3%	-18.2%
2000 Tech bubble	-6.8%	-21.2%	3.8%	-12.2%
2007 Financial Crisis	27.0%	11.3%	47.0%	28.9%

Inflation adjustment based on the Consumer Price Index

For a better sense of how these cycles figure into a larger historical context, here's a long-term view of secular bull and bear markets, adjusted for inflation, in the S&P Composite since 1871.

These charts are not intended as a forecast but rather as a way to study the current market in relation to historic market cycles.

Where are the bubbles forming next?

Auto loans heat up, with emerging market corporate debt also expanding fast

Where is the next bubble going to form? And will it hurt when it bursts?

After all the bubbles of the past two decades, it is tempting to find them everywhere. But even if stocks are overpriced, it is hard to call them a bubble. Low interest rates push investors into stocks, but the wild enthusiasm that accompanied history's classic bubbles is absent.

But the next bubbles do seem to be brewing in credit. The asset class that drove the financial crisis in 2008, has been inflated again, by the same heady mixture of ingredients.

The knock-on effects for the economy should be far less severe than they were after the US housing bubble burst; but the trend is still alarming.

The most worrying place to look is in US auto loans. The Great Recession of 2008 and 2009 was driven by a fall in US house prices that inflicted levered losses, and not by the subsequent banking crisis.

Those levered losses were driven by excessive lending to "sub prime" borrowers with poor credit histories, which in turn was encouraged by rising securitisation and the need to offer low-risk products with a high yield.

The good news is that there is no repeat of this pathology in the housing market, even with house prices rising. Spending on home appliances and furniture has grown far less than spending as a whole over the past five years. And the use of houses as "ATMs" for equity withdrawal via second mortgages is minimal, running at barely a fifth the rate seen before the credit crisis. So unlike the boom of the last decade, the recent rise in house prices has not spurred excessive credit.

In the auto loans market, however, it seems that lenders are staging a rerun of the credit crisis. Sales of sub prime auto loans were higher last year than in 2007, as were sales of prime auto loans.

Auto sales tanked in 2009, to hit a level lower than they had seen a decade earlier. Their subsequent rebound has been central to the US economic recovery.

US sales of new cars in the first four months of this year rose more than twice as fast in the districts with poorest credit histories than in the areas where people had the best credit history. There are also reports that defaults are rising.

To be clear, the subprime auto loan boom cannot cause as much damage as the subprime housing boom. The sums involved are much smaller, people do not expect their cars to rise in value and cars are easily repossessed. There is no equivalent of the costly dramas of foreclosure.

There is still reason to fear that a burst auto bubble would have serious economic consequences. Credit's problems are not limited to car loans.

Some growth might even be healthy – fleets are ageing, and many deferred car purchases during the recession, and so this may be in part a healthy catch-up. We will soon know; the longer the growth in auto loans goes on, the harder it is to view it as anything other than a bubble.

But there is still reason to fear that a burst auto bubble would have serious economic consequences. Stripping out spending on cars, the US may well have had negative real sales growth in the first half of this year. The recovery in the auto sector may well have been helped by the cheap finance that is available – which implies that a burst bubble in the sector would hurt.

Credit's problems are not limited to car loans. Future bubbles often appear in asset classes that have expanded the fastest.

On this basis, corporate emerging market debt has expanded far more than any other asset class since the close of 2008; by some fivefold. US high-yield or "junk" bonds and emerging market government debt are next on the list.

All have expanded far faster than commodities or equities. Like equities, the price of these asset classes has been helped by the rock bottom rates available from "risk-free" bonds, making investors far more willing to take a risk and look elsewhere.

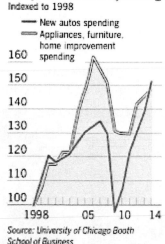

Subprime drives spending
Indexed to 1998

——— New autos spending
══════ Appliances, furniture, home improvement spending

Source: University of Chicago Booth School of Business

There is ample room for emerging market corporate debt to grow. Companies need more financing, and their economies are growing faster than in the developed world. But these are just the conditions in which bubbles can form. The internet drove much real growth, but it still created one of history's greatest bubbles because people grew excited and overestimated that growth.

There is further reason to worry about debt. When the balloon went up in 2007, credit was a vehicle used mostly by institutions. Now, thanks to exchange traded funds, credit is available at a low price to retail investors.

Even though corporate debt in emerging markets tends to be much less liquid than equities, it is available through ETFs, which promise to be as liquid as any stock. What would happen if large numbers of investors tried to head for the exits at the same time?

Credit is still a long way from the mad overextension it had reached by 2007. But some corners of the credit market are bubbling over and that should cause concern.

It is a global world

According to Chaos Theory; if a butterfly flaps its wings Tokyo, we can see the impact in another part of the world, such as in Texas.

Even financial practices in one part of the world impact the rest of the world. (Note: Sub-prime loans in the USA which lead to the 'Great Recession').

In a global world, one country learns from practices in another part. Each country or continent has its own idiosyncrasies. Some practices benefit the world; others like leverage come with their own complications.

What FedEx needs to learn from Mumbai's dabbawallas

In Lower Manhattan, a busy banker stuffs herself with overly rich restaurant fare ordered off **Seamless.com**. In Frankfurt, a manager slops generous portions of the canteen's stew onto his lunch plate.

In Mumbai, an insurance analyst sits down to a healthy home-cooked meal, still warm from the stove where it was prepared by his wife or mother.

Indian dabbawallas push their carts laden with food, on their way to make lunch time food deliveries, through the streets of Mumbai.

India's commercial capital is a teeming metropolis of nearly 20 million, boasting a sparkling international air terminal and a sleek new metro system, swanky furniture stores and Bollywood starlets. It's a city constantly striving, yearning for the future.

Remarkably, its age-old tradition of home-cooked meals — delivered on wheels — has resisted the momentum of change.

The dabbawallas, as they're known, are the men who make it possible.

They have cemented their place in Mumbai's colorful tapestry. They deliver lunch from home to the office or school every day, monsoon or shine.

The dabbawallas take great pride in ensuring delivery even against great odds: They worked through the floods in 2005 and the terrorist attack on Mumbai in November 2008 when most of the city had come to a standstill.

The dabbawallas are a common sight in Mumbai: men clad in white kurtas, weaving their bikes through impossible traffic and swarming throngs, juggling multiple tiffins — circular silver tins with four to five compartments, each packed with food — that are destined for office buildings and school courtyards.

Transporting lunches may sound simple but what the dabbawallas do every day is a remarkable feat — one so impressive, in fact, that professors from Harvard Business School have traveled to India to study it.

Some 5,000 men dole out over 200,000 meals a day, picking up the tiffins in the morning from women, typically, who have packed steaming, spicy dishes into each compartment: a curry, vegetables, dal (lentils), and flatbread (with some variations).

For many Mumbai residents, this is the only way to lunch — on a feast, made with the love of a mother or wife.

The dabbawallas sort the various lunches according to where they came from, and where they are intended to go, labeling each tiffin with an alpha numeric code. The tins are then loaded onto city trains, transported through the city's maze and handed off to local dabbawallas who complete the last leg of the route.

At lunchtime, the sharp aromas of turmeric, cumin and chili fill the office as workers deftly mop up their curries with bread. After the food is eaten and the tiffins packed back in their bags, the dabbawallas return the boxes to their respective homes, their loads a bit lighter.

Adding to the physical demands and challenge of precision, the large majority of the dabbawallas are semi-literate or illiterate, mostly hailing from small villages near the city of Pune in Maharashtra state. Their trade first started 125 years ago, in much simpler times. But as Mumbai has grown and transformed rapidly, adding new districts and train lines, the dabbawallas have adapted.

So deeply imprinted that the dabbawallas rarely, if ever, make a mistake. Their delivery system has been awarded a **six sigma level of efficiency.** That means they make around one mistake in every six million deliveries.

Their delivery system has garnered international fame as a highly specialized trade, attracting Prince Charles and Richard Branson and warranting a case-study at Harvard Business School, visits from global delivery giant FedEx, and a series of documentaries.

The dabbawallas' lore even spawned a critically-acclaimed movie last year. In **"The Lunchbox,"** a mistaken dabbawala delivery sparks an unlikely romance between a young housewife and an office worker nearing retirement.

The biggest challenges to dabbawallas are cultural ones, like changing family roles. As women shed their aprons and head to their own workplaces, nobody is left behind to cook lunch at home. Solution is to have the dabbawallas' wives take over the cooking, closing the catering circle.

Others have lamented the growing taste for Western standards, for business lunches and quick fast food fixes. Yet the dabbawallas say nothing, not even McDonald's, has managed to put a dent in their business.

Many people in this city prefer their lunch fresh, prepared lovingly by their wives or mothers--This is why despite so many restaurants cropping up all over the city, the business of dabbawallas still sees a 5-10 % growth each year.

What's more, the dabbawallas are part of the Mumbai's identity.

Mumbai is recognized, identified by the dabbawallas — all over India, all over the world they feel proud. They are learning from this business, the values, and the culture.

Disconnect between corporate earnings and stock markets

As amazing as it seems, over 5 years have now passed since the market hit "bottom" at the end of the 2008 "Great Recession." Since then, the stock market has delivered **phenomenal** performance – especially in the last few years.

But has the stock market "disconnected" from the realities in the underlying economy? Are companies really making enough profits to merit the **224.4% stock market rally** we've had from the March 9, 2009, low point, through June 30, 2014 (including dividend re-investment)?

The table below shows that companies have indeed enjoyed some good, steady earnings growth over the past 48 months.**

The table also shows the stock market has gone *completely crazy*, far outpacing profit growth... especially in the last 2 years (as shown in red)!

	Last 12 mos. (7/1/13-6/30/14)	2 years ago (7/1/12-6/30/13)	3 years ago (7/1/11-6/30/12)	4 years ago (7/1/10-6/30/11)
Earnings	12.69% (est.)	3.45%	4.83%	24.99%
Stock market	24.61%	20.60%	5.45%	30.69%

Stock returns include re-invested dividends, but do not reflect investment fees or expenses.
Ignores taxes & inflation. You can't invest directly in an index like the S&P 500.

In total, **earnings** have increased by about a **53%** over the past 48 months (or about an **11% annualized compound rate**). In dollars, using data from Standard & Poor's, earnings have grown from $67.10 per share for the 12-months ending in June 2010, to an estimated $102.49 per share for the most recent 12 months.

Stocks, on the other hand, have increased by **over 107%** during that same 4-year period (or nearly **18% annualized**, including dividend re-investment)!

So stocks have gone up by 107% when earnings have increased by only 53%.

The graph below makes the disparity even more clear – and reveals that **the "disconnect" has been most pronounced since about 10/1/2011.**

I've highlighted the last 4 years using thicker lines. You can see steadily rising profits, or "earnings" (depicted by the thick blue line). You can also see a skyrocketing stock market – especially in the 2 years 9 months since about 10/1/2011 (depicted by the red line).

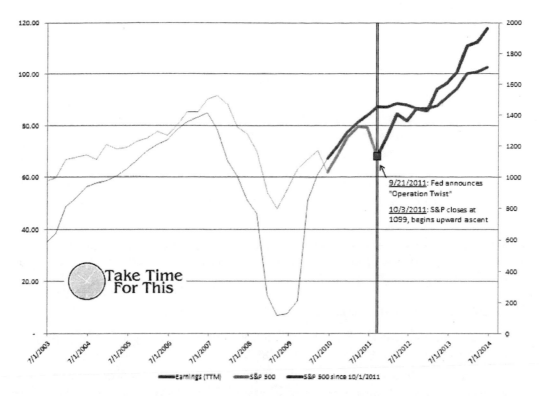

9/21/2011: Fed announces "Operation Twist"

10/3/2011: S&P closes at 1099, begins upward ascent

Take Time For This

Earnings (TTM)   S&P 500   S&P 500 since 10/1/2011

Since 10/1/2011, earnings have increased by about 17.8% (or about a 6.2% annualized compound rate). Stock returns in the same 33-month period have totaled 89.4% (or about 26.1% annualized compound rate, including dividends).***

Sometime in 2011 – which was coincidentally (?) the last time the stock market has experienced any volatility at all – **the normally similar "shape" of the "earnings" line and the "stock market" line *separated*?** Actually, the "shapes" of the lines diverged in the Spring and Summer of 2011, as the markets took a tumble that coincided with the end of the Federal Reserve's (Fed's) so-called "QE2" money-printing program. Then, just after the Fed announced another program known as "Operation Twist" (on 9/21/2011), the stock market took off, departing from the earnings line in a significant way. Earnings have risen… but the stock market has accelerated into the stratosphere!

It could be that the stock market is *predicting* higher earnings over the next few quarters… and indeed, analysts project accelerating earnings growth later this year. From my vantage point, though, additional factors certainly appear to be in play.

What's the "mystery booster"?

For a clue about the "mystery booster" that has propelled stocks since 2011, consider what the Fed's "Operation Twist" was all about. In a nutshell, the Fed began buying longer-term bonds and securities *in an effort to keep interest rates low* (…in an effort to stimulate the economy).

How do you suppose investors reacted to these Fed-induced low interest rates?

The answer seems to be that investors finally began shifting money away from low-interest-rate bonds and into – you guessed it – the stock market... thus driving stock prices higher & higher. (Note: Fund flows data suggests this migration from bonds to stocks shifted into overdrive in 2013, but with a particularly heavy flow going into foreign-stock investments... which wouldn't affect the S&P 500, which is an index of U.S. stocks; interesting).

The "mystery booster," in my view, has really been investors' willingness to continue buying more and more stocks – at higher & higher prices.

Of course, in my view, the Fed's actions have heavily influenced those investor behaviors. So credit a major "assist" to the Fed for today's stock prices that are now ahead of earnings, and probably ahead of where prices should be given the underlying fundamentals of the economy.

Wall Street VS Main Street

Call it the **'Derek Smalls Recovery'**, named after the Spinal Tap bass player in the famed mockumentary who strove to be "kind of like lukewarm water."

It's a time in which consumers and companies cut back on spending rather than make investments, where technology leaders fail to innovate and deflation and increased regulation become ever-larger threats.

It all adds up to a world where Wall Street and the owners of capital boom while Main Street and the workers struggle.

The greatest risk of all is that Wall Street excesses rather than Main Street recovery forces the Fed to tighten. More than five years after the global financial crisis it's still a 'lukewarm' recovery. The 'fire' of zero interest rates and central bank liquidity continues to be doused by the 'ice' of de-leveraging, regulation and deflationary tech innovation. Meanwhile Wall Street booms.

Indeed, signs continue of an uneven recovery.

For the first time in three years, nonfarm payrolls growth has topped 200,000 for five-straight months. Yet consumer confidence continues to meander, even dipping slightly in June as those in the lower income brackets feel pinched.

Economists are pushing hard on the belief that gross domestic product gains will improve dramatically for the rest of the year after the first-quarter's 1 percent drop—a number that Goldman Sachs predicts would be revised to a -1.8 percent by the time all is said and done.

It may be worth noting that during the past five years, nominal GDP growth has been just 19 percent compared with the 45 percent that has been typical in recoveries.

Meanwhile; the stock market booms, with S&P 500 up 190 % from the lows it hit in March 2009, thanks largely to easy Federal Reserve policy that remains vigorous even as it continues to unwind.

The longer it takes for growth and rates to normalize, the greater the risk of speculative excesses and ultimately a policy response aimed at curbing speculation in asset markets before the economy has fully healed.

Reference may be made to David Bowie's 1974 post-apocalyptic album **"Diamond Dogs."**

The recovery in U.S. employment is now one of the longest labor market expansions since the war.

That expansion started from a dreadful base, thanks to the recession that followed the 2008 financial crisis. But at last the unemployment rate, at 6.1 %, has dipped below its peak from the previous cycle, a decade ago. The number of new jobs has exceeded 200,000 for the fifth month in succession, the longest streak of this recovery.

The recovery has been slower than many wished, and has tested Americans' tolerance for economic pain. But the signs of approaching normality can no longer be ignored.

But when it comes to investment, not all are celebrating. US stocks have rallied, with only one brief interruption in the summer of 2011, ever since the crisis hit rock bottom in early 2009. Wall Street has been wildly out of sync with Main Street.

The Dow Jones Industrial Average, an outdated measure that still commands much attention, has topped 17,000 for the first time; the S&P 500, now the world's most widely followed index, is closing in on 2,000. Volatility, as measured by the VIX index, is at a seven-year low.

But they face a difficult question. As Main Street finally tastes recovery, where does Wall Street stand? It is the way of the economic cycle that growth prompts rate rises as central banks try to avert overheating. Rates are historically low and have offered critical support to stocks.

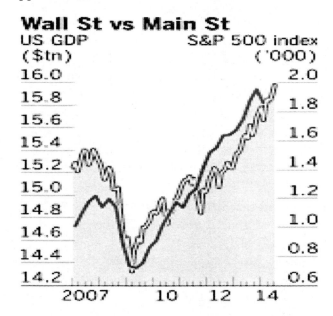

While the economy trundled on anemically, things were great for stock investors. Companies were able to generate profits but conditions were too weak to provoke higher rates from the Fed. Cuts in growth estimates this year as a bad US winter drove a contraction in the economy, helped to ensure that the Fed talked down the possibility of rate rises, pushed bond yields down – and propelled the stock market further.

Now, optimists for the economy expect that rates will rise, and so stocks will at last run into trouble. Some such as Jim Paulsen, chief equity strategist for Wells Capital and an inveterate bull warn that wage inflation is picking up. Non-supervisory wage inflation is now 2.5 %, above the Fed's target of 2 % for the headline consumer price index. How, he asks, would the Fed respond to a pick up in inflation to 3 %?

He remains a "bull" in that he has confidence that the economic recovery is real and that we are at the start of a more normal economic cycle. But this bullishness means that he is braced for an imminent sell-off, as confusion over the Fed's response breeds uncertainty and volatility.

It is a given that the Fed will make a mistake – perfectly judging a retreat from these exceptional policies is not possible. But will it make a hawkish error, and raise rates too soon, or a dovish error, and raise them too late?

Following the lesson of 1937, when the Fed raised too early and triggered a second leg to the Great Depression, many assume that the Fed would carry on too long. Janet Yellen, the Fed chairwoman, appeared to confirm this recently when she dismissed an uptick in inflation as "noise".

Such expectations are embedded in markets. So a hawkish mistake could be nastier, as it would come as a greater surprise. Even a hint of one could push stocks down – as shown last year by the sell-off in emerging market stocks when the Fed talked about "tapering off" its stimulus.

And any Fed move must be refracted through the bond market. In all seven periods of Fed tightening since the war, Treasury yields started to rise an average of seven months ahead of the first rate rise. So if the Fed starts tightening early next year, Treasury yields should begin their decisive ascent very soon.

That is what the bulls will worry about over their summer barbecues. Meanwhile, bears think the Fed is more likely to make a dovish mistake, that the market rally has only ever been about assistance from the Fed, and that the economy is still weak. They suspect the market will instead surge into a "melt-up," sucking in all those who have held out so far – before crashing when the Fed realizes its mistake and raises rates far faster than it wants, in a bid to head off inflation.

Years without any 5 per cent S&P corrections are rare. 1995 is the only one since 1970. With several indicators showing growing optimism among investors – the risk of a 10-15% correction in stock prices over the next few weeks has increased dramatically.

On the positive side, an earlier correction in asset prices would be healthier than a continued rally and a later crash.

I belong to the former correction and believe a short-term correction in stock prices is clearly on the cards.

Where does the 'Market Cap to GDP' or 'Buffett Valuation Indicator' stand currently?

Market Cap to GDP is a long-term valuation indicator that has become popular in recent years, thanks to Warren Buffett. Back in 2001 he remarked in a Fortune Magazine interview that "it is probably the best single measure of where valuations stand at any given moment."

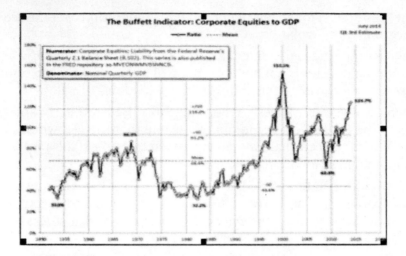

Here is a more transparent alternate snapshot over a shorter timeframe using the Wilshire 5000 Full Cap Price Index divided by GDP. I've used the FRED data for the stock index numerator (WILL5000PRFC).

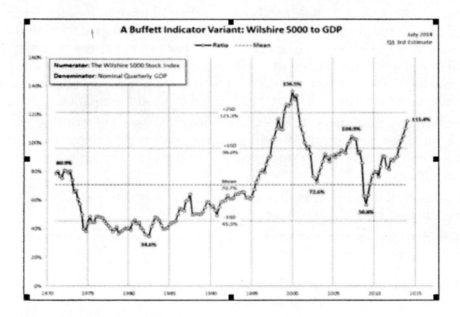

How Well do the Two Views Match?

The first of the two charts above appears to show a significantly greater overvaluation. Here are the two versions side-by-side. The one on the left shows the latest valuation over two standard deviations (SD) above the mean. The other one is noticeably lower. Why does one look so much more expensive than the other? One uses Fed data back to the middle of the last century for the numerator, the other uses the Wilshire 5000, the data for which only goes back to 1971. The Wilshire is the more familiar numerator, but the Fed data gives us a longer timeframe. And those early decades, when the ratio was substantially lower, have definitely impacted the mean and SDs.

To illustrate my point, here is an overlay of the two versions over the same timeframe. The one with the Fed numerator has a tad more upside volatility, but they're singing pretty much in harmony.

What Do These Charts Tell Us?

In a CNBC interview earlier this spring CNBC interview (April 23rd), Warren Buffett expressed his view that stocks aren't "too frothy". However, both the "Buffett Index" and the Wilshire 5000 variant suggest that today's market is indeed at lofty valuations, now above the housing-bubble peak in 2007. In fact, the more timely of the two (Wilshire / GDP) has risen for eight consecutive quarters and is now approaching two standard deviations above its mean -- a level exceeded for six quarters during the dot.com bubble.

Wouldn't GNP Give a More Accurate Picture?

Here is the same calculation with Gross National Product as the denominator; the two versions differ very little from their Gross Domestic Product counterparts.

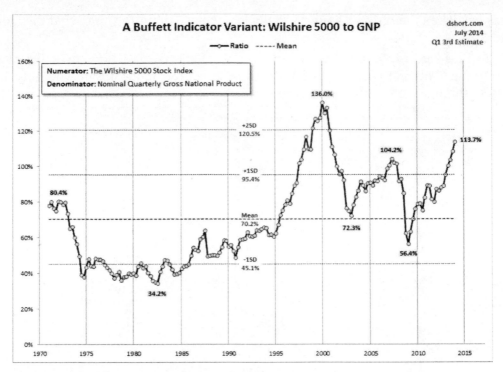

Here is an overlay of the two GNP versions -- again, very similar.

Estimating Stock Market Returns to 2020 and Beyond: Update

Will the bull market continue?

From the real price of the S&P-Composite with dividends re-invested (S&P-real) one finds that the best fit line from January 1871 onward is a straight line when plotted to a semi-log scale. There is no reason to believe that this long-term trend of S&P-real will be interrupted. S&P-real and the best fit line together with its prediction band are shown in Figure-1, updated to Jun-2014. (See appendix A for the equations.)

Also shown is the Cyclically Adjusted Price to Earnings Ratio P/E5 (which is the real price of the S&P divided by the average of the real earnings over the preceding 5 years), it is currently at a level of 23.9, down from Jan-2014 level of 26.1.

One observes that whenever S&P-real "bounced-off" the lower extreme of the prediction band and P/E5 moved from below to above 13.4 a bull market always followed. The last time this occurred was in March 2009. Since then S&P-real has "only" gained about 150%. Comparing this to previous post-bounce-off-gains (which ranged from 300% to 1720%) then the possibility exists of further gains to come.

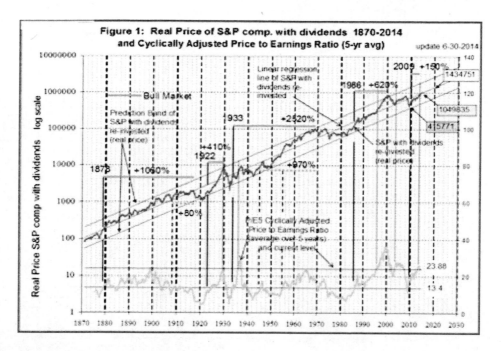

Figure 1: Real Price of S&P comp. with dividends 1870-2014 and Cyclically Adjusted Price to Earnings Ratio (5-yr avg)

What gains (if any) can we expect?

Extending the best fit line and the prediction band to 2020 provides a glimpse into the future which enables us to estimate the change of S&P-real from the current level of about 1,049,835. In 2020, the value of S&P-real as indicated by the best fit line is about 1,430,000, while the lowest and highest values shown by the prediction band are 740,000 and 2,770,000, respectively.

Thus the historic trend forecasts a probable gain of about 35% for S&P-real over the next five years. The worst scenario would be a possible loss of about 30%, and the best outcome would be a 160% increase.

What other analysts expected

Commentators, such as Butler|Philbrick and Hussman warned us in December 2011 that the markets then were expensive and overbought, and that one could only expect very low returns going forward over periods as long as 20 years. Figure-2 shows the current situation in more detail and also includes the levels of S&P-real as per Butler|Philbrick (B|P) forecast, indicated by the red markers connected by the dashed red line.

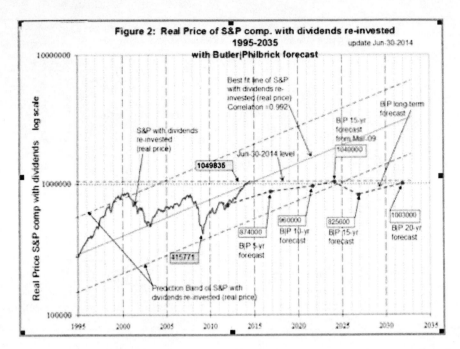

Figure 2: Real Price of S&P comp. with dividends re-invested 1995-2035 with Butler|Philbrick forecast

From December 2011 onward B|P predicted a real annual return for the stock market of only 1.46% for 15 years, and 2.08% for 20 years (Appendix B below). Also they forecasted a 6.48% annual return from Mar-2009 to Mar-2024. One can see that the March 2024 level is quite possible as it is just above the lower extreme of the prediction band, but it would appear that the December 2026 and 2031 forecasts are overly pessimistic.

One can see from Figure-2 that the current level of SP-real is already higher than all the forecast levels. This shows that long-term forecasts are unreliable and it would be better for financial experts to predict a range for returns than absolute values. However, the forecasts should not be discarded lightly.

Is the market overvalued?

One observes from Figure-1 that presently S&P-real is where it should be; its level still borders on its long-time historic trend line.

The P/E5 is at a high level of 23.9 but it is lower than the Jan-2014 level of 26.1. The relatively high level may indicate an overvalued market, and the graph of P/E5 has also now a downward slope. Similar conditions prevailed only four times in the past: in 1929, 1937, 2002 and 2008. Only after one occasion, in 2002, was it followed by a continuous market advance. However, at that time the S&P-real had been declining for several years from the upper extreme of its prediction band. At the three other occasions the S&P-real had previously peaked, and the market continued to decline for several years thereafter.

Long-term investors should also heed Shiller's Dec-2013 warning, and consider the high level of the Shiller P/E10 ratio, currently at 26.5. He states that the plot of P/E10 "confirms that ......Long-term investors would be well advised, individually, to lower their exposure to the stock market when it is high, and get into the market when it is low." The plot shows that for a P/E10 of 25 one can expect a 10-year annualized return of between -5% and +5%. So caution is certainly indicated and one should consider market-timing models, on which my book is premised, to time one's exposure to the stock market.

Appendix A

The best fit line and prediction band were calculated using statistical software from PSI-Plot. There were 1699 data points from Jan-1871 to July-2012. The SP-real values for the period after July-2012 are "out of sample" and were not included in the regression analysis.

The equation of the best fit line is $y = 10^{(ax+b)}$.

y = is the dependent variable of the best fit line. x = are the number of months from January 1871 onwards. a = 0.0023112648 b = 2.02423522

The Pearson correlation coefficient is 0.992. This number is most appropriately applied to linear regression as an indication of how closely the two variables approximate a linear relationship to each other. A perfect fit would have a correlation coefficient of 1.000.

The equation of the upper and lower extremes of the prediction band is $y = 10^{(ax+b)}$ with parameters 'y', 'x', and 'a' as before, but with

$b = 2.31005634$ for the upper extreme line, and $b = 1.73841411$ for the lower extreme line of the prediction band.

Appendix B

Butler|Philbrick real returns forecast for the stock market from December 2011.

Source: Butler|Philbrick & Associates

Investment Horizon	20-Years	15 Years	10-Years	5-Years
Forecast Real Returns	2.08%	1.46%	3.75%	5.64%

Financial Implications of FIFA World Cup victory: Buy Brazil?

Christ, the Redeemer

Christ the Redeemer is an Art Deco **statue** of Jesus **Christ** in Rio de Janeiro, Brazil. It was considered the largest **Christ statue** in the world from 1931 until 2010 when it was topped by the **Christ** the King **statue** in Poland. It is 30 metres (98 ft) tall, not including its 8 metres (26 ft) pedestal, and its arms stretch 28 metres (92 ft) wide.

The **statue** weighs 635 tonnes (625 long, 700 short tons), and is located at the peak of the 700-metre (2,300 ft) Corcovado mountain in the Tijuca Forest National Park overlooking the city. A symbol of Brazilian Christianity, the **statue** has become an icon for Rio de Janeiro and Brazil. It is made of reinforced concrete and soapstone, and was constructed between 1922 and 1931.

According to Goldman Sachs model, Brazil was the overwhelming favorite to win the FIFA football World Cup.

Goldman looked at history of football—40,000 observations and various other parameters beginning 1960. They noted goals scored each time against the opposition and weighted it with the most recent performance. Using Probability analysis, they obtained a distribution which is reflected in the chart below:

Of course, their model was a pretty dynamic one and kept changing as the tournament progressed.

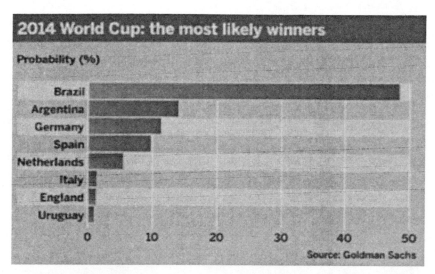

And according to Goldman research, in the short term, the country's stock markets stood to some advantage.

If Brazil had won; in my opinion, other than the very short-term positive effect, playing host to the tournament would not necessarily have boosted the winning country's economy or its shares.

The World Cup would not have made it for Brazil, as had not been the case for South Africa or others before. One learns from experience that the boost from World Cups and Olympic games is relatively limited.

The boost to Brazil's gross domestic product (GDP) this year will add up to less than half a percentage point, leading to a total economic growth forecast of 1.5 percent.

Surely, playing host will boost the tourism sector. But tourism is a small share of GDP in Brazil, unfortunately

A woman chooses from colored garlands, some of which are in the colors of World Cup football team national flags, amongst German flags

One could have expected a boost in consumption if Brazil wins the World Cup.

Now that Brazil has not succeeded in winning the World Cup, we might even see a worsening of the current situation--declining consumption has been behind the country's very poor economic data over the past year or so.

Hosting the World Cup brings with it higher inflation, higher labor costs and all kinds of other things, which is exactly what Brazil didn't need at this point.

Brazil's Bovespa index has recovered around 7 percent so far this year, after falling over 15 percent last year. Brazil's stock market is expensive, offering a risk premium of only 0.7 percent, below its average of 2.3 percent.

While the country offers positives from a 200 million populations, ample farmland and water as well as self-sufficiently on food and fuel, investors don't like the government intervention into business. They don't like the history of hyperinflation and what they really don't like is the expectation that the economy is going to grow 1.7 % this year and 2 % next year.

All roads seemed to lead to Brazil winning the World Cup. Home advantage, past record, and form were but a few of the tailwinds.

Financial markets as a predictor of Germany's football win over Brazil

A Brazil fan looks dejected following the 2014 FIFA World Cup Brazil Semi Final match between Brazil and Germany.

Brazil suffered a crushing 7-1 defeat to Germany in the World Cup semi-final on July 8, but the Germans haven't only been thrashing the Brazilians on the football pitch.

Germany's equity, currency and government bond markets have long been trumping the beleaguered Latin American country, which now has a World Cup defeat to contend with on top of its economic woes.

To illustrate this trend, I divided the **Brazilian Bovespa's** daily close over the past five years by the **German Dax's** daily close. A higher number therefore reflected stronger performance for Brazilian stocks and a lower number illustrates

German stock market strength. Since 2010, the ratio of the Brazilian Bovespa to that of the DAX has fallen from 12 times to now stand at 5.4 times.

Also, just comparing performances between both markets over the last five years is telling enough. The Dax has risen 79 % in the period, while the Bovespa declined 5 %.

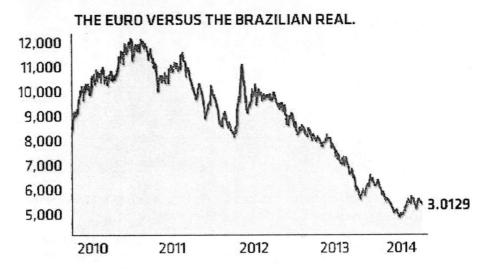

THE EURO VERSUS THE BRAZILIAN REAL.

On the currency front, Germany's **euro** currency has vastly outperformed the **Brazilian real** as well.

Euro-real has come off a touch of late, but is still up 40 percent from the 2010 low. The Brazilian real may have seen renewed strength in recent months after the Brazilian central bank took steps to shore up losses following the heavy sell off in the emerging market rout earlier this year, but the currency still is still down 11 percent against the U.S. dollar over the past five years.

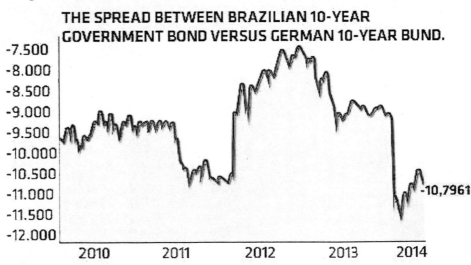

THE SPREAD BETWEEN BRAZILIAN 10-YEAR GOVERNMENT BOND VERSUS GERMAN 10-YEAR BUND.

Meanwhile, comparing the performances of the German and Brazilian government bond market also offers striking disparity.

German 10-year government bond yields have seen a dramatic fall to 1.21 percent from 1.91 percent over the past six months, as geopolitical tensions in Iraq and Ukraine fueled demand for safe haven assets.

By contrast, Brazilian government bonds are yielding over 12 percent. Brazil's economic growth plummeted to 2.3 percent in 2013, down from 7.5 percent in 2010.

Lower yields reflect higher prices and investor demand in the fixed income market.

Thus, clues as to who would win the Brazil-Germany football encounter could best have been traced to the two countries financial markets' performance themselves.

Why oil is on the boil, yet again

Iraq has become an important swing player with big promise in the global energy market, and the widening conflict has experts worried any supply disruptions could lead to a sharp oil price spike.

The outbreak of violence in Iraq in recent weeks, which has led to hard-line Islamic militants getting closer and closer to its capital Baghdad, has "rekindled market concerns," according to the International Energy Agency.

Fighting in the country has intensified this week, with the Islamic State of Iraq and al-Sham (Isis), a breakaway group from al-Qaeda, making further inroads into Iraqi Kurdistan, the autonomous region in the north of the country, and even approaching its capital.

This has sent the price of oil soaring to new highs for the year. This had been set to be Iraq's best year for oil production in three decades, but that now looks under threat.

Iraq is projected to provide roughly 60 % of the growth in crude production capacity for Organisation of Petroleum Exporting Countries (OPEC) for the rest of this decade, according to the oil cartel.

If the situation is contained, the impact on the price of oil may be relatively muted, according to the IEA. Production from the north has been off the market since early March due to the earlier violence in the west of the country, and disruption to the region's ability to get its oil to the market via Turkey. Supply had been on the rise from the south of the country, however.

There is now an elevated risk of opportunistic combined armed attacks by ISIL targeting energy assets in southern provinces, particularly given their presence in northern Babil province overlooking Highways 1 and 8, two of the three main highways connecting Baghdad and Basra.

Iraq itself is a relatively small part of the OPEC output, and other oil exporters could potentially meet any losses from its supply. However, there are also concerns that heightened risk in Iraq could further destabilize the rest of the region.

Perception of heightened political risk in North Africa and the Middle East and chronic disruptions in Libyan exports have been a feature of the market for some time, but so far have been largely offset by record growth in non-OPEC supply.

As violence in Iraq has escalated, oil futures climbed to $106 per barrel -- a 2% increase and the highest level since September 2013.

The price of gas typically rises about 2 to 2.5 cents per gallon for every dollar that crude rises.

If oil prices keep heading higher that could translate into a jump of more than 20 cents at the pump within the next couple weeks— currently, the US national average of gasoline is $3.65 per gallon.

The issue is supply: The market is already missing Libyan oil, and the market has been able to compensate -- but now if you add in a loss of Iraqi exports, that is certainly a concern and should logically push oil prices higher.

One needs to be cautious about the threshold of $4, which can spark outrage, malaise, and a bit of demand destruction.

Iraq produces about 3.3 million barrels a day, and so far the only reported disruption is the flow of oil through the 600,000 barrel Kirkuk-Ceyhan pipeline, which runs from Kirkuk to Turkey. The Kirkuk fields produce about 400,000 to 500,000 barrels a day, while the major fields in the Basra area produce about 2.6 to 2.7 million barrels a day.

If it spreads to the south or threatens the south, I think the anxiety is going to be reflected in the oil market--the recovery of Iraq was kind of key to the future of the world oil market.

Iraq is one of the largest sources of growth for the global oil market going into the future. U.S. oil production is more than double Iraq's, but it is expected to plateau by early to mid 2020s, while Iraq has the potential to add about 200,000 a year into 2040.

Although OPEC is producing 30 million barrels a day, supply disruptions in other parts of the world make Iraq's growing production all the more important. Increasing U.S. oil production also has helped offset the loss of oil from places like Iran and Libya, and it has risen to 8.5 million barrels a day, up 1.2 million barrels in just the last year.

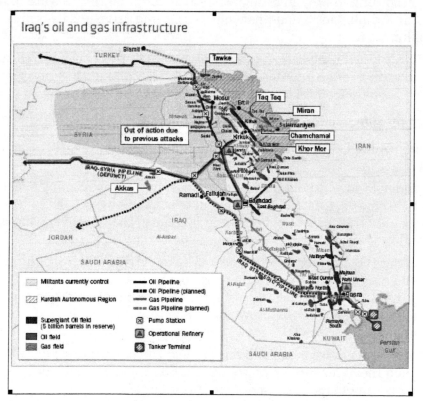

The U.S. imports about 300,000 barrels of Iraqi crude a day or about 4 percent of total imports.

That loss of Iraqi oil directly, you could argue is not going to have much of an impact on the U.S. but the fact that 2 million barrels of Iraqi oil is going to Europe and Asia means world supply could tighten.

If the violence were to spread to the south and disrupt even a half million barrels of production, on top of the 1 million lost from Libya and oil lost from Iraq, it would jolt the oil market.

You could easily see oil prices jumping $20 a barrel if we lose a significant amount of Iraqi oil.

The quick moves by Islamist militants ISIS, a Sunni group known as the Islamic State of Iraq and Syria, has put the Shiite-led government of Prime Minister Nouiri al-Maliki at risk of collapse if it does not get assistance.

Iran has sent fighters into Iraq to help its government, and Francona said the two countries have been much more closely allied since Maliki was elected.

If Iraq were split along sectarian lines, with Shiites controlling the southern region, and the Sunnis holding central areas, and Kurds holding the north, the oil riches would be disproportionately split with the Shiites holding most of it.

The southern part of Iraq has the most promise for expanding production since the five super giant fields in the south account for 60 percent of the country's proven reserves. According to EIA, an estimated 17 percent of oil reserves are in the north of Iraq, near Kirkuk, Mosul and Khanaqin. It said Iraq estimates its proven reserves at 141 billion barrels.

The Kurdistan Regional Government area contains about 4 billion of proven reserves according to the International Energy Agency, though EIA says KRG reports that number could be tenfold.

Gold went up $50 on June 17, 2014 and the big rally is yet to come

Gold bullion rallied just under $50.00 an ounce on June 17, 2014 and nobody expected it.

Let's understand why gold is smiling bright. Inflation is becoming a real problem in America. Years ago, I started writing about how all this money the Federal Reserve is creating out of thin air would become inflationary. That's exactly what is starting to happen now.

Why is the Fed starting to pull back on its money printing operation with the goal of being out of the money printing business by the end of this year? Why is the Fed telling us that after keeping interest rates near zero for years, by the end of next year, the federal funds rate will move up to 1.13% and by the end of the following year, it will move to 2.5%?

In my opinion, we are being told this because the powers that be see inflation in the cards, and they are working on trying to curb rapid inflation before it happens. And if there is something gold thrives on, it is inflation.

The Bureau of Labor Statistics reports prices in the U.S. economy increased by 0.4% in May after increasing 0.3% in April. *(Source: **Bureau of Labor Statistics, June 17, 2014.**)* This increase in the Consumer Price Index (CPI) was the biggest since February of 2013.

With this rise in prices, inflation in the past 12 months was 2.1%. If we assume that going forward, the new monthly norm for inflation will be 0.3%–0.4%, then in the next 12 months, we are looking at inflation of 3.6%–4.8%. Gold loves inflation, plain and simple!

The more there is of a currency in a financial system, the higher the chances of inflation; and the velocity of money is a big part of that.

Without getting too technical, the velocity of money is simply how many times one dollar is used in an economy. And the more that dollar is used, the greater the chance of inflation.

As it stands, we see the velocity of money is sitting at its lowest level ever recorded. In the first quarter of 2014, velocity of money in the U.S. economy was 1.4. This means one dollar was used only 1.4 times. Back in the 1980s, the velocity of money was 3.0. *(Source: Federal Reserve Bank of St. Louis web site, last accessed June 17, 2014.)*

Why has the velocity of money been so low? When the Federal Reserve started printing money in 2009 and giving it to the big banks in hopes they would lend it out to customers, the banks (being too worried about the U.S. economy) didn't lend the money out. Instead, they took the money and bought safe government bonds.

But finally, after five years, banks are loosening up and lending again. Last month, commercial and industrial loans at all commercial banks in the U.S. economy stood at $1.69 trillion. This was the highest amount in years. *(Source: Federal Reserve Bank of St. Louis web site, last accessed June 17, 2014.)*

As the banks start lending, the velocity of money increases and that just brings more inflation.

I have said it many times before: inflation in the U.S. economy is going to be a major problem. And after roughly five years, inflation is picking up. The perfect inflation storm is brewing up as even the velocity of money picks up.

Gold is the best hedge against inflation. That's why it's an important part of any investment portfolio. And those gold mining stocks...they are still looking very cheap.

Oil and El Nino could be the party pooper for high-flying Indian stocks

Emerging economies such as India, which is a net oil importer, and continues to face the malaise of sticky inflation, could be impacted in the short-term by oil prices shooting up, thanks to the Iraq conflict.

Higher oil prices coupled with higher food prices, thanks to the El Nino Effect, which the IMD (Indian Meteoroligical Department) which has a 70% chance of occurring in July or early August.

IMD expects below-normal precipitation for the June to September period at 93% of the long-period average.

This comes at a wrong time for Indian stock markets, which were hoping for stable or lower interest rates to revive growth.

Higher inflation and higher interest rates could just be the recipe for a sudden and 15% correction in Indian stocks, which have been among the best performing global stock markets thanks to a reformist pro-growth government led by Narendra Modi taking charge at the centre.

Onion prices could bring tears in the eyes of Indian stock markets

An eye-watering rise in the price of onions has contributed to an unexpected surge in Indian inflation that could along with high crude and other food prices rattle the country's financial markets in the near term.

Onion prices have shot up 40% in the last two weeks to Rs 18.50 per kg at Lasalgaon, the country's largest wholesale market for the edible bulb, despite the imposition of minimum export price on the vegetable to check its domestic rates from going up.

Prices have increased due to speculation amid anticipation of weak monsoon affecting Kharif (summer-sown) crops.

On June 17, 2014; the Centre had imposed a minimum export price (MEP) of USD 300 per tonne on onion to curb overseas sales and control rising retail prices.

Onion prices have gone up purely on anticipation of drought as there has not been any decline in the supplies.

About 39 lakh tonnes of rabi onion is stored in the country but that may not be sufficient if Kharif crop gets affected on account of deficient monsoon.

The Indian Met department has predicted a below normal monsoon this year, posing threat to Kharif crops including rice. Monsoon rains are the key for the farm sector as about 40 per of agriculture land is irrigated through rain water.

The domestic demand during the lean period from June to November is met through stored rabi (winter) crops and fresh kharif (summer) crops.

Onion production is estimated to have risen to 192 lakh tonne during 2013-14 crop year (July-June), from 168 lakh tonne in 2012-13. Exports meanwhile fell to 13.58 lakh tonnes last fiscal from 18.22 lakh tonnes in 2012-13.

Onion is predominantly a rabi crop grown throughout India. During the kharif season it is grown mainly in Maharashtra, Karnataka, Gujarat and Andhra Pradesh.

India produces about 15m tonnes of onions a year, and the vegetable is regarded as an essential part of almost every meal.

Onion shortages have been credited with bringing down two Indian governments since 1980, and ministers usually try to avert price spikes and the ensuing public anger by outlawing hoarding and hurriedly approving imports, even from India's regional rival Pakistan.

It's obviously something that could have political implications given that you can't make a good curry without onions.

Although the poor monsoons are to blame, underlying problems include bad roads and the country's poor infrastructure for storage and distribution of fresh produce.

What has been a key concern for a long time now is that [the] rise in food prices continues to contribute strongly to overall inflation. It is therefore imperative that structural factors affecting food inflation are addressed on a priority basis.

Increased inflation makes it less likely that the Reserve Bank of India, under its governor Raghuram Rajan, will contemplate lowering interest rates any time soon.

Rising wholesale price inflation will take rate cuts off the agenda until well into next year. Policy makers also cannot ignore the elevated level of consumer price inflation.

WPI, which is consistently on the rise, is used by Indian officials as the "headline" inflation rate; although policy makers have begun to accept that the consumer price index is a more realistic measure that reflects what Indians actually experience in the market.

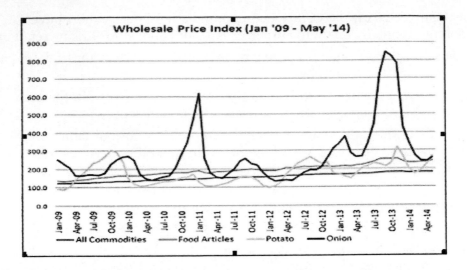

India's annual rate of inflation, based on its monthly Wholesale Price Index, climbed to 6.01 per cent for the month of May 2014, as against 5.20 per cent for the previous month and 4.58 per cent during the corresponding month of the previous year, setting off alarm bells among the ruling establishment.

The official WPI for 'all commodities' for the month of May rose by 0.8 percent to 181.7, from 180.2 in the previous month.

I found it curious that while the onion and potato indices are parallel at most times, sharp surges in the former are not extended to the latter.

We found it curious that while the onion and potato indices are parallel at most times, sharp surges in the former are not extended to the latter.

Monthly Wholesale Price Index
(Base Year: 2004-05 = 100)

	All Comm.	Food Art.	Potato	Onion
Apr-04	97.5	97.5	78.7	107.8
May-04	98.0	98.5	98.9	97.6
Jun-04	98.3	98.8	107.3	94.2
Jul-04	99.2	100.7	110.4	98.7
Aug-04	100.6	103.0	125.3	106.6
Sep-04	100.5	101.1	126.8	108.2
Oct-04	100.7	102.4	130.0	107.5
Nov-04	101.5	105.2	116.5	108.0
Dec-04	100.5	99.4	79.8	92.3
Jan-05	101.0	97.7	73.5	96.6
Feb-05	101.1	97.6	72.0	94.5
Mar-05	101.4	97.9	77.7	88.0
Apr-05	102.7	100.4	99.9	85.3
May-05	102.5	100.3	109.8	83.3
Jun-05	102.9	102.3	116.5	84.0
Jul-05	104.0	106.5	121.1	97.5
Aug-05	104.1	106.2	116.4	122.0
Sep-05	104.9	106.7	109.2	172.4
Oct-05	105.4	109.0	118.2	209.5
Nov-05	105.5	109.9	149.9	222.6
Dec-05	104.9	105.5	137.3	163.4
Jan-06	105.4	106.7	126.9	113.4
Feb-06	105.6	106.1	103.9	85.9
Mar-06	105.7	105.0	113.0	80.1
Apr-06	107.8	106.4	116.6	75.0
May-06	108.7	108.3	128.6	79.0
Jun-06	109.9	111.8	146.5	84.9
Jul-06	110.8	112.2	148.8	89.4
Aug-06	111.5	114.9	146.6	95.1
Sep-06	112.2	118.1	157.8	101.1
Oct-06	112.7	119.8	180.4	103.0
Nov-06	112.6	119.9	180.0	109.8
Dec-06	112.2	117.8	113.8	122.0
Jan-07	112.4	118.9	85.1	174.8

Feb-07	112.6	119.2	84.8	189.5
Mar-07	112.8	118.9	102.1	167.2
Apr-07	114.5	121.5	115.3	138.7
May-07	114.7	122.3	133.7	130.9
Jun-07	114.8	121.8	150.4	155.5
Jul-07	115.7	124.8	164.1	186.1
Aug-07	116.0	126.1	169.4	209.9
Sep-07	116.0	125.5	169.9	255.5
Oct-07	116.3	126.0	176.5	260.4
Nov-07	116.8	125.2	174.2	230.5
Dec-07	116.7	121.6	153.3	179.8
Jan-08	117.5	119.9	131.5	120.5
Feb-08	119.0	122.5	114.1	114.0
Mar-08	121.5	125.6	109.8	114.4
Apr-08	123.5	128.9	102.7	113.3
May-08	124.1	130.2	104.0	107.8
Jun-08	127.3	130.3	106.9	126.5
Jul-08	128.6	133.4	117.3	144.1
Aug-08	128.9	134.4	118.9	170.3
Sep-08	128.5	135.8	127.0	169.1
Oct-08	128.7	140.3	128.2	171.4
Nov-08	126.9	141.1	128.5	211.9
Dec-08	124.5	136.3	105.6	227.9
Jan-09	124.4	137.2	92.7	252.8
Feb-09	123.3	134.1	88.5	230.4
Mar-09	123.5	135.6	103.2	207.5
Apr-09	125.0	140.1	143.5	164.5
May-09	125.9	141.8	172.2	163.6
Jun-09	126.8	145.0	199.8	171.0
Jul-09	128.2	150.4	232.7	170.8
Aug-09	129.6	153.7	244.5	166.8
Sep-09	130.3	154.7	268.7	178.3
Oct-09	131.0	157.8	303.6	227.7
Nov-09	132.9	164.7	293.6	251.2

Dec-09	133.4	164.6	240.1	268.2
Jan-10	135.2	164.9	149.3	270.4
Feb-10	135.2	163.4	121.5	247.8
Mar-10	136.3	163.6	105.4	171.3
Apr-10	138.6	168.8	110.3	148.0
May-10	139.1	172.1	118.1	139.0
Jun-10	139.8	175.4	125.3	150.2
Jul-10	141.0	178.2	133.7	158.0
Aug-10	141.1	176.7	133.3	164.7
Sep-10	142.0	179.9	139.3	204.8
Oct-10	142.9	180.9	153.3	278.4
Nov-10	143.8	181.4	154.7	343.7
Dec-10	146.0	189.4	171.5	469.3
Jan-11	148.0	192.4	128.7	619.4
Feb-11	148.1	181.3	108.3	260.6
Mar-11	149.5	179.0	106.9	179.1
Apr-11	152.1	186.8	109.1	156.9
May-11	152.4	186.3	118.2	150.3
Jun-11	153.1	188.8	125.9	174.4
Jul-11	154.2	192.8	143.1	200.9
Aug-11	154.9	193.7	154.8	244.8
Sep-11	156.2	197.2	159.2	257.6
Oct-11	157.0	199.3	154.9	231.3
Nov-11	157.4	196.5	140.3	222.9
Dec-11	157.3	190.9	110.8	180.1
Jan-12	158.7	191.1	98.9	151.0
Feb-12	159.3	192.4	105.9	133.8
Mar-12	161.0	197.1	126.6	136.0
Apr-12	163.5	207.2	173.8	139.6
May-12	163.9	206.1	203.5	138.2
Jun-12	164.7	209.4	232.8	157.9
Jul-12	165.8	212.4	247.9	180.7
Aug-12	167.3	211.8	264.3	194.1
Sep-12	168.8	213.1	242.7	194.0
Oct-12	168.5	212.7	231.0	210.2
Nov-12	168.8	213.8	235.5	259.8
Dec-12	168.8	211.2	175.1	311.2
Jan-13	170.3	214.7	171.2	340.0

Feb-13	170.9	215.4	159.0	377.8
Mar-13	170.1	214.1	146.6	286.6
Apr-13	171.3	219.8	172.7	266.4
May-13	171.4	223.1	206.1	268.5
Jun-13	173.2	230.9	213.3	339.1
Jul-13	175.5	238.5	232.7	445.3
Aug-13	179.0	252.4	224.0	723.1
Sep-13	180.7	252.9	212.9	845.6
Oct-13	180.7	251.7	231.4	826.7
Nov-13	181.5	255.9	317.9	782.4
Dec-13	179.6	240.2	267.5	430.4
Jan-14	179.0	233.7	198.6	341.6
Feb-14	179.5	232.5	171.3	273.9
Mar-14	180.3	234.6	192.6	243.6
Apr-14	180.2	238.8	227.2	240.4
May-14	181.7	244.3	270.9	260.9

Use India's 'Onion Approach' to make money in stocks

In India's retail market, onions are now trading around Rs 30 per kg up from Rs 20 per kg just a few weeks back.

How to Buy Stocks

I just wanted to illustrate a very important aspect of Behavioural **Finance.**

One did not look at Buying MORE Onions when the price touched Rs 80+. Families which purchased 2 kilos of onions purchased only 1.5 kilos or even lesser.

In fact one looked at alternative choices, like the hotels which served cucumbers or cabbage for onions.

When it comes to the Stock Markets it is the opposite

When the SENSEX touched a new high of 21000, everyone was queuing to buy stocks.

When the markets corrected a few weeks later, no one wanted to even look at buying the same stocks.

If one uses the **Onion approach** to buy Stocks, we will be very successful in creating Wealth in Equities.

Yet, Bullish on emerging markets

In 2014, EM is beginning to outperform the developed countries. EMs have a lot going for them, they have high growth, they have low government debt to Gross Domestic Product (GDP) and they have incredible increase in farm reserves.

Besides, if you look at the commercial banks in the US, in Europe, Japan and China, they have an awful lot of money on their balance sheets ready to be invested because the loan/deposit ratios of these banks are going down not up. So, I see a very bullish environment for EMs in general and India in particular.

Flows into Indian stock markets could easily double from here

Currently, there are limitations on how much foreigners can buy of Indian companies. There is a likelihood of the government reducing these limitations, which could easily double inflows into the Indian stock markets.

This could also force an increase in the weighting of the indices for Indian and of course an increase in weighting of the various emerging market indices would again force the various index funds, the ETFs to increase their weightings in India. This could cause a big flow of money going into India.

Besides, there is a lot of pressure on the Indian government to change the rules as regards to institutional investors having to reveal their underlying shareholders. I for one do not think the government should change these rules. There is already misuse of hot moneys coming though tax havens and this adds to the volatility in the Indian stock markets.

India figures high in the pecking order of EMs

Right now, China is at the top because China is going through a lot of very significant reforms but longer term, India has got to be at the top of the list simply because of the demographic advantage it enjoys.

India has a very regular pyramid shaped structure where there are lots of young people coming into the work force. That mean that going forward, India has the potential to outpace China in terms of growth. Of course, China cannot continue their very high growth rates because the base of the economy is so large, India is just beginning that process.

So, double digit GDP growth rates in India are certainly possible and this is going to start reflecting in exceptional Indian stock market performance.

Amazon ups its ante on India with $2bn investment

Amazon, the US *ecommerce* pioneer, is to invest an additional $2bn in its operations in India, highlighting the rising stakes in the country's small but fast-growing internet retailing market.

Amazon expects growth in India to be among the fastest it had seen in any of its markets.

At current scale and growth rates, India is on track to be the fastest country to a $1bn in gross sales according to Amazon's chief executive Jeff Bezos.

Amazon's India plans come a day after Flipkart, an eight-year-old Indian version of the US ecommerce company, said it had raised $1bn in fresh capital to upgrade its mobile technology platforms.

Analysts said the timing of the announcement reflected Amazon's intensifying rivalry with Flipkart, which is India's largest *internet retailer* by sales, and whose two youthful founders both began as Amazon employees.

Amazon launched its operations in India a year ago, and has since aggressively built its profile, with slick television advertisements and offers of guaranteed same-day delivery for customers in selected cities.

The US-based company is establishing five new warehouses to facilitate expansion of its same-day *delivery services*.

Indians are expected to buy about $2.3bn worth of merchandise over the internet this year, *accounting* for just 0.4 per cent of all retail sales. But with the expansion of modern brick-and-mortar retail chains stymied by high real estate costs and logistical difficulties, ecommerce is growing in importance and popularity, aided by the rapid growth of smartphone use in the country.

Merchandise sales over the internet in India will rise to $32bn, and about 3 per cent of all retail sales, within the next six years.

Companies such as Amazon, Flipkart and local rival Snapdeal, which is backed by eBay, are expanding and refining their operations as they compete for leadership in the huge potential market, though profitability appears to be some way off.

India's ecommerce moment

The online retail market in India is relatively tiny today — with $3.2 billion in sales estimated for this year — but it is ramping up quickly, with at least 50 percent year-over-year growth expected in each of the next four years. Here's what its growth looks like.

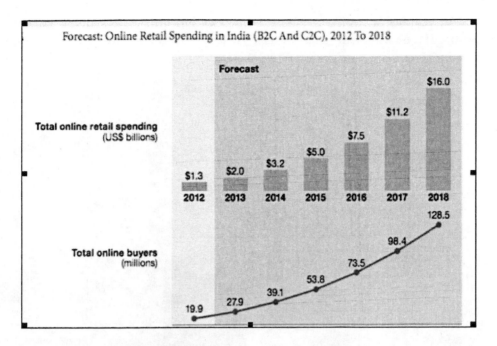

Source: Forrester Research

That growth in e-commerce sales is expected to be fueled in a big way by a boom in shopping on mobile devices. Snapdeal says that about 30 % of the company's gross sales were taking place via mobile phones. The number is expected to only grow as the pace of smartphone adoption increases in the country.

Despite a population about four times the size of the U.S., India still lags the U.S. in smartphone users. But as the chart below shows, that trend is expected to change considerably over the next five years. By 2016, India is slated to surpass the U.S. in smartphone users and tally about 50 million more smartphone owners than the U.S. by 2018. Here's a look at the country's coming smartphone boom.

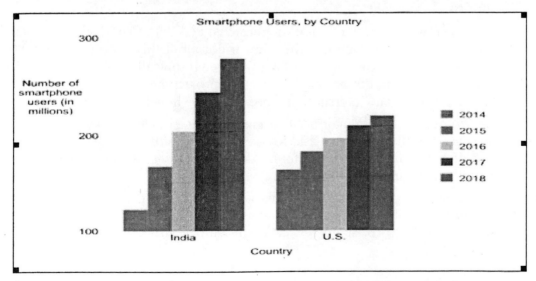

And, of course, in order to shop online, Indian consumers need an Internet connection. Here's a look at Internet user growth over the next five years compared to the U.S.

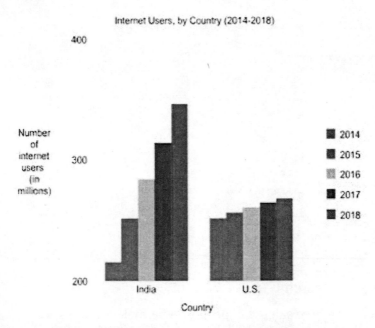

Internet Users, by Country (2014-2018)

India's e-commerce moment appears to be approaching. And Amazon, eBay and India's biggest homegrown sites are amassing war chests for the minds and wallets of the next great online retail market.

How Iraq insurrection changes the world of managing money

At the outset of this year, many alerted against a real risk of a fall in the oil price, which at that point had been stable for several years. Shale gas was entering the equation, while political problems across the Middle East stood to be resolved, easing pressure on supply.

The success of the insurrection in Iraq has changed that. Crude oil prices have surged to their highest in nine months. Most if not all of this bad news is now in the price; the rebels in Iraq are still a long way geographically from upsetting the country's oil production. But as Iraq is central to projections of rising oil supply in the next two decades, any interruption there would be hugely important.

So far, crude oil prices remain well within the range in which they have traded for some years. But the balance of risks for the future has shifted, with a sharp break to the upside far more likely than before. As with bond yields, this obliges equity investors to look again at their positioning.

At a sectoral or geographic level, this is not difficult. Russian stocks, out of favour thanks to political events, would stand to win. But beyond oil companies themselves, there are surprisingly few clear-cut winners from an oil spike.

Absolute Strategy Research says sectors that were in the past positively correlated by 50 per cent or more to the oil price include not only Russian or Norwegian stocks, but surprising names such as the Polish stock market (which, as measured by Datastream, has a 51 per cent correlation with the oil price).

The sector most negatively affected by an oil price spike is global retail, with a negative correlation of -72 per cent. High oil prices effectively act as an inhibiting tax on economic activity. Healthcare, telecoms, food and beverages and travel and leisure (affected via prices of airline fuel) are all negatively correlated by more than 60 per cent to the oil price.

Iraq supply shock may send Brent to $150

Brent crude oil may "spike" to $150 a barrel briefly if the conflict in Iraq hits operations at the main southern oil fields which supply export terminals on the Persian Gulf.

Such a supply shock could affect up to 2.6 million barrels a day in Iraqi oil exports. A disruption of that scale would trigger a coordinated release of strategic oil reserves by member states belonging to the International Energy Agency. Swing producer Saudi Arabia would also put more oil onto the market to mitigate the impact on the global economy.

Pump jacks and wells on the Monterey Shale formation in California

The more probable scenario is an "extended de facto sectarian civil war" in Iraq lasting one or two years creating "intermittent and moderate" supply disruptions of up to 500,000 barrels a day.

To date, Sunni militants have not yet built the military capability to push their advance south to threaten the strategically-critical oil fields which contain almost three-quarters of Iraq's reserves.

'Fear premium'

The bulk of supply comes from the South (80 percent) and the Kurdish-controlled north (12 percent), which is not yet at risk from ISIS's advances--- since the ISIS is not strong enough to move into these oil producing areas, Iraqi oil supply should largely be stable.

Nevertheless, the pot should continue to boil, with surprises still to the upside.

One cannot rule out the risk of attacks by Sunni militants using "unconventional" tactics including car or truck bomb attacks and sabotage. Such disruptions of up to half a million barrels a day could push Brent crude $10 higher to the $120-125 range.

Such a 'supply shock' I believe is very much possible over the next few months which could end up roiling global financial markets.

Style effects

So this suggests that anyone who believes the insurgents will drive on and threaten Iraqi oil production should short-sell consumer cyclicals. In other words, an oil spike would be fresh reason to stick with stocks that have already surprised the consensus by outperforming so far this year, on the back of falling bond yields.

Style effects are harder to deduce. Most recent rises in oil were driven by demand (and a strong economy) not supply. When oil price rises denote growth then the value style tends to work well (because value is in short supply). An Iraq oil shock would be different.

Therefore, the best bet is to focus on "quality" stocks, with strong profit margins that can withstand a battering from high oil prices. That entails going with stocks that had been punished for 18 months until the spring rotations.

With growth figures looking better than had been feared in the US, and the Bank of England hinting at raising rates sooner rather than later, many will be tempted to double down on their bet on higher bond yields. That would mean buying the cyclical stocks that would be most hurt by an oil price spike. Such a spike would be deflationary, leading to lower bond yields still, and to more money pouring in to utility stocks and high dividend-payers.

It is a nasty environment for managing money – even with stocks at all-time highs.

When will the US Fed raise rates

Last year, US bond yields rose rapidly after Ben Bernanke, the then Fed chairman, speculated about a possible "tapering off" of bond purchases. What ensued is now known as the "taper tantrum" as a group of emerging markets with high current account deficits (the "Fragile Five") saw their currencies come under attack.

With rates returning to normal in the US, traders no longer needed to take a risk on the higher yields on offer in the emerging world, and exited.

That episode ended when the Fed surprised everyone by not tapering in September. When the Fed eventually tapered in December, it had changed the mood music, trying to emphasise that higher rates were a long way off.

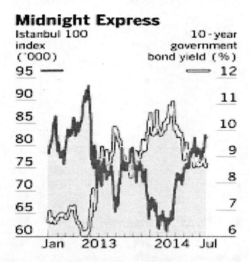

Midnight Express

What then happened in Turkey in January is instructive. The Turkish lira came under further pressure. To defend it, the central bank announced, at midnight, that it was more than doubling its core interest rates.

Then bond yields in the US started their steady drift down, and relieved the pressure. How has Turkey responded? Under political pressure, the bank has cut rates repeatedly, showing that the midnight hike was an aberration. That has been enough to push the Borsa Istanbul index up 44 per cent from its January low. It remains 24 per cent below its pre-taper tantrum high, but the effect has been dramatic. Thanks to falling US bond yields, the lira remains stronger than it was in January.

Federal Reserve officials publish their forecasts for the central bank's key interest rate on a chart known as the 'dot plot.' Below, we've highlighted the median forecast in orange. The predictions are going up, which means Fed officials think the interest rate will be higher in the coming years than previously thought.

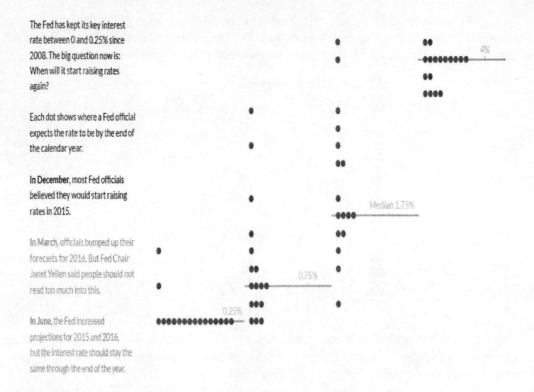

The Fed has kept its key interest rate between 0 and 0.25% since 2008. The big question now is: When will it start raising rates again?

Each dot shows where a Fed official expects the rate to be by the end of the calendar year.

In December, most Fed officials believed they would start raising rates in 2015.

In March, officials bumped up their forecasts for 2016. But Fed Chair Janet Yellen said people should not read too much into this.

In June, the Fed increased projections for 2015 and 2016, but the interest rate should stay the same through the end of the year.

Economic "Hope" vs. Indicators of Economic Reality

There is much hope that after a dismal Q1 GDP report of -1% annualized growth in the domestic economy, that Q2 will see a sharp rebound of between 3-4% according to the bulk of economists. The Federal Reserve is predicting that the U.S. economy will grow as strongly as 2.8% in real terms for the entirety of 2014. The achievement of the Fed's rather lofty goal would require a real 4% annualized growth in each of the next three quarters. The problem with this assumption is that the last time that the U.S. economy grew at 4% or more, over three consecutive quarters, was in 1983.

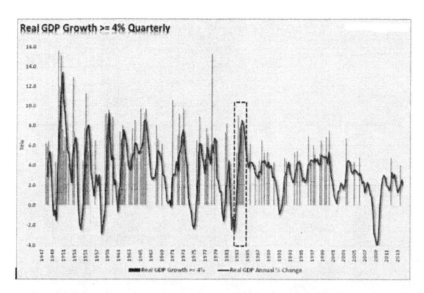

Real GDP Growth >= 4% Quarterly

It is very likely that the Federal Reserve will curtail their GDP growth forecast at their next meeting. However, this should come as no surprise as this has been the "modus operandi" of the Federal Reserve since they began publishing their economic and policy forecasts 2011. The chart below shows the history of the average range of their forecasts versus actual economic outcomes.

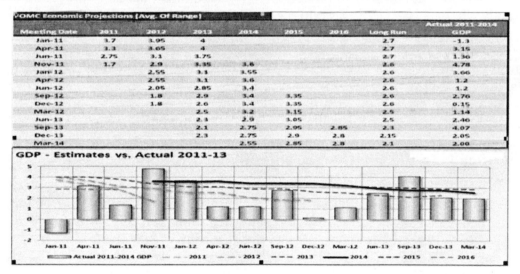

FOMC Economic Projections [Avg. Of Range]

Meeting Date	2011	2012	2013	2014	2015	2016	Long Run	Actual 2011-2014 GDP
Jan-11	3.7	3.95	4				2.7	-1.3
Apr-11	3.3	3.65	4				2.7	3.15
Jun-11	2.75	3.1	3.75				2.7	1.36
Nov-11	1.7	2.9	3.35				2.6	4.78
Jan-12		2.55	3.1	3.55			2.6	3.06
Apr-12		2.55	3.1	3.6			2.6	1.2
Jun-12		2.05	2.85	3.4			2.6	1.2
Sep-12		1.8	2.9	3.4	3.35		2.6	2.76
Dec-12		1.8	2.6	3.4	3.35		2.6	0.1%
Mar-12			2.5	3.2	3.15		2.5	1.14
Jun-13			2.3	2.9	3.05		2.5	2.46
Sep-13			2.1	2.75	2.95	2.85	2.1	4.07
Dec-13			2.3	2.75	2.9	2.8	2.15	2.05
Mar-14				2.55	2.85	2.8	2.1	2.00

GDP - Estimates vs. Actual 2011-13

The current economic recovery is starting to show signs of age. What most economists and analysts have failed to include in their ever ebullient forecasts is the lifespan of an economic and business cycle.

The Economic Cycle

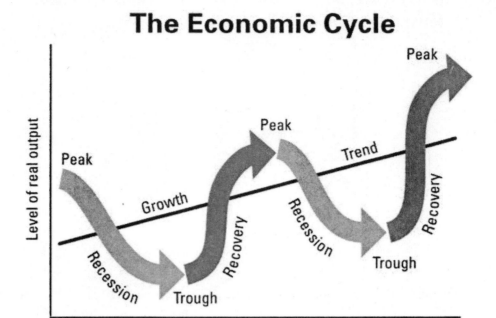

Economies and businesses do not operate on a rational basis of only producing exactly what is necessary to sustain the current demand. Instead, as demand rises, supply is rapidly increased to the point of excess. At some point the excess supply, or supply glut, leads to a down cycle until that excess is reduced to excessively low levels. It is at this point that the cycle renews as demand exceeds supply creating the next up cycle.

There are a few important indicators, in my opinion, that reflect upon the actual strength of economic activity. Rail traffic, shipping of bulk dry goods, and some very specific commodities such as lumber and copper. **The two I want to focus on specifically in this missive are shipping and copper.**

According to Wikipedia:

"The Baltic Dry Index (BDI) is a number (in USD) issued daily by the London-based Baltic Exchange. Not restricted to Baltic Sea countries, **the index provides 'an assessment of the price of moving the major raw materials by sea. Taking in 23 shipping routes measured on a timecharter basis, the index covers Handysize, Supramax, Panamax, and Capesize dry bulk carriers carrying a range of commodities including coal, iron ore and grain.'"**

Since this is not a *"traded"* index, it is void of the volatility that can be created by financial market activity. Most directly, the Baltic Dry Index measures the demand for **shipping capacity versus the supply of dry bulk carriers.** *The demand for shipping varies with the amount of cargo that is being traded or moved in various markets (supply and demand).*

"The supply of cargo ships is generally both tight and inelastic—it takes two years to build a new ship, and a ship's fixed costs are too expensive to take out of circulation the way airlines park unneeded jets in deserts. So, marginal increases in demand can push the index higher quickly, **and marginal demand decreases can cause the index to fall rapidly.**

Because dry bulk primarily consists of materials that function as raw material inputs to the production of intermediate or finished goods, such as concrete, electricity, steel, and food; the index is also seen as an efficient economic indicator of future economic growth and production.

People don't book freighters unless they have cargo to move. Therefore, it would seem to be a reasonable assumption that IF economic growth was indeed on the cusp of rapid acceleration, that the demand for raw materials would be rising thereby increases the cost of shipping. The chart below shows the Baltic Dry Index *(monthly basis)* as compared to real, inflation adjusted, gross domestic product.

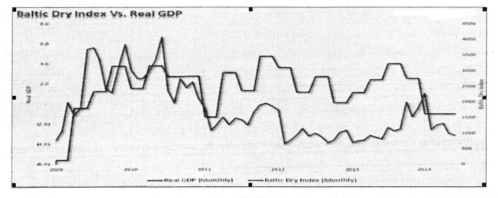

The currently declining levels of the index confirm much of the recent economic data that has been a continuation of the *"struggle through"* economy rather than an acceleration of organic economic growth.

The same holds true for copper. Because of copper's widespread applications in most sectors of the economy - from homes and factories to electronics and power generation and transmission - demand for copper is often viewed as a reliable leading indicator of economic health. This demand is reflected in the market price of copper. Generally, rising copper prices suggest strong copper demand and hence a growing global economy, while declining copper prices may indicate sluggish demand and an imminent economic slowdown.

The chart below is a comparison between spot copper pricing and real GDP.

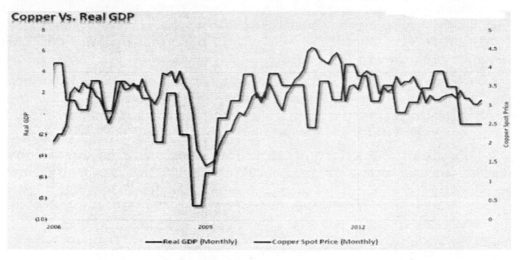

Like shipping prices, copper prices are also suggesting that current economic data may also be overstating the actual underlying economic activity.

If this is indeed the case, this could present a potential issue for the Federal Reserve as it reduces its economic support due to the statistical strength in government produced data. It is highly likely that at the next FOMC meeting there could be an acceleration of the *"taper"* from $10 billion per meeting since the beginning of the year to $15 billion. This would also move up the actual termination date of the program to September from October.

The chart below shows the historical correlation between increases in the Fed's balance sheet and the S&P 500. I have also projected the **theoretical conclusion** of the Fed's program by assuming a continued reduction in purchases of $10 billion at each of the future FOMC meetings.

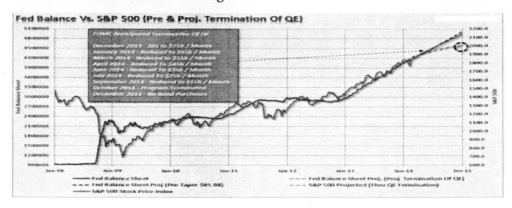

If the current pace of reductions continues it is reasonable to assume that the Fed will terminate the current QE program by the October meeting. If we assume the current correlation remains intact, it projects an advance of the S&P 500 to roughly 2000 by the end of the year. This would imply an 8% advance for the market for the entirety of 2014.

Such an advance would correspond with an economy that is modestly expanding at a time where the Federal Reserve has begun tightening monetary policy.

With the market already approaching the 2000 mark currently, the Fed reducing support, and market exuberance hitting levels normally associated with bull market peaks, any disappointment in actual economic activity could lead to a fairly sharp correction in the financial markets. While I **AM NOT** suggesting that the Baltic Dry Index or Copper prices are predicting an economic *"disaster,"* **I am suggesting** that there is an increased risk of disappointment in the coming months.

Considering that the markets have now gone 26 months without a correction of 10% or more, a historically long span, the probability of such is exceedingly high. All that is lacking is the catalyst to induce *"fear"* into an overly complacent marketplace.

Yield Spreads & Market Reversions

The *"chase for yield"* was the desired result by the Federal Reserve when they dropped rates to record lows and announced, in 2010, that supporting asset prices to boost consumer confidence had become a *"third mandate."* However, they may have gotten more than they bargained for as several Fed officials have now voiced concerns over potential financial instability. To wit:

Fed's Kocherlakota Urges 5 More Years Of Low Interest Rates via Reuters

Kocherlakota acknowledged that keeping rates low for so long can lead to conditions that signal financial instability, including high asset prices, volatile returns on assets, and frantic levels of merger activity as businesses and individuals strive to take advantage of low interest rates.

But that is a risk, he suggested, the Fed should be willing to take.

In a world of rational expectations, asset prices adjust and that's it, but if one allows for limited information, **the resulting bull market may cause investors to get 'carried away' over time and confuse what is a one-time, perhaps transitory, shift in fundamentals for a new paradigm of rising asset prices.**

This *"exuberance"* can be clearly seen in bond yields. In normal times, the interest rate paid on a loan is driven by the potential for a default on repayment of the principal. For example, a person with a credit score of 500 is going to pay a substantially higher interest rate on a loan than an individual with a 700+ credit score. The *"risk"* of a potential repayment default is offset to some degree by a higher interest rate. If a loan of $100,000 is made with an interest rate of 10% for 30 years, the principal is recouped after the first 10 years. The real risk is that the loan defaults within the first 1/3 of its term.

Currently, investors are assigning only 1/2% difference in interest rates between loaning money to a highly credit worthy borrower and one that is only marginally so. This is shown in the chart below which is the spread between AAA and BAA rated bonds from 1919-present.

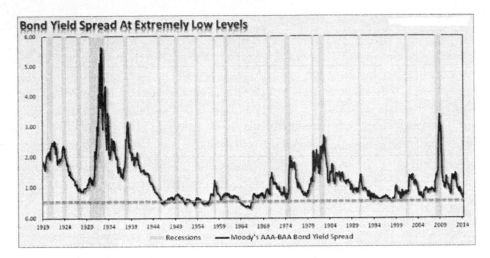

There have been precious few times in history that the spread between interest rates have been so low. Importantly, extremely low yield spreads are not a precursor to an extended economic recovery but rather a sign of a mature economic cycle.

The Federal Reserve officials have very good reason to be concerned about the potential for *"financial instability"* as extremely low thin yield spreads have also been indicative of both minor and major financial market corrections and crashes.

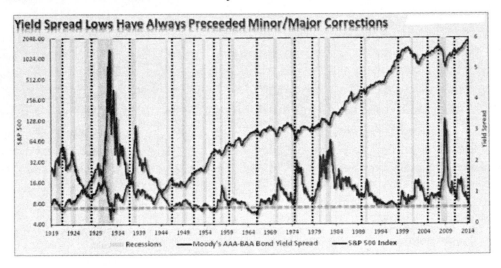

I have zoomed into the chart above to show just 1960-present in order to provide a bit more clarity.

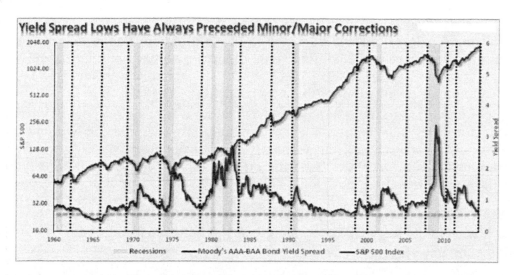

What investors need to be watching for is a *"widening"* of the spread between yields. The decline in the yield spread shows the rise of investor *"complacency."* However, the *"lack of fear"* is a late-cycle development and not one seen at the beginning of economic upswings. Importantly, when the yield spread begins to rise, it tends to do so rapidly leading to a reversion in asset prices.

Currently, the ongoing *"chase for yield"* has led investors to take on much more *"credit risk"* in portfolios than they most likely realize. When *"fear"* is introduced into the financial markets, the subsequent *"instability"* will lead to far greater losses than most individuals are prepared for.

The chart below is a comparison between "junk bond" yields, the least credit worth borrowers, versus the S&P 500.

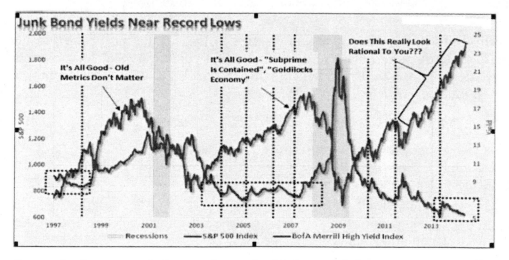

Currently, loans are being made to the highest risk borrowers at an effective interest rate of just 5% as compared to the *"risk free"* rate of 2.6% for a 10-year Government bond.

We have seen this exuberance before. In 1999, the old valuation metrics no longer mattered as it was *"clicks per page."* In 2007, there was NO concern over subprime mortgages as the housing boom fostered a new era of financial stability. Today, it is the Federal Reserve *"put"* which is unanimously believed to be the backstop to any potential shock that may occur.

It is important to understand that it is not the DECLINE in interest rates and yield spread that is important, but it is the REVERSAL that must be watched for. I point out these issues of risk only to make you aware of them as the always bullishly biased media tends to ignore *"risks"* until it is far too late to matter. It is likely that it will be no different this time.

In the minutes of its June meeting the Federal Reserve has indicated that it will end its huge QE3 program of asset purchases in October if the economy stays on track.

The Fed also made significant steps on agreeing its "exit strategy" when the time does come to raise interest rates. These decisions will shape how future Fed policy is communicated to financial markets.

According to the minutes, "many" Fed officials want to keep reinvesting income into their asset purchases until at or after the time that interest rates rise. That would be a change to the current strategy of stopping reinvestment before raising rates.

When the Fed does start to raise rates, it is likely to express its target Federal Funds rate as a range, like the current 0 – 0.25 per cent, instead of giving a single number as it did in the past. That will allow the Fed to make only minimum use of its new reverse repo facility – a way for non-bank players such as money market funds to make deposits at the Fed – in order to minimise any distortion to financial markets.

The Fed also looked at possible changes to the calculation of the Fed Funds rate to make it more reflective of bank lending conditions and take account of international efforts to reform benchmarks such as the LIBOR (London Interbank Offered Rate).

How will markets react when the Fed's "QE" program ends?

In the last 6 years, the Fed has introduced the world to QE1, QE2, and QE3, which are essentially **massive** attempts to inject money (liquidity) into the economy, purportedly as a "stimulus."

The sheer magnitude of these 3 "QE" money-printing programs has been staggering; although unfortunately, all the money printing has led to anemic results in terms of stimulating real economic growth.

How much money printing are we talking? Before QE1, the Fed owned about **$900 Billion** in assets on its books – which was already an all-time record high. Here's what happened next:

Program	Duration	Amount
QE1	11/25/2008 – 03/31/2010 (16 mos.)	An additional **$1,725 Billion**
QE2	11/03/2010 – 6/30/2011 (8 mos.)	An additional **$ 600 Billion**
QE3*	09/13/2012 – present (22 mos. so far)	An additional **$1,855 Billion so far**

* This chart ignores another Fed program known as "Operation Twist," which began 9/21/2011.

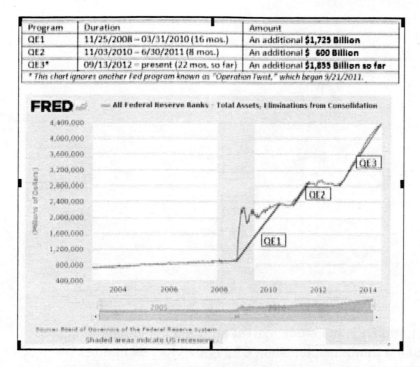

As the charts above show, the Fed has printed enough money in the last 6 years to increase its own assets **from a record $900 Billion to a new record of about $4,400 Billion.**

So how have markets behaved in the midst of all this unprecedented monetary meddling?

This 1st chart shows a history of the stock market – along with the Fed's "QE" programs – beginning in 2007.

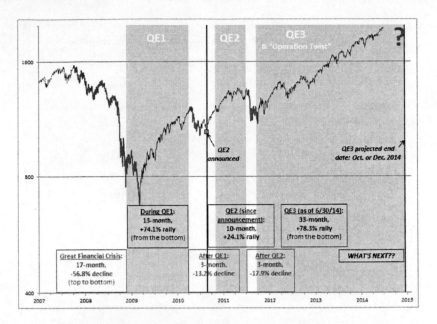

After QE1 and QE2, the stock market suffered immediate declines!
Will the same thing happen when QE3 ends in a few months?

Certainly, the Fed's actions have *heavily influenced* the markets in recent years. HOWEVER, trying to predict the market's corresponding reaction to a single, predetermined event has NEVER been a winning strategy. Bottom line: I believe the end of QE3 will probably play out somewhat differently than either QE1 or QE2.

How does "QE" impact interest rates?

The "QE" experiments have also whipsawed interest rates – in fact, even more so than the stock market. This next chart shows interest rates for 10-year US Treasury bonds.

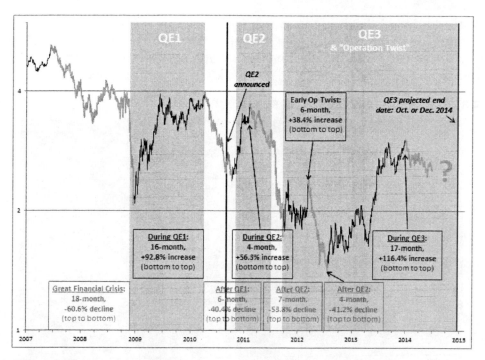

It is pertinent to note that:

- Interest rates have been even more volatile than the stock market.
- Rates crashed with the stock market before QE1, then skyrocketed during QE1... then plummeted again as soon as QE1 ended! And that was just the beginning....
- Rates hit an all-time record low of 1.4% in July 2012 (in the midst of "Operation Twist," about 2 months before the start of QE3). Over the next 17 months, rates shot higher, hitting an interim high of 3.03% on 12/31/2013, before dropping slightly in 2014.

Indian stock markets hold the most potential but have run ahead of themselves

Narendra Modi's landslide victory in India's elections spurred hopes that Asia's third-largest economy would soon see growth-supportive policies. Stocks rose sharply in the run-up to the elections and while post-election sentiment may see stocks rise further charts indicate that a quick retracement is possible.

India stocks' rapid rally faces this speed bump

Indian office workers walk past the bronze bull outside the Bombay Stock Exchange

India stocks have sped ahead with a more than 23 percent so far this year, but with valuations becoming less compelling, a potential speed bump from looming share sales is on the cards.

With the government's aggressive divestment plans and ongoing corporate equity raisings, we think the demand/supply balance can turn less favorable in the coming months.

The government is targeting divestments of almost $10 billion worth of shares this fiscal year, with some of the stake sales potentially fast-tracked. In addition, private-sector companies have raised $3.8 billion of fresh equity so far this year, with the trend set to continue. I estimate a pipeline of around $3.1 billion of new and secondary offerings already announced for the rest of the year.

While the divestments will help India achieve the much needed fiscal consolidation and the corporate capital raising improves balance sheets, history suggests excess equity supply is likely to act as an overhang for the markets until demand catches up.

The new equity supply comes as valuations are already looking less appealing-- on an equal-weighted basis, the MSCI India is trading at 20.5 times forward earnings, the highest in Asia.

In March 2014 the NIFTY 50 broke decisively above 6350, which had been a major resistance level since January 2008. It was previously tested in November 2010, and more recently acted as a strong resistance level from November 2013 to January 2014.

The NIFTY had formed a very wide trading band with support located near 4650. Support was tested in December 2009, February 2010 and again in December 2011. The width of the trading band is measured and this measurement is projected upwards to give a breakout target near 8000.

The key concern is the nature of the breakout. The NIFTY has developed a parabolic trend. These trends are found most frequently in bull markets, or markets showing volatile rebounds. While parabolic trends are usually seen in fast-moving stocks, they are also present in fast-moving index areas or markets.

Parabolic trends are best described using an arc, or a segment of an ellipse. They start slowly then accelerate very rapidly until activity on the price chart is almost vertical. They cannot be adequately described by straight edge trend lines; instead the price action uses a parabolic curve as a support level.

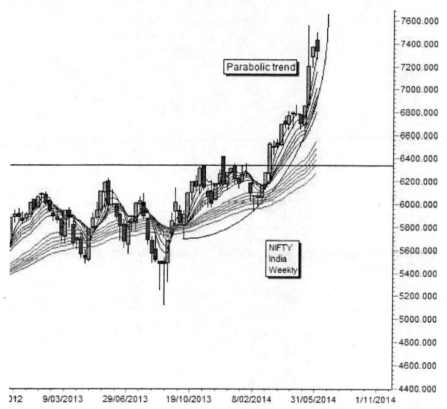

The key problem with parabolic trends is the way they end – (usually) rapidly and with a substantial fall. The trend line approaches vertical so there comes a point when the next candle will inevitably move to the right of the parabolic trend line. This is the signal for the end of the trend; often the price will gap down and then fall dramatically.

The retracement in this trend is usually between 50 percent and 100 percent of the original rise. For the NIFTY that's a potential retreat to below 6600 on current index values. However, combined with the trading band analysis, which suggests an upside target near 8000, a 50 percent retracement would have a target below 6800.

In either case there is potential for a major trend retreat. Traders will protect profits as the NIFTY moves towards the 8000 target level and will close positions and go short when the index moves to the right of the parabolic trend line.

Parabolic trends offer fast-moving momentum profits, but they carry the danger of rapid and significant trend retracement.

Yet, Indian stocks will be the best asset class to invest in over the next 10 years

India story all set to gather momentum

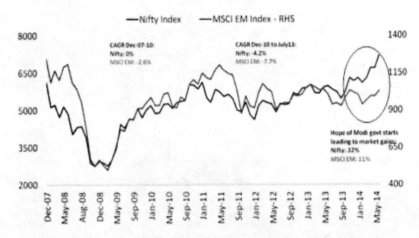

We can see similar change in the growth of our country if desired expectations are delivered.

Pillar of future growth

Key drivers:

1. *Politics – stable, strong Government, after 30 years*

2. Investment cycle: policy push + cyclical upswing

3. Inflation and interest rates to cool down

4. Current Account and Currency have stabilized

5. Budget Expectations

Why is a stable government so important?

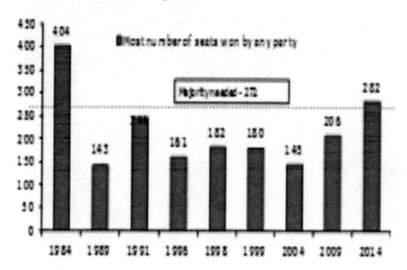

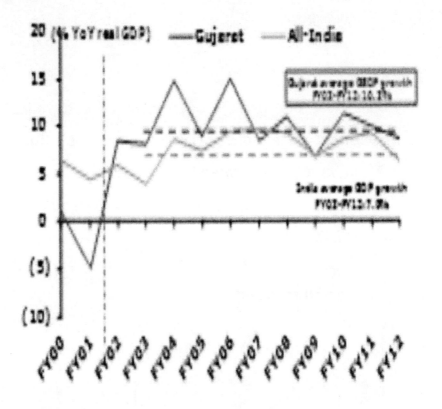

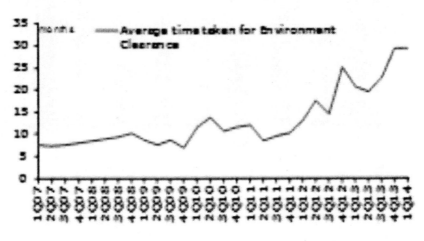

GDP Growth : Pvt. + Public Consumption, Net Exports and others

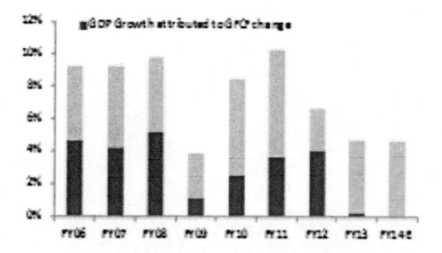

Priorities of the new regime

1. **Reduce Inflation** - Release food stock, Restructure APMC laws
2. **Improve Governance, decision-making**
3. **Job creation by stimulating manufacturing investments** - liberalize FDI limits and law, create industrial clusters
4. **Reforms in mining, power sectors and land acquisition**
5. **PSU reforms** - Holding company structure
6. **Accelerate infrastructure creation**
   - Dedicated Freight Corridor, 100 new cities, River-linking, Road and Rail Diamond Quadrilateral, National Gas Grid, Strengthen Power Grid, High Speed Rail, Alternate Energy

Indian Investment cycle: Policy push + Cyclical upswing

The story so far: As bad as it gets: USD 130 Billion
Indian capital projects stalled under the previous regime

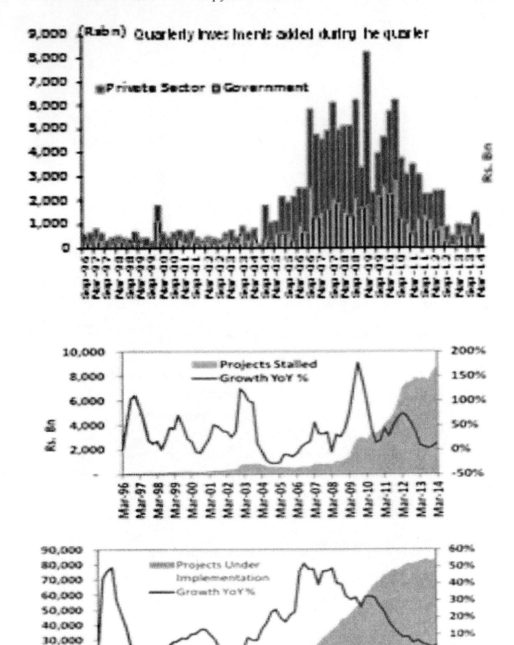

- Investment cycle suffered a virtual collapse. Corporate sentiments were impaired due to lack of clear road map, slowing GDP growth and elevated cost of capital.

- Projects worth INR 8,000 bn got stalled – due to Fuel linkages /EC/FC/Regulatory Clearances, creating a large back log of capital work in progress.

- Better policy framework and governance to revive investments.

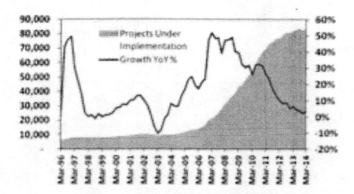

- Investment cycle suffered a virtual collapse. Corporate sentiments were impaired due to lack of clear road map, slowing GDP growth and elevated cost of capital.

- Projects worth INR 8,000 bn got stalled – due to Fuel linkages /EC/FC/Regulatory Clearances, creating a large back log of capital work in progress.

- Better policy framework and governance to revive investments.

Indian Investment cycle: The opportunity

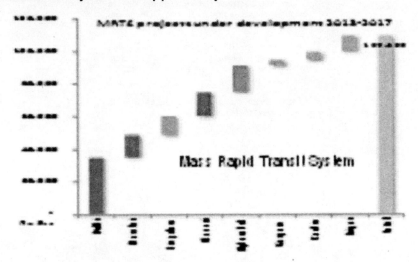

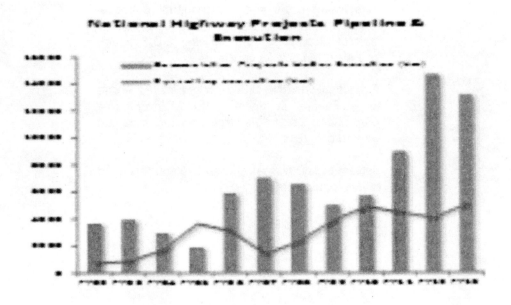

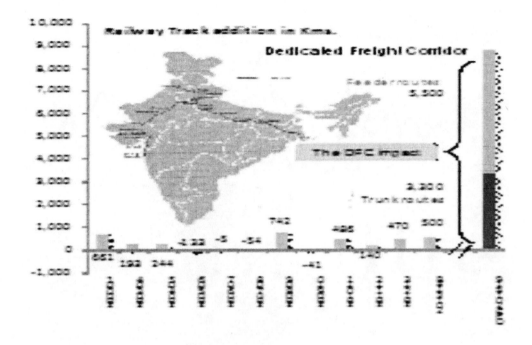

- FDI in critical sectors like defense, media

- Policy for labor-intensive sectors like textiles and construction are likely

Today, Indian Current account deficit and currency have stabilized

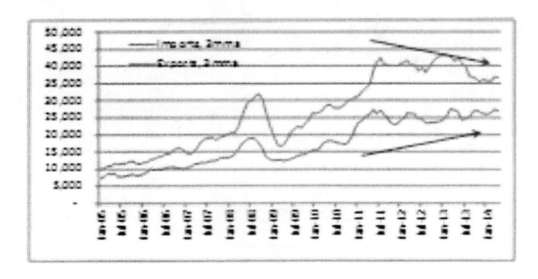

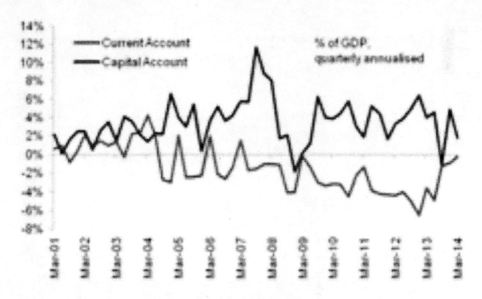

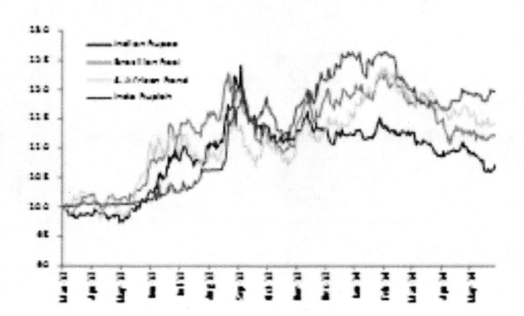

- Dramatic reduction seen in India's trade deficit due to falling imports and rising imports
- Gold imports are down 70%. Non Oil, Non Gold imports also down. Current account deficit for quarter ended March 14 is the lowest in 4 years
- Indian Rupee is amongst the best performing in the past 9 months

What are the Indian Budget expectations?

Financial Budget in early July is a crucial event which will reflect the intent of the new government and draw up expectations on the pace of economic recovery and shape market sentiments

•With limited scope of increase on revenue side, the budget is more likely on reforms in expenditure side

(i) Curtailing fuel subsidy

(ii) Cutting on social/populist scheme and channeling efforts on capex/productive measures.

•On the revenue side-

(i) Excise rationalization to the headline rate on range of sectors.

(ii) Narrowing negative service tax list

•Road map for disinvestments, financial sector reforms, DTC and GST guidelines, Fuel security measures , FDI would be laid out.

Overall the budget would be a balanced act, ahead of some important state elections, and will highlight structural roadmap on important economic areas.

I believe we have reached a cyclical bottom in GDP growth rates

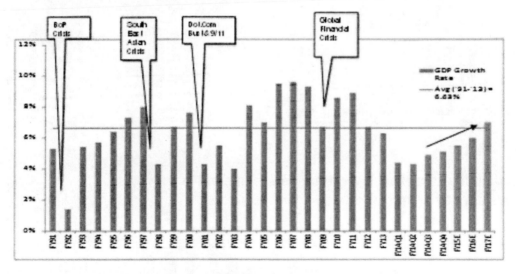

Since '91 India's growth has averaged 6.6%. We believe GDP growth has bottomed out in 2014

Sales and margins—slow recovery has begun

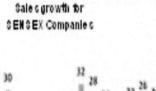

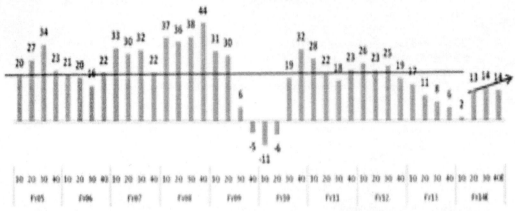

Profitability at cyclical lows: Margins and interest costs are Key drivers of profits

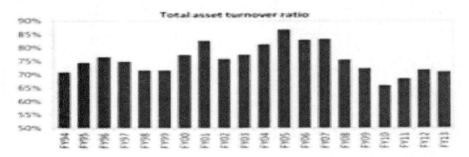

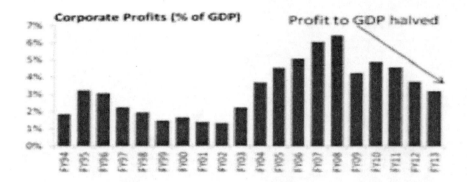

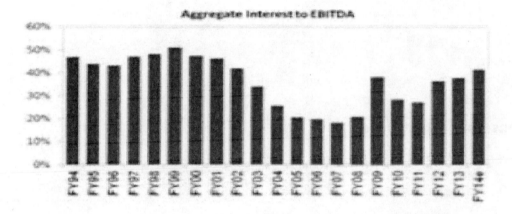

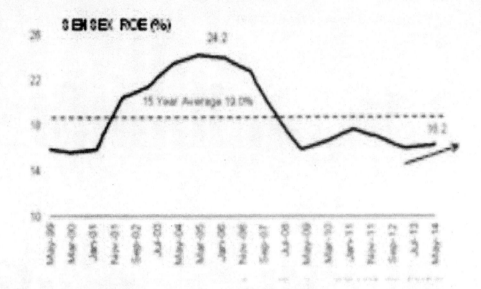

Consensus expectations are still low

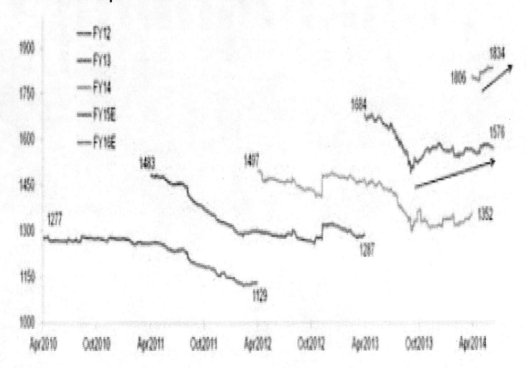

- Over the last four years we have seen an earning decline cycle. In FY12, FY13, FY14 we saw sharp cuts in Sensex earnings estimates.

- From Dec 2013 we saw consensus earning revision towards the positive side.

- Historically, analyst estimates for earning growth tends to lag in accelerating GDP growth environment,. Over the course of next few years we expect upwards revision in estimates

Markets at all time High.. Where are Valuations

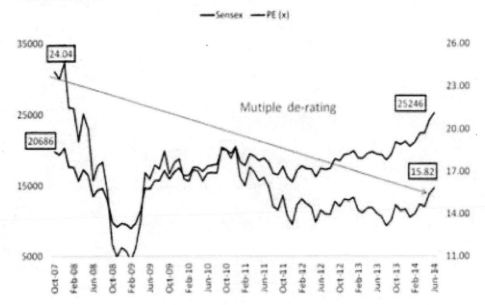

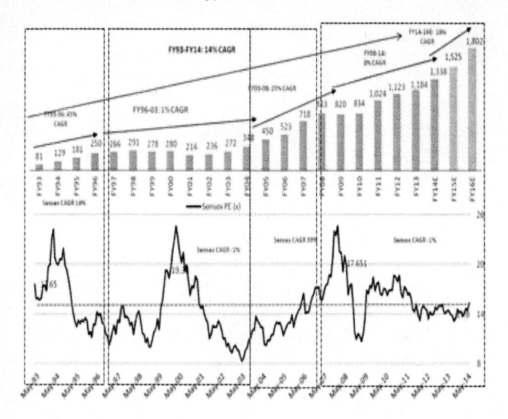

Market valuations are still reasonable

- Valuations are slightly above the Long term averages of 15.1x. Currently Sensex trades at 15.8x 1 Year forward PE.

- Even as indices are trading near all-time high levels, valuation parameters are comfortably below the 2008 highs.

- The current PE are on moderate earnings growth estimates. As earning upgrades cycle sets in on visibility in reform process, valuations will provide further comfort.

Opportunities in valuation gaps, cyclical more headroom..

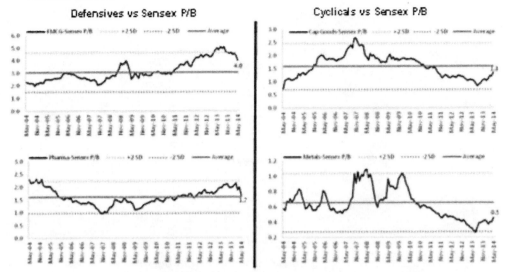

Cyclical sectors trading below their LT average levels makes a compelling case for mean reversion as outlook improves.

Why India could be the star-performer over the next 10 years?

Equity markets have rallied on decisive election outcome leading to hopes of improving pace and quality of economic recovery.

• A pro-reform government coupled with decisive leadership will accelerate the reforms and growth process.

• The depressed corporate profitability will improve over the next couple of years as the economy sees a cyclical uptick, clocking CAGR of 18-21% - driven by higher revenues, operating leverage and interest costs savings.

• Even post the sharp run up- Sensex trades at 1year forward PE of 15.8x, a tad higher than the 15 year average of 15.1x. Earning upgrades cycle on visibility in reform process will provide further support to market and valuations.

• As economy see significant acceleration of growth in the next 3 years – equity returns will be driven both by earning growth and valuation re-rating providing investor a good investment opportunity.

• In the current scenario, equity investments provide a compelling case over other asset classes. Indian investors should increase their equity allocations and benefit from Indian growth story.

Yet, Why emerging markets are here to stay?

From time to time, emerging markets bashing has become a fshion.

Commentators forget that Emerging nations like China, Brazil, Russia and especially India after the victory of Narendra Modi — are experiencing economic and social change that won't be reversed.

After a brief panic earlier this year, many money managers have been putting cash back to work in such unpredictable markets, lured by cheap stocks and strong measures taken by local policy makers. But few are committing significant funds to Turkey, spooked by the autocratic tendencies of Prime Minister Mr. Erdogan and the economy's dependence on volatile investment flows.

My biggest investment successes — from Internet stocks in China and Russia, to housing finance companies in India — have sprung from my ability to ignore the passing wisdoms of the market. So it may be prudent to buy Turkish stocks, based on the conviction that over the long-term, Mr. Erdogan's radical reform ambitions will transform Turkey.

Today we can invest in a wide variety of emerging markets around the world, as well as a host of "frontier markets," a designation given to the lesser-developed subsector of emerging markets, which includes the majority of the African continent. We are very excited about the potential for these frontier countries in the next 25 years, as many are growing at a rapid pace and quickly assimilating the latest technological advancements, particularly in mobile finance and e-commerce. Generally more youthful and growing populations mean consumer power has been on the rise, with a growing middle class.

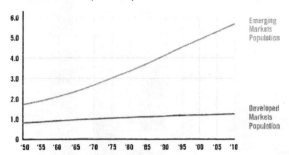

Emerging vs. Developed Countries: Population
1950 – 2010 (#Billion)

Source: Population Division of the Department of Economic and Social Affairs of the United Nations Secretariat, World Population Prospects: The 2010 Revision. Emerging Markets as represented by the MSCI Emerging Markets Index; Developed Markets as represented by the MSCI All-Country World Index. MSCI makes no express or implied warranties or representations and shall have no liability whatsoever with respect to any MSCI data contained herein. The MSCI data may not be further redistributed or used as a basis for other indices or any securities or financial products.

Reasons for Optimism

There will always be challenges in any country; developed countries certainly aren't immune to issues like corruption, and temporary market and economic setbacks. Throughout short-term challenges, I have remained focused on the long term and on my conviction of the potential I believe emerging markets hold. I also believe in the importance of being on the ground, assessing the situation first-hand and talking to individual businesses within a country to determine their distinct fundamentals and potential. This can bring valuable insights you can't get by analyzing reams of data.

- Emerging markets in general have been growing 3-5 times faster than developed countries; many frontier markets have seen even higher growth.
- Emerging markets generally have greater foreign reserves than most developed countries.
- Emerging markets' debt-to-gross domestic product (GDP) ratios are generally much lower than developed markets.

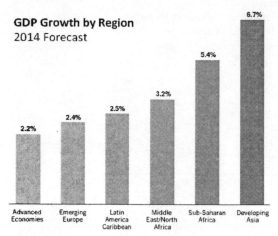

GDP Growth by Region
2014 Forecast

Put all this together, and I believe there's a good case to be optimistic about the future for emerging and frontier markets, and I believe their share of the global investable universe will continue to grow. Just imagine what the next 25 years could bring!

The best way to play emerging markets

Dividend payers and China A-shares are undervalued

Retail investors again seem to think they can make money in the emerging world, and have sent money pouring back in. But where, exactly, can they find value?

Most emerging markets were inefficient and illiquid in the first place (earning them the "emerging" tag), and the indiscriminate waves in and out of the sector over the last decade should have created some inefficiencies along the way.

Here are two possible systematic mispricings. First, there is the disjunction between the Chinese A-share market, largely restricted to domestic investors but opening slowly, and the market for H-shares, quoted in Hong Kong and available for international consumption.

Second, there is the issue of dividend yield. The developed world's "hunt for yield" has passed the emerging world by – now, dividend-payers seem too cheap. Dividend income might even provide much-needed insurance for those diving into markets that will continue to be volatile.

Chinese A-shares

The A-share market was grotesquely inefficient for years, thanks to crude interventions by the Chinese authorities. At the height of a short-lived 2007 bubble, A-shares traded for twice the valuation that the same companies traded at in Hong Kong. They are now at a slight discount.

Gaining access to A-shares for foreigners as a QFII (qualified foreign institutional investor) is cumbersome, but western access to A-shares has slowly widened. Domestic investors are sour on the market since the bubble burst – and that allows entry at favourable valuations. The CSI 300 index, covering Shanghai and Shenzhen, trades at a multiple of less than 10 times earnings, its lowest in more than a decade.

A-shares include smaller companies that are not available in Hong Kong, while the consumer-driven sectors that have sparked the greatest hopes for growth in China are better represented.

One can look at Midea Group, an appliance maker that employs 126,000. Its stock trades at 8 times this year's earnings forecasts, while yielding more than 4 per cent. Fuyao Glass, an auto-glass maker that recently bought a General Motors factory in Ohio, trades on a similar multiple while yielding 6 per cent.

There are risks in investing in a market where access is heavily regulated, and where past volatility has been extreme. Profound macroeconomic questions about China, and its overextended property market, remain unanswered. But it is fair for those with a long investment horizon to hope that, as the market liberalises, so valuations will steadily grow richer.

High-yielding stocks

Over the last two decades, emerging companies have managed to raise their dividends far faster than their developed world counterparts. There are reasons in many jurisdictions to question whether companies truly respect the interests of minority shareholders – but dividend payout ratios have increased and stabilised, as companies take shareholders' interests more seriously.

There is an interesting investment opportunity because high dividend-yielders are not as highly valued as they are in developed markets. MSCI's index of the highest yielding emerging markets companies is trading at a 17 per cent discount to the emerging markets as a whole, in terms of earnings multiples, while high-yielders in the US and Europe trade at a premium. So this suggests that investing for yield in emerging markets could be a good way to search for value.

There are arguments why yield may seem so cheap. High-yielding stocks tend to come from sectors like utilities, which when investing in EM means committing to large formerly state-owned monopolies. Many do not look appetising, and their yields may now be so high in large part because state-owned enterprises have sold off aggressively in recent years. But even if this is so, the high yield offers some additional protection for investors.

Emerging markets with a strong dividend-paying culture are a disparate bunch. For example, Taiwan has the strongest dividend-paying culture, thanks to the law introduced in 1998 that taxed companies' retained earnings, giving them a strong incentive to make a high payout ratio. South Korea, in other ways very similar to Taiwan, has low payout ratios, with companies often opting to keep cash within the *chaebol* conglomerate structure.

Other countries with a strong dividend yield include Saudi Arabia, South Africa and Turkey, while sectors with high yields including telecoms, consumer discretionary, and industrials – which should all benefit from the hoped-for growth in the middle class.

If the investor return to emerging markets continues, all stocks stand to benefit. But the evidence is plausible that dividend-paying stocks, and Chinese A-shares, are systematically undervalued. They look as good a way to play the emerging markets as any.

Janet Yellen and the business of bursting bubbles

Fed Chariman Janet Yellen says Fed is not in the business of bursting bubbles. Central banks have a poor record of anticipating asset bubbles, let alone preventing them. There is no reason to suppose that their foresight has improved. In contrast, it is within the Fed's power to bolster the economy's resilience to bursting bubbles via tougher macroprudential controls.

Bubbles will always be with us, argues Janet Yellen. The goal should be to make them less explosive.

Ms Yellen is in good company. On July 3, Sweden's central bank reversed its stance of tightening interest rates to head off asset price bubbles by slashing them to just 0.25 per cent.

Far from rebuilding confidence, the Riksbank's strategy of "leaning into the wind" had brought Sweden to the brink of outright deflation. In place of the blunt monetary instrument, the Riksbank will look at further toughening banks' capital requirements.

At the Bank of England, Mark Carney has taken macroprudential policy a step further by promising to vary the loan-to-value ratio on mortgages with the housing boom cycle. Central banks everywhere are starting to vary their bank stress tests to take the asset price cycle into account.

The debate is far from settled. This week the Bank for International Settlements threw a contrarian straw into the wind by insisting that central banks should tighten early and clearly to stave off another cycle of bubbles. Ms Yellen is wise to ignore their advice.

Without easy monetary policy, the US, the UK and other leading economies would have grown by far less in recent years. Premature tightening would have reduced growth, risked deflation and increased the value of the debt burden that the BIS so fears.

The BIS was right to warn of the dangers of "balance sheet depression", which can persist for years. Alas, its remedy would worsen the disease. Without growth, the balance sheet can only deteriorate further.

That said, there are grounds to worry that the Fed is not doing enough to limit the impact of future asset price shocks. Unlike the BoE, which seems serious about counteracting the UK's chronic housing boom-bust cycle, the Fed's macro prudential tool kit is limited.

Ms Yellen has made it clear the Fed will increase capital cushions as conditions demand. But almost all the onus is on the formal banking sector. Much of the risk, however, has shifted into shadow banking. There are real concerns the Fed is behind the curve. Regulators are almost never as nimble as the markets they regulate. Ms Yellen must do more to demonstrate that the Fed, and its sister agencies, will follow the search for yield into whichever asset classes it goes, and via whichever entities.

On the bright side, the US economy's strong labour market numbers in June – with 288,000 new jobs added – is another signpost on the way to ending the historically easy monetary policy of the past few years. The Fed's taper will almost certainly be completed by the autumn. And there is a rising chance that it will begin to raise interest rates in late 2015 if not before.

For six years, the Fed has done its best to boost asset prices to rekindle the real economy. The path was ugly but undoubtedly the lesser of two evils. At some point, US interest rates will begin to normalise and the search for yield may go into reverse. Volatility will return to the markets and risks will rise. It is imperative the Fed makes use of every macroprudential tool it has to protect the US recovery from the bubbles it has helped create.

781,000 Jobs to Go Until Full U.S. Unemployment Recovery to pre-crisis levels

Perhaps the biggest reaction from the May 2014 U.S. employment situation report is that the number of non-farm payroll jobs recorded as part of the establishment survey portion of the report has finally recovered to pre-recession levels.

But what about the household survey portion of the employment situation report? Well, as it happens, about 781,000 jobs have to be filled before it recovers to its pre-recession peak.

Meanwhile, if we dig deeper into the household survey portion of the report, we find that compared to the peak in total employment that was recorded in November 2007, we find that the news is especially dire for one particular demographic group of the potential U.S. labor force:

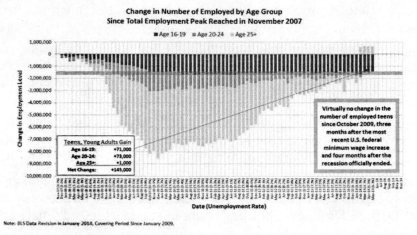

Change in Number of Employed by Age Group
Since Total Employment Peak Reached in November 2007

Note: BLS Data Revision in January 2014, Covering Period Since January 2009.

Since October 2009, three months after the last federal minimum wage increase, there has been virtually no jobs recovery for American teens. For May 2014, the official count puts the number of teens with jobs at a level that's 1,377,000 lower than the 5,927,000 teens who were counted as being employed in November 2007.

Inspired by Bill McBride, who has long predicted that the number of non-farm jobs reported in the establishment survey portion of the U.S. employment situation report would exceed its pre-recession level this year, we'll offer this prediction: the number of teens counted as being employed in the household survey portion of the employment situation report will begin falling after July 2014.

The U.S. Unemployment Rate Is Not Signaling a Recession

A reliable source for recession forecasting is the unemployment rate, which can provide signals for the beginnings and ends of recessions. The unemployment rate model, updated with the June figure of 6.1%, does not signal a recession now.

The model relies on four indicators to signal recessions:

♦ A short 12-period and a long 60-period exponential moving average (EMA) of the unemployment rate (UER),

♦ The 8-month smoothed annualized growth rate of the UER (UERg).

♦ The 19-week rate of change of the UER.

The criteria for the model to signal the start of recessions are given in the original article and repeated in the Appendix.

Referring to the chart below, and looking at the end portion of it, one can see that none of the conditions for a recession start are currently present.

♦ The UER is not forming a trough and its short EMA is well below its long EMA - the blue and red graphs, respectively, the spread being -0.59%.

- UERg is currently at a low level, minus 17.7% – the green graph.
- Also the 19-week rate of change of the UER is now at about minus 8.7%, far below the critical level of plus 8% - the black graph.

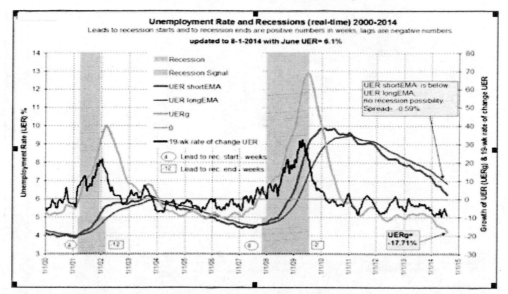

For a recession signal, the short EMA of the UER would have to form a trough and then cross its long EMA to the upside. Alternatively, the UERg graph would have to turn upwards and rise above zero, or the 19-week rate of change of the UER would have to be above 8%. Currently the trajectories of the unemployment rate's short- and long EMA are still downwards - none having a positive slope, UERg is far below zero, and the 19-week rate of change of the UER is also way below the critical level.

Based on the historic patterns of the unemployment rate indicators prior to recessions one can reasonably conclude that the U.S. economy is not likely to go into recession anytime soon.

With an improvement in US macro data in the past quarter, there is a concern that high interest rates are both imminent and a threat to equities. This should not be a concern.

The 10-year yield is currently 2.65%. A rise in yields from a low level like this has not, in the past, been a headwind for equity appreciation. The chart below shows a positive correlation between rising rates from a low level and equity appreciation.

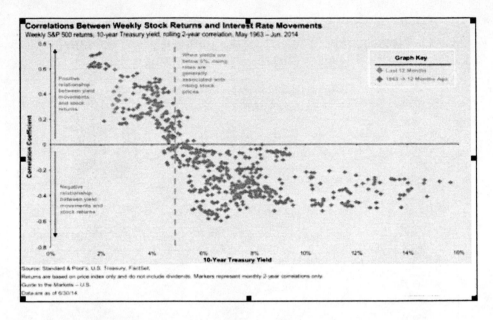

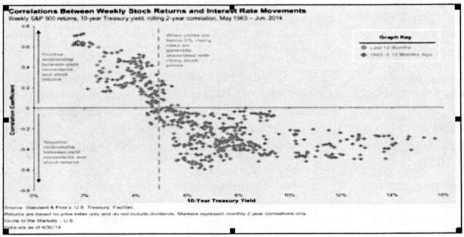

Intuitively, that makes sense. Better growth is associated with higher equity prices and higher rates. It also improves valuations.

There's a similar concern that better data implies the end of QE in the autumn, and that this presents a threat to equities. The end of prior QE programs in 2010 and 2011 did, in fact, precipitate a fall in equity prices.

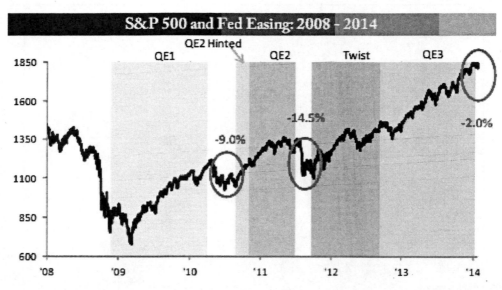

The assumption at the time was that interest rates would rise when the Fed stopped their QE programs; instead, they fell. Why? Because investors feared growth slowdown. This led to a fall in rates and equity prices. If the market now anticipates better growth, rendering stimulative QE purchases superfluous, then ending those purchases should not precipitate a fall in prices.

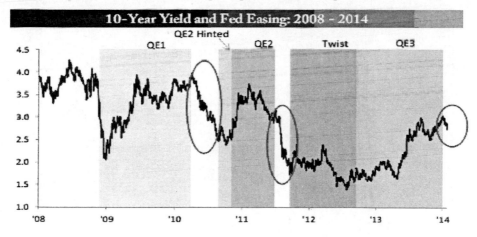

Net, a small bump higher in rates and the end of Fed stimulus in themselves are not things with which to be concerned.

The caveat and this is key, is that macro growth, and therefore SPX revenue growth, must now pick up. These are the things with which to be concerned.

More than 5 years into expansion, revenue growth is not driving earnings. It's been mostly margins. Margins have benefited from low labor and interest costs. But history shows that sustainable earnings growth in prior bull markets, especially after several years into a recovery, are instead driven by revenues (light blue bars)

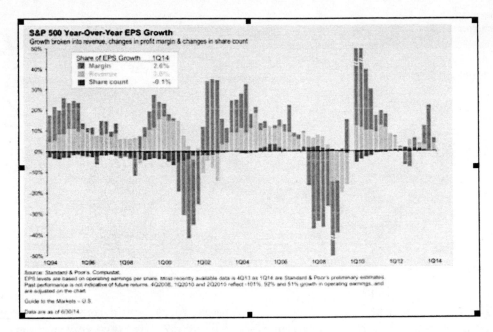

Revenue growth matters because total equity returns are still being driven not by earnings but by multiple expansion (dark bars, below). This is in contrast to the prior bull market.

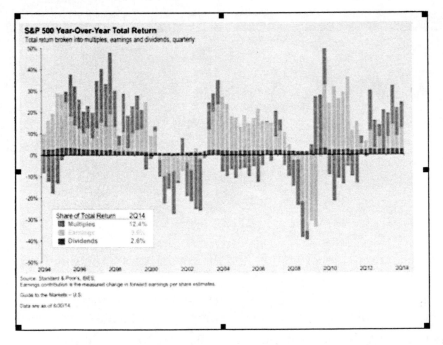

In the first half of 2014, SPX rose 6%. If the consensus is right, EPS (TTM) rose 2.6% from the end of 2013. That means 57% of the year-to-date gains in SPX are from multiple expansion.

This follows the pattern of the last two years. In 2013, 80% of the gain in SPX was from multiple expansions. This pattern is beginning to resemble the final years of the tech bubble of the late 1990s. Asset prices are rising because someone else is an assumed buyer at a higher price, not because of underlying fundamentals.

Sales growth in 2013 was a paltry 2% but the consensus expects this to improve to 3% in 2014. We agree. But the current rate of appreciation in SPX (12% annualized) will be difficult to sustain when revenues are growing at just 3%.

This would not be an issue if multiples were lower, but price/sales for SPX is now 1.72 times, 8% above their peak in 2007 and more than 20% above their past 15-year median.

So the key remains growth. Did the U.S. June 2014 employment data indicate faster than 3-4% nominal growth is imminent?

Here is a column chart of monthly percent change for this indicator over the past fifty years. I've also included a 12-month moving average. We can see that consecutive MoM declines outside of recessions are quite rare. Recessions, other than the second half of the early 1980s double-dip, have followed a distinct downtrend in the 12-month moving average -- not something we're currently seeing.

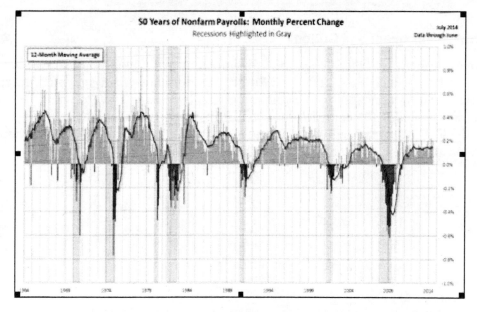

The chart and table below illustrate the performance of the Big Four with an overlay of a simple average of the four since the end of the Great Recession. The data points show the cumulative percent change from a zero starting point for June 2009. We now have the first indicator update for the 60th month following the recession. The Big Four Average (gray line below).

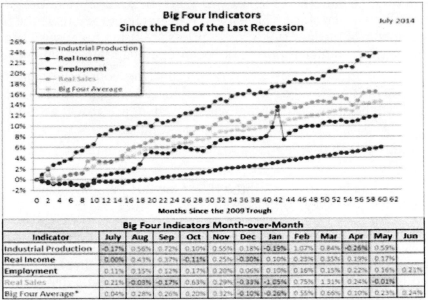

Indicator	July	Aug	Sep	Oct	Nov	Dec	Jan	Feb	Mar	Apr	May	Jun
Industrial Production	-0.17%	0.56%	0.72%	0.10%	0.55%	0.18%	-0.19%	1.07%	0.84%	-0.26%	0.59%	
Real Income	0.00%	0.43%	0.37%	-0.11%	0.25%	-0.30%	0.10%	0.23%	0.35%	0.19%	0.17%	
Employment	0.11%	0.15%	0.12%	0.17%	0.20%	0.06%	0.10%	0.16%	0.15%	0.22%	0.16%	0.21%
Real Sales	0.21%	-0.03%	-0.17%	0.63%	0.29%	-0.33%	-1.05%	0.75%	1.31%	0.24%	-0.01%	
Big Four Average*	0.04%	0.28%	0.26%	0.20%	0.32%	-0.10%	-0.26%	0.55%	0.66%	0.10%	0.23%	0.24%

Employment is released the first week of the month, income the last week, Industrial Production and Sales mid-month.
*The Big Four Average is calculated with the most recent unrounded data point for each series.

Current Assessment and Outlook

The overall picture of the US economy had been one of a ploddingly slow recovery from the Great Recession, and the Winter data documented a sharp contraction. The early Spring appeared to support the general view that severe winter weather was responsible for the contraction -- that it was **not** the beginnings of a business cycle decline. The May Industrial Production strengthened the optimistic view, as has release of the U.S. June Nonfarm new jobs data.

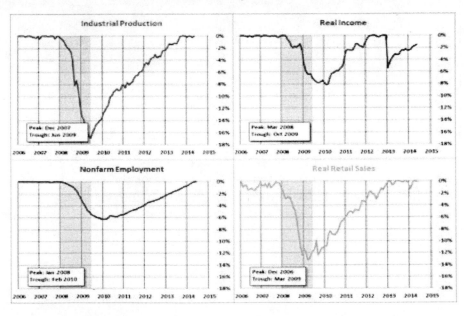

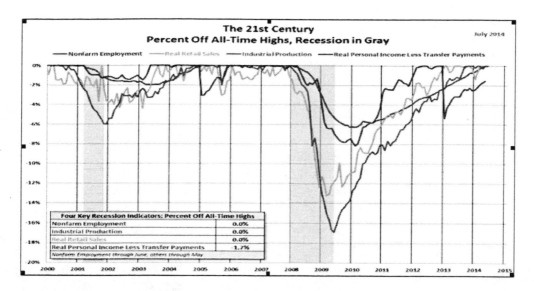

The 21st Century
Percent Off All-Time Highs, Recession in Gray

Four Key Recession Indicators: Percent Off All-Time Highs	
Nonfarm Employment	0.0%
Industrial Production	0.0%
Real Retail Sales	0.0%
Real Personal Income Less Transfer Payments	-1.7%

On Mario Draghi's 'Negative Interest Rates' decision

The European Central Bank's decision to reduce the interest rate on deposits at the central bank to (-) 0.10 % went as far as even the most ardent doves could reasonably have expected. Rates can probably fall no further.

There was a €400bn injection of liquidity, in what the ECB called a "targeted longer-term refinancing operation" – a near copy of the Bank of England's 'Funding for Lending Scheme'. There was a form of quantitative easing, in which the central bank will buy securities backed by private sector loans. And there was the cessation of a "sterilisation" exercise, which had previously damped the monetary effect of the ECB's purchases of government bonds.

Unlike the interest rate, which is now as low as it can go, all of these measures could be intensified if the eurozone recovery continues to disappoint. Is this a "big bazooka"? It clearly falls some way short of a broad asset purchase programme of the kind pursued by the Federal Reserve and the Bank of Japan. None of the measures introduced on June 5, 2014 will produce a transformation in monetary conditions.

After all, Denmark cut the interest rate on deposits at the central bank below zero a couple of years ago, with only moderate effects. True, the ECB carries more sway than the Danish central bank.

A negative interest rate is, in effect, a levy on banks: instead of receiving interest on their deposits at the ECB, they will watch them shrink. But the TLTRO and liquidity injections cut the other way, perpetuating the ECB's recent efforts to provide extremely easy conditions in the money markets. So, banks should gain more from easy money than they lose through negative interest rates.

The decision no longer to sterilise the central bank's earlier purchases of government debt is a signal of intent, even if its direct effect is not very large. For the first time, the ECB is financing these purchases by creating money. The course pioneered by Haruhiko Kuroda at the Bank of Japan can no longer be assumed to be entirely out of the ECB president's reach.

The TLTRO is designed to encourage banks to increase their lending to the private sector, in sectors other than housing. The BoE has had some success with this approach. But in Europe, as in Britain, a lack of demand for loans may limit its effectiveness.

Inflation in the euro area has fallen to about 0.5 % – and much lower in some countries. To many outside observers, it already looks extraordinary that the ECB has drifted so far from its inflation target of just below 2 % without adopting some form of QE. High unemployment in the eurozone is an indication that inflation is unlikely to return quickly.

The ECB's balance sheet has been shrinking recently, as previous LTROs were paid off; now it will probably grow once again.

Could fund managers turn into dinosaurs?

According to a recent KMPG study, 50% of global asset management firms will be gone by the year 2030 because new technology and social habits are changing the industry.

It is true that today, even boutique investment managers have a role to play in serving various investor expectations.

Because of new technology and changing social habits, there will be a requirement of so many new people to fill in those niches.

For example, new generation does not need personal touch any more. With the DNC (Do Not Call) which the FTC put out few years ago, you cannot cold call anymore.

So, Bud Fox's tryst with destiny in the movie Wall Street (1987) is unlikely to be repeated anymore.

For the uninitiated, Wall Street is a 1987 American drama film, directed and co-written by Oliver Stone, which stars Michael Douglas, Charlie Sheen, Daryl Hannah and Martin Sheen. The film tells the story of Bud Fox (Sheen), a young stockbroker desperate to succeed who becomes involved with his hero, Gordon Gekko (Douglas), a wealthy, unscrupulous corporate raider.

Also, with changing demographic trends; the role of women as head of households and as ones making financial decisions is increasing.

Are Robo-Advisors Warning of a Late Stage Bull Market?

Behavioral science talks about the many shortcomings of human psychology when it comes to investing. The emotions of *"greed"* and *"fear"* are the predominant drivers of not only investor behavior over time but also the development and delivery of the financial products that they use. As markets rise and fall, investors consume products and services accordingly. During strongly rising markets the demand for "risk" related products rise. Conversely, as markets fall the demand for safety and income rises and "risk" related losses mount. Of course, the business of Wall Street is to provide those *"products"* to the consumers they serve.

It is from this perspective that as we see the financial markets cycle from *"boom"* to *"bust,"* that we have seen a series of product and services offerings come and go in the financial marketplace. In the early 80's, we saw the rise of *"portfolio insurance"* which eventually gave way in the *"Crash of '87."* As the bull market gained momentum in the 90's the proliferation of mutual funds exploded on Wall Street as the demand by individual investors grew. Wall Street quickly figured out that it was far more lucrative to collect ongoing fees rather than a one-time trading commission. The age of the *"stock broker"* was officially dead as the rise of the asset-gathering *"financial consultant"* gained traction. The mutual fund business was booming, and business was *"brisk"* on Wall Street as profits surged.

However, as the internet was developed, the next major financial innovation occurred - *"online trading."* For the first time, Wall Street could tap directly into the masses and the *"Wall Street Casino"* officially opened. The marketplace for the delivery of products and services exploded, and Wall Street was happy to deliver a steady stream of new offerings to the newly minted *"investing geniuses."* The "financial consultants" were deemed *"hooligans"* for charging fees for *"advice"* for something that a *"trained monkey"* could do online.

"Why would anyone pay an advisor and reduce their returns when all one had to do was point-and-click their way to wealth."

Day trading shops were set up around the country along with videos, seminars and academies all designed to teach individuals the *"art of trading their way to wealth."*

That, of course, was the late 90's and soon thereafter not much was left but broken homes and empty bank accounts. The demand for *"advice"* surged as individuals, desperate for hope, clung to the *"words of wisdom"* from the very individuals that they had chastised during the preceding bull market.

As shown in the chart below, the cycle continues to repeat itself.

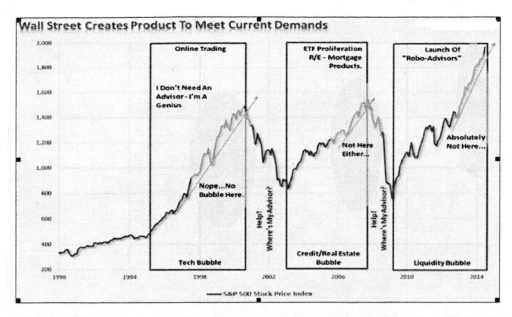

Wall Street Creates Product To Meet Current Demands

After the devastating crash of *"dot-com"* bubble, individuals shunned stocks to jump into real estate. This was surely a *"can't lose"* proposition as *"everyone needs a house,"* right? As the demand for real estate grew, Wall Street once again responded with a litany of products from Real Estate Investment Trusts (REIT's) to private real estate investment vehicles and, of course, the infamous mortgage-backed security and derivative products.

As the liquidity fueled real estate market gained traction, the liquidity derived from low interest rates, cash-out refinancings and mortgage-ATM's were dumped back into the financial markets. Making money was so easy - why would anyone ever pay a financial advisor a *"fee"* to manage their money for them. Once again, the mainstream media jumped into the fray touting low costs investing, indexing and launching a series of *"investing contests."* There was once again nothing to worry about in the financial markets - valuations were reasonable due to low interest rates, *"subprime was contained,"* and it was the advent of Bernanke's *"Goldilocks"* economy. What could possibly go wrong?

Of course, by the time that individuals figured out the party was over; Wall Street had already left without having to clean up the mess. For a second time, emotionally battered and financially crushed, individuals rushed to seek out the human contact of financial advisors. The need to commiserate, hear words of encouragement and be shown signs of hope were worth the *"fees."* Individuals were no longer concerned with *"beating some index"* but rather how to protect what they had left.

Human psychology and emotional behaviors *are* critically important to understand as they are the one constant in an ever changing financial landscape. I have shown the following chart before which is not a new concept by any means.

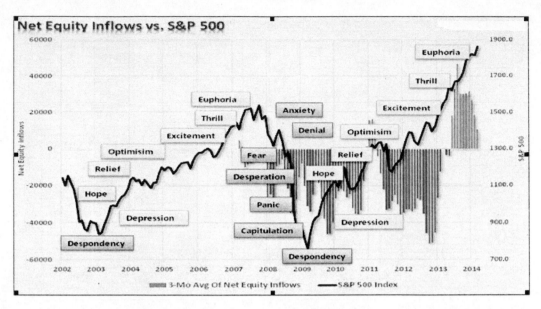

The emotions of *"greed"* and *"fear"* continually dominate investor behavior. It is due to these emotional biases that instead of *"buying low and selling high"* the vast majority of individuals do the opposite. After the end of a correction process in the markets, individuals' appetite for *"risk"* is extremely limited. The previous losses of personal wealth have left most anchored in despondency. As markets begin to recover individuals do not perceive the initial recovery as the return of an investible cycle, but rather an opportunity to *"get out"* of the financial markets and promising *"never to return."*

It is not until very late in the *"bull market"* cycle that individuals return to the *"casino."* Of course, this is after a long period of being chastised by the mainstream media *"for missing the rally"* and admonishing advisors for not *"beating the market."* After all, at this point who needs an advisor anyway? Everyone should just buy an index fund because *"this time is different"* and **there is an overwhelming perception that there is *"no risk"* of chasing *"risk."***

The Next Innovation That Will Likely Mark The Top

Near each major market peak throughout history, there has been some *"new"* innovation in the financial markets to take advantage of individual's investment *"greed."* In 1929, Charles Ponzi created the first *"Ponzi"* scheme. In the 1600's, it was *"Tulip Bulbs."* Whenever, and where ever, there has ever been a peak in *"investor insanity,"* there has always been someone there to meet that need. In that past it was railroads, real estate, commodities, or emerging market debt; today it is investment advice.

The latest innovation to come to market is what is termed *"Robo-Advisors."* Robo-Advisors are a breed on online investment services that allow individuals to attach their investment accounts to *"buy and hold"* portfolio allocation models of low cost index funds with an automated rebalancing process. On the surface, it sounds like a winning idea with low cost portfolio management, index based performance, and immediate online access.

Due to the liquidity driven surge in the markets over the last five years, the increased optimism has once again created the belief that *"monkeys throwing darts"* can pick stocks as well as a veteran investment advisor. Therefore, why pay the fee for an advisor when buying a very low cost index fund will give you better performance? It is a valid question. History, however, has the answer.

The problem for Robo-Advisors is yet to come as there is a *"duration"* mismatch between Robo-advisors and individual's emotional behavior. The investment time frame for Robo-Advisors is very long term based on historical returns of markets over time. In theory, the model is sound. *"If"* **an individual indeed invested in the model, *"if"* they rebalanced regularly and *"if"* they held for a 20-30 year period, depending on where in the market cycle they began, they would indeed perform very well. There are a lot of *"IF's"* in that statement.**

Unfortunately, as discussed above, despite most individuals best intentions of being a long term investor, **the reality is that their *"long-term"* time frame is only from today until the next major market correction begins.** To put this into context, in the 1960's the average hold time for stocks was roughly six years. Today that hold time is from six weeks to six months. When the next downturn begins, as it eventually will, money will flee Robo-advisors in search of human contact, advice and hope.

That is the cycle of innovation in the financial market place. Despite the best of intentions, and advances in innovation, humans will always seek out the comfort of other humans in times of distress. The rising notoriety of Robo-advisors is very likely the symbol of the current late stage *"market exuberance."*

I have been around long enough to see many things come and go in the financial world, and there is only one truth: *"The more things change, the more they stay the same."*

Global stock markets are seeing a rotation from the U.S. and India into China and Korea

Spurt in oil prices is threatening to throw India's inflation figures out of control.

The Indian stock markets have registered a gain of around 20% this year; so is it fair to now book profits and move out?

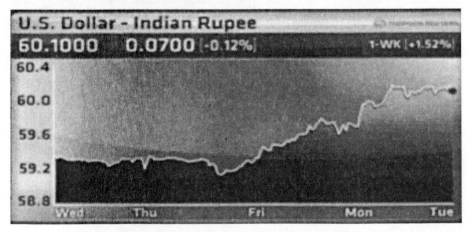

Lot of money is moving into China which is being widely perceived to be an undervalued market. The reserve ratio is widely perceived as being good for Chinese financials. The interest in Chinese shares in Asia is because they are discounted cheaper than 'H' shares in Hong Kong.

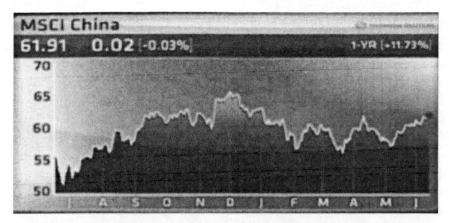

Some months back, the PBoC (People's Bank of China) was fighting shadow banking with higher interest rates; now, they appear more dovish.

The Chinese authorities do not want to see a spike in interest rates.

CHINA MARKETS (30-DAYS)

Hang Seng	23,300.67 ▲	587.76	[+2.59%]
H-Shares	10,522.13 ▲	566.78	[+5.69%]
Shanghai Comp	2,084.63950 ▲	58.13600	[+2.87%]
Taiex	9,217.18 ▲	328.73	[+3.70%]

CHINA MARKETS (YTD)

Hang Seng	23,300.67 ▼	5.72	[-0.02%]
H-Shares	10,522.13 ▼	294.01	[-2.72%]
Shanghai Comp	2,084.63950 ▼	31.33800	[-1.48%]
Taiex	9,217.18 ▲	605.67	[+7.03%]

2014 is also the year which will see the FATCA come into existence on July 1:

What is FATCA and what it means for the world of finance

The **U.S. Foreign Account Tax Compliance Act** or **FATCA** comes into effect on July 1, 2014 to target those who evade paying U.S. taxes by hiding assets in undisclosed foreign bank accounts.

FATCA requires foreign financial institutions (FFI) of broad scope - banks, stock brokers, hedge funds, pension funds, insurance companies, trusts - to report directly to the IRS all clients' accounts owned by U.S. Citizens and U.S. persons (Green Card holders).

If an institution does not comply, the U.S. will impose a 30% withholding tax on all its transactions concerning U.S. securities, including the proceeds of sale of securities.

In addition, FATCA requires any foreign company not listed on a stock exchange or any foreign partnership which has 10% U.S. ownership to report to the IRS the names and tax I.D. number (TIN) of any U.S. owner.

FATCA also requires U.S. citizens and green card holders who have foreign financial assets in excess of $50,000 (higher for those who are bona-fide residents abroad) to complete a new Form 8938 to be filed with the 1040 tax return, starting with fiscal year 2011.

Risk of funds withdrawal from U.S. bank deposits held by non-resident aliens

In addition to investments in securities, foreigners hold over $1 trillion on bank deposit in the United States because those deposits are tax free and the United States represents a safe haven for non-resident aliens. Congress has deliberately established this policy to attract foreign funds so necessary to the U.S. economy. But if a 30% withholding tax may potentially be applied upon transfer of those deposits to an overseas account, the attractiveness of United States banking services disappears.

Foreign divestment of U.S. investments is a serious risk

The FATCA threat of a 30% withholding tax and the potential exposure to transfer of personal data is inciting foreigners to divest out of U.S. securities and investments. Some foreign banks throughout the world have already indicated their intention to do so and have advised their institutional and private clients accordingly.

The foreign direct investment component is also vulnerable

If future financial transfers out of the United States are perturbed by FATCA, the direct investment component of the U.S. economy may suffer as well. A pull back in foreign direct investment in the U.S., which now represents an accumulated $2.7 trillion, would negatively impact the growth of the economy. Attracting foreign companies to invest in the United States requires not only good business prospects but also a free flow of capital both into and out of the country. With the economy seriously underperforming, unemployment high and budget and trade deficits ballooning, this is not a time when the U.S. can afford to lose any kind of investment in its economy, but that is exactly what FATCA will provoke.

The huge potential foreign investment losses largely outweigh FATCA revenues

The U.S. financial industry is one of the nation's most competitive sectors in world markets today, and the open access and ability to freely transfer funds into and out of U.S. financial markets has historically been a key reason for that strength. This competitive position will be diminished by FATCA. The U.S. financial industry will find itself isolated from many international transactions. Foreign investors will avoid U.S.-based hedge funds. Foreign hedge funds will avoid investing in U.S. securities and will refuse U.S. clients.

IMF US GDP downgrade: What it means for interest rate outlook

Recent economic data from the U.S. indicate that the world's largest economy could see growth of 3 percent in 2014.

A sharp downward revision to the International Monetary Fund's (IMF) U.S. growth forecast is a surprise but doesn't necessarily mean that interest rates in the world's number one economy will stay low for longer than anticipated.

The IMF recently cut its U.S. gross domestic product (GDP) growth forecast to 2 percent for 2014 from 2.8 percent, estimated that U.S. inflation will stay below the Federal Reserve's 2 percent target through 2017 and said the Fed should keep its key rate near zero longer than markets expect.

Some analysts challenged that view saying signs of stronger-than-expected growth in the U.S. economy pointed to monetary tightening sooner rather than later.

Clearly those IMF comments hit a little bit of a nerve but if you look at the incoming data flow, especially the numbers we got recently on production, home builder sentiment and the Empire State survey, they all paint a picture of an economy growing close to a 3 percent clip.

This is above trend for the U.S. so I'm not sure these downgrades to the outlook are warranted.

Data released showed May U.S. industrial production increased a monthly 0.6 percent, home builder sentiment surged in June and the New York Federal Reserve's Empire State index of business conditions in June rose to a four-year high.

Is London closing in on Silicon Valley?

The U.K.'s tech scene is snapping at the heels of its stateside counterparts, growing faster – and employing more people - than its Californian rival, according to a new report.

As the first London Technology Week gets underway, the research bolsters London's case to become a key global digital hub.

Some 744,000 technology and information workers are employed across London and the U.K.'s east and southeast regions (including Oxford and Cambridge), according to a report by South Mountain Economics' Michael Mandel. This figure has shot up by 76,000 since 2009.

Old Street roundabout, in the area known as London's Tech City

This is larger than California's infamous tech sector, which employs 692,000, South Mountain Economics found. And even taking into account the rapid growth of San Francisco's digital scene, the sector in London and its surrounding areas is expanding faster than its Californian rival, according to the research.

To keep ahead of the game, however, London has some significant hurdles to overcome, according to a survey of fast-growing businesses published by Tech London Advocates last month.

The biggest impediment to the capital's digital future is a shortage of talent, according to 43 percent of those questioned. While some 10 percent highlighted issues with the U.K.'s immigration legislation.

The challenges holding back London are the same as New York's, they're the same as San Francisco's. When you're building a robust digital and internet economy, you need more talent, and you have to make sure skills keep up with the pace of technology.

One way Britain was working to overcome these challenges was by introducing things like the "Exceptional Talent" visa for international leaders in science, engineering and tech.

Tech City UK is trying to look at this case by case and to help companies get those visas.

Economic boost

Taken alone, London's tech sector employs only slightly fewer workers than those in New York and San Francisco/Silicon Valley, according to South Mountain Economics.

London has around 382,000 workers in the sector, just below San Francisco/ Silicon Valley's 397,000 and New York's 411,000. Nonetheless, report author Mandel said the figures places "the city within the top echelon of global tech regions today."

Separate research by Oxford Economics, also published recently, found that London's digital tech sector is expected to grow at a rate of 5.1 % per year.

This will boost Britain's gross domestic product by £12 billion ($20.37 billion) over the next decade, according to the report, creating 46,000 new jobs in the capital.

Speaking at the launch of London Technology Week, Mayor of London, Boris Johnson, said these forecasts were realistic. However, he stressed it was time to question why London – as Europe's biggest digital hub - hadn't yet produced a tech giant like Twitter, Google or Facebook.

"Is it because of a British diffidence about making billions of pounds? Is it because we don't have the right kind of kick-ass business people here in London? Is it that the banks and venture capitalist industry aren't as imaginative and proactive as they could be?" Borris Johnson asked.

Why Ukraine still matters?

The market seems to have shrugged off recent troubles in Ukraine. Yields on the country's ten year bonds are now down to 8.8%, about 2% lower than at the start if May.

A new President, billionaire chocolatier Petro Poroshenko is taking charge amidst optimism about his ability to solve the military conflicts over Ukraine's borders.

Yet, there are plenty of potential mis-steps and risks that lie ahead. Unrest in eastern Ukraine, and Ukraine's own position in the world order are biggest risks to its return to normality.

Ukraine is close to signing a trade deal with the European Union to remove customs duties on some of its exports, which could benefit agriculture in particular, according to Khramov. Yet this could in turn lead to further action in terms of trade sanctions from Russia, previously its biggest export partner, against Ukraine.

The price for gas from Russia is set to rise by 40 percent in May next year, which will further squeeze Ukrainians.

A bailout from the International Monetary Fund has been well received, but comes with plenty of conditions attached.

And several of the country's banks are facing the process of recapitalization.

There is also plenty of potential for political unrest with elections for the new Rada (the Ukrainian parliament), likely to be called earlier than planned (the last election was in 2012).

With violence still erupting in eastern Ukraine, this could be an extremely contentious election.

There are also still significant risks attached to investing in neighboring Russia.

Russia's conduct in the past few months has signaled the power shift away from liberalism towards the 'siloviki' faction in the top echelons of government. While this has been in progress for a while, recent appointments in the army and regions suggest the faction is gaining strength as Russia feels more threatened – and this is unlikely to be good news if Ukraine is trying to establish itself as more than a Russian satellite.

The risks of expropriation and nationalization – especially in response to Western sanctions – are likely to rise.

Is the Michael Jackson resurrection good for US bonds?

There is little that is new or thrilling about either the US music industry or corporate America

The resurrection of Michael Jackson

The recent Jacksonian resurrection, of course, was an illusion. The biological Michael left us nearly five years ago at the age of 50. The Billboard Music Awards audience was treated to a hologram – a three-dimensional image – miming a song that was recorded by Jackson nearly a quarter century ago and released this month.

The Sin City crowd loved it. Michael Jackson is still a great showman even if his heart is not beating anymore.

The music world folks or the US corporate world are simply less interesting than a fixed-income instrument backed by the full faith and credit of the federal government in Washington. Jack Lew, the US Treasury secretary does offer a future. It is measured in basis points, for the most part, which is pretty depressing, but at least it is real.

The music industry, by contrast, has retreated from its traditional role as the purveyor of the Next Big Thing. That was its old product: Crosby, then Sinatra, Presley, The Beatles, The Rolling Stones, Motown, James Brown, Madonna and Michael himself. Jazz gave way to rock and then to the twist, folk, rock again, soul, funk, heavy metal, disco, punk, reggae, hip-hop and so on.

Consider, if you will, that Jackson's career peaked not so long after the release of his album Thriller – in 1982. In other words, nearly 32 years have passed since that moment. If the music business had been so backward-looking in the year of Thriller's debut, the awards shows then would have featured holograms of Patti Page, Phil Harris or Sammy Kaye (some of the chart toppers of 1950).

The harrowing thing for investors is that creativity shortages of this kind are becoming common in US business. Check out the front pages and you'll see what I mean.

One recent example is Pfizer's bid for its UK rival, AstraZeneca. The US pharmaceutical company would most likely lower its tax rate if it succeeds. But I doubt it would be much closer to healing the world, to paraphrase one of Jackson's more popular songs.

Similarly, AT&T's agreed deal to buy satellite television service provider DirecTV has struck more than a few industry analysts as lacking a clear strategic rationale.

As businesses grow more complex, their managers are increasingly drawn from the ranks of lawyers and financial engineers. That crowds out the freewheeling sorts with the ability to appreciate talents such as those possessed by the Jackson family of Gary, Indiana.

Music industry executives lacking fresh ideas are trying to reinstitute such odd ideas as the Jackson hologram. After all, seen purely from a balance- sheet perspective, Michael is in a far better place. He's no longer the amortising asset of his later years. He's an annuity now.

Investors manic for 'disrupter' stocks

Euphoria is a typical late-cycle signal. Investors throw caution to the wind and try to maximise upside returns. Pension funds overweight equities at the expense of prudent asset allocation, individual investors rush into hot equity mutual funds, Wall Street's strategists recommend overweighting equities and hedge funds lever long positions substantially.

We can find no data that conclusively support the notion that the US stock market is in such a euphoric stage.

Credit Suisse data indicate US pension funds have among the lowest equity allocations in more than 30 years and remain focused on alternatives rather than conventional equities.

A Bank of America Merrill Lynch indicator shows Wall Street strategists are recommending an underweight of equities relative to the traditional 60/30/10 stocks/bond/cash benchmark. International Strategy and Investment's hedge fund survey shows hedge funds are neutrally positioned. ICI data show net outflows from US equity funds for seven straight weeks.

The current IPO market certainly seems frothy, but that frothiness is unique and does not reflect investors' sentiment towards the broader equity market. Whereas speculative IPO markets often mirror overall stock market valuation, the current cycle's speculation, much like that during the late-1990s technology bubble, seems limited to a relatively narrow universe of stocks. Detailed valuation data continue to suggest considerable fear of traditional equities.

Bubble-like 'disrupters'

Investors rationalised lofty valuations during the technology bubble with theories regarding the "new economy". "Disrupter" companies are today's rationalisation. Investors seem willing to pay outrageous valuations for disrupter companies because the companies are supposedly changing the world and have no relationship to the economic cycle, to Washington or to geopolitical events. It seems hard to fathom how an auto company, an energy company or a limousine service is not connected to the economy, but investors nonetheless appear giddy regarding disrupters' potential returns.

Many of the disrupters sell at bubble-like valuations because of this enthusiasm. According to Bloomberg, Tesla Motors, perhaps the best known of the disrupter companies, sells for more than 850 times enterprise value to earnings before taxes, interest, depreciation and amortisation. The S&P 600 biotechnology index sells for 350 times. For comparison, the S&P 500's enterprise value to ebitda is 11 times and the Russell 2000's is about 15 times. One would think the deflation of the technology bubble would have taught investors the lessons of avoiding super-speculative stocks, but apparently not.

Beta is a standard measurement of a stock's sensitivity to the movement of the stock market. A stock with a higher beta will tend to move in an exaggerated way relative to the movement in the market, whereas a lower beta stock's movements will tend to be less pronounced. Most disrupter stocks are considered higher beta stocks.

An axiom of basic financial theory states that investors should pay a premium for safety, but demand compensation for taking risk. Investors should generally pay premium valuations for lower beta stocks as they offer relative safety and discounted valuations for higher beta stocks as compensation for accepting those stocks' risk. Within this context, the disrupter group's valuations seem especially speculative.

High beta cheap

Whereas disrupter stocks sell at huge premiums to the overall market because investors believe the stocks' successes are assured, traditional high beta stocks within the S&P 500 are selling at the cheapest relative valuations in the almost 30-year history of our data. Judging by these data, investors are historically scared about traditional market risk.

High beta S&P 500 portfolios were historically dominated by technology shares, but that is no longer the case. Currently, the quintile of S&P 500 stocks with the highest betas is a mixture of many cyclical sectors. Technology comprises only 15 per cent of today's high beta group. Financials are 23 per cent, consumer cyclicals are 24 per cent and industrials are 15 per cent.

Further, my research indicates earnings surprise statistics for the traditional high beta group are among the world's best. Only 17 per cent of the S&P 500's high beta quintile reported negative earnings surprises in the last reporting period. That compares with the S&P 500's 25 per cent, Europe's 48 per cent and emerging markets' 49 per cent. The IPO market seems very speculative, but one must take care in extrapolating those lofty valuations to the broader market.

The enthusiasm for disrupter stocks seems manic, but the lack of enthusiasm for traditional equity risk presents opportunity.

Why Abenomics and Modinomics are poles apart

My view is that India and Japan face very different sets of problems, so 'Modinomics' and 'Abenomics' cannot be readily compared. Two leaders with clear economic agendas to revive their country's economic prospects, and stock markets riding high on waves of optimism. It's not too difficult to see the similarities between India's Prime Minister Narendra Modi and his Japanese counterpart Shinzo Abe, but perhaps the links end there.

India and Japan face very different sets of problems, so 'Modinomics' and 'Abenomics' cannot be readily compared. India is country trying to "fight" inflation whereas Japan is a country which is trying to "increase" inflation.

India's biggest problem is a massive infrastructure deficit - it needs power plants, highways, railways, clean water. It has a growing population with rising incomes, but the infrastructure deficit constrains Indian growth. By contrast, Japan's biggest problem is a zero-growth, aging population.

Abe came to power roughly 18 months ago, determined to end a cycle of deflation and lackluster growth in the world's third biggest economy through a three-pronged strategy involving monetary and fiscal stimulus and long-term structural reforms.

Monetary stimulus and optimism about Abenomics fuelled a 57 % rally in the blue-chip Nikkei stock index last year. India's stock market meanwhile surged to a record high after last month's landslide win for the pro-business Modi, triggering comparisons between Abenomics and Modinomics.

Commentators have been quick to conclude that the rally in Tokyo's stock exchange that followed Japan Prime Minister Shinzo Abe's victory, could be mimicked by the Indian markets. While the upgrades/re-rating to the Indian equity markets is not surprising, the comparison ignores some ground realities. Of all the catalysts that triggered the surge in Japanese stock markets last year, only one is applicable to India's situation: a stable government at the center.

Because India is decentralized, Modi is constrained in what he can do to at a national level to boost the long-term growth prospects of an economy hampered by high inflation. By contrast, Japan is highly centralized, so Abe can achieve a lot with monetary policy, taxes, and incentives, if he can obtain political backing at the national level. The Bank of Japan is committed to pumping 60-70 trillion yen ($589-$687 billion) into the economy a year to boost inflation and Tokyo just announced plans to cut the corporate tax rate to 30 % in the years ahead from around 36 % now.

Honeymoon over Abe, however, has also come under criticism for not doing more in terms of long-term structural reforms. Some of what Abe may be doing are half measures and may not be going far enough. By contrast, what is Modi doing in

India. India was rated by the World Bank as the 134th best place to do business in the world out of 189 countries. It came in just in front of the West Bank and Gaza and Modi recognized that -- just recently he increased rail fares 14 percent, freight rates 6.5 percent. These are typically hot topics politically in India – everybody stays away from rail fares. I think Abe needs to do some of the same things in Japan. In addition to last week's hike in rail passenger to help fund investment, Modi's government has cheered markets with taking immediate steps to help contain inflation such as ordered a crackdown on hording to contain rising food prices.

The danger for Modi, is that a failure to maintain the reform agenda could lead to the same disappointment that has undermined Abenomics and the Nikkei's stellar rally. The Modi government is still in the honeymoon phase, while Abe's government no longer enjoys that advantage.

US Q2 2014 GDP Economic "Hope" Misses the Point

The release of the final estimate of the Q1-2014 Gross Domestic Product report took most everyone by surprise by plunging to a negative 2.9% versus a negative 1.8% consensus. However, not to fear, the ever bullish media spin machine quickly stepped in to assuage fears by stating:

"If GDP were truly so weak, we would not expect aggregate hours worked to climb 3.7% annualized through May, jobless claims to remain near cycle lows, consumer confidence to hit a cycle high, industrial production to climb 5.0% at an annual rate over the first five months of the year, core capital goods orders to be up 5.8%, ISM to be above 55, and vehicle sales to hit their strongest annualized selling pace for the year. GDP is the outlier in these data points. I will roll my eyes and move on. Most of the data we just mentioned is consistent with underlying growth over 3.0%.

This is a problem with the majority of economic analysis. Blinded by the ever pressing need to take a *"bullish spin"* on the data *(negative spins do not attract advertisers, readers or viewers)* more important structural analysis is missed. Let's break down that statement above into its parts.

Aggregate hours worked climbed 3.7% *annualized* through May.

Annualizing data is the worst offense in economic analysis. It is extremely deceptive as it assumes that every single month going forward will produce a similar result which, especially with economic data, is rarely the case. The reality is that a rebound in activity following the Q1 slump creating a pickup in hours worked. While the 3.7% annualized rate sounds extremely positively and exciting, the reality is that average weekly hours worked was 34.4 in January, slumped to 34.3 in February, and rose to 34.5 in March, April and May. Working 1/10 of an hour longer than in January doesn't sound nearly as optimistic.

Jobless Claims

Jobless claims are indeed near cycle lows, as they should be at this point in the economic cycle. However, first-time claims are a function of layoffs, terminations and separations. As shown in the chart below, there are only so many employees that businesses can terminate and still maintain operations and at some point will have to *"hoard"* what labor they have left. This does not mean that businesses are increasing employment due to a stronger business cycle.

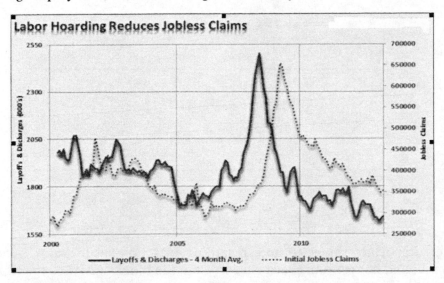

Consumer Confidence, ISM

The Consumer Confidence and ISM surveys are good coincident indicators as they tell us much about what business owners and consumers are feeling *"right now."* Since these surveys are primarily *"sentiment"* based, rather than *"data based,"* there is less reliability as a forward looking indicator. Sentiment can, and does, change course very rapidly which makes this data much less important for investment purposes.

The ISM Composite Index *(an average of the manufacturing and services surveys)* shows the high volatility of the data. After a sharp drop in sentiment in Q1, there has been a sharp rebound over the last few months. This is as expected due to rebound in activity as an inventory restocking cycle proceeds.

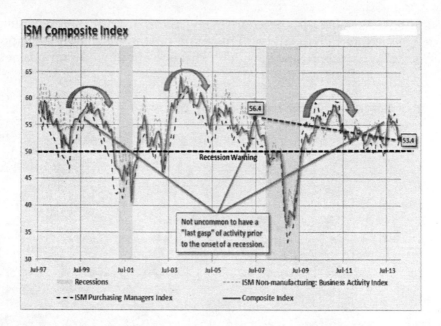

A few important things to note regarding ISM Composite Index. While the current rebound has certainly been encouraging, the index has failed to eclipse any of the old highs since the financial crisis. The entire recovery has been a systemic run of declines and rebounds which has been the hallmark of the overall anemic recovery. Secondly, notice that activity tends to rebound just before the onset of a recession as a *"last gasp"* of activity occurs. It is important NOT to get lost in a single data point but putting the data into context.

The context of these ongoing *"recovery seizures"* are more clearly shown in the following chart of the Chicago Fed National Activity Index *(one of the most overlooked economic indicators)* which is a broad national composite of 85 subcomponents. Each stint of *"recovery"* has given way to the underlying weakness in the ongoing *"struggle through"* economy.

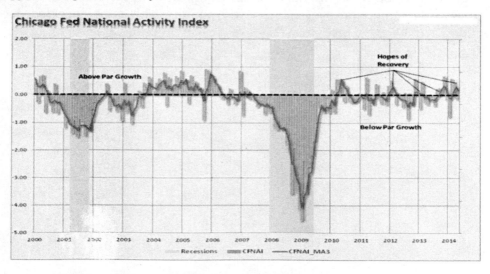

Auto Sales

Lastly, auto sales are no longer as much of a leading indicator as they once were historically. In the 1970's automobile sales made a much large percentage of the economy than they do today. Furthermore, as I addressed at length in "Auto Sales - Hype vs. Reality:"

"The current level of unit sales has risen from its lows but now appears to be reaching a potential saturation point. At the bottom of the financial crisis, the quantity of sales suggested that the average American would keep their existing vehicle for 25 years. Today, that is no longer the case and much of that excess replacement need is likely filled.

Furthermore, with dealer inventories reaching extreme levels, financial incentives to move cars out of the showroom will continue to become an ever more pressing need. Subprime auto loans are already back in vogue along with little or no money down deals. Since that worked out so well last time, why not do it all over again?"

Economics Vs. Investing

All of this analysis and *"spin"* on the economic data misses the real point. As individuals, we are investing capital in business models that should produce an expected return over time based on several factors: 1) the price paid 2) projected future cash flows, and 3) the point within the current business cycle.

If we pay too much for a projected stream of cash flows at a very late point in a normal business cycle - the net return will be extremely low, if not negative.

The only reason that we care about economic data is solely to determine the current point within any given economic or business cycle. In the financial markets, our sole job as investors is to *"buy low and sell high"* and those *"low points"* highly correspond to the lows in the economic cycle as shown in the chart below.

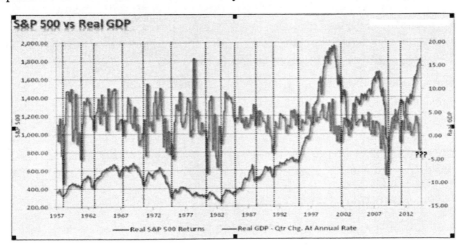

Currently, the parabolic rise in the markets, extreme bullish optimism, and high levels of complacency are *"trumping"* the drop the Q1 GDP in *"hopes"* that it was indeed just a *"weather related anomaly."* This is very similar to what happened in late 1999 as the economy began its slip into a recession. The initial drops in GDP were disregarded by analysts and economists until it was far too late. The same thing occurred again in 2007 with Bernanke's call of a *"Goldilocks Economy."*

When it comes to evaluating the underlying strength of the economy, one of the most important measures is the level of *"final sales."* While GDP measures total domestic production, **final sales reflect the demand by consumers, businesses, and government.** Since the economy is almost 70% driven by consumption this number is far more important in determining what is happening beneath the headline GDP report. The chart below shows real, inflation adjusted, final sales.

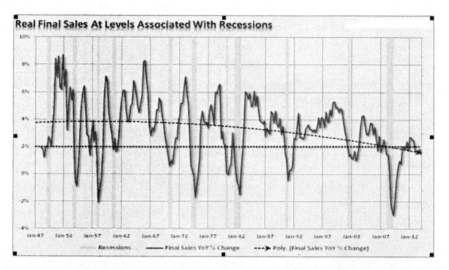

The current downturn in real final sales suggests that the underlying strength in the economy remains extremely fragile. More importantly, with final sales below levels normally associated with the onset of recessions, it suggests that the current rebound in activity from the sharp decline in Q1 could be transient. This is particularly the case with energy, gasoline and food costs rising sharply which saps discretionary spending capability of consumers.

Furthermore, a major problem with economic analysis overall, from an investment standpoint, is that the data is highly subject to revisions, manipulation and subjectivity. Making investment decisions today based on data that could be sharply revised over the next year is extremely dangerous. This is why economic data is only useful in determining the potential point within a given economic cycle that an investment is being made. Given that the current economic recovery is more than 60 months old, which is extremely long by historical measures, the odds of substantial investment growth from this point in the cycle are very low.

As individuals, it is entirely acceptable to be *"optimistic"* about the future. However, *"optimism"* and *"pessimism"* are emotional biases that tend to obfuscate the critical thinking required to effectively assess the *"risks"* related to making investment and portfolios related decisions. The current *"hope"* that Q1 was simply a *"weather related"* anomaly is also an emotionally driven skew. The underlying data suggests that while *"weather"* did play a role in the sluggishness of the economy, it was also just a reflection of the continued *"boom bust"* cycle that has existed since the end of the financial crisis.

Does Sweden household debt pose contagion risk?

Sweden may have managed to come out of the financial crisis much stronger than some of its European peers, but its ballooning level of household debt poses a serious threat to its economy and its neighbors, the International Monetary Fund (IMF) has warned.

Property prices in Sweden have risen sharply, rising 5 % between March and May compared to the same period last year. In Stockholm, prices rose 7 % year-on-year, with average house prices in the city now at $660,000. A recent SEB survey published last month showed 66 % of households expect house prices to rise in the coming year. The booming housing market has encouraged Swedes to take on more mortgage debt, but concerns are growing over the risks this poses to banks.

Following its annual visit to Sweden, the IMF said sudden drop in house prices could hit the banking system in the same way overleveraged households and sub prime mortgages sparked the financial crisis in 2007.

Even though Sweden is not a member of the euro zone, analysts are now comparing Sweden's contagion risk to southern Europe, where heavily indebted Greece helped trigger the euro zone debt crisis.

Low interest rates and easy monetary policy have helped household debt in Sweden grow to 175 percent of disposable income in 2013, the fund said. The figure rose to 19 percent if tenant-owned housing associations are included.

The benchmark interest rate currently has stood at 0.75 percent since December, when it was cut from 1 percent.

At the same time, inflation has fallen way short of the central bank's target of 2 percent for over a year. The country fell into deflation in May, when prices fell 0.2 percent, but the central bank has been reluctant to respond by cutting rates, fearing that might encourage households to take on even more debt.

Nordic economies are all very intertwined, much more so than those of southern Europe and we saw how effective contagion was in those markets a couple of years ago.

The central bank in Sweden, Riksbank, is now facing intense pressure to act after the IMF's warning that "financial instability in Sweden would quickly spread to other Nordic and Baltic countries" and annual CPI inflation fell further in May.

The fall in inflation in May from 0 percent to -0.2 percent will deepen fears that Sweden is falling into a "damaging bout of deflation."

Headline inflation has been weak in Sweden for more than a year now, but the central bank has been slow to respond to the disinflation trend for fear that lower rates would encourage highly indebted households to take on yet more debt.

But the onset of falling prices will add to the growing pressure on the central bank for more action. I continue to expect the policy rate to be lowered by another 25bp, possibly as soon as next month.

Why the equity bull market is intact?

Retail investors raised cash allocations to 40% in 2014.

It is an immutable truth of investing that you should sell at the top and buy at the bottom. And it is almost as immutable a truth that most of us do exactly the opposite, buying at the top and selling at the bottom.

Professional investors are prone to this. But nobody suffers it worse than retail investors. Over history, they tend to be sucked in at the top of a bull market, turning optimism into euphoria; and to give up just when all hope has been lost and the foundations for a fresh rally have thus been built.

In the US, mutual funds took in $259.5bn in 2000, when the market peaked and crashed. In 2002, a great time to buy on the verge of a strong recovery, investors removed $24.7bn.

These basic facts are well known. They do not necessarily suggest that retail investors are stupid. At market bottoms, families tend to be cash-strapped. It is harder to put money away in long-term stock plans. Stock markets, in which only the affluent can participate, become an engine to drive inequality even further.

One new survey suggests the problem is even worse in this post-crisis environment. This bull market has endured for more than five years but has not made people happier.

The reason, it appears, is that many stayed out of the market. Indeed, as the rally has continued, the proportion of savings that investors park in cash has significantly increased.

That is the core finding of a survey of retail investors in 16 countries by State Street. Globally, retail investors have raised their cash allocations from 31 per cent in 2012 to 40 % in 2014. In the US, where rising share prices should directly reduce the share of cash in portfolios, cash allocations jumped from 26 to 36 per cent.

As stocks have risen far faster than bank deposits, it is hard to see any good reason for cash reserves to rise in this way

Japan had the highest cash allocation at 57 %, so a jaded public failed to enjoy the stock market boom sparked by Abenomics. This also implies that the rise in asset prices will not have the hoped-for "wealth effect" and prompt consumers to spend more.

Other results speak badly both of consumers and of their advisers. Some two-thirds of investors globally said they did not know the fees they paid for their investment because it was too difficult to find out.

Most spent more time reading free catalogues than reading investment statements. Almost two decades after Arthur Levitt, then head of the US Securities and Exchange Commission, attacked the prose in mutual fund prospectuses for "flowing like peanut butter", basic communications to retail investors are no better.

There are two powerful implications for people in financial services. The first is that nobody trusts them. Trust, even more than credit, is the essential lubricant for capitalism, so this is a serious problem. The second implication is rosier. If retail investors are still in cash, and do not believe this rally, then the bull market has longer to run, even though stocks are already expensive. For years now, the greatest reason for optimism has been that so many remain dubious. If so much has stayed in cash, then greed has not yet swamped fear and an overpriced stock market has not yet turned into an exuberant bubble.

That could yet happen if, as in 1999 and 2000, retail investors at last decide to flock into stocks.

It is not inevitable. The Bank of England's warning that the UK could see rate rises earlier than expected is a reminder that the Fed could do the same and suck life out of the stock market. What appears to be turning into an outright war in Iraq, not at all on investors' radar screens even weeks ago, could also change the calculus.

But if retail investors still have so much in cash, then the conditions for a future stock market "melt-up" are in place.

Why England's football team needs to embrace yoga and meditation?

The words 'penalty shoot-out' are guaranteed to strike fear in the heart of all England fans. It's time the team realised it's not about football, but psychology

West Germany v England, July 4 1990. West Germany won 4-3 on penalties

England travels to the World Cup in Brazil in fear of the penalty shoot-out. The team has lost six out of seven shoot-outs in major tournaments. Going into this competition, all conversations about England's chances end with the rider: "But what if it goes to penalties?"

The answer to England's problems may be found in Oslo, in an unprepossessing office next to Norway's Olympiatoppen training centre. Here sits Geir Jordet, a former footballer who is director of psychology at the Norwegian Centre of Football Excellence. To understand their anxieties, Jordet interviewed 10 of the 14 players who took penalties for either Holland or Sweden in their Euro 2004 quarterfinal shoot-out (which Holland won, its first and only shoot-out success; the Dutch rival England for incompetence from the spot). The results, published as an academic study, were fascinating.

For the purpose of his interviews, Jordet broke up the shoot-out into four phases:

Phase One: the break after extra-time

Phase Two: the centre circle

Phase Three: the walk

Phase Four: at the penalty mark.

He then assessed each player's reaction at each phase. Six interviewees knew before Phase One that they would be taking a penalty; two specifically did not want to take one and another was annoyed that three other teammates had, during Phase One, expressly ruled themselves out. Four players felt more stressed when they were told what number they would be shooting, as they didn't know – and therefore couldn't prepare for – what the shoot-out situation would then be; another four were calm because they knew when they would be shooting.

Surprisingly, it was Phase Two that was the most stressful, particularly for the players on the losing side (Sweden), who were not standing in the centre circle as a group.

For three players, the loneliness of the walk, Phase Three, was the toughest part of the process. By Phase Four, when the players were at the ball itself, only two were expressing anxiety. Jordet concluded that coaches could learn something about every phase of the shoot-out. From Phase One: that players like to know the order they will be kicking as early as possible – and don't like surprises (or teammates bailing on them). From Phase Two: that waiting alone for your turn throws up negative emotions. From Phase Three: that the solitude of the walk calls for a coping mechanism. And from Phase Four: how best to face the goalkeeper in a psychological confrontation.

When Jordet was asked why England lose so often on penalties, he came up with several explanations. He'd looked at whether you should shoot high or low, strike with power or go for accuracy, and found no significant effects. The big effects were all about pressure and how you deal with stress. It was not about football but psychology.

All-Time Penalty Shoot-out Table				
Country	**P-W-L**	**Scored-Missed**	**Goal %**	**Win %**
Germany	6-5-1	26-2	93	83
Paraguay	5-3-2	19-3	86	60
Brazil	10-6-4	36-11	76	60
Spain	7-4-3	25-8	76	57
Uruguay	9-5-4	38-7	84	56
Argentina	9-5-4	33-10	77	56
France	6-3-3	25-6	81	50
Mexico	7-3-4	18-11	62	43
Italy	8-3-5	30-12	71	38
Holland	5-1-4	16-8	67	20
England	7-1-6	23-12	66	14

I have advocated yoga and transcendental meditations for professionals on Wall Street. Maybe, England's football team needs to embrace the same as well.

From an investment standpoint:

Brazil's experience in hosting high-profile sporting events could ultimately prove an example of how the acceleration of change can take place when people have a greater voice. The rise of the Internet, and more importantly the rise of cell phones and smartphones, has played a key part. It remains to be seen how the people's discontent will play out at the polls during Brazil's general election in October, but we will be watching. We believe the inverse correlation of Brazilian equities with President Rousseff's popularity demonstrates how populist government intervention in markets can be detrimental to growth. If the opposition party is victorious in the next election, there could be dramatic changes for the better, particularly in the area of encouraging greater private enterprise. But even if the current government remains, people are demanding change, so I think we could very well see it regardless.

A key point to consider is that while international sporting events may not provide the kick-start to growth for a country that many hope for, they can provide an opportunity for the people to demonstrate to the world that they are unhappy with their government. We've seen that in the case of Brazil.

There are a number of key elections coming up in emerging markets that could prove quite revolutionary. In India, Narendra Modi's landslide victory proved within a short period how quickly sentiment and stock prices can change. We believe the reform outlook for many emerging markets looks the brightest it has in years. China's government under President Xi has signaled its intention to embark upon extensive reform, and in Indonesia, presidential frontrunner Joko Widodo has announced ambitious plans to cut subsidies and increase investment. These are just a few examples.

World Cup could add to stock market woes

As World Cup fever heats up, a note of caution: the world's most widely viewed sporting event could spell trouble for markets. For many, the soccer World Cup is a time of anxiousness and suffering, followed by chaotic collapse (usually on penalties to Germany). England fans have come to expect this but, as a client recently pointed out, the pain doesn't always stop there. Markets also suffer around World Cup time.

The international football tournament, held every four years, kicks off in Brazil on June 12 and runs for four weeks. The inaugural competition was in 1930, the first full year of the Great Depression. More recently, it coincided with the U.S. recession in 1990, a bond market crash that started in the U.S. and spread across developed markets in 1994, the Asian Financial Crisis and collapse of Connecticut-based hedge fund Long Term Capital Management (LTCM) in 1998, a U.S. housing market crash in 2006 and the beginning of the euro zone crisis in 2010.

Based on past episodes, we should start by looking for bubbles. Abenomics - the name given to Japanese Prime Minister Shinzo Abe's economic revival plan - is one of these potential bubbles.

Aggressive monetary easing in Japan triggered a huge surge in the Nikkei and a collapse in the yen, in the expectation that the Japanese authorities could kill deflation and shift their economy onto a better medium-term growth path. But now these policies seem to be running out of steam.

The benchmark Nikkei 225 has rallied over 40 percent since Abe took office in December 2012. However, sportswear manufacturers and food and beverage stand to gain from Brazil's upcoming World Cup.

With the economy slowing in response to the April tax hike and the central bank apparently unwilling to ramp up QE [quantitative easing] again, there is a risk the Abenomics effect begins to unravel. A stalling U.S. economic recovery reflecting in falling U.S. bond yields is another key risk for markets.

Doubts linger about whether the economic recovery will gain traction. We think it will, but the housing market has shown a disturbingly large response to just a modest rise in mortgage rates over the past year. Sales of new homes tumbled to their lowest level in eight months in March, dashing hopes for a quick turnaround for the sector.

Over the past few years, the market might have expected the Fed to respond to such an outcome by stepping up its stimulus. However, with central bank determined to end QE, the extra stimulus might not be forthcoming this time.

We could be left with a stagnant economy and a feeling of vertigo in stock markets. And last but not least, China's economy is in a precarious position.

We are assuming a persistent slowdown in China and a gradual intensification of financial-sector pain, but after five years of credit-fuelled investment, the economy could unravel faster than we expect.

Cracks in the country's real estate market - a pillar of the world's second largest economy - have started to deepen in the recent months, with home prices falling sharply in third- and fourth-tier cities as a result of excess capacity.

The Russia-Ukraine crisis

Tensions between Russia and Ukraine remain high, and have spilled onto the international stage. The Western world seemed to be caught off guard by Russian President Putin's reaction to civil unrest in Ukraine, leading to Russia's annexation of Crimea and spreading into a broader question of regional sovereignty.

The United States has imposed a number of sanctions on Russia and has taken a stronger and harsher stance than the European Union (EU) simply because Europe would suffer more if it did the same.

The West has held off on true "sectoral" sanctions – applying sanctions to every company in an industry sector. However, should Russia intervene militarily, that position could change. Sectoral sanctions could cut the Russian economy off from the US dollar-based global financial system, but would be extremely challenging to implement and could cause collateral damage to Western economies, particularly the Eurozone. Sectoral sanctions also could play into Putin's hands, increasing his control over the oligarchs and their enterprises, resulting in the oligarchs' moving money outside of Western control, perhaps to China.

It may be prudent to envision an agreement whereby the Ukrainian government agrees to a federal system giving the Russian-speaking areas of the country considerable autonomy.

Business on both sides – Ukraine and Russia—should be able to continue despite the conflict. There is considerable trade and investment flow that won't be interrupted, even with some sanctions. Russia is a major supplier of oil to Germany and the Netherlands in particular, and of natural gas to Western Europe generally. Disruption to energy trade would be in neither side's interest.

Ukraine's finances, although under pressure, are likely to be supported by the EU, United States and World Bank. There is a possibility of Russia being able to achieve some financial benefits as well, including gas contracts.

Russian equities have often presented themselves as potential bargains during various stressful points in time. This is true even more so today.

The message of falling US bond yields

Global bond yields are in a deep slide, taking the 10-year U.S. Treasury to a level not seen since October 2013—well before the Fed began winding down its easy money program.

The common themes are accommodating central bankers and concerns about growth. In the U.S. a short position in Treasurys continues to support the market as investors are forced to cover with each notch higher in price and lower in yield. Yields were lower across the curve, but the 10-year yield broke below a range that it has held since the end of October, touching a low yield of 2.52 percent.

Reports that the European Central Bank has a road map for new stimulus, following ECB President Mario Draghi's recent dovish words has sent sovereign yields in Europe lower with some hitting all-time lows. The 10-year German bund yield has touched 1.36 percent.

The biggest bond markets cannot really disconnect from each other. Global bond investors are looking across and saying 'Treasurys are cheap compared to bunds".

Meanwhile, the 10-year gilt was as low as 2.57 % after the Bank of England's inflation forecast and comments from Bank of England Governor Mark Carney suggested the BOE may not raise rates as soon as markets expected.

I think the market's in a bit of a shell shock...People were expecting certainly in the 10-year sector of the range to hold.

The catalyst is the more dovish stance on European monetary policy, the weaker data in Europe a combined with less ambitious hiking expectations in the U.K. They didn't pull forward hiking expectations.

One should also refer to headlines on the Peoples Bank of China encouraging banks to loosen mortgage lending. Concerns about Ukraine are also putting a bid in Treasurys, in a flight-to-safety trade.

Another side of the global rate story is the worry about global growth. Retail sales in the U.S. have fallen short of expectations, while Chinese industrial production and retail sales are below forecast, and inflation readings in France of late have been flat and negative in Germany.

Coming into this year, and especially where we are now within the year, the market was positioned to be much further along in the curve of fiscal and economic reforms, coupled with global growth patterns, and consequently there was this view we were going to have higher rates associated with those developments.

There was an air pocket created post the June 2013 FOMC meeting-that unleashed the selling pressure that moved us from 2.25 to 2.50 in a heart beat...In October we got to 2.47. We have to break under 2.50 and see if we can purge the 2.25/2.50 range. We have to go into that range to see if the rally is over. We have to see the capitulation trade.

As the Fed tapered, the market overshot and the 10-year yield was at 3 % at the end of the year. The Fed first tapered its bond-buying program in December, trimming $10 billion from every meeting since then.

The Fed also competes with the market for securites at the long end of the curve, as it continues to buy, and that is also helping send rates lower.

Global yields:

Global yields are at historical lows. Recently, Ben Bernanke has indicated in comments to a group of investors that rates will be staying low for a considerable amount of time longer as economic conditions don't warrant tightening. The ECB has also hinted the same. With Japan's 10yr Bond now below 1.0% and pushing within 20 basis points of its 144 year history low, I would have to imagine we are heading very much in the same direction.

The US 10yr Bond in its nearly 250 year existence has an average yield of 6.24% over that time span -- hence the expectation that rates can and should claw back close to its historical average.

I believe that although global growth has not revived even with all the massive quantitative easing by world central banks, growth should begin to return back on the global stage beginning mid-July 2014. This could lead to gradual rise in interest rates as well.

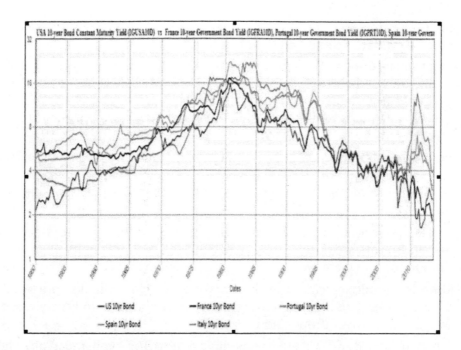

What are low U.S. bond yields suggesting?

The most important question to ask at the moment is whether the US bond market is telling us something negative about a change in the macro landscape.

US bond markets lead all markets because they act as the risk-free rate for all risk assets. Where bond markets lead, equity markets generally follow.

The current challenge for investors is to decide whether lower bond yields reflect a downbeat shift in the fundamental economic outlook or a combination of a weak macro start to the year and market technicalities that keep interest rates well supported.

Cheap US Treasuries

Ten-year US Treasury bonds are still in the same trading range they have been in since last summer. But something has changed. Markets price on a fundamental but also on a relative basis and European bond yields have recently collapsed. That in turn has made US Treasuries look cheap versus European and Japanese government bonds.

For sovereign wealth funds, global institutional investors and even central banks, US Treasuries are the least expensive developed market government bond to be investing in currently.

Lower US bond yields are not signalling a collapse in US growth. There is potential for full-year US growth of between 2.5 and 3 per cent over the next 12 months – growth that is good not great, mid-cycle in recovery, and sustainable.

However, there is concern whether disinflationary pressures will weigh negatively on growth ahead, particularly in Europe and Japan. Europe is pulling itself out of recession and its recovery is still close to stall speed; we are not back to what can be considered trend and sustainable growth levels.

The European Central Bank has been the most able of the developed market central banks. It has been able to accomplish the most, doing the least. But there is a rising sense from markets that the ECB needs to act. That is what the collapse in European bond yields is telling us – and US bonds are along for the ride. That is what has changed.

In general, the fall this year in government bond yields has weighed on investor sentiment and left equity markets largely rangebound. Year to date, investment flows into fixed income assets have outweighed flows into equity markets globally by two to one.

Investors lose money in equity markets when leading indicators are falling. When such indicators are decelerating, you want to hold less equity exposure, so it is crucial to focus on where we are in the investment cycle.

Leading economic indicators in the US have been flat thanks to a weak first quarter, but are trending higher. Across the G7, they continue to accelerate due to the recovery both across Europe and in Japan.

If you believe the macro environment is improving, you must also believe interest rates are gradually moving higher. That should not be as contrarian a view as markets are currently making it out to be.

However, the story is different in the short haul where a summer correction in global stocks is clearly on the cards.

NYSE Margin Debt Rose Slightly in May; Leading Indicator for a Market Correction?

The New York Stock Exchange publishes end-of-month data for margin debt on the NYXdata website, where we can also find historical data back to 1959. Let's examine the numbers and study the relationship between margin debt and the market, using the S&P 500 as the surrogate for the latter.

The first chart shows the two series in real terms — adjusted for inflation to today's dollar using the Consumer Price Index as the deflator. I picked 1995 as an arbitrary start date. We were well into the Boomer Bull Market that began in 1982 and approaching the start of the Tech Bubble that shaped investor sentiment during the second half of the decade. The astonishing surge in leverage in late 1999 peaked in March 2000, the same month that the S&P 500 hit its all-time daily high, although the highest monthly close for that year was five months later in August. A similar surge began in 2006, peaking in July 2007, three months before the market peak.

The latest data puts margin debt in its second month of decline following a record high.

The next chart shows the percentage growth of the two data series from the same 1995 starting date, again based on real (inflation-adjusted) data. I've added markers to show the precise monthly values and added callouts to show the month. Margin debt grew at a rate comparable to the market from 1995 to late summer of 2000 before soaring into the stratosphere. The two synchronized in their rate of contraction in early 2001. But with recovery after the Tech Crash, margin debt gradually returned to a growth rate closer to its former self in the second half of the 1990s rather than the more restrained real growth of the S&P 500. But by September of 2006, margin again went ballistic. It finally peaked in the summer of 2007, about three months before the market.

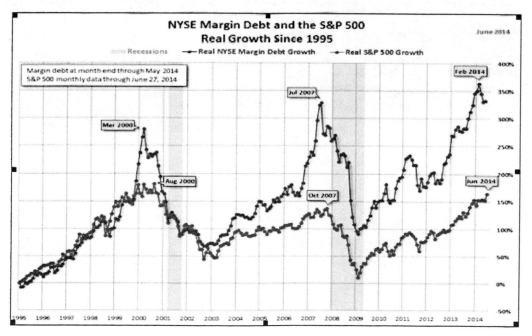

After the market low of 2009, margin debt again went on a tear until the contraction in late spring of 2010. The summer doldrums promptly ended when Chairman Bernanke hinted of more quantitative easing in his August, 2010 Jackson Hole speech. The appetite for margin instantly returned, and the Fed periodically increased the easing until the beginning of tapering purchases now underway.

The latest Margin Data

Unfortunately, the NYSE margin debt data is about a month old when it is published. Following its February peak, real margin declined sharply for two months, -3.9% in March -3.2% in April. However the May data shows a slight increase, 0.3%, in the debt level. It will be interesting to determine in the months ahead if February remain the all-time high or the May reversal will pick up steam.

NYSE Investor Credit

In the following graph, margin debt is analyzed in the larger context that includes free cash accounts and credit balances in margin accounts. Essentially, he calculates the *Credit Balance* as the sum of *Free Credit Cash Accounts* and *Credit Balances in Margin Accounts* minus *Margin Debt*. The chart below illustrates the mathematics of Credit Balance with an overlay of the S&P 500. Note that the chart below is based on nominal data, not adjusted for inflation.

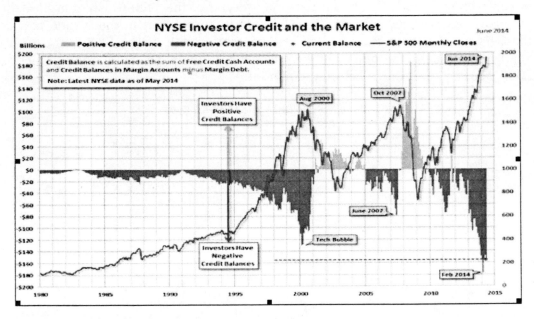

Here's a slightly closer look at the data, starting with 1995. Also, I've inverted the S&P 500 monthly closes and used markers to pinpoint the monthly close values.

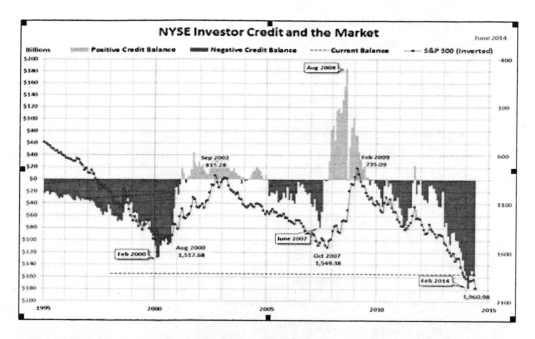

As I pointed out above, the NYSE margin debt data is a several weeks old when it is published. Thus, even though it may in theory be a leading indicator, a major shift in margin debt isn't immediately evident. Nevertheless, we see that the troughs in the monthly net credit balance preceded peaks in the monthly S&P 500 closes by six months in 2000 and four months in 2007. The most recent S&P 500 correction greater than 10% was the 19.39% sell off in 2011 from April 29th to October 3rd. Investor Credit hit a negative extreme in March 2011.

Bank of England's role in the UK housing bubble

UK's housing market must still face rising interest rates

When the US housing and credit bubble burst in 2008, there were some hard lessons, but they were clear. Asset bubbles are dangerous, particularly when they affect property prices. The best way to deal with a bubble is to stop it from inflating in the first place.

After all, we only use the word "bubble" to describe speculative manias because a bubble cannot be deflated gently; it bursts.

So preventing asset price bubbles is a challenge for policy makers. Rather than just try to regulate inflation and growth, they must also head off speculative excess.

This week saw the first attempt by a large western economy to do just that. The Bank of England is leaving its base rate at 0.5 per cent for now – although perhaps for not much longer. But it announced measures specifically designed to stop a bubble in the UK housing market through its regulation of the lending sector.

It has put a cap on the proportion of mortgages that can cover more than 4.5 times the borrower's income. Such mortgages will now be capped at 15 per cent of the total. Further, lenders must also carry out a new test of affordability in which they work out whether the borrowers could still service their mortgages if interest rates were to rise 3 percentage points.

The BoE was at pains to stress that this was not a stringent cap and it is unquestionably right about this. A loan of 4.5 times income is potentially an enormous burden, so this is not a huge restriction. At present, only about 10 per cent of overall mortgage lending is at this threshold, so the cap allows lending to become even more excessive before the limit is reached.

And there is no differentiation between regions. In London, some 20 per cent of lending exceeds the 4.5 times limit. But as the cap is national, not regional, there is no compulsion on the capital's borrowers to start tightening.

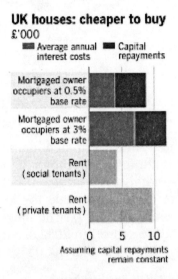

UK houses: cheaper to buy

The BoE plainly believes there is not yet a bubble in UK house prices. Indeed, it says the cap will only take effect if house prices rise another 20 per cent nationally over the next three years.

The bank does not want to scare people unduly, or cause a sudden stop in the economy, as the UK's recovery remains anaemic. The rise in sterling that followed the announcement showed great confidence in the forex market that the BoE had achieved this.

But in the process, it has let the housing and banking sectors off the hook – as could be seen in sharp rises for UK housebuilding stocks.

Specific factors driving the London property market, such as foreign demand, mean that one large sector of UK property is far closer to a bubble than the rest.

But the biggest problem is one of its own making: the environment of exceptionally low interest rates that was fostered by its "QE" bond purchases. There is a decent argument that QE was a necessary evil when it was adopted amid the crisis in 2009. But it is now distorting the housing market in damaging ways.

Price indices have presented wildly contrasting pictures of the health of the housing market – according to some the boom is back, while to others the slump staggers on.

Judged by price/earnings multiples, comparing house prices with average earnings, UK houses are already in a bubble. But judged by affordability, how much houses cost to finance in relation to earnings – UK housing actually looks cheap, thanks to low rates.

Meanwhile, low interest rates have helped to change the nature of the market. Owner-occupiers now pay less in mortgage interest than social housing tenants pay in rent (and vastly less than private tenants pay). This is wholly an effect of cheap interest rates and its effects are very unfair. Meanwhile, judged by comparison with rents, another classic valuation tool for housing, UK houses look expensive.

A return to normal base rates would change these calculations utterly. Average mortgage payments are a little less than £4,000 a month. By the time base rates hit 3 per cent (still low), this would rise to £7,000. Most mortgages now sold are at a fixed rate but some two-thirds of outstanding UK mortgages are at a variable rate, making the housing market very vulnerable to rate rises. No wonder the BoE wants to test this.

Ultimately, QE creates an environment that is already a bubble by some measures but not close to a bubble by others. There is none of the speculative excitement normally associated with bubbles and yet the risk of one remains clear. The problem for policy makers, investors, or just normal people wanting to find accommodation, is acute.

UK housing is not the only asset class that suffers from these issues. Stocks in the US, still setting records, continue to look cheap with respect to bonds. They look unambiguously expensive compared with their own earnings and with respect to their own history. Can this really be called a bubble? What will happen when rates rise?

The BoE is right to be trying to avert a property bubble without hurting the rest of the economy. But until rates start to rise, it is difficult to tell whether they are right that there is not already a bubble.

On Exotic Exchange Trade Funds (ETFs)

With more than 1,600 ETFs available for purchase in the U.S., one of the daunting issues investors face is one of quantity: Just because there's an ETF for something doesn't mean you should buy it.

Many niche ETFs have only a few million dollars in assets under management—asset size can have a big impact on an ETF's ability to track an index and trade efficiently. Smaller ETFs also have a history of disappearing rather quickly if they don't gain traction with investors.

Many of the trends that the niche ETFs are chasing are actually part of boom-and-bust cycles—meaning they could suffer at the wrong time—shortly after the ETF is created. Or they can be too early to capitalize on a long-term trend.

Consider the **Market Vectors Rare Earth** and **Strategic Metals ETF (REMX).** Launched in October 2010, it targets special industrial metals that are hard to extract and are used in everything from from flat-screen TVs to electric cars and jetliners. The market boomed when China—which produces a majority of rare earths—tightened controls over export in 2009. Many people thought that these commodities would continue to see their prices skyrocket, but this ETF is down about 57 percent since its launch—it peaked in April 2011, and it's been all downhill since then.

The rare earth metals ETF could still be a good long-term bet—providing a niche way to target the global adoption of personal technology—but it also gave us the idea to put some of the newest oddball ETFs to the recent performance test, because ETFs aren't just getting into more market niches but slicing those niches finer.

We've taken three niche ETFs—**LocalShares Nasville Area ETF (NASH),** the **Forensic Accounting ETF (FLAG)** and the **Global Robotics & Automation Index ETF (ROBO)**—and looked at what they target and whether it's worked so far. All three ETFs were launched in 2013.

Who will win the battle of the oddball ETFs? One ETF will be eliminated in each preliminary round; the other two will move on in the Battle of the Oddball ETFs to face new challengers in subsequent rounds.

Minimum Volatility Stocks: Better Tax-Efficient Returns, Also During Rising Markets

Minimum volatility ETFs should provide exposure to stocks with potentially less risk. They track indexes that try to capture the broad equity market with a reduced amount of volatility, seeking to benefit from what is known as low-volatility anomaly. Consequently they should show reduced losses during declining markets, but also reduced gains during rising markets. However, better returns with simultaneous tax efficiency can be obtained also during rising markets by selecting a number of the highest ranked stocks of a minimum volatility ETF and holding those positions for at least one year before new trades are initiated.

One of the largest minimum volatility funds is the **iShares MSCI USA Minimum Volatility ETF USMV** which provided an annualized return of 17.75% from inception Oct-20-2011 to Jun-18-2014, whereas **SPY**, the ETF tracking the S&P500, had a higher return of 22.06% over the same period. USMV's lower performance did not deter its growth, as evidenced by the fund's current net assets of about $2.7-billion. Investors seem to assume that they are incurring less risk by investing in this fund and that any potential downside will also be lower relative to the broader equity market, just as the upside has been so far.

USMV tracks the hypothetical investment results of the MSCI USA Minimum Volatility (USD) Index. The parameters for this index are not publicly available, making it impossible to reconstruct a similar index to verify historic performance. The best one can do is to use the current holdings of USMV for back testing. The back test results should not be significantly affected by survivorship bias, because the fund's annual portfolio turnover rate is low and the back test period is relatively short.

Back testing Performance

USMV currently holds 150 large-cap stocks (market cap ranging from $4- to $445-billion) of which 148 were listed at the inception of the fund on Oct-20-2011. Using these stocks as the universe, back tests were performed on an online portfolio simulation platform assuming an initial investment of $100,000.

Back test period Oct-20-2011 to March-31-2014.

1. All stocks held continuously over period, no buy/sell rules applied.
2. 12 stocks selected by a ranking system, with buy/sell rules.

Ranking System:

As for the Best10(S&P1500) portfolio management system.

Buy Rules:

- Sector Weight <30%,
- and Industry Weight <20%,
- and exclude some of the largest market cap stocks from being selected.

Sell Rules:

- Hold position at least 1-year,
- or sell when price declines more than 15% from the most recent high since the position was opened.

Results of back test (1) with all the stocks of USMV's current holdings:

Had one at inception invested equal weight in all the stocks and applied the same expense ratio as for USVM, then to Mar-31-2014 the annualized return would have been 19.9%. Over the same period USMV produced 17.9% according to the fund's fact sheet. The 2% higher annualized return of the simulation can be attributed to back testing with an equal weighted universe, whereas the fund has weighted holdings. (Similarly, annualized return from equal weight ETF RSP for this period was 23.08% versus 21.03% for SPY.) The results confirm that using the current holdings for the entire back test period is a legitimate technique when back testing over shorter periods.

In the figures below the red graph represents the model and the blue graph shows the performance of benchmark SPY.

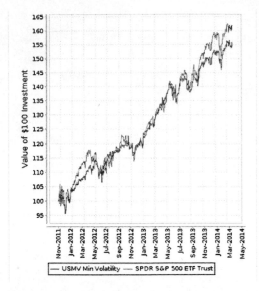

Inception Date	10/20/11
Last Rebalance Date	03/29/14
Days Since Last Rebalance	83
Rebalance Frequency	Weekly
Benchmark	SPDR S&P 500 ETF Trust
Universe	USMV
Ranking System	USMV1

Quick Stats as of 3/31/2014

Total Market Value (inc. Cash)	$ 155,843.39
Cash	$ 6,365.08
Number of Positions	150
Total Return	55.84%
Benchmark Return	62.03%
Active Return	-6.18%
Annualized Return	19.87%
Annual Turnover	0.64%
Max Drawdown	-6.48%
Benchmark Max Drawdown	-9.69%
Overall Winners	(144/152) 94.74%
Sharpe Ratio	1.69
Correlation with SPDR S&P 500 ETF Trust	0.96

Results for backtest (2) with selected stocks from USMV's current holdings:

Had one at inception invested equal weight in the 12 highest ranked stocks and applied the buy/sell rules, then to March 31, 2014 the annualized return would have been 34.6 %. Allowance was made for an expense ratio of 0.15% as applied by the fund and slippage of 0.1% of the transaction price when stocks were bought and sold.

This strategy would have provided much higher returns than SPY and USMV, and the simulation shows that minimum volatility stocks can outperform the broader market also during up-market periods.

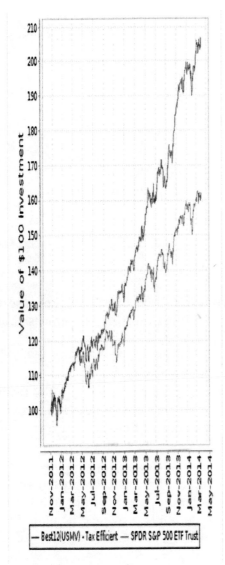

Inception Date	10/20/11
Last Rebalance Date	03/29/14
Days Since Last Rebalance	87
Rebalance Frequency	Weekly
Benchmark	SPDR S&P 500 ETF Trust
Universe	USMV
Ranking System	USMV1

Quick Stats as of 3/31/2014

Total Market Value (inc. Cash)	$ 206,637.38
Cash	$ 1,979.52
Number of Positions	12
Total Return	106.64%
Benchmark Return	62.03%
Active Return	44.61%
Annualized Return	34.56%
Annual Turnover	88.65%
Max Drawdown	-6.73%
Benchmark Max Drawdown	-9.69%
Overall Winners	(33/36) 91.67%
Sharpe Ratio	2.65
Correlation with SPDR S&P 500 ETF Trust	0.90

Conclusion

Using a ranking system to rank the stock holdings of USMV and only investing periodically in the 12 highest ranked stocks according to the buy/sell rules would have produced the best returns, as demonstrated by the results for backtests (2). The performance from 2011 to 2014 is shown in Figure-1 together with the sector allocation of current holdings. One can see that the model's holdings are well diversified.

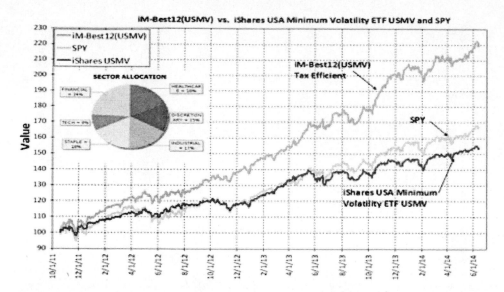

Also the model's annual portfolio turnover rate is only 89% because of the specified minimum one year holding period, making most of the returns subject to long-term capital gains tax only.

Performance of four displaced models

A simulation of performance for four models, displaced by 3 months from each other (starting dates Oct-20-11, Jan-20-12, Apr-20-12 and Jul-20-12), provided an internal rate of return of 31.6% to Jun-18-14, with most of the returns classified as long-term capital gains

The combined holdings at the end consisted of 48 positions of which 23 stocks were represented once, 2 were represented twice, and 7 were represented 3 times. Thus there were 32 different stocks in the holdings with only a 28% overlap between the four models. Using four displaced models provides the ability to stage one's investments over a year with trades occurring approximately every 3 months thereafter.

Although more than 20% of USMV's 150 holdings are held by the four models, the combination still showed a 31.6% annualized return, almost twice the 17.8% return of the ETF. A shadow ETF consisting of four displaced models could accommodate about 20% of USMV's assets, and should at the same time produce significantly higher returns than USMV.

Following the 12-position model

As demonstrated, a 12-stock model should significantly outperform USMV and SPY.

Gold, I believe, will the comeback kid of 2014.

Beginning the last week of May and extending right upto November of 2014, we could see huge upside in gold prices. The same could rise by 20 to 25% making it a much favored asset class for investors in 2014.

In Portuguese bullfight, the forcados try to subdue the animal by lining up in front of its charge and leaping on to it. Horrible injuries aside, they are usually successful. In the equity markets right now, the bull is winning - in spite of the slowing down of China, the emerging economies not doing well.

Developed market valuations have reached historic highs and deserve caution, especially in view of the froth generated by the poster boys whose valuations are not commensurate with their revenues.

Innocent tech investors could get whipsawed unexpectedly.

If you're holding certain tech stocks, you could be in for an unexpected wild ride but not because of some major new invention or life-changing discovery

After digging down into the market and examining flows, I am convinced money managers are funding their IPO investments by selling tech as well as biotech. Firms that chase these kinds of momentum IPOs tend to be involved in both groups.

Although I believe the phenomenon will end (and I fear it could end very badly when it does end—I believe from May2014 you could see this IPO fever begin to wane with even greater velocity—already more than six tech IPOs are already in the pipeline).

Therefore, with some major new IPOs on the horizon, if you hold technology stocks, investors to be prepared. They could swoon, unexpectedly.

As long as big money senses that there are rabid buyers for certain IPOs I would expect to see more selling pressure in other areas of the market. Hedge funds are looking for a pop, and, even if the opportunity is outrageous, the money has to come from somewhere.

And when the downturn comes, you could other areas of the market hit as well as investors rush in to take profits where they are in the green.

Having resorted to quantitative easing to bail out of the Great Financial Crisis, central banks are now beginning to withdraw the stimulus led by the US Fed. True economic health will be known only when stimulus is removed

The current state of US financial markets might be best described with the help of a dead Austrian physicist and a logic-defying feline of unknown vital status.

Schrödinger's cat is a thought experiment designed by Erwin Schrödinger to highlight the apparent absurdity of one particular interpretation of quantum mechanics when transposed to everyday objects.

The theoretical cat sits in a sealed box containing a flask of poison and a radioactive source. The poison is released at essentially a random time determined by the decay (or not) of a single atom. Once the poison is released the cat dies. Otherwise the cat lives.

The prevailing theory of quantum mechanics at the time implied that, since the probability of an atom of the radioactive substance decaying is equal, until someone opens the box the cat is both alive and dead.

The moment the box is opened and the cat observed, the two "states" – living cat and moribund cat – collapse into one that is either dead or alive (but in both cases presumably quite annoyed).

Such an experiment, intended to demonstrate the eccentricity of a certain school of quantum physics, makes a satisfying analogy for the state of markets after five years of quantitative easing by the Federal Reserve.

Central banks have flooded the financial system with cash, driving investors to park their money in higher-yielding securities and largely obfuscating the true state of underlying markets.

As the sound of guns from Ukraine grow louder, the markets start dipping. As S&P cuts Russia's rating to junk, funds flee Japan.

History shows that markets are cheap when bullets are flying, and by the time peace arrives it has been priced in.

Unfortunately, the timing is harder than it sounds. Iraq invaded Kuwait in August 1990; US, developed and emerging market equities dropped for the next two to six months. All bounced the day the US-led Operation Desert Storm began. US cannons seemed to matter more to investors than Iraq's.

Russia seems so far to have avoided firing a shot, unlike in its invasion of Georgia in 2008. The war then was short, and had less effect on relations with the west than so far in Ukraine. The lesson was quite different to the Gulf, too: investors had to buy in early to profit from the bounce.

Georgia may be an outlier. As researchers GaveKal point out, the 1938 Sudetenland crisis prompted widespread price falls, which only bottomed out when Britain and France made the strategic error of handing the territory to Germany. The same applied in the Cuban missile crisis, as prices fell almost to the end.

So long as the Ukraine standoff continues, early bargain hunters might find they lose money. But Russian stocks, almost painfully cheap already, continue to fall whenever the Ukraine crisis roars its ugly head again. They might well lose more, but unless the cannons sound, it is worth buying to profit from eventual trumpets.

Ask a broker about where he sees markets going ahead and this is what he shows you:

Fortunes fluctuate commitment doesn't!

I still remember a mutual fund who every time a positive news would emerge in the stock markets would send me a text message why investing in it's fund makes sense.

And when there would be negative news, it would just keep mum.

Over the last year, investors have been lulled to sleep wrapped in the warmth of complacency as the Federal Reserve stoked the fires of the market with $85 billion a month in liquidity injections.

Eurozone continues to present good growth opportunities for investors. The inventory build-up and capex cycle has been so much lagging behind that a 5% growth in the Eurozone is not off the track.

Doomsday Sayers and perma-bulls have been both off the track in predicting future market behavior.

To be successful as investors we can't fixate on the recent past, nor complain about what should be happening, but rather focus on what is expected to take place and why.

We have had two real market crashes occur in the last 100 years, which works out to about one every 50 years. If they are so infrequent, then why do we hear so much about them? I'll give two reasons: One, people often crave attention and can easily gain it by making bold forecasts (whether they turn out incorrect or not) and, two, people assign a higher probability to market crashes now than they have in the past.

For example, shown below is the S&P 500 along with a Bloomberg story count for articles that have the words "market crash" in them. Since the early 1990s, we saw a spike on the 10-year anniversary of the 1987 market crash, then another around the September 11th 2001 terrorist attacks, and then again on the big October swoon of 2008. I want to draw your attention to the first two spikes in 1997 and 2001 and point out that, once they calmed down, fears over a "market crash" returned to normal levels. However, after 2008, there has been a continual and ongoing spike in calls for a market crash unlike anything we've seen over the prior two decades.

Where should you invest in the remainder of 2014?

This is the common question haunting most investors and investment managers alike. Stocks? Bonds? Precious metals? Real estate? Or all of the above as some professional money managers profess so that they can average out the returns from these asset classes, as they know not which way these markets are headed.

Some believe you should always be invested because it is never easy to time the market. After 5 years, Dow Jones and many other global stock indices reclaimed their former peak. So if you had remained invested all the time, you would be where you were in 2008 (unless you had special stock-picking abilities).

There is no need to get hysterical and start throwing things around so that you reach that state of nirvana, which helps you become a real 'Guru' of investing. You are not Aristotle and your hysterical moment is certainly not 'Eureka'.

Instead of getting hysterical, you would be better off doing some meditation which would definitely help you clear your vision and advance your financial goals better.

I have no intention to bore you by extolling the virtues of long-term equity investing. You are all familiar with the virtues of long-term investing. Equities historically, no doubt, give the best returns, when looked at over a long period of time. You have seen several such presentations in your life.

One thing is for sure; it is hard to believe that stocks will continue to out perform all other asset classes indefinitely. All assets take turns whether they are outperforming or under-performing, as liquidity constantly shifts from overvalued to undervalued assets. Contrarians tend to buy value in anticipation of a trend change, while trend followers chase momentum. Contrarians are usually early to the game, while trend followers are late leaving it.

Is the dress for success different in politics than that in economics?

There is one other major difference between Kejriwal and Modi, which is in their sartorial preferences. While the AAP leader Kejriwal prefers the crumpled white shirt and Gandhi cap, Narendra Modi likes well-starched expensive kurtas and varied headgear. In politics, there is no set wardrobe for success!

Positive benefits of meditation on investing

There is no need to get hysterical and start throwing things around so that you reach that state of nirvana which helps you become a real 'Guru' of investing. You are not Aristotle and your hysterical moment is certainly not 'Eureka'.

Instead of getting hysterical, you would be better off doing some meditation which would definitely help you clear your vision and advance your financial goals better.

The role of print and electronic media in dissemination of information is laudable. At the same time, when we read newspapers, watch TV we imbibe impressions about scandals, problems and difficulties. Even the financial reporting tends to add too much data and create too much noise, which an ordinary investor is unable to filter out.

This creates agitation and brings out negative tendencies in the mind, which remains tense and disturbed. It is like throwing a rock into still water and creating ripples.

When the mind is peaceful and quiet, sensitive and receptive, positive seeds can be planted in the subconscious. This in turn leads to greater positivity and can help in investing more wisely. (Read '***Why transcendental meditation is the latest buzzwords on Wall Street*** *later in this book*).

I have no intention to bore you by extolling the virtues of long-term equity investing. You are all familiar with the virtues of long-term investing. Equities historically, no doubt, give the best returns, when looked at over a long period of time. You have seen several such presentations in your life.

One thing is for sure; it is hard to believe that stocks will continue to out perform all other asset classes indefinitely. All assets take turns whether they are outperforming or under-performing, as liquidity constantly shifts from overvalued to undervalued assets. Contrarians tend to buy value in anticipation of a trend change, while trend followers chase momentum. Contrarians are usually early to the game, while trend followers are late leaving it.

I have included a roadmap for investors in 2014. What are the factors that have enabled me to draw this roadmap for investors I have indicated in the latter half of my book? I have brought all these factors to work together in making my forecasts for what could turn out to be a turbulent year for investors—2014.

Any professional advisor will tell you it is not possible to time the market. It is frequently said "A drop of 20% in just over two months? But what if a recovery came just as fast—and the rally continued from there to end a 24% up for the year?"

If you understood the factors, this is not a 24% up move, but a 64% movement in indices. Even if you can capture 50% of this movement, you would still outbeat the market model by 12% (not a mean outperformance).

Naturally therefore, I have to stick my nick out and make several hard predictions for 2014 and beyond. This, I believe, would be more value for money for an investor and professional alike.

Instead, this book is a handy guide to investors as to how they should approach 2014, what investment ideas would be most productive.

As you talk with your stockbroker, you obviously would want to discuss the S&P 500 at an all-time high and whether a correction could be round the corner.

To which your broker tells you it is impossible to time the market.

In which case, he asks you to dollar cost average. To buy stocks in installments so that you don't buy all the stocks at the peak.

You ask him why. He says he does not have a crystal ball.

Yet, he could do his homework. He could look at emerging trends, comparison with past behavior, with valuations in the past and see how different they are today.

He could look at GDP of different countries, whether inventory additions or inventory drawdowns are taking place, whether governments are responsive in terms of encouraging growth or decelerating growth.

Chinese depreciation of the renminbi could be sending messages of change in government policy towards slowing of growth.

It would definitely be better to do some homework than make blind guesses.

There are talks of credit bubble in China and other emerging markets.

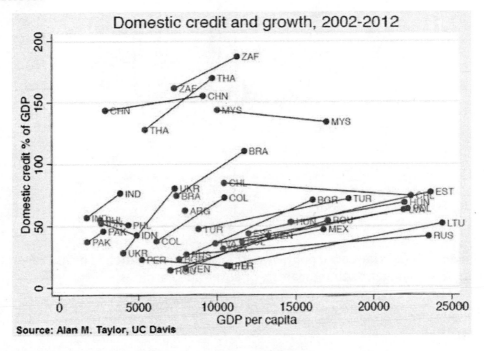

Source: Alan M. Taylor, UC Davis

Indian stock markets currently look over-stretched

India looks overvalued relative to other global emerging markets, saying valuations, after a sharp rally on Bharatiya Janata Party's (BJP) decisive election win, appear "very stretched" against lower GDP growth. The Nifty has risen 24.4 percent since September 13 when Narendra Modi was declared as BJP's prime ministerial candidate, with overseas funds pumping over USD 14 billion in the cash shares over that period.

Foreign flows have certainly proved plentiful, with $2.4bn coming into equities during May and a further $1.5bn already so far during June – comfortably the largest in emerging Asian markets.

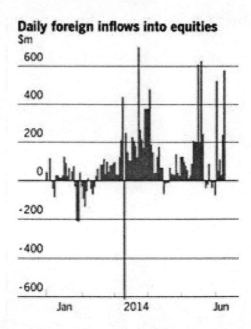

However, India's improved political outlook is yet to be matched by improvements in many underlying growth indicators, or corporate earnings.

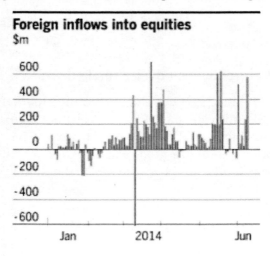

Source: *Thomson Reuters Datastream*

Other factors may come to weigh on India's rise. The country's lofty inflation rate shows only marginal signs of abating, probably precluding cuts in interest rates until well into next year, while the possibility of a weaker than usual monsoon could undermine growth in 2015.

Recent increases in overall share levels also disguise sharper movements within industries, with particularly heady re-ratings in sectors such as metals and power, which are expected to benefit from higher industrial investment.

Lumbering state-owned businesses have performed especially strongly too, with public sector energy explorer Oil & Natural Gas Corporation jumping 25 per cent over the past month.

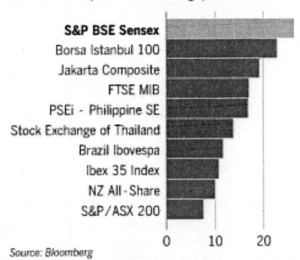

Top performing major stock markets
Year-to-date ($ terms, % change)

Source: Bloomberg

Thus far, the new government has done little wrong, but equally given few hints as to how bold it plans to be in moving forward with measures to fix politically sensitive problems, like its undercapitalised state-owned banks, or excessively complex labour laws.

Narendra Modi has the electoral mandate to repeat the type of liberalising reforms introduced in India more than two decades ago although the effect of such measures would take many years to be felt, and thus to justify such immediate and short-term rise in stock prices.

There is the potential for massive long-term upside and a long-term bull story in India has just started, but I suspect there needs to be further economic pain before the agenda for more fundamental reform to governance practices becomes clearer. Mexico and China have also witnessed similar selloff in the past as reform euphoria in both markets waned, while Modi's comparison with Margaret Thatcher raises short to medium term risks. Although I prefer India to the other BRICs, I advise non-emerging market investors to wait for a better buying opportunity – around mid-July 2014.

Indian stock markets are already discounting FY2016 earnings, and are no longer cheap. Valuations will however remain expensive because of the positive sentiment among investors.

Earnings upgrades look difficult in the short term. Thus, economic reforms that can drive economic and earnings growth in the medium term will be critical.

Investors would be better off taking some money off the table in sectors like banking, capital goods, cement, and metals & mining where investors appear to be expecting too much too soon.

Here's why:

Banking: The steep increase in stock prices of banks suggests that the market is no longer worried about the NPL (non-performing loan) problem in the banking sector. However, this is a serious issue and banks, particularly PSU banks, continue to report very high slippages. Even assuming that the NPL problem is contained and book values of banks reflect the true value of the book (adjusted basis), many PSU banks now trade close to or above book value despite quite low RoEs (return on equity).

Cement: Valuations of cement stocks are quite expensive even after factoring in a strong recovery in their volumes and profitability over the next two years. Even assuming near-peak profitability for cement companies in FY2016, cement stocks trade at 7-11 times FY2016E EBITDA and 15-21 times FY2016E EPS, 50-70% higher than mid-cycle multiples.

Capital goods: I do not doubt a recovery in the investment cycle in India over the next few months. In fact, the order booking of companies over the past few quarters already signals an improvement. However, valuations are quite stiff for capital goods companies after factoring a significant recovery in their earnings.

Metals & Mining: It is difficult to fathom whether the new government can award coal blocks or mineral ore mines in a discretionary fashion, given allegations of corruption in previous such allocations. Even assuming the government is able to kick-start the process of allocation quickly; it will take a few years to develop the new mines. Market is ignoring the risk of market-related pricing of resources through price discovery in auctions. The government could also increase the royalty on coal and mineral ores, which is quite low compared to the royalty on other resources, such as oil and gas

Can Modi make India the new China?

Narendra Modi is being swept into office as India's prime minister on a wave of optimism about his ability to restore the fortunes of Asia's third biggest economy.

But is he the leader to haul India out of its funk, and put the world's second most populous nation back on track to rival China?

Investors think so. The prospect of a government led by Modi has boosted Indian stocks by 15% so far this year. The rupee has responded too, gaining 6% against the dollar after a dismal performance in 2013.

An economic turnaround will be more difficult to execute. It will require a level of political skill and collaboration that has eluded top Indian policymakers for years.

India's growth potential was once mentioned in the same breath as that of China. But the world's biggest democracy has failed to deliver and its economy is just a fifth the size of its Asian rival.

Growth has fallen below 5%, and inflation is now running above 8%. Manufacturing has slowed and the country's fiscal deficit has ballooned.

Structural reforms have fallen foul of political gridlock. Analysts say India needs to simplify its tax code, encourage foreign investment and streamline agricultural production. Modi will have to move fast.

Modi likes to emphasize his management credentials. He campaigned on a record of low unemployment and high foreign investment in Gujarat, the state he has led since 2001.

He has promised to end policy paralysis, reduce inflation and tackle corruption. He also pledged to establish manufacturing hubs and industrial corridors, improve the tax code and reform the banking sector.

It is likely Modi will try to get some quick wins under his belt by pursuing reforms that can be implemented through executive action.

Although the BJP's hugely impressive victory means that Modi will be much less dependent on partnerships and alliances than we had envisioned, it does not in and of itself fundamentally change the fractious nature of India's political landscape.

INDIA WILL LEAD EMERGING
MARKET REVIVAL

The global advantage is shifting back to American shores

Antoine van Agtmael, for many years an official of the International Finance Corporation, coined the term "emerging markets" in 1982. He wanted to foster equity investing in the developing world, and end a dangerous addiction to debt.

His proposed response was for the IFC to sponsor the first ever emerging markets equity fund. Most investors, even at large institutions, lacked the resources to hunt bargains in distant markets. But a diversified portfolio of stocks from across the emerging world might solve this problem.

Mr Van Agtmael himself has been an evangelist of emerging markets, ardently suggesting that the most successful companies in EM have the smarts, after learning to survive in their home countries, to become dominant multinationals.

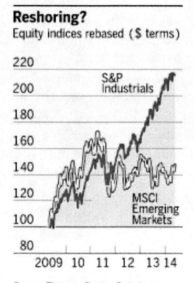

Reshoring?
Equity indices rebased ($ terms)

Source: Thomson Reuters Datastream

There is symbolism, then, in his new project to document how and why the global advantage is shifting back to the US.

There are complaints in Asia about competition from the US. Manufacturers that had moved to China are moving back to Mexico, or even to the US itself. In China, where the priority is to raise real wages (and erode competitiveness), he points out that self-satisfaction after the 2008 crisis has given way to unease. Wages have risen 400 per cent since 2001, according to Ernst & Young, while US unit labour costs have dropped 12 per cent since 1995.

Fundamentally, the US is more competitive than had been thought, while China is less so. What Mr Van Agtmael calls the "creative response" from the west has come sooner than he anticipated. The advent of robotics, 3D printing and the like, he suggests, have moved the west from manufacturing to "brainfacturing".

As this plays out, investors are rediscovering political risk (and singling out state-owned companies for punishment), and drastically reappraising their projections for the emerging market future.

Has he given up on his positive thesis for the emerging markets? Certainly not. As he points out, long-term potential is always ignored when markets come down (just as problems are ignored when prices are rising).

It is still the emerging, and not the American, consumer who will steadily become king. Already, he points out, more cars, washing machines, televisions and mobile phones are sold in the Bric countries (Brazil, Russia, India and China) than in either the EU or the US.

He also contends that slower emerging growth is not a problem – for China, it is an advantage – and he denies that the inevitable unwinding of quantitative easing in the US need cause anything like the panic that briefly gripped emerging bond and currency markets last year.

But the enthusiasm with which he charts the growth of a US "Brain Belt" to supplant its old "Rust Belt" is reminiscent of the excitement with which he once charted the rise of emerging multinationals. Innovation centres are sprouting up across the US, he points out, in places like Minneapolis, Akron or Boulder, as well as around prestigious universities. He charts more than 200 examples of "re-shoring" as companies like GE return to the US, while Apple makes Macs in the US for the first time.

For the next decade he expects growing confidence in the US (like post-1970s Japan), more innovation in manufacturing, and an epic "battle for the billions of emerging consumers". He still expects emerging markets to grow faster.

The notion of a Brain Belt might yet be as catchy as the notion of "emerging markets". Is that a good thing?

Van Agtmael's "emerging markets" certainly aided his aim of opening up new markets to equity finance. It also had some negative consequences, such as a succession of attempts to impose brands on new markets with increasingly absurd results. Think of acronyms, from Brics to Civets, Mints and Biits.

This is part of a broader trend to oversimplification. People lazily assumed that all "emerging" markets would indeed emerge, that they would outperform the existing developed markets, and that they would grow in a straight line.

None of these ideas is necessarily true. There is no cause to abandon carefully chosen positions in EM (or to invest mindlessly in the "Brain Belt"). But, three decades after "emerging markets" arrived on the scene, should all investors should follow Van Agtmael in accepting that the game is changing.

I don't think so. May emerging markets such as Egypt, Turkey and India have faced uprisings and are emerging from the shadows of corrupt governments.

This itself lays the foundation for high growth as energies of people are channelized to more productive and creative purposes.

In India, growth has lagged behind due to various bottlenecks. The new government led by Narendra Modi has a track record of fast growth and this could set the stage for economic revival in the Indian sub-continent.

Once India revives, other emerging economies on fear of being left behind will also follow in India's footsteps.

So, do not as yet write out emerging economies. They are on a comeback trail.

Why Indian stocks?

Extreme under-allocation to equities

Period	Gross Domestic Product Rs Lakh Cr	Gross domestic savings Rs Lakh Cr	Households savings Rs Lakh Cr	Financial household Savings Rs Lakh Cr	Physical assets savings of households Rs Lakh Cr
FY00	20.1	5.2	4.4	2.1	2.3
FY01	21.7	5.2	4.6	2.2	2.6
FY02	23.5	5.9	5.5	2.5	3.0
FY03	25.3	6.6	5.8	2.5	3.1
FY04	28.4	8.2	6.6	3.1	3.4
FY05	32.4	10.5	7.5	3.3	4.4
FY06	36.9	12.4	8.7	4.4	4.3
FY07	42.9	14.9	9.9	4.8	5.1
FY08	49.9	18.4	11.2	5.8	5.4
FY09	56.3	19.0	13.3	5.7	7.6
FY10	64.8	21.8	16.3	7.7	8.6
FY11	78.0	26.6	18.3	8.1	10.2
FY12	80.7	27.7	20.0	7.2	12.8
FY13 E	101.0	31.1	22.5	8.1	14.6
FY14 E	114.1	35.2	26.5	9.1	16.3
FY15 E	129.0	39.7	28.3	10.3	18.6
FY16 E	145.7	44.9	32.5	11.7	20.9

❏   Indian households own a whopping USD 1.5 trillion of Gold and Silver
❏   Yearly Household Savings into Financial Assets like Bank Deposits is more than double the collective holding in equities (March 2013)
❏   Retail Public holding of equities is <6% (USD 72 Bn / Rs. 4.3 Lk Crs) of Total Market Cap of BSE 100
❏   FIIs alone have invested more than USD 90 Bn in Indian Equity Markets in the last 5 years (CY 09-13)

Economic re-rating of India could lead due to huge upside in Indian equities

	March 2014	March 2013
Corporate Results	Dec-2013 marginally higher than expectations	Disappointed
Global Outlook	Markets remain strong despite 3 QE tapering steps	Fears of QE tapering, fiscal cliff etc.
FII Inflows	Decisively strong	Indecisive & weak
Returns	1.)Higher Equity Returns* 2.) Alternatives like real estate and gold remain weak 3.)Fixed income only other viable option	1.) Low Equity returns* 2.) Other asset classes doing well

Market valuations are at discount to averages; similar are RoEs

12-month forward Sensex P/E (x)

12-month forward Sensex P/B (x)

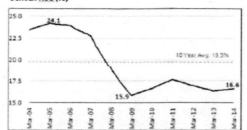

Sensex RoE (%)

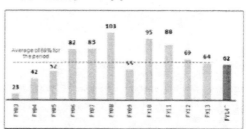

India's Market Cap to GDP (%)

Companies With Sound Fundamentals...

... Available At Attractive Valuations

Price to Book Value (P/BV)

■ Upto 1   ■ Between 1.1 to 2   ■ Between 2.1 to 5   ■ Greater than 5

Price to Earning(P/E)

■ Less than 5   ■ Between 5 to 10   ■ Between 10.1 to 20   ■ > 20

❑ **From Price/Book Value perspective,**
  ✓ 46% of companies are traded at P/BV of 1 or less
  ✓ Another 23% of companies are traded at P/BV of between 1.1 to 2.0

❑ **In terms of PE**
  ✓ 50% of companies in the universe^ are traded at PE of less than 10x on TTM** Earnings
  ✓ 75% of companies in the universe^ are traded at PE of less than 20X on TTM** Earning
  ✓ Assuming improved earnings going ahead, forward P/Es would be even more attractive

The road ahead for India

US revival will be an aid to recovery of other developed & emerging economies

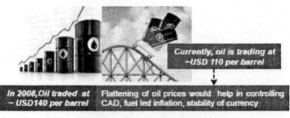

Currently, oil is trading at ~USD 110 per barrel

| In 2008, Oil traded at ~ USD140 per barrel | Flattening of oil prices would help in controlling CAD, fuel led inflation, stability of currency |

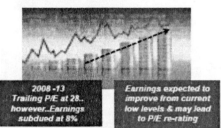

| 2008 -13 Trailing P/E at 28... however...Earnings subdued at 8% | Earnings expected to improve from current low levels & may lead to P/E re-rating |

| 2008 -13 Policy log jam | Several policies cleared & key Bills passed in recent times |

Prime Minister's Project Monitoring Group has cleared 147 projects, entailing a total investment of around Rs 5 lakh crore

Scalable Opportunities:

Themes like Retail, Media, Hospitals, etc., which are essentially high-growth themes

Contra Strategy:

A contra theme, which would make investments into sectors / stocks which are significantly below their normal valuations. Eg., Sectors like Engineering, Capital Goods, etc.,

Opportunities in the current market context

Established business at discounted valuations:

Investments into companies which are trading at distressed valuations due to specific events like mandatory OFS, PSU disinvestment, etc.

Corporate Actions:

Promoter's increasing stake and/or buyback candidates, acquisitions possibilities.

1. Scalable Opportunities

__Long Term Growth Prospects undermined due to near term challenges__

❑ Currently small in India vs. Globally

❑ However, with current growth rates it will take critical mass in future…

❑ A few examples :-

- Insurance
- Media
- Hospitals
- Retail and Franchising
- Internet Business

2. Established business at discounted valuations

❑ Companies impacted due to non-fundamental reasons

- Mandatory offer for sale
- Divestment by government

3. Contra Strategy

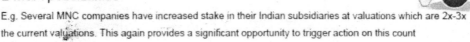

__Sustainable business models – ignored currently__

❑ **Leaders**- Companies which are leaders in their segments i.e. top 2-3 companies, which are out of favor.

❑ **Long History** - Companies which have had 15-20 years of operating history.

❑ Low **near term visibility & hence low expectations**

❑ Lack of street coverage

- Coverage has reduced from over 300 companies to about 100 companies

4. Corporate Action Candidates

❑ Promoters increasing stake and/or buyback candidates

❑ M&A possibilities

E.g. Several MNC companies have increased stake in their Indian subsidiaries at valuations which are 2x-3x the current valuations. This again provides a significant opportunity to trigger action on this count

SUMMER 2014 CORRECTION ON THE CARDS

Capitalism is back – alive and kicking. That, at least, is the impression created by the rush of companies debuting on the world's share markets.

Global "initial public offering" volumes have already exceeded $38bn in 2014, more than twice as high as in the same period last year. European IPOs have tripled, according to Thomson Reuters data.

Twitter debuted late last year; the IPO highlight of 2014 is likely to be the US listing of Alibaba, the Chinese ecommerce giant, which might be the biggest yet.

IPOs are the lifeblood of equity markets: they replenish share supplies and invigorate investors – as well as provide finance for companies to expand. So their revival is a sign of a return of Keynesian "animal spirits" – or commercial risk-taking – and of financial markets functioning efficiently again after almost seven years of crises.

Or is it? Amid all the hype that makes IPOs so headline grabbing, there are reasons for caution. The animal spirits may be more those of bigger companies, bankers and financiers, rather than the smaller beasts in the jungle that will provide the economic growth of the future.

A broader economic worry is that the IPO market is still not serving the smallest companies. A few months back; at the top of IPO fever, even as volumes were near record highs, the number of IPOs were on a long term downward trend – which means the average size was rising. The first months of 2014 saw about 200 IPOs globally. The same period in 1996 saw almost 700, although that was in the run up to the dotcom bust.

In the US, the Jobs Act, which was intended to help funding of smaller businesses, is encouraging companies to the market, although it is too early to quantify its impact. Otherwise, the impression remains that illiquid markets, new ways of trading equities and constraints faced by banks and brokers have scared entrepreneurial companies off IPOs.

Of late, it has been a turbulent ride for US equity investors and they remain none the wiser as to whether another stretch of rapids or calmer water beckons.

With the Fed steadily withdrawing its monetary stimulus, it is hardly surprising that some investors have questioned sky-high valuations in certain areas of the equity market and are headed for the exit.

A rotation into defensive areas of the market, away from the higher octane growth stocks, mainly in biotechnology, social media and large internet names helps explain why the broad market market as represented by the S&P 500 is still just marginally below its all-time record high.

What has started from correction in technology and biotechnology stocks will spread into banking and financial sector stocks by the middle of May 2014 which are then expected to lose momentum.

What lies ahead? As shown by Google's revenue miss due to declining ad prices, which has prompted a renewed drop in its shares, earnings do matter.

First quarter earnings growth is currently running at minus 1.3 %, well shy of Wall Street's sunny forecast of 4.4 % gain back in January. It may be noted that not since the third quarter of 2012 have year-over-year quarterly earnings registered a negative performance.

The broad S&P 500 currently trades at 15.2 times its estimated forward 12-month earnings. Although this is down from a recent peak of 15.4 times, the market remains well above its 10-year average of 13.8 times and looks vulnerable, particularly as cost-cutting and not revenue growth has defined the current US earnings cycle.

The US earnings cycle is the weakest in 55 years with annualized growth of 2.8% from the prior-cycle peak in the second quarter of 2007 through the first quarter of 2014.

In previous cycles, earnings had already rsen 50% to 70% above their prior peak by this stage, whereas we are only up 20% from 2007.

A renewed focus on whether the economy delivers stronger growth is translating into more market volatility.

If Wall Street's rosy earnings forecasts don't materialize in the coming quarters and the Fed ends QE, rougher water could be the destination for equity bulls.

Reasons for recent NASDAQ selloff

Some playing were playing and playing hard with liquidity. There are worries about a "contagion" which ae helping to deflate the NASDAQ.

The hedge funds and others had bought into easy stocks, the momentum stocks and are now having to pay dearly for being in them.

Correlation between US Treasury yields and stock prices

Even as Fed tapers its bond purchase program, US bond yields were expected to rise. Owever, the US bond yields have been falling instead in tune with falling growth parameters raising questions about the durability of the stock market rally.

The 10-year Treasury bonds serve as the "orchestra conductor" leading the selloff.

In a Pavlovian fashion, equities are responding to it.

The technical underpinnings of the market are not as strong as I would like to see, given the nominal new highs in the market. Seasonal factors are about to run negative and geopolitical and global economic concerns continue to linger.

Also, in the wake of Michael Lewis's "Flash Boys" hitting store shelves, moves by regulators to slow down high-frequency trading (HFT) could also affect the market at some juncture. Witness the current FBI investigation into the HFT arena.

My call for a correction is a shorter call. I am a major believer that we are in a secular bull market that will last for several years to come, though this market remains stretched here and now.

A major reason why the market is going through a "rotational correction" as opposed to a more broad one is that central banks, around the world, appear to be getting out their bazookas again for another, potentially, significant amount of stimulus.

China's weak manufacturing data may be setting the stage for another round of easing by both the People's Bank of China and a blast of fiscal stimulus from the central planners.

This is a kind of a lull in an ongoing bull market and as a result there is some sensitivity to subtle bits of bad news. While the markets are not quite too sure, not quite too confident in themselves, this is the time we might have a little (rapid correction).

The Dow Jones Industrial Average is off around 1 percent this year, after climbing over 22 percent last year.

The market could "take fright" from any number of factors, such as an escalation of tensions in Ukraine, deleveraging in China or even if the Federal Reserve's moves to taper its asset purchases prove to be too fast.

The correction could be as much as 15 percent over a four to six week period, thereafter presenting a nice buying opportunity.

What we've seen over the past few weeks is a narrowing of leadership in the market--Fewer and fewer stocks are participating on the upside. The underlying market is deteriorating.

Earlier in April, high-flying momentum names in biotech, Internet and social media sectors sold off sharply, with the Nasdaq index dropping as much as 9.7 percent from its March high, flirting with the "official" correction level of 10 percent, before retracing some losses. The index is still down nearly 4 percent from its early April high.

Many U.S.-listed technology stocks entered bear-market territory – or a loss of at least 20 percent.

Valuations are no longer cheap--more funds are flowing into stocks considered defensive or lower risk. We see a bit more flight to safety.

If conditions deteriorate, the Fed would hold off on tapering and that would, of course, boost prices again—note that the correlation between the Fed's moves to increase its balance sheet by buying assets and gains in stocks is around 90 %.

Where should you invest in 2014? This is the common question haunting most investors and investment managers alike. Stocks? Bonds? Precious metals? Real estate? Or all of the above as some professional money managers profess so that they can average out the returns from these asset classes, as they know not which way these markets are headed.

Some believe you should always be invested because it is never easy to time the market. After 5 years, Dow Jones and many other global stock indices reclaimed their former peak. So if you had remained invested all the time, you would be where you were in 2008 (unless you had special stock-picking abilities).

There is no need to get hysterical and start throwing things around so that you reach that state of nirvana which helps you become a real 'Guru' of investing. You are not Aristotle and your hysterical moment is certainly not 'Eureka'.

Instead of getting hysterical, you would be better off doing some meditation which would definitely help you clear your vision and advance your financial goals better.

I have no intention to bore you by extolling the virtues of long-term equity investing. You are all familiar with the virtues of long-term investing. Equities historically, no doubt, give the best returns, when looked at over a long period of time. You have seen several such presentations in your life.

One thing is for sure, it is hard to believe that stocks will continue to out perform all other asset classes indefinitely. As Chart One shows perfectly well, all assets take turns whether they are outperforming or under-performing, as liquidity constantly shifts from overvalued to undervalued assets. Contrarians tend to buy value in anticipation of a trend change, while trend followers chase momentum. Contrarians are usually early to the game, while trend followers are late leaving it.

I have included a roadmap for investors in 2014. What are the factors that have enabled me to draw this roadmap for investors I have indicated in the latter half of my book. I have brought all these factors to work together in making my forecasts for what could turn out to be a turbulent year for investors—2014.

Any professional advisor will tell you it is not possible to time the market. It is frequently said "A drop of 20% in just over two months? But what if a recovery came just as fast—and the rally continued from there to end a 24% up for the year?"

If you understood the factors, this is not a 24% up move, but a 64% movement in indices. Even if you can capture 50% of this movement, you would still outbeat the market model by 12% (not a mean outperformance).

The start of 2014 saw the global markets decisively in risk-off mode, with global equities falling, government bonds rallying and many emerging market currencies collapsing.

Economic fundamentals in the DM's have not really changed. There have been some mildly disappointing data releases in the US, but these have been mostly due to an excessive build-up in manufacturing inventories since mid 2013, and the prospects for final demand seem firm.

Furthermore, the Fed's tapering of asset purchases has now been clearly separated from its intentions on short rates, which remain extremely dovish. So far, the decline in developed market equities has been very minor compared with the rises seen last year, and do not even constitute a normal pull-back in a bull market.

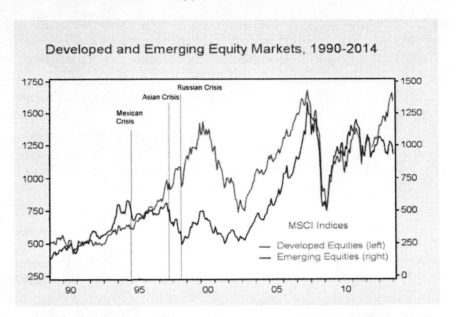

In the emerging markets (EM's), however, there is much greater cause for concern. As the graph above shows, the EM crises in the late 1990s did not, in the end, prove fatal for equities in the US and Europe, but they did cause occasional air pockets, notably in 1998. This is why investors are focused on whether the current EM crises will deteriorate further, and whether they will eventually take the DM's down with them.

The causes of the crises are not hard to discern, and are familiar from the 1990s. After 2008, many of the EM's tried to avoid the consequences of the Great Recession in the DM's by adopting aggressively expansionary fiscal and monetary policies, believing that their growth miracles of the 2000s could continue.

They were pushed in this direction by the capital inflows that followed quantitative easing by the Fed. Classic, and severe, credit bubbles ensued, with current account deficits widening rapidly in a group of countries that last summer became known as the 'fragile 5' – India, Indonesia, Brazil, Turkey and South Africa. These five have remained fragile, and have now been joined by Argentina, Russia, and Chile. So now we have the 'fragile 8', and the number could grow further.

These countries have many differences, but they also have something in common: a requirement to improve deteriorating balance of payments positions, which are much harder to finance now that the Fed is withdrawing QE. Some of them are inclined to blame the Fed for their predicament, but this is cutting very little ice in Washington. Unlike the onset of the EM crises last summer, the latest bout has not coincided with any change of opinion about monetary policy in the DM's.

Instead, the markets seem to be reacting to the fact that many of these countries need to undertake several difficult policy steps, all at the same time: lower real exchange rates, higher real interest rates, fiscal tightening in some, and structural reforms in many.

In other words, the economic problems of the 'fragile 8' are increasingly being viewed as internal to them, and there is scepticism about the ability of their political systems to deliver the necessary policy adjustments. (Paul Krugman points to the dangers of "economic populism" [1], and makes the case for restrictive policies in some EM's.)

Of course, the slowdown in China has not helped the fragile group, especially those that are dependent on commodity exports. But a dangerous dynamic is now in place, familiar to those who remember the melt-down of the emerging Asian economies after the financial crisis of 1997. Then, China remained immune from the worst features of the crisis, but that did not prevent the rest of Asia from experiencing severe recessions as "sudden stops" in capital inflows forced them to adjust their balance of payments deficits very abruptly.

The decades-long consequences of these sudden stops included a decline in the investment/GDP ratio of 9 percentage points, and a drop in trend GDP growth of 3.3 per cent. (See Carmen Reinhart and Takeshi Tashiro). As the DM's are now discovering, financial shocks have exceptionally long-term effects on economic performance. It is a serious mistake to expect any of this to blow over rapidly.

Optimists claim that there are grounds for hoping that some or all of the fragile group may ultimately avoid the worst fate of the Asian tigers.

Foreign currency debt as % GDP

Troubled currencies			
	1996	2007	Sep-13
Brazil	26%	15% ↓	17% ↓
India	7%	16% ↑	14% ↑
Russia	19%	19% ↑	13% ↓
South Africa	15%	20% ↑	16% ↑
Turkey	17%	28% ↑	30% ↑
Average	17%	20% ↑	18% ↑

More robust currencies			
	1996	2007	Sep-13
Chile		35%	45%
China	9%	7% ↓	10% ↑
Colombia	22%	16% ↓	17% ↑
Czech Republic	17%	29% ↑	40% ↑
Hungary	67%	97% ↑	83% ↑
Indonesia	30%	16% ↓	20% ↓
Israel	9%	61% ↑	20% ↑
Korea	27%	32% ↑	31% ↑
Malaysia	31%	43% ↑	39% ↑
Mexico	47%	20% ↓	30% ↓
Philippines	30%	41% ↑	29% ↓
Poland	19%	37% ↑	40% ↑
Thailand	51%	13% ↓	19% ↓
Average	30%	34% ↑	33% ↑

Source: Nomura, Bloomberg. Note: Arrows indicate increase or decrease since 1996.

One difference is that exchange rates have been much more flexible during the onset of the crisis this time than they were in the 1990s, when most of the relevant economies were trying to run fixed exchange rates against the dollar.

This encouraged an even bigger build-up in external debt in the severe 1990s cases than has happened now (though many EM's do look vulnerable on this score). And the collapse in confidence was all the more sudden, because banking sectors were much more severely exposed to the revaluation of large foreign debts.

This time, the more gradual adjustment of EM exchange rates – upwards before the crisis and downwards later on – provided a shock absorber. Still, the consequences in terms of imported inflation, declining domestic demand and imploding credit bubbles will inevitably be very challenging for policy makers, many of whom have become hubristic after the EM miracle years in the 2000s.

Some will be able to meet the challenge. India, for example, is now doing much better with Raghuram Rajan at the central bank. But others may choose to follow Argentina by refusing to accept the laws of market economics. They will be tempted to monetise the fiscal deficits that will follow economic slow-downs, thus feeding a downward spiral in nominal exchange rates. They cannot realistically hope to be rescued from this fate by "policy co-operation" from the Fed or the IMF; it is largely up to them.

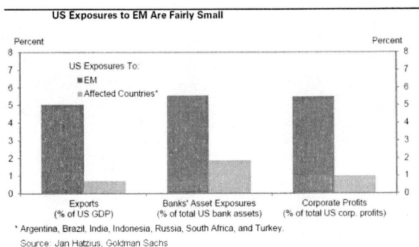

US Exposures to EM Are Fairly Small

US Exposures To:
- ■ EM
- ▪ Affected Countries*

Exports (% of US GDP) | Banks' Asset Exposures (% of total US bank assets) | Corporate Profits (% of total US corp. profits)

* Argentina, Brazil, India, Indonesia, Russia, South Africa, and Turkey.

Source: Jan Hatzius, Goldman Sachs

Could all this develop into a major global shock? Exports to the 'fragile 8' still represent only 0.7 percent of US GDP, so a damaging trade shock is not on the cards. The exports of the euro area are about twice as vulnerable to the 'fragile 8' as the US, and a small number of euro area banks (especially in Spain) are very exposed to loan losses in the EMs. This means that there could be contagion to southern Europe, where some banks may already need to raise large amounts of new capital after the ECB's stress tests.

But the overall consequences for the developed economies still seem largely manageable – always assuming, of course, that China does not hard land.

FOOTNOTES

[1] Rudi Dornbush and Sebastian Edwards' paper in 1991: "Our purpose in setting out these experiences, those of Chile under Allende and of Peru under Garcia, is not a righteous assertion of conservative economics, but rather a warning that populist policies do ultimately fail; and when they fail it is always at a frightening cost to the very groups who were supposed to be favored. Our central thesis is that the macroeconomics of various experiences is very much the same, even if the politics differed greatly."

WHAT THE CLUB SANDWICH
SAYS ABOUT YOUR LIVING COSTS

The Swiss capital of Geneva is home to the world's most expensive sandwich, according to Hotels.com's latest 'Club Sandwich Index.'

The firm claims that looking at the cost of a classic hotel sandwich made of chicken, bacon, egg, lettuce and mayonnaise as a barometer of affordability offers travelers an indication of the costs associated with their destination of choice.

Now in its third year, the Club Sandwich Index (CSI) is calculated from the prices guests paid for a club sandwich in 30 hotels, across five, four and three-star categories, in either the capital or an important tourist city in 28 surveyed countries. In total 840 hotels were canvassed globally.

And according to the 2014 CSI, Geneva has retained its top spot as home of the most expensive club sandwich in the world at $32.60.

Other pricey tourism hotspots include the gastronomic hub of Paris, which held on to the number two spot with an average price of $29.36, followed by Finland's Helsinki, where the price rose to $24.35 from $19.74 in 2013, knocking Norway's Oslo out of the top three.

Average price for a club sandwich in 28 cities

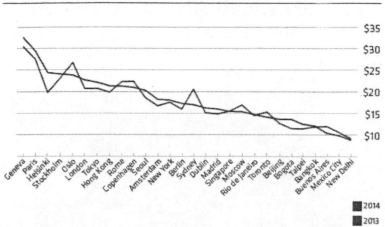

The Hotels.com Club Sandwich Index

In the U.S., New York City had the priciest sandwich at $17.99, and ranked 13 for the send straight year.

Meanwhile, the cheapest place for a club sandwich in the U.S. was Orlando, where the average of $10.68 was just above that of Buenos Aires at $10.37, which ranked 26th globally.

India's New Delhi remained the cheapest destination among cities surveyed, with the average price for a club sandwich at $8.78, while Mexico City also offered a bargain at $9.78.

Australia's Sydney saw the greatest decrease in average prices, falling to $16.93 in 2014 from $20.53 in 2013.

INFLATION, CPI AND THE BIG MAC:
BITE OF REALITY

From my research, I have determined that the average price of a Big Mac is $4.45 (the range was $3.78 to $5.28), atn increase of $0.09, or 2.0% from what I obtained in January. While it increased during the past three months, annualized, this is a decline of 2.4% over the last 12 months.

This compares to the Consumer Price Index (CPI) reported today by the Bureau of Labor Statistics. The CPI increased 2.0% year-over-year.

We are seeing a reverse of what we saw last year. Big Mac prices rose more than CPI last year. This year the reverse is true–CPI is rising more than the price of a Big Mac.

The Big Mac provides a better indication of price movements than the government compiled CPI. Many of us can neither follow nor actually experience what the CPI means or how it moves. Conversely, the Big Mac is consumed constantly, and we shell out hard-earned dollars to purchase the sandwich. Thus, it is a real-time metric of our economy.

Individuals eat 17 Big Macs a second. This means Big Macs are eaten at a rate of 1,200 a minute, 61,200 an hour, 1,468,800 each day and 536,112,000 a year. At $4.45, the current average price of a Big Mac generated $2.4 billion in revenue for McDonald's from Big Macs sold in the U.S. alone.

People experience the change in the price of the Big Mac daily. It is tangible. Consequently, it is a good way to view inflation.

While I have just observed why the Big Mac makes for a good inflation gauge, it also is important to relate it to the financial advisor profession, and how we communicate the impact of inflation to individual clients.

Bet on the Big Mac

The level of inflation – to a great extent – drives the valuation of the stock market. Mild inflation (1-3%) is typical, and relates to the highest of valuations. However, when inflation is above 3% and the market multiples, the amount that investors are willing to pay for each dollar of earnings declines. Market valuations also decline with inflation below 1% and even further when prices decline outright.

CPI has a longer history to track than the Big Mac. However, CPI has changed over time as the weighting for different components has shifted. So, essentially, the calculation for CPI has changed. That said, are we not better off using the Big Mac to measure inflation? The formula for the Big Mac hasn't changed.

Implications for Financial Advisors

There are two main implications for financial advisors. First, realize that costs are increasing faster for clients than the government suggests. Therefore, individuals need more income to sustain the same level of consumption they have had in the past.

Second, value of the stock market is predicated on the level of inflation. However if inflation is higher, or lower, than what is reported, does that make valuations of the stock market unstable than they already are?

Now, finally, the stock market is fairly valued for conditions of low inflation and low interest rates (assuming average long-term economic growth in the future). But what lies ahead? If inflation remains low and stable indefinitely, then this secular bear will remain in hibernation until the inflation rate runs away in either direction.

What if inflation is already above the level to support heightened valuations for the stock market? Does that mean that the stock market could lose its lofty stance quicker?

Certainly this is a possibility and further justifies ongoing tracking of the Big Mac as the inflation measure of choice for financial advisors to use with your clients.

THE IMPORTANCE OF PROTECTING JAPANESE RICE OVER SUSHI AT 'SUKIYABASHI JIRO'

Obama Tells Japan's Abe: 'Best Sushi I've Ever Had'

Entire blocks of Japan's famed Ginza shopping and entertainment district were closed off Wednesday night, as Prime Minister Shinzo Abe welcomed President Barack Obama to what may be Tokyo's most celebrated sushi restaurant, the Michelin three-starred **Sukiyabashi Jiro**.

After the 90-minute meal, Mr. Abe quoted the president as saying, "It's the best sushi I've ever had."

The prime minister, speaking outside the much-ballyhooed restaurant, said the successful sushi dinner vindicated his "cool Japan" policy of promoting Japanese cultural assets such as food.

The president arrived at the tiny restaurant, featured in the documentary ***"Jiro Dreams of Sushi,"*** just 90 minutes after landing in Tokyo. He was accompanied by the U.S. Ambassador to Japan, Caroline Kennedy and National Security Adviser Susan Rice, and he was welcomed by Mr. Abe at the entrance.

Japanese officials said that the informal and intimate dinner was designed to promote a "frank exchange of ideas" between the two leaders, who have not developed a particularly close relationship since Mr. Abe took office in December 2012.

Maybe Mr. Abe can stress the importance of protecting Japanese rice over sushi-I am apparently referring to the contentious trade talk even as Japan hopes to protect its agricultural products.

WHAT AMERICA'S APRIL 2014 UNEMPLOYMENT IS TELLING US?

The headline number from the payroll survey beat expectations by a mile with 288,000 jobs, but beneath the surface, the household survey shows employment *declined* by 73,000.

Total nonfarm payroll employment rose by 288,000, and the unemployment rate fell by 0.4 percentage point to 6.3 percent in April, the U.S. Bureau of Labor Statistics reported today. Employment gains were widespread, led by job growth in professional and business services, retail trade, food services and drinking places, and construction.

Unemployment Rate - Seasonally Adjusted

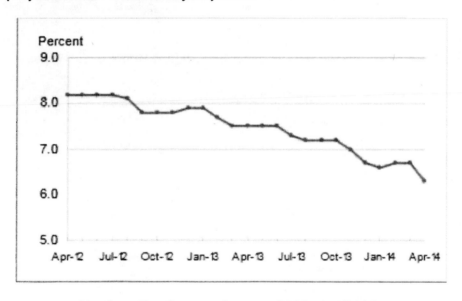

Nonfarm Employment January 2011 - April 2014

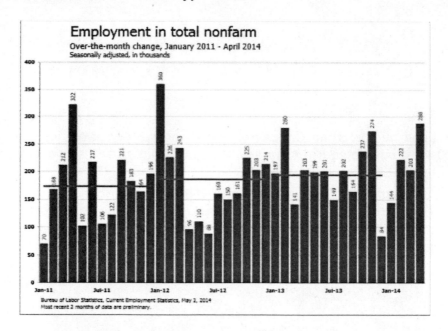

Nonfarm Employment Change from Previous Month by Job Type

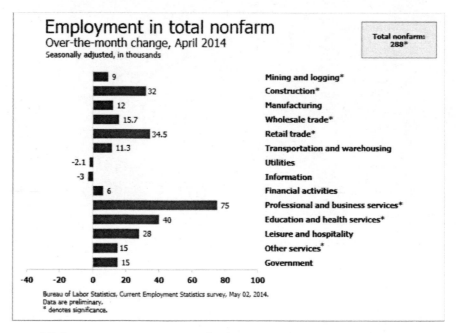

The establishment survey gain is the largest 1-month gain since January 2012. Nonfarm employment remains just 113,000 below its January 2008 peak.

Hours and Wages

The Average weekly hours of all private employees was flat at 34.5 hours. The Average weekly hours of all private service-providing employees was flat at 33.3 hours.

Average hourly earnings of private workers rose $0.03 to $20.50. Average hourly earnings of private service-providing employees rose $0.02 to $20.28.

Birth Death Model

Starting January, I dropped the Birth/Death Model charts from this report. For those who follow the numbers, I keep this caution: Do not subtract the reported Birth-Death number from the reported headline number. That approach is statistically invalid. Should anything interesting arise in the Birth/Death numbers, I will add the charts back.

Table 15 BLS Alternate Measures of Unemployment

Measure	Not seasonally adjusted			Seasonally adjusted					
	Apr. 2013	Mar. 2014	Apr. 2014	Apr. 2013	Dec. 2013	Jan. 2014	Feb. 2014	Mar. 2014	Apr. 2014
U-1 Persons unemployed 15 weeks or longer, as a percent of the civilian labor force	4.3	3.7	3.3	4.1	3.6	3.4	3.5	3.5	3.2
U-2 Job losers and persons who completed temporary jobs, as a percent of the civilian labor force	3.9	3.7	3.2	4.1	3.5	3.5	3.5	3.5	3.4
U-3 Total unemployed, as a percent of the civilian labor force (official unemployment rate)	7.1	6.8	5.9	7.5	6.7	6.6	6.7	6.7	6.3
U-4 Total unemployed plus discouraged workers, as a percent of the civilian labor force plus discouraged workers	7.6	7.2	6.3	8.0	7.2	7.1	7.2	7.1	6.7
U-5 Total unemployed, plus discouraged workers, plus all other persons marginally attached to the labor force, as a percent of the civilian labor force plus all persons marginally attached to the labor force	8.5	8.1	7.2	8.9	8.1	8.1	8.1	8.0	7.6
U-6 Total unemployed, plus all persons marginally attached to the labor force, plus total employed part time for economic reasons, as a percent of the civilian labor force plus all persons marginally attached to the labor force	13.4	12.8	11.8	13.9	13.1	12.7	12.6	12.7	12.3

Table A-15 is where one can find a better approximation of what the unemployment rate really is.

Notice I said "better" approximation not to be confused with "good" approximation.

The official unemployment rate is 6.3%. However, if you start counting all the people who want a job but gave up, all the people with part-time jobs that want a full-time job, all the people who dropped off the unemployment rolls because their unemployment benefits ran out, etc., you get a closer picture of what the unemployment rate is. That number is in the last row labeled U-6.

U-6 is much higher at 12.3%. Both numbers would be way higher still, were it not for millions dropping out of the labor force over the past few years.

Labor Force Factors

1. Discouraged workers stop looking for jobs
2. People retire because they cannot find jobs
3. People go back to school hoping it will improve their chances of getting a job
4. People stay in school longer because they cannot find a job
5. Disability and disability fraud

Were it not for people dropping out of the labor force, the unemployment rate would be well over 9%.

Synopsis

Last month, weather-related effects were taken back and then some. This month we see a return to the divergence between the household survey and the establishment survey. +288,000 vs. -73,000 is massive. So is the decline in labor force of 800,000. That is the only reason the unemployment rate declined.

WHY INDIAN MANGOES COULD
TURN SOUR IN EUROPE?

An Indian fruit vendor displays mangoes

The European Union's ban on mango imports from India is unlikely to dent Asia's third-largest economy, but it could create trade friction between the two economies.

The ban on mangos, along with aubergines, two types of squash and patra – a type of leaf used in Indian cooking – until the end of next year, came into force this week after consignments were found to be infested with fruit flies in 2013.

Although European countries import a hefty number of the exotic fruit, with U.K. imports surmising £6.3 million ($10.64 million) annually, the overall impact on India's economy would be small. Fresh fruits only account for around 0.2 percent of India's global exports – or $2.5 billion's worth. Mangos account for 5 percent of India's fresh fruit exports to the E.U. While the impact is likely to be marginal, the ban has increased trade friction between India and the E.U., which could have negative implications down the road given that Europe is India's largest export market.

Total Indian exports to the E.U. surmise €38 billion ($52.68 billion) annually, of which 7.5 percent are agricultural products.

Following the discovery of the infested mango consignments in 2013, the E.U. has asked India to improve their standards to comply with E.U. regulations, which the body is set to review in 2014.

The E.U. and India are in the process of negotiating a Free Trade Agreement, and escalating bilateral trade tensions could hurt the progress of bilateral trade negotiations when the next Indian government takes office after the Indian elections end in mid-May.

The mango ban could damage India's global reputation in terms of its health and safety standards. Furthermore, Indian grown premium Alphonso mangoes, which are popular in the U.K., are in season as the ban comes into force.

Was the March 2009 low the end of a secular bear market and the beginning of a secular bull?

The key word on the chart above is **secular**. The implicit rule I'm following is that blue shows secular trends that lead to new all-time real highs. Periods in between are secular bear markets, regardless of their cyclical rallies. For example, the rally from 1932 to 1937, despite its strength, remains a cycle in a secular bear market. At its peak in 1937, the index was 29% below the real all-time high of 1929. For a scholarly study of secular bear markets, which highlights the same key turning points, see Russell Napier's Anatomy of the Bear: Lessons from Wall Street's Four Great Bottoms.

If we study the data underlying the chart, we can extract a number of interesting facts about these secular patterns (note that for the table below I am including the 1932-1937 rally):

Year	Market Milestone	Percent Change	Number of Years	Annualized Return, No Dividends	Annualized Return with Dividends
1877	Low	-	-	-	-
1906	High	378%	29.3	5.1%	10.1%
1921	Low	-69%	14.9	-7.5%	-2.0%
1929	High	396%	8.1	21.9%	28.4%
1932	Low	-81%	2.7	-44.9%	-41.2%
1937	High	266%	4.7	32.1%	38.7%
1949	Low	-54%	12.3	-6.2%	-0.8%
1968	High	413%	19.5	8.8%	13.3%
1982	Low	-63%	13.6	-7.0%	-3.0%
2000	High	666%	18.1	11.9%	15.3%
2009	Low	-59%	8.5	-9.8%	-8.1%
Now	-	122%	5.0	N/A	N/A

Based on inflation-adjusted S&P Composite monthly averages of daily closes.

The annualized rate of growth from 1871 through the end of January (using extrapolated CPI data for the most recent month) is 2.07%. If that seems incredibly low, remember that the chart shows "real" price growth, excluding inflation and dividends. If we factor in the dividend yield, we get an annualized return of 6.81%. Yes, dividends make a difference. Unfortunately that has been less true during the past three decades than in earlier times. When we let Excel draw a regression through the data, the slope is an even lower annualized rate of 1.75% (see the regression section below for further explanation).

If we added in the value lost from inflation, the "nominal" annualized return comes to 9.02% — the number commonly reported in the popular press. But for a more accurate view of the purchasing power of the market dollars, we'll stick to "real" numbers.

Since that first trough in 1877 to the March 2009 low:

Secular bull gains totaled 2075% for an average of 415%.

Secular bear losses totaled -329% for an average of -65%.

Secular bull years total 80 versus 52 for the bears, a 60:40 ratio.

This last bullet probably comes as a surprise to many people. The finance industry and media have conditioned us to view every dip as a buying opportunity. If we realize that bear markets have accounted for about 40% of the highlighted time frame, we can better understand the two massive selloffs of the 21st century.

Based on the real (inflation-adjusted) S&P Composite monthly averages of daily closes, the S&P is 122% above the 2009 low, which is still 8% below the 2000 high.

Add a Regression Trend Line

Let's review the same chart, this time with a regression trend line through the data.

This line is a "best fit" that essentially divides the monthly values so that the total distance of the data points above the line equals the total distance below. The slope of this line, an annualized rate of 1.75%, approximates that number. Remember that 2.07% annualized rate of growth since 1871? The difference is the current above-trend market value

The chart below creates a channel for the S&P Composite. The two dotted lines have the same slope as the regression, as calculated in Excel, with the top of the channel based on the peak of the Tech Bubble and the low is based on the 1932 trough.

Historically, regression to trend often means overshooting to the other side. The latest monthly average of daily closes is 76% above trend after having fallen only 12% below trend in March of 2009. Previous bottoms were considerably further below trend.

Will the March 2009 bottom be different? Perhaps. But only time will tell.

I include some interesting demographic analysis based on the ratio of the higher earning, bigger spending age 35-49 cohort to less financially empowered age 20-34 cohort. Unfortunately this ratio is being savagely trumped by a far more powerful demographic shift: The ratio of the elderly (65 and over) to the peak earning cohort (age 45-54). The next chart, based on Census Bureau historical data and mid-year population forecasts to 2060, illustrates this rather amazing shift.

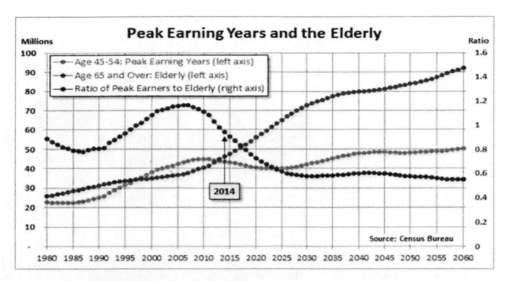

In the chart above, the elderly cohort (red series) is dramatically increasing in numbers. The ratio of the two, the blue line in the chart, peaked in 2007 and began its long rollover in 2008, coincident with the beginning of the last recession. We have many years to go before this ratio approximately levels out around 2030.

Even more disturbing is the elderly dependency ratio, the label given by demographers to the ratio of the 65 and older population to the productive workforce, which for developed economies is usually identified as ages 20-64. The next chart illustrates the elderly dependency ratio with Census Bureau forecasts to 2060. Note that in this chart I've followed the general practice in demographic research of multiplying the percent by 100 (e.g., the estimated mid-year 2014 elderly dependency ratio is 24.3% x 100 = 24.3).

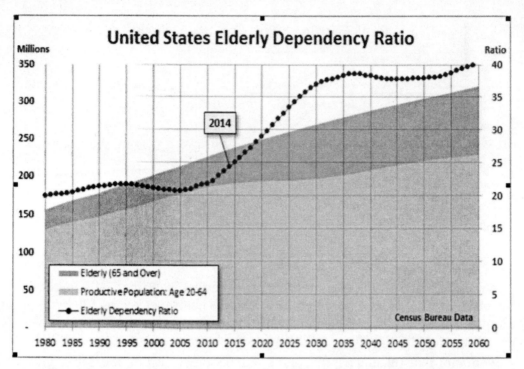

As the chart painfully illustrates, the elderly dependency ratio is in the early stages of a relentless rise that doesn't hit an interim peak until around 2036, over two decades from now. Given the unprecedented demographic headwinds for today's investors, it is always a matter of conjecture whether we are truly in a secular bull market.

PHARMA M&A: IS IT BACK?

Two important M&A deals have struck the world of Pharma.

Glaxo Smithkline (GSK) and Novartis have announced a $ 16 Billion commercial tie-up. GSK will get most of its Swiss rival's vaccines business and its consumer healthcare, while Novartis will pay up to $ 16 Billion for GSK's oncology business. In the meantime, Eli Lilly of the U.S. is to pay $ 5.4 Billion for Novartis' animal health division.

There are a lot of synergies between animal health and human health. This deal presents Eli Lilly a great market opportunity as people around the world look to put more protein into their diets—safe, nutritious, affordable food.

The deals reflect how industry players need to be positioned over the next dcade. They are trying to look forward 10-20 years ahead rather than 2-3 years.

In a second deal, Valeant, alongwith activist investor Bill Ackman is pitching $ 50 Billion pitch for Botox maker Allergan.

There are several factors driving companies to make deals at the moment, such as the sector's well-publicized difficulties with developing new products and pricing as well as a move to exploit a U.S. tax law.

The M&A deals shows that management will not sit idly by waiting for the pipeline to mature but will take brave decisions to unlock shareholder value.

U.S. tax law is one of the key factors driving companies to make deals. If at least 20% of a U.S. company's shares are hold overseas, it can re-domicile its tax base and make savings on its tax bill. Buying a foreign domiciled company can be a quick wn for U.S. pharma groups, which mostly have a solidly American shareholder base, to bring in more overseas shareholders.

The future of pharma lies in research, not cuts

In the first deal, pharma companies that invest heavily in research and development on cancer drugs and vaccines have discovered a way to specialise in the things they do best without resorting to large mergers. In the second, constant dealmaking, accompanied by the cutting of R&D to save cash and please Wall Street, produces new types of cream for acne and athlete's foot.

The pharma industry – having endured years of poor productivity and falling returns, not helped by companies formed in past mergers struggling to sort themselves out – is stirring. New drugs for cancer and other serious illnesses are emerging, along with the appetite and the financing for deals.

Some would like to restart where the industry was forced to halt in 2009 with the last wave of mergers, such as Pfizer's $68bn acquisition of Wyeth. That produced dubious results but, nothing daunted, Pfizer has suggested a $100bn merger to AstraZeneca of the UK.

The beauty of the Novartis/GSK deal is that it shows what can be done by precision and determination, rather than the usual Wall Street prescription of a big premium (and large fees to advisers and banks) for a mixed bag of assets. Instead of paying a lot for everything, including medicines that do not fit well, both sides can be choosy.

There are assets embedded in most companies that are worth more to others. Acquirers deal with this by taking a sledgehammer to the whole and extracting the good parts. This deal lets Novartis give up vaccines while gaining most of GSK's oncology arm, and a joint venture in consumer medicine.

Such exchanges are difficult to pull off – you have to find a suitable partner, agree on asset valuations, structure deals to suit both sides and do the whole thing at once. But when they occur, as they have done in the energy and food industries, they are very efficient.

They suit pharma companies, which often pursue a wide variety of research projects and medicines but benefit by specialising. They are not keen to sell their small divisions for cash, since they have plenty of that, but they want to bulk up their larger ones. An asset swap is rather less glamorous than an acquisition, but equally less wasteful.

This brings us to Valeant. The group has been growing so rapidly since Michael Pearson, the former head of McKinsey's pharma practice, became its chief executive in 2008 that it is easy to have missed it.

But Mr Pearson, now a billionaire thanks to a performance-based bonus scheme, has no intention of slowing down – he wants to break into the industry's top five by 2016.

Valeant's business model is as simple as its accounting and tax structure are complex. While at McKinsey, Mr Pearson concluded that the industry he advised was spendthrift, not only in the sums it spent on headquarters and staff but in its investment in drug discovery. Employing scientists to search for new drugs was a waste of money because they often failed.

When he got the chance to put his ideas into practice he cut Valeant's research to 3 per cent of revenues – compared with about 19 per cent at big pharma companies – and acquired products by buying other companies with debt. Valeant has taken over more than 35 companies since 2008, including Bausch & Lomb, which it acquired for $8.7bn last year.

Botox would fit with Mr Pearson's approach. He likes well-known brands in areas such as dermatology and ophthalmology, where patients and doctors are the buyers, rather than cost-conscious insurers and health systems. He plans to cut Allergan's $1.1bn research budget by $900m and focus on low-risk projects.

His partner in this adventure is Bill Ackman, founder of Pershing Square Capital, the activist hedge fund, which rapidly acquired a 9.7 per cent stake in Allergan.

Mr Pearson has so far generated big profits for his shareholders and himself, and it may not matter too much if a combined Valeant-Allergan invests more in variations of Botox than finding an innovative cosmetic chemical. But if the entire pharma industry adopted his approach, drug discovery would grind to a halt.

One future is for companies to intensify research in areas of need such as oncology, exchanging assets in order to concentrate on what they do best. The other is to succumb to cost-stripping backed by hedge funds for whom five years is a long time. It is a moral choice.

ELECTION YEAR FOR EMERGING MARKETS: WHAT TO EXPECT

It's election year for major emerging market economies from India to Brazil.

And political risk falls at a time when investors are assessing just what an unwinding of U.S. monetary stimulus means for the developing world.

The so-called 'Fragile Five' – India, Indonesia, Brazil, South Africa and Turkey – are all holding elections in the months ahead, with corruption just one theme expected to be feature highly.

There has been a notable shift in market concerns about emerging markets over the past month or so. While the May to August 2013 phase of the sell-off was dominated by fears about balance of payments weaknesses, the current phase is about a broader set of risks, in particular growth, the credibility of the policy-making regime and the political climate in general.

In each of these countries, we are seeing very heavy voter turnout, thus indicating anti-incumbency factor will play key role in the election results.

India

India's performance has really been a disappointment. The outgoing government could definitely have done better.

Other than the various scams which kept rolling out, even at the mundane level, their performance left much to be desired.

Look at the dismal **traffic situation**. After so many years, the traffic offender can go scot-free by merely paying a bribe. If in something as important as traffic violation you can get away by paying a bribe, would this not percolate down below. Can the government not install CCTV cameras to monitor this?

Look at the **plethora of tax forms** an Indian taxpayer has to fill out. The government keeps increasing compliance.

When the country was not doing well over the last few years, all that the government needed to do was to allow entrepreeneurs to go the 'innovation way' rather than waste their time indulging in wasteful and lengthy tax compliance.

A whole body of accounting professionals has grown just to cater to the new compliance requirements.

Reach the **Indian airport** and there is some porter prompting you would you like your bags out quickly (Speed money?). Why does it have to start right from the time one reaches the airport?

And it would be always nice if the **leader of the country is vocal** and one who can talk with the nation and galvanize the population when the need arises.

India has felt this vacuum despite having the best brains and people educated in the top U.K. and American Ivy League universities.

Indian politics has been subject to a roughly 20-year cycle for the last 100 years.

Whichever way one looks at it, there is no denying that Arvind Kejriwal and Narendra Modi have changed Indian politics in a fundamental way. But they are not the first to do so.

If you look at Indian politics since it started in earnest in the mid-1890s, you will find that it has a roughly 20-year cycle. Approximately after every two or so decades it undergoes a convulsion that changes it forever.

The key dates are 1916-1920, 1937-1940, 1952-1956, 1969-1972, 1987-1991 and now.

On each of these occasions, except 1952-1956, a new player came along and changed the paradigm for ever.

1952-1956 was an exception because then it was not a new person but two new ideas that came along. These continue to be with us till date.

Histoy has repeated itself in 2014 in the Indian general elections.

Is there a wardrobe for success?

There is one other major difference between Kejriwal of AAP and Modi of BJP (two of the strong contenders in the Indian elections) which is in their sartorial preferences. While the AAP leader prefers the crumpled white shirt and Gandhi topi, Modi likes well-starched expensive kurtas and varied headgear. In politics as in economics, there is no set wardrobe for success!

Election Results: The country's 815 million voters cast their ballots from April 7 to May 12 and results were declared on May 16. A pro-growth Narendra Modi-led government has been installed at the centre.

India's opportunity comes from being uniquely young – a large majority of the population is of working age. This promises a surge in economic growth, as gains from those of productive age outweigh the burden of supporting the old and the very young. Such a demographic dividend could add 2 percentage points to per capita growth. The country cannot afford to let this potential slip away. Each year, 9m people enter India's job market and a 1 % point rise in gross domestic product adds about 1.5m direct jobs. Thus, restoring growth to 8 % from 4.5 % today would do it. Failure to do so risks confronting India with a demographic disaster, as the great hope of youth turns into despair.

Backdrop: India, Asia's third-biggest economy and the world's largest democracy, kicked off 2014 on a gloomy note, with growth expected to drop below 5 percent for the 2013-14 year as the country battles the worst slowdown since the 1980s. The economy's trade gap in March widened to $10.51 billion, its highest since October 2013, while industrial output has fallen in four of the last five months.

However, a strengthening currency has provided some relief for investors although this has been achieved by artificially curbing gold imports. The rupee is over 12 percent higher since hitting an all-time low in August 2013. Meanwhile, the government in its budget earlier this year unveiled indirect tax cuts to help woo voters.

Key election themes: Consumer inflation, running at an annual rate above 9 percent, and rampant corruption.

The road ahead for India:

Hundreds of public and private sector projects are stuck. Given clarity of purpose, Indian bureaucracy is capable of high performance, and we saw this during Prime Minister Narasimha Rao's first two years from 1991 to 1993.

India's pugnacious press, fearless judiciary and a hugely diverse, disobedient people make dictatorship a tall order

Is this India's Margaret Thatcher moment? This is a discontented and politically troubled nation, similar in some ways to Britain in the late 1970s with high inflation, declining growth, high fiscal deficits and a government in denial. Britain yearned for a strong leader then, and in Mrs Thatcher it got one. In Mr Modi Indians, too, have chosen a strong leader. His Thatcherite rhetoric of "less government and more governance" resonates with the aspiring young middle class, as does his language of "outcomes", "accountability" and "unbureaucratic service".

But Mrs Thatcher did not merely restore the British economy to health through right-of-centre policies. She also reformed the institutions of governance, bringing more accountability to the state. This is what India needs as well – to reform its bureaucracy, police and judiciary. Mr Modi would thus have to go beyond the economy and show himself an ambitious reformist, if this were indeed to be India's Margaret Thatcher moment.

Indonesia

Jakarta governor Joko Widodo.

Election due: The results of April's legislative elections are due in early May, followed by a presidential election in July. If there is no clear winner in the first round of voting in the presidential election, a second round is expected to take place in September.

Backdrop: Like its emerging market peers, Indonesia has come under pressure from an unwinding of U.S. monetary stimulus that has exposed economic weaknesses such as a wide current-account deficit. After seeing its deficit narrow to 1.98 percent of gross domestic product (GDP) in the fourth quarter of 2013, the government now expects a figure of less than 3 percent for the first three months of 2014. The central bank has hiked rates five times since the middle of last year to prop up a crumbling rupiah.

While the economy – the biggest in Southeast Asia – grew a better-than-expected 5.72 percent on year in the fourth quarter, economists say political uncertainty, the impact of monetary tightening and a controversial mineral export ban will all be headwinds in the coming months.

Key election themes: Endemic corruption, poor infrastructure, under investment in health and education.

Expected outcome: Early tallies from April's legislative vote showed the Indonesian Democratic Party-Struggle (the PDI-P) won around 19 percent of votes, the biggest share of any party but well below the 25 percent needed to nominate candidate Jakarta Governor Joko "Jokowi" Widodo, viewed as a favorite to win, for president.

To resolve that, PDI-P and smaller National Democrat party (NasDem) struck an alliance during the weekend of April 14. Since the National Democratic Party won about 7 percent of votes in the legislative polls, the coalition effectively clears the way for Widodo to run for presidency in July. May 10 is the deadline for parties to nominate their candidates for president.

The wild card: Watch the youth vote. Of the projected 187 million eligible voters in this year's elections, over a third will be between the age of 16 and 20. Indonesia's politicians face a young electorate that is increasingly online and this could well shape the political landscape in the years ahead, analysts say.

View from the experts: Regardless of the election results, the general belief is that the new administration will maintain the major economic policy initiatives of the previous government with further legislation in the mining and agribusiness sectors set to materialize.

Turkey

Prime Minister Tayyip Erdogan

Election due: Municipal elections on March 30 declared Prime Minister Tayyip Erdogan's Justice and Development Party (AKP) triumphant. Presidential elections are set for August and parliamentary elections are due in 2015.

Backdrop: The ruling AKP, which has been in power since 2003, has been hit by a high-level bribery and corruption scandal that sparked street protests late last year. Most recently, Erdogan imposed a ban on social media site Twitter, invoking backlash about the country's control on freedom of expression.

Moody's has since cut the outlook of Turkey's sovereign rating to negative while the International Monetary Fund revised its real gross domestic product forecast to 2.3 percent this year, from 3.5 percent. Meanwhile, the Turkish lira continues to fall after hitting a record low against the dollar in January, which forced the country's central bank to hike interest rates.

Key election themes: Corruption, inflation

Expected outcome: Erdogan is widely seen as winning the presidential elections later this year after the AKP secured 45 percent of the vote in March's municipal elections, compared with 28 percent for the main opposition Republican People's Party (CHP). The CHP has since called for a recount, citing irregularities, but it's demand was refused by High Election Board.

Foreign investors are happy with the outcome of the Turkish local elections because "they like stability."

Erdogan has dominated Turkish politics for more than a decade and won credibility for delivering economic stability. A survey by SONAR research, one of Turkey's main pollsters, earlier this year put support for the AK Party at 42.3 percent, two percentage points below its last poll in August 2013 and below the 50 percent won by the AK in the 2011 election, Reuters reported.

The wild card: The controversial Gülen Movement, an Islamist group led by U.S.-based preacher Fethullah Gulen, has been trying to ruin the AKP's image ever since implicating the prime minister in a bribery scandal last year. Having emerged as a powerful force in the months after, the group is known for its deliberate attempts to infiltrate government structures.

View from the experts: March's election result "is a bullish outcome for the local market simply because investors are not keen on heightened political uncertainty and instability".

Brazil

Street scene in Belem, Brazil

Election due: Elections for a new president and parliament are expected on October 5.

Backdrop: Brazil, the biggest economy in Latin America, faces an uncertain election year. Its stock market, down more than seven percent so far this year, has been battered by Federal Reserve tapering fears. A severe drought is stretching the country's finances, the central bank has hiked interest rates by 325 basis points since April last year to contain inflation and last year a small demonstration against a 50-cent rise in bus fares exploded into the biggest street protest Brazil has witnessed in years.

In March, Standard & Poor's (S&P) downgraded Brazil's long-term debt rating to BBB minus, one notch above "junk" status. It is the latest blow to Rousseff who has struggled to revive the economy since the 2011 slowdown that has plagued her presidency since she succeeded Lula da Silva.

Key election themes: Poor public services, rising living costs and deteriorating public finances and corruption.

Brazil has strong macroeconomic fundamentals, after the country suffered a credit rating downgrade on Tuesday.

Expected outcome: President Dilma Rousseff from the Workers' Party is running for re-election and despite the weak economic backdrop she is the favorite to win. The latest poll by Ibope showed Rousseff with 43 percent of the electorate's support.

The outcome however, could still be a close call, analysts say. Other candidates include Marina Silva, an environmentalist and former environment minister.

The wild card: The World Cup. What exactly does soccer have to do with an election? Well, potentially a great deal if shutdowns associated with preparing or hosting the sporting event takes a toll on the economy. A law passed last year gives the 12 cities hosting matches and the states in which they are located the right to declare special holidays on game days. While it's not yet clear whether these holidays will go ahead, the impact is certainly something to watch.

View from the experts: The poorer have tended to be loyal supporters of [former President Luiz Inacio Lula da Silva] Lula/Dilma, since the government's social programs benefited them. It's also the case that the support of the Workers Party has shifted over the last decade, from its core base in the industrial urban heartland and trade union movement of the south, including Sao Paulo to the poorer, rural, less educated and marginal Northeast.

South Africa

Table Mountain, Cape Town, South Africa

Election due: General election scheduled for May 7.

Backdrop: South Africa's economy grew 0.7 percent on quarter in the third quarter of 2013, the slowest pace in more than four years, and sticky inflation stood at an annual 5.4 percent on year in December. Its currency, the rand, hit a five-year low against the dollar in January, exacerbating labor disputes and a wide current-account deficit.

Key election themes: Unemployment running at about 24 percent, poor infrastructure, labor unrest, a weak economy and corruption.

Expected outcome: The African National Congress (ANC) is expected to extend its 20-year hold on power but with a reduced minority in the 400-seat parliament amid corruption scandals and civil unrest. The ANC has won each of the last four elections by a landslide, winning more than 60 percent of the popular vote. The Democratic Alliance is the official opposition and currently holds 67 seats to the ANC's 264.

The wild card: According to the Council on Foreign Relations (CFR), a think tank, the Economic Freedom Fighters (EEF), founded by former head of the ANC's youth wing Julius Malema is something to watch. The EEF favors wholesale nationalization of land and industry and appeals directly to the poor in townships and rural areas. Some analysts say the EEF could win as much as 10 percent of the vote – a development that would be an "earthquake," the CFR said.

View from the experts: Conventional wisdom is that this will be the most competitive election in the country's post-apartheid history. Should the ANC's share of parliamentary seats fall below 60 percent, there likely will be a strong move to replace [President Jacob] Zuma as party leader–and as chief of state. However, it is difficult to imagine that the ANC will 'lose' its majority in parliament.

ARE GLOBAL STOCK MARKETS IN A BUBBLE?

First of all, bubbles only occur when no one is looking for them. Bubbles form when greed runs rampant and there is a mass hypnotic state that the current ride will never end. The shear fact that multitudes of articles are being written about *"market bubbles"* is a sign that we are likely not there, yet.

Is This a Bubble Market? There's One Way to Tell

Is Financial Media Warding Off Stock 'Bubble'?

The Upside of Speculative Market 'Bubbles'

Yellen: Bubbles? What Bubbles?

I read with interest a recent piece on Bloomberg entitled *5 Reasons We're Not In a 2000 Bubble Redux,* which I have summarized for you:

- Volume of IPO's is less than half of the first quarter of 2000.

- First-day returns of IPO's are just 1/5th of the first 1st quarter of 2000.

- Speculative companies carried a 43% higher valuation to dividend paying companies in 2000 versus just 26% today.

- Cash derived from equity issuance was 20% in 2000 versus just 11% today.

- Share turnover in 2000 was an annualized 89% rate versus 58% today.

While these are certainly some interesting arguments, the comparison between now and the turn of the century peak is virtually meaningless. Why? Because no two major market peaks *(speculative bubble or otherwise)* have ever been the same. Let me explain.

In late October of 2007, I gave a seminar to about 300 investors discussing why I believed that we were rapidly approaching the end of the bull market and that 2008 would likely be bad, really bad. Part of that discussion focused on market bubbles and what caused them. The following two slides are from that presentation:

IS THIS TIME DIFFERENT?

× All the previous traits in some form or fashion we found in EVERY previous market bubble and collapse.

+ Tulip Bubble - 1600
+ Exchange Alley - 1690
+ South Sea Bubble - 1750
+ Emerging Markets – 1820
+ Railroads – 1845
+ The Gilded Age – 1907
+ The New Era – 1929
+ Commodities – 1973
+ Portfolio Insurance – 1987
+ LTCM – 1997
+ The New Era In Technology – 2000
+ Real Estate / Subprime Lending - 2008

ALL BUBBLES REVOLVED AROUND SPECULATION IN SOMETHING?

× Precious Metals
× Debt / Leverage
× Selected Companies
× Commodities
× Banks
× Real Estate
× Export Goods
× Foreign Bonds
× Foreign Direct Investment
× Mutual Funds

× Agricultural Land
× Public Land
× Railroads
× IPO's In Speculative Co's.
× LBO / M&A
× Foreign Exchange
× Hedge Funds
× Derivatives
× New Technology
× Art / Collectibles

Every major market peak, and subsequent devastating mean reverting correction, has ever been the result of the exact ingredients seen previously. Only the ignorance of its existence has been a common theme.

The reason that investors **ALWAYS fail to recognize** the major turning points in the markets is because they allow emotional *"greed"* to keep them looking backward rather than forward.

Of course, the media foster's much of this *"willful"* blindness by dismissing, and chastising, opposing views generally until it is too late for their acknowledgement to be of any real use.

The next chart shows every major bubble and bust in the U.S. financial markets since 1871 *(Source: Robert Shiller)*

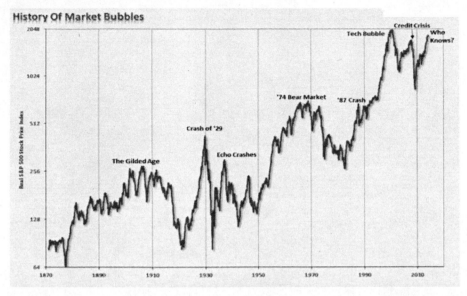

At the peak of each one of these markets, there was no one claiming that a crash was imminent. It was always the contrary, with market pundits waging war against those nagging naysayers of the bullish mantra. Yet, in the end, it was something that was unexpected, unknown or simply dismissed that yanked the proverbial rug from beneath investors.

What will spark the next mean reverting event? No one knows for sure butthe catalysts are present from:

Excess leverage,

IPO's of negligible companies,

Companies using cheap debt to complete stock buybacks and pay dividends, or

High levels of investor complacency.

Either individually, or in combination, these issues are all inert. Much like pouring gasoline on a pile of wood, the fire will not start without a proper catalyst. **What we do know is that an event WILL occur; it is only a function of "when."**

The discussion of why *"this time is not like the last time"* is largely irrelevant. Whatever gains that investors garner in the between now and the next correction by chasing the *"bullish thesis"* will be wiped away in a swift and brutal downdraft. Of course, this is the sad history of individual investors in the financial markets as they are always *"told to buy"* but never *"when to sell."*

For now, the *"bullish case"* remains alive and well. The media will go on berating those heretics who dare to point out the risks that prevail. However, the one simple truth is *"this time is indeed different."* When the crash ultimately comes, the reasons will be different than they were in the past - only the outcome will remain same.

Why a mean reversion would be mean to the stock market

If the benchmarks used to determine the value of securities were to suddenly reverse course, the "new normal" could soon be history.

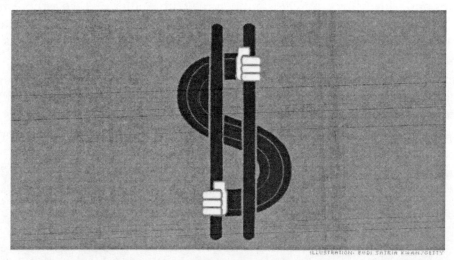

ILLUSTRATION: BUDI SATRIA KWAN/GETTY

Seldom have so many of the metrics that influence stock prices strayed so far from the long-term trends we've come to consider "normal." Corporate earnings are far above what's normal historically, interest rates are way below normal because of Fed intervention, and bond prices that wax when rates wane are hovering at seemingly unnatural heights.

The typical investor might echo something Yogi Berra could have said: "I'm confused by the 'new normal' because it's so unusual."

Because so many influential factors are so unusual, investors struggle to determine if stocks are really cheap or at least reasonably priced, or extremely expensive. Wall Street mavens generally argue that equities are a bargain, and urge you to buy more, while usually prescient, quantitative benchmarks show extra-rich valuations, and urge caution. What to believe?

To clear the confusion, let's compare the likely future equity returns from two scenarios. In the first, we assume that the current metrics will remain in place, so that the "new normal" persists for years to come. In the second, we predict that the metrics that have prevailed during most of the past half-century return in force. That's called "mean reversion," the tendency for market rates and ratios to go back to their historic norms, tugged by a kind of gravitational economic force.

To set the framework, it's important to gauge where earnings, dividends, and prices, the determinants of future returns, sit right now. Then we'll examine where they're likely to go in 10 years under the two sets of assumptions. An excellent starting point is the CAPE, or cyclically adjusted price-earnings ratio, developed by 2013 Nobel laureate Robert Shiller of Yale. Instead of using current profits, a highly erratic measure, Shiller employs a 10-year average of inflation-adjusted earnings per share that smoothes the constantly-shifting peaks and valleys -- right now we're at a historic peak. He divides that adjusted earnings number into the current S&P average to arrive at the CAPE.

Why trust the CAPE? Two of the best minds investing, Rob Arnott of Research Affiliates and Cliff Asness of AQR Capital agree with Shiller that it's either the best, or one of the best, measures of whether stocks are cheap or dear, and an excellent guide to future returns. Put simply, the lower the CAPE, the better the gains in the decade to come, WI.

Today, the CAPE stands at 25.4. Like almost every market metric out there, the current CAPE is way out of the ordinary -- on the high side. The average CAPE over the last two decades is around 18, and for the past century, a couple of points lower.

For our first, "now is our future" assumption, we'll project that the CAPE stays at its current level for the next decade. That means investors will get an inflation-adjusted return equal to the inverse of the CAPE, or the "earnings yield," of 3.93%, let's call it 4%. (If a company's PE or CAPE is 25, its earnings yield must be 4%.)

The total expected return is that 4% plus inflation of around 2%, or a total of 6%. That return comes in two parts. The first is the dividend yield of around 1.6% a year (large companies today pay out about 40% of their profits), and the second is earnings-per-share growth of 4.4% annually. Keep in mind that earnings per share increase at a far slower rate than overall corporate earnings that over long periods track GDP, because companies typically issue large numbers of shares each year, in excess of buybacks, to fund their plans for expansion.

That's hardly a wonderful outlook, and it's a long way from bountiful future Wall Street expects. But the second scenario is far more daunting. It demonstrates the dastardly meanness in mean reversion.

Now we'll project that the CAPE reverts to recent average of 18 in by 2024. EPS will be 57% higher than today at our 4.4% growth rate, but because the multiple will drop, the stock will post a capital gain of only 8% over that entire period. Dividends, collected each year, will deliver another 16% or so, for a total return of 24%. That's an annual gain of just 2.15%, a number that should pretty much match inflation, and nothing more.

Our exercise reveals a big surprise. The most important measure in all of equity analysis *is* actually normal. It's the equity risk premium, the extra return investors demand over and above the rate on U.S. government bonds -- it amounts to the compensation for the additional risk of holding stocks. Today, the ERP is a robust 3.5%. That's the 4% earnings yield, minus the inflation-adjusted rate on 10-year treasuries of around 0.5%. We're in a situation where the level of earnings yield is extraordinarily low, but because of extraordinary monetary policy, the real rates are extraordinarily low. Subtract the low real rate from the extra-low yield, and you have a perfectly good looking ERP.

Blame it on the Fed. In the "new normal," no mean reversion scenario, the total return is the risk premium of 3.5% plus the real yield of 0.5% plus inflation. For that 6% scenario to triumph, the real yield needs to stay puny. Staying puny means more of the same, so that low-yielding bonds will continue providing weak competition even for expensive stocks. Hence, investors will make do with low returns on stocks because the alternatives are so unattractive.

In fact, for real rates to remain that low, the U.S. would need to go into a prolonged period of economic stagnation such as the malaise that's long inflicted Japan, says Brightman. In that case, it's highly possible that the mid-single digit returns we forecast could be far too optimistic.

In the second scenario, everything returns to normal. But the risk premium *already is* normal. What's far from the mean, and threatens to revert, is the real interest rate. Over the past two decades, inflation-adjusted rates have averaged around 2%. If they return to that level, then our mean, mean reversion scenario is the one that wins. It's important to point out that the change may not come quickly. But if the U.S. economy shows any kind of vitality, it will arrive eventually. Then returns will barely beat inflation. And 10 years in the wilderness is a long, parched journey.

The abnormally low real rates are the work of the Fed. They cannot last. Once demand for capital supplants money supply creation as the principal force driving rates, as it must, real rates are bound to rise sharply, restoring the trend that began in mid-2013. That's why the mean-reversion scenario is the most likely, if not inevitable, outcome. One scenario is fair, the other is poor, and the poor one will probably reign. The Wall Street pundits can't stop thanking the Fed. They should reconsider.

How The 'Truman Show' hits global stock markets

In the *Truman Show*, the late nineties Hollywood film, the eponymous character lives a seemingly charmed world, snuggled comfortably into an American suburbia of white picket fences and crisply cut lawns.

But gradually Truman starts to notice something is not quite right. He is actually trapped inside a film set controlled by hidden directors, and discovers to his horror that he is the unknowing star of the world's most popular reality TV show.

Biotech groups and junk bond yields

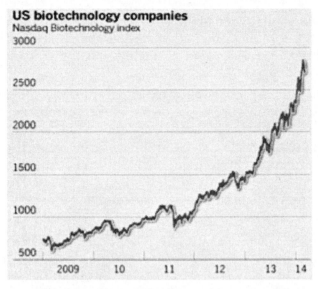

US biotechnology companies
Nasdaq Biotechnology index

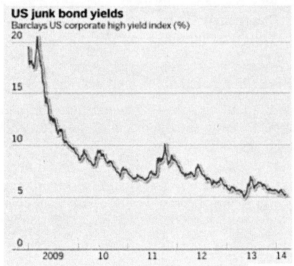

US junk bond yields
Barclays US corporate high yield index (%)

The question some of the world's biggest hedge funds are starting to ask is whether overly placid investors will also wake up to discover they are living in a "Truman Show market" – where central bankers' ultra loose monetary policy has manufactured a fake reality that is bound to end.

Investors have been lulled into a false sense of security that is creating an ever greater risk of a sharp correction.

All the Trumans – the economists, fund managers, traders, market pundits – know at some level that the environment in which they operate is not what it seems on the surface. But the zeitgeist is so damn pleasant, the days so resplendent, the mood so euphoric, the returns so irresistible, that no one wants it to end.

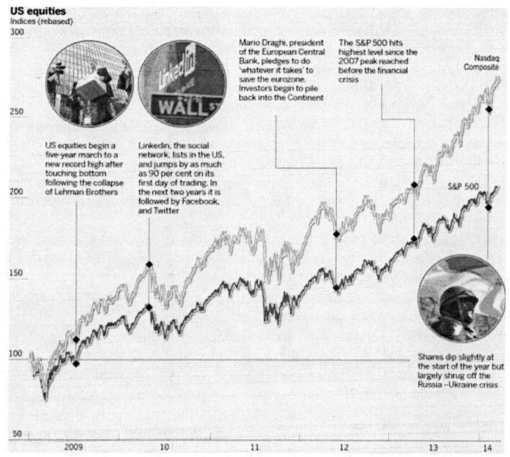

US equities
Indices (rebased)

300

250

Mario Draghi, president
of the European Central
Bank, pledges to do
'whatever it takes' to
save the eurozone.
Investors begin to pile
back into the Continent

The S&P 500 hits
highest level since the
2007 peak reached
before the financial
crisis

Nasdaq
Composite

US equities begin a
five-year march to a
new record high after
touching bottom
following the collapse
of Lehman Brothers

Linkedin, the social
network, lists in the US,
and jumps by as much
as 90 per cent on its
first day of trading. In
the next two years it is
followed by Facebook,
and Twitter

200

S&P 500

150

100

Shares dip slightly at
the start of the year but
largely shrug off the
Russia–Ukraine crisis

50

2009   10   11   12   13   14

No matter how sceptical hedge fund managers may be, they find themselves in a bind. While the assumption that central bank bond-buying will continue for the foreseeable future has been a boon to broader markets, indiscriminately surging equities have made life frustrating for most specialised stock pickers.

At the same time other hedge fund strategies, such as making bets on interest rates and currencies according to views on the direction of the global economy, have faltered as markets have refused to obey previously presumed iron rules, such as money printing leading to devaluation. Of late these so-called global macro funds have retreated from such trades as their performance has suffered.

Many hedge funds continue to predict this ongoing drift upwards in asset prices due to an implicit backstop from central banks, who want to believe they are omnipotent, and that when data is bad they can just turn on the taps again and make it go away.

As a result, while many managers feel deeply uneasy with the lofty valuations attached to certain parts of the US stock market, and low returns offered by risky assets such as junk bonds, few are willing to step out just yet.

More recently, encouragement has been taken from falling correlations between assets, meaning some portfolio managers are confident they can start to exploit more effectively the pricing anomalies between better and worse quality securities.

The number of individual stocks mispriced to each other is high, there are some trading on vapour whilst others are still trading on reasonable valuations. Are there lots of cheap stocks? No, but on a long short basis there are opportunities.

The big question is when this is all going to change. From a purely intellectual point of view, it is interesting how central banks will reverse their policies. From a market point of view, it is uncertain and complicated.

Loose central banks have actually increased the riskiness of markets as a result of their policies forcing too much money into the same assets, meaning any corrections are likely to be sharper than normal.

Everyone is thinking the same and being driven into the same trade. Shifts when moving from one state to another can be difficult and abrupt. It is not healthy to have a 'rigged' market".

Yet, for now, as long as markets continue to believe in the willingness and ability of central bankers to maintain current conditions, few hedge fund managers are ready to make any big bets against a reversal.

Few argue that equities are cheap on any metric, but the majority of hedge fund managers are opting to remain invested.

The *Truman Show* market looks set to continue, even if an increasing number of participants have started to spot the cameras hidden behind the trees.

Take, for instance, the corporate default rate and the analytical models that are supposed to help forecast it.

The one-year default rate for US and European junk-rated companies currently stands at about 3 per cent, according to the quarterly review from the **Bank for International Settlements** released recently, just 1 percentage point above its average during the boom-era years of 2005 to 2008.

With default rates so low, the strategy of investing in higher-yielding, but riskier corporate bonds has paid off. Corporate credit spreads, or the additional yield investors demand to hold riskier securities, are hovering at a historical nadir, indicating that investors have been keen to take advantage of the low default rate and increase their holdings of corporate bonds.

In fact, as the BIS notes, "in addition to reflecting perceptions of credit risk, spreads may also drive default rates." In an era of cheap and easy money, investors are encouraged to buy bonds from troubled companies and thereby suppress the default rate.

The overwhelming effect of QE on corporate defaults and spreads has, perhaps unsurprisingly, led to all sorts of modelling difficulties. Even top-tier analysts will sometimes (quietly) confess they are at a loss when it comes to estimating future corporate defaults.

Models that incorporate QE extending for the foreseeable future tend to predict that corporate defaults will continue to occur only infrequently. Meanwhile, models that attempt to incorporate some sort of "tapering" of central bank support show sharp increases in default.

Which to choose? What's really in the box – living, functioning companies or ones that are flatlining?

The same comparison could be applied to the state of the broader US economy.

Deutsche Bank, for instance, writes this week that the current economic expansion in the US economy will be 54 months old by the end of the year. The average expansion since 1854 has totalled just 39 months by the bank's calculations.

That means the current expansion – hot on the heels of one of the worst recessions on record – is now the seventh longest of the 34 expansionary economic cycles to have occurred in the US over the past one and a half centuries.

The US appears to have "just about escaped [a correction] due to extraordinary monetary and fiscal stimulus".

This time really is different. Or, it isn't.

We will only know for sure when we open the box – once the extraordinary central bank policies have been unwound – and peer in to see whether the cat is dead or alive. At that point the US economy, and the state of its many companies, will reveal themselves to be in reasonable health, or stubbornly inert.

Take, for instance, the corporate default rate and the analytical models that are supposed to help forecast it.

The one-year default rate for US and European junk-rated companies currently stands at about 3 per cent, according to the quarterly review from the **Bank for International Settlements** released recently, just 1 percentage point above its average during the boom-era years of 2005 to 2008.

With default rates so low, the strategy of investing in higher-yielding, but riskier corporate bonds has paid off. Corporate credit spreads, or the additional yield investors demand to hold riskier securities, are hovering at a historical nadir, indicating that investors have been keen to take advantage of the low default rate and increase their holdings of corporate bonds.

In fact, as the BIS notes, "in addition to reflecting perceptions of credit risk, spreads may also drive default rates." In an era of cheap and easy money, investors are encouraged to buy bonds from troubled companies and thereby suppress the default rate.

The overwhelming effect of QE on corporate defaults and spreads has, perhaps unsurprisingly, led to all sorts of modelling difficulties. Even top-tier analysts will sometimes (quietly) confess they are at a loss when it comes to estimating future corporate defaults.

Models that incorporate QE extending for the foreseeable future tend to predict that corporate defaults will continue to occur only infrequently. Meanwhile, models that attempt to incorporate some sort of "tapering" of central bank support show sharp increases in default.

Which to choose? What's really in the box – living, functioning companies or ones that are flatlining?

The same comparison could be applied to the state of the broader US economy.

Deutsche Bank, for instance, writes this week that the current economic expansion in the US economy will be 54 months old by the end of the year. The average expansion since 1854 has totalled just 39 months by the bank's calculations.

That means the current expansion – hot on the heels of one of the worst recessions on record – is now the seventh longest of the 34 expansionary economic cycles to have occurred in the US over the past one and a half centuries.

The US appears to have "just about escaped [a correction] due to extraordinary monetary and fiscal stimulus".

This time really is different. Or, it isn't.

We will only know for sure when we open the box – once the extraordinary central bank policies have been unwound – and peer in to see whether the cat is dead or alive. At that point the US economy, and the state of its many companies, will reveal themselves to be in reasonable health, or stubbornly inert.

THE WOLF OF WALL STREET: IS HE STILL ROAMING AROUND?

The Wolf of Wall Street: Fact vs. Fiction

If you've seen Martin Scorcese's *The Wolf of Wall Street*, based on the book by Jordan Belfort of the same name, you most likely hold one of two diametrically opposed opinions on the film. Either you think it's a hilarious, over-the-top re-enactment of Wall Street's party culture of the 90s, or a dark and debauched look at men who had no shame in committing securities fraud, as well as checking their morals at the office door.

Judging by box office numbers, the film starring Leonardo DiCaprio and Jonah Hill has been soaring like a high-flying technology stock, and has also been a big winner for Scorcese's portfolio, as it is now his top-grossing film.

One man who knew some of the players in the boiler room known as Stratton Oakmont depicted in *The Wolf of Wall Street* is Josh Brown, known these days as the Reformed Broker. Brown tackles the questions many people are asking regarding Belfort's portrayal of a wild and out of control Stratton Oakmont in the movie and book.

The Real Stratton Oakmont

Brown maintains that some exaggerations exist in the movie, but the company culture was pretty spot on. "When I started in the business ... a year or two after Stratton went down, they busted all these firms, and the survivors set up their own firms. They decided they would do this [business] without 'chop stocks' (AKA pink slips, or penny stocks), we're going to do this with legitimate stocks, but maintain the same Stratton culture of aggressive sales, and working all day," among other things.

Brown recalls that 20 years ago the fraternity-based, debauched culture was alive and well, but what enabled this behavior was a lack of mobile phones and the Internet to disseminate images of scandalous activities like "dwarf tossing" and exotic dancers working the trading floors. If anyone saw anything risqué happening now, "they could capture it on video, and upload it to the web, they don't need any media connections… it takes five seconds. Back then people could deny everything," without video proof, he says.

Brown also notes it wasn't just the smaller shops engaging in this behavior, as "you had the 'boom boom room' in Solomon Smith Barney," a notorious basement below the trading floor which was the source of much litigation in later years.

The Clients, the Money and the Retail Broker

As the movie's success grew, stories started emerging of clients who were ripped off by Belfort's brokers, left with nothing in their retirement accounts. "You can't care about your clients in that environment and actually thrive, you're going to get fired," Brown recalls.

Based on the commission system in place at these brokerages, brokers were given bigger percentages the more money they made in each month, so they were incentivized to make more trades at the end of the month to hit the next commission percentage tier. This of course would be to the detriment of clients buying worthless stocks. The big money was too hard for the brokers to ignore; however, as the movie depicts the 300-foot yachts, Lamborghini Countaches, and pharmaceutical-grade quaaludes don't grow on trees.

Present day "Wall Street," according to Brown, is a totally different place. The retail brokerage has gone the way of the dodo, as the days of brokers cold-calling plumbers and electricians is over. These days most individuals are trading their own accounts using online brokers. The issue now according to Brown is that people are 'blowing themselves up,' meaning going bankrupt in the stock market on their own. People are churning their own accounts, day in day out—in a way, they [investors] are their own wolves these days, according to Brown.

Yet, I disagree. In emerging and relatively less regulated markets such as India, salaries of staff working for brokers is still based on volume of business they bring to the organization.

So, the Wolf of Wall Street, athough has mellowed down in the corridors of Wall Street, continues to rule high elsewhere.

ARROGANT EXECUTIVES AND NARCISSISTIC TEACHERS

Over the past decade, academics have produced a steady stream of research on the problems posed by narcissistic executives. Narcissists create toxic work environments, spend more lavishly, and tend toward risky decision-making. They're also more likely to engage in white-collar crime. Research has also shown that business school students are more narcissistic than students in other disciplines. Not all research points to narcissism as a bad thing in a business setting, but the question remains: **What should management programs do to develop less self-involved students?**

A team of researchers from Appalachian State University in Boone, N.C., believe one solution can be found at the front of the classroom---if you want less narcissistic business grads, it might help you to hire less narcissistic faculty according to Jim Westerman, one of the authors.

To reach that conclusion, Westerman and his colleagues collected a survey called the Narcissistic Personality Inventory from 536 students and 16 instructors at a public university in the southeastern U.S. They cross-referenced the results with the final grades and students' subjective assessments of instructors and courses. It turned out that those students who scored more highly on the narcissism test got better grades in courses taught by highly narcissistic professors. Students with lower narcissism scores got lower grades and found courses taught by narcissists more difficult.

The more narcissistic faculty seemed to have a dual effect that is of dismay to those who desire reduced levels of narcissism in business education. They discouraged less narcissistic students, yet rewarded and provided a potential model for future behavior for more highly narcissistic students through their enhanced status.

This isn't the Appalachian State researchers' first attempt to find a solution to B-school narcissism. In a 2010 article published on *Businessweek*'s website, Daly and Westerman suggested that MBA programs should screen out narcissists in the application process, rein in grade inflation, and require students to study abroad in hopes of making them less self-absorbed.

Now Westerman wants to expand the faculty-narcissism study to more universities and reach deeper into the role of instructors, which sounds like a good idea. Research has shown that the millennial generation is more narcissistic than previous generations, and the members are beginning to enter the professorial ranks.

GUESS WHAT DOES THE 'WOLF OF WALL STREET' WANT TO TEACH YOU NEXT - 'ETHICAL PERSUASION'

Jordan Belfort and Leonardo DiCaprio

Jordan Belfort is back. Now that "The Wolf of Wall Street" is a certified hit, the man whose life the film is based on is back selling something. This time, however, it's all legal.

Belfort is selling a program on how to be a successful salesperson using "ethical persuasion." "Success in the absence of ethics... is failure, it's not success at all," according to Belfort.

'Real' Wolf of Wall Street

Belfort was interviewed on the Web by Mike Koenigs, the creator of Instant Customer. The convicted former broker, who made millions manipulating stock offerings, described his own career arc. He became a self-taught "closer," succeeding through use of the right "tonality." "Tonality is the secret language of influence," said Belfort, adding, "it gives you control of the conversation."

Such insights are part of a sales program Belfort is selling called "Straight Line." "You only have about four seconds on a phone call to be perceived as sharp as a tack, enthusiastic as hell and an expert in your field," according to Belfort. Part of succeeding is being an active listener. "Bill Clinton was the best." Another important rule: "Don't say stupid s---."

The webinar Wednesday went on for more than two hours, as an energetic Belfort talked about everything from going bankrupt to Wall Street salaries. "Everyone on Wall Street tells you what they make," he laughed. "Everyone else thinks it's rude."

He didn't flinch from admitting he broke the law and deserved to go to prison.

"I never felt good. People asked, 'Why did you do all those drugs?' Why do you think?'" However, he made one claim his former clients might disagree with. "If you were to have invested $10,000 in every one of Stratton's new issues, my guess is you'd be up 100 times on your money, because a couple of them were wild successes." Belfort's firm profiled in the film was Stratton Oakmont. New issues were stocks Belfort was taking public which they manipulated.

Belfort looks at his own life as a success, having survived drug abuse, ripping people off, prison and several broken relationships. These days, the man portrayed on the big screen by Leonard DiCaprio is now getting calls from celebrities to "do lunch." He still owes victims nearly $100 million in restitution.

"Buy these books, all the money goes to investors," Belfort said.

Additional online training programs are available, valued around at least $297.

WHY YOGA AND TRANSCENDENTAL MEDITATION ARE THE LATEST BUZZWORDS ON WALL STREET NOW?

Benefits of Surya Namaskar: Improves awareness, increases flexibility and strength, relieves lethargy and tensions, reduces weight, enhances agility and grace.

Scientists link stress hormone to financial crisis

The stress that financial traders suffer during periods of high volatility in the markets reduces their appetite for risk, according to a study led by Cambridge university neuroscientist and former Wall Street trader John Coates. This may prolong financial crises.

The research, published in Proceedings of the National Academy of Sciences, combines field and lab work. Prof Coates and colleagues discovered that levels of the stress hormone cortisol increased by 68 per cent on average in a group of City of London traders over eight days in which market volatility increased.

The scientists took this finding to Addenbrooke's Hospital in Cambridge where they used pharmacology – hydrocortisone tablets – to raise cortisol levels in volunteers, also by 68 per cent over eight days. Participants then played an incentivised risk-taking game. The appetite for risk collapsed, by as much as 44 per cent according to one measure, in those with raised cortisol. (The study was double-blinded with a control group taking dummy tablets.)

Prof Coates believes the implications are important for the financial world. Subclinical stress affects people's risk-taking behaviour, in a way that conventional metrics cannot detect. There is a powerful physiological mechanism at work in the markets, and no one – not the traders, not the risk managers, not the policy makers – is aware of it.

The study also throws doubt on the assumption embedded in economics that risk preferences are stable. This assumption, mostly hidden from view, underlies almost every economic model and, it turns out, every indicator of market sentiment.

In fact individuals and companies tend to freeze up during crises, just when the markets offer the most attractive opportunities. During a financial crisis, the economy most needs risk takers but rising stress hormones contribute to the widespread risk aversion sometimes called irrational pessimism. The stress response may thereby exacerbate market instability and prolong crises.

Bankers and lawyers are on an unhealthy treadmill

While long hours are not worth the effort, those able to effect change do not care

For years, getting a job at a Wall Street bank, a Magic Circle law firm or a blue-chip management consultancy was a route to a very rewarding career in return for an awful lot of work. Lately, the bargain has lost some of its appeal to the best and the brightest.

The death last year of Moritz Erhardt, a German student who was interning at Bank of America in London, was one prompt for a rethink among investment banks about how they treat young employees. So too, is growing competition for talent from technology companies that offer equity, informality and less relentless work demands.

Both Bank of America and Credit Suisse have announced measures to curb the tradition of making young bankers work into the early hours and through weekends on spreadsheets and pitch books. Law firms are trying to curb attempts by juniors to shine by billing incredible numbers of hours. Consulting firms are telling partners to show a little respect for their juniors.

There is no simple fix for an entrenched culture of overwork at professional services firms. The fact that an entry-level analyst at a Wall Street bank is required to sacrifice his or her personal life to the job – sitting at a desk until dawn, eating order-in food and correcting invisible errors in spreadsheets – has been built into the system.

They know they have signed up for long hours but, until they get there, they don't realise how disruptive it is. Your friendships deteriorate and your boyfriend or girlfriend is angry because they have not had a meal with you for a month. You lose touch with your family. It's miserable.

It is, of course, an elite problem. Despite everything, thousands compete for such jobs, hoping the Faustian pact will pay off. Goldman Sachs, which has tried to reform how it treats junior employees, received 17,000 applications for its 2014 intake of analysts and recruited 330.

In some ways, those jobs have become more attractive as other industries have reduced recruitment of young people, instead taking on unpaid interns who must work for nothing, relying on parental subsidies. The deal-related professions not only pay well but train their recruits.

There is, however, a flaw in the all-or-nothing choice. The imposition of long hours on analysts and associates is not simply a rite of passage, a military-style effort to destroy resistance and inculcate loyalty to the organisation. It is a symptom of a problem with work in professional services in the 21st century – it is unhealthy.

Erhardt's death may have been an extreme example – the cause was an epileptic fit that a coroner said could have been triggered by overwork. But many bankers, lawyers and consultants face the stress of not being able to set any boundary between work and home. It ripples down the chain of command, starting from the top.

For a generation, occupational psychologists have viewed the most stressful kind of work as that with high demands and no autonomy: for example, a factory worker who has to follow a strict routine but is given little time to do it. Such employees face higher risks of heart disease and stress-related illness.

Professional services jobs are not like that – consultants and lawyers have a lot of autonomy and tend to work independently. The difficulty is that clients pay large amounts of money to firms for deal-related advice – often running into millions of dollars. In return, they expect high levels of service delivered seamlessly and without delay.

This has always involved working on deals late or on weekends. But technology and globalisation have now lowered the barriers to working around the clock routinely. A banker or consultant is always available to be pulled into a conference call in any timezone.

It is not enough for your health to limit your work stress. You also need to control your time strain. The easiest way for senior bankers or lawyers to do that is by handing out-of-hours work over to juniors and disrupting their lives instead.

Many junior bankers end up working in the evening because a partner who has been out pitching to potential clients all day returns to the bank late in the afternoon, and tells them to prepare a document immediately based on the sortie. Although they have been at their desks for hours, they start to work intensively only then.

The good news is that this method of organising work is inefficient and thus ripe for reform. The bad news is that many lawyers or bankers do not care much about that. Not only do they feel, like senior doctors, that they too were juniors once and this generation deserves to suffer equally, but the status quo is easier for them.

It is thus tougher to change than declaring officially that juniors really ought not to work so hard. If you simply tell people not to work on Tuesday nights, they will work on Saturdays instead--You must fix the whole organisation, not just individual behaviour.

BCG has instituted a policy of giving its employees predictable times off – an evening or a day at the weekend when they will not be contacted and they can switch off the phone. It hardly sounds like a revolution to place some border between work and home but, for many firms, it is.

A string of recent deaths within the banking world have brought global attention to the stressful conditions that financiers work in and around. Large banks have attempted to respond to the problem by limiting working hours on the weekends but the effectiveness and ability to enforce those rules have come into question. Studies have found that stockbrokers are three times more likely to suffer from depression than the general adult population. Excess stress is a leading cause of heart and brain disease. So what's a banker to do?

Some prominent investors have taken to transcendental meditation (TM). Some teach the relaxation method to their entire company. The technique requires 20 minutes of silent meditation two times a day and is popular with folks like Bridgewater's Ray Dalio (who offers TM to his 400 employees), Bill Gross, Dan Loeb, Nigol Koulajian (Quest Partners) and Kevin Kimberlin (Spencer Trask & Co).

Transcendental meditation is often thought of as a remnant of the hippie culture of the 1960s-- images of Maharishi Mahesh Yogi and The Beatles wearing necklaces of flowers come to mind. The David Lynch Foundation is attempting to reinvent the TM image.

Today typical TM practitioners are people on Wall Street, whole schools, architects or mothers at home. These days everybody is a typical transcendental meditation practitioner because everybody suffers from stress.

The non-profit readily points to a slew of scientific studies that prove TM reduces health risks and enhances brain functioning.

Blue Cross and other insurance giants are under pressure to get TM covered. Stress is a huge problem -- one of the top HR companies in the UK has called workplace stress the black plague of the 21st century. It costs American business over $300 billion a year and there was a recent study that came out saying 83% of American workers feel high levels of stress on the job...who wants to live the rest of their life on Xanax of Prozac?"

With the use of transcendental meditation, evidence shows that [bankers] think more clearly, that they make better decisions, plan better and solve more problems and if you do that the chances of making money are far greater...you have a leg up and a competitive edge.

HOW SHAKING OFF ITS REPUTATION FOR CORRUPTION WILL HELP INDIA

Are Indian stock markets efficient?

With the large number of players and companies, they have gained efficiency. I would however, still request SEBI, the market regulator to go into unusual movements in stock prices exactly half an hour before expiry (at 3 p.m.) on every options expiration day, which is the last Thursday of every month.

WHAT HAPPENS AT 3 P.M. ON EVERY OPTIONS EXPIRATION DAY? IS INDIA'S SEBI WATCHING?

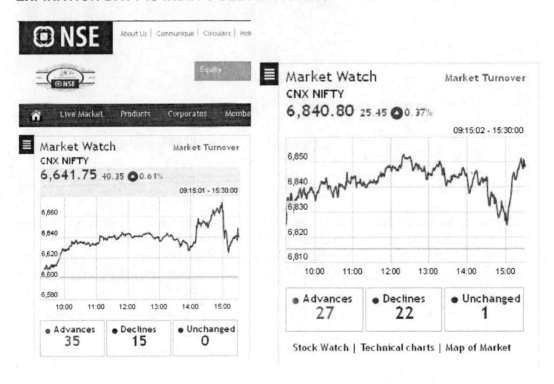

NSE INDIA MARCH 25, 2014   NSE INDIA APRIL 23, 2014

Indian National Stock Exchange

June 26, 2014

Reducing the scope and scale of corruption is the most important reform India can bring about. Corruption serves to divert resources in a highly distorted and inefficient manner. Structural deficits resulting from leakages and corruption impede growth, fiscal sustainability and acceptable norms of distribution of income and wealth.

Policy errors that lead to slower growth mean rapid adjustments are required to avoid a downward spiral. Besides, statistics reveal that as a country shakes off a reputation for corruption, its economy tends to grow and its capital markets tend to rise.

Prime Minister Dr Manmohan Singh has said that the Right to Information Act is not being used to its full potential. "This important legislation should not be only about criticising, ridiculing, and running down public authorities," he said. "RTI should be more about promoting transparency and accountability, spreading information and awareness and empowering the citizen."

Dr Singh has expressed concerns about "frivolous" applications and the invasion of privacy, adding that "the potential for good, constructive use of the Right to Information is perhaps far greater than what its current status would indicate."

Earlier last week, Dr Manmohan Singh, whose government is being targeted for intractable corruption, said that a "mindless atmosphere of negativity" over corruption was damaging the country and he feared for the morale of civil servants.

Correlation or causation? The link means emerging market investors should be watching how effective countries are not just in reforming, but in convincing the world that they're reforming.

It's not surprising that countries thought to be corrupt do less well than countries thought to be clean. The enclosed charts show a surprisingly tight correlation – for better and for worse – between perceptions of corruption and investment as a percentage of GDP.

In Indonesia's case, perceptions that the current government has been reforming the country's endemic corruption have helped shore up arguments for investing in its rapidly growing economy:

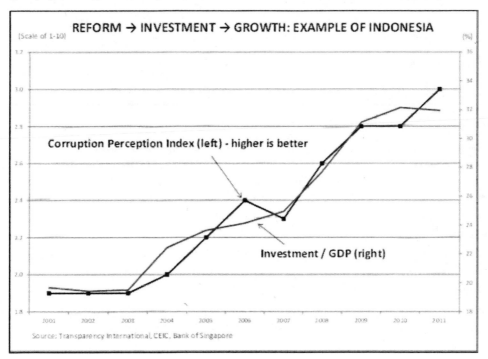

Source: Bank of Singapore

In India's case, by comparison, it appears that a perception that corruption is re-emerging has been accompanied by an almost equally steep drop in foreign direct investment:

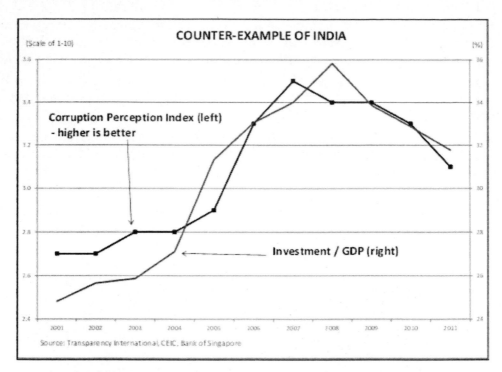

COUNTER-EXAMPLE OF INDIA

Source: Transparency International, CEIC, Bank of Singapore

Source: Bank of Singapore

India's economy is still growing slightly more quickly than Indonesia's – an expected 5.5 %, versus 5 % in Indonesia – but it is not just direct investors who have become wary. Its equity markets are still below where they were in 2008, while Indonesia's have risen 40 per cent since then. In part, the fall-off in investment in India has contributed to its infrastructure bottlenecks, high inflation and slowing growth rate, all of which have worried portfolio investors.

The apparent link between corruption and investment, even as growth stays relatively strong illustrates that "the quality of growth is important and not just the absolute speed."

Where is corruption most rife: in India, the country from which, between $500bn and $1.5tr in illicit funds have been spirited overseas since 1947; or the countries in which those funds are deposited?

That was the question raised by AP Singh, the head of India's Central Bureau of Investigation, in a speech to the first-ever Interpol Global Programme on Anti-Corruption and Asset Recovery, organized sometime back in Delhi. Singh pegged the amount of illegal Indian money held abroad at $500bn, or nearly 30 per cent of India's 2010 GDP.

According to Transparency International's Corruption Perception Index 2011, the answer to our question is clear. In TI's ranking from best to worst, India clocks in at 96 out of 192 countries, while Switzerland sits pretty at number nine.

But A P Singh took issue with that ranking while discussing the nature of corruption and graft: does the recipient of stolen goods – in this case, tax haven countries like Switzerland, the Cayman Islands and Dubai – bear any responsibility for the theft? Is Switzerland, where Singh said Indians were the biggest foreign depositors, any less responsible for the "black money" it holds for powerful Indian politicians, industrialists and billionaires than India?

Fifty-three per cent of the countries said to be least corrupt by the Transparency International Index are offshore tax havens, where most of the corrupt money goes. The tax havens include New Zealand which is ranked as the least corrupt country, Singapore ranked number five and Switzerland ranked number [nine].

There is a lack of political will in the leading tax haven States to part with information required to trace such assets as they are all too aware of the extent to which their own economies have become geared to this flow of illegal capital from the poorer countries. India in particular has suffered from the flow of illegal funds to tax havens such as Mauritius, Switzerland, Lichtenstein, British Virgin Islands, etc.

But A P Singh might be letting India off lightly at the expense of the Swiss and others. In 2008, when the German government offered to provide the names of foreign citizens with money deposited in Lichtenstein's LTG bank, countries like the Czech Republic, Spain, Italy and Finland accepted.

India declined to pursue the accounts of its citizens, prompting Transparency International India to report allegations "that this money belongs to the rich and powerful politicians, industrialists and stock brokers and that is [the reason for] the reluctance on the part of Government of India."

In August 2011, the French government handed over a list of 700 HSBC bank accounts held by Indians in Switzerland. Details of HSBC's Indian account holders have emerged because a former employee stole data in 2008 and later handed these over to French authorities. Several countries including UK, Spain, Italy and France itself have used this data for tax evasion investigations.

An amended double taxation avoidance agreement with Switzerland as proposed would, according to India's finance ministry, "allow India to obtain banking information (as well as information without domestic interest) from Switzerland in specific cases for a period starting from 1st April 2011."

Indeed, A P Singh noted in his speech that the money stolen in many of the country's most recent, epic government graft scandals – including the 2G telecom spectrum scam that robbed the exchequer of an estimated $39bn, the 2010 Commonwealth Games debacle infamous for $80 rolls of toilet paper and the case of the now-jailed chief minister who racked up $660m in illegal income – found its way to Dubai, Singapore and Mauritius before traveling to Switzerland, the British Virgin Islands and the Cayman Islands.

Mainland China's massive outflows were predominantly the result of trade mispricing – a common practice whereby multinational corporations manipulate figures on commerce and earnings to minimise tax liabilities. A popular means of tax evasion for companies, trade mispricing is the driving force behind most of the illicit capital exiting developing countries.

Second-ranked Saudi Arabia and fourth-ranked Russia were exceptions to the trade mispricing rule because of their status as oil exporters, oil being difficult to misprice.

What needs to happen now is for the G20 to broaden its dialogue on information exchange agreements, international co-operation and international financial protocols. Most effective in curtailing the massive illicit outflows from developing countries would be a requirement for automatic cross-border exchange of tax information on personal and business accounts and country-by-country reporting of sales, profits and taxes paid by multinationals.

The global recession is expected to have a severe impact on developing economies and undo years of poverty alleviation efforts and economic gains. The desire to offset this predicted impact is sincere. But until efforts are made to dismantle the shadow financial system and mandate more co-operative and rigorous reporting, success will remain as elusive as India's missing black money.

Investors cheer India election's reform potential

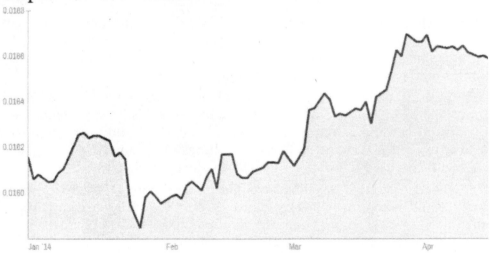

Rupee vs. U.S. dollar

Indian markets are riding high as investors bet that an election and new administration will cure some of the country's economic ills.

Mumbai's benchmark Sensex index has trounced its Asian peers in recent months, hitting a record high last week and gaining 15% since the start of the year. The rupee has strengthened too, clawing its way back from a dismal performance in 2013.

Victory for a Modi-led coalition has paved the way for end of the Congress Party's dominance, and created an opening for a new government to implement economic reforms.

India would benefit greatly from changes to its tax code, a reduction in excessive bureaucracy and more efficient agricultural policies. Momentum on these long-promised reforms stalled under the leadership of the Congress Party.

India's potential for growth was once mentioned in the same breath as that of China. But the world's second most populous nation and biggest democracy has failed to deliver and its economy is just a fifth the size of its Asian rival.

Economic growth has fallen below 5% in recent quarters, some of the lowest levels in years. The currency has lost more than a third of its value since 2011.

Observers don't expect much improvement for some more time until the policies of the new government begin to bear fruit, a troubling sign for one of the world's top 10 economies.

Modi presented himself as a candidate in the mold of a CEO, campaigning on his economic record as head of Gujarat state. Investors are hoping that he will be able to conjure some of the same magic on a bigger stage. Hence the run-away rise in the Mumbai SENSEX.

Some analysts expect only "piecemeal improvements," believing that the BJP is not resolutely free-market oriented.

WHY I BELIEVE INDIA COULD OUTPERFORM THE WORLD AFTER AUGUST 26, 2014

I believe India will outperform as a destination of choice for investors in 2014. Reasons are manifold:

Indian Equities: an opportunity, not to be missed!

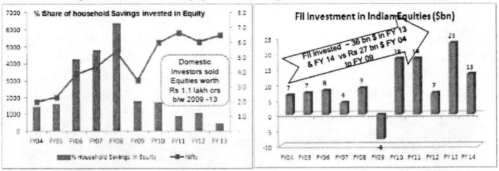

- Household savings into equity dropped sharply from 7.3% in FY '08 to 0.5% in FY'13 while CNX Nifty gained over 20% (CAGR) during the same period
- FII Investors on the contrary have made significant investment in Indian Equities and benefited from the market rally
- Even a small improvement in Household Allocation to equities can result in significant inflows to equity markets

a) The country has already gone through flat stock market indices due to policy paralysis over the last five years—the worst is, so as to say, if not already then almost behind India

b) Election results have been announced mid-May 2014—since there is a stable government which has been formed at the centre with decisiveness coming into power, Indian stocks have take off; however, I believe we could soon see a selloff as markets have run ahead of themselves. Indian stocks should rebound strongly after mid-August 2014.

c) Fiscal deficit + Current Deficit + Inflation was closer to 20% in March 2013, has now subsided to 15%

d) 175 companies in the BSE-500 are trading at 7-year lows in the last six months

e) 200 companies in BSE 500 are trading below their book values

f) Drug companies in India, their skills honed by years of manufacturing generic versions of brand name drugs are now expanding into drug innovation and some even challenging existing patents.

g) Long years of flat markets (5 years in the case of India) have been followed by sharp bull phases

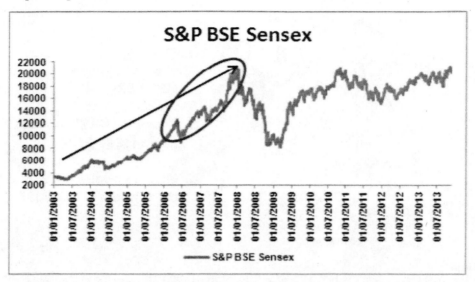

h) India is well diversified in terms of size and demographics. When growth comes, companies with additional capacity will do exceedingly well

i) US recover expected to be in full swing by 2015—expected to benefit emerging economies like India

k) Flattening of oil prices in contrast to rising oil prices would relive India's Current Account Deficit problem

k) Foreign Institutional Investors have invested $ 60 Billion in Indian stocks. They can buy upto $ 100 Billion, as per current regulations. If they do put in so much money, which is likely considering India could become the darling of foreign investors soon, not much of stock will be available for the retail population.

l) 90% of global funds have 'ZERO' exposure to India so far

m) India has 15% of world population, 5% of world GDP on Purchasing Power Parity Basis, 2.5% even without Purchasing Power Parity Basis.

n) Operating Leverage would be very high for companies in India in the event of an eventual upturn as is expected beginning the second half of 2014.

India could clearly turn out to be an outperformer and it would be prudent to put your bets on India around August 18, 2014. Happy investing!

Within India, the banking sector is likely to outperform. Multiple headwinds such as high Current Account Deficit and Fiscal Deficit, rising NPA levels and slowdown in the general economy have taken India's GDP growth to decade-low. Historically, banking sector has lead the economic recovery and been the biggest participant in the recovery of the economic cycle. Hence, banking stocks are expected to clearly outperform the rest of the market.

Phases of Indian Bull Markets – Born From Pessimism

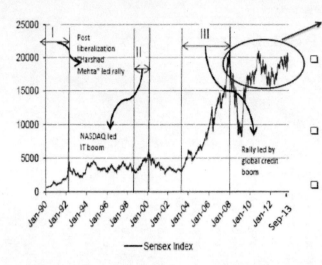

Long periods of 'flat' markets?

❑ Phase I - Post liberalization "Harshad Mehta" led rally (1990-92)

❑ Phase II - NASDAQ led IT boom (1998-2000)

❑ Multi-year rally led by global credit boom (2003-2007)

Long periods of flat markets have been typically followed by sharp bull phases.

Significant polarization in Markets

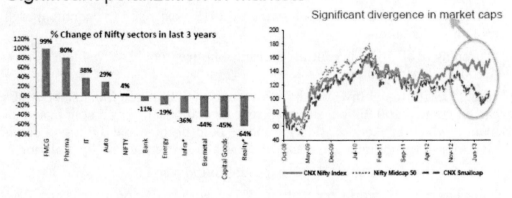

❑ Huge divergence across sectors and market caps

❑ Some sectors / stocks are trading at all time high while many have witnessed flat / negative growth

❑ Opportunities exist across market-caps and sectors

Equity Was The Biggest Wealth Creator

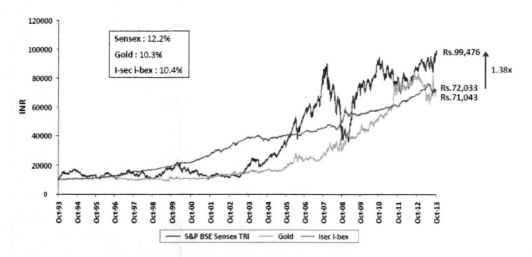

India Economy – Growth Low, But Set To Improve

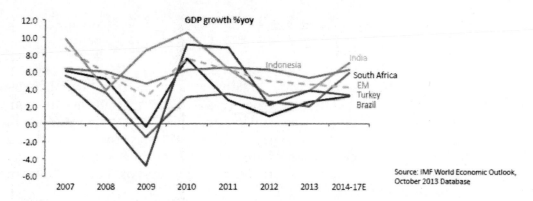

Source: IMF World Economic Outlook, October 2013 Database

- Like other EMs, experiencing a growth slowdown –
  - A mix of cyclical and structural factors underpin this decline
- Macro adjustment underway – remedial policy measures, corporate de-leveraging, etc.
- Improved farm production and election spending expected to lead a cyclical recovery over the near term

India Markets – Valuations Still Reasonable

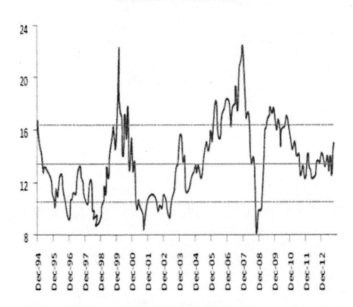

MSCI India – 12M Forward PE

A couple of months back there was a big divergence which was there between the defensives - fast moving consumer goods (FMCG), pharmaceuticals and some of the cyclical sectors which could be banking and financials, metals and capital goods sector. That divergence is now trying to compress because there is lot of value in some of the sectors where the immediate outlook is not that great. If we see a cyclical recovery from here, then these are the sectors which could do well over the next two-three years timeframe.

In the last two years the market has started to recognise that a bit, we have seen some outperformance in some of the cyclical stocks and it remains to be seen whether we see this recovery sustaining. More importantly general elections which are there next year will be the key in terms of how the pace for the recovery will be, especially on the investment side, which got impacted severely in the last two years.

Some of the cyclical is where one should tactically start looking at it. In this space there are lots of companies which have got high leverage. I do not think those are the stocks which one would look at, at this point in time because interest rates do not seem to be coming down in a hurry though we expect them to come down eventually because inflation would come down especially when we have seen slowdown in the broader economy but there are still better quality companies.

Yes. If one would take a medium-term or a long-term view then that is the area one would see outperformance from that perspective. However, at the moment there is no clarity so one would look at cues both from macro standpoint in terms of where interest rates are headed to be slightly oriented because there are lot of underweight positions which is there across fund managers in this sector. Defensives while they look good, the valuations especially in the consumer staple space is at an all time high.

Multiplex operators strike gold in Bollywood-mad India

PVR, Inox, Reliance Mediaworks are scrambling to set up theatres to cater to rapidly growing Indian middle-class

For a country that produces twice as many movies a year as Hollywood, India has a problem that's making cinema theatre operators beam: a shortage of modern multi-screen cinemas and plenty of increasingly affluent film fans.

Multiplex operators like PVR Ltd, Inox Leisure, Reliance Mediaworks and Mexican chain Cinepolis are scrambling to set up theatres targeting the rapidly growing number of middle-class Indians willing to pay to watch Bollywood movies in more comfortable surroundings.

These plush theatres, often in big city shopping malls, are a far cry from the single-screen cinemas most Indians still frequent and which range from huge, purpose-built halls to sheds where the deluxe seats are wooden benches.

The potential is huge, provided operators can find the right location in a country where prime urban real estate is costly and in short supply.

Multiplexes account for just 8% of India's 12,000 screens but rake in a third of total box office receipts, according to the Single Screen Association of India and a report by consultants KPMG and the Federation of Indian Chambers of Commerce and Industry (FICCI).

Averaging Rs 160 each, tickets at Indian multiplexes cost almost three times more than a ticket at single-screen cinemas, the KPMG-FICCI report said. At the Inox multiplex in a prime Mumbai area, tickets for a recent showing of blockbuster "Krrish 3" sold for as much as Rs 380 each.

"Indians love their movies, their Bollywood stars and the middle class is increasingly ready to spend on a better movie-watching experience"--believes Pramod Arora, president of India's biggest movie theatre operator PVR, which expects revenue growth of 25% a year for the next three years.

By comparison, KPMG forecasts overall film industry revenues to grow 10.8% a year through to 2017.

PVR wants to grow in the bigger metro areas as they have limited real estate available and wants to capture all that first because that represents the prime consumption story in India.

MOVIE MADNESS

Multiplexes made it to India with the advent of modern shopping malls in the past decade or so.

PVR set up India's first multiplex in 1997. Last year, it acquired rival Cinemax and has seen its share price double this year. India has just 8 screens per million people, far less than the 117 per million in the United States and 31 per million in China, according to the KPMG-FICCI report.

PVR runs 398 screens and plans to open another 300-360 in the next three years. Cinepolis, the world's fifth-largest operator, plans to have 500 screens in India by the end of 2017 from 68 now.

Finding the right location, however, is a challenge for multiplex operators as mall development slows along with the economy. Economic growth this fiscal year is expected to be well below the decade-low rate of a year ago.

Debt is another issue for the industry. PVR is the most leveraged of the listed Indian multiplex operators, according to Thomson Reuters StarMine data, with Rs 600 crore in debt for a debt-equity ratio of one.

Some investors, however, are cautious.

The business model of PVR is reasonably good--but debt is a big concern for the company and the industry in general. It is fairly high and if say for some reason several movies in a row flop then there might be concerns.

WHY DOWNSIDE OUTWEIGHS THE UPSIDE IN THE SHORT TERM FOR GLOBAL STOCKS

Further upsets could provide excuse for global market correction.

Anyone who doubts the efficiency of financial markets should watch how quickly they reduce complex geopolitical conflicts to simple stories. Russia's creeping invasion of Ukraine's Crimean peninsula is a case in point.

Sudden fears of a regional war sent shares tumbling globally Russia's Micex stock index saw its biggest daily fall since the 2008 financial crisis. Then, almost as rapidly, markets decided the situation had stabilised, the economic repercussions would be limited, and it was not yet time for a global sell-off.

Equities regained lost ground; the US S&P 500 hit another all-time high. The consensus view of how 2014 will pan out – a gradual world economic recovery punctuated by bouts of emerging market volatility – remained intact. But for how long?

The relative calm observed reflects investors' calculations that a balance of economic interests between Russia and the west will prevent the crisis becoming a systemic threat to the global economy, even if it develops into a prolonged, 21st century version of the Cold War.

Huffing and puffing

Russia's actions have emboldened the US and Europe to shore up rapidly Ukraine's finances, averting economic collapse. With Russia's economy weakening, meanwhile, Moscow will not want to jeopardise global trade and financial links. That gives the west leverage, the argument goes.

Vice versa, from the west's point of view, exports to Russia are not so hugely important and the country's image as an investment destination was already poor. But Russian energy supplies are vital for continental Europe.

The bottom line is that, apart from all the huffing and puffing, it is not really in anybody's interest to impose sanctions.

True, memories remain fresh of Russia's dramatic default in 1998, part of a broader emerging market panic. Some $50bn of domestic debt was affected, and, in a precursor to the global financial crisis almost a decade later, the event led to the near-collapse of the Long Term Capital Management hedge fund. But a longer term perspective adds weight to the argument that a "balance of economic interest" will limit fallout from the Crimea confrontation.

After repudiating Tsarist-era bonds in 1917, the Soviet Union had a strong record in meeting its debt obligations. That is not very relevant to Russia's position today and S&P has on April 25, 2014 downgraded Russia's foreign currency rating to one notch above "junk" status to 'BBB-A-3' from 'BBB/A-2' as well as cutting local currency long term rating to 'BBB' from 'BBB+'.

The 1998 default took place at an exceptional moment in Russia's post-Cold War history and is ill-suited as an example in the current situation "during which Russia's foreign policy is returning to a non-ideological version of the Brezhnev doctrine".

Overnight risk

The problem with such "balance of interest" arguments is that they suppose market thinking by politicians. Markets tend to view events "through the lens of rational self-interest". That leads to negative surprises when politicians turn out to have other motivations. Ukraine is an example of how a country-specific risk became, overnight, a geopolitical risk.

An immediate danger is that further shocks provide the excuse for a global market correction, seen as overdue by some investment strategists. World equities are arguably vulnerable because improvements in developed market economic data had not kept pace with share price rises.

That has not happened so far – although it still could. A longer term worry, however, is that events in Ukraine have a corrosive impact on investors' attitudes. This year we have seen a crisis in Argentina switch to worries about other emerging markets around the globe – whether South Africa, Turkey, Brazil or Indonesia. For each there were individual reasons for concern, but the impact on perceptions is cumulative.

Exacerbating the potential for volatility are historically low interest rates and "quantitative easing" by central banks, which have eroded the risk premiums demanded by investors on emerging market assets. At some point, Ukraine – or another unexpected geopolitical shock – could trigger a global re-pricing that results in severe losses on investment portfolios. For now, however, it is simpler for markets to ignore such possibilities.

The Divergent trend: Bad for stocks

In the hit movie and novel "Divergent", people are divided into different tribes based on their personalities. If you don't fit in somewhere you're considered "divergent", and that's where the trouble starts for the young heroine Beatrice Prior.

So what does that have to do with the stock market?

There's a "divergent trend" happening right now, and investors need to take note.

When the bull market is in full force, you see a lot of new highs for both individual stocks and the overall market indexes.

To put that in plain speak, when the stock prices of companies like Google (GOOGL), Yahoo (YHOO, Fortune 500) and Coke (KO, Fortune 500) are reaching new highs, you would expect to see lots of record setting days for the S&P 500 and Nasdaq as well.

Everyone wins, basically.

But a telling trend happens when the tide is about to turn: We still see the overall indexes like the S&P 500 hitting new highs, but we don't see as many individual stocks peaking anymore.

That's the divergence factor. It's a sign the market upswing is losing steam.

Here's where it gets scary: The number of individual stocks hitting new highs peaked last May when there were over 900.

Last month there were only 500.

The bull market looks tired.

The number of 52 week highs

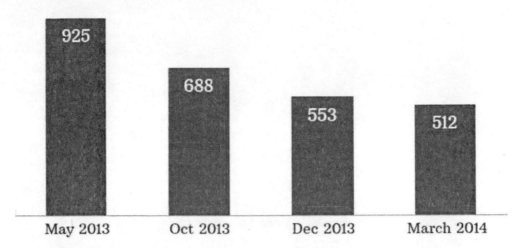

Those of you who watch the market closely will recall that the overall market hasn't slowed down just yet.

The Nasdaq closed at a 14-year high on March 5, and the S&P 500 closed at an all-time peak on April 2.

History backs up this divergence theory. If you look at 15 stock market highs since 1962 you will find that the peak in new highs for individual stocks precedes the peak in the overall markets by 9 to 11 months.

If that holds true this time around, we're about done with the bull run.

We're 11 months past the May 2013 peak of new highs in individual stocks.

Beatrice Prior in the "Divergent" film would be looking worried with dark mood lighting about now.

Gretz adds that the current climate is somewhat out of synch.

Usually stocks like Caterpillar and the oil companies come down before the averages, but in this market the leaders like Netflix are coming down first. Leaders usually come down last, but now they're first.

Why global stocks are due for correction?

Most global indices are at or have surpassed their all-time highs.

It is interesting that, as humans, we fail to pay attention to the warnings signs as long as we see no immediate danger. Yet, when the inevitable occurs, we refuse to accept responsibility for the consequences.

Over the last year, investors have been lulled to sleep wrapped in the warmth of complacency as the Federal Reserve stoked the fires of the market with $85 billion a month in liquidity injections.

Eurozone continues to present good growth opportunities for investors. The inventory build-up and capex cycle has been so much lagging behind that a 5% growth in the Eurozone is not off the track.

Doomsdaysayers and perma-bulls have been both off the track in predicting future market behavior.

I would like to detail the 10 typical warning signs of stock market exuberance.

(1) Expected strong OR acceleration of GDP and EPS (40% of 2013's EPS increase occurred in the 4th quarter)

(2) Large number of IPOs of unprofitable AND speculative companies

(3) Parabolic move up in stock prices of hot industries (not just individual stocks)

(4) High valuations (many metrics are at near-record highs, a few at record highs)

(5) Fantastic high valuation of some large mergers (e.g., Facebook & WhatsApp)

(6) High NYSE margin debt

   Margin debt/gdp (March 2000: 2.7%, July 2007: 2.6%, Jan 2014: 2.6%) Margin debt/market cap (March 2000: 1.8%, July 2007: 2.3%, Jan 2014: 2.0%)

(7) Household direct holdings of equities as % of total financial assets at 24%, second-highest level (data back to 1953, highest was 1998-2000)

(8) Highly bullish sentiment (down slightly from year-end peaks; still high or near record high, depending on the source)

(9) Unusually high ratio of selling to buying by corporate senior managers (the buy/sell ratio of senior corporate officers is now at the record post-1990 lows seen in Summer 2007 and Spring 2011)

(10) Stock prices rise following speculative press releases (e.g., Tesla will dominate battery business after they get partner who knows how to build batteries and they build a big factory. This also assumes that NO ONE else will enter into that business such as GM, Ford or GE.)

All are true today, and it is the third time in the last 15 years these factors have occurred simultaneously which is the most remarkable aspect of the situation.

The following evidence is presented to support the above claim.

Exhibit #1: Parabolic Price Movements

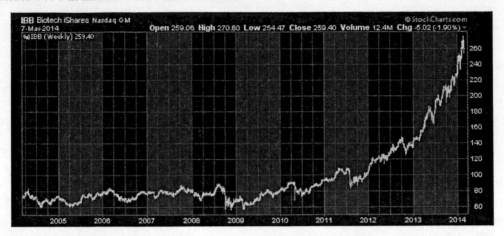

Exhibit #2: Valuation

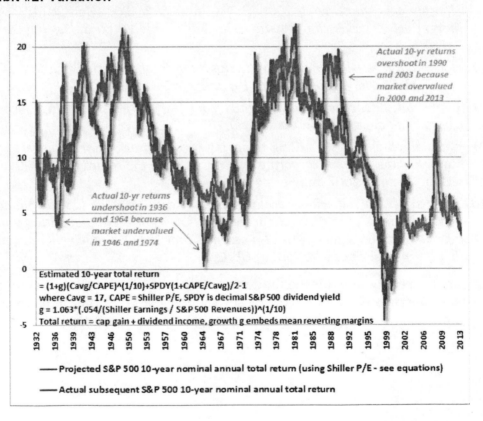

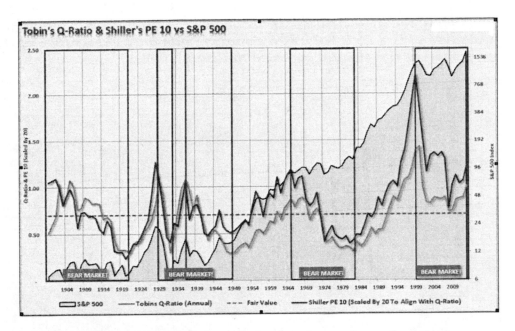

The current valuation of the S&P 500 is lofty by almost any measure, both for the aggregate market as well as the median stock:

(1) The P/E ratio;

(2) the current P/E expansion cycle;

(3) EV/Sales;

(4) EV/EBITDA;

(5) Free Cash Flow yield;

(6) Price/Book as well as the ROE and P/B relationship; and compared with the levels of inflation; nominal 10-year Treasury yields; and real interest rates.

Furthermore, the cyclically-adjusted P/E ratio suggests the S&P 500 is currently 30% overvalued in terms of Operating EPS and about 45% overvalued using As Reported earnings.

The **biggest surprise is how many investors expect the forward P/E multiple to expand to 17x or 18x**. For some reason, many market participants believe the P/E multiple has a long-term average of 15x and therefore expansion to 17-18x seems reasonable. **But the common perception is wrong**. The forward P/E ratio for the S&P 500 during the past 5-year, 10-year, and 35- year periods has averaged 13.2x, 14.1x, and 13.0x, respectively. At 15.9x, the current aggregate forward P/E multiple is high by historical standards.

Most investors are surprised to learn that since 1976 the S&P 500 P/E multiple has only exceeded 17x during the 1997-2000 Tech Bubble and a brief four-month period in 2003-04. Other than those two episodes, the US stock market has never traded at a P/E of 17x or above.

A graph of the historical distribution of P/E ratios clearly highlights that outside of the Tech Bubble, the market has only rarely (5% of the time) traded at the current forward multiple of 16x.

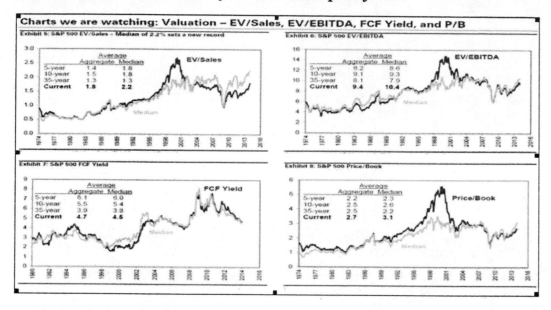

The elevated market multiple is even more apparent when viewed on a median basis. At 16.8x, the current multiple is at the high end of its historical distribution.

The multiple expansion cycle provides another lens through which we view equity valuation. There have been nine multiple expansion cycles during the past 30 years. The P/E troughed at a median value of 10.5x and peaked at a median value of 15.0x, an increase of roughly 50%. **The current expansion cycle began in September 2011 when the market traded at 10.6x forward EPS and it currently trades at 15.9x, an expansion of 50%.** However, during most (7 of the 9) of the cycles the backdrop included falling bond yields and declining inflation. In contrast, bond yields are now increasing and inflation is low but expected to rise.

Incorporating inflation into our valuation analysis suggests S&P 500 is slightly overvalued. When real interest rates have been in the 1%-2% band, the P/E has averaged 15.0x. Nominal rates of 3%-4% have been associated with P/E multiples averaging 14.2x, nearly two points below today. **As noted earlier, S&P 500 is overvalued on both an aggregate and median basis on many classic metrics, including EV/EBITDA, FCF, and P/B.**

Exhibit #3: Selling Of Company Stock By Senior Managers

Prof. Seyhun - who is one of the leading experts on interpreting the behavior of corporate insiders - has found that when the transactions of the largest shareholders are stripped out, insiders do have impressive forecasting abilities. In the summer of 2007, for example, his adjusted insider sell-to-buy ratio was more bearish than at any time since 1990, which is how far back his analyses extended.

Ominously, that degree of bearish sentiment is where the insider ratio stands today.

Note carefully that even if the insiders turn out to be right and the bull market is coming to an end, this doesn't have to mean that the U.S. market averages are about to fall as much as they did in 2008 and early 2009. The one other time since that bear market when Prof. Seyhun's adjusted sell-buy ratio sunk as low as it was in 2007 and is today, the market subsequently fell by 'just' 20%.

That other occasion was in early 2011. Stocks' drop at that time did satisfy the unofficial definition of a bear market, and the insiders' pessimism was vindicated.

Exhibit #4: Investor's Confidence

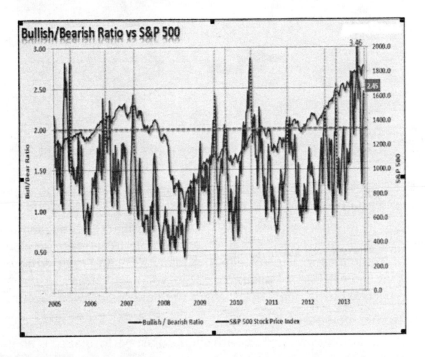

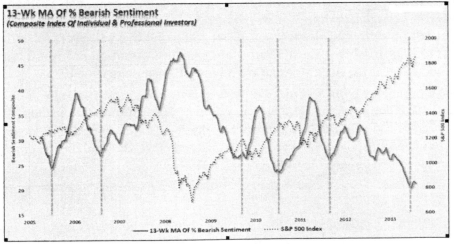

Exhibit #5: Ownership Of Stocks As % Total Financial Assets

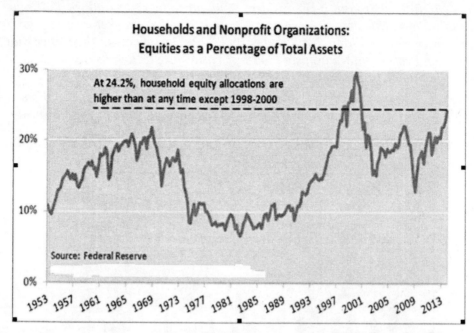

Thus, the *""warning signs"* are all there. However, since the road ahead seems clear, it is human nature that we keep our foot pressed on the accelerator.

As the Federal Reserve extracts liquidity from the markets, the *"Bernanke Put"* is being removed which leaves the markets vulnerable to a *"mean reverting event"* at some point in the future. The mistake that many investors are currently making is believing that since it hasn't happened yet, it won't. This time is only *"different"* from the perspective of the *"why"* and *"when"* the next major event occurs.

1) The Delusions Of Real Returns

This is a topic that I discuss very often with clients. Past performance is no guarantee of future results, and making investment decisions based on such is likely going to leave you very disappointed. Extrapolating 110 year historical average returns going forward is extremely dangerous. First, you won't live 110 years from the time you start saving to achieve those results, and starting valuation levels are critical to your expected returns. Brett does an excellent job discussing this issue.

Money managers point to historical data going back to the 1920s to show that in the past stocks have produced total returns of about 10% a year over the long term and bonds, about 5%—meaning a standard "balanced" portfolio of 60% stocks and 40% bonds would earn just over 8% a year. (Naturally, their legal departments quickly add that the past is no guide to the future.)

Are these forecasts realistic? Are they sensible? Are they even based on actual logic or a correct reading of the past data?

A close look at the data reveals a number of disturbing errors and logical flaws. There is a serious danger that investors are deluding themselves and that returns from here on may prove far more disappointing than many hope or believe.

This has happened before. Money invested in a balanced fund of stocks and bonds at certain points in the past—such as in the late 1930s, or during the 1960s and 1970s—ended up losing money for many years, after accounting for inflation.

Far from making an annual profit, investors went backward in real, purchasing-power terms. And those losses were even before deducting costs or taxes."

2) Lessons From The Bull Market by Jason Zweig, Joe Light and Liam Pleven

Every day, in the newspapers, on financial-news shows and online, dozens of market strategists make bold predictions about the direction stocks are heading. **Take their forecasts with a mound of salt.** *After all, current prices already reflect the sum of stock-market buyers' and sellers' opinions. If one investor is bullish, there must be another investor on the other side at the current price.*

In a speech about intellectual honesty 40 years ago, Nobel Prize-winning physicist Richard Feynman said, 'The first principle is that you must not fool yourself—and you are the easiest person to fool.'

What they should be asking is this: Am I fooling myself into remembering my losses as less painful than they were? Am I itching to take risks that my own history should warn me I will end up regretting? Am I counting on willpower alone to enable me to stay invested and to rebalance through another crash?"

Investors who hear the phrase 'bull market' might decide it is time to get in on the rally. On the other hand, investors who hear the current bull market in stocks has been running for five years might worry it will soon end. In either case, investors would do better to tune out the chatter. The definition of a bull market is arbitrary, and the term tells investors little about what will happen next.

3) How Market Tops Are Made

Rather than focus on the usual noise, Desmond suggests anyone concerned about a top should be watching for very specific warning signs. He notes the health of a bull market can be observed by watching internal indicators that provide insight into the overall appetite for equity accumulation.

These four include:

1. *New 52-Week Highs*
2. *Market Breadth (Advanced/Decline Line)*
3. *Capitalization: Small Cap, Mid Cap, Large Cap*
4. *Percentage of Stocks at 20 percent or greater from their recent highs"*

4) New All Time Highs = Secular Bull Market?

If the current cyclical bull unfolds into a secular one that is perfectly average in duration and magnitude (a very tall achievement, in our book), the annualized total return over the next ten years will still be a bit below the long-term average return of 10%. *Frankly, we don't find this all that compelling, considering all that must go according to plan for the market to achieve it (i.e. sustained EPS growth at a healthy 6% and an inflated terminal P/E multiple).*

Based on the relative positions of these time-tested measures, secular bulls seem to be implicitly betting on the reflation of a multi-generational stock bubble less than 15 years after it popped. The pathology of 'busted bubbles'—which we've detailed at length in the past—doesn't support that bet.

If **we are indeed seeing a new secular bull market, the extraordinary measures undertaken by global central banks in the wake of the Lehman Crisis has front-end loaded many of the gains to be realized in this bull.**

5) Does Shiller's CAPE Still Work?

It is becoming more difficult for more mainstream commentators, analysts and managers to justify their arguments for a continued bull market when having to contend with rising valuation levels. However, as would be expected, at the peak of every major bull market in history there have always been those that have suggested *"this time is different."* In 1929, stocks had reached a new permanent plateau. In 1999, old valuation measures didn't matter as it was about *"clicks per page."* In 2007, subprime credit was *"contained"* and it was a *"goldilocks economy."* In 2014, old valuation metrics simply don't account for the new economy. We have always heard the same *"sirens song"* during every major bull market cycle and, as the sailors of the past, we are ultimately lured toward our demise. Bill Hester does an excellent job breaking down the arguments against Shiller's CAPE valuation metrics.

More recently the ratio has undergone an attack from some widely-followed analysts, questioning its validity and offering up attempts to adjust the ratio. This may be a reaction to its new-found notoriety, but more likely it's because the CAPE is suggesting that US stocks are significantly overvalued. All of the adjustments analysts have made so far imply that stocks are **less overvalued than the traditional CAPE would suggest.**

We feel no particular obligation defend the CAPE ratio. It has a strong long-term relationship to subsequent 10-year market returns. And it's only one of numerous valuation indicators that we use in our work – many which are considerably more reliable. All of these valuation indicators – particularly when record-high profit margins are accounted for – are sending the same message: **The market is steeply overvalued, leaving investors with the prospect of low, single-digit long-term expected returns.** *But we decided to come to the aid of the CAPE ratio in this case because a few errors have slipped into the debate, and it's important for investors who have previously relied on this ratio to understand these errors so they can judge the valuation metric fairly.*

Importantly, **the primary error that is being made is not even the fault of those making the arguments against the CAPE ratio. The fault lies at the feet of a misleading data series.**

Of course, despite the repeated warning signs, the next correction will leave investors devastated looking to point blame at everyone other than themselves. The question will simply be *"why no one saw it coming?"*

Have Indian stock markets have gone ahead of themselves?

The real threat's external

A slowing China, weak global demand and investor pessimism over emerging markets should worry the next government more than domestic economic problems

Narendra Modi may be able to fix India's ailing domestic economy, but it's the sorry state of world demand that will pose a bigger and more intractable challenge to the country's prime ministerial hopeful.

India's stock market is not only starting to price in a victory for the opposition leader, it's also anticipating that Mr Modi will end the domestic investment slump fairly easily. Equity benchmarks that track banks and machine and equipment manufacturers - both of which serve as proxies for investment - are up 13 per cent since the beginning of March. The broader market has risen by just 4 % over the same period.

Investors' hopes are not unfounded. Indian companies have already done quite a bit to shrink their balance sheets and cut debt. As fewer loans go bad, state-owned banks will face less pressure to write off or restructure debts. That could signal a recovery in credit-fuelled investment, especially if a Modi victory makes it easier for companies and lenders to raise equity on the stock market.

Then there's cost of capital to consider. India's real interest rates, adjusted for producer price inflation, are now about 3.5 per cent, a massive jump from their 2010-2012 average.

However, debt will not become less expensive as the Reserve Bank of India will not succeed in so easily controlling inflation. There is forecast of a poor monsoon that could once again lead to rise in food inflation.

While India's domestic investment slump is likely to abate after the elections, the global economy will continue to pose a formidable challenge.

Start with exports, which did well for a few months last year due to the weak rupee but are now losing steam because world demand is too frail to provide a boost to suppliers in emerging markets. Particularly worrying is the decline in India's engineering exports in February. Industry association EEPC says the fall may have had something to do with the "drop in the value of renminbi being calibrated by the Chinese authorities." While those concerns are overblown for now, Beijing's decision to widen the yuan's daily trading band against the US dollar has raised fears that China might indeed prefer a cheaper currency. That could spell trouble for Indian exporters.

Meanwhile, lacklustre US demand is having more immediate effects. Infosys recently lowered its revenue guidance for the year because global technology firms aren't spending as much on computer software. US retailers, too, are responding to margin pressure by paring back their 2014 capital expenditures.

If India's exports keep losing steam but domestic demand revives, the nation's current account deficit, which has been artificially suppressed by the present government's crackdown on gold imports, may once again start to rise. The gap between what India pays for imports, including energy, and what it earns from exports may also widen if the stand-off between Russia and the West over Crimea keeps crude oil prices elevated.

Financing the deficit became a challenge for New Delhi last summer after the US Federal Reserve said it would end its quantitative easing programme, reducing the worldwide supply of excess dollars. Unless the general election produces a business-unfriendly outcome that prompts investors to take flight, a repeat of last year's rupee crisis is unlikely. The more likely scenario is the opposite: a surge in hot money inflows following a Modi victory, which will allow India to run higher trade deficits.

But euphoria about India's new government is unlikely to outweigh broader pessimism about emerging markets for long. The CBOE index for volatility in emerging market exchange traded funds - a good proxy for investors' nerves - is 49 per cent higher now than in October last year. This isn't an environment in which Mr Modi can consider pursuing a risky, high-growth strategy with short-term funds borrowed from foreigners. To permanently lower the risk of a future balance-of-payment crisis, the new Indian government will need to implement a plan to boost the country's exports - a complicated task when the US, which is still the world's most important source of demand, hasn't increased its imports for two years.

Mr Modi's businessmen backers want the Indian economy to grow by eight to nine per cent a year so they can boost revenue and earnings and reclaim the international adulation they enjoyed before 2008. He won't find that easy to deliver. The financial crisis has made the global economy more treacherous. Indeed, a slowdown in China could tip a global economy already grappling with disinflation into outright deflation.

If that happens, India will feel some benefits. The current government's obsession with paying villagers to stay where they are has stunted the country's much-needed urbanisation drive. If it gets underway, the steel, copper, aluminium and power required will cost less than in the early 2000s when a fast-growing China elevated the prices of all commodities. At the same time, though, global deflation will put Indian exporters' prices under pressure. It would take a big surge in domestic labour productivity to counter that squeeze. One part of those productivity gains would compensate companies for their lack of pricing power; the other part would boost labour incomes.

In a difficult global environment, a sustainable expansion of India's economy can only come from productivity-driven increases in domestic employment and wages. And that means launching a bold reform programme. A new credit binge could well end up becoming Mr Modi's shortcut to growth. But with the world economy mired in stagnation, any artificial boost will run out of steam even more quickly than it did in the previous decade.

EMERGING MARKET REVIVAL:
FLASH IN THE PAN?

According to *Quantum Theory*, an act of locating an article a particle in space tends to change its position and the act of locating the position of an article in space tends to change its location.

After last year's rout, emerging markets have charged ahead recently but the rally should shortly run out of steam.

The catalyst for the rally has been te ending of an unprecedented period of fund outflows from the asset class (22 weeks, 7 % of assets under management) rather than an improvement in fundamentals.

Although, there are pockets of strength such as improvement in India's current account position although that is also due to artificially reining in gold imports.

Fund flows so far this year are still negative, with bond funds shedding $ 9.33 Billion and $ 25.55 Billion fleeing equity funds till date. This followed a tough 2013, which saw $ 14.1 Billion exit emerging markets.

Emerging markets' upcoming earnings reports are likely to miss consensus estimates, which would mark the ninth quarterly miss out of the past 11 quarters.

In addition, continuing strength in U.S. data and rising U.S. bond yields will spur U.S. dollar strength, pushing down emerging market currencies through the third quarter.

Emerging markets have seen a brutal sell-off earlier this year and last year after sharp falls in the value of th Argentine peso, Turkish lira, South African rand and Brazilian real triggered panic selling across the asset class, with analysts largely blaming the turbulence on the Federal Reserve's move to begin tapering its asset purchases.

In the backdrop of great expectations of commencement of tapering by the US Fed; on September 18, 2013; the US Fed refrained from reducing its experimental bond purchase program, thus maintaining its unconventional support for markets and the economy. This has led to fuelling the risk-on rally in emerging markets which began a fortnight back.

Although the Fed mentioned that unemployment rate remains high in the backdrop of a benign inflation rate, the true reason for Fed's backing off could be the debt ceiling that the United States was going to hit in October that year and the gyrations that could cause in world financial markets.

The Fed's greatest challenge was not in deciding on the optimal month to start the taper but in balancing its focus on a carefully-crafted journey (namely a gradual, measured and conditional normalization of monetary policy) with the markets' natural inclination to jump quickly to the destination (thereby risking to pre-emptively impose market-determined terminal values on a still-fragile economy).

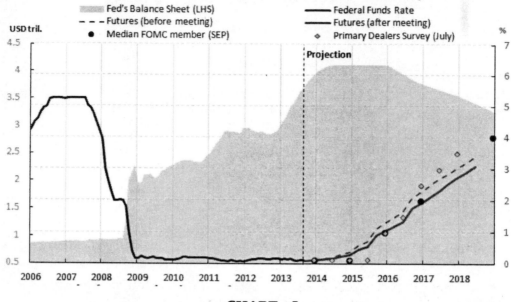

CHART I

At the time of publishing this book, Emerging market stocks are coming back in favour with a vengeance. Some call it the revival of growth. Some call it the favourable effect of currency depreciation. In India, analysts laud what they call the 'Raghuram Rajan effect'.

Emerging markets had seen a broad selloff since the Fed tapering talks first gripped markets over three months ago. The Indonesian rupiah lost 16.5 % since late May, while the Indian rupee plummeted to a record low of 68.8 against the dollar on August 28.

The ongoing revival in sentiment is not only with respect to India but emerging markets in general.

Data emanating from the Emerging markets suggests that their growth has slowed significantly, and the onset of tapering speculation drove a sharp fall in stocks and currencies, particularly for countries with big current account deficits such as India or Turkey.

The rally that ensued has been purely a global phenomenon. Lot of analysts term it as the 'Raghuram Rajan rally', but that's putting the cart before the horse. It is an emerging market rally because those had got terribly oversold (see Chart II)

GLOBAL EMERGING MARKET PRICE-TO-BOOK RATIO
1993 TO 2014

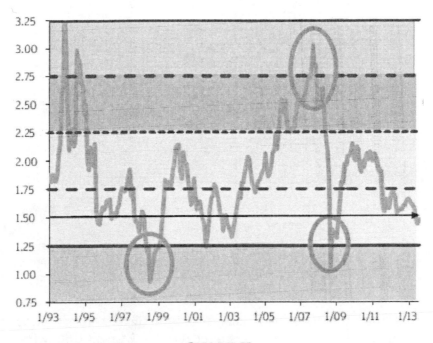

CHART II

Emerging markets had got terribly oversold over the last couple of months, nobody wanted to buy them and voila, the sentiment towards emerging markets changed from August 28, 2013.

The global liquidity phenomenon led to an aggressive pricing or even mispricing of emerging market assets and currencies, which suddenly appear overheated.

In this heated debate of how much credence to give to the emerging markets rally, some important points have been lost: That in the past any change in the chair of the Fed was associated with an unusual time of a more tight monetary policy and that this time again the stage has been set for the end of the current extremely expansive monetary policy.

There seems to be a clear pattern in the timeline of the past Fed Chairmen in the last decades: The monetary policy during their tenure was mostly rather dovish, but every time they passed the torch to next one, they seemed obliged to bring it back to a more neutral or even hawkish level, a change in course that was often picked up by the next person at the start of his first term, until things became more rocky and he switched back to a more expansive course in the later years. So it seems that Fed chairmen tended to press the pedal to the metal most of the time, but before the captain passed the helm he tried to reduce the speed almost to a standstill. Not without dangers, as I will show.

Now here is the evidence: I plotted the yield of the Fed Fund rate and the 10-year Treasury together with the changes in the chair of the Federal Reserve and important (negative) events taking place soon after the change:

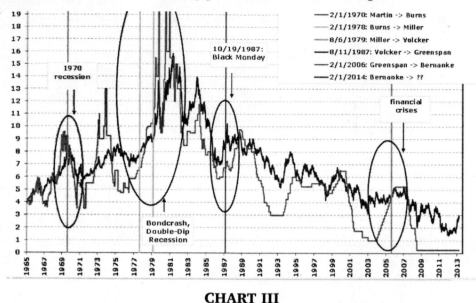

CHART III

Could this time be different?   Let us look at history to get some answers. Chart II compares the market responses after the Great Crash (following a peak in September 1929), the crash of Japan's stock market from New Year's eve 1989, and the bursting of the Nasdaq bubble in 2000.

Each time, after the crash, stocks found a level, and enjoyed a few rallies, while moving crab-like, sideways for many years.

The Lehman crash, however, bears no similarity to any of these previous incidents. A different dynamic is plainly at work. The extra ingredient has come from the Federal Reserve, and also the US government.

The S&P500 hit bottom in March 2009 when it became clear that the TARP (Troubled Assets Relief Program – the US government's single most contentious act that requisitioned $800bn in public money to shore up the banks) was beginning to work. This was when Citigroup and Bank of America, the focus of the greatest concern, announced that they were trading profitably.

Rises in the S&P500 have correlated almost perfectly with injections of money from the Federal Reserve, which has stimulated markets by buying bonds in a policy now universally known as QE. Lulls in the stock market's recovery overlap with lulls in QE.

If the pattern of markets after previous crises has been breached, the pattern of economies has not.

Thanks to the time former Fed Chairman Ben Bernanke bought the US with the QE money, many good things happened: banks have recapitalized; house prices have hit a floor and begun to recover; inflation never reared its ugly head; unemployment is less worse than it was.

But here, things grow problematic. The hit to the world economy has, in the event, fallen far short of a replay of the 1930s Great Depression. This is thanks to China and the emerging markets. After falling by less than 1 % in 2009, world gross domestic product has grown at an annual clip of 3 % or more ever since.

But in the western world, this recovery is still anaemic. If the pattern of markets after previous crises has been breached, the pattern of economies has not. Outside Germany, unemployment remains at politically unacceptable levels throughout the western world. But at some point, the monetary stimulus must end.

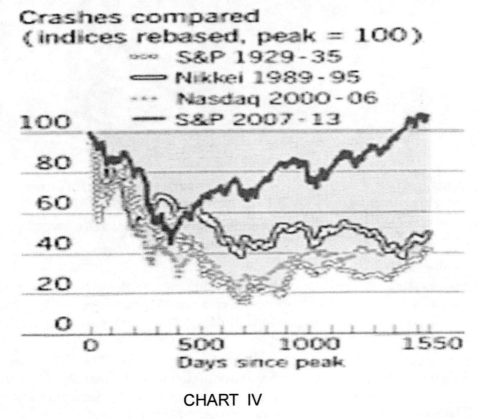

CHART IV

Is the economy strong enough to survive QE's removal? And can market gains remain intact?

US experience suggests that markets should be fine. Bond yields have been rising since July last year, anticipating the end of QE. Those yields have not pushed stocks down.

The great post-Lehman rally is facing its critical test.

Is the emerging market rally a flash in the pan?

Emerging markets of late are shaking off last year's rout, but it isn't clear if the rally has staying power or if it's just a flash in the pan.

Investors were overly negative on emerging markets and it was a crowded short. Some of those shorts have now been unwound.

It isn't clear if those trades will stay unwound.

It remains fashionable to be bearish on emerging markets. Less than a few weeks ago, the questions were still all about an emerging market blow up, banking crisis, currency collapse, and earnings disappointments. Now that emerging markets [have] rallied off the lows, the perception is that it is clearly not sustainable.

Over the past two weeks, emerging market bond funds saw $2.85 billion worth of inflows while around $4.80 billion has flowed into emerging market stock funds over the past three weeks, although the two segments have still seen net outflows of $9.33 billion and $25.55 billion respectively so far this year.

In 2013, $14.1 billion exited emerging market equity funds, while $14.04 billion said good-bye to the segment's bond funds.

The Indonesian rupiah, Singapore dollar, Philippine peso and Malaysian ringgit have short-term buying opportunities.

The segment faced a brutal sell-off last year and earlier this year after sharp falls in the value of the Argentine peso, Turkish lira, South African rand and Brazilian real triggered panic selling across the asset class, with analysts largely blaming the turbulence on the Federal Reserve's move to begin tapering its asset purchases.

Investors have been too negative on emerging markets, noting that the segment's earnings forecast revisions are no longer worse than the developed market counterparts'. In addition, emerging markets still appear cheap compared with historical levels and developed markets.

That should continue to lend support to those wishing to allocate more toward emerging markets.

But it added, for the rally to continue, the earnings environment will need to remain supportive.

Export momentum will also need to continue improving.

Better exports means better earnings and better earnings means greater willingness on the part of investors to become buyers of equities.

Investors appear to have been covering shorts on emerging market bond ETFs (exchange-traded funds) almost uninterrupted since last August-- the value of the ETFs on loan as an indicator of "fast-money" investors' appetite for short selling.

Others aren't certain whether emerging markets are really all that cheap.

While the cheap names in emerging markets are "very cheap and unloved," the growth stocks are trading at high price-to-book levels.

If indeed we have seen the peak in growth stock multiples, the declines are not done yet.

Emerging market growth stocks, especially in the consumer, tech and healthcare sectors, have benefited from the Federal Reserve's quantitative easing measures, which have kept the cost of equity low. As the Fed tapers, that source of sustenance and mojo is going to be gone soon.

EM consumer stocks hit as retail dream fades

A BYD, or 'Build Your Dreams', electric car

The emerging market consumer, so the narrative went, would dazzle the global investor as they indulged their retail dreams, buying everything from designer T-shirts in Brazil to convenience store goods in Russia and cars in China made by a company known as BYD, which stands for "Build Your Dreams".

Investors who rode such aspirations have seen stellar returns. The MSCI Emerging Markets Consumer Discretionary index, which aggregates the share prices of leading EM consumer companies, has risen 250 per cent since its 2009 trough. By contrast, the broader MSCI emerging markets index has risen only 69.61 per cent in the same period.

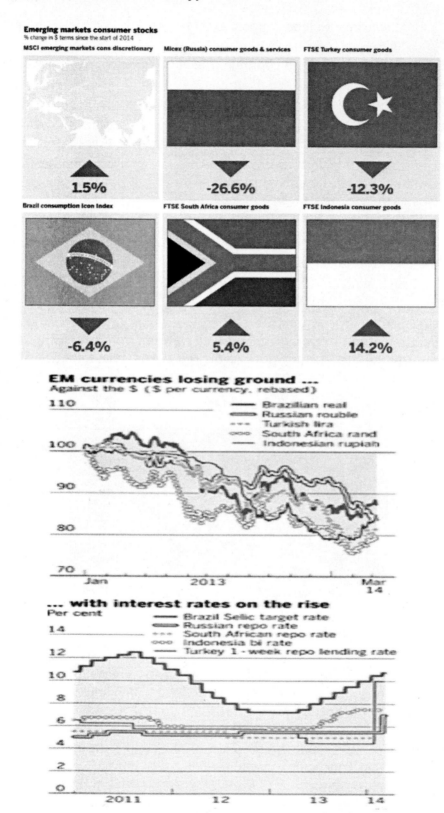

Now, however, one of the most successful investor narratives since the 2008 financial crisis is coming back down to earth, according to consumer surveys in several emerging markets, investment bank analysts and some fund managers.

There isn't much fundamental reason in the very near term to be optimistic about consumer spending in emerging markets.

A spreading dynamic is responsible for the more sober outlook. Central banks have hiked interest rates to defend their depreciating currencies, reducing the willingness of consumers to borrow to buy consumer goods. That, in turn, has hit consumer stocks.

The impact of higher interest rates is likely to be most pronounced and protracted in countries that run current account deficits and are vulnerable to the slacker global demand for commodities that is flowing from China's economic slowdown.

These countries include Brazil and Turkey, which have seen their respective consumer stock indices fall 6.4 per cent and 12.3 per cent so far this year. In Turkey consumer credit growth seems poised for a very sharp slowdown in the wake of the January rate hike.

South Africa, which also falls into this category, has performed somewhat better – with its consumer stocks rising 5.4 per cent – partly because the rebound in the rand's value against the dollar has helped shore up sentiment.

Russia, where the consumer stock index has fallen 26.6 per cent so far this year, is the worst EM performer. Investor sentiment has, of course, been rattled by geopolitical nervousness over the future of Ukraine, but economic issues are also contributing to the sell-off in Russian equities. A sharp hike in interest rates to defend the rouble is seen as likely to hit consumer spending in coming weeks, fund managers say.

Indonesia, which runs a current account deficit and has exposure to the Chinese economy, has bucked the trend this year, with its consumer goods index rising 14.2 per cent so far this year. One reason, analysts say, is that its central bank – encouraged by an improving current account picture – has held rates steady this year.

According to survey of consumers in Indonesia by Asean Confidential, a research service at the Financial Times, consumer sentiment in Indonesia is holding up. Asean Confidential's discretionary spending index for Indonesia went to 88.3 in February, up from 87.9 in December – marking a break with the wider Asean region, which saw a slight easing in consumer sentiment. Malaysia and Thailand look particularly reluctant to maintain the high pitch of credit-fuelled spending of the past few years.

China, too, shows signs of slowing consumer credit absorption. A China Confidential survey showed a fall in its future discretionary spending index in February to 74.8, down from 75.5 in January, signifying a moderation in spending plans. The consumer borrowing index also eased to 72.5 in February from 75.9 in January, suggesting households are increasingly cautious over consumer credit.

This may account for some of the souring sentiment around Chinese car companies, many of which are among the poorest performing stocks in the MSCI consumer index this year. Geely cars is down 27 per cent and Great Wall cars is down 23 per cent.

In my view, the emerging consumer story is a long-range, structural shift, which is not going to be thrown off course by cyclical issues that the market is currently encountering.

Original sin in emerging markets: it's back

Is it 1997 all over again? EM bulls scoff at the idea: this time, they say, is different, and for solid reasons.

Two things especially have changed, according to this view. Emerging markets no longer have such high levels of debt relative to GDP. And whereas in the 90s many EMs had a lot of dollar-denominated debt backed by local-currency revenues (the so-called "original sin"), much of this has been replaced by local-currency debt.

But have things really changed that much?

Let's look first at debt levels.

Fig. 5 EM balance sheet generally in decent shape

Foreign currency debt as % GDP

Troubled currencies			
	1996	2007	Sep-13
Brazil	26%	15% ↓	17% ↓
India	7%	16% ↑	14% ↑
Russia	19%	19% ↑	13% ↓
South Africa	15%	20% ↑	16% ↑
Turkey	17%	28% ↑	30% ↑
Average	**17%**	**20%** ↑	**18%** ↑

More robust currencies			
	1996	2007	Sep-13
Chile		35%	45%
China	9%	7% ↓	10% ↑
Colombia	22%	16% ↓	17% ↓
Czech Republic	17%	29% ↑	40% ↑
Hungary	67%	97% ↑	83% ↑
Indonesia	30%	16% ↓	20% ↓
Israel	9%	61% ↑	20% ↑
Korea	27%	32% ↑	31% ↑
Malaysia	31%	43% ↑	39% ↑
Mexico	47%	20% ↓	30% ↓
Philippines	30%	41% ↑	29% ↓
Poland	19%	37% ↑	40% ↑
Thailand	51%	13% ↓	19% ↓
Average	**30%**	**34%** ↑	**33%** ↑

Source: Nomura, Bloomberg, Note: Arrows indicate increase or decrease since 1996.

Many of these countries are in decent shape. But not that decent. On average, in fact, the two groups have more foreign currency debt today than they did on the eve of the 1997 Asian crisis – although those averages are skewed by the two outliers in red, Turkey and Hungary. But is this the full picture?

Next, let's look at the composition of debt. Our first set of charts below shows the amount of cross-border bank lending to Nomura's troubled countries, plus China.

All of these counties have enjoyed rapid economic growth during the past two decades so a run-up in external liabilities by their banks may not come as a surprise. Nevertheless, we can see that in many countries, original sin is alive and kicking.

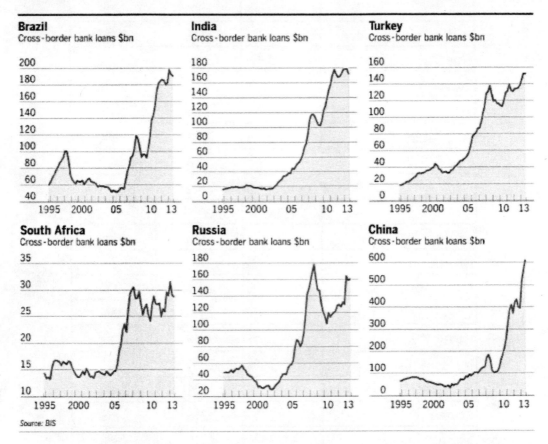

Brazil
Cross-border bank loans $bn

India
Cross-border bank loans $bn

Turkey
Cross-border bank loans $bn

South Africa
Cross-border bank loans $bn

Russia
Cross-border bank loans $bn

China
Cross-border bank loans $bn

Source: BIS

But there is more to FX debt than bank lending. A flurry of recent working papers, from the IMF, Princeton University and others, point to a rapid expansion of bond issuance by the private sector in emerging markets and to a structural change in the way those bonds are issued.

Our next group of charts shows the amount of money raised through foreign currency debt securities by our selected countries, grouped according to residence and nationality of issuer.

Figures such as those collated by Bloomberg (and used in Normura's chart above) generally rely on balance of payments data from central banks. It is standard practice for central banks to identify issuers by country of residence rather than nationality – so that if the Brazilian subsidiary of Banco Santander, for example, issues a bond, it will appear as part of the private sector debt of Brazil rather than of Spain. And if an overseas subsidiary of a Brazilian company issues a bond in, say, the Cayman Islands, it will appear in the debt of the Cayman Islands, not of Brazil. In the data commonly used to assess FX liabilities, in other words, debt issued by non-resident nationals does not show up.

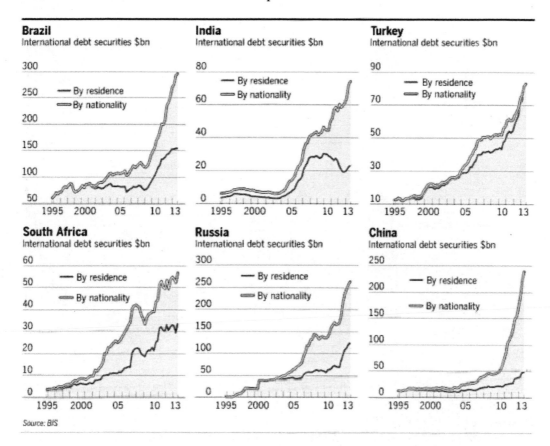

Source: BIS

For many years, this distinction was not significant. But over the past decade, as our charts show, the amount of debt issued by EM corporations through overseas subsidiaries has grown quickly – adding substantially to the stock of original sin. Pretending it is not there does nothing to reduce the vulnerability of the ultimate issuing nation.

Drilling down a bit further, we see that while the bulk of such issuance has come from governments and banks, in some countries – India and China stand out in our sample – a significant part of the increase has come from non-financial corporations (NFCs).

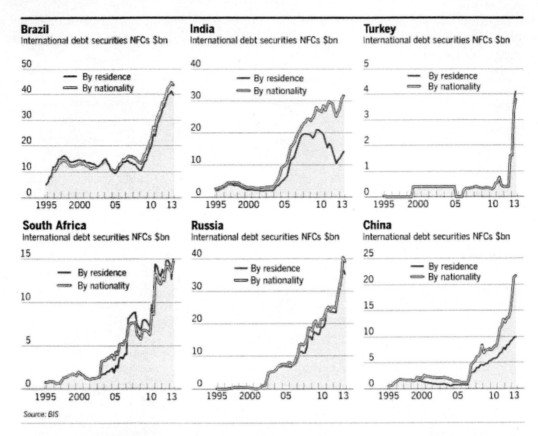

Source: BIS

Hyun Song Shin and Laura Yi Zhao, in a recent paper from Princeton, argue that, especially in China but also in other countries such as India, Indonesia and South Korea, such issuance constitutes surrogate financial intermediation and has contributed to the stock of credit available in those countries.

As Kyuil Chung, Jong-Eun Lee, Elena Loukoianova, Hail Park and Hyun Song Shin put it in a paper on similar lines from the IMF:

One conceptual challenge has been to reconcile what appears to be the small net external debt position of many EM economies with the apparently disproportionate impact of tighter global monetary conditions on their currencies and financial markets... One piece in the puzzle may be the role of NFCs that operate across borders.

As an old proverb says, "commit a sin twice and it will not seem a crime". Financial markets may take a different view.

EMs are paying the price of ETF liquidity

Volatility inflamed by ability of exchange traded funds to exit quickly

Are exchange traded funds the best way to invest in emerging market equities?

The structure of ETFs allows trading through the day and have contributed significantly to the scale of the recent sell-off in emerging markets besides helping make the sector more volatile.

The two main counter-arguments are that other macro factors were more important to the sell-off, which is true – but still avoids the issue of whether ETFs have accelerated volatility. The second complaint is that ETFs are far cheaper in terms of the fees they charge than alternative open-ended or closed-end funds. This is also undeniably true.

So let me address both issues. First, ETFs now dominate flows in and out of emerging markets, and the money held in them is plainly flightier than money held in other instruments. According to Strategic Insight Simfund, since the beginning of 2009 there have been six separate quarters in which emerging market ETFs have suffered net outflows. There have been no such quarters for actively managed funds in the sector, while the far smaller flows into open-ended funds have also been steady.

While it is true that ETF investors are responding to macroeconomic and corporate fundamental factors when they make buying and selling decisions, the money they hold is plainly impatient. This is not surprising, as a key advantage of ETFs is that they are liquid – hold assets in an ETF and you know that you can sell quickly. At the margin, this money helps to accelerate boom-and-bust cycles in emerging asset markets – and this in itself may not help their plans to grow.

Cost matters

For investors, though, the issue of fees should be critical. Arguably, the case for index investing rests on low fees. After all, future performance is unknown, but fees can be guaranteed to eat into return. All other things equal, therefore, investors should opt for the lower-cost vehicle.

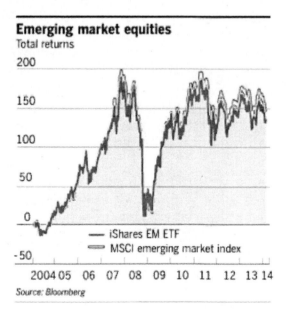

Many argue that the case for index investing comes from the efficient markets hypothesis (EMH), which holds in its strongest form that as all information is already incorporated in share prices, it will be difficult or impossible to beat the market.

Jack Bogle, the founder of Vanguard and generally regarded as the godfather of index investing, suggests that the case rests on the CMH, or Cost Matters Hypothesis.

Normally, he is unquestionably right about this. But if a market is inefficient, it is easier to outperform an index, even after fees. And that is happening to ETFs in emerging markets. Compared with the developed world, they find it far harder to match their benchmark indices, while active funds find it far easier to beat them.

The iShares ETF that tracks the MSCI emerging markets index has underperformed its benchmark by 12.3 percentage points over the last decade, meaning an annual return of 8.73 per cent, against 9.31 per cent for the index – 58 basis points per year. For the main ETF tracking the S&P 500 the tracking error has been 7 bps; for the Russell 2000 index of smaller companies, 2 bps; and for the S&P 350 index it has been negligible.

There are reasons for this: it is often difficult to access markets; markets are open at different times, and the range of different countries means that using futures to help replicate the index is not practical.

He points out that tracking errors are reducing over time, as access to markets such as Chile and Colombia, or even Russia, grows easier. But they weaken the case for passive investing in emerging markets.

Liquid stocks more volatile

Why do active managers fare so well? Their fees should be an insuperable disadvantage as ETFs are virtually costless for those who already have a brokerage account. Active managers need to cover the considerable cost of attempting to pick stocks in far-flung corners of the world.

And yet in emerging markets, even after fees, active funds tend to be better. According to Morningstar, while the iShares EM ETF has dropped 10.88 per cent over the past year, the average active diversified EM fund shed only 7.5 per cent. Over five years, active mutual funds beat the ETF by 13.21 to 11.32 per cent. It appears there really are bargains to be found in EM, and that active investors find them.

What is going on? One argument is that the two percentage points of underperformance with ETFs represent the premium for their liquidity. You can always get out in a hurry, which is not true of a direct investment in shares in some emerging stock exchanges.

As further evidence, note that hedge funds – which force investors to tie up their money for long periods – perform well in emerging markets. According to EurekaHedge, Latin America specialist hedge funds gained 1.83 per cent last year, while the MSCI Latin America index fell 15.59 per cent. In the first month of this year they dropped 1.95 per cent, against an 11.88 per cent fall in the index.

Another perverse effect of ETFs' search for liquidity is that in emerging markets, it is the most liquid stocks that tend to be the most volatile. Brazil, Russia, India and China are four of the five most volatile markets in the EM universe. A "Beyond Brics" index that excludes them (along with South Korea and Taiwan) has a standard deviation of 14.7 percentage points, compared to 19.3 percentage points for the main MSCI EM index. Indices of domestic consumer stocks, also relatively illiquid and under-represented in the indices, also show lower volatility.

Why could this be? It may well be because ETFs congregate in the large stocks that are the most liquid, and move in and out frequently; less liquid stocks are traded less regularly in consequence, and hence give investors a less bumpy ride.

Many of these problems can be addressed without jettisoning the ETF structure altogether. ETFs aimed at specific sectors or following particular styles or strategies – far less common than in developed markets – would help address the problem, and are beginning to take off. As emerging markets grow more efficient, some of these issues will fade, and ETFs' cost advantages will grow stronger.

For now it appears that both investors and, arguably, the emerging markets themselves are paying a price for ETFs' liquidity.

Is there more EM drama to come?

The good times were very good for emerging markets prior to mid-last year. Capital inflows led to currency appreciation which provided the liquidity for domestic investment and consumption booms.

Since the 2008 financial crisis, emerging market foreign exchange reserves have increased by US$2.7 trillion, their monetary bases are up US$3.2 trillion and money supply (M2) has risen by US$14.9 trillion.

Unsurprisingly, that's fueled mammoth property booms. Hong Kong and Chinese residential real estate prices have doubled over the past five years, while Singapore's are up 70%.

Carry trades have partly financed the asset booms. Bank of America Merrill Lynch estimates that emerging market external loan and bond issuance has increased by US$1.9 trillion since the third quarter of 2008.

And the banks are at the heart of this and other financing. Thus, Hong Kong banks have been the go-to for the China carry trade. And their net lending to China itself has increased from 18% of Hong Kong GDP in 2007 to 148% now.

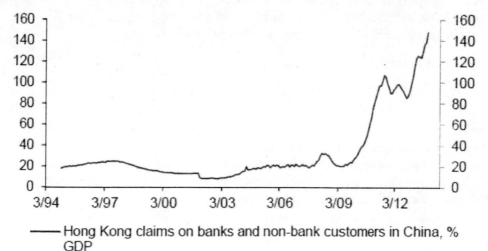

——— Hong Kong claims on banks and non-bank customers in China, % GDP

Source: BofA Merrill Lynch Global Research, HKMA

QE is the trigger for an unwinding of all this. The weakest links, those countries with chronic current account deficits such as Turkey, have been hit first. *Asia Confidential* believes the next in line will be the countries where the largest credit bubbles have occurred.

And that's where China comes into play. Those who insist that China doesn't have a debt problem don't get it. History shows that it isn't the amount of debt, but the pace it's gathered which matters when it comes to potential financial crises.

With this, China is in a league of its own. Since 2008, Chinese total outstanding credit has more than doubled. Its banking assets having grown by US$14 trillion, or the equivalent of the entire US commercial banking sector. Credit growth in the years leading to the bursting of previous credit bubbles - such as the US pre-2008, Japan pre-1990 and South Korea pre-1997 - has been 40-50%. China's credit growth has dwarfed this and it's easy to see the dangers that represents.

I believe the next phase of this crisis will be felt in the banking systems of several countries. China is the obvious one and that's already begun (with some defaults).

Hong Kong banks are among the most vulnerable outside of China. That's not only because of the exposure to lending to the mainland. But overall bank assets now total around 800% of GDP. It doesn't take a genius to work out the disproportionate impact that even a small percentage of those assets going bad would have on the city's GDP.

Australia and Singapore don't have the same direct China lending exposure but the risks to their respective banking systems are high also. The Australian economy is highly dependent on Chinese commodity imports and the country's big four banks have financed a monstrous property bubble off the back of the decade-long mining boom. Moreover, the Australian banks rely on short-term external financing as loan-to-deposit ratios are close to 120%.

The Singapore banking sector is also at risk given its domestic credit boom which has seen bank assets increase to total 650% of the country's GDP. Yes, Singaporean banks have large capital buffers but significant risk remains.

Winners and losers

There are a number of commentators, particularly out of the US, who suggest that the emerging market crisis won't have any impact on developed market economies. They're deluded.

Emerging markets account for more than 50% of global GDP. Moreover, emerging markets ex-China represent a third of global imports. Including China, they account for 43% of imports. An slowdown in emerging markets will hurt their imports and therefore exporters in the developed world.

In addition, the profits of many US and European companies depend on overseas markets, particularly in the developing world. For instance, more than 50% of S&P 500 profits are generated outside of the US.

So the emerging market crisis will substantially impact global economic growth. And stock markets, particularly elevated ones such as the US, are most vulnerable.

Commodities are likely to be hit too. China is the largest consumer of most commodities and a downturn there will reduce their previously insatiable consumption. Even precious metals may be impacted given the deflationary consequences of a China slowdown. Though bullish on gold, we suspect it may break key US$1,180/ounce levels and have a further lurch down before climbing again.

As for the likely winners as the emerging market crisis deepens, *Asia Confidential* would put the US dollar at the top. The reason is that a reduction in the exporting of US dollars will result in less supply amid growing demand. This could well result in a sharp spike in the dollar.

The fate of US treasury bonds is an interesting one. Declining foreign exchange reserves of emerging markets should mean reduced demand for treasuries. In theory, this should put pressure of bond prices. However, given accelerating deflationary forces, we'd suggest Europe and the US central bank will step in to plug the demand gap.

EMERGING MARKETS ARE THE PLACE TO BE BUT AFTER AUGUST 26, 2014

The start of 2014 has seen the global markets decisively in risk-off mode, with global equities falling, government bonds rallying and many emerging market currencies collapsing. Yet few investors currently believe that the risk-off pattern will continue in the developed markets (DM's) for the year as a whole. The bullish consensus for developed equities remains firmly intact, for now.

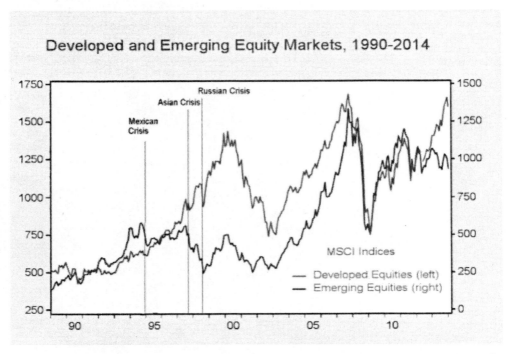

Economic fundamentals in the DM's have not really changed. There have been some mildly disappointing data releases in the US, but these have been mostly due to an excessive build-up in manufacturing inventories since mid 2013, and the prospects for final demand seem firm.

Furthermore, the Fed's tapering of asset purchases has now been clearly separated from its intentions on short rates, which remain extremely dovish. So far, the decline in developed market equities has been very minor compared with the rises seen last year, and do not even constitute a normal pull-back in a bull market.

In the emerging markets (EM's), however, there is much greater cause for concern. As the graph above shows, the EM crises in the late 1990s did not, in the end, prove fatal for equities in the US and Europe, but they did cause occasional air pockets, notably in 1998. This is why investors are focused on whether the current EM crises will deteriorate further, and whether they will eventually take the DM's down with them.

The causes of the crises are not hard to discern, and are familiar from the 1990s. After 2008, many of the EM's tried to avoid the consequences of the Great Recession in the DM's by adopting aggressively expansionary fiscal and monetary policies, believing that their growth miracles of the 2000s could continue.

They were pushed in this direction by the capital inflows that followed quantitative easing by the Fed. Classic, and severe, credit bubbles ensued, with current account deficits widening rapidly in a group of countries that last summer became known as the 'fragile 5' – India, Indonesia, Brazil, Turkey and South Africa (although they have reduced their current account deficit but it is not in the right way). These five remain fragile (although their intensity has reduced), and have now been joined by Argentina, Russia, and Chile. So now we have the 'fragile 8', and the number could grow further.

These countries have many differences, but they also have something in common: a requirement to improve deteriorating balance of payments positions, which are much harder to finance now that the Fed is withdrawing QE. Some of them are inclined to blame the Fed for their predicament, but this is cutting very little ice in Washington. Unlike the onset of the EM crises last summer, the latest bout has not coincided with any change of opinion about monetary policy in the DM's.

Instead, the markets seem to be reacting to the fact that many of these countries need to undertake several difficult policy steps, all at the same time: lower real exchange rates, higher real interest rates, fiscal tightening in some, and structural reforms in many.

In other words, the economic problems of the 'fragile 8' are increasingly being viewed as internal to them, and there is scepticism about the ability of their political systems to deliver the necessary policy adjustments. (Paul Krugman points to the dangers of "economic populism" [1], and makes the case for restrictive policies in some EM's.)

Of course, the slowdown in China has not helped the fragile group, especially those that are dependent on commodity exports. But a dangerous dynamic is now in place, familiar to those who remember the melt-down of the emerging Asian economies after the financial crisis of 1997. Then, China remained immune from the worst features of the crisis, but that did not prevent the rest of Asia from experiencing severe recessions as "sudden stops" in capital inflows forced them to adjust their balance of payments deficits very abruptly.

The decades-long consequences of these sudden stops included a decline in the investment/GDP ratio of 9 percentage points, and a drop in trend GDP growth of 3.3 per cent. **(See Carmen Reinhart and Takeshi Tashiro.)** As the DM's are now discovering, financial shocks have exceptionally long-term effects on economic performance. It is a serious mistake to expect any of this to blow over rapidly.

Optimists claim that there are grounds for hoping that some or all of the fragile group may ultimately avoid the worst fate of the Asian tigers.

Foreign currency debt as % GDP

Troubled currencies			
	1996	2007	Sep-13
Brazil	26%	15% ↓	17% ↓
India	7%	16% ↑	14% ↑
Russia	19%	19% ↑	13% ↓
South Africa	15%	20% ↑	16% ↑
Turkey	17%	28% ↑	30% ↑
Average	17%	20% ↑	18% ↑

More robust currencies			
	1996	2007	Sep-13
Chile		35%	45%
China	9%	7% ↓	10% ↑
Colombia	22%	16% ↓	17% ↓
Czech Republic	17%	29% ↑	40% ↑
Hungary	67%	97% ↑	83% ↑
Indonesia	30%	16% ↓	20% ↓
Israel	9%	61% ↑	20% ↑
Korea	27%	32% ↑	31% ↑
Malaysia	31%	43% ↑	39% ↑
Mexico	47%	20% ↓	30% ↓
Philippines	30%	41% ↑	29% ↓
Poland	19%	37% ↑	40% ↑
Thailand	51%	13% ↓	19% ↓
Average	30%	34% ↑	33% ↑

Source: Nomura, Bloomberg

Note: Arrows indicate increase or decrease since 1996.

One difference is that exchange rates have been much more flexible during the onset of the crisis this time than they were in the 1990s, when most of the relevant economies were trying to run fixed exchange rates against the dollar.

This encouraged an even bigger build-up in external debt in the severe 1990s cases than has happened now (though many EM's do look vulnerable on this score – see Jens Nordvig's table on the left). And the collapse in confidence was all the more sudden, because banking sectors were much more severely exposed to the revaluation of large foreign debts.

This time, the more gradual adjustment of EM exchange rates – upwards before the crisis and downwards now – may provide a shock absorber. Still, the consequences in terms of imported inflation, declining domestic demand and imploding credit bubbles will inevitably be very challenging for policy makers, many of whom have become hubristic after the EM miracle years in the 2000s.

Some will be able to meet the challenge. India, for example, is now doing much better with Raghuram Rajan at the central bank. But others may choose to follow Argentina by refusing to accept the laws of market economics. They will be tempted to monetise the fiscal deficits that will follow economic slowdowns, thus feeding a downward spiral in nominal exchange rates. They cannot realistically hope to be rescued from this fate by "policy co-operation" from the Fed or the IMF; it is largely up to them.

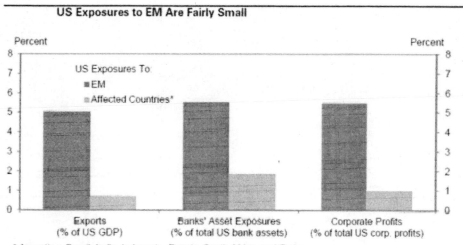

US Exposures to EM Are Fairly Small

* Argentina, Brazil, India, Indonesia, Russia, South Africa, and Turkey.

Source: Jan Hatzius, Goldman Sachs

Could all this develop into a major global shock? Exports to the 'fragile 8' still represent only 0.7 percent of US GDP, so a damaging trade shock is not on the cards. The exports of the euro area are about twice as vulnerable to the 'fragile 8' as the US, and a small number of euro area banks (especially in Spain) are very exposed to loan losses in the EMs. This means that there could be contagion to southern Europe, where some banks may already need to raise large amounts of new capital after the ECB's stress tests.

But the overall consequences for the developed economies still seem largely manageable – always assuming, of course, that China does not hard land.

FOOTNOTES

[1] *Rudi Dornbush and Sebastian Edwards' paper in 1991: "Our purpose in setting out these experiences, those of Chile under Allende and of Peru under Garcia, is not a righteous assertion of conservative economics, but rather a warning that populist policies do ultimately fail; and when they fail it is always at a frightening cost to the very groups who were supposed to be favored. Our central thesis is that the macroeconomics of various experiences is very much the same, even if the politics differed greatly."*

ARE U.K. HOUSE PRICES IN A BUBBLE?

UK house price increases accelerated to 11.1 per cent in May, according to data from Nationwide, a figure that adds fuel to the debate over whether a bubble is developing in the market.

The growth comes a day after the European Commission added its voice to warnings that Britain's housing market– particularly in London – is posing a threat to the UK's economic stability, and urged George Osborne, the chancellor, to act.

The EU executive wants Mr Osborne to calm the capital's housing market by reining in his Help to Buy scheme and increasing council tax on more expensive properties.

Nationwide's price rise last month, measured on an annual basis, compared with a 10.9 per cent rise in April. On a monthly basis, prices rose 0.7 per cent in May. The rapid rises run counter to other indicators that have suggested the market is cooling slightly. The Bank of England says that the number of mortgage approvals had fallen for the third successive month, and stood 17 per cent lower than in January.

On first thought, this could be due to banks changing lending criteria and practices ahead of the introduction of the Mortgage Market Review at the end of April that tightened affordability standards.

The European Commission's report echoes the concerns of Mark Carney, the Bank of England governor, of the potential risks posed by the housing market. It recommends adjusting the second stage of the Help to Buy mortgage guarantee scheme, which is not restricted to new builds, and mitigating risks related to high mortgage indebtedness.

On the shortage of new houses, Brussels said the government has failed to adequately address the "structural phenomenon" of the lack of new houses that is "likely to extend into the medium term".

According to the report, action is needed to further boost the supply of houses – by creating appropriate incentives to raise supply at the local level.

Nationwide data shows that in the first quarter the ratio of house prices for first-time buyers had reached 4.7 times that of their earnings, the highest level since the third quarter of 2008.

However, 'Help to Buy' was by itself, not responsible for driving up prices—the combination of low mortgage rates and growing confidence on the back of improving labour market conditions and the brighter economic outlook are probably playing a much greater role in stimulating buyer demand.

Senior figures at the Bank of England have warned that the housing market now poses the biggest domestic risk to financial stability. But a rate rise is unlikely to be on the agenda for its interest rate setting Monetary Policy Committee.

Action is more likely to come from the Financial Policy Committee that meets at the end of June and which is in charge of maintaining financial stability.

THE EL NIÑO EFFECT: WHAT IT MEANS FOR COMMODITIES

The odds of extreme weather this year have crept up to around 80 percent in favor, according to forecasters, posing a very serious risk to the price of soft commodities.

EL Niño, a climatic phenomenon caused by warm waters in the tropical Pacific Ocean can trigger downpours or droughts and affect temperatures, threatening crop yields and prices.

Investors are now weighing how to be positioned ahead of a possible event.

El Nino related flooding, Salinas, California, February 1998

The International Research Institute for Climate and Society at Columbia University reported a 70 percent chance of El Niño occurring in August, rising to a 75-80 percent probability by October. That could result in weather conditions likely to affect commodity prices generally, particularly softs such as cocoa, coffee, cotton and sugar.

Analysts have been using the ENSO (the El Niño Southern Oscillation Index) an indicator of El Niño events which measures the surface air pressure, as a gauge. Commodity strategists at Societe Generale have found a correlation between commodity prices and the index.

El Niño events tend to develop between April and June and reach their maximum strength during December and February.

Conditions usually persist for nine-12 months, but can occasionally last for up to two years, according to Columbia University.

Sugar, cotton and cocoa prices all respond positively within the first month of a weather shock--all increasing roughly 1 percent immediately.

Sugar prices after that are set to be volatile for six months. Dry weather in India and Thailand, brought by El Niño conditions, often threatens the sugar crops there, reducing global production.

Current price forecasts have us neutral on sugar prices in the current quarter, but bullish in the second half of the year. If an El Niño does materialize, this would add additional support to sugar prices from July to December.

Using the index price movements as a benchmark; Arabica coffee beans, the base for most coffee drinks and which have doubled in price since December, are expected to fall after a shock. Their price will not return to pre El Niño event levels until nine months later.

Investors are seeking agricultural exposure ahead of sowing season as the probability of an El Niño weather event continues to increase.

Earlier this month the Australian Bureau of Meteorology forecast there is a 70 percent chance Australia will be affected by this summer for the first time in four years. With prices of many agricultural commodities likely to rise as weather extremes disrupt production, investors favored positions in diversified Exchange Traded Products (ETPs).

Cocoa prices, which have surged to near record highs this year, are also expected to firm in the second half of the year. Drier weather in West Africa as a result of El Niño and a second consecutive global deficit in excess of 100,000 metric tons set to be recorded for 2013/2014 means prices are likely to strengthen.

The group where I think there is the biggest single factor risk is the palm oil growers and traders. It is concentrated so heavily around Malaysia and Indonesia that they cannot be impacted one way or another, whether that is lower yields or higher prices.

Coffee futures have risen some 20 cents per pound since early November—a 19 percent rise that nearly puts the commodity in technical bull market territory. But that doesn't mean the price of your morning latte is about to skyrocket.

First of all, November's $1.01 marked a seven-year low for coffee futures. Coffee has been under pressure due to high levels of production out of the world's largest coffee grower, Brazil. But supply is expected to be lower in 2014, particularly due to recent inclement weather.

December 2013 was "an extremely wet month" for many parts of Brazil, the NASA Earth Observatory reported. And rain can damage coffee plants, reducing output and consequently boosting price.

At this point, short-term price action is expected to depend on expectations of 2014 supply. But the broader story behind the long decline in prices—which have dropped from $3 in mid-2011—is that producers are finally growing enough coffee to match demand.

Demand for coffee has expanded dramatically for four or five years, and it's taken a while for global supply to catch up.

The increase in demand can be traced to the growing middle classes in emerging markets as well as on consumption in the U.S. that continues to increase. But even as the price has plunged over the past three years, consumers have rarely seen lower prices.

Consumer prices have underpaced the drop, which is of course a boon to companies like J.M. Smucker that produce coffee.

Still, a lot goes into the price of a cup of coffee, or a bag of roasted coffee, besides the beans themselves. That's why coffee that trades on the futures market for $1.20 per pound is sold in Starbucks for $12 per pound, or by specialty coffee roasters like Blue Bottle for as much as $26 per pound.

What you're paying for is the brand, the quality of the roasting and the selection of the beans. There's also a pretty healthy profit margin.

For those who drink more expensive coffee, the price fluctuations in the futures market are unlikely to have much impact at all.

Volatility will persist but unless the early summer harvest falls well short of the expected surplus of 60 million bags, prices will have a hard time getting above $1.50.

WHY U.K. HAS BECOME A TAX HAVEN?

U.S. firms are increasingly eyeing up London for takeover targets to benefit from low U.K. corporate tax rates.

U.S. companies are increasingly viewing the U.K. as a place to relocate to pare their tax bills.

Why? Relatively low tax rates and a business-friendly environment.

Pfizer (PFE, Fortune 500) was the latest high-profile example; it tried to take over the British pharmaceutical firm AstraZeneca (AZN).

American and French media giants Omnicom (OMC, Fortune 500) and Publicis (PGPEF) also planned a mega-merger that would have seen the new firm domiciled in the U.K., though the deal was scuppered.

A U.S. suitor trying to take advantage of a more favorable U.K. tax system has approached the British InterContinental Hotels (IHG).

British corporate tax rates are near 20%. In the U.S., rates are closer to 40% -- among the highest in the developed world. The U.S. also levies high taxes on income that's earned abroad and brought back -- or repatriated -- to the States.

The U.K. rules are not as strict, allowing money to flow home without so many tax hassles. The basic point is that the U.S. corporate tax system is the most onerous amongst the advanced countries. About $1.6 trillion in foreign earnings have been left overseas to avoid U.S. taxes.

Companies find London attractive because of its thriving business and financial scene, a close timezone between Asia and the United States, and easy access via air travel. Comfort with language and culture make a transition to the U.K. easy.

But moving to the U.K. is not as simple as opening an office in London and telling authorities your tax base has changed. The U.S. has blocked this strategy, so a corporate takeover is required.

Today, a U.S. company can only really move to a more tax-friendly nation through a process known as "inversion," where acquisition activity leads a foreign partner to own more than 20% of the stock in the merged entity, among other requirements.

This rule has spurred U.S. companies to consider big British takeover plans, but it's also created a backlash in Washington.

But various proposals in Congress to make it harder for companies haven't advanced. Meantime, companies are scrambling to make a move.

People are trying to get in before the door gets shut--while the opportunity is there, people are taking the chance.

Other companies have passed over the U.K. entirely in favor of even more tax-friendly places.

The U.S. banana producer Chiquita Brands International (CQB) has plans to go to Ireland, where corporate tax rates are about 12.5%. Chiquita agreed to take over Ireland's Fyffes, and the newly merged company will put its legal headquarters in Ireland.

Other countries that are known for low corporate taxes are Switzerland, Singapore and Luxembourg. On the other hand, most companies veer away from France because of its historically high taxes.

WHY QATAR AND UAE ARE ABOUT TO GET MAJOR UPGRADE

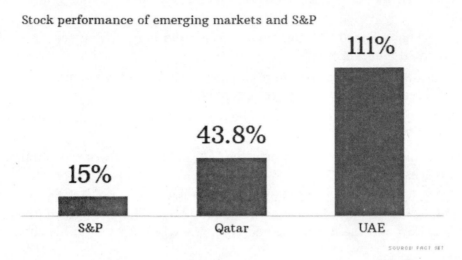

Stock performance of emerging markets and S&P

SOURCE: FACT SET

Think of Qatar and what probably comes to mind is the 2022 World Cup. For the United Arab Emirates, many Westerners likely think of Dubai, the world's tallest building or the setting for the film "Sex and the City 2".

But these two Persian Gulf countries are starting to make a name for themselves for their economies and stock markets.

Both countries will soon be upgraded to "emerging market" status, a step up from their classification as "frontier markets," a demarcation that's not too far off from the Wild West of the investing world.

The change in status by the MSCI will put Qatar and the UAE in the same league as countries like China and Brazil. It will also likely increase the flow of American investment dollars into these Gulf States.

Why does it matter?

When an organization like the MSCI shifts a country between the frontier and emerging categories, it's like a real estate agent tagging a neighborhood as hip or up-and-coming.

The MSCI unveiled the upgrades for Qatar and the UAE a year ago, but the official switch is expected to take place in June this year.

Investors who put money into funds that track the popular MSCI Emerging Markets Index are likely to own more stocks from these Gulf States soon.

The Gulf state growth story

Between 2008 and 2012, Qatar saw its GDP grow an astounding 86%, according to the World Bank, rocketing past other frontier nations like Nigeria and Saudi Arabia. The UAE's economy has grown more modestly over the same period, although still twice as quickly as the U.S.

Emerging market GDP percent growth

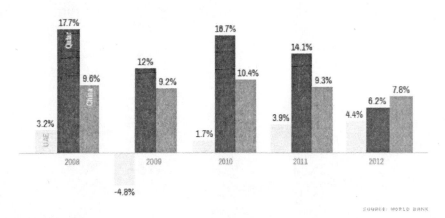

Additionally, the index move announcement last year is part of the reason both nations' stock markets have had such impressive gains. The Qatar Exchange Index is up 44% over the last year, and the UAE's Dubai Financial Market General Index has more than doubled.

Compare that to the S&P 500, a popular American stock market index. It's up 15% in the last 12 months.

Bigger fish, smaller pond

The trick for Qatar and the UAE will be to keep the excitement -- and growth -- up to draw investors when they stop being the big fish of the frontier markets pond. Now these two Gulf states will be in the "big leagues".

Investors looking for emerging markets exposure tend to focus on economies like China. Companies in Qatar and the UAE might only get 1% of the popular emerging market index's weight allocation.

That said, 1% of a larger pie could still leave the Gulf states better off. Around $1.4 trillion is invested in the funds that mimic the MSCI's Emerging Markets Index. That dwarfs the funds tied to the MSCI Frontier Markets Index by a factor of 100.

A word of caution

Keep in mind, however, that the impressive gains in many emerging markets are due in part to risk-chasing "hot money" driven by foreign investors seeking higher yields on their investments. What goes up can quickly go down -- dramatically.

When former Federal Reserve Chairman Ben Bernanke unexpectedly announced last May that the Fed would soon begin winding down its bond-buying program, Brazil's stock market fell nearly 20% over the next two months.

Another risk is that the fortunes of both countries are closely intertwined with energy prices, specifically oil. Energy and financial firms are big players in both economies.

The hope for Qatar, the UAE and other emerging markets countries is that the hot money subsides over time as investors get more comfortable with their underlying economies.

WHY JUNE 4, 2014 WAS A SPECIAL DAY FOR U.K.?

Pomp and pageantry returned to the streets of London on June 4, 2014 as the Queen laid out a package of reforms at the State Opening of Parliament, highlighting a continued path towards energy independence for the country.

The historic ceremony at the Houses of Parliament marked the formal start of the political year. In a speech written by the government, the Queen outlined the legislative program for the coming months which included plans to bolster investment in infrastructure, reform planning laws and opening up sites for potential hydraulic fracturing, known as fracking.

These investment plans, seen as controversial by some campaign groups, will enhance the United Kingdom's energy independency and security by opening up access to shale and geothermal sites and maximizing North Sea resources.

The process of fracking has helped lead a revival in the manufacturing industry in the U.S. with cheaper oil prices, also helping the country to rely less on foreign nations for oil and gas. The U.K. coalition government has seized upon the idea in recent years, using the crisis in Ukraine to show why the country must "urgently diversify" its energy.

The plans have come up against fierce resistance in some areas with campaigners concerned at the demolition of the natural landscape as well as highlighting allegations that it can contaminate water supplies. Greenpeace used the Queen's speech to launch a protest against the fracking laws.

The Queen's speech was the last one of its kind before next year's General Election and Cameron and his deputy Nick Clegg called it "unashamedly pro-work, pro-business and pro-aspiration." The Queen, speaking in front of the House of Lords, said that new laws would make the U.K. the "most attractive place for business" and would promote fairness for low paid workers.

Pensions reform was also high on the list with the coalition government set to allow more freedom and flexibility for people reaching retirement age. Plans are expected to allow pensioners total control over their money and will no longer force them to buy an annuity - an annual retirement income - despite concerns that this will be less secure and promote uncontrolled spending.

Also mentioned in the speech was a law imposing a 5 pence (8 cents) charge on the plastic bags given out by supermarkets.

Low on ideas?

The June 4, 2014 event is one of the highlights of the Westminster calendar and the Queen arrived at Parliament in a new coach marking hundreds of years of U.K. history. The new carriage contains in its bodywork fragments of Henry VIII's warship the Mary Rose, Isaac Newton's apple tree and the Stone of Destiny - used for centuries in the coronation of the monarchs of Scotland.

The first coach of the procession left Buckingham Palace at around 10:40 a.m. London time, which contained the the Imperial State Crown, the Sword of State and the Cap of Maintenance. The third coach transported the Queen and arrived at the Houses of Parliament just after 11 a.m. London time.

Many political analysts have seen the Queen's Speech as a chance for the government to prove that it has not become low on ideas. Ed Miliband, the leader of the opposition Labour Party called for reforms of the country's banks, a freeze in energy bills, wage rises and an increase in homebuilding. Business lobby group The Institute of Directors has meanwhile called for a simplification of the U.K.'s "excessively complex tax system" but applauded the overall message of the Queen's words.

IS INVESTMENT STYLE EMBEDDED IN YOUR GENES?

Warren Buffett and Carl Icahn have been much envied for their investing skills, but new research argues that your genes play a significant part in determining the type of investor you become.

Up to 25 % of investment decisions are down to genetics, according to economists Henrik Cronqvist and Frank Yu from China Europe International Business School (CEIBS), and Stephan Siegel from the University of Washington.

They conducted a study of 35,000 identical and non-identical twins in Sweden to look at what determines an individual's "investment style" – whether they are value or growth investors. Identical twins, which are genetically identical, were used to find out if any difference in investment style would be due to environmental factors, while the non-identical twins were used as a control.

What they found is that it is nature and nurture – it's both your genes and your environment that affect how you invest.

With regards to nature, the economists argue that investing style has a biological basis, with a preference for value versus growth stocks partially ingrained from birth.

'Warren Buffett gene'

There is such a thing as the 'value gene' - or the Warren Buffett gene – but this a bit of an oversimplification--It's probably not one gene, it's probably a complex set of different genes that are involved.

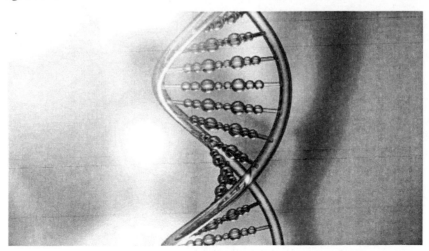

The economists looked at the differences in the investment portfolios of the twins – both identical and non-identical - in an attempt to devise what percentage of investment decisions are affected by an individual's genetic makeup.

Some 18 % of variations in investment styles were down to genetics if price-earnings ratios were used as a measure, according to the economists. This rises to 25 % if Morningstar's Value-Growth Score (which enables investors to choose a fund with their preferred style) is used as an investment style measure.

Everyone's DNA forms the framework from which they can develop, and investors certainly have different categories of risk - some people are naturally risk-takers and others are much more cautious.

Compared to the average person I think I am more willing to take certain risks – although I couldn't say how much of that is down to my DNA.

Next generation of cautious investors

When it comes to nurture, the study found that an investor's style is also affected by their experiences, both earlier and later in life.

Those investors that have had tougher upbringings, that were poorer - for example, Great Depression babies - are more likely to develop a value-orientated investment style later on in life.

As such, today's budding investors in Europe, for example – whose "impressionable years" have been spent in the midst of an economic downturn – were most likely to have stronger preferences for value investing.

If you get your first job in that period of time, when there's tough economic times, then later on we find that you're more likely to be a value-orientated investor, rather than a more glamorous, growth-orientated investor.

If you came from a background where there wasn't money to splash around, you're not going to be an extreme risk-taker.

SHOULD YOU COMBINE VALUE AND GROWTH STOCKS IN YOUR PORTFOLIO

Fortune favours the brave. And everything comes to he who waits. In these two well-worn phrases lie differing justifications for two different approaches to value investing. Both have merit, but the trick is to combine them.

Value investing has been popular ever since it was promulgated by US academic Benjamin Graham in the 1930s. His idea was that many companies had grown so cheap in the wake of the Great Crash and the subsequent economic depression that it was possible to buy them for less than their intrinsic value.

It received a separate and very different impetus in the 1970s, when a vast research project by two more academics, Eugene Fama and Kenneth French, showed that over time, cheap stocks – which they measured by price-to-book ratio – did indeed outperform. They labelled this the "value" effect.

These approaches are different. But there is also an academic debate over how to explain the Fama and French findings which leads, in turn, to two different kinds of "value" investing. Mr Fama himself, who was made a Nobel economics laureate last year, explains the value premium in terms of risk. Cheap stocks are generally cheap because they are in bad shape and face big risks. Therefore a value effect over time is just what would be expected in an efficient market – higher risk is related to higher long-term returns.

A second explanation comes from behavioural finance, and suggests that markets are inefficient. As humans we get excited about stocks with a great story to tell, and tend to ignore the more humdrum boring stocks that plug away producing predictable profits and dividends. Buying such stocks is a way of taking advantage of inefficiency and in the long run it will pay off. Both approaches are about "value", but they are different.

Brave and patient approach

The effort is now on to systematise both strategies. I label the approaches "brave" and "patient" value, and have a strategy for each. The patient approach involves buying stocks with strong balance sheets and regular dividend yields. This strategy is also called "quality income" and will work well in the long run. The disadvantage is that stolid dividend-payers tend to underperform in a strong bull market, as we have had for five years.

The "brave" approach involves buying the 200 cheapest stocks, relative to their own sectors, in the developed world. This compensates for the fact that some sectors will naturally look "cheaper" on basic metrics than others, and uses a weighted combination of five value measures – price/earnings, forward price/earnings and price/book multiples as well as, for non-financial companies only, free cash flow to price, and earnings before interest, tax, depreciation and amortisation to enterprise value. These companies are reshuffled every quarter, so the index will not ride for long with its "winners" whose share price takes off. It is now available as the SG Value Beta index.

Tying to it might make it a little easier psychologically to do the things that deep value investors need to do, such as buy shares in BP while its oil was still pumping into the Gulf of Mexico.

As Mr Lapthorne points out, the two strategies prove to be remarkably complementary. The "brave" value index has a high "beta", meaning that its fate is linked to the market. It outperforms in good times, and will suffer far greater falls in a downturn. Its ultimate gains come from a rising share price. Meanwhile, "patient" value is less correlated to the market, and delivers its returns by compounding dividends in the long term.

Over the last 20 years, patient value returned 11.9 per cent per year, while brave value gained 14.3 per cent per year, with far higher volatility. In combination they returned 13.4 per cent per year, with lower volatility than that achieved by an equal-weighted market index, which returned a compound 8.4 per cent per year. Wherever the returns from value come from, they mount up in the long run.

Shortage of value stocks

This is far removed from the original Graham approach of buying stocks so cheap that they virtually pay for themselves. But sometimes there are few such stocks. By Mr Lapthorne's own screen, using Graham criteria, barely more than 20 stocks in the MSCI World index now qualify. These do include intriguing names like Intel, BHP Billiton and Vodafone, along with a raft of large Japanese groups, and there is always the option of staying in cash if stocks look too expensive – but it does suggest limitations to the original Graham approach.

And maybe the later Graham would approve. In the 1950s, in retirement, he said he was "no longer an advocate of elaborate techniques of security analysis to find superior value opportunities". He proposed a screen based only on historic p/e, the AAA-rated corporate bond yield, and a test of balance sheet strength.

This seems to be practically a foolproof way of getting good results out of common stock investment with a minimum of work. That could be a good description for the value screens of today.

CHANGING FACE OF AFRICA INC.

Foreign investors pouring money into Africa are increasingly turning away from commodities-led projects to tap into the growing consumer market, while smaller, less-established countries are also getting a bigger lion's share.

The African continent became the world's second-most attractive investment destination in 2013, just behind North America. In addition, Africa's share of global foreign direct investment (FDI) reached its highest level in a decade, at 5.7 percent, while capital investments grew by 12.9 percent in the same period.

But 2013 also saw some major shifts in investment trends on the continent. Mining and metals, for instance, are no longer the main beneficiaries of FDI and the list of the top 10 countries in FDI projects showed some surprising trends.

Forget mining?

While there is a "dramatic improvement" in perceptions of Africa over the last four years, the usual magnets for foreign investment are losing momentum. FDI flows into mining and metals, coal, oil and natural gas have become less prominent, with their share of overall FDI projects at the lowest-ever level in 2013.

Instead, investors are turning to service- and consumer-related industries. The top three sectors – technology, media and telecommunications, retail and consumer products (RCP) and financial services – accounted for more than 50 %of total FDI projects last year.

The expanding but still underpenetrated consumer market and the improving communication infrastructure boosted investments in RCP, which accounted for 17.5 percent of FDI projects last year.

Although the African consumer market was largely still for basic goods and services; however, this was changing as citizens became richer. More than half of African households are forecast to have discretionary income by 2020.

Nigeria is one of the countries likely to see increasingly diversified FDI flows, despite concerns about political instability and terrorism activities, such as the recent kidnapping of nearly 300 schoolgirls.

Nigeria recently overtook South Africa to become the continent's fastest-growing economy. Nigeria's high birth rate would also boost consumer demand. Already there are more Nigerian babies born every year than there are in the whole of Europe.

Watch out for...Zambia

However, for Africa's less well-established countries, the story may still be about commodities. For small economies, the stuff that will really move the dial is resources. Ghana, Mozambique, Uganda and Zambia continue to be"resource stories".

Zambia is the world's third-largest copper producer and output is expected to double by 2020. The country is also rich in other natural resources, with fertile lands and hydro power, and is considered politically stable.

The Zambian government is also taking steps to develop various sectors beyond the mining industry, by setting up a sovereign wealth fund and boosting investment in infrastructure to develop tourism and agricultural industries.

As for Uganda, investors are attracted by the solid economic growth record, rapid population expansion and currently low per capita consumption. Uganda has also discovered oil, and is on track to become an oil producer by 2017.

Like Uganda, both Ghana and Mozambique have been boosted by recent energy discoveries – oil for Ghana, coal and gas for Mozambique – and the accompanying boom in infrastructure development.

Between 2014 and 2018, Mozambique's economy is seen expanding by 8 percent per year on average. "Mozambique has very strong growth prospects.

WHY EUROPE'S ECONOMY STILL CONTINUES IN THE DANGER ZONE

The latest economic growth figures from the European Union confirm that most of its member nations are struggling. It's time to make some tough, painful choices.

ADAM BERRY/GETTY IMAGES

For the past year, we've been hearing that global growth, and the world's equity markets, will get a major lift from a gradual recovery in Europe.

Indeed, Ireland and Portugal recently returned to the debt markets with well-received offerings, and the Greek government claims it will soon be in a position to issue bonds. Yields on sovereign debt remain remarkably low and stable. It's indisputable that a mood of tranquility has returned to the Eurozone.

But tranquility is not the same thing as progress, as the GDP figures released on May 15 by the Statistical Office of The European Union (Eurostat) alarmingly demonstrate. The 18-nation Eurozone expanded by just 0.2% in the first quarter of 2014, half the figure economists were projecting.

Germany, as usual, was the leader, posting a gain of 0.8%. The problem spots are precisely the places where the comeback is supposedly underway: the beleaguered nations of Europe's southern tier, as well as that tamed tiger, Ireland.

The latest figures confirm that most of these countries aren't improving at all. Italy's economy shrank by 0.1% in the first three months of 2014, matching the average of the three previous quarters. After expanding 0.6% in Q2 2013, France recorded zero growth. Portugal shrank 0.7%, following positive numbers in the preceding nine months. While figures weren't available for Greece and Ireland in Q1, neither country is showing progress. Greek GDP dropped 2.5% in the final three months of last year, and Ireland limped ahead at 0.2%.

The lone nation demonstrating a sustained upward trend, however modest, is Spain. It grew at 0.4% in the first quarter of 2014 after pretty much flat lining for the last nine months of 2013.

It's crucial to understand the divergent courses taken by Germany and the southern nations since the Euro's introduction in 1999, and how those policies have led to the disparate economic outcomes in these nations today. Inflation had always been a big problem in southern Europe. Rates were high, and they also carried a big 'risk premium' because you couldn't be sure that the separate central banks wouldn't do something crazy, causing moreinflation.

The institution of a single currency in Europe led to the creation of a Bundesbank-like European Central Bank that then and now sets monetary policy in a rigorous, predictable fashion. Rates dropped, and government and consumer spending exploded, driving high growth rates. What's often overlooked is that Germany didn't join the party. Germany was the 'sick man' of Europe. It suffered when the Euro was introduced, in contrast to the southern countries. Germany posted miserable GDP numbers in the early 2000s, while Ireland, Greece, and Spain all roared ahead.

Then, Germany made a turn that, in retrospect, seems astounding. Chancellor Gerhard Schroder (who served from 1998 to 2005) championed reforms designed to create a far more flexible labor market. His model was the U.S.

Schroder decisively lowered pension costs and unemployment compensation, and he gave companies more flexibility with hiring and layoffs.

Schroder lost the chancellorship to Angela Merkel in 2005. The fruits of his reforms didn't surface until around 2006, when the German economy emerged as the strongest player in Europe, as demonstrated by its resurgence from the financial crisis.

Big spending inflated wages in southern Europe, and productivity gains couldn't keep up, meaning labor costs in Spain and France for each unit of autos or steel produced grew at a faster rate than in Germany or the U.S. The crash exposed the competitiveness gap in southern Europe and Ireland. Global customers bought less and less of pricey exports from southern Europe.

So, what can these nations do now? It can be solved in one of two ways—one is exiting the Euro so that costs decline in the new currency compared to costs in other nations. The other is a combination of productivity gains and labor cost reductions. That would be the far better course.

The issue is that the troubled nations have done little to unshackle labor markets along the lines of Schroder's reforms of a decade ago.

Europe used to have two great stabilizers, France and Germany. Now it has one. In France, the retirement age is too low, and companies are often run by former government figures and are too politically connected, so that it's difficult for entrepreneurs to challenge entrenched companies. Ths the future of the Eurozone is increasingly on the shoulders of just one stabilizer, Germany.

The severe recession and high jobless rates have not done nearly enough to lower labor costs. In Spain, labor costs are still too high. The southern countries haven't solved the problem of letting wage costs run far ahead of gains in productivity.

Europe's period of economic calm hasn't been put to good use. It hasn't been used for the types of reforms that are needed. The attitude is, the Euro-crisis is over, yields are still fairly low, and we don't have to do anything.

Of particular concern is potential triggers that might undermine confidence in the credit markets. If Greece defaults, it could set off a contagion that would raise rates for the other nations, causing more defaults and a possible exit from the Euro. One would Euro stay in place, and the problem be addressed by the Schroder method.

Southern Europe may have missed its chance. The best time to reform was when times were flush in the mid-2000s. It's far more difficult to undo regulations and restrictions imposed over decades when economies are stalled and budgets are stretched to the limit, making a fiscal spending jolt highly risky.

Europe's leaders keep careening from one "solution" to another, fixating on the German elections, then on asset quality reviews for banks, then on huge monetary stimulus programs to prevent potential deflation. They're missing what really needs to be done. If Europe doesn't make some tough decisions, the market will make choices for them. That would deliver a giant, cracking sound heard round the world.

FASHION COMES FULL CIRCLE

Yesterday's posterboys are getting a hard knock. Biotechnology and internet, the posterboys of the stock market's rise to all-time highs are beginning to come down.

Biotechnology provided the spark, after a complaint in Congress about the price of a drug from Gilead Sciences, the sector heavyweight. This led the entire biotechnology sector lower.

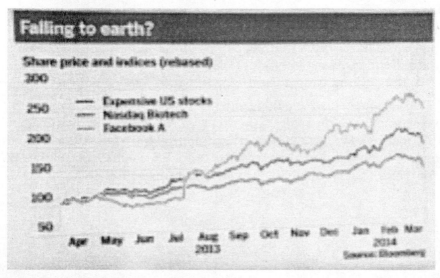

The conflagration spread across all the "story" stocks, those reliant on a tale of growth to justify their hefty valuations. Facebook had its biggest fall of the year, while eight of the biggest fallers in the S&P 500 – itself down, but by less than 1 % – were biotech or internet related.

Having bought expensive shares on the basis that they would get more expensive, when momentum faltered, it is only natural that investors should sell. The unanswerable question is whether downward momentum will build, or if last year's stunning rises can resume and make the shares even more wildly overpriced.

The scale of the fall remains small so far; biotech is down 14 per cent from last month's peak, compared with a 12-month gain of 92 per cent up to the peak. Leading dotcoms and other uber-growth stocks, such as electric carmaker Tesla, are suffering similarly.

Forecasting momentum is a mug's game, but the prospect of earlier rate rises looks like bad news for these shares. In principle, these stocks are most sensitive to interest rates, as profits are discounted back from the far future; in practice, the stronger economy usually pushing rates up more than offsets higher rates. This time might be different, as US bond markets price in higher 2-year and 5-year yields, but keep the economic outlook, and 10-year yields, barely changed. More pain may await.

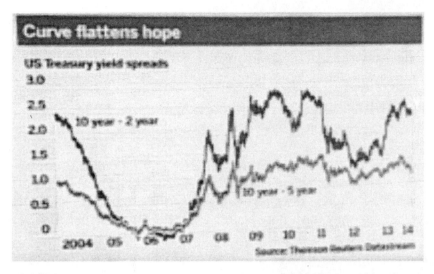

Candy CRUSHED

'Fruity' tech stocks lose their flavor

The makers of the mobile game Candy Crush insist a secret sauce justifies their Multibillion-dollar valuation.

Frankly, if you fill the floor of the New York Stock Exchange with people dressed as large pieces of fruit, you should not expect a welcome. King Digital, maker of the Candy Crush Saga game, was itself crushed on the day of listing and fell more that 15 per cent.

The fall fits the broad pattern of the past month: dotcoms, biotechs and other stocks driven to extreme valuations by stunning performances last year have since plunged. A quarter of the 121 members of the Nasdaq Biotech index lost more than a fifth in a month, with only 21 stocks avoiding a fall.

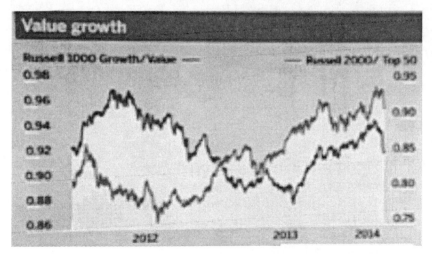

In the above chart, red line indicates relative performance of US growth stocks versus value or expensive versus cheap shares. Higher the line goes, the better the expensive stocks are doing and the lower the line goes, the worse those expensive stocks are doing.

It was not only the extraordinarily expensive shares that were hit, but broader "growth" stocks in general. Value stocks – those cheap on measures such as price to book or price to earnings – have sharply outperformed expensive "growth" stocks. The US Russell 1000 value index hit a new high on Wednesday, even as growth stocks fell again; value stocks have beaten growth by the most over a month since the autumn of 2012.

This switch to value has been accompanied by another move: strong performance of US banks. When Janet Yellen, chairwoman of the US Federal Reserve, raised the prospect of higher interest rates arriving earlier than expected, bank shares leapt. For the year so far they have now beaten biotechs and internet stocks, as well as the wider market.

The jump is natural: the Fed still offers banks free money, and they can now charge more for lending it for a few years.

The question is what can lead the market higher if the dotcom/biotech story is coming to an end. Cheap stocks tend to outperform over the long run, but many are low-quality; a dash for trash often ends badly. Banks offer some hope. They are the most reliant on confidence, so if they take over leadership of the market it would be a solid sign that investors see a return to some sort of pre-crisis normality. They would represent shift from growth into value.

Whether they are right to do so, of course, depends on what happens in the real economy.

Over 93m people play 'Candy Crush Saga' every day. Hundreds of millions of players are familiar with the lollipop hammer in the mobile game *Candy Crush Saga*, which is capable of crushing any of the sweets in the puzzle. But few players understand quite why they find crushing a jelly bean with the lollipop hammer so satisfying – which is the secret this audience at the Game Developers Conference comes to learn.

However, very few players understand quite why they find crushing a jelly bean with the lollipop hammer so satisfying. Is it the sense of gratification from unleashing the pink hammer?

"At the peak of frustration, offer a way to relieve it," seems to be the mantra. Neuroscience teaches that emotions help us to focus our attention and to remember.

The company behind *Candy Crush*, King Digital Entertainment, made 78 % of its $2bn in customer expenditure last year from the game.

King became the hero of these aspiring game makers when it listed on the New York Stock Exchange this. Its justification for a valuation of up to $7.6bn, largely on the back of the success of just one game, rests on its claim that it has discovered the "secret sauce" to creating yet more *Candy Crush*-style hits.

King believed they had a repeatable and scalable game development process that is unparalleled in the industry.

This development process – a blend of creativity, programming prowess and perhaps a little bottled lightning – will be familiar to Hollywood producers, songwriters and novelists in the established media industries.

Yet for investors in the newly hot market of mobile gaming, the question is whether creating a hit-driven yet sustainable business is truly a science. As with playing *Candy Crush* itself, it can sometimes be hard to tell how much of its success is skill and how much is down to pure luck.

It's very similar to movie studios. There are movie studios that have been around for 60-plus years that still can't manufacture blockbusters. They can still screw up.

So, what is the future of Candy Crush? Who are its parallels?

Zynga is another digital game maker that promised Wall Street it had found a data-driven formula for lucrative popularity. But its success was tied to Facebook when gamers' attention was shifting to mobile, and suddenly Zynga's luck ran out. Its stock price remains at little over half 2011's IPO price and a third of its 2012 peak.

King's advocates say that it designs its games with more finesse than Zynga used with *FarmVille* or *Mafia Wars*.

Supercell games include Clash of the Clans and Hay Day

2013 revenues	$892m
EBITDA	$464m

Even its critics agree that Candy Crush is an extraordinarily polished and beautiful game-When you learn how to tap into Pavlovian response patterns in a beautifully sophisticated way, we are hard wired to respond to it.

As its reach grew to 93m daily players, *Candy Crush* struck a cultural nerve.

But if designing the game is where creative talents let rip, keeping players engaged for months is where the science comes in. You can't design fun on a spreadsheet. Once you've found something that is fun then you can actually make it better by just looking at the data and analysing it.

Supercell made $5.2m a day in February from just two games – *Clash of Clans* and *Hay Day*.

To keep players interested, game designers constantly tweak and fine-tune their games. If too many players are turning off at a particular point, they add something new to make it more exciting. Tasks are made easier or harder, while tools can be made more or less expensive to keep players hooked.

Data: you can think of it like the speedometer of your car. Knowing how fast you are going is immensely useful. But you can't use it to set the direction. King argues that it has mastered such data analysis. Its highly tuned marketing machine – into which it pumped more than $300m last year – runs thousands of online advertising campaigns every day in what it says is a highly granular and data-driven way.

Not everyone agrees this is possible – *Angry Birds* maker Rovio has failed to launch new franchises despite its huge installed base – but there are signs that this is working for King.

They have three top 10 hits right now--The problem is that their second hit might be 10 times smaller but that's only because the first one *Candy Crush* is so abnormally enormous.

The business model of mobile gaming has already shifted significantly within the short life of the iPhone. Three years ago a paid-for mobile game such as *Angry Birds* would have been tested extensively and then released in as near to perfect state as possible.

Now, all "freemium" games – which charge nothing to download and play but hope to nudge keen players to pay for extras and power-ups – are released in beta mode, allowing them to be tested in small markets such as Canada, Australia or Finland. The launch is only the beginning and then you keep building and building. The interesting part about it is that it's almost like doing live focus testing with an audience of tens of thousands or almost millions sometimes.

At the heart of how these games make money are a few simple ideas or "mechanics". It's good for people to fail early on in the game. People get enraged: that drives monetisation.

An important ingredient of success is social networking: to encourage players to compete or at the very least co-operate with friends. In *Candy Crush*, getting beyond level 35 (out of 530) requires money, logging into Facebook and asking a friend for help, or waiting several days. Many choose a combination of all three.

Mobile game designers talk endlessly about the "core loop" of a game. This is the fundamental process at the heart of a game that the player will repeat over and over. In *Hay Day*, players first plant crops, before harvesting them, using them to feed animals or start making products, collect the products, sell them and then buy more animals or equipment.

Wooga, the Berlin-based makers of *Jelly Splash*, another popular cartoony mobile puzzler, found that pacing the difficulty of its levels was crucial to retaining players – and monetizing revenue.

The trick is to make the player believe that there is more skill involved than there really is – so it feels more like a simpler version of chess even if it is actually little more sophisticated than a slot machine.

As in casinos, these people are known in the mobile games business as "whales", and they are both lucrative and a concern for many in the industry.

Chasing whales presents own risks for developers. Casual players might be scared off the game entirely if they see that others are spending $50 on a virtual item, while people who spend time rather than money on a game can be angered when others simply buy their way to victory.

The secret of making so much money with games: You need to create a game that people play for years, not months, and those people have to play it a lot...nine or 10 times a day.

And you need to keep bringing in new games frequently. This is the reason why Kings Entertainments' reliance on one game—Candy Crush threatens to jeopardize its market valuations.

WHAT THE TECH CORRECTION MEANS FOR THE WORLD OF IPOS

The boom and now sudden gloom for dozens of newly listed US technology companies is perfectly illustrated by the case of Dicerna Pharmaceuticals.

Three months ago the Massachusetts-based laboratory raised $90m from an initial public offering, with its shares more than tripling on its first trading day to give it a market capitalisation of $816m.

US biotechnology and technology/internet IPOs for 2014, selected
% movement

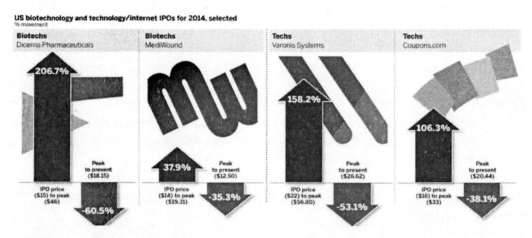

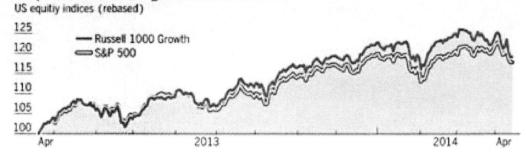

Outperformance of US growth stocks fades ...
US equitiy indices (rebased)

— Russell 1000 Growth
— S&P 500

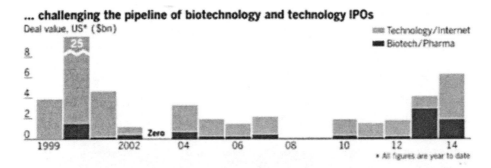

... challenging the pipeline of biotechnology and technology IPOs

Deal value, US* ($bn)

Technology/Internet
Biotech/Pharma

* All figures are year to date

The rush of equity market riches came despite the fact that Dicerna did not have a drug ready for early-stage clinical trials and its IPO featured one of the weakest lock-ups on its existing shareholders in recent memory.

Now, a savage correction in biotechnology, internet and cloud technology companies over the past month has left dozens of companies reeling, including Dicerna, which has slumped 63 % from its peak.

The Nasdaq Biotech index, which rose 65.6 % last year, surged a further 20 % to a record by late February. This collection of 121 companies has subsequently declined more than 20 per cent from that peak, officially satisfying the definition of a bear market.

It leaves bankers and investors grappling with the possibility that the most attractive window since the dotcom era to lure stock buyers with ultra-speculative start-ups has slammed shut.

Last week four companies, including two early-stage biotechs, delayed or postponed their listings.

Beyond biotechs, the sharp market sell-off has also afflicted some of the most high-profile internet and social media companies like Google, Facebook and Twitter, which have all suffered share price tumbles. Concerns are growing that the loss of faith in high valuations from these sectors may spread into other parts of the US market, including into the high-yield bond market.

Investors say the setback is fundamentally changing the landscape for companies preparing to pursue an IPO on the US market.

The escalation in risk aversion is likely to be more severe among investors when they gauge the prospects for the next batch of fast-growing companies seeking to go public before they have managed to turn a profit.

Historically, IPOs without positive earnings have produced lower long-run returns for investors than profitable companies have, so it is understandable that the deals most at risk are those of companies that have not yet achieved profitability.

Of the 48 biotech or tech companies to go public in 2014, only five had been profitable. So far this year, that group has averaged an impressive first day "pop" of 26 per cent, but have dropped 6 per cent on average after their respective first day of trading, according to data provider Dealogic.

One test for the IPO market came recently as lossmaking Sina Weibo, China's answer to Twitter, sought to raise up to $437m from a US listing. Sina, its parent company, has already cut its valuation expectations as tech stocks have plummeted.

Sina Weibo sees shares jump 19 percent on first day of trading

Billed as China's Twitter service, Sina Weibo has debuted on the US Nasdaq exchange. Depsite a less than desired IPO, shares jumped 19 percent in its first day of trade on Wall Street.

Weibo stock soars after Nasdaq IPO

Weibo stock soars after Nasdaq IPO

Ahead of its debut on the Nasdaq stock exchange, China's Twitter equivalent Sina Weibo sold 16.8 million US depository shares at $17 (12.3 euros) each, raising $258.6 million.

The IPO was less than the company had hoped for, however once the bell rang Thursday, a spate of buying suggested that Wall Street is still welcoming loss-making technology companies. Weibo shares rose from $17 to as high as $24.28, before ending the day at $20.24 (14.65 euros).

Weibo plans to use the IPO's proceeds to repay loans and invest in its business.

Growth potential

Sina Weibo was launched in 2009 to provide services akin to Twitter which is banned in China. Last year, the firm tripled its revenues to almost $188 million, while still incurring losses to the tune of $38 million. It's reported to now have about 144 million active users.

But Weibo has been facing questions about the growth potential of its user base as well as rising competition from domestic rivals including Tencent's WeChat, an instant messaging platform allowing users to send text, photos, videos and voice messages over mobile devices.

Chinese tech companies are increasingly eager to go public in the US. According to media reports, the country's huge Alibaba online retailer is going to present its US IPO project shortly. It could become the biggest tech IPO of all times, even eclipsing Facebook.

Bankers say the reception of the Weibo deal will probably set the tone for how a handful of lossmaking tech groups that are preparing second-quarter listings will fare. That includes Box, the enterprise software company, and JD.com, widely considered China's main rival to Alibaba, the e-commerce giant preparing a listing for later this year.

The Russell Growth 1000 is under particularly close surveillance, as the index, which favours high-growth companies, had outperformed the S&P 500 by 4.3 per cent over the past year at its peak in early March. That gap has narrowed to just 1 per cent after the recent sell-off.

For Dicerna, the change in tech stock fortunes means the pressure to make real progress on its treatments has intensified. As for lossmaking private companies, patience may become a virtue that they have to develop before investors are willing to supply them with fresh capital.

THE LISTING OF ALIBABA.COM

In weeks or perhaps days, investors will have an answer to the most popular guessing game in the world's markets right now: just what is Alibaba really worth and on what basis are those numbers calculated? The Chinese ecommerce giant is expected soon to file its initial documents for a public offering in the US, revealing for the first time what goes on inside a company estimated to control 80 per cent of China's ecommerce market.

Calling Alibaba China's Amazon.com is misleading—as the Chinese company's business model is different from Amazon, e-Bay or any other U.S. e-commerce competitors. In some ways, the Chinese company, which serves as an advertising platform for numerous entrepreneurs that rely heavily on Alibaba to generate traffic for their online retail operations bears some similarities to Google Inc.

The tech company behind the largest and most-anticipated IPO of the year doesn't trace its roots to Silicon Valley, a Harvard dorm room or MIT lab.

Alibaba was founded 15 years ago in the modest Hangzhou, China apartment of Jack Ma -- a former English teacher who started the company with an initial investment of $60,000 kicked in by 18 friends.

The company has since evolved into the dominant force in China's e-commerce industry, a market with so much potential that Alibaba's IPO may be the largest ever by a tech company -- surpassing even the $16 billion raised by Facebook.

Alibaba is often described as a combination of Amazon (AMZN, Fortune 500) and eBay (EBAY, Fortune 500), with some PayPal sprinkled in to boot. But the shorthand fails to capture the breadth of the business model dreamed up by Ma.

By one estimate, almost four out of every five dollars spent online in China are spent in Alibaba's marketplaces.

On last year's Singles Day -- China's version of Cyber Monday -- sales on Alibaba's shopping sites clocked in at $5.7 billion, more than double America's Cyber Monday figure.

The company's top two e-commerce sites, Taobao and Tmall, attract more than 100 million unique visitors each day, on par with what Twitter (TWTR) reported before its IPO.

Unlike Amazon, the company does not sell directly to consumers. Instead, it allows users to search the merchandise offered by sellers in thousands of digital stores.

The website design is distinctly Chinese. Each page is crammed with products in an effort to mimic a crowded Chinese market. Buyers and sellers often use a built-in messaging service to chat with each other, and haggling over prices is standard.

Alibaba is more than its flagship marketplaces. It also runs a wholesale operation, a cloud computing business, and Alipay -- a digital payment service. In a first step into finance, the company has started to offer investment funds.

The scale of the business is massive -- and profitable.

Yahoo has a 24% stake in Alibaba, and its financial reports offer a peak at the company's earnings. Alibaba's sales rose 66% in the fourth quarter of 2013 versus the year prior, while earnings surged 110% to $1.4 billion. In the most recent quarter, Facebook (FB, Fortune 500) reported income of $523 million and Amazon earned $177 million. Twitter has yet to post a profit.

The results have led analysts to produce sky-high forecasts for Alibaba's valuation, with some reaching more than $170 billion. One of Alibaba's biggest assets is Ma, who has stepped down as CEO but remains chairman of the company. He's a charismatic leader with a reputation for bold ideas.

Before founding Alibaba, Ma was twice rejected from a teaching college and was even turned away by a local KFC restaurant. But he has flourished as a tech executive, surviving a series of challenges from companies including eBay, which bought Chinese auction competitor EachNet in 2003.

Ma attributed his triumph in that case to Alibaba's home field advantage.

"I know the Chinese user market and users better than [former eBay CEO] Meg Whitman," Ma told the Wall Street Journal in 2005 as he stole market share from the American firm. Now, Ma and other Alibaba stakeholders are eager to retain their control over the company, something that complicated its search for a suitable listing exchange.

Hong Kong is the preferred destination for many of China's top companies seeking to go public, but Alibaba chose to list in New York after Hong Kong regulators refused to allow the company's partners to appoint board members. Other challenges are on the horizon, especially from rival Chinese firm Tencent, which has been spinning a web of mobile, telecom and online retail businesses that rank among the largest in the world.

It's best known as the operator of QQ, a desktop messaging service, and mobile messaging app WeChat.

Tencent is already public, and one of the best performing stocks of the past decade, increasing almost 13,000% since listing in Hong Kong in 2004. The firm now boasts a market cap of $125 billion -- more than McDonald's (MCD, Fortune 500) or Boeing (BA, Fortune 500).

Alibaba's revenue is much smaller than Amazon, because Alibaba itself dosen't sell products. Alibaba dosen't operate its own online store; instead, the company runs websites where millions of merchants can sell products to consumers and business customers.

Like ebay, Alibaba's online shopping sites are marketplaces where many merchants come in and sell their products directly to customers. But Taobao, Alibaba's biggest shopping site with more than 7 million sellers and 800 million product listings dosen't charge any commission fees on transactions.

Taobao makes mone because many merchants pay to advertise on the site as they try to stand out among several million merchants and attract consumers. Many of those ads are linked to Taobao's own search engine. When consumers type in keywords in the search box to look for certain items, the site shows not only search results but also ads for products related to the keywords.

As Taobao launched in 2003, has grown exponentially over the past decade, the site's revenue has grown with merchants spending more on ads to secure page views for their item listings.

Other than Yaobao, Alibaba also runs another site called Tmall, a marketplace for larger merchants and major brands like Nike Inc. and Gap Inc., where each seller pays a deposit as well as a commission fee on each transaction.

Last year, combined total volume of merchandise handled by Taobao and Tmall surpassed 1 Trillion yuan, or about $ 160 Billion, according to Alibaba. That figure was larger than Amazon's 86 Billion or eBay's 67.8 Billion.

The Chinese ecommerce giant has yet to choose a stock market venue but that does nothing to diminish its status as the world's hottest big listing-in-waiting. Most polls of analysts give Alibaba a market capitalisation above $100bn and, increasingly, north of $150bn. Pricing a company where so little information is available is more like a party game than a serious exercise.

Even so, hand over that blindfold. Combing through filings by Yahoo, a 24 per cent owner, gives Alibaba-watchers numbers for sales, gross profit, operating profit and net profit. Sales rose 65 per cent in the year to end-September 2013, while profits jumped fourfold – an increase not explained. Alibaba has only produced net profits from operations since 2011.

Try predicting earnings with any degree of confidence off that. Assume, say, that sales this year continue to grow at their most recent rate of 51 per cent. Use a net margin of 14 per cent – the rate in 2011 and 2012 – and full-year net profits by September 2014 would be $1.42bn. But use instead last year's $2.85bn profits, raise that by 51 per cent, and net income reaches $4.3bn.

Choosing comparisons to provide market-sanctioned multiples is as tough as predicting profits. Rakuten, arguably Alibaba's closest peer, given its similar model, trades on 33 times forecast earnings – racy for Japan but so-so for hot internet stocks in Asia.

Tencent, the Hong Kong-listed Chinese internet giant, trades on 38 times. In the US, valuations are far higher: Facebook trades on 53 while Amazon offers a mind-boggling 185. Applying those multiples to the two profit figures gives a range of $46bn to $795bn. It is not hard to come up with $100bn-plus. Still, hand over the pin and point out the donkey, please.

Unusually for such a large and visible company, current estimates of its value range from the $80bn implied by some synthetic securities to the $150bn-plus suggested by optimistic analysts comparing it with other highly valued internet stocks – and come in spite of the drubbing technology stocks have suffered in the past month.

The true valuation of Alibaba.com

Noble.

It works by taking long positions in Alibaba's main listed shareholders – Japan's SoftBank and Yahoo of the US – and then trying to isolate their stake in Alibaba through short positions. For example, SoftBank, which holds more than a third of Alibaba, also owns a sizeable chunk of US mobile operator Sprint as well as online gaming companies GungHo and Supercell.

For unlisted businesses – such as SoftBank's main telecoms unit – investors short out a similar publicly traded entity, such as Japanese rival KDDI. The process is part art, part science, and ultimately educated guess work.

The value implied by at least one version of these certificates was just over $80bn when Alibaba finally announced its intention to list in the US last month, according to a simple index put together by Bank of America Merrill Lynch.

However, analysts at the bank believe there to be a roughly 20 per cent discount to the true value of an Alibaba holding company, which would bring the valuation closer to $100bn.

Either way, the instrument is highly volatile. In the past year, the yen-denominated index has been almost double the current level, and almost half it – largely because of swings in the Japanese stock market rather than expectations over Alibaba's true size. But thanks to the mix of long and short positions it has not tumbled in line with global tech sector stocks over the past two months.

Even after recent falls, SoftBank and Yahoo have both enjoyed share price rallies of around 130 per cent since Alibaba sold its convertible bond in September 2012.

Convertible bonds

Would-be buyers of Alibaba's unlisted shares and convertible bonds have recently been making offers that value the group at $120bn-$150bn, according to bondholders and others involved in the market, write Sarah Mishkin, Naomi Rovnick and Arash Massoudi.

That is a sharp contrast with 2012, when Alibaba issued the $1.6bn convertible bond to a small group of investors including Singapore's Temasek and GIC.

At the time, Alibaba was valued at less than $40bn, two people with direct knowledge of the situation said. Under the terms of the deal, the bond will convert into equity upon completion of an IPO.

One share sale in February showed how dramatically its valuation has already changed. US investment fund Tiger Global bought a stake in Alibaba from Giant Interactive Group, a Chinese games developer. The sale valued Alibaba at around $128bn, according to calculations by Reuters. Investors with knowledge of the transaction say the actual valuation was slightly higher after accounting for fees and the structure of the deal, which went in part through Yunfeng Capital, a private equity fund co-founded by Alibaba's founder Jack Ma.

However, the valuation reflected by such share sales is complicated by the fact that the market is highly illiquid. Investors say many hedge funds trying to buy shares are unable to find a seller, even at valuations close to $150bn.

Still, the implied threefold gain in Alibaba's valuation follows a substantial rise in the share prices of its publicly traded rivals such as Tencent and Baidu. Much of those gains, equity analysts say, are because investors are increasingly confident that tech companies in the US and elsewhere have proven that they can profit from smartphone users.

Multiples

Comparing Alibaba to its peers is in theory the most simple and reliable form of valuation. The problem is the lack of information on Alibaba – and a dearth of truly comparable companies.

The most cited examples are Facebook, Tencent and Amazon. The first is the least similar business but like Alibaba it is something of a phenomenon, the second works if investors believe that all big Chinese internet companies are similar and the last actually sells goods but using a very different model to Alibaba. Rakuten, the Japanese online retailer, is probably the straightest comparison because, like Alibaba, it operates a marketplace in which it charges fees, rather than selling its own goods – the model that makes up the bulk of Amazon's business. It does, however, own a baseball team.

The only information investors have on Alibaba, until it files with the US Securities and Exchange Commission, come from the quarterly updates of Yahoo, its one-quarter owner. These give basic profit details. Yahoo's latest update shows that Alibaba had a bumper end to 2013, a year in which it produced $3.5bn in profits.

Facebook trades on 100 times last year's earnings while Amazon is valued at a dizzying 500 times. Tencent and Rakuten are on 50 and 40 times, respectively. Applying those multiples to Alibaba's 2013 earnings makes it worth between $141bn and $1.76tn. That last number is ridiculous. But comparing Alibaba to Rakuten produces $141bn and $176bn – bang in the range that the more optimistic analysts have bandied about.

"FRAGILE FIVE" OR "HIGH FIVE" CURRENCIES

Forget 'fragile', these are 'high five' currencies. **The so-called "fragile five" currencies are instead "fabulous," and investors should buy into them.**

The strong performance of the so-called "fragile five" currencies has marked a return to favor for the so-called carry trade, so much so that currency traders have re branded the group the "high five".

The five currencies -- made up of the Brazilian real, Indian rupee, Turkish lira, Indonesian rupiah, and South African rand -- are among the top-performing currencies since the end of February and are the best way to play lower volatility in currency markets this year, analysts have said.

An employee uses a machine to count a bundle of 100 Turkish lira banknotes inside a currency exchange office in Istanbul, Turkey.

What is the answer in FX to low volatility – buy carry, and that is what we have been suggesting since February. Buy the fabulous five or the high five – these aren't the fragile five anymore.

The carry trade, the strategy of borrowing in low yielding currencies to buy assets that yield a higher rate, was shunned last year as volatility in emerging market currencies spiked over fears of the winding down of U.S. stimulus.

But U.S. Federal Reserve chair Janet Yellen's reassurance that the Fed's unprecedented bond-buying program would be needed for "some time" has supported EM currency and encouraged investors to take on more risk.

Big swings in foreign exchange rates can make carry trades very risky, but the current low volatility is near record lows for developed market currencies, supporting the carry trade and EM currencies.

Interest rate volatility and demand for protection against extreme moves in the dollar have dropped significantly, with the JP Morgan FX volatility index at it lowest levels since 2007.

What you do is you pick up these currencies in Brazil, India, Turkey, Indonesia and South Africa and you just sit there and if there no volatility, you just take that yield on. In a low volatility environment, there is an answer in terms of trading and that is to buy the fabulous or high five.

Current account deficits in EM countries, a key concern for investors, have "melted away" in recent months. Since last year, the current account deficit for the five-country group has made a "remarkable adjustment".

It now stands at some 4.2 % of GDP (as of Q4-2013), against 6.2 % six months earlier providing an opportunity for investors to be long the currencies.

Given the sharp recovery in risk appetite, we would argue that those currencies that were targeted by aggressive speculative attacks last year now present a buying opportunity.

The Indonesian rupiah has been the best-performing currency of the year despite being among the "fragile five" -- but carry traders needed to be selective.

Recent hikes in interest rates by EM central banks have taken carry to attractive levels. However, any carry longs will need to be selective, with local growth and competitiveness stories and sensitivities to Fed tightening still very heterogeneous.

The concept of the "fragile-five" emerging markets is somewhat "misguided," as many of the countries have shrunk their current account deficits.

I use the word "somewhat" because countries like India have curbed their current account deficit by artificially curbing gold imports. Once they return to normal, there could once again be pressure on their currency.

Concerns about these five currencies grew in January and February of this year, when a combination of Fed tapering and slower growth in China sparked a selloff of emerging market currencies and stocks that had investors drawing parallels to the 1997 Asian financial crisis.

Fast-forward fourmonths, however, and those countries' currencies are looking anything but fragile. Bloomberg's index of 20 developing-country currencies has fully regained its losses from earlier this year. By April 10, the Turkish lira had surged 10.2 percent from its 2014 low on January 24, the Brazilian real 9.8 percent from February 3, and the Indonesian Rupiah 7.2 percent from January 27. And the South Korean won is at its strongest level against the dollar in more than five years.

The Fragile Five countries now boast five of the six most attractive emerging market carry-to-volatility ratios, an indicator that measures the attractiveness of a carry trade given its underlying risk. The fragile five could transition into the formidable five.

Why the quick turnaround? Most importantly, the fundamentals look good. At the height of the emerging markets rout in February, I had written that a full-blown crisis was unlikely because developing economies were stronger than in previous panics. This is still the case. Emerging markets have lower levels of external debt (25 percent of GDP compared to 40 percent in the 1990s), healthier trade balances, and higher levels of foreign exchange reserves (30 percent of GDP compared to 10 percent in the 1990s).

Another factor is that long-term U.S. yields have been more stable than markets appear to have been anticipating. Yields increased last month after Fed Chair Janet Yellen suggested policymakers could raise interest rates as early as the spring of 2015. But subsequent assurances by Yellen that the central bank intends to keep rates low for quite some time have eased concerns of a sooner-than-expected rate hike.

At the same time, some emerging market central banks, such as South Africa and Turkey, have raised interest rates this year, making their currencies more attractive relative to near-zero U.S. rates. Finally, global business activity, as measured the Purchasing Managers' Index, grew in the first quarter, helping emerging market sentiment.

If U.S. yields stay steady, I see potential out-performance by the Russian ruble and Turkish lira among emerging market currencies in Europe and the Middle East. Russia's fourth-quarter current account surplus was revised upwards while Turkey's foreign trade deficit was narrower than the market expected, and both of their central banks have tightened significantly. Any signs of easing by policymakers would jeopardize that outlook, although that looks unlikely to occur in the coming weeks. Turkey's trade deficit was narrower than expected in February

In Latin America, I am bullish on the currencies of both Mexico and Colombia. The Colombian peso is attractive in part because JPMorgan increased the country's weight in two of its local-currency bond indices, a move that should fuel more demand for its bonds and thereby increase currency inflows. As for Mexico, the country's strong credit standing makes its peso attractive. In Asia, the South Korean won seems likely to continue to shine. The Indian rupee, while currently attractive, is also more vulnerable to an eventual increase in U.S. yields.

However, a word of caution: there may not be much life left in the carry trade, as U.S. rates are still expected to start heading upward at some point in the coming months. Yields on 2-year notes could rise to 0.5 percent by summer (up from 0.36 percent on April 9), and 10-year yields to increase to 3.1 percent from 2.7 percent. That suggests the need for caution in chasing the carry trade.

CHINA'S TWO STOCK MARKETS

China's stock market may have spiraled downward for years, but new economy shares have actually surged, creating opportunities in more traditional sectors.

It's been a tale of two markets.

We've had a big flurry in the new economy stocks--see outsized gains in some shares of clean technology, green energy and solar companies.

For example, the Hong Kong-listed shares of wind-farm operator China Longyuan Power surged over 85 percent in 2013, although it's shed a bit more than 12 percent so far this year. Likewise, GCL-Poly Energy, a producer of solar-grade polysilicon and an operator of co-generation plants, saw its Hong Kong-listed shares climb more than 60 percent in 2013 before tacking on nearly 9 percent so far this year.

At the same time, the Shanghai Composite has shed nearly 6 % since the beginning of 2013.

Since the beginning of this year, around $6.48 billion has flowed out of China equity funds, with another $1.48 billion leaving Hong Kong funds, according to data from Jefferies.

The traditional economy stocks -- the industrials, the banks -- all of that kind of stuff has been left behind and that's created a lot of opportunities in the market-- these are stocks that are cheap and very profitable. And you don't normally get to say those two things at the same time.

The selloff has left the MSCI China index trading at around 8.8 times 12-month forward earnings, a near 27 percent discount to its long-term average of 12 times.

Among the traditional economy sectors, banks are trading at 4.7 times earnings, a more than 50 % discount to long-term averages, while property shares are at 6 times, a more than 40 % discount, the data show.

To be sure, not everyone sees the valuations as a buy signal.

How can China achieve sustainable growth?

China needs structural reforms that can correct imbalances in its economy.

People are concerned about the credit quality. People are concerned about the future movement of housing prices-- property transaction volume and sometimes prices have been declining in some cities. There are cases of defaults (on) trust products (and) corporate bonds. So people are concerned about the quality of the bank loans. That's why we're seeing this low valuation.

At the same time, we know that there's a credit issue. We know roughly where that credit is - it's in the local government financing vehicles, it's in the SOEs (state-owned enterprises). There are some great opportunities in the financial sector now. Valuations are cheap and attractive.

IS MORE AGGRESSIVE MONETARY STIMULUS ON THE WAY FOR CHINA?

China's decision to lower the reserve requirement ratio (RRR) for some county-level rural commercial banks recently has led investors to question whether broader monetary stimulus is in the offing.

Following the release of softer-than-expected March activity data, the State Council announced that it was cutting the amount of cash that village commercial lenders must hold as reserves in an effort to increase financial support for the agricultural sector. It did not specify when or by how much the RRR would be cut, saying only that an appropriate reduction would be made for qualifying banks.

I don't expect the amount of liquidity released to be significant for the economy. Nonetheless, this is another loosening signal from the government, which suggests it is probably more concerned about the economic outlook.

I continue to expect the government to cut the RRR for the whole banking sector in May or June.

How big is China's bad debt situation?

The amount of non-performing loans in China may be three times larger than what lenders have been reporting.

Decreasing the reserve requirement ratio tends to stimulate economic activity as lenders have more assets to loan out. The central bank last cut its reserve ratio for all banks in May 2012. It now stands at 20 %, near its record level of 21.5 % in 2011 amid an aggressive monetary tightening cycle.

The case for a universal RRR cut - which merely increases interbank liquidity - is "quite weak" as money market rates remain low.

The 7-day repo rate - viewed as a key gauge of confidence to lend in the interbank markets - stands at 2.7 % - far below the 10-plus percent levels seen last June amid a severe liquidity strain in the economy.

The likelihood of a system-wide cut remains low.

The cut in RRR for certain county-level rural banks might be viewed as the rumored RRR cut coming true. But this is an extremely limited targeted loosening as rural commercial banks are a very small part of the overall financial system.

Why you should stay invested in China

China's first-quarter GDP data is "reasonably accurate" and reflects ongoing transition in its economy.

Further very limited and targeted cuts similar to today's cut may happen, but we believe the impact on the overall economy will be too small to be meaningful.

Nevertheless, the bank expects further policy measures to be rolled out in the coming weeks until there are clear signs that the economy is on a stronger footing.

China's economy registered growth of 7.4 % in the first quarter, slowing from 7.7 % in the previous three months, but beating market expectations of 7.3 %. Data released alongside the gross domestic product (GDP), showed industrial output and asset investment for March underperformed market expectations.

I expect these measures will provide support for short-term domestic demand growth in the coming months. I continue to expect second quarter sequential growth to be stronger than first quarter as a result of these loosening measures and the seasonal dissipation of the impact of the anti-corruption campaign.

Towers where no lights burn at heart of China's puzzle

In a steel and coal-mining region of 5m people in the Chinese heartland, signs of economic slowdown are everywhere.

Forests of newly built but nearly abandoned apartment complexes with names such as Fortune Plaza and Golden Riverside ring central Yuncheng while, on the outskirts of town, the district's largest steel mill has gone bust, leaving mountains of unpaid debt and nearly 10,000 idle workers.

Local peasant farmers or debt collectors are the only ones to visit these plants now.

China's economy expanded 7.4 % in the first quarter of the year from the same period a year earlier, a sharp slowdown from 7.7 % growth in the fourth quarter of 2013.

That is still an enviable rate by the standard of most countries but in Yuncheng and other cities across China, the headline figure masks a multitude of growing problems.

The main reason for the slowdown is a slump in fixed asset investment, the biggest driver of the Chinese economy.

In the first three months of the year, investment grew 17.6 % from the same period a year earlier, the slowest pace since late 2002.

The slide was largely owing to declining real estate investment, which also experienced its weakest growth in more than a decade. The situation is certain to get worse in the coming months as new housing floor space under construction contracted 27.2 % in the first quarter.

That was largely a reaction to declining sales, which fell 5.7 % in terms of floor space in the first quarter from a year earlier, with the fall especially pronounced in smaller inland cities such as Yuncheng.

Surveys show clear divergence in price trends with first-tier major cities experiencing mildly rising housing prices. In some second-tier cities prices are shaky and in third and fourth-tier cities, especially those with ample supply, prices have come down.

The fate of China's overheated real estate market is absolutely critical to the health of the overall economy.

Real estate construction directly accounted for 16 per cent of GDP in 2013, according to estimates from Nomura.

At that level China is approaching a dependence on property last seen in Ireland and Spain before the bursting of their bubbles.

Many of the industries already suffering from severe overcapacity in China, such as steel, cement and glass, are heavily indebted and reliant on continued rapid growth in property construction for their survival.

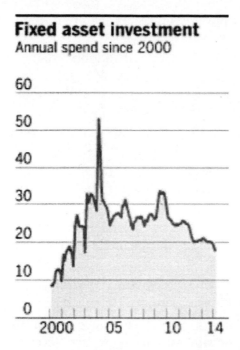

Fixed asset investment
Annual spend since 2000

Source: National Statistic Bureau

Land sales and property-related taxes accounted for 38 % of total government revenue in 2013 and heavily indebted local governments have used highly priced land as collateral for the vast majority of their loans.

A property crash would not only lead to collapsing growth in the world's second-largest economy and largest commodity consumer but would also have a huge impact on Chinese households, which have an estimated two-thirds of their assets tied up in real estate.

In numerous places such as Yuncheng, the crash has already begun. Prices are falling and sales are really terrible because too many apartments have been built and so many of them are empty--Even in a situation like this they are still building new housing complexes.

In the district where the Highsee steel mill has gone out of business, the local government approved 800,000 square meters of new construction last year even though the district's total population is only 300,000.

As night falls in the neighbourhoods of Yuncheng, the nightmare facing the Chinese government is the very few lights blinking on in newly constructed apartment towers.

In the past, and particularly after the 2008 global financial crisis, Beijing has turned to credit-fuelled property construction as the quickest and easiest way to boost flagging growth.

It is the lack of final demand, existence of excess capacities and barriers to private investment that have curbed China's corporate investment and overall growth--Against this background, stronger credit growth will not lead to sustained stronger corporate investment growth, but would likely lead to a continued build-up of unsustainable leverage levels in China's problematic local government debt and property sectors.

Fears grow over China property flameout

There are signs that China's housing market may be significantly overheated.

The risks of a blow up in China's property market are rising, threatening a slowdown that could hurt global growth.

The sector is second only to the related problem of credit growth on a list of threats to China's economy.

Talk of a property bubble in China is nothing new -- economists have long fretted over the meteoric rise of home prices, and the runaway pace of new construction.

Media reports on "ghost cities" -- newly constructed Chinese municipalities that were never occupied -- led to frequent warnings of a crisis, which has not yet materialized.

The sector's continued strength results in a kind of Rorschach test, where the same image is perceived very differently: Pessimists say real estate is emblematic of problems such as rapid credit growth and backward economic incentives. Bulls counter that the boom is sustainable, especially as hundreds of millions of Chinese migrate into urban areas.

The sheer size of the real estate sector -- some 16% of GDP -- underscores the importance of the debate for a world economy that is increasingly connected to China.

The fears of a slowdown have now returned, sparked by a flurry of reports from third and fourth-tier cities that suggest ailing developers are offering big discounts to unload property quickly. Even in some major cities, sales have slowed and homeowners are fretting over lower demand.

The far flung smaller cities account for almost 70% of all home sales, according to Japanese brokerage Nomura.

In China, the true risks of a sharp correction in the property market fall in third- and fourth-tier cities, which are not on investors' radar screens.

Yet it is difficult to make a definitive case that trouble is ahead.

Some statistics point to resilience. One indicator tracked closely by Beijing is the labor market, and that is holding up. Developers may be under stress, but there's no sign yet of a wave of defaults or bailouts.

Official data released by the Chinese government is largely unhelpful in gauging market risk. Prices are only offered for the largest cities, and home ownership statistics are not published.

The lack of data has produced a bevy of "known unknowns" -- or potential problem areas that are known to researchers, but remain clouded in mystery.

How much excess inventory currently exists? To what extent is the banking system exposed? How might Beijing respond in a crisis? Will developers receive government bailouts?

Foreign investors would likely be insulated in the short term because China's equity and property markets are largely closed to outsiders.

The immediate pain would be felt much closer to home. Many Chinese view their property as investments, and huge amounts of household wealth are tied up in real estate. Down payments of 30% are common.

But a housing shock could ripple out to the broader economy, especially the banking sector -- which provides financing to many developers. In addition, real estate is closely tied to the manufacturing and services sectors.

Property sector over investment is the top macro risk because the property sector is currently the keystone of China's economy -- if it slows, systemic risks rise.

Beijing would have numerous cards to play in response to a crisis. Banks and developers could be bailed out, and toxic loans corralled and sealed off from the financial system.

And there's another reason to think the fallout could be contained: Unlike in the United States prior to 2008, China has not chopped up and securitized its mortgages, lowering the risk of contagion.

IS THIS THE END OF 'CURRENCY WARS' ?

Policy shifts in China and Russia are offering hope. This year is likely to bring a significant easing of currency restrictions in the developing world. In particular, policy shifts in China and Russia offer the hope that the much discussed "currency wars" are finally drawing to a close, despite a recent complaint from a US official.

China announced plans for major currency reform during its Third Plenum, a decadal economic planning forum, in November. Zhou Xiaochuan, governor of the People's Bank of China, subsequently said the bank would increase the role of market exchange rates, refrain from normal foreign exchange market intervention, and establish a managed floating exchange rate system based on market supply and demand.

Last month, the central bank announced a further relaxation, widening the amount by which the renminbi can move up or down each day against the US dollar from 1 % to 2 %.

The calls for currency reform have become increasingly familiar since the 2011 debt ceiling crisis in the US. The reason for the pressure last year to pick up the pace of reform was revealed on November 20 when Yi Gang, head of the State Administration of Foreign Exchange which manages China's reserves, said it was "no longer in China's favour to accumulate foreign exchange reserves".

The country had accumulated a further $324bn in reserves in the second half of 2013 (a 9.2 % jump).

Note that China intends to manage the renminbi via a managed float rather than introduce a free floating currency. As a result it is possible the country will still experience intermittent increases (or, indeed, decreases) in its foreign exchange reserves.

In addition the country still has $3.82tn of existing reserves that it needs to manage. As a result no one should expect SAFE to retreat from the markets any time soon. Nevertheless, the pace of reserve growth will probably slow down over the next few years.

Russia is also looking to change currency policy. Announcements from the central bank in October and January made clear its intentions to float the rouble and abandon the current trading band in 2015.

The reform of currency policy in nations such as China and Russia might lead to some bumps along the way for the developed world.

It remains to be seen whether the recent sharp slide in the value of the rouble has dented the bank's drive towards currency liberalisation or whether, in the aftermath of the recent events in Ukraine, the Russian authorities might prove rather more reluctant to continue accumulating assets in overseas markets.

The key question is what impact these changes in policy will have on international markets.

To understand what this might mean it is worth highlighting that by January China had amassed $1.273tn of US Treasury securities, having accumulated an average of $4.9bn a month over the previous 12 months as its forex reserves grew.

Given this, it seems likely that a retreat by China from accumulating fresh currency reserves would also lead to a modest "tapering" of its purchases in a range of government bond markets in the developed world.

The split of China's holdings is a state secret, but International Monetary Fund data reveals the split for around 75 per cent of the reserves held by other emerging market nations.

The numbers show that, as of the end of the third quarter of last year, around 23.7 per cent of these reserves had been diversified into the euro, about 5 per cent into sterling and smaller amounts into the yen, Australian dollar, Canadian dollar and other currencies, while about 61 per cent had been left in the US dollar.

Even if these numbers do not reflect the current split in China's holdings it still seems reasonable to assume that a reduction in reserve growth will lead to declining demand for alternative reserve currencies such as the euro.

So the reform of currency policy in nations such as China and Russia might lead to some bumps along the way for the developed world, including the possibility of a slight rise in borrowing costs for their governments. There is also a possibility that geopolitical issues might muddy the waters. But overall, the liberalisation drive should be seen as good news.

From a domestic perspective it means the central banks of Russia and China can focus far more clearly on battling inflationary pressures when they emerge.

In the international sphere, it is unlikely these forces will have a major influence in the shorter term. Indeed, there are some signs of a fresh flare-up in the "currency wars" right now. However, in years to come these policy shifts mean many currencies whose value has been buoyed by demand from foreign exchange reserve managers, such as the euro and the Australian and Canadian dollars, may finally trade at more reasonable prices.

THE US ECONOMY IN PICTURES

With the economy now more than 5 years into an expansion, which is long by historical standards, the question for you to answer by looking at the charts below is:

"Are we closer to an economic recession or a continued expansion?"

How you answer that question should have a significant impact on your investment outlook as financial markets tend to lose roughly 30% on average during recessionary periods. However, with margin debt at record levels, earnings deteriorating and junk bond yields near all-time lows, this is hardly a normal market environment within which we are currently invested.

Therefore, I present a series of charts which view the overall economy from the same perspective utilizing an annualized rate of change. In some cases, where the data is extremely volatile, I have used a 3-month average to expose the underlying data trend. Any other special data adjustments are noted below.

Leading Economic Indicators

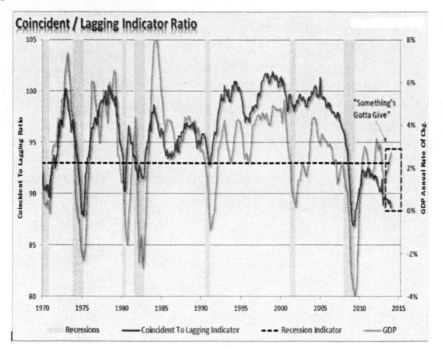

Durable Goods

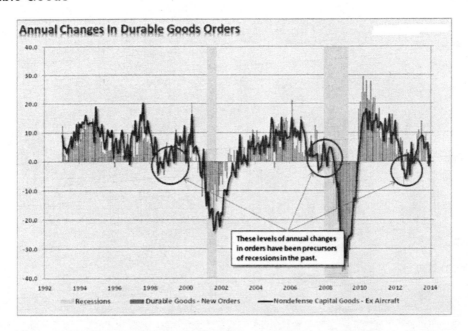

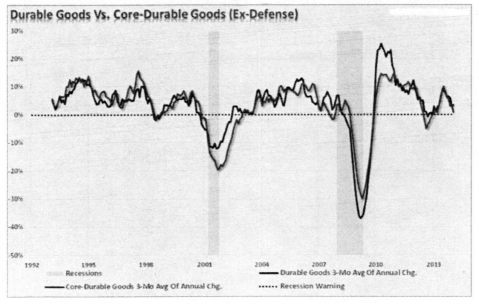

Investment

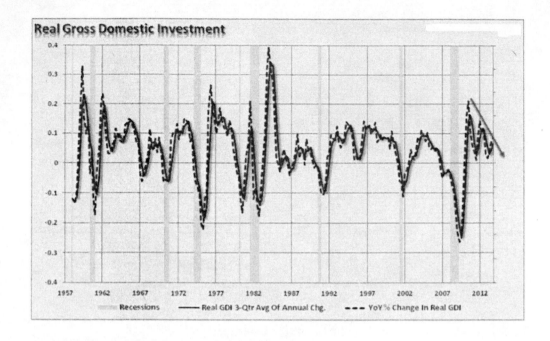

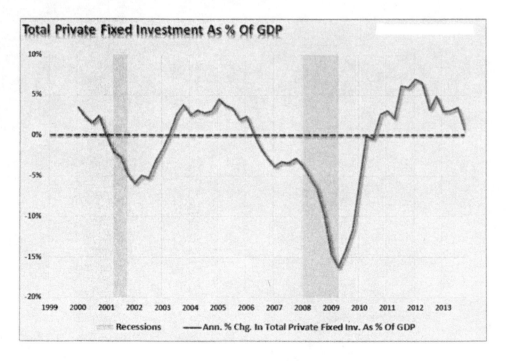

ISM Composite Index

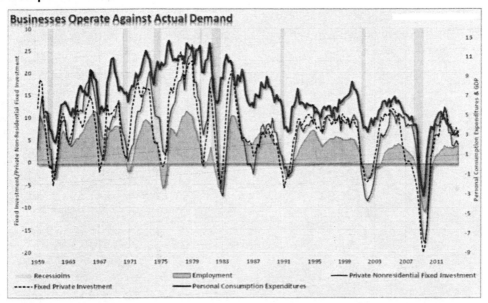

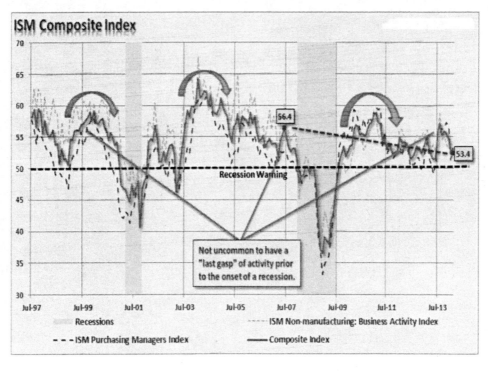

Employment & Industrial Production

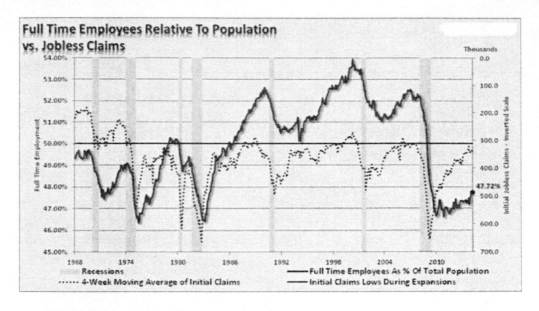

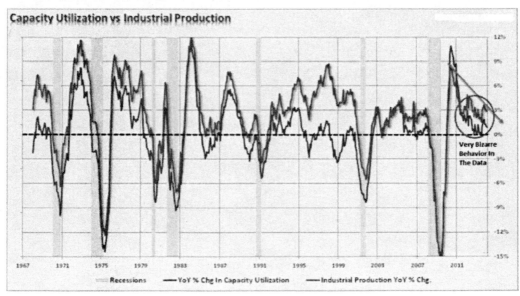

Retail Sales

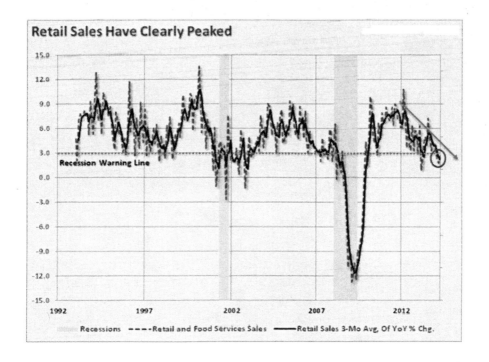

Social Welfare

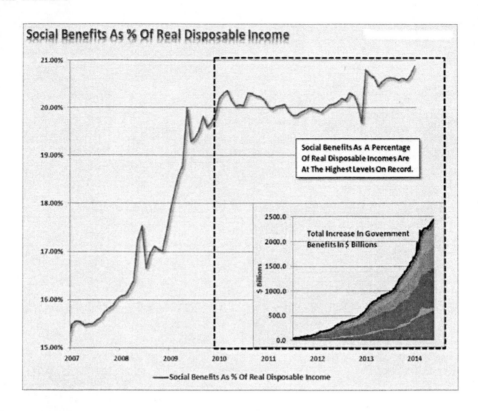

The Broad View

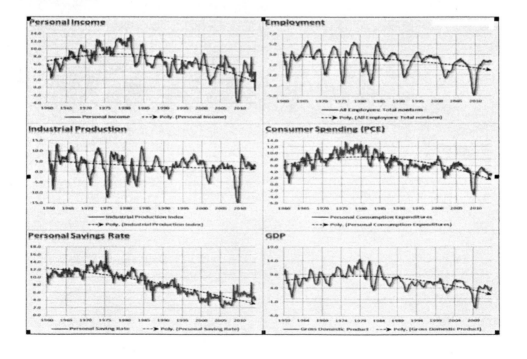

Economic Composite

(**Note**: *The Economic Composite is a weighted index of multiple economic survey and indicators -*)

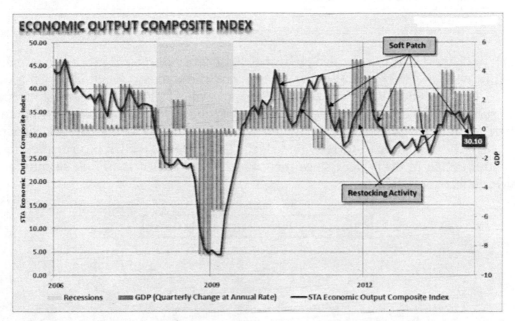

If you are expecting an economic recovery, and a continuation of the bull market, then the economic data must begin to improve markedly in the months ahead. The problem has been that each bounce in the economic data has failed within the context of a declining trend. This is not a good thing and is why we continue to witness an erosion in the growth rates of corporate earnings and profitability. Eventually, that erosion combined, with excessive valuations, will weigh on the financial markets.

For the Federal Reserve, these charts make the case that continued monetary interventions are not healing the economy, but rather just keeping it afloat by dragging forward future consumption. The problem is that it leaves a void in the future that must be continually filled.

In my opinion, the economy is far too weak to stand on its own two feet. With the Fed easing off the current rate of bond purchases, it will be interesting to see what happens in the months to come. While there will certainly be positive bumps in the data, as pent up demand is released back into the economy, the inability to sustain growth is most concerning.

CAN A LOWER STERLING CAN
HELP CUT U.K. DEFICITS?

Last year, the UK ran a fiscal deficit of 6 % of gross domestic product. Its main counterpart, as chart one (below) shows, was the current account deficit – ie, 70 % of the deficit was financed by foreign savings (RoW). (Due to statistical discrepancies, which I have added to the rest of the world, the figures shown in the chart for foreign inflows are almost but not exactly equal to the current account deficit.) The data go back to 1987 and, as the chart shows, the UK has run a current account deficit in every year since then. If the fiscal deficit is to fall, so must the current account deficit.

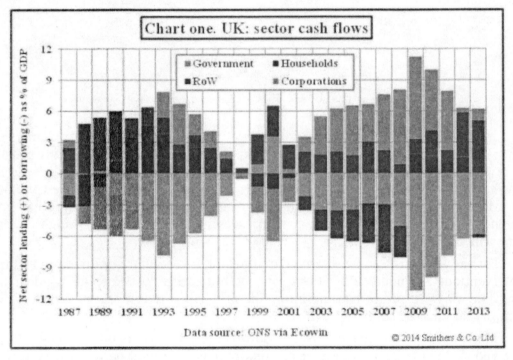

The current account deficit is greater than the trade deficit, but the two move together (see chart two, below). A large improvement in the latter is therefore needed and it is hard to believe that this can be achieved at today's exchange rates.

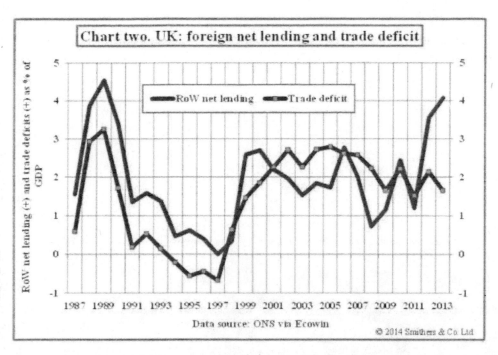

About 70 per cent of the UK's international trade is in goods and 30 per cent in services, whereas goods only constitute about 15 per cent of the UK's total output. Furthermore, what little improvement in the UK's exports that there has been since 2010 has been mainly in goods (chart three).

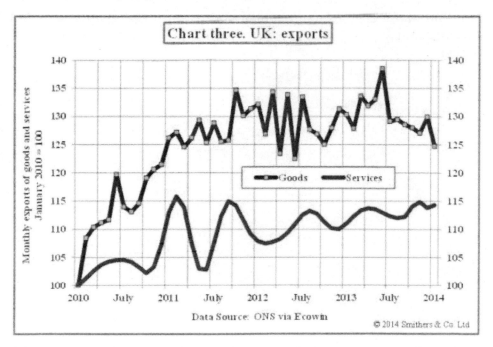

If the UK is to achieve a substantial increase in its net exports, then, there will need to be a significant increase in manufacturing output and, for this to occur, manufacturing must be adequately profitable. Chart four, which compares returns for the output of services (excluding finance) and manufacturing, shows that this is not the case today.

Goods are more open to international price competition than services, so the lower returns that are earned on goods' production points strongly to sterling being overvalued.

WHAT THE WORLD MUST DO TO KICKSTART GROWTH

The post-crisis panic might be subsiding but medium-term prospects are problematic

The medium-term prospects for the global economy have not been so problematic for a long time.

The IMF in its current World Economic Outlook essentially endorses the "secular stagnation" hypothesis, noting that the real interest rate necessary to bring about enough demand for full employment is likely to remain depressed for a substantial period. This is manifest by the fact that inflation is well below target throughout the developed world and is likely to decline further this year. Without robust growth in, and greater demand from, these markets, growth in emerging economies is likely to subside. That is even without considering the political challenges facing countries as diverse as Brazil, China, South Africa, Russia and Turkey.

In the face of inadequate demand, the world's primary strategy is easy money. Base interest rates remain at floor levels throughout the developed world and central banks signal that they are unlikely to rise soon. While the US is tapering quantitative easing, Japan continues to ease on a large scale, and the eurozone seems to be moving closer to this. This is all better than the tight money that in the 1930s made the Depression the Great Depression. But it has problems as a growth strategy.

We do not have a strong basis for supposing that reductions in interest rates from very low levels have a big impact on spending decisions. Any spending they do induce tends to represent a pulling forward rather than an augmentation of demand. We do know they strongly encourage economic actors to take on debt; that they place pressure on return-seeking investors to take increased risk; that they inflate asset values and reward financial activity. And we cannot confidently predict the ultimate impact on markets or the confidence of investors of the unwinding of central bank balance sheets.

While monetary policies lower capital costs and so encourage spending that businesses and households judge unworthwhile even at rock-bottom interest rates, many elements of investment exist that can be increased and that also have high returns but are held back by misguided public policies.

In the US the case for substantial investment promotion is overwhelming. Increased infrastructure spending would reduce burdens on future generations, not just by spurring growth but also by expanding the economy's capacity and reducing deferred maintenance obligations. For example: can it be rational in the 21st century for the US air traffic control system to rely on paper tracking of flight paths?

Japan, with the increase in value added tax on April 1, is engaged in a major fiscal contraction at a time when it is far from clear whether last year's progress in reversing deflation is durable or a reflection of one-off exchange rate movements. A return to stagnation and deflation could rapidly call its solvency into question. Japan takes a dangerous risk if it waits to observe the consequences before enacting fiscal and structural reform measures to promote spending.

Europe has moved back from the brink, with defaults or devaluations now remote as possibilities. But no strategy for durable growth is yet in place and the slide towards deflation continues. Strong actions to restore the banking system so that it can be a conduit for a robust flow of credit, as well as measures to promote demand in the countries of the periphery where competitiveness challenges remain, are imperative.

If emerging markets' capital inflows fall off substantially, and so they move further towards being net exporters, it is hard to see where in the developed world can take up the slack by accepting trade balance deterioration. So measures to bolster capital flows and exports to emerging markets are essential. Most important are political steps to reassure about populist threats in a number of countries, such as where authoritarian governments give signs of disregarding contracts and property rights, and provide investor protection and backstop finance. In this regard passage by the US Congress of authorisation for the IMF to enhance its ability to provide backstop finance, is imperative.

Creative consideration should also be given to ways of mobilising the trillions of dollars in public assets held by central banks and sovereign wealth funds largely in the form of safe liquid assets to promote growth.

In a globalised economy, the impact of these steps taken together is likely to be substantially greater than the sum of their individual impacts. And the consequences of national policy failures are likely to cascade. That is why a global growth strategy framed to resist secular stagnation rather than just muddle through with the palliative of easy money should be the need of the hour.

WHY THE U.S. DOLLAR IS HEADED HIGHER?

Dollar dissonance

I must admit that I have been bewitched, bothered and bewildered by the dissonant messages being sent by the U.S. dollar.

The dollar has declined roughly 7 percent in the last nine months, but without a good fundamental reason behind the drop. The dollar index topped out at about 85 last July, falling to 79 at the end of last week. It's hardly a crash, but it is very much worth watching.

In the context of all of the events taking place in the world, the dollar should be getting stronger, not weaker, against most of the world's major currencies.

With that as background, I ticked off a mental check list that included the typical reasons a currency falls in value, asking myself whether the checklist was applicable to the dollar's recent descent:

Weak economic data? Maybe, but not really. There has been weather-related softness in the data, but the labor markets are improving and we are likely to see more "green shoots" in second- quarter economic numbers here at home.

Easier monetary policy? Federal Reserve policy is still very easy, but quantitative easing is being reined in, leaving U.S. monetary policy a bit "tighter" than that of most other central banks, save for the Bank of England.

Rising domestic inflation? Nope.

Ballooning budget and trade deficits? They are all declining faster than anticipated, reducing the need to borrow money from abroad and reducing the risk of a fiscal crisis in the U.S.

Falling U.S. asset prices? Yes, but that typically prompts a flight to quality in the U.S. dollar, as we saw from 2008 to 2009, and during other major market declines of recent vintage.

Mass selling of U.S. assets by overseas investors? Possibly. However, that phenomenon would typically also be accompanied by rising interest rates, as U.S. Treasury holders dumped bonds, prompting a decline in bond prices and an accompanying jump in yields. Even if Russian and Chinese investors are reducing their bond holdings, and we're certainly not sure the Chinese are doing that, it's not showing up in the bond market, so it's a dubious explanation, at best.

So, as I ran through the list, nothing stood to me out as a good, or even typical, reason that would explain the dollar's persistent weakness. That led me to a few other possibilities: It may be geopolitical risk or even the risk of recession.

Geopolitical risk is a clear and present danger, as we have seen for months now, not just between Russia and Ukraine, but also within Turkey, Thailand, Venezuela and South Africa. There is also increasing tension between China and Japan over territorial issues in the South China Sea, something that has foreign policy experts concerned that it could lead to a military "mistake" between Asia's largest superpowers. However, In the event of a shooting war between Moscow and Kiev, or Beijing and Tokyo, the dollar, gold, oil, and U.S. Treasury bonds, would be safe-haven beneficiaries of such ominous, and dangerous, developments.

The dollar's weakness would be likely if, and only if, the U.S. were severely harmed by a geopolitical risk taking place overseas.

Then, there is the possibility of recession. When the dollar, U.S. interest rates and U.S. stocks fall in tandem, it could be a yellow — if not red — flag that implies U.S. economic growth has not JUST been hampered by the worst winter weather we have seen in years, but by something far more fundamental and threatening.

Assuming there is not an imminent recession, or major market catastrophe on the horizon (and recall that I am calling for a 10- to 20-percent correction in U.S. stocks, but not a "crash"), a sharp dollar rebound is possible in the weeks and months ahead.

Easier money in Europe and Japan, or an escalation of violence between Russia and Ukraine, some of which we saw over the weekend, could be the catalysts for just such a move upward in the U.S. dollar.

ECB President, Mario Draghi, said over the weekend, that persistent strength in the euro could prompt the ECB to launch a negative interest-rate policy and quantitative easing! A recent meeting between Japan's Prime Minister, Shinzo Abe, and the Bank of Japan may also produce easier monetary policy in Tokyo, both of which could suggest that the dollar is undervalued against the yen and euro.

Rather noteworthy is the fact that long-term interest rates, around the world, are falling toward U.S. levels, narrowing the differential between U.S. 10-year bond yields and other sovereign yields, from Germany (below that of the U.S.), to Greece, which has narrowed the rate gap considerably, despite its well-known economic and fiscal troubles.

Everywhere you look in Europe, for example, rates are falling, and yet, the euro is rallying.

At the moment, I am ready to bet that the dollar is ready to run on the upside. It will be a small bet to start, but could build as various scenarios begin to materialize.

CAN PIGS FLY?

Do art and economics go hand in hand?

Art and Economics at the Athens Biennale

The massive colonnaded building at 8-10 Sofokleous Street in the heart of Athens' grimy business district has enormous meaning in Greece: it is the National Bank of Greece building, the former home of the Athens stock exchange. This largely abandoned building has new meaning: it is the setting for this year's Athens Biennale, titled **AGORA, (Sept. 29th -Dec 1).**

The visuals of AGORA are spectacular: most performances took place in the derelict yet elegant former stock exchange trading floor, dominated by the George Harvalias' found installation piece **June 26th 2007,** the price board of the last day of trading here. The mood in this voluminous room was warm but essentially ominous: a repeating 80 minute sonic work **Diluvial,** about the dynamics of floods, propelled a feeling of dread.

The Biennale was curated this year was by a 30 person interdisciplinary team including social theorists, political scientists, and those with an art background. It is heavily tilted to performance, lectures, and workshops, often with a crisis theme. The Biennale's co-directors and co-founders are Xenia Kalpatsoglou and Poka-Yio.

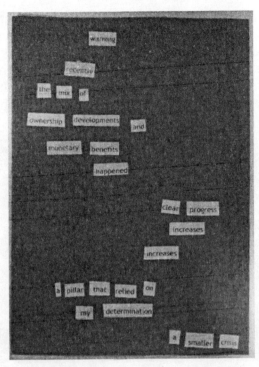

The economics of the Eurozone crisis are in some ways surprisingly simple. The peripheral countries after joining the Euro, enjoyed, at first, an illusory boom. This was followed by bust everywhere, not just in Greece (Portugal never even got to the boom stage). All suffered a decline in competitiveness and a collapse in industrialization There are many stories by economists as to why this occurred, often related to capital flow reversals, inappropriate interest rates, and the overall problems associated with giving up monetary independence. And there is theoretical as well political uncertainty as how to best proceed.

Economists have many prescriptions. One divide is whether the best way forward is for the peripheral countries to reform, or whether this is merely a second order issue compared to problems at the EU-wide level such as the need for a banking union.

Performance and fixed works suggest a creative way forward or of interpreting the crisis. "Performance lectures" by Norwegian artist A. S. Sveen offer his take on economics and the possible connection between money and happiness and an exploration of art's potential to change the world. Also noteworthy is Rainer Ganahl's installation **Credit Crunch** consisting of pottery inspired by the financial crisis, with some of the plates combining Greek mythology and contemporary figures, such as **"Medusa Merkel."**

What is notable about works like **Credit Crunch** is they provide effective, formal, visual solutions – in addition to the pure activism favoured by many — *as to how an artist can address an economic crisis. This is harder than it looks: the underlying mechanics of the crisis are highly abstract and hard even for economists to articulate except using advanced math.*

Athens is one of the most exciting cities in the world right now to see art being created and debated. This isn't escapist art but instead art trying to address one of the largest man-made disasters of our time. And if Greece is the epicenter of the crisis, **AGORA** might be the epicenter of a nascent yet global art movement that has arisen in response, one that is now exploring creative alternatives not just to the state of bankruptcy, but to the bankrupt economic and political policies that led to this situation.

A Greek national flag flies beneath the Parthenon temple on Acropolis hill in Athens, Greece

Volatile countries on the edge of Europe have long been out of favour with investors, but interest is reviving in these markets as share prices rise and economic conditions continue to improve.

In the past year, companies in Europe's periphery, including Portugal, Ireland, Greece and Spain – dubbed the "Pigs", or "Piigs" if Italy is included – have seen shares either outperform broader European stocks, or move in tandem.

The MSCI Ireland index, for example, has returned 47 per cent over the past 12 months, while MSCI Italy has returned 56 per cent. By comparison, MSCI Europe has returned 22 per cent in this time.

Peripheral European economies had been in recession for five or six years and as a result, companies had to cut costs and restructure to survive.

They have now regained their competitiveness and are attracting foreign investment. Over the next five years, we think the periphery will grow faster than economies in northern Europe.

Mr Norris has increased his holdings in peripheral European shares – specifically Piigs – to nearly 50 per cent because of his view that the region is now entering a period of "exceptional" performance.

Experts suggest the recent equity rally has been preceded by a recovery in the bond markets, as European corporates have been reducing more of their "bad" debts.

The concept of risk is also shifting, which is renewing interest in Europe; investors who turned to the less-indebted emerging markets a few years ago have been pulling out in recent months, largely due to the US signalling the end of quantitative easing. This end of "easy money" chasing higher yields has seen a retreat from riskier assets, such as the emerging economies and commodities.

The improvement in sentiment towards peripheral Europe can also be seen in bond markets. Yields rocketed during the eurozone crisis; Greece's 10-year borrowing costs reached 28 per cent in 2012. But yields have fallen sharply; 10-year Greek debt now yields 6.19 per cent, the lowest level in four years.

As a result, some investors are looking to European companies positioned to benefit from domestic growth, as opposed to those exposed to growth in the emerging markets.

It may also be worth investing in companies with a focus on domestic-facing companies such as utility firms and Italian banks, instead of "safer" German export companies.

It would have been great to have invested in Piigs early when it was extremely cheap, unloved and pretty risky; now it feels a lot more comfortable.

Similarly, one needs to be averse to those European-based companies geared towards emerging market growth, which he believes has been "over-extrapolated" and where market profit expectations remain "unrealistic."

This "rebound" in peripheral Europe is reflected in corporate profitability. Research from Swiss investment bank UBS shows corporate return on equity in Portugal was 25 per cent in 2007, but now stands at 4 per cent. By comparison, RoE in Belgium was 16 per cent and is now 14 per cent.

What excites us is where we see potential for a company to earn significantly more in terms of profit. In peripheral Europe, it can easily go from 4 per cent to 8 per cent, or even 12 per cent and above.

The cheapest areas in Europe are domestic-focused companies and those based on the periphery.

The intersection of these two trends – domestic bias and peripheral listing – did look very cheap, and continue to offer good value even after their performance over 2013.

Some of the favoured funds include Artemis European Growth, Invesco Perpetual European Equity and Schroder European Alpha Income.

However, peripheral Europe comes with risks. Spanish unemployment is still extremely high and Greece is still in recession – although some economists forecast it will exit this quarter.

Political risks are also a problem, as is the threat of deflation, often associated with severe weakness in equities. However, others point out that these risks are already priced in and that the European Central Bank would act if it thought deflation was a serious risk; its president, Mario Draghi, certainly appeared to leave the door open to further stimulus measures.

PONDERABLES FOR THE STOCK MARKETS

Why are Treasury yields falling even as the US Federal Reserve is preparing to raise interest rates?

The question is more baffling even than this. Treasury bonds have been in a bull market, meaning that their prices have steadily increased and their yields decreased, for more than three decades. Ten-year yields hit a low of below 2 per cent in the summer of 2012. Big investment institutions hold historically enormous allocations in bonds, and few equities – at a time when bonds look expensive and equities cheap by comparison. So all was set up for a "great rotation" out of bonds and back into stocks.

Last year, bond yields leapt as the Fed talked of "tapering" off its monthly bond purchases, which have been supporting yields. But 10-year yields only briefly exceeded 3 %. The Fed is now well locked in to a steady tapering that will phase out bond purchases altogether later this year. Yet yields have fallen back to 2.64 %.

Why? Institutions still need to buy bonds, to meet guarantees to future pensioners. So they are buying them now as they are available more cheaply. And Treasuries still serve as a "haven". Some of these flows reflect money being repatriated or "taken off the table" as investors grow more nervous about emerging markets.

How can Greece successfully borrow on the markets once more when it is barely two years since it partially defaulted and nearly left the euro?

Central bankers' words are powerful. Mario Draghi of the European Central Bank promised to do "whatever it takes" to save the euro, and those words alone have been enough to resolve confidence in peripheral countries' debt.

As for political concerns, the popular anger at the austerity measures forced on Greece, and other countries, is obvious and understandable. Greece's bond issue came at the same time as a general strike. But investors have learnt the lesson that political turmoil in many eurozone countries has not been enough to topple pro-euro governments so far (against expectations). They are now extrapolating political acquiescence into the future. The premium they require for this seems very low.

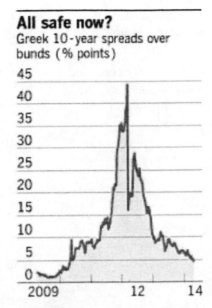

All safe now?
Greek 10-year spreads over
bunds (% points)

Source: Thomson Reuters Datastream

Why are emerging markets now looking their cheapest compared with the developing world in more than a decade, even though their economies are still growing faster?

Markets and economic growth do not go together. And then there are concerns about China, which is trying to manage a transition in the way it manages its economy. It is also trying to deflate a bubble in its credit market. Bubbles are difficult to deflate without bursting, and everyone knows this.

Further, investors are nervous that rising rates will put pressure on those countries that have a high current account deficit, and are therefore particularly reliant on inflows of "hot money".

Finally, emerging markets might well be a bargain, but because of superior future growth not any narrowing of their discount to developed markets. Investors, worrying about state interference, now believe there is a reason for a discount. There has been civil unrest in such important markets as Thailand, Turkey and Brazil. And, of course, there is the situation in Ukraine.

Why is the US stock market still close to all-time highs when so many remain negative about the economy, and when there is geopolitical risk arising from the situation in Ukraine?

The Ukrainian and Russian currencies had recently devalued, and Russia was already by far the world's cheapest major stock market. Investors must think that the crisis in Ukraine has been priced in (which is reasonable) and that there is no need to price in the risk of further escalation (which looks more tenuous).

For the stock market, the bottom line is earnings. They remain strong, and the expectation is for an 8.2 per cent rise in earnings in the first quarter. There is no obvious catalyst that would push them down.

The Fed is still buying bonds and its likely trajectory involves slow, predictable rate rise – just the conditions under which, in the middle of the last decade, the US housing and credit bubbles inflated.

Faith in central banks remains deep, and there is a shortage of other things to invest in. It is not a healthy basis on which to buy stocks that now look very expensive. If earnings disappoint, watch out.

WHY THE INTEREST RATE RISE PATTERN IS DIFFERENT THIS TIME

Higher Treasury yields with low policy rate heightens risks

The US Federal Reserve's forward guidance last May that it would soon begin to "taper" its asset purchases marked the start of a new phase of global monetary normalisation.

- ◆ The prolonged period of bond market volatility that followed surprised many by its intensity. Yields on US Treasuries rose, and have remained well above the exceptionally low levels of early 2013. But the Federal funds rate, and indeed the policy rate in all large advanced economies, was held close to zero.

This pattern is almost the exact opposite of the 2004-06 tightening, when the Federal funds rate rose by 425 basis points but the long-term rate barely moved. It is also quite unlike the 1994 tightening cycle, when it was changes in expectations about future policy rates that drove the bond market sell-off.

There are several implications of this new pattern at the outset of tightening. One is a more powerful transmission to interest rates in other countries.

Long-term interest rates are more correlated across countries than short-term rates. A central bank operating under a flexible exchange rate regime can set its policy rate independently of the Fed funds rate.

But it has much less power over the long-term rate in its own currency because yields in all bond markets integrated into the financial system tend to rise whenever US yields jump. Bond yields in countries with weaker macroeconomic or financial fundamentals often rise even more.

EM not alone

The recent squall hitting the emerging markets was intensified when non-resident investors realised they were holding larger interest rate risk in emerging market currencies than usual. Sharp currency depreciations also reminded them of their exchange rate exposures.

The risks are not confined to emerging markets. The huge issuance of low-yielding long-term debt by advanced economy governments over the past five years means portfolios holding such bonds are carrying much higher interest rate risk.

Much of this exposure is with financial institutions such as pension funds, banks and insurance companies. How they react to a larger than expected rise in interest rates could add to market pressures. Another amplification channel could be increased credit risk as higher rates make some borrowers less creditworthy.

The second implication is that short-term funding costs are still being kept very low. The steeper yield curve means banks earn more profits from borrowing short and lending long.

In addition, carry trades remain cheap, inevitably tempting some investors to take leveraged positions in risky assets. Financial stability risks have probably increased.

At present, markets believe short-term rates in the large advanced economies are likely to remain close to zero at least until the end of this year, and then rise only gradually. But for how long will markets continue to believe this?

A number of central banks have been making forecasts of their own policy rate for some years. A recent study showed their forecasts are good for two quarters ahead but are less reliable beyond about six months or so.

Wrong reading

Of particular relevance to the current situation is the finding that central banks under-predicted increases in the policy rate in the early stages of an upturn. Their monetary policy framework had not changed but stronger than forecast macroeconomic developments led them to move the policy rate sooner than expected.

A further uncertainty is how central banks will seek to shrink their balance sheets when the recovery gathers strength. The more quickly they choose to sell assets, the more spreads on longer term debt may rise. Because this will tend to be contractionary, the less short-term rates may rise.

The decision on when and how to shrink their balance sheets will not be easy. A policy of just allowing bonds to run off as they mature might attract less opposition but would not be neutral economically: the pace of balance sheet reduction, determined only by the path of past purchases, would be independent of prevailing conditions and could even continue into the next recession.

An additional consideration is that the main counterpart of increased central bank assets is massive bank reserves; either these will have to be reduced, or rates payable on them will have to rise in line with policy rates. Either route will take us into unknown territory.

The problems of trying to normalise monetary policy after the long period of aggressive and unconventional expansion will be difficult to solve. Look out for bumps ahead.

IS THE WORLD READY FOR HIGHER INTEREST RATES?

As the movement of central banks becomes more unpredicatable (with the goalposts changing, as Fed chairperson Janet Yellen seems to be suggesting), the stock markets could become more volatile.

The labor force participation is still falling—there are still no signs of recovery.

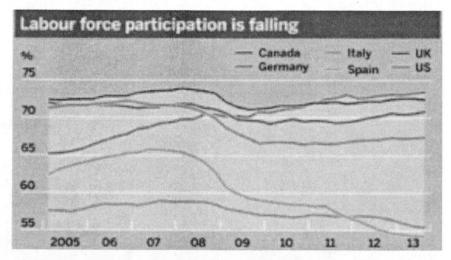

Secondly, not only has the inflation rate failed to keep pace with GDP growth, there is still lot of excess capacity floating around. Central banks are not going to be able to face a growth-inflation tradeoff anytime soon.

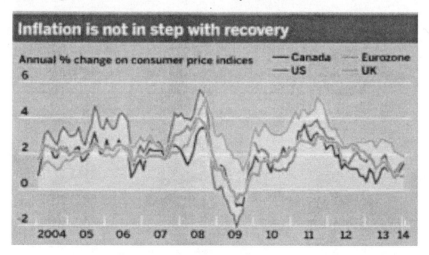

Productivity like inflation and labor force participation has not kept pace. So, real wages are also not rising.

Besides, leverage has come back.

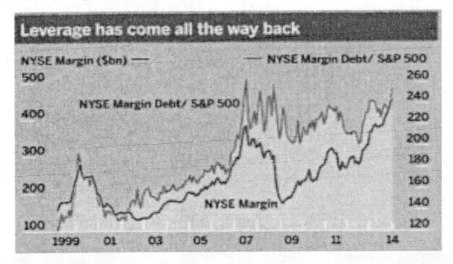

Therefore, premature rise in interest rates to fight the ghost of inflation may result in asset deflation.

IS THE U.S. DOLLAR'S FATE TIED TO THE YIELD CURVE?

A sharp flattening in the U.S. government bond yield curve this week could be a bearish sign for the dollar, currency analysts say.

Yields on five-year Treasurys have shot up since last week's Federal Reserve meeting raised the prospect of interest rates rising sooner rather than later, narrowing the gap with 30-year bond yields to their tightest spread since 2009.

Although a rise in yields at the short-end of the yield curve usually boosts the appeal of the dollar, a fall in yields at the long-end reflects concerns about the economic outlook and this is weighing on the currency.

The dollar is down more than three percent since the start of the year.

Part of the currency pair's weakness can be attributed to one of biggest stories in the financial market this week which is that the U.S. yield curve is flattening at an alarmingly rapid pace.

Typically yield curves flatten when inflation expectations are falling or investors are worried about slower growth but in this case, short-term rates are rising as long-term rates are falling.

The charts show a clear correlation between dollar/yen and the yield curve, suggesting the dollar could head lower against the yen if the yield curve flattens some more.

Recent comments by new Fed chief Janet Yellen suggesting interest rates could start to rise six months after the scaling back of monetary stimulus ends took markets by surprise, sparking a sharp rise in short-dated Treasury yields. Two-year yields for instance have risen to about 0.48 percent on, their highest level since last September.

The curve has been flattening and we've seen two-year yields really move up, especially after the Fed last week because of shifting expectations that maybe rates could move higher sooner than expected.

The attraction with [long-dated] U.S. Treasuries also has to do with the risk-on, risk-off dynamic and when you have geopolitical tensions in Eastern Europe or concerns about growth because we've had disappointing data in China.

It was the way in which the U.S. yield curve has flattened that was impacting dollar/yen. The underlying message in the data is that the economy is still not gaining momentum, so it may be a case that this is reflected at the long-end of the curve.

Data shows orders for U.S. durable goods rose 2.2 percent in February from a month earlier after two straight months of falls. But the data also showed a surprise drop in core capital goods, a gauge of planned spending on capital goods.

WHY TEA PRICES COULD RISE?

Asia's tea-growing regions, namely Sri Lanka and Malaysia, have been impacted by a recent drought that could lead to a rise in tea prices.

A long dry season in the East has left Asia's premier tea-growing regions parched and could lead to a rise in tea prices.

The drought across Sri Lanka in the first three months of 2014 has contributed to a 50 percent fall in tea production on previously corresponding period, industry sources said. Some 400,000 small tea holders in Ratnapura, Kalutara, Galle and Matara districts are among the worst affected, according to The Sri Lanka Tea Board.

Sri Lanka is the second largest exporter of tea at 300 million tonnes. In a context where tea prices have been falling – last year tea prices fell 40 percent which was the most precipitous fall in the history of the commodity – it's conceivable that tea prices are going to ascend in this context.

Tea producers in Malaysia have also been hit by drought. At the Boh Plantations in the Cameron Highlands, February's crop declined 50 percent on previously corresponding period.

Changing weather a concern

There's evidence to suggest weather patterns are becoming more volatile.

A Sri Lankan tea picker works on a plantation in the central town of Kandy

I think longer term there is a worry about climate change. The view is that in the tropics it is going to create greater levels of inconsistency in rainfall. One will encounter periods that are much drier and periods that are much wetter. Your total annual rainfall may not change very dramatically in the tropics. However, its distribution will and that will have very serious effects on us.

In the dry periods, we would see crop yields fall but the concern in very wet periods is that we would see slope instability because we are growing tea on quite steep terrain. Of course you have incidents of landslides under those kinds of conditions, particularly if it comes after a very dry period.

Changing tastes

Agricultural over-development in the Cameron Highlands could also have a lasting impact on the flavor of Boh Tea.

There's been a lot of land clearance for agriculture. This undoubtedly is impacting temperatures. Monitoring has shown a rise in temperatures in the Cameron Highlands, and while it isn't having a direct impact onto us immediately, in the longer term it potentially could. Ultimately one could anticipate that your flavors would be impacted.

But as consumption increasingly shifts to instant tea and tea mixes at the expense of traditional brews, such subtle changes in flavor are becoming less obvious.

In today's context, particularly here in Malaysia, consumer lifestyles are changing so much that people don't have the same downtime. So, quite a lot of the growth areas in the tea market are in arenas of convenience.

We see instant tea, for example, and mixes of tea (tea combined with sugars and milk, already packaged) that you merely add hot water to, is a burgeoning market. You might say: 'well now that's not real tea', but there's no right and wrong with tea. Tea is an intensely personal product.

SHOULD YOU SHORT THE AUSSIE?

Are currencies living in an alternate world?

The resilience of the euro and the Australian dollar has stumped analysts, with one saying that currency markets are now living in an alternative world.

The Australian dollar, also known as the Aussie has risen to $0.9158, its highest level this year. It is closely tied to the health of China's economy and the fact that the rally has come amid signs of weakness in China, Australia's biggest trading partner, has taken analysts by surprise.

Meanwhile, the euro has also proved resilient in the face of weak manufacturing activity data from China and a dip in European factory activity data on Monday. It currently trades around $1.3829.

Australian Currency.

The Aussie's jump is "bizarre" given China's bleak manufacturing data—but the move may reflect investors starting to view China data and its relation to the Aussie differently.

China's manufacturing activity contracted for a third straight month in March, a Markit/HSBC survey showed recently.

In the world we live in at the moment bad news out of China is actually good for the Aussie because it has stoked chatter that Beijing is moving closer to unleashing monetary and potentially fiscal stimulus measures as soon as next quarter.

Yet, I'm not sure I'm confident in that story... given weaker commodity prices... it's difficult to get too upbeat on the outlook for Aussie.

The price of copper and iron ore - both of which are major exports out of Australia - have tanked in recent weeks, further confounding analysts as to why the Aussie is staying strong.

There are basically three reasons for Australian dollar's resilience.

Firstly, the market was "massively short" the Australian dollar at the moment.

Secondly, the Reserve Bank of Australia's transition from a dovish to neutral bias has led to a significant jump in the nominal yield versus real yields in Australian government bonds, boosting the appeal of the Aussie.

Finally, Asian central banks have started to become slightly more positive and reallocated funds into the Aussie.

But I do not expect the Aussie's resilience to continue, as weaker commodity prices and a mixed picture for the domestic economy starts to be priced in. The country's central bank could start talking it down again soon as well.

In the past, comments from Governor Glen Stevens, who previously said he would prefer to see the currency at 85 cents, have helped push the currency lower.

Why Australia's luck is running out as China slows?

Australia's slowing resource economy - in charts

As China's growth engine slows, Australia's "iron man" economy will soften, these charts produced by the Australian government show.

Back in 2009, when China was spending heavily to stimulate economic growth, Australia's miners were swept up by widespread enthusiasm in the financial industry for the concept of a "commodities supercycle" and invested heavily in new projects.

The supercycle idea has been punctured since the Beijing government accepted credit-fuelled growth cannot continue forever.

But many of the projects miners began work on in 2009 are now coming on stream.

That is hurting commodities prices already, a report by the Australian government's Bureau of Resources and Energy Economics says that this is hurting commodities prices.

Meanwhile, as mining investment is cooling off, there could be "sustained pressure" on employment growth, the report adds, saying:

The decline in commodity prices can more accurately be attributed to the strong growth in world supply that is the product of substantial global investment in commodity production capacity since the GFC.

The report goes on to forecast a short-term decline in Australia's economic growth due to falling investment in new mining projects. From the report:

Over the outlook period to 2018–19, Australia's GDP growth rate is assumed to decline over the next two years, before recovering to trend growth in 2018–19. Capital expenditure, particularly in the mining and energy sectors, has been an important driver of economic growth in Australia since the GFC.

Continued structural change in the Australian economy and the transition from the mining construction phase to the production phase has the potential to place sustained pressure on employment growth

Australia's exports of resources are also going to decline this year, the below chart shows.

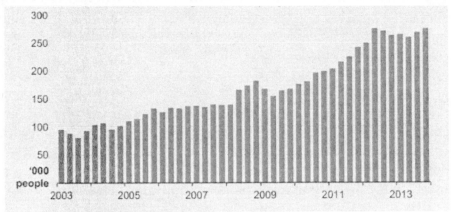

Figure 3   Quarterly Australian sector employment

Reasons to be bearish on currency and country grow daily

There is only one good reason not to short the Aussie dollar: it is expensive. But the grounds for taking a bearish view on both the currency and the country become more compelling by the day.

Australia has long been the land of coal, iron and liquefied natural gas (LNG), which is even better than being the land of milk and honey thanks to the demand for these resources from China.

Australia was among the biggest beneficiaries of China's voracious appetite for iron to turn into the steel skeletons of everything from cars and railroads to flats and office towers, as well as coal for the country's power plants. As China prospered, demand for gold to decorate the necks, wrists and fingers of China's plutocrats and their wives also soared.

China was a big reason why Australia's economy has grown by 4 per cent a year for about 20 years. It escaped the Asian financial crisis 15 years ago and the global financial crisis five years ago. But last year, growth was only 2.4 per cent.

The Lucky Country may not be as lucky in future as it has been in the past two decades.

Contagion danger

As China gradually both slows and shifts underpinned by urban services, there will be less demand for Australia's resources. "Almost all economic figures released so far this year were weaker than consensus," China research from HSBC noted on March 21. "China's manufacturing sector is losing momentum."

The growth in industrial production slowed to the lowest reading in nearly five years for the first two months of 2014, according to HSBC.

When China's growth rate slows by 1 per cent, emerging markets suffer a slowdown of 0.7 per cent. Australia is not an emerging market but it will also suffer disproportionately from any slowdown in China, along with Indonesia, Brazil, Chile and Peru, according to JPMorgan.

Recently, an official at one Asian sovereign wealth fund with a $30bn portfolio of Chinese shares sought advice from a big Hong Kong-based hedge fund manager on how to hedge that portfolio in the face of falling growth on the mainland. One answer: short Aussie dollars.

Today, the Australian dollar is the most exposed of the G-10 currencies to China.

Australia is plagued by a currency that is so overvalued it makes oil-rich Norway's currency look cheap. But the price of oil is high while the prices of Australian commodities are under downward pressure, leading to deteriorating fundamentals.

The contribution of capital spending to GDP was negative in 2013 and is expected to remain negative this year--we are facing the mining investment cliff.

Bechtel, the big US engineering and construction company, has three large LNG export terminals projects in Australia – contracts worth tens of billions of dollars. But everything is so expensive and the shortage of skilled labour so acute that people familiar with the projects say the company is unlikely to do much more in Australia when these projects are completed. Over A$110bn worth of resources related projects were cancelled last year alone.

Meanwhile, the people who manage KKR's new $2bn special situations fund say they are spending much of their time in Australia, meeting with the owners of smaller mines who need capital as their cash flow dries up, in the face of rising costs and weaker demand.

Manufacturing is not going to pick up the slack. Surveys of Australian business show no intention to increase spending in non-mining sectors of the economy. Toyota became the last car company to say it planned to stop making cars in the country.

Private investment will be a material drag on growth in the next fiscal year and probably much longer.

Safe bets are off

Meanwhile, sitting in Hong Kong, it is easy to feel a mix of emotions at the prospect of a real slowdown in China. Hong Kong will be even more vulnerable than Australia if this happens. Residents of this Chinese territory have long maintained renminbi accounts on both sides of the border and enjoyed higher interest rates on their Chinese currency accounts than they could get on either US or Hong Kong dollar accounts as the renminbi appreciated.

Now, suddenly everything is going into reverse as China slows and its currency weakens – by about 2 % in the past few weeks. If that continues, it may be a better hedge for a big portfolio of Chinese equities to short the renminbi than to short Aussie dollars (and much less costly). The authorities in Beijing have indeed succeeded in their goal of injecting uncertainty into the trajectory of the Chinese currency.

Sadly, it is not clear what the safe bets are any longer.

GAMECHANGER FOR ASIA'S BOND MARKETS

Asia's corporate bond markets remain relatively underdeveloped compared to their Western peers, but a plan from the Asian Development Bank (ADB) to "harmonize" the region's regulations could be a gamechanger.

Right now, it's really hard for a Malaysian company to issue Thai baht bonds. Or a Philippine company (to issue) an Indonesian rupiah bond – partly because the rules are different and partly because they just don't know how to do it.

That's why the ADB is trying to standardize bond-issuance across the Asean plus-three region, which includes the eight Southeast Asian markets as well as Japan, South Korea and China.

Asia's bond markets have seen rapid growth since the global financial crisis, rising to 24.2 percent of Asian gross domestic product (GDP) in 2012 from just 16.7 percent in 2008, Deutsche Bank said in a January note.

Indonesia is vulnerable to the Fed's rate hikes, due to a high foreign ownership of its sovereign bonds.

Asia's corporate bond markets remain, with few exceptions, small and illiquid, with the region's corporate funding still overwhelmingly bank-based. In addition, despite the region's pickup in bond issuance, secondary markets have low trading volume and the segment lacks investor diversity.

Bond issuance in many markets is dominated by a handful of players, it said, noting that in Taiwan and Indonesia, the ten largest issuers were responsible for more than 80 percent of the total bond issuance last year.

The Asian bond market initiative is to promote greater investment by making it easier for the region's investors' to invest in each other's bond markets. They try to work together with both market regulators and participants to harmonize rules in the region for issuing bonds.

It's a change that would likely be met enthusiastically.

A single rule for all of Asia would be fantastic. It would make trading easier--each country currently has its own rules and regulations and different withholding taxes.

The change also would make it easier to develop benchmarks as well as create a yield curve with similar maturities. Currently, it's difficult because when you look at all the issues, they are all in different currencies and denominations. The covenants are not the same. It would make liquidity a lot better and transparency a lot better.

Developing the region's bond markets may be key to continuing economic growth. For a consumer-based high-income economy, consumers and businesses need to have improved access to capital and modern financial products.

Many Asian central banks have a buildup of foreign exchange reserves due to high savings rates across the region and controlled financial systems.

This has meant that the Asian surplus of the past 15 years has been 'recycled' back into the international financial system via official portfolio flows,with central banks buying developed-nation government bonds.

The 'trapping' of the Asian surplus in FX reserve portfolios has resulted in a much slower financial development than would have been the case if the private sector had played the primary role in allocating those savings.

I estimate reforms would result in the total Asian financial system accounting for half of the global system by 2030, up from around 22 percent currently.

ARE BRITONS FINALLY GETTING RICHER AGAIN?

The UK's labour market figures have sparked a lot of excitement – and a certain amount of confusion – on the hot topic of real wage growth. Here are six charts that explain what has happened and what it means.

1. Have Britons had their first pay rise since 2008?

Not quite. The annual increase in UK average weekly earnings was 1.7 per cent in February. Inflation as measured by the consumer price index was also 1.7 per cent in February. That means the average worker's pay has stopped falling in real terms for the first time since 2008 (if you ignore a bonus-related blip in 2010)

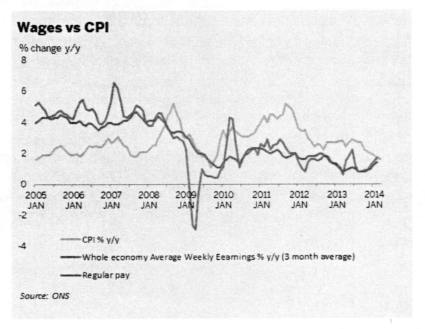

It is too soon to say for sure that real wages have started to rise again (CPI in March was 1.6 per cent; we won't have the March wage data for another month). But it seems very likely. Meanwhile, today marks the end of the UK's six-year slide in real wages – a significant moment.

2. Setting aside the politics, is this really a big deal economically?

Context is important. Average real wages have fallen about 10 per cent since 2008 to their lowest in a decade; that is a big hole out of which to climb. But today does mark a turning point after one of the weirdest and most painful periods in the history of wages in Britain, as this long-term historical chart shows.

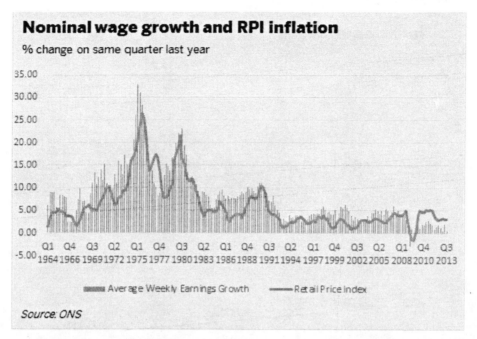

Nominal wage growth and RPI inflation

% change on same quarter last year

Source: ONS

Until now, shoppers have been propelling the economic recovery – in spite of their falling salaries – by simply saving less. Even anaemic growth in real wages should put the recovery on a firmer foundation.

3. Can I trust these numbers?

There is more than one way to measure people's earnings. This is the official Average Weekly Earnings dataset, based on a monthly survey of about 9,000 businesses. It doesn't capture the 15 per cent of workers who are self-employed. But it is the most up-to-date data we have.

There are also several different ways to measure inflation. The CPI doesn't capture owner-occupiers' housing costs, for example. This chart shows the other measures of inflation (CPIH is the CPI with a measure of owner-occupier housing costs, RPIJ is the RPI with a better formula). Real wages are rising on the CPIH measure and still falling on the others. But the direction of travel is the same.

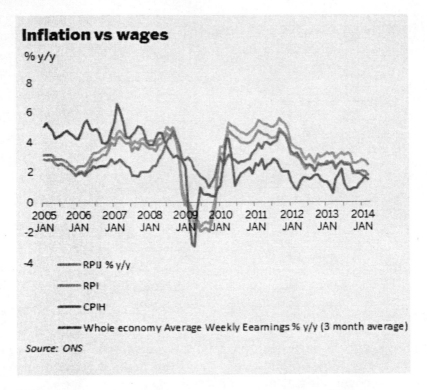

Inflation vs wages

%y/y

Source: ONS

4. We're just talking about "average" wages here. Doesn't that conceal big differences in the fortunes of the rich and the poor?

Actually it doesn't. The pain of falling real wages has been shared remarkably evenly across high, middle and low earners.

The real disparity has been between the young and the old, as this chart from the Resolution Foundation shows.

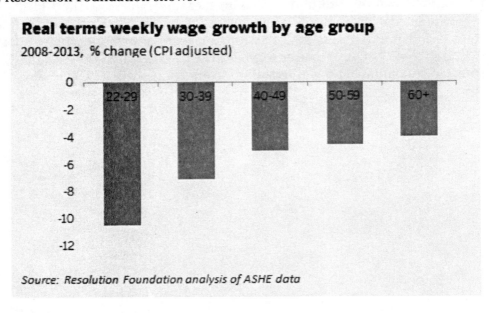

Real terms weekly wage growth by age group

2008-2013, % change (CPI adjusted)

Source: Resolution Foundation analysis of ASHE data

5. Does today's news mean living standards have stopped falling?

There's an important distinction between real wages and living standards. Wages are only one source of income – they do not tell you anything about how tax and benefit changes have affected people's incomes. They also don't tell you how households are doing; they only tell you about individuals.

The best measure of living standards comes from a huge government survey of households that happens once a year. Unfortunately the latest data is for 2011-12, but modelling by the Institute for Fiscal Studies suggests living standards too should start to improve this year.

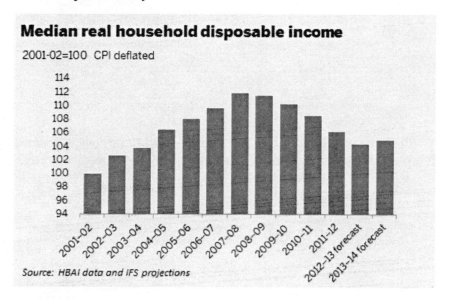

Median real household disposable income

2001-02=100 CPI deflated

Source: HBAI data and IFS projections

6. What happens now?

Most economists expect both real wages and living standards to start to rise gently. Inflation is subdued and earnings growth should start to improve as the labour market recovers. But few expect a very rapid recovery in wages: productivity is still weak and companies will be keen to repair their profit margins after such a long downturn. Meanwhile, the government is less than half way through its planned spending cuts: benefit cuts will drag on the incomes of poorer people in the next few years.

So people will almost certainly still be poorer when they go to the polls next year than they were in 2010. This OBR forecast suggests it will be late 2016 before wages regain their 2010 levels.

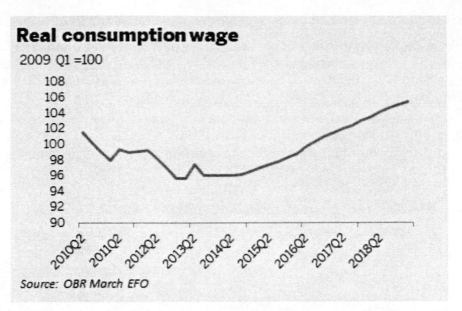

Real consumption wage

2009 Q1 =100

Source: OBR March EFO

What will that mean for the election result? It all depends on whether people care more about where they are now – or where they feel they are going.

JAPANESE DEBT: STILL CLIMBING

Despite 'Abenomics', government bonds have stayed calm – but critics say Tokyo cannot ignore its debt mountain forever

Heading higher: A worker climbs up a tower of a conveyor carrying excavated soil to a residential area under construction in Rikuzentakata, Iwate Prefecture

No one disputes that Japan's debt is worryingly high. The International Monetary Fund and OECD both warn that deep cuts to spending must be made, beyond the government's basic pledge to balance its books – excluding debt-servicing costs – by 2020.

Japan's finance ministry seems to take a perverse delight in pointing out the world's worst debt optics: gross central government borrowings equivalent to 24 years of tax receipts, or about $80,000 for every man, woman and child. (The next worst is Ireland, with $60,000, according to Bloomberg.)

Japan has recently suffered its largest ever trade deficit last fiscal year, underlining a wrenching structural shift for an economy long renowned as an export powerhouse. The gap between the value of Japan's exports and that of its imports grew by more than two-thirds in the 12 months through March to Y13.7tn ($ 134Bn) –the third consecutive fiscal year of deficits, the longest streak since comparable records began in the 1970s.

Toyota, Hitachi and other large Japanese companies enjoyed soaring profits as a result of the weaker yen, which has fallen by a fifth against major currencies since November 2012.

But the improvement has come less from increased exports than from depreciating exchange rates. A steady outflow of Japanese manufacturing jobs to low-cost destinations and declining competitiveness in some sectors, such as consumer electronics, has limited the power of a cheap yen to life exports.

Shinzo Abe, the prime minister, is determined to change direction. If Japan can succeed in igniting nominal growth and inflation, the theory goes, the debt will instantly start to look less formidable. Hence the triple stimulus unleashed almost 18 months ago, via the "three arrows" of a flexible fiscal policy, more aggressive monetary easing from the Bank of Japan and various structural reforms to boost competitiveness.

But that plan depends on maintaining order in the bond market – an outcome that is by no means assured. Critics say that rather than fixing Japan's economy, "Abenomics" could be storing up trouble. All Mr Abe has done is to pile debt upon debt, they claim, while flunking more difficult growth initiatives such as Japan's entry into the Trans-Pacific Partnership free-trade agreement.

Last year the Diet signed off on two spending packages on top of the regular budget – one to jump-start growth and another to smooth over the impact of the first rise in consumption taxes for 17 years, effective in April. And last week the Diet waved through its biggest budget for the fiscal year ahead. Gross debt issuance comes to a record Y182tn ($1.78tn), about the same size as the economy of India.

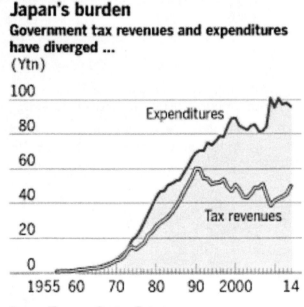

Japan's burden
Government tax revenues and expenditures have diverged ...
(Ytn)

Source: Thomson Reuters Datastream

So far the bond market seems untroubled. Even as Abenomics has shaken up other assets such as stocks and property, Japanese government bonds (JGBs) continue to sail on serenely, giving the government with the highest debts the lowest borrowing costs in the world.

But many wonder how much longer the game can go on. Because fiscal stimulus borrows income from the future for immediate consumption, such policies only compound Japan's already huge public debt, thereby increasing the risk of fiscal chaos. Are we trying to see how far we can push things before fiscal collapse?

Mr Abe is going all-out for growth because he has to. Barring the type of scenario outlined by Mr Fujimaki, only growth can fix its debt problem.

State finances have deteriorated partly because of demography. Social security payments to a fast-ageing population have nearly tripled since 1990 to Y31tn – about a third of the total budget – in the fiscal year beginning in April.

But the real problem is that as the economy languished, Japan collected less and less tax, forcing the state to borrow to plug gaps between income and expenditure.

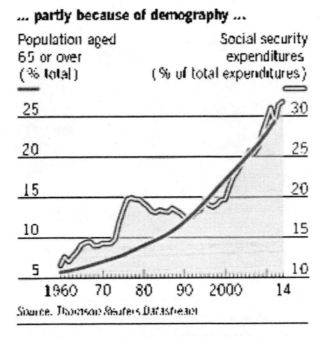

... partly because of demography ...

During the high-growth 1980s, tax revenues rose more quickly than spending, keeping total borrowing at less than 60 per cent of gross domestic product in 1990. But those two lines began to diverge in the early 1990s when nominal growth began to sputter, and they spread further apart as Japan tipped into deflation in 1997. Annual deficits narrowed a little in the mid-2000s. But the huge extra budgets to cope with the Lehman crisis, followed by the clean-up after the March 2011 tsunami, pushed them wider still.

Until now, the finance ministry has had few problems selling its debt domestically, which means it has not been at the mercy of overseas bond vigilantes. Commercial banks were stuffed with deposits from companies and households and had limited opportunities to lend. Where better to put all that cash than the ultra-liquid JGB market, which requires no capital to be set against it?

Insurers, too, had to match yen liabilities with yen assets, while the vast Japan Post group kept buying more JGBs than anybody. Entirely owned by the finance ministry, it was hardly in a position to do otherwise.

As long as prices were falling, bonds were a fair bet. A 10-year bond bearing a coupon of, say, 1.5 % had a real yield of 2.5 %, if deflation was at minus 1 %.

But now that the fall in the yen has pushed up inflation, real yields have turned negative for the first time in decades and are putting one of the objectives of Abenomics to the test. Under the plan drawn up by Haruhiko Kuroda, the BoJ governor, bond-heavy investors are now supposed to shed JGBs so they can put cash to work in riskier assets, supporting the broader drive towards growth.

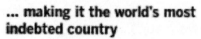

... making it the world's most indebted country

Government debt as % of GDP, top advanced countries

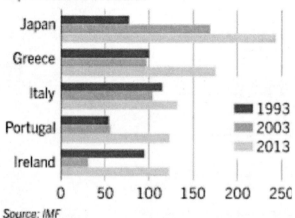

Source: IMF

As long as the BoJ can be counted on to soak up the bonds they do not want, all will be well. So far that theory has held, as the big banks have sold big chunks of their bonds to the BoJ while yields have remained low.

The Abe-Kuroda double act deserves credit for "masterfully" holding confidence together--But if they do get to north of 2 per cent inflation, then all investors will have to question whether they want to stay in the game.

I continue to bet on further weakening in the yen while positioning for a huge rise in bond yields by buying cheap options on interest rates.

Even bond bulls accept that relying so much on the BoJ is risky.

The more government debt a central bank buys, the greater the appearance of "fiscal dominance" – where monetary policy essentially becomes a ruse to keep the state solvent.

The boundaries are already blurred. Dealers talk about "the BoJ trade" – buying bonds at auction from the finance ministry then flipping them immediately to the central bank to bag a few basis points of profit. One issue of 30-year bonds on February 6 was almost 90 per cent owned by the BoJ a month later. We are buying tonnes of JGBs; we are monopolising the market.

The BoJ's grip on the market is nothing more or less than central bank financing of the fiscal deficit

A senior finance ministry official says that it is true that "the BoJ is financing the government, in a way". But, it is important to recognise that the BoJ is buying assets for similar reasons as the US Federal Reserve: to keep downward pressure on bond yields and promote a stronger recovery.—refer to a pact drawn up in October 2012 under the previous government and endorsed by Mr Abe in January last year, under which the BoJ and the government pledged to work together to revive Japan.

The BoJ will fight deflation and we will continue our efforts on fiscal consolidation--That is the agreement.

But many suspect that the pair will be bound together for longer than the two-year period outlined last April.

And the more long-term bonds the BoJ buys, the trickier its exit. More than 80 per cent of its assets are now in JGBs – much higher than the Fed, with about 55 per cent in US Treasuries – with an average maturity near the maximum eight years. A simple withdrawal of stimulus like in 2006, when the BoJ allowed its shorter-term debt to run off, looks impossible.

The BoJ's grip on the market represents nothing more or less than central bank financing of the fiscal deficit, and could ultimately lead to market turmoil.

The finance ministry knows the situation is delicate. Its debt-raising strategy for the year ahead is based on locking in low rates on longer-term bonds, while giving investors more latitude to set maturities themselves.

The ministry also claims to have one eye on deficit reduction, noting that the first of two increases in consumption tax in April should allow it to cut new bond issuance by about Y1.6tn in the year ahead.

It admits, though, that its long-term targets for cutting debt are unlikely to be hit. For the past few years, the official line has been that the government plans to erase its primary deficit – the gap between revenues and expenditure, excluding debt payments and bond issuance – by 2020.

But last summer the cabinet office sketched out projections that implied that the government would miss the target. In February the finance ministry added colour, saying that even with the most optimistic assumptions for growth and cuts to spending, it would fall about Y6.6tn short.

Claims of fiscal discipline are a charade. If you really look into next year's revenues and expenditures, they're spending Y23.3tn on debt service and Y31tn on social security, and getting Y50tn in tax. Before they even run the government they've already spent the money.

One former BoJ official draws a parallel to spending on social security now and spending on the military in 1945, which accounted for a similar share of tax revenues. It is unmanageable. Someone needs to make brave decision to cut it.

Mr Fujimaki cannot see a painless way out. His Japan Restoration party is a motley group spanning Toru Hashimoto, the gaffe-prone mayor of Osaka, and Kanji

"Antonio" Inoki, a former wrestler. But the third-biggest force in the more powerful lower house of parliament is united, Mr Fujimaki says, by a belief that years of "socialist" rule have led Japan astray.

A rebirth is possible, once hyperinflation reduces the government's quadrillion-yen debt to "peanuts" and a radically weaker currency draws manufacturers back home, he says.

But something has to give. Maybe we'll be OK today or tomorrow. Abenomics is weighing down the axle on a car with no brakes.

CHINA'S FINANCIAL DISTRESS ALL TOO VISIBLE

Country's economic change will have deflationary consequences

Investors have a lot to worry about without cause to fret about China, but now they have that too. Trend growth is slowing down, and markets have been shaken up by the actions of the People's Bank of China (PBoC), which is trying to tame a virulent credit boom.

The incidence of financial distress is rising and becoming more visible. The recent drop in the renminbi, and the sharp fall in copper and iron ore prices are the latest high-profile manifestations of China's changing outlook. These are not random developments or bad luck, but connected parts of a complex economic transformation with deflationary consequences for the world economy and skittish financial markets.

In the first two months of 2014, industrial confidence and output indices, retail sales, fixed asset investment, and credit creation were all weaker than expected. A slowdown in economic growth at the start of the year, coinciding with the Chinese new year holidays, is not unusual, but in each of the past two years, the government sanctioned faster credit growth and infrastructure spending to compensate. This time, those options are not available, or much riskier, because the government is trying to change China's economic development model.

Change is mostly visible in finance, where market forces are slowly being brought to bear. The PBoC has announced the goals of full interest rate liberalisation by 2016, and of admitting private firms into the financial sector. It has introduced a two-way market in renminbi trading, and widened the trading band to plus or minus 2 per cent around a daily reference rate. These and other policy changes affecting shadow banking may already be damping the credit, currency and interest rate arbitrage behaviour of local banks, state enterprises and private companies.

Premier Li Keqiang confirmed a change in attitude last week when he said people should be prepared for bond and financial product defaults as the government proceeded with financial deregulation. He spoke in the wake of the country's first corporate bond default and the failure of a significant steel mill to repay loans that fell due.

Slowing economic growth, chronic overcapacity and rising debt service problems in key industries are becoming more common, raising the risk of chain defaults involving suppliers and purchasers. Overcapacity recently prompted a senior executive in the Chinese Iron and Steel Association, Li Xinchuang, to say the problem was so severe it was "probably beyond anyone's imagination".

In an industry survey by the State Council, 71 per cent of respondents said overcapacity in iron and steel, aluminium, cement, coal, solar panels and shipbuilding was very serious.

Copper has fallen nearly 15 % this year, and by more than a third from its 2011 peak. Falling prices have embraced a swath of both ferrous and non-ferrous metals, sending ripples from Perth to Peru.

The underlying reason for the base metals shake-out is the mirror image of the prior boom, in which China's voracious appetite raised its consumption to about 40 per cent of global production. Its per capita consumption is far higher than any other emerging country, regardless of income per head.

In short, what China gave producers and miners on the way up, it is taking away as the commodity composition and intensity of GDP growth tail off.

Large swings in market prices are happening also for murkier – and largely speculative – reasons that hinge on the use of copper and ore as collateral for loans, and as a means of raising finance abroad and bringing it onshore to spend or lend. As the authorities clamp down on credit creation and shadow financing, falling prices, including that of collateral, will expose participants to losses, and markets to the risk of distress selling.

The transmission effects of lower prices into emerging markets and the global economy are most likely to prove disruptive, even if the positive real income effects for consumers eventually win out.

China's economic transformation is happening regardless. Its leaders have choices only about how to manage it, and when to accommodate what is likely to be a painful adjustment. Sage advice would be to grin and bear it now, so as to avoid harsher outcomes later. But the political willingness and capacity to do so is unpredictable.

It is still possible that China will blink, raise infrastructure and housing spending and new credit creation, and lower bank reserve requirements and the renminbi. This would introduce a sharp twist to the underlying plot, but lead to a more dramatic conclusion.

THE FUTURE OF LONDON HOUSING

Political and financial upheaval in some of the world's largest emerging economies is driving a new wave of rich migrants to London's supercharged property market as a place to park their wealth.

Knight Frank, a specialist in upmarket properties, said it had seen online enquiries about British homes from crisis -hit countries such as Argentina, Ukraine and Turkey soar over the past year.

There is potentially a further wave of investment headed for the prime central London property market.

This is despite prices in London already having risen sharply after a rush of foreign buyers of London mansions, prompted by the Eurozone debt crisis and the Arab spring, along with Britain's political stability and benign property taxes.

Prices in London overall in the last 12 months have risen an average of 18% and some top-end values have inflated even more, driving prices in Britain's capital beyond the reach of most residents and making it a hot political topic.

Finance Minister George Osborne said in December he would impose a capital gains tax on foreign property investors from 2015 in a bid to allay fears that wealthy foreign buyers are driving a property bubble.

Knight Frank, which sells homes worth at least 1 million pounds ($1.6 million) and is marketing a 15 bedroom house on The Bishop's Avenue, London's "billionaires row", at 65 million, said the bulk of those enquiries were for homes in the capital.

If you invest in high-end London property you probably feel you have a degree of certainty - it's like a safe currency.

The biggest rise in interest came from Brazil, with a 115 percent spike over the 12 months to the end of January, compared with a year before.

Brazil is one of the so-called "fragile five" economies seen as vulnerable to the U.S. Federal Reserve scaling back monetary stimulus, because of its large current account deficit and reliance on outside capital.

The next biggest increases in enquiries came from Argentina, in the midst of a currency crisis, and Ukraine, which is reeling from a wave of political unrest. Enquiries from both countries spiked 67 percent.

Other members of the fragile five group also saw a pickup in internet house hunting in London's plushest neighbourhoods. Enquiries from Indonesia and Turkey, which have both endured weeks of capital flight and falling currencies, rose 10 percent, while South African interest climbed 9 percent and Indian interest was up 3 percent.

London and the top end of its property market is a well established harbor for money fleeing economic and political instability, because of Britain's relative stability and a tax regime that historically goes easy on foreign residents' overseas wealth.

However the issue of foreign property purchases is politically controversial, with many media reports saying expensive houses and apartments are often bought only as investments and are left unoccupied. Several mansions on The Bishops Avenue had been left empty and were falling into disrepair.

Population growth is central to any attempt to speculate on London's distant future. Already nearing historic highs at 8.3m, the populace is expected to rise to 10m by 2031 – equivalent to adding an extra three boroughs. It had already grown by 12 per cent in the decade to 2011, compared with 7 per cent in the UK as a whole.

The capital's schools and hospitals will feel the strain, with most of the rise expected to come from a growing number of births rather than immigration. But perhaps the greatest challenge facing the city in the coming decades is the question of where the extra people will live.

London housebuilding rates are at half the level needed to meet demand – put by Mr Johnson at 42,000 a year for at least the next decade. There is already evidence of overpopulation: some 12 per cent of people live in overcrowded conditions, as defined by the standard number of bedrooms per head. London's average household size rose from 2.35 to 2.47 people over the decade to 2011, while the national average remained flat.

This mismatch of supply and demand has led to steep rises in the capital's house prices. Figures last month from the Office for National Statistics put the rise in the year to September at 9.4 per cent, compared with a national figure of 3.8 per cent. A London home costs £434,000, on average, compared with £245,000 across the UK.

Mr Johnson last month launched a long-term strategy, proposing new incentives and powers to kick-start stalled housing schemes and encourage more low-cost homes – both to buy and rent – for low and middle income Londoners.

But with a recovery in the mortgage market, and London property continuing to attract foreign investment, the city is already undergoing a building boom across many areas. King's Cross and the Nine Elms project around Battersea are two of the biggest brownfield sites. But another area of vibrant growth is east London, where the regeneration triggered by the Olympics – still a work in progress – has been followed by a string of proposed business and residential schemes.

East London's Royal Docks, which fell into decline in the 1970s, is the centre of several projects, including the creation of an "Asian business port" by Chinese developers ABP. Oxley Holdings, a Singapore developer, last month bought the Royal Wharf site with permission to build 3,385 homes on the land, which agent Knight Frank said was the biggest site to come on the market since Battersea Power Station.

East of the City of London, Irish property developer Tom Ryan is proposing Europe's tallest residential tower, a 74-storey skyscraper on the western side of Canary Wharf; to its east is Wood Wharf, an area for which 1,600 homes are planned, as well as retail and office space.

In spite of this acceleration of development, Newham is not yet Chiswick. Tony Travers, an expert on the capital at the London School of Economics and Political Science, says the old image of the East End as unfashionable and threatening has been dispelled. But if you compare the perfectly nice terraced housing in east London with its equivalent in outer west London, it is still seen as less desirable.

Population growth may change this, he adds, as young people will be forced to buy in the east. The young are going to start living in Leyton and Ilford in a way that they used to live in Shepherds Bush or West Hampstead.

The extent to which they are pushed further out of the centre – in whichever direction – will be influenced in part by the flow of foreign capital into London housing. Concentrated at the top end of the market, overseas demand has prised London further apart from the rest of the country in terms of property values.

London Transport imagines the future from 1926

Making predictions is a perilous business. In a poster produced by London Transport in 1926, an artist imagined how the UK capital would look a century later: in this unrecognisable vista, the skies are filled with a multitude of small aeroplanes and airships, and the streets are overshadowed by unlikely brick-built skyscrapers.

The poster was included by Boris Johnson in his "2020 Vision", a document setting out the long-term strategic needs of the city. While the London mayor pointed out where the early 20th-century transport planners went awry, he agreed with them in one important respect: London in 2026 is likely to be far more crowded, and its public services far more pressed, than its current inhabitants have ever experienced.

According to figures from Savills, the estate agent, the 10 most expensive boroughs in London have a total property worth of £552bn, the same as Scotland, Wales and Northern Ireland combined. More than £7bn of overseas money went into prime London property last year, the agent said. The Treasury is watching the trend closely: last month it was considering taxing capital gains on foreign sales of British property, which UK citizens, but not foreigners, pay on any home that is not their primary residence.

But the role of overseas investment is hotly contested. Many believe there would be a price to pay if its flow were stemmed. A study for Berkeley Group, the developer, by Mr Travers and Professor Christine Whitehead of the LSE, said such investment was essential to the supply of affordable housing. Its loss would threaten improved infrastructure funded through planning obligations. In short, international investors generate additional housebuilding, which relieves rather than exacerbates the pressure on housing supply.

The world has recognised London's myriad qualities as a solid investment: but its appetite for the city may end up being something London can neither live with, nor without.

Sale of HSBC tower hints at return to property boom times

London's biggest and most expensive office building, HSBC's global headquarters, is up for sale at what would be a record price for the British market, in a sign that the capital's commercial property market is booming again.

The 44-storey, 1.1m sq ft building in Canary Wharf, east London, is being marketed by the estate agents JLL and GM Real Estate for offers above £1.1bn, say sources with knowledge of the property.

The HSBC tower became the most expensive building in London when it sold for £1.09bn at the height of the UK property boom in 2007.

HSBC has a 13-year lease on the building and is committed to annual upward-only inflation-linked rent reviews, according to sources familiar with the tenancy arrangements. This would make it an attractive proposition for investors seeking a hedge against inflation.

Where is London in this world?

Some cities, such as Brasília and Washington, are the political capitals of their countries but not their business and financial centres. For others, such as Istanbul and Milan, the reverse is true. London performs both roles. London leads and shapes the nation of which it forms part in a way that only Moscow and Paris, among large European capitals, come close to matching.

But London's significance to Britain, Europe and the world extends further than that. More than in any other European city, London life is seamlessly woven into the global economy, global population movements and global culture.

This brings both advantages and disadvantages. On the positive side, London generates much of the wealth that helps to protect and raise living standards elsewhere in Britain. According to the Centre for Economics and Business Research, a British-based independent forecaster, London will record economic growth next year of 3.8 %, accounting for almost a third of Britain's entire economic expansion.

By 2018 the capital's output will be 16 % higher than it was before the financial crash of 2008, the CEBR says.

On the other hand, London's dominance means that other British cities, including once great imperial commercial and manufacturing centres such as Birmingham, Bristol and Liverpool, struggle to emerge from the capital's shadow.

This is not true in Germany, where Berlin is the nation's political nerve centre but Frankfurt is the financial capital, Hamburg is the media capital and other cities, such as Düsseldorf and Munich, compete with Berlin as dynamic business hubs. Neither is it true in Italy, where the glorious artistic heritage and local identities of Florence, Naples and Venice place them beside rather than below Rome in importance.

London's centrality to British economic performance, and its role as the nation's chief gateway for trade and investment, will not change in the foreseeable future. But in transport, education and housing, this will present policy makers with great challenges as well as opportunities, as is being discovered by Britain's Conservative-Liberal Democrat coalition government and Boris Johnson, the Conservative mayor of Greater London since 2008.

The debate over whether to construct a new airport for London, or just to add a third runway at Heathrow airport west of the capital, is a good example. European cities such as Berlin, Istanbul, Milan and Moscow have responded to the boom in international demand for business and leisure travel either by upgrading old airports or by making plans for new ones.

British politicians recognise that new investment in airport capacity is essential to London's future, but they seem unable to make up their minds about which option to take. The cost of a new airport, plus the necessary transport links to London, would run into tens of billions of pounds. It would be an expensive choice for a country whose public finances are stretched and which is already investing very large sums in modernising the capital's creaking overground and underground rail networks.

In education and housing, the task is to maintain London's attractiveness and reputation for quality, while not crowding out native Britons. Many Americans, Arabs, Chinese and Russians, not to mention French, Germans, Italians and Scandinavians, want their children to study at top-ranked universities and schools. The wealthiest revel in their sumptuous properties in Kensington, Mayfair and at Tower Bridge.

But the impact on Londoners has been enormous. Non-Britons now account for more than one in two students at the London School of Economics, one in three at University College London, and lesser but still sizeable numbers at the finest private schools such as St Paul's and Westminster. High tuition fees and accommodation costs, not easily affordable for many British families, are driving this trend.

Meanwhile, London house prices, especially in the most exclusive districts, are soaring thanks to what appears to be the insatiable appetite of the world's most affluent people for a property in the British capital. On the website of Berkeley

Homes, the developers who built One Tower Bridge, a luxury complex due to open in 2014, buyers are wooed in Arabic, Chinese, French, Hindi, Russian and Turkish as well as English.

London politicians such as Simon Hughes, the MP for Bermondsey and Old Southwark, on the south bank of the Thames, want restrictions on foreigners' property investments in order to free up homes for local buyers, many of which cannot possibly afford today's prices. Eric Pickles, the UK minister for local government, points out the legal drawbacks: "You certainly couldn't do it for EU citizens, and it would be dubious in terms of anyone else … I'm more concerned about getting affordable housing into London."

In certain respects, expensive housing and living costs are the price Londoners pay for hosting one of the world's largest financial industries and displaying an open attitude to globalisation in all its forms, including foreign investment. The beneficial effects are considerable, as demonstrated in a report by Startup Genome, a private sector project that sought out the world's most favourable locations for innovative entrepreneurship. Top of its list was Silicon Valley. Then came Tel Aviv, Los Angeles, Seattle, New York, Boston and London. Paris, Moscow and Berlin were the only other European cities in the top 20, each well below the UK capital.

Berlin is these days the EU's most important capital in terms of political weight. But it will not match London as a business and finance hub as long as Frankfurt remains Germany's financial centre. Arguably, London will face more serious competition over the medium term from rising cities such as Dubai, Shanghai and Singapore than from Europe. New York and Tokyo will still be alive and strong.

London will have to keep raising its game to stay at the heart of the world economy.

'Ghost gazumping' haunts London housing market

Property buyers in London are increasingly being asked to pay tens of thousands of pounds extra at the last minute, in a new, more aggressive form of "gazumping" that does not feature a rival bidder.

In a sign of the frenzied state of the capital's housing market, estate agents say many sellers are raising the price of their homes days before the exchange of contracts.

Unlike the gazumping of the 1980s, when rival buyers stepped in at the last minute with a higher offer, this trend involves sellers increasing the price because they can – because there is so much demand for a small number of properties.

It's now very common and a depressing factor of a market with low supply and monster demand.

This "ghost gazumping" typically happens several weeks after an initial offer is accepted, as rival estate agents door-knock sellers and tell them they have agreed to too low a price.

This was a "new phenomenon" that had not been seen before, even during the property bubbles of the 1980s and the mid-2000s.

The trend was increasingly common in London suburbs including Dulwich, Twickenham, Shepherd's Bush and Kensal Rise.

We've just seen it happen with one house, where the deal was struck at £1m but the sellers have gone back and asked for £1.1m. The buyers are paying the higher amount.

UK house prices

Price indices have presented wildly contrasting pictures of the health of the housing market – according to some the boom is back, while to others the slump staggers on.

Many buyers are paying the extra sums, in some cases in six figures, to avoid having to find a new house as prices keep rising.

The phenomenon illustrates how much the housing market has strengthened since the credit crunch, when prices fell sharply in some boroughs of London.

Prices in the capital were 14.9 per cent higher year-on-year in the fourth quarter of 2013.

The trend was a symptom of a huge demand for property but not enough homes on the market.

Vendors are very good at looking at good news, but they don't read bad news. So they will see statistics showing house prices are up 10 per cent in a year and they think they rose by that amount in February alone--They think, therefore, their house must suddenly be worth 10 per cent more.

At some point interest rates are going to go up and it will be a wake-up call

Unscrupulous agents were approaching homeowners whose properties had been under offer for more than eight weeks and urging them to leave their current agent and put their house back on the market at a higher price.

In the 1980s and 2000s you had gazumping, where it was someone coming in and they could offer more money. What now seems to be happening is where the price is going up without any rival bid at all. It's not necessarily greed; if people think they can get more, they will try.

One in three UK homes purchased by cash buyers

The number of people buying their home in the UK without a mortgage has hit the highest level since 2007, with one in three purchases being made outright with cash, according to researchers.

Cash buyers spent £90bn last year on 350,000 homes, a study by estate agents Hamptons International showed. Buy-to-let investors and second homeowners rushed to sink their money into the rapidly rising market, with the number of cash buyers increasing by a third year-on-year.

The influx of cash buyers has sucked supply out of the market, Hamptons said, leading to the number of homes on the market falling by 5 per cent year-on-year nationally and by a fifth in London.

Price indices have presented contrasting pictures of the health of the housing market; according to some the boom is back while to others the slump staggers on

Cash buyers have been at the vanguard of the housing market recovery in recent months, with the number increasing at a faster rate than those purchasing with a mortgage.

Low levels of stock have been a factor driving rapid price increases, particularly in the south of England. Until we see more owners moving home, who have properties to sell as well as buy, the shortage of homes for sale is likely to continue.

In London alone, more than £18bn was spent on cash-only house purchases. In the wider southeast a further £27bn was spent on outright purchases.

How Hong Kong buyers have sent London real estate soaring

Foreign buyers are snapping up central London homes, distorting prices and forcing policymakers to levy new taxes in an attempt to control the market.

London real estate is among the most desirable in the world, attracting wealthy investors looking for high returns -- often at the expense of city natives who are being priced out of many neighborhoods.

Foreign money so dominates that nearly 70% of newly built properties in primeareas of central London were bought by foreign nationals between 2011 and 2013, according to realtor Knight Frank.

And nowhere is the frenetic race for London real estate more evident than in Hong Kong, where newspapers regularly feature full-page advertisements for new buildings and developers host sales events in swanky hotels.

Hong Kong's marquee Mandarin Oriental hotel is transformed into a showroom for London properties on most weekends, with realtors including Knight Frank and Colliers seeking to attract buyers -- many of whom are willing to shell out for an apartment sight unseen.

Competition for these buyers is intense, so much so that sellers even do battle over securing the best function rooms at the Mandarin.

The buyers we are dealing with are very experienced investors. There are also people who come every week to look at the projects that are on offer, so they understand what's good value.

130 to 140 potential investors come through the doors on a typical weekend at the Mandarin. The would-be buyers are met with floor plans, view books with glossy images of Buckingham Palace, as well as a sizable supply of dim sum, croissants and coffee.

Buying at the Mandarin is a full-service experience. As a deal is signed, investors can meet with lawyers or discuss furniture options with interior designers.

Some investors hope to rent out the property to tenants. Others buy for their children studying at boarding schools and universities across the UK. Most sign up for developments that won't be completed for years.

Asian buyers are very savvy and are used to reading plans. They are able to visualize what they are getting in the end.

Others value London real estate for its raw earning power, and see property as a stable alternative to stocks.

If you look at the performance of the stock market over the last 10 years compared to central London, I think that most people would come out worse if they were in the stock market.

There's just a feeling that people would rather have a stake in something that they own outright.

For developers, selling in Hong Kong is a matter of going where the money is. Euroterra co-founder Pantazis Therianos said he chose to focus on Asia after observing the success that other developers were having in the region.

But some developers fear the appetite for London properties may slow as the government prepares to tax future investment gains made by non-residents.

Currently, only UK residents are subject to capital gains tax on their second homes -- a tax that is usually levied at 28%.

The capital gains tax change, due to take effect in April 2015, will require overseas buyers to surrender some of the profits they make on UK property.

Some foreign buyers will be affected by another tax change. From this month, the government is applying stamp duty at a rate of 15% to any purchase of residential property worth £500,000 or more made through a company.

And pressure is building for measures to prevent foreign investors being offered first refusal on prime London real estate. The city's mayor has urged developers to stop marketing new homes to overseas buyers before they've been made available to Londoners.

THE ROAD AHEAD FOR FACEBOOK

Why Zuckerberg had to buy Whatsapp

With 450 million active users each month, a million new sign-ups per day and a whopping 72% of its users active on the service every day, handling about 50 billion messages and 500 million pictures, Whatsapp has rapidly grown to become the biggest messaging service in the world, with massive penetration in large developed markets such as India.

The clearest illustration of its phenomenal gowth came earlier this year, when the number of messages sent on Whatsapp every day overtook the number of plain old SMS text messages sent all over the globe. What's more, the company is the very epitome of "fast and nimble"—Whatsapp at age five has just 55 employees.

Is Facebook playing platform catch-up with $2bn Oculus deal

What is Facebook? To many of its 1.2bn regular users, it is a place to share photos and chat with friends.

To its founder Mark Zuckerberg, it is a virtual world where members could eventually spend most of their daily lives. That is the vision behind Mr Zuckerberg's $2bn acquisition of Oculus VR, a pioneer in the long-promised but newly resurgent realm of virtual reality.

Every 10 or 15 years there's a major new computing platform.

To me, by far the most exciting platform is around vision...It's different from anything I've ever experienced in my life. Whoever builds and defines the next generation's technology platform would benefit financially and strategically.

In the current mobile era, Facebook missed out on creating its own platform, leaving Apple and Google, which developed the iOS and Android smartphone operating systems respectively, to dominate.

Mr Zuckerberg believes Oculus would boost Facebook's goals of connecting everyone, understanding the world and building the knowledge economy.

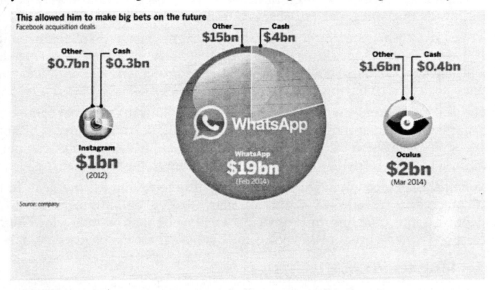

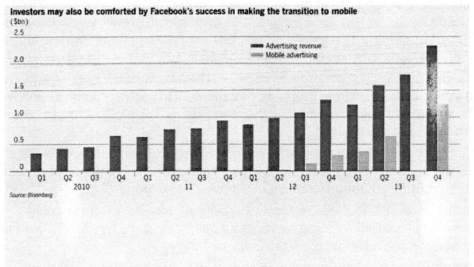

Recently, at a Game Developers Conference in San Francisco, Oculus and its new rival from Sony PlayStation, dubbed Project Morpheus, stole the show. Developers were abuzz with excitement about the potential of the new technology.

Not so many years ago, Facebook itself was in that position, as games makers such as Zynga were propelled to huge riches through its viral distribution platform. Now, although more than 375m people still log into games through Facebook every month, it is a distant priority for developers behind Apple's App Store and Google Play for Android devices. Even Zynga is trying to loosen its ties with Facebook.

The world is moving mobile--Facebook is part of the ecosystem, rather than the platform.

In the realm of Apple and Google, Facebook is just another app.

Owning Oculus puts Facebook back into focus for games developers. Oculus's chief technology officer is John Carmack, who as founder of id Software created pioneering 3D PC games such as *Doom* and *Quake* in the 1990s.

It does give them an opportunity to explore what the next level of gaming might be. However, Facebook could have achieved that through a simple partnership, without having to spend a dollar. That could have brought "some data and some evidence it was worth buying".

The deal risks scaring them off both the platforms. Many in the games community were alarmed that their darling had sold to Facebook, posting hundreds of angry messages on Oculus's website. Several backers of Oculus's Kickstarter campaign, which raised $2.4m in 2012, are also upset, according to posts on that site.

Nonetheless, Facebook might have another near-term aim for the deal. In the hyper-competitive recruitment market of Silicon Valley, building a virtual world could prove more tempting to prospective employees than working for Google, Pinterest or Twitter – even if Facebook cannot deliver it for many years.

In the long term . . .

Mr Zuckerberg is fond of calling Facebook a "utility" that should be viewed more like electricity than a flash-in-the-pan fad of a social network. Until he bought Oculus, some thought that was a convenient way of explaining why it had fallen out of favour with teenagers.

But the $2bn deal shows something else: the kernel of a virtual world created entirely by Facebook – where users can visit their doctor on Facebook, attend lessons in a classroom on the other side of the world using Facebook and yes, shop in a Facebook megastore.

That may sound like a nightmare for privacy campaigners, who have long criticised the company, or regulators, who are already struggling to apply the law to the internet on computers and smartphones.

But those were all examples Mr Zuckerberg gave of how Oculus could be used in the longer term. Calling it the "most social platform ever", he said Oculus had the potential to be the technology platform of the future.

Ensuring that Facebook can evolve as new platforms evolve makes sense to us.

Yet $2bn seems like a significant amount of money for a problem that has yet to emerge. Assuming that developers paid Oculus at least $300 for each of the 75,000 headsets it has sold to date, Mr Zuckerberg is paying a hefty 90 times its revenues for the company.

Virtual reality could become the next stage of Silicon Valley's transformation of other industries, from transport to fashion. If Facebook can actually own the platform of the future, $2bn – more than three-quarters of which is paid in its high-flying stock – might come to look like a bargain.

It is hard to imagine a world in which people regularly interact in a digital 3D environment but by the same token if you asked me before smartphones became popular, did I imagine I would be standing in line in Starbucks scanning Facebook and using my phone to pay? I wouldn't have been able to.

As this world Mr Zuckerberg envisages is probably at least a decade off, he held back from explaining exactly how Facebook would profit from it. There might be advertising in the [virtual] world but we'll have to figure that out down the line, among other possible moneymaking opportunities.

Many marketers poured money into virtual worlds such as Second Life in the years when social networking was taking off. In the mid-2000s, companies such as IBM and American Apparel created giant virtual pavilions where Second Life users could interact. The experience had a "lot of limitations".

Also note the technical challenges facing virtual reality. Many users of Oculus's prototype experience feelings of nausea and questions are already being raised about the longer-term health effects of prolonged exposure to screens resting just inches from the eyes.

Similar concerns were once raised about television and cell phones. For now, people who want to live in Facebook full-time must do so by staring at glowing rectangles held at arm's length from their faces.

WHAT HISTORY SAYS ABOUT FED RATE HIKES

Recently, Janet Yellen gave her first post-FOMC meeting press conference. In her prepared statement, she stated exactly what was already expected:

1) *accommodative policy will remain in place for a considerable amount of time after the current quantitative easing program ends this fall,*

2) *employment is improving,*

3) *the economy is recovering but has more work to do, and;*

4) *the current quantitative easing program would be "tapered" from $65 to $55 billion per month beginning in April.*

The problem for the markets came during her press conference when she was asked what a *"considerable amount of time"* between the end of the current QE program and the first rate hike would be. She replied: *"About six months."* It took the markets about 5-seconds to understand exactly what that meant: *"Rate hike in early 2015."* If you want to know the precise moment that those words were uttered, just look at the chart below to see if you can figure it out.

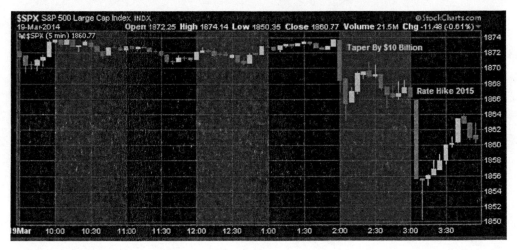

The question is this:

"If the Fed begins to hike interest rates, what effect does that have on the economy and the markets?"

Prima facie, the idea of rising interest rates shocked the markets, however, in the long-term it's a positive sign. Rates rise as the economy does better.

The assumption he makes is that as the economy *"catches fire"* and corporate profits increase, then it is natural for interest rates to rise also. If a growing economy is a function of expanding profitability, then what is wrong with the chart below?

"The chart below shows corporate profits, per the BEA, divided by GDP. (You can substitute GNP but the result is virtually identical between the two measures.)"

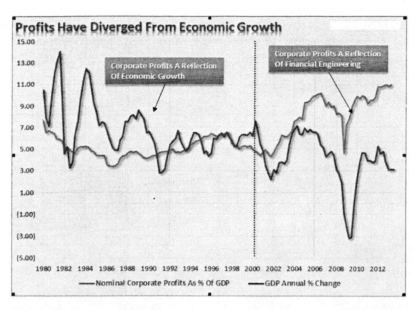

The current levels of profits, as a share of GDP, are at record levels. This is interesting because corporate profits should be a reflection of the underlying economic strength. However, in recent years, due to financial engineering, wage and employment suppression and increase in productivity, corporate profits have become extremely deviated.

Much of the profitability increases for corporations have come from stock buybacks and cost cutting. However, many of those stock buybacks and dividend increases *(as with AAPL)* have been financed with low interest rate debt issuance. If rates rise, this is no longer an option. The *"cash on the sidelines"* story is true to some degree as total liquid assets as a percentage of total assets is near all-time highs. However, corporations have relevered balance sheets to a large degree due to the cheap cost of debt. The chart below shows the ratio of cash to debt.

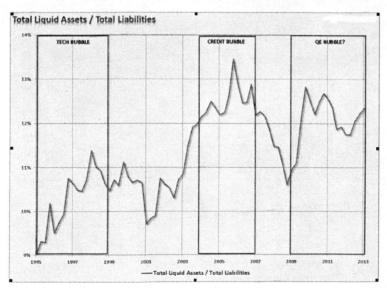

As far as cost cutting goes, much of that has come from reducing employment. However, as the chart below of full-time employment relative to the population shows, corporations have likely *"milked that cow dry."*

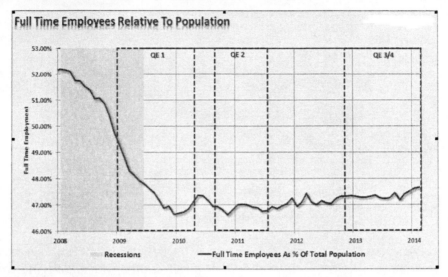

The problem is that the data suggests that artificially low interest rates and ongoing monetary interventions have been a key driver of both market returns and corporate profitability. However, what has been lacking is sustainable, organic, economic growth.

With this background, the consequence of a hike in overnight lending rates *(Fed funds rate)* will likely have far more significant impact on corporate profitability, economic growth and market returns than currently believed.

In order to support that conclusion a historical look at Federal Reserve actions can give us clues about future outcomes. The first chart below shows the fed funds rate as compared to economic growth.

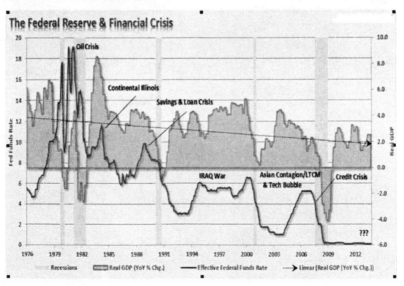

What is interesting is that a case can be made that the Federal Reserve's monetary policies are potentially complicit in both economic booms and busts. When the Federal Reserve has historically begun raising interest rates the economy has slowed down, or worse. Subsequently, the Fed has to reverse its policies to restart economic growth.

It is significant that each time the Fed has lowered the overnight lending rate, the next set of increases have never exceeded the previous peak. This is due to the fact, that over the last 35 years, economic growth has been on a continued decline. I have detailed this declining trend in the Fed funds rate below as compared to the S&P 500.

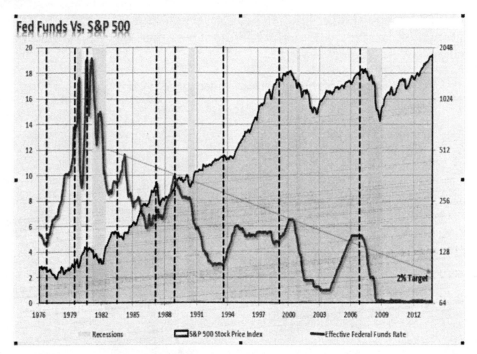

Increases in interest rates are not kind to the markets either. I have highlighted, with the vertical dashed black lines, each time the Fed has started increasing the overnight lending rates. Each time has seen either market stagnation, declines, or crashes. Furthermore, it is currently implied that the Fed funds rate will increase to 3% in the future, yet the current downtrend suggests that an increase to 2% is likely all that can be withstood.

Rising interest rates are generally perceived to negatively impact earnings as borrowing costs rise, housing as mortgage costs increase, disposable incomes as debt costs rise, etc. With an economy that is nearly 70% driven by consumption there is little wiggle room for increased costs when incomes remain primarily stagnant.

THE JOBS AND THE JOB SEEKERS
HAVE BOTH DISAPPEARED

The Economic Policy Institute (EPI) had an interesting chart and comments in its report The Vast Majority of the 5.8 Million Missing Workers Are Under Age 55.

Since the start of the Great Recession over six years ago, labor force participation has dropped significantly. Most of the drop—roughly three-quarters—was due to the lack of job opportunities in the Great Recession and its aftermath. There are now 5.8 million workers who are not in the labor force but who would be if job opportunities were strong.

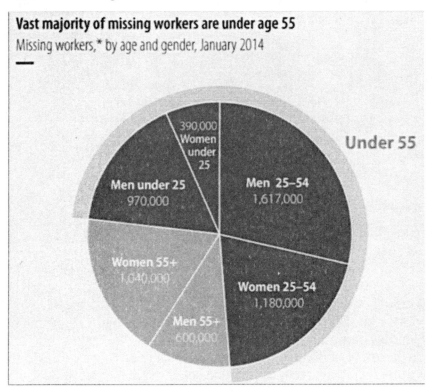

Vast majority of missing workers are under age 55

Missing workers,* by age and gender, January 2014

It is possible that some of these missing workers who are at or near retirement age have given up hope of ever finding decent work again and decided to retire early. Such workers may not ever be drawn back into the labor market, even when labor market conditions substantially improve. It is important to note, however, that more than 70 percent of the 5.8 million missing workers are under age 55. These missing workers under age 55—4.2 million of them—are extremely unlikely to have retired and are therefore likely to enter or reenter the labor force when job opportunities substantially improve.

If the missing workers were in the labor market looking for work, the unemployment rate right now would be 10.0 percent instead of 6.6 percent.

Core 25-54 Age Group

I like the above idea but a chart that shows changes over time would be better. Also, let's take out those under the age of 25 to see trends in the core 25-54 age group.

In general, those in age group 25-54 should be working, not retired, and not still in school.

Age 25-55 Employment Data

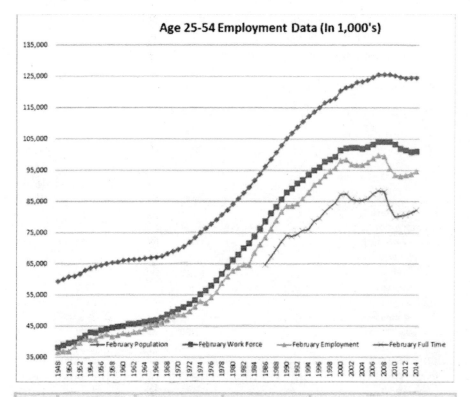

Year	Population	Labor Force	Employment	Full Time Employment
2007	125,456	104,160	99,849	88,374
2008	125,440	104,021	99,503	88,101
2009	125,498	104,018	95,530	82,935
2010	125,178	103,191	93,348	79,948
2011	124,647	101,774	93,017	80,368
2012	124,341	101,276	93,346	80,721
2013	124,354	100,761	93,736	81,264
2014	124,439	100,904	94,666	82,248

Since February 2007....

- Population of age group 25-54 declined by 1,107,000
- Labor Force declined by 3,256,000
- Employment declined by 5,183,000
- Full-Time Employment declined by 6,126,000

The loss in employment in the core 25-54 age group is a whopping 5,183,000. Factoring in the decline in population, that is an excess job loss of 4,076,000!

The labor force should have declined by 1,107,000. Instead, it declined by 3,256,000. That is an excess labor force decline of 2,149,000.

Calculating a More Realistic Unemployment Rate

Here are the figures from the Latest Jobs Report. (Numbers in Thousands)

Category	Feb. 2013	Dec. 2013	Jan. 2014	Feb. 2014	Change from: Jan. 2014- Feb. 2014
Employment status					
Civilian noninstitutional population	244,828	246,745	246,915	247,085	170
Civilian labor force	155,511	154,937	155,460	155,724	264
Participation rate	63.5	62.8	63.0	63.0	0.0
Employed	143,464	144,586	145,224	145,266	42
Employment-population ratio	58.6	58.6	58.8	58.8	0.0
Unemployed	12,047	10,351	10,236	10,459	223
Unemployment rate	7.7	6.7	6.6	6.7	0.1
Not in labor force	89,317	91,808	91,455	91,361	-94

To calculate an more realistic unemployment rate, all we need to do is adjust the labor force then run the math. Adding 2,149,000 back to the labor force we get 157,873,000. The number of employed is 145,266,000 as shown above. The ratio of employed to the labor force is 92.01 percent.

Via the above method, the unemployment rate would be 7.99 percent, not the 10 percent calculated by the EPI. Regardless, 7.99 percent is way higher than the reported 6.7 percent.

Moreover, that 7.99 % unemployment rate assumes everyone else who dropped out of the labor force either retired or is genuinely disabled (an admittedly ridiculous assumption, yet one that makes things seem better that they are).

Taking other age groups into consideration, I estimate the true unemployment rate (not counting part-time employment) is somewhere between 8.5 and 9 percent.

Demographic Trends in the 50-and-Older Work Force

The overall LFPR is a simple computation: You take the Civilian Labor Force (people age 16 and over employed or seeking employment) and divide it by the Civilian

Noninstitutional Population (those 16 and over not in the military and or committed to an institution). The result is the participation rate expressed as a percent.

For the larger context, here is a snapshot of the monthly LFPR for age 16 and over stretching back to the Bureau of Labor Statistics' starting point in 1948, the blue line in the chart below, along with the unemployment rate.

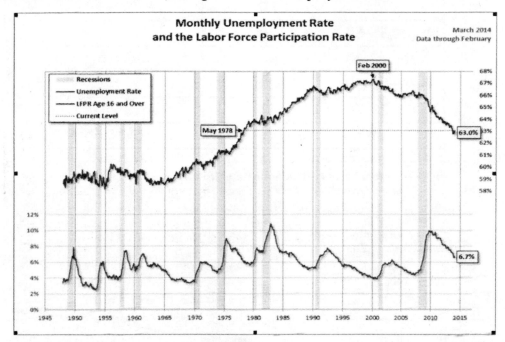

The overall LFPR peaked in February 2000 at 67.3% and gradually began falling. The rate leveled out from 2004 to 2007, but in 2008, with onset of the Great Recession, the rate began to accelerate. The latest rate is 63.0%, back to a level first seen in 1978. The demography of our aging workforce has been a major contributor to this trend. The oldest Baby Boomers, those born between 1946 and 1964, began becoming eligible for reduced Social Security benefits in 2008 and full benefits in 2012. Job cuts during the Great Recession certainly strengthened the trend.

The Growing Ratios of Older Workers

It might seem intuitive that the participation rate for the older workers would have declined the fastest. But exactly the opposite has been the case. The chart below illustrates the growth of the LFPR for six age 50-plus cohorts since the turn of the century. I've divided them into five-year cohorts from ages 50 through 74 and an open-ended age 75 and older. The pattern is clear: The older the cohort, the greater the growth.

Cohort	Employed per hundred in January 2000	Employed per hundred in February 2014
Ages 50-54	80	78
Ages 55-59	70	72
Ages 60-64	46	55
Ages 65-69	23	32
Ages 70-74	13	19
Age 75 plus	5	8

Another Way to Envision the Data

The table inset in the chart above shows the participation rate for the latest month and the percentage growth since January 2000. The adjacent table rounds the rates to integers for January 2000 and for the latest month. Essentially this table gives us two snapshots: The number of workers per hundred for each of the six cohorts at the turn of the century and the number of workers per hundred now. This is not the scenario that would have been envisioned a generation ago for the "Golden Years" of retirement. Consider: Today nearly one in three of the 65-69 cohort and almost one in five of the 70-74 cohort are in the labor force.

There is no question that the pace of Boomer retirement will accelerate in the years ahead. Just add about 65 years to the red dots in the chart below and you'll get some idea of the epic retirement wave that is just beginning (and note that the birth statistics below don't include immigration).

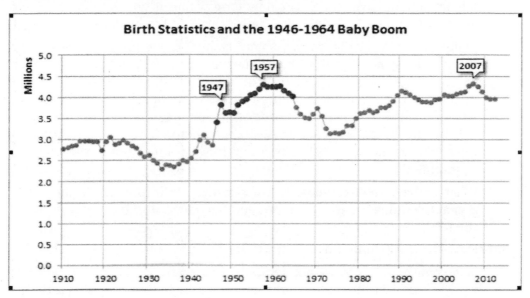

What's Ahead?

With the improvement in the market since the 2009 index lows, many households approaching the traditional retirement age are in better financial shape and with healthier nest eggs than was the case a few years ago. On the other hand, when we look at the age 65-69 cohort, the dark blue line in the second chart above, we see that it rose steadily between the last two recessions despite the market's improvement, although it appears to be leveling out over the past 18 or so months. If we can avoid a near-term recession and the economy continues to improve, perhaps the participation rates of the older cohorts will gradually reverse directions. That would certainly improve the job opportunities of younger generations.

Known unknowns about labour market slack

Here are questions to which the answers remain disputed:

1) To what extent will discouraged workers return to the labour force if the economic recovery accelerates?

2) Are part-time workers — and specifically those who became part-time after their (full-time) hours were cut — another kind of labour market slack? In other words, would companies choosing to increase the hours of these part-time workers, making them full-time again, slow the pace of hiring unemployed workers. By how much?

3) How many of the long-term unemployed now represent structural unemployment? Keep in mind that a) structural vs cyclical is a useful conceptual framework, but those are still categories invented by economists, and the real world is never so neat, and b) the share of long-term unemployed that rejoined the labour force spiked in the very tight labour market of the 1990s (see also here). Could that happen again? How tight would the labour market have to be? For how long would it be reasonable to allow above-target inflation while waiting for this trend to begin?

4) There are also likely to be some labour force dropouts who could hypothetically be coaxed back into the labour market, but whose switching costs are high — because they're on disability, say, or have enrolled in classes, or because they gave up and retired earlier than they'd expected. How high would wages have to climb in order to make the opportunity cost tradeoff worthwhile for them to return? Again, if higher wages drive inflation above the Fed's target, how much higher and for how long should this overshoot be tolerated?

5) What is the correct estimate of the natural rate of unemployment, or the non-accelerating inflation rate of unemployment, or whatever you want to call it?

6) How much will inflation climb this year relative to last year?

7) Is the hourly wage growth acceleration of recent months the result of shorter work weeks caused by the winter, and will thus flatten out, or is it the start or a self-sustaining rise?

8) Longer-term secular inflationary forces *appear* to be pushing in the opposite direction as they were in the 1970s. In other words, they appear anti-inflationary, making it far less likely now that the central bank will lose real or perceived control over inflation. Back then: massive labour force participation growth; pressure on policymakers to accommodate new entrants by keeping real wages low (through high inflation); two supply-side shocks to the energy landscape. Demographic-driven labour force participation decline; stronger constituency to keep inflation low (retirees, "savers"); positive supply-side shock to energy landscape. This seems like a plausible story to us. But is it true? And how much should it matter?

9) What's the output gap? How useful a concept is it? What about sectoral shifts and automation and outsourcing and are good and evil mere human constructs or were they passed along to us by a benevolent superbeing?

For monetary policy, what matters are inflation and unemployment, expectations of what they'll be in the future, and the variables that influence them. Different subcategories that constitute labour market slack are obviously a big part of that debate, but given the lack of clarity about the trends mentioned above, we think it best to focus on the overarching goals — and, crucially, on the relative costs and benefits of missing on one side versus the other side of those goals.

THIS BASE METAL IS WEATHERING THE ROUT

Amid a brutal rout in base metals this year, one commodity is standing out from the crowd and has even further to run this year.

Prices of nickel, a metal used in the production of stainless steel, have been soaring in recent months, up roughly 17 percent year to date and trading at approximately $16,300 per metric ton.

Its peers however, including copper, iron ore, aluminum and zinc, have been tanking alongside. Copper, for example, has lost around 12 percent year to date, as worries over the use of copper in Chinese trade financing deals panicked investors.

It's [nickel] been a little bit of a slow burner though obviously it's one of the only commodities that's up on the year. The whole issue surrounding the Indonesian ban on raw materials is at the crux of this.

Indonesia - the world's largest miner of nickel - imposed an export ban on mineral ores in January, in an effort to boost profits at home as miners are forced to process their ore domestically before exporting it. The ban specifically targeted the nickel and bauxite industries and will affect more than $2 billion in annual shipments.

Worker on staircase leading to processing platform at nickel refinery

The full effect of the export ban has yet to be felt, meaning nickel prices could run up further.

At the moment, we're not seeing the real impact of that being played out in China as Chinese steel makers still have high inventories.

But inventories are starting to fall in China, and we expect that to really kick in the second quarter into the second half. That's when I expect the nickel price to really react to the upside.

Nickel prices could climb to around $9.50 a pound ($19,000 per metric ton) by the year end, if we consider tensions in Russia and developments in the global steel industry, on top of Indonesia's export ban on mineral ores as key drivers.

In the recent past, the European Union stepped up sanctions on Russia over its annexation of Crimea, and warns it would move to impose trade and economic measures if Russia moves beyond Crimea into southern and eastern Ukraine.

Russia represents roughly 28 % of global nickel mine supply. In addition, the global steel industry will see a strong uptick in demand this year, which is seen as a boon for nickel.

The steel industry is reaching the end of three years of destocking (a process of reducing inventory), while demand for steel from countries outside of China is improving. Furthermore, economic growth in China to come in at healthy levels this year, despite worries of a slowdown.

We are seeing talk of shrinking lead times for stainless makers in Europe, but Chinese steel makers are still talking of depressed demand mode, but I expect this to change soon. Shrinking lead times - which are the time difference between delivery and order - are often an indication of renewed demand.

Indonesia is a known story and factored in. It is only the potential for escalation of sanctions against Russian nickel exports that has pushed the price higher.

WHAT THE BREAKOUT IN THE GOLD-TO-COPPER RATIO IS TELLING US

Copper is considered an industrial metal, used in industries across the board. When copper prices fall, it's usually an indicator of slowdown in the global economy. On the contrary, gold bullion isn't much of an industrial metal; rather, it is used as a hedge against uncertainty in the global economy.

When you look at these two metals together, often referred to as the gold-to-copper ratio, they tell us something very important: the ratio of how many pounds of copper it takes to buy one ounce of gold bullion has long been an indicator of sentiment in the global economy.

If the gold-to-copper ratio is in a downtrend, it means investors are betting on the global economy to grow. In contrast, if it is increasing (if the number of pounds of copper it costs to buy an ounce of gold is rising), it tells us investors are concerned about protecting their wealth in a slowing global economy.

Below, you'll find a chart of the gold-to-copper ratio.

Chart courtesy of www.StockCharts.com

Looking at the chart above, it is clear something happened at the beginning of 2014. Investors became very worried. Since the beginning of the year, the gold-to-copper ratio has increased more than 28%—the steepest increase in more than two years.

And the weekly chart of copper prices looks terrible too:

Chart courtesy of www.StockCharts.com

Copper prices have been trending downward since 2011. In 2013, these prices broke below their 200-day moving average and recently, they broke below a very critical support level at $3.00. While all of this was happening, on the chart, there was also a formation of a pattern called the "descending triangle." It's a bearish breakdown pattern that suggests prices are going to head much lower.

One must wonder how low copper prices can actually go. Just by looking at the descending triangle pattern, technical analysts usually target the price by measuring the widest distance on the pattern and subtracting it from where the price broke below. In simple terms, by that measure, copper prices may be heading toward the $2.00 level or lower, another 33% below where they are today.

After the financial crisis, the easy money supplied by the central banks in the global economy created the illusion that there was economic growth. But the reality was the complete opposite.

Now, the Federal Reserve is pulling back on its printing program. We recently heard that the central bank will be printing $55.0 billion a month in new paper money instead of the $65.0 billion it printed last month and the $85.0 billion it printed each month for most of 2013. (Source: Federal Reserve, March 19, 2014.)

Add to the Fed's pullback on quantitative easing the troubles coming out of the Chinese economy, and it looks to me as if the global economy is going the wrong way. While politicians will simply choose not to talk about it, the mainstream media is directing investors the wrong way, just as the bear wishes; it's leading investors back into the stock market, as if it's a safe place to be again.

Dear readers, in the short term, the truth is that the global economy isn't getting better; it's getting worse.

WILL AMERICAN GAS SCARE RUSSIA

As the Ukranian crisis gathers momentum, calls are mounting for the US to export shale gas to Europe to help free the continent from Russian influence. Observers are right to focus on Moscow's energy leverage but they are prescribing the wrong response. The most useful thing that Europe could import is not American gas itself but the open economic model that has enabled the US natural gas industry to thrive.

Europe buys nearly 30 per cent of its natural gas from Russia. This has led to concern that President Vladimir Putin might turn off a few taps to gain leverage in the confrontation with Ukraine. For now, these fears are overblown – among other things, Europe has a lot of natural gas in storage – but the fundamental worry is well founded.

Yet US natural gas exports would do little to reduce Russian leverage. They cannot replace Russian gas in the current crisis since it will be more than a year until any US export terminals are built. Even once these facilities are up and running, the economics of sending shale gas to Europe are unlikely to make much sense. Once the cost of shipping is included, Russian gas is far cheaper; Moscow's share of the European market is not likely to change much. Instead, American gas will flow mainly to Asia.

This is not to say that US exports would not hurt Mr Putin. They would push down the price of gas in Europe, which is one of the many reasons why they should be allowed. But it is fanciful to suppose that they could provide a decisive edge against Moscow in a future crisis.

Europe's politicians should instead put their energy into copying the successful US policies that laid the groundwork for a spectacular boom in natural gas production. This might allow Europeans to produce more gas at home instead of buying it from Russia.

The US Energy Information Administration estimates that Europe has 598tn cubic feet of technically recoverable shale gas, roughly half as much as the US. Yet almost none of this is being exploited. In part, that is because the continent is playing catch-up with a boom that started elsewhere. But there are deeper reasons, too. Many European countries have banned shale gas production. Those that allow development have slapped on taxes and government royalties that do much to deter it.

The US has lessons to offer on both fronts. Most gas-rich US states have rejected calls to prohibit shale gas production; instead, they have allowed development subject to robust environmental safeguards. The specifics vary from state to state. In Texas, a longtime energy producer, the industry has won public acceptance with less oversight than elsewhere. In Ohio or Illinois, which are new to the natural gas game, regulation is more stringent. Europeans would be wise to draw lessons from US states that have struck a balance between development and the environment.

The American shale gas industry has flourished on private land, where property owners are susceptible to commercial incentives. In Europe, mineral rights are generally publicly owned and unlikely to be privatised. Still, the more basic lessons – that government policy should be careful not to undermine the economics of gas development, and that care should be taken to ensure that local communities benefit from development – should be listened to carefully.

The US can also export lessons about gas markets. The US market responds efficiently to disruptions because regulators insist on open access to infrastructure such as pipelines, and enforce standards of transparency that ensure market participants are adequately informed. Europe has moved in this direction. Unlike the US, it needs to protect itself against foreign producers that might manipulate liberalised markets. Still, it has room to improve.

Focusing on steps such as these may be less attractive than talking up US natural gas exports: it denies America a chance to brag about its strategic influence and forces Europeans to grapple with their own political problems. The biggest opportunity to improve European security, though, comes from exporting the US model, not selling American gas.

SELF-RELIANCE

Political risk works both ways on gas price increases

Phrases you do not want to hear if you own stock in an Indian energy conglomerate right before a national election: "Common Man party."

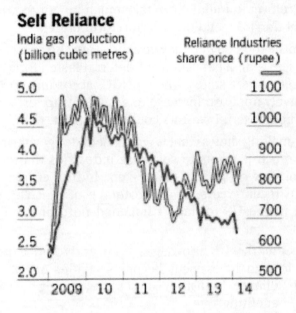

Self Reliance

India gas production (billion cubic metres)

Reliance Industries share price (rupee)

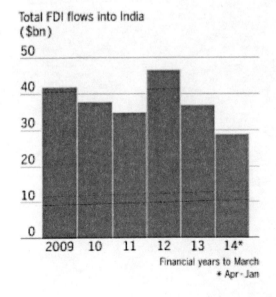

Total FDI flows into India ($bn)

Financial years to March
* Apr - Jan

Source: Ministry of Commerce and Industry

Recently the deferral of plans to double prices for more than four-fifths of India's domestic gas shows why not. An increase to $8 per million metric British thermal units from April would have helped Reliance Industries. It owns KG-D6, a field atop India's largest natural gas reserves in the Bay of Bengal. Boosting production there is difficult at low prices. But then an increase would not have got incumbent politicians re-elected. They see the anti-establishment threat of the Common Man party, which has promised to lower prices.

When populism leaks into the portfolio, is it time to sell? Never hang an investment case on reform in India: it can take much longer to arrive than investors can stay solvent. But don't depend on lack of reform either.

If market reformists took power, they could restore the price formula. Reliance's earnings would fall less than 2 per cent if the deferral lasted for a quarter, compared with a 7 to 8 per cent hit at state-owned ONGC, according to Nomura. Reliance could even retroactively apply an increase to gas it sells to fertiliser producers (the government bears their costs). Investors could hang tight, then.

Except fertiliser-making shows what is wrong here, longer-term. The government has to decide how much it wants to subsidise industries that use a lot of gas. In the meantime imports of oil and gas have kept India's current account running persistent deficits in recent years, as a percentage of its GDP. Asian nations pay three times pricing in the US to import liquefied natural gas (partly because of shipping costs).

India needs looser markets in its own gas, then, and to price the gas with enough stability such that foreign investment becomes viable. At 12 times its forward earnings, buyers of Reliance Industries shares are pricing in fair chances of the company eventually benefiting.

WHATSAPP AND THE FUTURE OF VOICE CALLS

Whatsapp, the instant messaging service has already been eating into the margins of telecom companies by providing instant messaging to its millions of consumers. The telecom industry has already been nervous about the strengthened competition from its low-cost messaging platform.

From next quarter, the company's 465m users will be able to make calls to each other, opening a new threat to the traditional revenues generated by telecoms groups that have seen their SMS cash cow slain by the rise of messaging platforms such as WhatsApp.

And WhatsApp will not stop there. It wants to have a voice service bigger than any of the existing mobile players, with a goal of 1bn users. The company is adding more than 1m customers a day, and has needed to double its servers every year to keep up with "insane" demand from emerging market economies such as Russia, India and Brazil, as more people owned smartphones.

But it is not all bad news for mobile operators – WhatsApp subscribers will need mobile data access, which means revenues for telecoms groups and the potential to move customers to tariffs based purely around data rather than voice and SMS.

Mr Koum said carriers were keen to work with WhatsApp to drive customers on to data plans, and pointed to a deal it had struck with KPN's E-Plus service to a co-branded mobile service in Germany.

The world is moving to data. Carriers partner with us to drive usage of data plans. The core of the partnership is data plans. The world is going to data, bits and bytes, zeros and ones. Not just us, all these apps are using data not just for communications, to watch a movie or tweet news. We are a small part of it.

The deal with Facebook has already helped WhatsApp, which does not publish its revenues, to add 15m new users in less than a week.

WhatsApp is the world's most popular mobile chat app but some smaller competitors have seen an increase in uptake, perhaps from people nervous that Facebook's acquisition will change the service.

People talk about bubble but I want to talk about potential – 5bn people with an always-on device with all the world's information at their fingertips. You can talk about bubbles and economics, but that's not interesting. It's interesting to talk about how the world is changing because of the smartphone.

IS BRAZIL ABOUT TO BE DOWNGRADED TO JUNK STATUS?

Standard & Poor's, the international rating agency, cut Brazil to one notch above junk on Monday evening, adding to a chorus of complaints from many in the investment community, not to mention ordinary Brazilians, that the country's once-promising growth story is currently shot to pieces.

No prizes for guessing how that went down in Brasília. As if to remove any doubt, the finance ministry put out a strongly-worded statement, rubbishing S&P's decision point by point. But the ministry hasn't done itself any favours.

First, the ministry says, the ratings agency "alleged" that Brazil's slow growth was one reason for its downgrade. The ministry points out that "during the period of the crisis that began in 2008" Brazil grew by 17.8 per cent. Leaving aside the possibility that this could lead the uninformed to think 17.8 % was Brazil's annual growth rate after 2008, this statement is unhelpfully backward looking. Nobody questions that Brazil's GDP grew by 7.5 % in 2010. The problem is that, this year, it is expected to grow just 1.7 % – far below Brazil's potential and its needs.

Second, the ministry says S&P is wrong in its assessment of Brazil's fiscal position, "taking into consideration that the country has generated one of the biggest primary surpluses in the world in the past 15 years."

This is asking for trouble. Last year, Brazil failed to meet its primary surplus goal, even though it was revised down to 2.3 per cent from 3.1 per cent. The government has also resorted to dubious methods to make ends meet over the past few years, including "creative accounting" and putting pressure on the tax authorities to settle multibillion-dollar back-tax disputes.

On its third point, the ministry is on firmer ground: Brazil continues to attract large volumes of foreign direct investment, with $65.8bn entering the country in the 12 months to February. (Though such investment has not always turned out well.)

But on point four, the ministry is right back in trouble. Brazil's external accounts, it says, are not a source of vulnerability, as the country has foreign exchange reserves equal to 10 times its short-term debt. Two comments are worth making here: first, that Brazil is not as well protected as it thinks; second, that official figures of Brazil's foreign debts ignore a mounting pile of original sin.

The ministry's fifth point is that S&P is wrong to complain about Brazil's low rate of investment, as the country has embarked on an ambitious $400m investment programme. Well, Brazil frequently embarks on investment programmes worth hundreds of millions of dollars, not all of which materialise. The fact is, its investment rate is stuck at 18 % of GDP: not nearly enough.

Finally, the ministry turns to S&P's reasons for maintaining Brazil at investment grade. Here, readers may be relieved to learn, the agency got everything right. By this point, however, few readers will be taking the ministry seriously.

Investing in Brazil: value creation and value destruction

If investing is all about value creation, the latest batch of figures from Brazil's central bank make for sobering reading. They show the rich returns you can make when investing in Brazil goes right – and the huge losses that result when it goes wrong. Over the past three years, foreign direct investors and buyers of Brazilian portfolio assets have suffered value destruction on a colossal scale.

An analysis of central bank figures by beyondbrics shows that, taken together, flows of foreign direct investment to Brazil and foreign investment in Brazilian portfolio assets were worth more than $260bn between January 2011 and November 2013. Over the same period, in spite of those inflows, the value of such assets held by foreigners fell from $1,351bn to $1,327bn, a loss of $24bn, implying value destruction of more than $284bn in less than three years.

This is not to say that individual investments have not made money – many have. And in previous years, Brazil has delivered enormous returns. During 2009, according to the central bank, the value of equities held by foreigners increased from $150bn to $376bn – a rise in value of nearly $227bn in a year that saw inflows of just $37bn, implying value creation of $190bn in equities alone during that year.

But in the past three years, value creation has turned into value destruction. Some of the blame lies with the global malaise afflicting emerging markets since the boom years before and immediately after the global financial crisis of 2008-09. But critics say Brazil has fared especially badly because of the rise of a local brand of state capitalism.

In part, this has its origins in the crisis itself. When the global recession threatened to derail Brazil's hitherto impressive record of growth, the government knew just what to do. It slashed banks' reserve requirements by nearly $50bn and offered $2bn of cheap loans to exporters. The stimulus worked. After a brief recession in 2009, Brazil returned to stellar growth of 7.5 % in 2010.

But it did not last. Growth has since slumped and stayed stubbornly below pre-crisis levels.

For investors, the results can be seen in the central bank figures. For much of the past decade, money has been flooding into Brazilian assets on all fronts. From January 1, 2003 to November 30, 2013, the total flows of FDI to Brazil were worth about $405bn. Over the same period, the total stock of FDI in the country increased from a little over $100bn to more than $725bn, as measured by the central bank. So over that period, investors got a pretty tidy return on their capital.

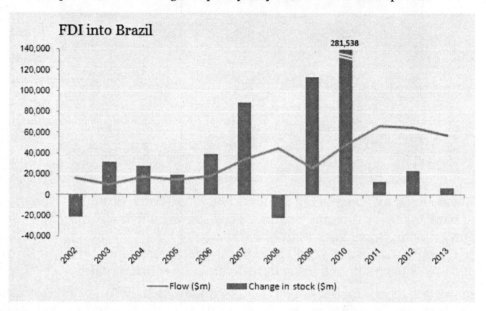

Source: central bank

But those returns were far from consistent. The stock of FDI increased by $113bn in 2009 and by $282bn in 2010, when FDI flows were $26bn and $48.5bn, respectively. But in the three years since then, direct investors sent $189bn to Brazil, only to see the value of the FDI stock increase by just $43bn. Ouch.

The discrepancy between flows and stocks is explained by variations in exchange rates and asset prices. Assets may (or not) be bought in Brazilian reals but their value on the central bank's accounts is expressed in US dollars. So variations in the exchange rate can have a big impact. In addition, assets are marked to market by the central bank, so the dollar amount of money sent to the country can change dramatically once it is spent as asset prices rise or fall.

Over the past three years, the exchange rate and asset prices have given foreign direct investors a hammering. True, many are in for the long term and will be more interested in the cash flows their investments generate in future than in whether the dollar value of their investments has changed. But others will be private equity investors looking for an exit. And nobody likes to think they have overpaid.

And what of portfolio investors?

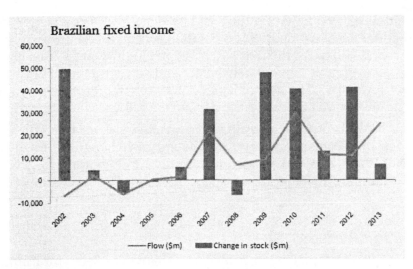

Source: central bank

On the fixed income side, the picture is relatively positive. Flows from January 2002 to November 2013 were worth $106bn. Over the same period, the value of the stock held by foreigners increased by $230bn. In the boom years of 2009-2010, flows were worth $39bn while the value of the stock increased by $89bn; since then, flows have been worth $47bn while the stock has increased in value by nearly $62bn (though there has been a downturn of late: In Jan-Nov last year, flows were $25bn while the rise in value of assets held was just $7bn).

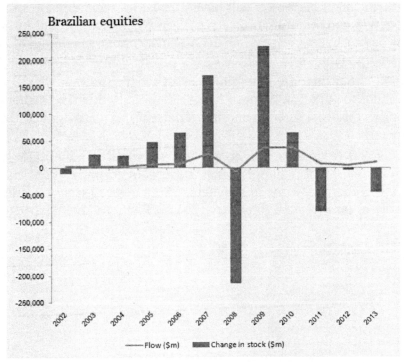

Source: central bank

For equity investors, however, the past few years have been traumatic. For the full period under examination, flows of $138bn accompanied a rise in the value of equities held of $275bn. For the 2009-10 boom, the figures are $75bn and a mighty $292bn, respectively. But immediately before and since, the numbers are frightful. In 2008, outflows of $7.5bn accompanied a fall in value of nearly $215bn. Since the boom, inflows of $23.5bn have accompanied a fall in value of nearly $130bn.

A casual analysis of what constitutes vulnerability is a large current account deficit funded by speculative inflows in a country with low interest rates and no forex reserves- Brazil does have a current account deficit, but it is largely funded by FDI, interest rates are high and rising, and it has about $360bn in foreign exchange reserves.

The problem facing investors is that it's difficult to come up with confidence about Brazil's growth model.

The fault lies with Brazil's state capitalism. This can be seen, for example, in the changing roles of private sector and public sector banks. In the boom years before the crisis, private banks accounted for about two thirds of credit in Brazil and public-sector banks, about one third. But as private banks became nervous about the extend of consumer borrowing and reined in lending, the government ordered public banks to step in. They now account for more than half of all credit – much of it in subsidised loans provided by the BNDES, the government development bank with a habit of trying to pick corporate winners.

Other examples are rule changes for the oil industry, in which Petrobras, the government-controlled oil major, will have a stake in every consortium exploring Brazil's big new-found oil and gas reserves. Even when government interference is perceived as having beneficial results – such as in a change of command at Vale, the privatised mining giant – it is resented by the private sector as interference.

Brazil is far from the only emerging market where the state has an expanded role. Lubin points to Turkey and South Africa. But he says Brazil is further hampered by its currency, still overvalued even after falling 30 per cent against the dollar in the past three years.

Brazilian assets risk falling prey to the "it's so bad, it's good" trade. A key thing in Brazil is to monitor what's happening at the level of corporate governance, in the relation of the corporate sector to the state. The danger is that any improvement could be a trigger for investors to pile in – risking further value destruction.

HAS JANNET YELLEN UNLEASHED THE DOLLAR BULLS?

The U.S. dollar will continue to strengthen if upcoming economic data confirms that recent weakness is weather-induced.

The rally in the U.S. dollar on the notion that U.S. interest rates could rise sooner rather than later may just be getting started.

The dollar soared more than 1 percent against the yen and almost 1 percent versus the euro after new Federal Reserve Chair Janet Yellen said interest rates could start to rise six months after the scaling back of monetary stimulus ends.

As long as upcoming U.S. economic data confirms the Fed's confidence that recent weakness in data is related to unusually cold weather, the dollar should head higher.

The Fed policymakers have not downgraded growth forecasts for this year or next and the fact they haven't done that is one reason why they are hawkish.

U.S. dollar index: Three month chart

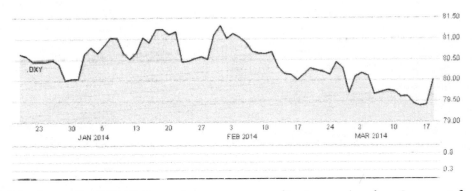

With the end of ZIRP [zero interest rate policy] now in play, I expect further gains in the dollar and yields.

A LONG-TERM LOOK AT INFLATION

The US June Consumer Price Index for Urban Consumers (CPI-U) released yesterday puts the May year-over-year inflation rate at 2.13%, a 19-month high, but well below the 3.88% average since the end of the Second World War and 11% below its 10-year moving average.

The Bureau of Labor Statistics (BLS) has compiled CPI data since 1913, and numbers are conveniently available from the FRED repository. My long-term inflation charts reach back to 1872 by adding Warren and Pearson's price index for the earlier years. The spliced series is available at Yale Professor (and Nobel laureate) Robert Shiller's website. This look further back into the past dramatically illustrates the extreme oscillation between inflation and deflation during the first 70 years of our timeline.

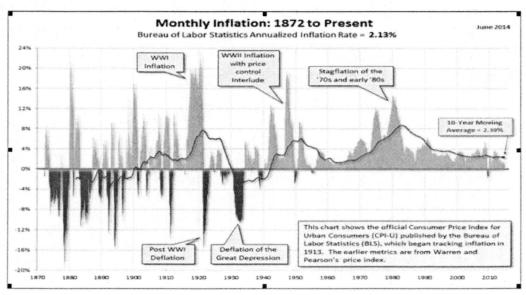

Alternate Inflation Data

The chart below includes an alternate look at inflation *without* the calculation modifications the 1980s and 1990s (Data from www.shadowstats.com).

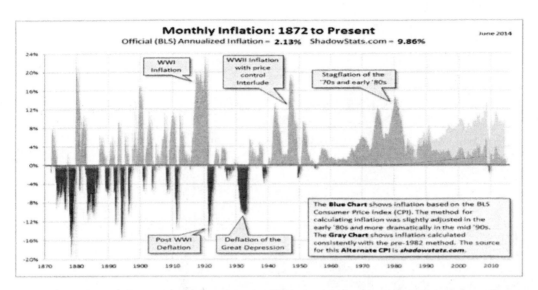

On a personal note, the more I study inflation the more convinced I am that the current BLS method of calculating inflation is reasonably sound. I see nothing today that is remotely like the inflation during the 1970s and 1980s. Moreover, government policy, the Federal Funds Rate, interest rates in general and decades of major business decisions have been fundamentally driven by the official BLS inflation data, not the alternate CPI.

For independent evidence that the Consumer Price Index is a reasonably accurate representation of the prices we pay, see the MIT Billion Prices Project US Daily Index.

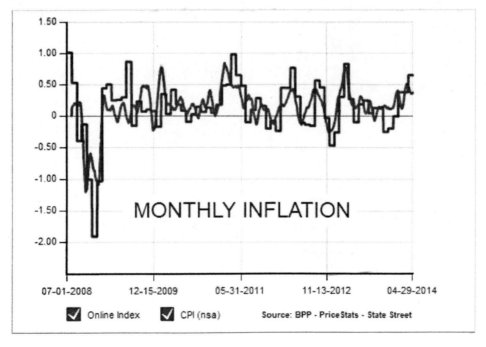

For a long-term look at the impact of inflation on the purchasing power of the dollar, check out this log-scale snapshot of fourteen-plus decades.

REAL RETAIL SALES PER CAPITA: ANOTHER PERSPECTIVE ON THE US ECONOMY

The Tech Crash that began in the spring of 2000 had relatively little impact on consumption. The Financial Crisis of 2008 has had a major impact. After the cliff-dive of the Great Recession, the recovery in retail sales has taken us (in nominal terms) 14.9% above the November 2007 pre-recession peak to a new high.

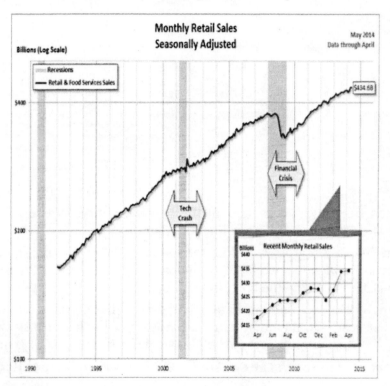

Here is the same chart with two trendlines added. These are linear regressions computed with the Excel Growth function.

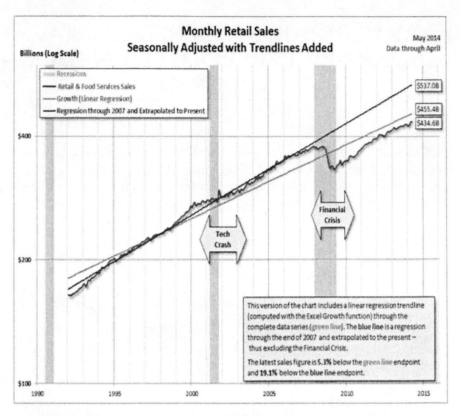

The green trendline is a regression through the entire data series. The latest sales figure is 4.6% below the green line end point.

The blue line is a regression through the end of 2007 and extrapolated to the present. Thus, the blue line excludes the impact of the Financial Crisis. The latest sales figure is 19.1% below the blue line end point.

We normally evaluate monthly data in nominal terms on a month-over-month or year-over-year basis. On the other hand, a snapshot of the larger historical context illustrates the devastating impact of the Financial Crisis on the U.S. economy.

The "Real" Retail Story: The Consumer Economy Remains at a Recessionary Level

How much insight into the US economy does the nominal retail sales report offer? The next chart gives us a perspective on the extent to which this indicator is skewed by inflation and population growth. The nominal sales number shows a cumulative growth of 164.8% since the beginning of this series. Adjust for population growth and the cumulative number drops to 112.5%. And when we adjust for both population growth and inflation, retail sales are up only 24.4% over the past two-plus decades. With this adjustment, we're now at a level we first reached over ten years ago in March 2004.

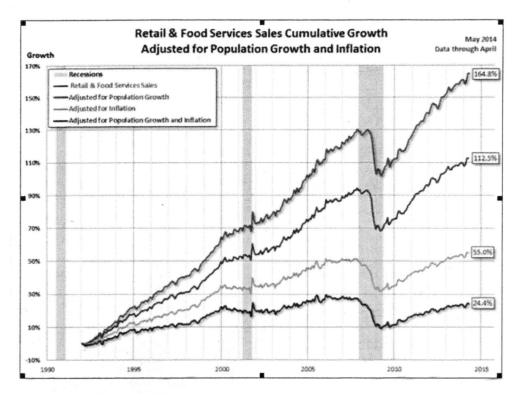

Let's continue in the same vein. The charts below give us a rather different view of the U.S. retail economy and the long-term behavior of the consumer. The sales numbers are adjusted for population growth and inflation. For the population data I've used the Bureau of Economic Analysis mid-month series available from the St. Louis FRED with a linear extrapolation for the latest month. Inflation is based on the latest Consumer Price Index. I've used the seasonally adjusted CPI as a best match for the seasonally adjusted retail sales data. The latest retail sales with the dual adjustment declined 0.2% month-over-month, and the adjusted data is only up 1.3% year-over-year.

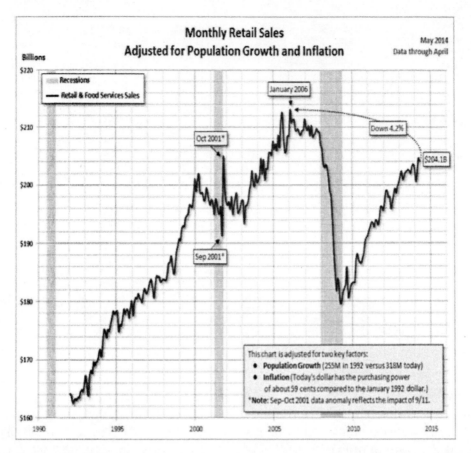

Consider: **Since** January 1992, the U.S. population has grown about 25% while the dollar has lost about 41% of its purchasing power to inflation. Retail sales have been recovering since the trough in 2009. But the "real" consumer economy, adjusted for population growth is still in recession territory — 4.2% below its all-time high in January 2006.

As I mentioned at the outset, month-over-month retail sales were up 0.1%. Let's now examine **Core** Retail Sales, a version that excludes auto purchases.

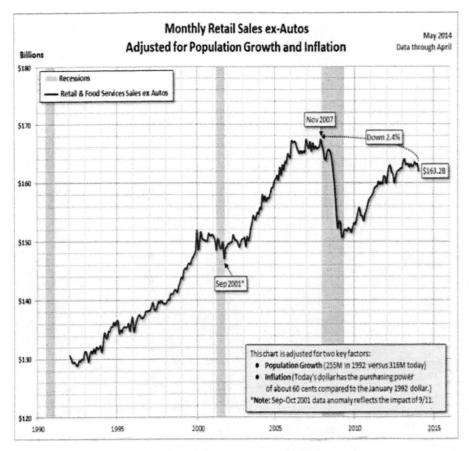

By this analysis, adjusted Core Retail Sales were down 0.3% in April from the previous month and flat year-over-year and down 2.4% from its record high in January 2006.

The Great Recession of the Financial Crisis is behind us, a close analysis of the adjusted data suggests that the recovery has been frustratingly slow. The sobering reality is that, in "real" terms — adjusted for population growth and inflation — consumer sales remain at the level we saw at the peak before the last recession.

U.S. HOUSING VS U.S. STOCKS

According to Gallup, Americans think real estate is the best long-term investment. Unfortunately, they're wrong.

As the real estate market recovers, so does America's faith in housing as an investment.

According to **a Gallup poll released recently,** a plurality of Americans now think of real estate as the "best" long-term investment, followed by gold, stocks and mutual funds, savings accounts/CDs, and bonds:

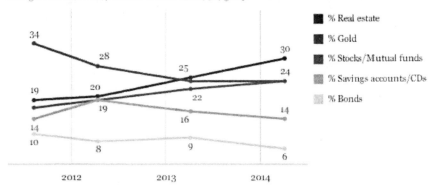

Americans Say Real Estate Is the Best Long-Term Investment

Which of the following do you think is the best long-term investment -- [ROTATED: bonds, real estate, savings accounts or CDs, stocks or mutual funds, (or) gold]?

- ■ % Real estate
- ■ % Gold
- ■ % Stocks/Mutual funds
- ■ % Savings accounts/CDs
- ■ % Bonds

34   28   25   30

24

19   20   22   14

19   16

14   10   8   9   6

2012   2013   2014

April 2012 question asked to a half sample

GALLUP

If one assumes "best" to mean the investment that offers the highest return, then Americans have things backwards. Real estate, on average actually returns very little when adjusted for inflation. Robert Shiller -- the economist famous for helping to create the widely cited Case-Shiller housing index **puts it** like this:

Home prices look remarkably stable when corrected for inflation. Over the 100 years ending in 1990 -- before the recent housing boom -- real home prices rose only 0.2 percent a year, on average. The smallness of that increase seems best explained by rising productivity in construction, which offset increasing costs of land and labor.

And since 1990, housing has continued to be a middling investment, when you take into account the bursting of the real estate bubble:

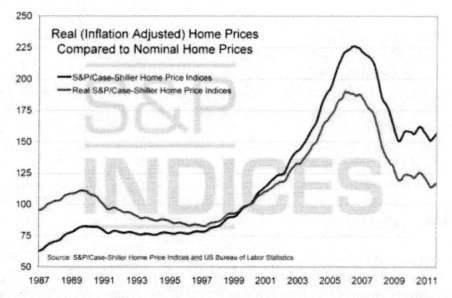

When adjusted for inflation, the average house has appreciated little since 1987. The picture looks a lot different for the other investments Gallup asked about it in its polls. The S&P 500, for instance, has produced an inflation-adjusted annual return **of 6.32%** since 1929, while investing in government debt would have returned roughly half that figure. Gold, interestingly enough, has performed pretty well on an inflation-adjusted basis, **averaging** a 4.12% return per year since the end of the Bretton-Woods monetary order in 1971.

If you break down the Gallup data into income groups, the answers are even more revealing. For one, wealthy Americans are more likely to pick stocks as the best investment than any other income group. This makes sense, as investing in the stock market is -- as the above data shows -- the best way to become wealthy.

Perceived Best Investment, by Income

Which of the following do you think is the best long-term investment -- [bonds, real estate, savings accounts or CDs, stocks or mutual funds, (or) gold]?

	Real estate	Gold	Stocks/ Mutual funds	Savings accounts/CDs	Bonds
	%	%	%	%	%
$75,000 and over	38	18	30	7	7
$30,000 to $74,999	26	26	25	16	6
Less than $30,000	28	31	13	17	7

April 3-6, 2014

GALLUP

Secondly, it appears as if people are likely to say investments they own are the "best." According to the Gallup report:

Upper-income Americans are much more likely to say real estate and stocks are the best investment, possibly because of their experience with these types of investments. Upper-income Americans are most likely to say they own their home, at 87%, followed by middle (66%) and lower-income Americans (36%). Gallup found that homeowners (33%) are slightly more likely than renters (24%) to say real estate is the best choice for long-term investments.

So wealthy Americans are the most likely to understand that stocks provide the best chance for a higher return, but they are also not free of the tendency to think that the thing they are doing (in this case, owning a home) is the intelligent thing to do.

Of course, this analysis takes for granted the idea that "best" necessarily means the investment that is most likely to make you the most money. There are, of course, other reasons why people might decide to invest in real estate. While it theoretically might make sense for an investor to rent his home and plow the money he saves on taxes, mortgage interest, and maintenance into the stock market, such a strategy might not work in the real world. First of all, people have limited time: They're going to spend a lot of energy choosing a good place to live, and might not also have the time to wisely manage securities investments too. Secondly, owning a home is a great way to force yourself to save money, as each mortgage payment is something you have to make, lest you risk losing your home.

Either way, if you decide to put your extra cash into real estate for these reasons, you should be aware that this is the reason you're doing it. As long as you don't expect your home to make you a lot of money on an inflation-adjusted basis, invest away.

COULD RISING INTEREST RATES DERAIL NASCENT U.S. HOUSING RECOVERY?

Now that the U.S. Census Bureau has finally posted the income data that it collected in January 2014 through the Current Population Survey (over a month late, the Bureau posted its data for February 2014 at the same time), we can now check in on the status of the second U.S. housing bubble. The chart below reveals what we find:

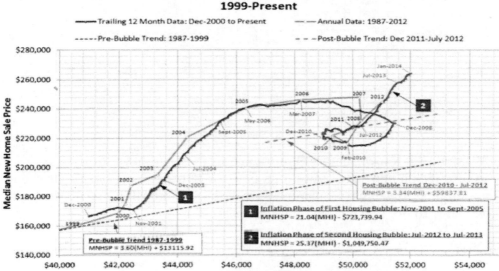

Here, we see that the second U.S. housing bubble continued to inflate through January 2014, although at a slower pace than it did during its initial phase, which ran from July 2012 through July 2013.

The pace of inflation would seem to affected by changes in U.S. mortgage rates, which spiked upward in mid-2013 as the Federal Reserve announced its decision to begin tapering its purchases of mortgage-backed securities and U.S. Treasuries, but which have since fluctuated between 4.3% and 4.5%.

That doesn't seem like a big range to drive the trend for median new home sale prices, but in the latter half of 2013 through January 2014, the rate of change of median new home sale prices would appear to be affected by those fluctuations, rising faster when mortgage rates drop to the low end of the range and rising at a slower pace when rates rise.

That, of course, is the result of median new home sale prices being very much at the economic margin, which is the reason why we pay such close attention to them.

We'll close with an updated look at the long-term trends in median new home sale prices in the U.S., which put the recent bubbles in U.S. new home sale prices into better context.

U.S. Median New Home Sale Prices vs Median Household Income, 1967-Present

We don't yet know what level mortgage rates would have to reach to send the trend for median new home sales on a downward trajectory to begin deflating the second bubble. Given how apparently weak the U.S. housing market continues to be, we hope to not find out anytime soon.

REFERENCES

U.S. Census Bureau. Median and Average Sales Prices of New Homes Sold in the United States. [Excel Spreadsheet]. Accessed 24 March 2014.

Sentier Research. Household Income Trends: January 2014. [PDF Document]. Accessed 20 March 2014. [Note: We've converted all data to be in terms of current (nominal) U.S. dollars.]

Board of Governors of the Federal Reserve System. H.15. Selected interest Rates. 30-Year Conventional Mortgage Rate. Not Seasonally Adjusted. [Online Database]. Accessed 24 March 2014.

FROM BUYBACKS TO M&A : SHAREHOLDERS RISK APPETITE GROWS

Shareholders support capital expenditure and M&A

The simplest good news scenario for US stocks to justify their high valuations involves a solid economic recovery and increased capital spending creating a positive feedback loop into rising sales. Valuations and profit margins can then gently fall back, even as earnings and shares rise.

Shareholders cannot make the economy do what they want. But they have influence over company spending – and there are encouraging signs.

Until last year, increase in share prices pushed management to use cash to buy back stock or pay dividends. By the end of last year, the benefits of a buyback announcement had almost vanished, although they have picked up a bit this year.

At the same time, a survey of fund managers shows near-record support for capital spending and plunging support for returning cash to shareholders. It is not a coincidence that this happened as the economy grew fast enough for the Federal Reserve to start tapering bond purchases. Bond yields rose alongside hopes of higher growth, and investors rotated from defensive dividend stocks to pick up more economically sensitive cyclicals.

Still, last year total US dividends and buybacks were higher than capital expenditure by listed companies. It is hard to measure appetite for capex, but shareholders appear to be more supportive of takeovers – also chasing growth – than they have been since before Lehman failed. Dealogic data shows the one-week share price reaction of US companies announcing a takeover worth $100m or more has recently been the best since 2006 (although sample sizes are small, so this should be treated with some caution).

Investors are sending the right signals to management. Whether management will read the signs, boost investment and M&A and cut down on buybacks remains to be seen.

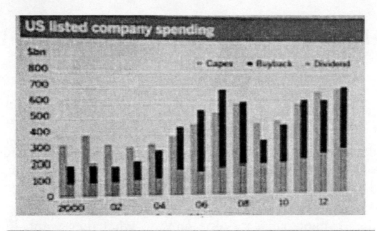

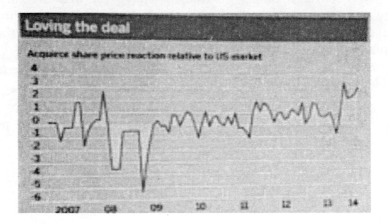

IS WEAK GLOBAL RECOVERY IMPACTING EMERGING MARKETS?

Economies with reliance on commodity exports remain fragile

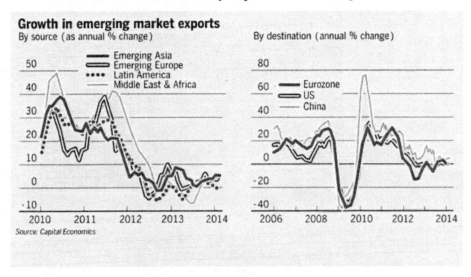

- Current account deficits in India, Indonesia and South Africa shrink but in Turkey it widens as a weakening currency fails to boost exports

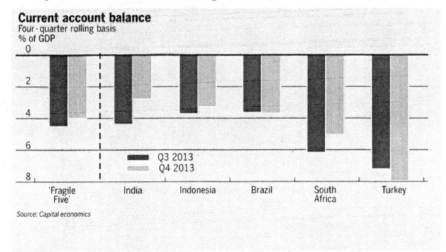

- Demand for exports from Latin America lags other emerging markets
- Turkey imports grow sharply, while India, Indonesia and South Africa reduce the number of imports

It was not supposed to happen this way. Swooning emerging market currencies last year were expected to boost exports to resurgent developed markets in Europe, the US and Japan.

The hoped-for export boom would then, so the theory went, help repair a key frailty of emerging economies such as the so-called "fragile five" of India, Indonesia, South Africa, Turkey and Brazil by narrowing their current account deficits.

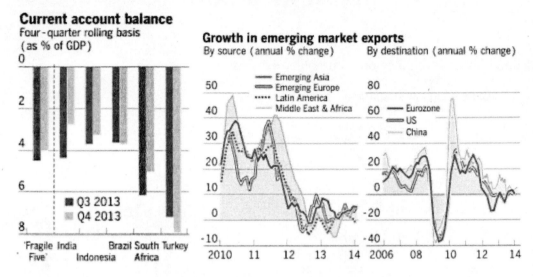

Change in imports/exports
Q3 to Q4 2013 (four-quarter rolling basis, % points of GDP)

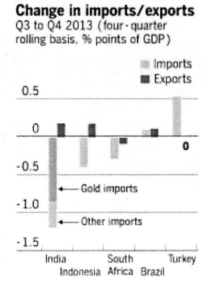

Vulnerable emerging markets

Years of coverage Ratio of foreign exchange reserves to 'gross external financing requirement', Q2 2013

Turkey	Chile	Indonesia	India	South Africa	Hungary	Brazil	Poland
0.9	1.0	1.1	1.2	1.2	1.7	2.0	2.1

HAS THE EMERGING WORLD DECOUPLED FROM THE DEVELOPED WORLD?

Emerging economies holding back global recovery - OECD

Just a few years back, in the midst of the Great Recession, it was expected that the emerging markets like China and India will help the world recover out of its misery.

How much the world economy has changed since then?

The recovery in developed economies has gathered momentum although slowing activity in big emerging markets means global growth will be only moderate at best in the near term, according to the OECD.

Exceptionally bad winter weather in North America and a sales tax hike in Japan are also disrupting the pace of recovery, the Paris-based Organisation for Economic Cooperation and Development said.

Against that backdrop, the OECD urged the European Central Bank and the Bank of Japan to keep up their monetary stimulus, if not increase it, while it said the U.S. Federal Reserve was right to begin winding down its bond-buying programme.

The gradual recovery in the advanced economies is encouraging, even if temporary factors have pushed down growth rates in the early months of this year, while the slowdown in emerging economies is likely to be a drag on global growth.

Growth for major advanced economies in the first half of 2014 will be slower than in the second half of 2013, but much improved from the sluggish rates of late 2012 and early 2013, the OECD said in an update of its views on the global economy.

Given that emerging economies now account for over half the world economy, continued sub-par economic performance for several of the major EMEs (emerging market economies) is likely to mean that global growth remains only moderate in the near term.

It estimated growth in the United States would slow to 1.7 percent in the first quarter from the previous three months on an annualised basis, down from 2.4 percent in the fourth quarter when exceptionally bad weather weighed on activity.

Japanese growth would surge 4.8 percent in the first quarter from the previous quarter as consumers brought forward purchases ahead of a sales tax increase on April 1.

The OECD gave its updated forecasts as part of an interim health-check for the global economy before its much more detailed Economic Outlook due in May. It did not update its estimates for U.S. and Japanese growth in the second quarter because one-off factors made it too problematic, it said.

Turning to Europe, the OECD saw Germany's quarter-on-quarter annualised growth rate reaching 3.7 percent in the first quarter before slowing to 2.5 %.

France, the euro zone's second biggest economy after Germany, was seen growing only 0.7 % in the first three months of the year, rising to 1 % in the second quarter.

Outside the euro zone, the British economy was seen growing 3.3 % in both the first and second quarters.

Turning to emerging market economies, the OECD said some were seeing a marked loss of momentum as capital outflows exposed vulnerabilities in some countries.

It noted that Brazil, India, South Africa and Turkey among others have been forced to raise interest rates to keep capital outflows in check.

Meanwhile, weak balance sheets in China raised the risk of a sharp slowdown there, the OECD said.

Yet, N.B.A. Looks to Asia for Next Growth Spurt

Fans cheer during a game between the Los Angeles Lakers and the Golden State Warriors in Beijing. The N.B.A. is one of the most popular brands in China. Credit Mark Ralston/ Agence France-Presse — Getty Images

When the National Basketball Association commissioner David Stern spent a week in Beijing in the winter of 1987, he had to plead with China Central Television to broadcast N.B.A. games — and he eventually offered to provide content free.

Now, the N.B.A. is one of the most popular brands in China, and the only American sports league with a significant following throughout Asia. The league has a combined 70 million followers on Sina Weibo and Tencent's microblog platforms, compared with fewer than 400,000 followers for the National Football League

The new commissioner, Adam Silver, who replaced Mr. Stern last month, is hoping to build off that success, with expansion plans across Asia. In China, the basketball league is expanding TV coverage and building lavish sports facilities. In

India, it is promoting the sport through after-school programs. In South Korea, it is trading on basketball's "swag."

He has big ambitions. Mr Silver believes that N.B.A. China, which had $150 million in revenue in 2012, enjoyed growth "greater than 10 %" last year, and that he expected double-digit growth for the foreseeable future. While revenue in China is a small fraction of the overall business — the league generated $5.6 billion in global revenue last year — Mr. Silver said the N.B.A. would eventually be bigger internationally than domestically, and Asia was the key factor.

The U.S. represents less than 5 percent of the world's population. And they have, along with soccer, the most popular sport in the world.

From the outset, the N.B.A. had to tweak its strategy for the Chinese market. Unlike in the United States, there have been no bidding wars for N.B.A. television rights in China, because CCTV is a monopoly there. Although the league and CCTV announced a multiyear deal in 2012 that offered more N.B.A. content to Chinese homes, it is unlikely ever to be as lucrative as the league's American deal, an eight-year, $7.4 billion contract that expires in 2016.

So the N.B.A. has largely had to rely on licensing and marketing deals. There are the digital operations, including partnerships with the Chinese Internet giants Sina Corporation and Tencent Holdings that provide live streams of games, and a popular online store on Alibaba's Tmall site.

It is building the N.B.A. Training Center, a $1.5 billion, 130,000-square-foot structure near Beijing set to open next year. The center will include a restaurant, merchandise store, fitness center and multiple full-size basketball courts.

N.B.A. have a very strong presence on the ground in China, but their biggest obstacle has been the state-owned media market, and that the China sports industry is state-controlled. But things are improving. China loves basketball too much to deny the N.B.A.

The league has also secured licensing deals with major companies. Anheuser-Busch InBev, which owns the Harbin beer brand in China, has N.B.A. logos on its Harbin bottles. They are also emblazoned on Mengniu Milk.

They've been making a lot of money from licensing its logo to a large variety of companies, and these products do very well because Chinese fans know the N.B.A. is the highest level of what they do, and not many brands can say that.

The league has used its experience in China as a jumping-off point to the rest of Asia.

In 1990, the league opened an office in Hong Kong to handle all business in Asia, including China, at the time just a single employee working out of an apartment. Today, N.B.A. Asia has a staff of more than 100 across offices in Hong Kong, Taiwan, South Korea and India.

The definition of Asia doesn't exist for N.B.A. --they look at each country and see what our strategy is there.

For example, the league focused on pop culture in South Korea. Three years ago, the league signed a deal with the South Korean apparel maker MK Trend and gave the Seoul-based company freedom to alter its team colors. MK Trend's N.B.A. apparel, with bright pastel colors and shiny "bling," became a top seller in the country, and can often be seen on South Korean television, in programming like Girls' Generation music videos and the hit show "Running Man."

The trick is to take advantage of the N.B.A.'s image as a hip lifestyle brand. Korean stars want to wear the N.B.A. gear, and that, in turn, leads to increased sales.

With South Korean pop culture influential throughout Asia, tourists from China and Japan turn up at his stores with photos of K-pop stars wearing N.B.A. caps and ask for the same item. MK Trend will branch out into China this May, with more stores in Macau and Hong Kong this year.

Across Asia, the league is relying on grass-roots projects to help build awareness.

Last month in China, the league began the N.B.A. Yao School, an after-school program named after the former basketball star Yao Ming that aims to teach basketball and life skills to children.

Sony India's chairman, Man Jit Sing, whose Sony Six channel broadcasts N.B.A. games, said the league had brought the game to Indians with Jr. N.B.A., which gives underprivileged children the opportunity to play basketball and aims to promote values like teamwork and sportsmanship.

The Jr. N.B.A. is in 150 schools right now, reaching over 200,000 children in India. N.B.A. programs are India's highest-rated programs behind cricket. They can't touch cricket in India — nothing can — but after that, they are the most popular.

Mr. Levy, who oversees the Jr. N.B.A. program in Asia, said the league was looking to expand such efforts.

The trick is that more people play basketball, because that will translate to more people following the N.B.. they have Jr. N.B.A. programs running all over Asia. We've been in the Philippines for seven years, and we're rolling out these programs to Vietnam, Indonesia and Malaysia this year. Sponsors have paid close attention to basketball's growing popularity in the region.

Nike and Adidas send their biggest N.B.A. stars on promotional tours in Asia every summer. Dunkin' Donuts hired LeBron James of the Miami Heat and Mercedes-Benz signed Kobe Bryant of the Los Angeles Lakers to promote their products in Asia; and Colin Currie, managing director of Adidas Group Greater China, said the company signed the Houston Rockets guard Jeremy Lin more for his Asian marketability than for his American appeal.

Another Houston Rockets guard, James Harden, said there was "no doubt" that playing for the Rockets — Mr. Yao's former team — had helped him and his teammates secure business deals in Asia. The ZTE Corporation, the Chinese smartphone maker, signed the Houston Rockets to a sponsorship deal last October.

BOEING, AIRBUS AND.. COMAC
YOU MAY FLY ON A MADE-IN-CHINA AIRCRAFT SOONER THAN YOU THINK

COMAC could dominate in 20 years: Airbus

Could Chinese plane maker COMAC start eating in Airbus' lunch?

While the Commercial Aircraft Corporation of China (Comac) has yet to win any big international orders with its C919 passenger airplane, you may be flying on an aircraft manufactured by China's state-owned commercial aerospace company sooner than you think.

John Leahy, chief operating officer of Airbus believes Comac will emerge as a serious competitor in the mainstream commercial aviation market over the next 20 years.

If you recollect, Airbus was started in 1970, it took 20 years before they were just being taken seriously, that would be the same with any manufacturer, no matter the country behind that.

The 'iron bird' test platform, a plane-like fuselage simulator, for the C919

So far, Comac has won 400 orders for the C919, the mainland's largest locally produced aircraft intended to compete with the **Boeing** 737 and 2014 a roadmap for investors.doc A320.

The majority of customers for the narrow bodied, single-aisle passenger airliner are still domestic carriers such as Air China, China Southern Airlines, China Eastern Airlines and Hainan Airlines.

The C919's will undertake its maiden test flight in 2015, one year later than originally planned, with the first delivery scheduled for 2016.

Even if the C919 doesn't gain traction outside of China, the next aircraft they manufacture will be a success.

The Chinese don't really worry about 10, or 20 years. It's where will they be in 50 years' time. They are on a learning curve, and it doesn't really matter to them how long it takes. **At some point there will be ABC - Airbus, Boeing, Comac.**

They will break out of China with the C919, because they know they have to develop their customer support infrastructure to be able to support planes outside of China.

It wouldn't be a surprise to see C919's flying in Africa. Beijing may make an investment into an African infrastructure project in exchange for orders of the aircraft for example. Africa could be a testing ground.

Comac's expansion into the global market, however, won't be without major challenges.

In addition to overcoming negative perceptions over the safety of products produced in the mainland, the company must set up a large amount of infrastructure in order to support its fleet.

Airlines exist on having a reliable operation. To do that you have to have spares and technical support in the right place, doing that in English, at a distance, they don't have any track record at all on that, so that's their biggest challenge.

... And Tesla is getting ready to build cars in China

At some point in the next three or four years Tesla will be establishing local manufacturing in China according to CEO Elon Musk who believes China is very important to the future of Tesla. Musk was in Beijing to mark the first deliveries of Tesla's Model S to customers in China, where the sports car sells for around $115,000.

Electric vehicle sales in the world's second biggest economy have been tepid so far, but many automakers see great potential. The country's middle class is expanding rapidly and is increasingly interested in luxury cars.

China also faces a growing air pollution problem, and the government is working to encourage the adoption of electric cars.

Yet much of China lacks the infrastructure needed to support them. State media reported that Tesla (TSLA) is ready to help change that, with Musk pledging to launch a nationwide battery charging and service network by 2015

Tesla is going to make a big investment in China in terms of charging infrastructure, according to Musk.

The automaker has already built a supercharger network in the United States, making it easier for Tesla drivers to travel between major cities.

China isn't the only place Tesla wants to build a new factory. It has plans for a massive U.S. facility that is expected to produce more lithium ion batteries annually by 2020 than were produced worldwide in 2013.

Tesla estimates the new factory will cost $4 billion to $5 billion and employ about 6,500 people. It could be located in either Arizona, Nevada, New Mexico or Texas.

Making more batteries, and reducing their cost, are vital to Tesla's ability to produce a cheaper car in numbers that could catapult the company into the ranks of the major automakers.

And Twitter is working on an Asian strategy

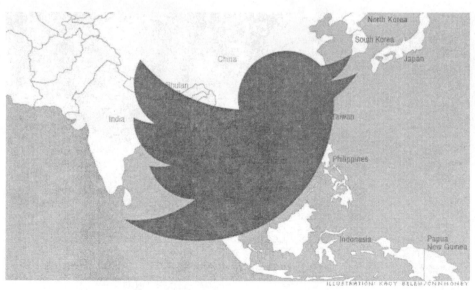

Twitter must target Asia more aggressively if it hopes to have long-term financial success.

Now that Twitter is a public company, investors want to know when the company will be profitable. Wall Street will also be keeping a close eye on its mobile strategy.

All social media companies need to emphasize mobile. Fortunately for Twitter (TWTR), it is already off to a good start: 75% of its users access the service via a mobile device, and mobile advertising accounts for around 55% of its revenue.

Twitter also announced the acquisition of mobile advertising company MoPub in September for a reported $350 million, an indication that the company realizes it needs to be an even bigger player in mobile.

But Twitter has a problem. It is not a major presence in Asia. And according to figures from tech research firm Gartner, the Asia Pacific region is the biggest mobile ad market, with an estimated $4.8 billion in revenues this year.

North America is second, with $3.8 billion in mobile ad sales. So for Twitter to realize its full potential, it will need to infiltrate the Asian market sooner rather than later.

At present, only a fraction of Twitter's users are based in the Asia-Pacific region. Twitter's current share of global mobile advertising revenue sits at about 2%, compared to Facebook's (FB, Fortune 500) 16% and Google's (GOOG, Fortune 500) 53%.

That's not great news for Twitter. But if the company can successfully grow its user base in Asia, there is a good chance that Twitter's total share of global mobile ad sales will increase dramatically.

So what stands in Twitter's way? Sina's (SINA) Twitter-like micro-blogging service Weibo, and voice and 'chat' messaging services such as Tencent's WeChat are the biggest obstacles.

Weibo has been successful gaining share in China. Net income in the third quarter for Weibo nearly tripled from a year ago while sales were up 21%.

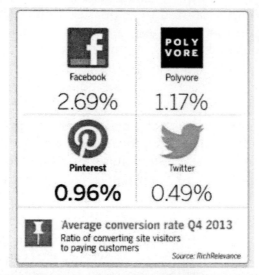

Facebook 2.69%   Polyvore 1.17%

Pinterest **0.96%**   Twitter 0.49%

Average conversion rate Q4 2013
Ratio of converting site visitors
to paying customers

Source: RichRelevance

Mobile social network apps
Photo: Alamy

China's Weibo a better bet than Twitter?

This growth has been fueled mostly by a strategic partnership with Alibaba, through which Weibo subscribers are able to purchase goods on the site using 'Alipay', Alibaba's third party payment system. In fact, Twitter might want to adopt a similar model in order to help it achieve profitability.

WeChat, on the other hand, has done a strong job of infiltrating the broader market outside of China, building a strong user base in countries such as India, Malaysia and Thailand.

Tencent (TCEHY) also used WeChat to boost sales in China through a collaboration with its own e-commerce website 51buy, and recently made headlines by generating HK$637 million (US$82 million) worth of sales through its service on November 11, which has become the Chinese equivalent of Cyber Monday in the United States.

So for Twitter to effectively grow its audience in Asia, it will be crucial to understand and appreciate the differences in user behavior between that region and the U.S. -- especially with regards to China. It may also need to follow some of the strategies that Weibo and WeChat have employed in their own quest for profitability.

Of course, it would help if Twitter figured out a way to be profitable from its existing user base. But expanding into what's already the world's largest market for mobile advertising will be key to Twitter's long-term success.

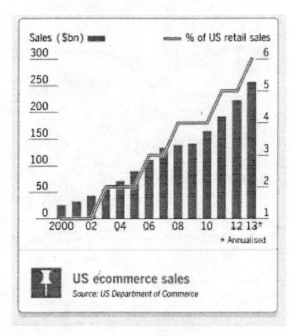

US ecommerce sales
Source: US Department of Commerce

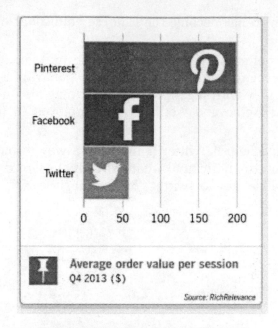

Average order value per session
Q4 2013 ($)

Source: RichRelevance

EMERGING MARKETS AREN'T ON SALE YET BUT COULD BE IN THE SECOND HALF OF 2014

ILLUSTRATION: JACOB THOMAS

Yes, Chinese and other emerging market stocks are down this year, but there's little reason to love them now.

When you fall in love with an investment, you can be blinded to fundamental shifts taking place before your eyes. Witness what's going on in the emerging markets.

The darling buys of the 2000s, shares of companies based in the developing world have had a tough two years because of both slowing growth in China and the end of cheap global credit that pumps up demand for risky assets.

To proponents, this merely means an attractive asset class is on sale. Recent declines were overdone and based largely on irrational investor panic.

That may be looking through rose-colored glasses. Here's what I see:

Valuations haven't improved

The price/earnings ratio for these shares, based on projected earnings over the next year, is 11.4. Because profits have fallen, that's higher than when the MSCI Emerging Markets Index peaked in May 2011, before tumbling 17%.

Tailwinds are fading

For decades, emerging economies benefited from an endless supply of young workers and weren't financially burdened by a large elderly population. No longer.

In China, the ratio of dependents to workers, which had been falling for years, is now rising -- as in the slower-growing U.S. The same goes for Russia, Eastern

Europe, and the Asian Tigers. Just as worrisome: China's working population, like the developed world's, has peaked and is likely to fall for the next three decades.

Expectations are diminishing

China's economy is not merely going through a temporary dip—the annual GDP growth could fall from 7% to 5% in the coming decade.

Crisis in emerging markets has also created opportunities

Emerging markets have been through the mill: a sharp sell-off in January that prompted emergency rate rises, followed by a bounce, and now, a renewed bout of geopolitical tension centred on Crimea.

Such confusion creates opportunities, but few seem to have taken them. The rules for extracting outperformance in the developed markets are now well-known and well tested. But while the same rules apply in emerging markets, they do so far more weakly.

That at least seems to be the main lesson from a huge historical study produced last month by Elroy Dimson, Paul Marsh and Mike Staunton, three London Business School academics, for their annual exhaustive research exercise, the *Credit Suisse Global Investment Returns Yearbook*.

They, like other academics, have identified three repetitive effects in developed markets that lead to outperformance in the long term. These are the value effect (cheaper stocks outperform); the size effect (smaller stocks outperform); and the momentum effect (winners tend to keep beating losers).

There is controversy over whether these effects are driven by human behavioural anomalies, or are a rational response to risk, but there is no doubt they exist.

In emerging markets, the value effect is even stronger than in the developed world. The Dimson/Marsh/Staunton research, going back to 2000, finds that companies that are cheap judging by their dividend yield outperformed by 4.3 percentage points per year, compared to 3.1 percentage points for developed markets.

But the size effect is very much weaker, with larger companies outperforming in six emerging markets over this period. Overall the "size" premium has only been 1.9 percentage points in emerging markets, compared to 6.6 percentage points in the developed world.

As for the momentum effect, a policy of buying the previous six months' "winners" while shorting the "losers" led to an outperformance of 0.78 per cent per month in the developed world, but only 0.24 per cent in emerging markets. Seven emerging markets had negative momentum returns.

Russia should be a buy

So the same basic effects are at work in emerging markets, but their strength is very different. Buying cheaply will eventually work out. Relying on momentum, given the choppiness of sentiment in these markets and their proneness to sudden reversals, is more awkward.

Similarly, buying smaller companies in markets that are often oligopolistic and dominated by a few big players can be a problem – or alternatively, the big emerging market players that have turned themselves into globalised conglomerates in recent years have proved prohibitively difficult to bear.

Amplifying the problem, emerging markets traders complain that over the past four years, neither value nor momentum has worked. Cheap stocks and countries have stayed cheap, while the markets have traded in a large range with no clear direction (although there has been a steady underperformance of the developed world).

The imbroglio over Russia is a perfect example. Russia has been a screaming "buy" on value screens for a while. Before the military escalation in Crimea, it was the cheapest of all emerging markets, according to MSCI, when measured by either earnings or book multiples (a few countries had higher dividend yields). Russian shares were available for less than 70 per cent of their book value.

This did not avert a savage sell-off, which brought the Russian stock market to barely half its post-crisis peak. This seems like clear downward momentum. Even momentum strategies would have been foiled by rapid switchbacks in prices at the peak of the Ukraine crisis. Russia's RTS index dropped 14 % at one point, and then gained 9.5 per cent from there over the following 24 hours.

Crises prompt higher rates

The momentum problem is not limited to Russia. Civil unrest has provoked crises of varying severity in three different countries within the last six months: Thailand, Turkey and Russia. In all cases, higher rates from central banks have been part of the response.

And the emerging market political timetable for the rest of the year offers little respite. Important elections have been or about to be conducted in Colombia, Turkey, Hungary, India, South Africa, Indonesia and Brazil. Expect populist rhetoric and perhaps fiscal pump-priming to increase in these countries.

Governance is the corollary of value in emerging markets. Companies may well trade at a discount to their replacement cost, or their intrinsic value. But if their managers are not working for minority shareholders, or are instead working for the government, shareholders cannot expect to see that value.

Governance has generally been worsening post-crisis.

The stocks most obviously cheap on value screens tend to include formerly nationalised energy groups, or Chinese banks, where the issue of governance is particularly acute.

Added to all of this, the macroeconomic backdrop for emerging markets is ugly. They face rising rates as the Federal Reserve slowly exits from quantitative easing, but also a slowdown in demand for their goods from China.

This makes emerging markets investing even harder than usual. Do enough homework on the intrinsic value of a company and you will ultimately be rewarded. Value works, if given long enough. But value investors in emerging markets also have to do extensive homework on governance issues.

Anyone patient enough to do this work will find some bargains. But none of them will be in Russia.

Size effect:

There is a much smaller advantage for size in emerging markets as compred to developed markets. To the extent it may not even be worth comparative investing in small companies. One reason could be that large companies in emerging markets did much better than small companies as they reached out to the globe.

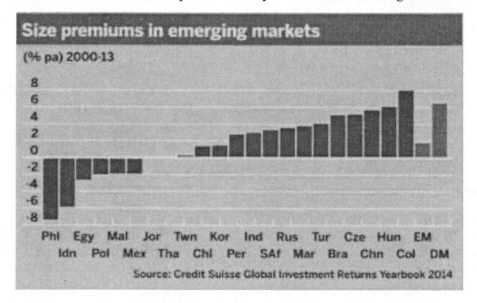

Value effect:

Using dividend yield as a parameter, there is greater value buying cheap companies in emerging markets as compared to developed markets.

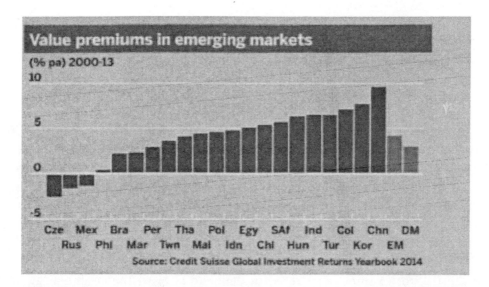

Momentum effect:

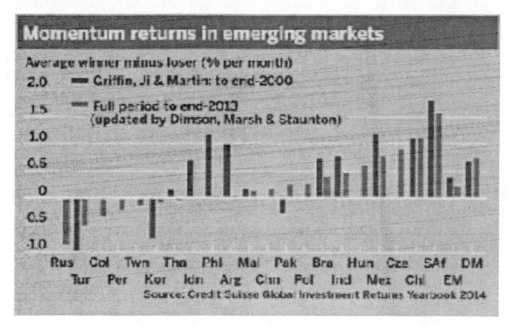

But reality so far is falling short of reason. "Most emerging market exports have been anaemic at best this year.

In aggregate, emerging market exports grew 4.3 % year-on-year in January, up from 4.2 % in December, but this meagre uptick masks a sharp divergence in fortunes between regions. Latin America and some parts of Africa have performed poorly, while emerging Asia and Eastern Europe have been relatively buoyant. Within regions, there have also been significant country-specific differences.

These discrepancies not only help to reveal the influences suppressing an export-led emerging market recovery, they also identify differing levels of vulnerability among fragile five and other emerging economies to further market turmoil.

On the optimistic side, India and Indonesia appear to be graduating if not quite yet from the fragile five then at least from the grouping's critical list. Their current account deficits have been shrinking as a percentage of GDP mostly because whopping currency depreciations last year – 28 per cent for the rupee and 20 per cent for the rupiah between May and August – have brought significant reductions in imports.

Stock, bond and currency markets in both countries are already rewarding this turnround, even at a time of instability in Ukraine and continued fears over the unwinding of US monetary stimulus. But these upbeat readings do not obscure the fact that such deficit reductions derive more from slumping domestic demand than from resurgence in developed world purchases of Indian and Indonesian exports.

In the US, for example, [there is] evidence to suggest that non-energy import growth has been considerably weaker than it was at similar stages of the US cycle at any time since 1980 and the persistence of the eurozone's current account surplus suggests that prospects for a sharp increase in import demand there are weak.

Part of the problem with US and EU demand is that it has not yet broadened out to include electronics, which account for between 30 to 60 per cent of total exports from countries such as Malaysia, Thailand and the Philippines.

Until such a broadening in US and EU demand takes place, the export fortunes of Southeast Asia will continue to be dictated by Japan – where demand has been relatively strong – and by China, where a slowdown in construction investment this year has sent non-food commodity markets into a tailspin.

The spectre of weakening Chinese imports of iron ore, copper and other resources looms large for Brazil, South Africa and Indonesia among the fragile five, but is also negative for Chile, Colombia, Russia and Peru, says Mr Botham, who has ranked emerging markets according to their vulnerability to a Chinese slowdown.

Exposure to China appears likely to preclude improvements in Latin America's average current account deficit for some time to come. Latin America has fared relatively poorly, in part to heavy dependence on commodity exports whose prices have been falling.

Indeed, the metrics are stark. Non-food commodity exports account for well over 80 per cent of total exports to China in Columbia, Chile, Brazil and Peru. The same is true in South Africa, Russia and Turkey, while in some frontier markets such as Zambia, reliance on copper exports to China is so heavy that the national currency, the kwacha, has depreciated against the US dollar by as much as 8 per cent in the past month.

The stresses afflicting China, therefore, add emphasis to hopes that a strong upsurge in US, EU and Japanese demand for emerging market exports will soon materialise. But in the absence of such a recovery, two fragile five members – Turkey and Brazil – appear particularly exposed because their current account deficits failed to improve in the fourth quarter of last year.

South Africa did manage to shrink its deficit but remains vulnerable because it did so largely by raising interest rates and hobbling its domestic economy to reduce imports. Overall then, the outlook for an export-led solution to emerging market woes appears remote. Looking ahead, in theory, the currency falls over the past year could – in time – support a rise in manufactured goods exports.

CHINA'S 'LEHMAN MOMENT'

Rarely a day has passed this month without news of another Chinese company on the brink of collapse. There are solar cell makers missing interest payments on bonds, steel mills defaulting on bank loans and property developers going bust.

Anyone hearing this steady drumbeat of disaster could be forgiven for thinking that China's star is fading, and fading fast.

It is certainly true that Chinese companies face serious challenges after a surge in their debt levels over the past five years. Coming down from their credit high was always going to be painful.

But some of the sensationalist shorthand for the adjustment now under way – "China's Lehman moment", "China's Bear Stearns moment", the collapse of "China's giant Ponzi scheme" – obfuscates more than it illuminates. Business is getting much tougher for Chinese companies from banks to property developers, but it is facile to think that they are headed for a replay of the 2008 financial crisis.

When encountering wildly bullish or deeply bearish views about China it is worth pausing for a moment to remember the country's most defining feature: its enormous size. This makes it fertile ground for what psychologists call "confirmation bias".

Want an example to show that the Chinese property market is in danger? Look no further than Zhejiang Xingrun Real Estate, a developer in a small eastern town that cannot repay Rmb3.5bn ($566mn) of debt. Or would you prefer to make the case that everything is just fine? Then point to Shanghai, where sales of new homes jumped 46 per cent by area last week, nearing a three-month high.

Of course, the scale of China's economy should not stop analysts, investors and journalists making useful generalisations, but any conclusions drawn from a handful of anecdotes should throw up red flags.

Taking a broader look at China's recent default scares, three observations stand out.

First, Chinese corporate debt has soared over the past five years. The debt of non-financial companies rose from about 85 per cent of gross domestic product in 2008 to closer to 120 per cent today. This is a very steep rise in a short time – something that has been a precursor to financial crises in other countries – and it puts Chinese companies at the high end of indebtedness among emerging markets.

To maintain its high levels of GDP growth in the wake of the global financial crisis, China instigated a huge financial stimulus. The problem of excess capacity is only going to get worse

Second, China's government is not blind to the dangers. The immediate trigger for the current corporate troubles was policy action.

When the central bank engineered a cash crunch last June and then allowed money market rates to drift higher in the second half of last year, it sent a message to banks about being more careful with their lending, and to companies about being less reliant on cheap credit.

By allowing Chaori Solar to miss an interest payment on a bond this month – the first true default in the modern era of China's bond market – regulators also sent a message to investors that they cannot count on bailouts. The hope is that this will force investors to assess risks more carefully before throwing their money at undeserving companies.

Third, there is reason to be cautiously optimistic that China's deleveraging will result in a slowdown, not a collapse. For better and for worse, the Chinese government still controls the economy's big levers. Interest rates, the exchange rate and bank lending remain in Beijing's hands to a significant degree – certainly far more than in any developed economy.

State control is part of what landed China in this predicament: too much cheap credit flowed to less-efficient government-owned companies. But state control also has advantages when trying to get out of the mess. Just as it kick-started the deleveraging process last year, China's central bank has relaxed its chokehold over the past month by easing monetary conditions. The seven-day bond repurchase rate – a gauge of short-term liquidity – has fallen 220 basis points from the start of this year to 2.9 per cent. This does not mean deleveraging has come to an end, but it is a sweetener to help companies through a painful period.

In addition, Beijing has been selective in introducing the concept of moral hazard to investors. It has let private companies fail, while standing behind government-backed companies. That approach would be highly worrisome if continued for too long – eventually, China has to allow ailing state companies to fail. But letting the air out gradually is preferable to shock therapy.

This is as far as China's Lehman moment goes. The country's corporate woes look more like a slow, managed wave of deleveraging than a sudden, unwanted financial tsunami.

BOOHOO: PLATFORM HEELS

Internet fast-fashion retailer's valuation teeters

Online fashion retailer Boohoo.com soared more than 50% on its stock market debut on London's AIM market, giving the firm value of around 870 million pounds. Fear not. The fast-fashion retailer Boohoo.com went public in the UK 14 years after internet fashion retailer Boo.com disappeared with hardly a whimper – but it is not related to its unlucky predecessor.

Boohoo aims to deliver the latest trends to 16- to 24-year-olds as cheaply as possible. It will offer about £300m in shares next week, if all goes well. The firm follows in the footsteps of internet darling Asos, which has seen its share price multiply 335 times since the IPO in 2001. Given that Boohoo targets a more price-sensitive demographic, it is surprising that its gross margin (60 per cent) is wider than Asos' (52). It may help that Boohoo does not push others' labels. It only sells its own brand and sources nearly three-quarters of its product in the UK, which shortens lead times.

Less inventory gets tied up in transport from foreign manufacturers. Their customers demand the latest – right now, please. Brands such as Zara and River Island offer this all along the high street. Boohoo, though, has no shops to stock. It delivers to all its customers worldwide from one warehouse in Burnley, not yet at full capacity. The funds from the IPO will go to expanding the warehouse and beefing up its IT system as the company enlarges its international offerings; over a third of Boohoo's sales arrive from abroad.

Also, Boohoo turns over its inventory much faster each year (about nine times) than Asos (five-and-a-half times). Good, but bear in mind that Boohoo for now generates only a eighth of Asos' revenue scale.

Be prepared for a valuation that teeters, like many of the firm's customers, on platform heels. The estimated ratio of enterprise value to earnings before interest, taxes, depreciation and amortisation multiple should be in the high-20s. Asos' ratio is around 45. Fast fashion, at these valuations, requires a slow, deliberate investment style.

WHERE DOES THE FROTH IN TECHNOLOGY STOCKS COME FROM?

The froth in technology stocks has been driven by revenue. That did not make it rational.

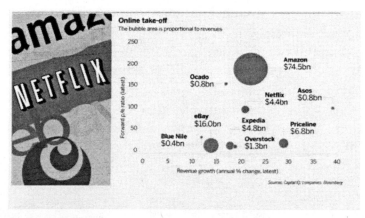

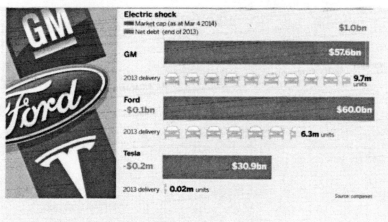

In the world of technology stocks, it was February 2000 deja vu – at least as measured by the Nasdaq Composite, the index preferred by tech investors. A week ago it hit a level topped only during the final month of dotcom insanity before that bubble burst in March 2000.

For sceptics, this was a sign of froth in high-growth shares. Companies such as Facebook, Twitter, Arm Holdings, Tesla and the biotechnology sector began trading at levels that many find hard to comprehend. Facebook paid $19bn for WhatsApp, a price of $345m per employee. The number of highly valued companies – worth more than 20 times expected earnings and more than 10 times both sales and book value – was the highest since the dotcom crash.

No surprise, then, that companies chose to cash in.

2014 had the strongest start for US listings since 2000. Biotech companies in particular rushed to take advantage of public demand for speculative stocks, while online retailers are among those floating in Europe.

Frequently founders and private equity backers merely wish to sell, with many companies raising little new cash. There is wide agreement on the explanation: years of weak economies left investors without the usual sources of growth from the economic cycle, so rising optimism was directed to new technology instead.

There has been some appetite from investors now to hope and dream rather than focus on the downside risks, and that naturally pointed them towards technology.

The hopes got focused in four areas: social media, biotech, online retail/payment and a handful of disruptive hardware technologies, in particular Tesla's electric cars, Arm's cheap processors and 3D printing.

All told solid stories. This, shareholders swore was not a repeat of the dotcom bubble years. Back then, listed companies that simply added.com to their name averaged a 74 per cent gain in 10 days, a post-bubble study showed. Business plans written on table napkins attracted venture investors.

THIS GLOBAL STOCK MARKET
RALLY HAS LEGS

Unlike in previous bubbles, today's companies have real revenues and are growing at the expense of slow-moving incumbents weighed down by old business models. The companies dominating Nasdaq as it approaches its 2000 highs are now mature businesses. Even among the new "story stocks", many – including Facebook, Arm and the bigger biotechs – are very profitable.

Clearly the future of retail is online. Social networks are used by hundreds of millions of people. Biotech is no longer purely promise. The future of the electric cars looks brighter than at any time since the early 20th century.

There was a solid story to tell about every bubble in history, from Dutch tulips in 1634 to the British railway mania of the 1840s, Florida land in the 1920s or the safety provided by portfolio insurance in 1987.

Dotcoms, too, had a tale: the internet has indeed proven to be a disruptive technology. The question is, will today's stocks reap big enough benefits from the disruption? Or are investors once again overexcited?

The case against is fairly simple. Easy money has encouraged speculation. Emerging markets were the initial beneficiaries; investors and companies even began to rebrand them as "growth markets". A mini-bubble inflated rare earth stocks fivefold in 2010 (they are now worth half their starting point). Apple and Samsung soared as investors latched on to the smartphone and tablet boom, before dropping back. The new tech stocks have been merely the latest fashion.

That does not mean every company will lose out or even that they are all overvalued. There is "massive upside" for many of the disruptive stocks, including Facebook, which GLG has owned since it listed. However, the number of investors chasing themes such as big data mean any company disappointing revenue expectations will suffer badly.

You have a lot of people interested in big data and you have got relatively few stocks so there's a rarity factor--There's lazy money in some of those [shares] because it is thematic.

Many fund managers are ditching traditional valuation tools, instead guesstimating how much of a total market – advertising, pharmaceuticals, cars – a company might grab in a decade, rather than focusing on growth rates or earnings.

As one hedge fund manager put it, if there's a 10 per cent chance that Tesla could take 10 per cent of the market value of the motor industry, it justifies its current price.

A frequent refrain was that "if [insert favoured company] can grow the way Google did, it is worth far more" than the current share price.

Valuations assumed that the new tech stocks will create an awful lot of disruption in traditional companies, that incumbents will fail to fight back effectively, and that yet more start-ups will not disrupt the new business models (as Facebook did to previous social networks). Some of these stocks might be the Google of retail or carmaking; others will be as valuable as a losing lottery ticket.

Online: a low-return game

Here's the case for owning Amazon's shares at $360.

The company's sales are growing at about 20 per cent a year. If this continues for 10 years it will have revenues of about $460bn (Walmart's current level – and who denies that Amazon is the next Walmart?).

Now assume that its operating margin goes to 10 per cent, from 1 or 2 per cent now. High for a mass- market retailer, sure, but Amazon has higher-margin businesses, too – cloud computing and all that.

At a 20 per cent tax rate (think Luxembourg, Ireland or Bermuda), 2022 profits are $71 a share. If the valuation is then 20 times earnings, it's a $1,600 stock. Buy!

Fast and loose? Sure. But a much more rigorous projection is hard to imagine. The crucial variable – what competition in internet retail will do to any one company's growth and margins – is unknowable.

So stress test the projection: plug in 15 per cent average growth, 7 per cent margin, a 30 per cent tax rate and a multiple of 15. On this view Amazon still doubles its sales twice in the next 10 years and its margin triples – but the stock remains under $500 in '22. That's a bond-like annual return of 3 per cent. Buy something else!

Bulls on Amazon and internet retail generally can point to one segment long penetrated by internet sales: travel. Margins, growth and valuations remain high for the leaders, Expedia and Priceline.

Remember, though, that these companies are exchanges that aggregate supply and demand, and exchanges enjoy powerful network effects. Everyone wants to be on an exchange (or, for that matter, a chat app) that has a lot of people on it already.

So don't confuse the travel sites with companies that are essentially old-fashioned retail operations – sourcing, selling and distributing physical goods – that happen to have digital storefronts. This group, which includes Ocado, AO World and big parts of Amazon, will compete on price, distribution and selection – a capital-intensive, low-return game.

Tesla: A bet on batteries

A company with a $30bn market cap does not get to sell niche products. Tesla Motors, after a 600 per cent run-up over the past two years, has been given credit for being a mass-market car company far in advance of moving mass-market volumes.

The company sold a grand total of 25,000 Model S sedans at $70,000 a pop. By 2020 the electric car revolutionary plans to sell 500,000 units a year – aggressive, but bordering on plausibility.

Audi, BMW and Mercedes together sell almost 6m cars annually. Can Tesla profitably deliver that many vehicles? If so, then its share price still looks pricey but not absurd.

Ramping up production of cutting-edge cars is much trickier than getting a few hundred million people to download an app.

By 2020, Tesla's "generation III" model will be available and selling at, say, $45,000 each. If 80 per cent of the company's volume targets are made up of these, with the rest being the plush Model S, Tesla will rake in $25bn in revenue.

At an 11 per cent operating margin (higher than what Ford and General Motors aim for) earnings per share could be $13. Applying a 30 times forward multiple, and then discounting back five years at a 15 per cent discount rate yields a stock price of about $200. This is about where Tesla shares were just before its recent earnings announcement.

(Its shares are now $250).

There is a hypothetical combination of price, margin and volume that justifies the share price. But investors are betting on Tesla's ability to overcome a non-financial hurdle: it must make breakthroughs in battery design and manufacture which bring the unit costs down dramatically while increasing the distance the cars can go on a charge and decreasing the time it takes to charge up. What's more, it is not enough for this technology to exist: Tesla must own it, or it will suddenly be on a level playing field with much larger competitors. Because Tesla has wisely tapped financing markets as its stock has soared, it won't be short of capital. It will need it.

Social media: the new, new thing

Go ahead, try saying social media is not the future of advertising and watch the reaction from the whippersnappers, *writes Nicole Bullock*. That #enthusiasm supports high growth expectations. Sales at Facebook rose 55 per cent to nearly $8bn in 2013 from a year ago. And it is wildly profitable: over a third of its revenues converted to free cash flow last year. At Twitter, revenue more than doubled, hitting $665m.

Both increased their share of worldwide digital advertising, too. At $119.5bn for 2013, the market expanded by 15 per cent, according to eMarketer. But what percentage of ad spend do they have to capture to justify the high hopes?

Take Facebook. Looking out to 2017, Wall Street expects Facebook will produce sales of about $23bn and earn $2.86 per share. For both sales and profits that comes to compound annual growth of about 30 per cent. At the current share price of $71, the multiple a few years out is then 25 times – not bad. Assume $20bn of sales comes from advertising. eMarketer forecasts worldwide digital ad spend of $179bn for 2017. Facebook would have to win an 11 per cent share; it has 6 per cent now. This doesn't seem a stretch for a company with 1.2bn monthly users.

For Twitter, 2017 sales forecasts of $4bn would equal nearly 60 per cent CAGR from 2013 and just 2 per cent of the digital ad market, against 0.5 per cent now. The multiple on expected 2017 earnings is about 50 – toppy, but Twitter is younger than Facebook.

The market is big enough that reasonable market share targets translate to big growth. The tricky bit is what these projections imply about the structure of the market: that a new disruptive competitor is unlikely to emerge quickly, as Twitter and Facebook did themselves.

One might argue that Facebook and Twitter cannot suffer the fate of MySpace. Their huge user bases mean that those who defect for the new new thing risk losing connections. And the companies have the money to buy the next new thing anyway. But if their business models turn out to be based on user inertia and pricey acquisitions, the market will rethink those valuations.

Biotech: real medicine, snake oil prices

Please don't wake, no don't shake me. Biotechnology investors are channelling John Lennon as they hope the "dream" stocks at the cross-section of medicine and innovation continue to float upstream. In three years, the sector has turned $100 into $284, humbling the $151 the S&P 500 returned. But the alarm is buzzing.

The sector has top-heavy DNA. A handful of large companies – Amgen, Biogen Idec, Celgene and Gilead – have seen their research come good, and amassed an arsenal of cash from a diverse drugs portfolio. Start-up labs, by contrast, are often experimenting with cures to ultra-rare "orphan" diseases. They depend on funding from private investors and venture capitalists that buy scientists time to tinker.

The hope is that good trial results will attract the big boys: Gilead's $11bn purchase of Pharmasset in 2011 laid the ground for the start-ups' incredible boom.

These companies are now creating more froth than medicine. Labs yet to begin trials are sizzling out of their test tubes to list their shares. In one case, investors waived important protections on insider share sales. It didn't matter; the pre-clinical issuer's shares more than tripled. Valuations for the smaller biotechs cannot be justified by anyone other than a gambling addict hoping they can spot the next Pharmasset.

Sure, management teams have learnt from mistakes that left shattered glass across the industry after the dotcom bubble burst. Regardless, most will still fail. These are stocks for thick-skinned professionals. Generalists should steer clear, but instead are investing willy-nilly; the sector's main exchange traded fund has seen inflows of $1.4bn over the past three years.

The case for the big four is different, and rests on earnings growth. So far, analysts have been forced to revise estimates higher and higher. Assuming operating profit growth of more than 20 per cent, the four trade at 18 times 2015 earnings and 15 times 2016. That compares pretty fairly with the broader healthcare sector. But the big four's halo effect on the start-ups makes no sense.

That is why some are hitting snooze.

WHY INFLATING THE ECONOMY
WILL NOT HELP JAPAN

A majority of market participants now expect no further action from the Bank of Japan. Here are four reasons why:

The economy seems to be holding up

Before Japan raised taxes on consumption for the first time in 17 years in April, there were fears that the move would trigger a slump, knocking the BoJ off course in its pursuit of its new 2 per cent inflation target. Some advisors to prime minister Shinzo Abe were asking for pre-emptive action from the central bank to make sure it stayed on course.

But so far at least, the data looks fairly solid. Core CPI data for the Tokyo area in April – showing a year-on-year rise of 2.7 per cent, only slightly less than expectations of 2.8 per cent – suggest that some retailers have used the tax to force through opportunistic price hikes, which will push inflation up.

BoJ-ers like what they're seeing.

Deputy BoJ governor Hiroshi Nakaso believes Japan was "resilient enough to absorb the effects" of the tax hike, citing better jobs and income data – along with a lack of a regional currency crisis or a domestic banking crisis, both of which dragged Japan down last time the sales tax went up in 1997.

Other countries wouldn't like it

There is a "palpable sense of trepidation" around the continent that "the emphasis on the BoJ to pull Japan out of its funk will have adverse global effects. Korea and Thailand, in particular, are worried about liquidity from QQE spilling across borders, driving up exchange rates.

Bonds are already looking peaky

The BoJ's commitment to buying just about every long-term government bond it can get its hands on in order to hit its base-money target of Y270tn by the end of this year has completely changed the character of the bond market. The bank used to wait a month before it would buy new issues from the ministry of finance; now the gap is down to a day.

Dealers' inventories are low and trading is thin, which makes the ministry of finance nervous about sudden rate spikes. One day last week the benchmark 10-year bond went completely untraded for the first time since Boxing Day 2000.

The BoJ could always buy more shorter-term debt to pump up the monetary base. Maybe by QQE5 we'll run out of T-bills. But the idea of QQE, as set out last April, was to bring down interest rates across the yield curve – hence the extension of the average remaining maturity of bond purchases from 3 years to 7 years. Mopping up more T-bills would effectively reverse that pledge.

More stock purchases are a possibility, and it is one that most economists have been flagging for months. But would a big round of ETF purchases – perhaps tripling or even quintupling from the current Y1tn a year – really quicken anyone's pulse?

Markets? What markets?

Yes, Japanese stocks have been weak – the third weakest in the world this year, after Russia and Venezuela. The yen, too, has strengthened against almost all of the major currencies – which is the main reason why investors have been "lusting" for more from the central bank, in the words of Mr Prasad.

But analysts have noticed a shift in the BoJ's communication. In recent months, Mr Kuroda and co have talked a lot less about assets or foreign-exchange rates and more about metrics from the real economy. One particular favourite is the unemployment rate, which at 3.6 per cent in February was nearing the mid-3 per cent level that the BoJ considers full employment.

The BoJ is becoming more data-dependent. They want to keep policy decision-making independent from developments in financial markets.

Which brings us back to reason one.

The BoJ and the government signed a pact last year to work together to unlock "sustainable" growth in the world's third largest economy.

Deflation provides a good example of economists' bad habits. They assume that people behave in the same way even if they live in different countries and that their behaviour does not change over time. They are sometimes right. But deflation and inflation show how misleading this tendency to generalise can be. Today deflation is a danger for the eurozone, but not for Japan.

Deflation can cause problems, but not always. Since its market crashed in 1990, Japan's gross domestic product grew more when prices fell than when they rose.

Deflation is usually bad for investment, but not for consumption. It is often believed that consumers postpone their spending when they expect prices to fall, (or increase their savings). The evidence is strongly against this.

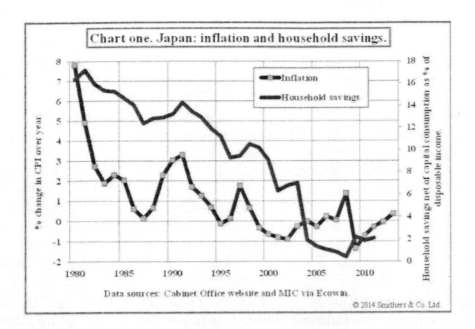

As chart one shows, Japanese households have reduced their savings as inflation has fallen. Not only has the general direction of both been the same, but so, more often than not, have the blips. For example, savings and inflation both rose from 1987 to 1991 and again from 1996 to 1998.

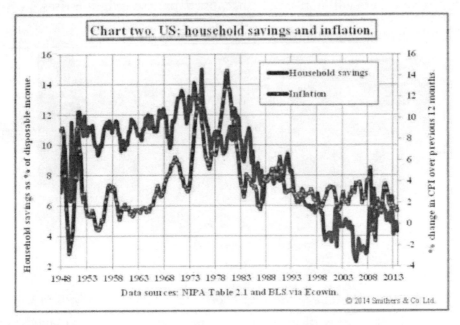

The tendency for inflation and savings to move in the same direction is not just true of Japan. Chart two shows that in the US savings have risen as inflation has picked up and fallen back with its decline.

As Japan needs more consumption and less investment, inflation is unlikely to help.

Another much misunderstood aspect of inflation is the claim that it helps reduce the national debt relative to GDP. This is true only under two conditions. First that debt is not much more than 100 per cent of GDP or second, that interest rates do not rise in line with inflation.

If real interest rates do not change, then nominal rates will rise by the same amount as inflation. If debt is below 100 per cent of GDP this will mean that interest payments rise more slowly than nominal GDP and, if debt is above 100 per cent, they will rise more rapidly.

In practice, the break-even point is often above 100 per cent of GDP as nominal interest rates may rise more slowly than inflation. This happened in the UK after the end of the second world war, when exchange controls limited the free movement of capital. This is known as financial repression and seems unlikely to work in Japan today.

Japan has a gross national debt of 230 % of GDP and is therefore likely to find that within a year or so inflation will increase rather than reduce the fiscal deficit. A small rise in inflation to, say, 2 per cent would probably have little impact. But anything above that is likely to cause a panic in the bond market.

In this context it is Japan's gross debt that matters. The foreign exchange reserves are huge and bring the net debt down to about 150 per cent of GDP, but interest rates on these will not rise just because Japanese inflation rises.

Does Sony's revamp signal a sea change for Japan Inc?

Sony Xperia Z1 smartphone in the Sony booth at the CES in Las Vegas in January.

The major restructuring of **Sony's** consumer electronics units may signal that a long-awaited shakeup to break Japan Inc. out of its doldrums has finally begun.

"Zombie" companies resisting change and offering little in the way of growth had long plagued Japan's moribund economy. In the wake of Abenomics – a series of policy measures unveiled under Prime Minister Shinzo Abe to jump start the economy – that may be changing, with more companies beginning to shake up their business models, especially in the face of increasing competition from abroad.

Sony swallows bitter pill for revival

There's a real feeling in corporate Japan that we have got to change. Evidence of that happening is most welcome.

At its quarterly earnings announcement Thursday, Sony said it would hack off its long-ailing computer and television businesses, stepping up its restructuring efforts. The turnaround efforts include plans to cut around 5,000 jobs, a once-taboo step in corporate Japan.

Sony isn't alone. **Panasonic** has emerged from a period of heavy losses after it sold off some units and shifted its focus toward industrial, rather than consumer, clients; its efforts also included reducing its workforce by more than 30,000 workers.

It's indicative of the wake-up call that Prime Minister Abe is having. It's really causing positive reverberations throughout corporate Japan.

Japan has rightly realized that if they don't do something, they're going to slowly sink into the Pacific Ocean and become vulnerable and irrelevant. In a way, Sony is a microcosm of that.

Others also see the crossing of former taboos could indicate Japan's corporate world is heading into a period of major changes.

Japan has been the last bastion of jobs for life. Maybe it does indicate a shift of structure in Japan.

Abe likely isn't a fan of the layoffs, as they will complicate his efforts to push companies for much-need wage increases.

One thing Japan needs is higher wages growth, but if other companies follow Sony's lead, it may not get that.

If Prime Minister Abe wants a new Japan, then some people will have to lose their jobs--ultimately, a stronger Japan will lead to more jobs.

Why is Sony lagging behind its Japanese peers? While some Japanese tech firms are forecasting record profits this year, there are some unique factors behind Sony's struggle.

To be sure, not everyone is convinced Japan Inc.'s moves indicate a drive for growth so much as a painful necessity. It's a painful adjustment to slower growth.

North Asia is a big loser from slower growth in China. The really beneficial effects of rapid growth in the early part of the century are running in reverse--Japan was a major beneficiary of China's rapid growth before the Global Financial Crisis.

(Sony) didn't want to do this. They're doing this to save the company. Other companies are going to be facing the same kind of pressures as Sony. There's a limited amount the (weaker) yen can do to help out there.

Sony itself may see its moves as only a retrenchment in the face of tough competition, rather than a springboard for growth.

Indeed, it's likely noteworthy that Sony's moves leave the company's basic structure intact. Last year, Sony rejected calls from billionaire investor Daniel for a breakup of the company, with spinoffs of the entertainment and insurance divisions.

WHERE IS THE U.S. GDP HEADED

The chart below is my way to visualize real GDP change since 2007. I've used a stacked column chart to segment the four major components of GDP with a dashed line overlay to show the sum of the four, which is real GDP itself. Here is the latest overview from the Bureau of Labor Statistics:

The decrease in real GDP in Q1 2014 primarily reflected negative contributions from private inventory investment, exports, state and local government spending, nonresidential fixed investment, and residential fixed investment that were partly offset by a positive contribution from PCE. Imports, which are a subtraction in the calculation of GDP, increased.

Let's take a closer look at the contributions of GDP of the four major subcomponents.

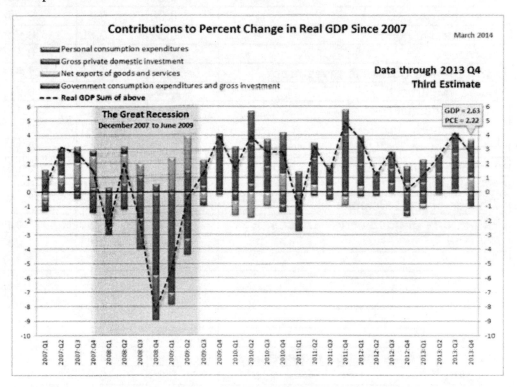

Note: *The conventional practice is to round GDP to one decimal place, the latest at -2.9. The -2.93 GDP in the chart above is the real GDP calculated to two decimal places based on the BEA chained 2009 dollar data series.*

Over the time frame of this chart, the Personal Consumption Expenditures (PCE) component has shown the most consistent correlation with real GDP itself. When PCE has been positive, GDP has usually been positive, and vice versa. In the latest GDP data, the contribution of PCE came at 0.71 of the -2.93 real GDP. The Q1 contribution from PCE decreased rather dramatically from Q4 2013.

Of course the general view is that the unusually severe winter was a transitory cause of weak GDP rather than fundamental weakness in the business cycle. In support of that view, note that the positive contribution from PCE was highly concentrated in services with the positive contribution from consumer goods being quite tiny.

Here is a side-by-side look of the Advance, Second and Third Estimates.

BEA Estimates of 2014 Q1 Contributions to GDP			
Category	Advance	Second	Third
Percent change at annual rate:			
Gross domestic product	0.1	-1	-2.9
Percentage points at annual rates:			
Personal consumption expenditures	2.04	2.09	0.71
Goods	0.08	0.16	0.04
Durable goods	0.06	0.11	0.09
Nondurable goods	0.02	0.06	-0.05
Services	1.96	1.93	0.67
Gross private domestic investment	-1.01	-1.98	-1.97
Fixed investment	-0.44	-0.36	-0.27
Nonresidential	-0.25	-0.2	-0.14
Structures	0	-0.21	-0.22
Equipment	-0.32	-0.18	-0.16
Intellectual property products	0.06	0.19	0.24
Residential	-0.18	-0.16	-0.13
Change in private inventories	-0.57	-1.62	-1.7
Net exports of goods and services	-0.83	-0.95	-1.53
Exports	-1.07	-0.83	-1.25
Goods	-1.19	-0.97	-1.12
Services	0.12	0.13	-0.12
Imports	0.24	-0.12	-0.29
Goods	0.21	-0.14	-0.25
Services	0.02	0.02	-0.03
Government consumption expenditures	-0.09	-0.15	-0.14
Federal	0.05	0.05	0.05
National defense	-0.11	-0.11	-0.11
Nondefense	0.16	0.16	0.16
State and local	-0.14	-0.2	-0.18

Here is a look at the contribution changes between over the past four quarters. The difference between the two rightmost columns was addressed in the GDP summary quoted above. I've added arrows to highlight the quarter-over-quarter change for the major components.

Contributions to GDP Percent Change: The Last Four Quarters	2013 Q2	2013 Q3	2013 Q4	2014 Q1
Percent change at annual rate:				
Gross domestic product	2.5	4.1	2.6	-2.9
Percentage points at annual rates:				
Personal consumption expenditures	**1.24**	**1.36**	**2.22**	**0.71** ◀
Goods	0.71	1.03	0.66	0.04
Durable goods	0.46	0.58	0.21	0.09
Nondurable goods	0.26	0.46	0.45	-0.05
Services	0.53	0.32	1.57	0.67
Gross private domestic investment	**1.38**	**2.56**	**0.41**	**-1.97** ◀
Fixed investment	0.96	0.89	0.43	-0.27
Nonresidential	0.56	0.58	0.68	-0.14
Structures	0.43	0.35	-0.05	-0.22
Equipment	0.18	0.02	0.58	-0.16
Intellectual property products	-0.06	0.22	0.15	0.24
Residential	0.4	0.31	-0.26	-0.13
Change in private inventories	0.41	1.67	-0.02	-1.7
Net exports of goods and services	**-0.07**	**0.14**	**0.99**	**-1.53** ◀
Exports	1.04	0.52	1.23	-1.25
Goods	0.84	0.52	1.06	-1.12
Services	0.2	0.01	0.17	-0.12
Imports	-1.1	-0.39	-0.24	-0.29
Goods	-1	-0.32	-0.18	-0.25
Services	-0.11	-0.07	-0.06	-0.03
Government consumption expenditures	**-0.07**	**0.08**	**-0.99**	**-0.14** ◀
Federal	-0.12	-0.11	-1	0.05
National defense	-0.03	-0.02	-0.7	-0.11
Nondefense	-0.09	-0.09	-0.29	0.16
State and local	0.05	0.19	0	-0.18

As for the role of Personal Consumption Expenditures (PCE) in GDP and how it has increased over time, here is a snapshot of the PCE-to-GDP ratio since the inception of quarterly GDP in 1947. The latest ratio is 68.6%, matching the all-time high of 68.6% in Q1 2011. From a theoretical perspective, there is a point at which personal consumption as a percent of GDP can't really go any higher. We may be hovering in that upper range.

Let's close with a look at the inverse behavior of PCE and Gross Private Domestic Investment (GPDI) during recessions. PCE generally increases as a percent of GDP whereas GPDI declines. That is not what we've been seeing in recent quarters, but Q1 GDP could be sounding a caution. Note that I've plotted the two with different vertical axes (PCE on left, GPDI on the right) to highlight the frequent inverse correlation.

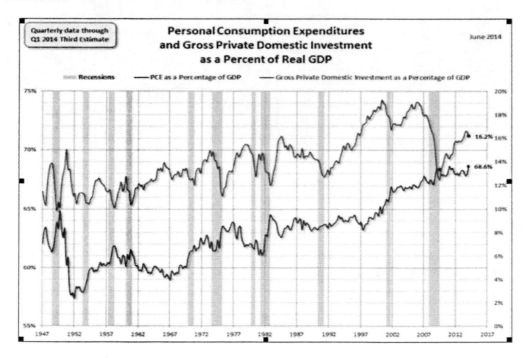

WHY GOOGLE IS LOOKING AT RAY-BANS TO GIVE GLASS SPECS APPEAL

Ray-Bans via Instagram

Google has been working hard lately to dampen the constant, rumbling criticism of Glass. First, it issued guidelines on etiquette for its pioneering wearable gadget, warning early adopters: "Don't be a glasshole."

Then last week, it decided that the people buying its $1,500 headset weren't glassholes after all, trying to dispel ten "myths" about the prototype product: Glass really isn't a "distraction from the real world" or "the perfect surveillance device", it insisted in a blogpost.

The ground suitably prepared, Google has now made a much more meaningful step towards mainstream acceptance: it is partnering with the maker of Ray-Ban and Oakley frames to make Glass fashionable.

Google Glass Titanium: AP

Many analysts now see design, rather than technology, as the biggest barrier to wearables' wider adoption. Google itself has already moved in the right direction with January's unveiling of its new "Titanium Collection" for Glass, which FT fashion editor Vanessa Friedman faintly praised as making "the leap from nerd-wear to pretty acceptable actual glasses".

It's more than a year since the *New York Times* reported that Google was working with hip online specs retailer Warby Parker to make Glass wearers "look less like cyborgs". However, that partnership never made the leap from rumour to actual announcement. Perhaps some in the fashion business remain wary of association with the controversial wearable.

So only time will tell if Luxottica, the Italian eyewear conglomerate, is brave or foolhardy in stepping up to the challenge of giving Glass specs appeal.

Its partnership with Google only extends to Ray-Ban and Oakley for now, but the Luxottica eyewear family also includes such fashionable licensees as Burberry, Chanel and Paul Smith, as well as its own Persol and Oliver Peoples.

Oakley Thump

Oakley, beloved of extreme sports fans, has already launched ski goggles with a heads-up display and "Thump" sunglasses with an MP3 player. Fitting Glass into Ray-Bans, the hipsters' favourite, might present a greater design challenge.

Luxottica, on its part is "thrilled" to be working with Google; they believe both have come to a point where both have a technology push and a consumer pull for wearable technology products and applications... it was high time to combine the unique expertise, deep knowledge and quality of our group with the cutting edge technology expertise of Google and give birth to a new generation of revolutionary devices.

Google's own post on the deal was equally bombastic, placing the development in the continuum of 700 years of spectacles' evolution to a "global phenomenon : Luxottica understands how to build, distribute and sell great products that their clients and consumers love – something we care deeply about at Glass, too. They'll bring design and manufacturing expertise to the mix, and, together, we'll bring even more Glass style choices to our Explorers. In addition, Luxottica's retail and wholesale distribution channels will serve us well when we make Glass available to more people down the road.

A Google spokesperson did not provide details about price or availability but emphasised Luxottica's central role in making and selling Glass (the group also owns the Sunglass Hut chain). The approach echoes Google's Nexus line of Android devices, which are made in close partnership with the likes of LG and Samsung.

Luxottica will manufacture these frames and lead distribution of Glass in the eyewear category (in optical shops, kiosks, etc.) and Glass will continue to sell the device online through the Explorer program.

REVISUALIZING THE SECOND
U.S. HOUSING BUBBLE

As we were looking at the current trends in U.S. median new home sale prices, we were forwarded the following question:

"Can you quickly and easily 'real dollar' this chart?"

By "this chart", our inquisitor is likely referring to the following chart, showing the overall trend for median new home sale prices with respect to median household income since 1967:

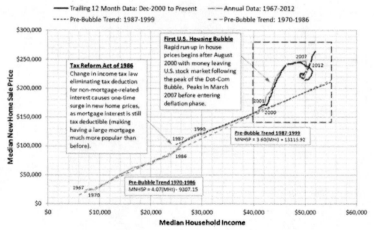

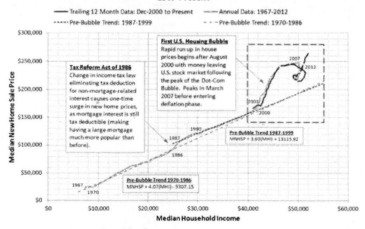

And the answer to their question is: "Why, yes we can!"

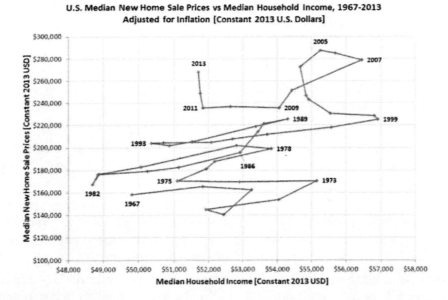

U.S. Median New Home Sale Prices vs Median Household Income, 1967-2013
Adjusted for Inflation [Constant 2013 U.S. Dollars]

It's not as pretty as our nominal value chart, which better describes the world in which people actually live and buy things, but it does clearly show housing prices defying the post-2000 recession as real median incomes fell during the first U.S. housing bubble, and again at present in the second U.S. housing bubble, as median new house prices began rising in 2011, but with no meaningful increase in median incomes to support them.

As for what a non-bubble driven housing market looks like, since we've already demonstrated that household income is *the* primary driver of home prices, we should see a close coupling between median incomes and median sale prices, with both either rising or falling at rates consistent with those observed over extended period of time.

That we're instead seeing nearly vertical movements for prices with respect to household income indicates that other factors have created a situation where housing is becoming increasingly unaffordable.

After all, if the families who earn the median household income are increasingly unable to afford the median price of new homes for sale, something other than the fundamental driver of house prices is seriously skewing the real estate market.

And history tells us that the other factors that can affect home prices do not have any significant "staying power".

WILL DIET COKE TAKE THE POP OUT OF COCA-COLA ?

Coca-Cola might look focused on conquering the world, but it has a nagging problem right at home: Selling Diet Coke to Americans.

Declining unit sales of fizzy drinks in the U.S. are nothing new for the likes of Coca-Cola and PepsiCo. Carbonated beverage volume fell every year between 2005 and 2012, according to Beverage Digest, which is expected to release 2013 data in the next several days.

Until recently, the beverage companies had a solution to the problem that allowed them to maintain steady revenue growth. Here's how it worked: Over the last few years, the volume of carbonated beverages sold in the U.S. would normally fall by a fraction of a percentage point if prices were held steady.

If companies increased prices by 1 percent, volumes would decline further, but by a smaller 0.8 percentage point. That allowed companies to boost revenue by raising prices, which they generally did.

What's changed recently is the baseline volume decline. In the period from last July through January, the average decline in volume would have been nearly 4 percentage points, assuming prices didn't change, Faucher said. The data in his study include large-format retailers like grocery chains but exclude some others like small shops and vending machines.

The likely culprit: Diet soda. While health concerns around calories are nothing new, there has recently been a pickup in negative publicity about artificial sweeteners. Indeed, Coca-Cola said on its last investor call that sparkling beverage volume in North America fell 2 percent in 2013, largely due to Diet Coke. Unlike 2012, when Coca-Cola was able to raise prices faster than volume fell, it was only able to keep sparkling revenue roughly flat for North America in 2013.

Weak U.S. soda sales, both regular and diet, pose a serious threat to Coca-Cola. North American sparkling beverages account for 30% of companywide revenue.

Diet Coke is the second-best selling carbonated drink in the country after regular Coke, according to Beverage Digest's latest data. And if concerns about the safety of Diet Coke take hold in the U.S., consumers in other major markets like Europe could soon take notice.

The obvious solution is to change consumer perception about health risks or introduce a new Coca-Cola product using non-chemical sweeteners. But both Coca-Cola and Pepsi have introduced many versions of their drinks over the years. Some, like Coke Zero, have been very successful, suggesting the company has a shot at coming up with an answer. But it's hard to guess how long that will take.

Another option is to reduce prices to keep volumes intact. But that is probably a short-term solution to a bigger problem. Even if it results in higher revenue, it hurts profit margins. And it can be tough to raise prices in the future if consumers grow accustomed to big promotions.

Large price cuts may not even stave off volume declines. Coca-Cola-owned sparkling beverage prices declined by 4.5 % from a year earlier in the four weeks through March 15, but volumes only rose 3.8 %, according to domestic Nielsen data. The overall impact was to increase market share slightly in sparkling drinks but revenue declined.

The better option is probably to continue on the path of price hikes, which Coca-Cola has indicated it wants to do. The tobacco industry went through a phase of aggressive discounting a couple of decades ago when health concerns impacted volumes. But Big Tobacco ultimately focused on boosting prices and the industry has largely been successful.

That said, soda and cigarettes are different because consumers can switch from Diet Coke to another non-cola beverage—even bottled water. The price premium of carbonated drinks over bottled water in the U.S. has increased from 125 % in 2010 to more than 150 % today. Any moves to widen that price gap further may make it more tempting to stop drinking soda.

All this comes as Coca-Cola has been through a rough patch. Since the start of 2012, Coca-Cola shares have risen 10 percent, compared with 25 % for PepsiCo and 47 % for S&P 500. And earlier, large Coca-Cola shareholder Wintergreen Advisers publicly complained about the company's 2014 executive compensation plan, which it argued could dilute shareholders by 14 %. The company disputed the claim, saying that the awards would only be paid if employees met specific goals.

Coca-Cola, given its global brand strength and pricing power in most markets, deserves to trade at a premium multiple. But it first needs to get its diet problem under control, else more investors may soon be up in arms.

HOW TO INVEST IN BOLLYWOOD –
THE LARGEST PRODUCER OF MOVIES
IN THE WORLD

Raja Harischandra

Directed by	Dadasaheb Phalke
Produced by	Dadasaheb Phalke for Phalke's Films
Written by	Dadasaheb Phalke
Story by	Ranchhodbai Udayram
Starring	D. D. Dabke
	P. G. Sane
Cinematography	Trymbak B. Telang
Release dates	3 May 1913
Running time	40 minutes
Country	India
Language	Silent film

A scene from **Raja Harishchandra (1913)** – credited as the first full-length Indian motion picture.

India is the largest producer of films in the world.[3][4] In 2009 India produced a total of 2,961 films on celluloid, that includes a staggering figure of 1,288 feature films.[5] Indian film industry is multi-lingual and the largest in the world in terms of ticket sales and number of films produced and 2nd largest in terms of revenue. The film industry is supported mainly by a vast film-going Indian public, and Indian films have been gaining increasing popularity in the rest of the world—notably in countries with large numbers of expatriate Indians. Largest film industry in India is the Hindi film industry mostly concentrated in Mumbai (Bombay),[6] and is commonly referred to as "Bollywood", an amalgamation of Bombay and Hollywood, which produces around 20% of films in India.

Soon, those not connected with the Hindi film segment in any way will also be able to reap the benefits of the sector's double-digit growth, with **Third Eye Cinema Fund** (TCEF), a Securities and Exchange Board of India (Sebi)-registered alternative investment fund, set to hit the market.

TCEF, which will target well-heeled investors, aims to generate about 25 per cent returns.

Given the growth of the Indian film industry, many individuals want to invest in it, but have no clue how to go about it.

Also, there are many myths such as the segment isn't professional and organised. With the digitisation of screens and the advent of a corporate structure in major studios/production houses, these myths are being busted.

What better time to enter the industry and make it more professional and transparent?

HOW COPPER'S DECLINE HAS SENT THE ZAMBIAN KWACHA INTO TAILSPIN

The Zambian kwacha has been one of the weakest currencies against the US dollar this year, losing more than 8 per cent of its value against the world's reserve currency during the past month alone.

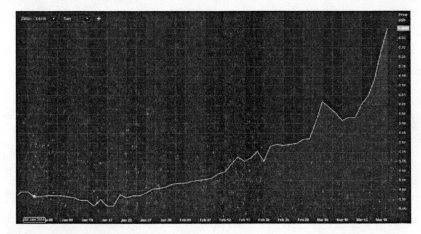

Source: Thomson Reuters

The blame lies with falling copper prices, driven down by a slowing Chinese economy. Negative sentiment towards emerging markets has only made things worse.

Copper is mainly used in infrastructure so with the world's second-biggest economy looking to reduce fixed investment and boost domestic consumption, the metal has lost fundamental support. Also affecting the metal's prospects are plans by global miners such as Glencore Xstrata and BHP Billiton to boost mine capacity and output this year.

Copper prices have fallen 14.4 % this year, including 10 % in the past month.

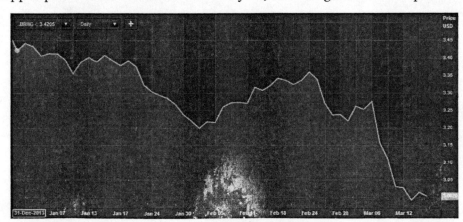

Zambia and the Democratic Republic of Congo are the biggest producers of the metal on the continent. Copper makes up 60 % of Zambia's exports.

That puts it in a similar position to Chile, where copper accounts for nearly 50 per cent of exports. Falling prices have put pressure on both countries' currencies, but the Chilean peso has some protection: profits at Codelco, Chile's state-owned copper miner, are stashed in a sovereign wealth fund that the country can dip into during lean times.

In Chile, sales are sterilised somewhat by a sovereign wealth fund but in Zambia this does not exist yet.

Nevertheless, the peso has fallen more than 8 per cent against the US dollar this year.

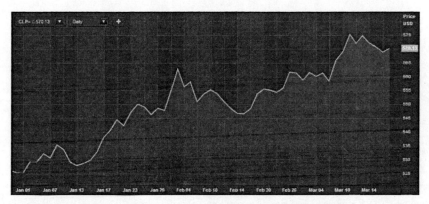

Source: Thomson Reuters

"Although clearly the fall in copper prices hasn't helped the kwacha it is also true that heightened local demand for the dollar and general emerging market tensions have weighed on the currency as well," said Lawrence.

Zambia's central bank has joined those in South Africa and Ghana by raising rates to support the currency. That will add to downward pressure on growth. Capital Economics sees GDP growth coming in at 4.5 per cent this year and next, down from an estimated 5.5 per cent last year and 7.2 per cent in 2012.

Further pressure should come in the form of a fiscal squeeze: Zambia's fiscal deficit widened to over 8.5 per cent of GDP in 2013 due to its bloated public sector wage bill and an expensive subsidy programme.

Capital warned: "…fiscal policy now needs to be tightened substantially. With government spending becoming less supportive, we think that Zambia is set for a period of weaker growth."

Fears over the government's commitment to fiscal prudence have sent Zambia's borrowing costs soaring. It was a darling of EM bond investors when it sold a $750m 10-year eurobond at a yield of just 5.625 per cent – famously, making it apparently less risky than Spain.

Along with those of Ghana and Nigeria, Zambian yields have taken off. The 2022 bond is now trading at a yield of about 8.3 per cent.

WHY THE 'INDIA GROWTH STORY' LOST ITS MOMENTUM?

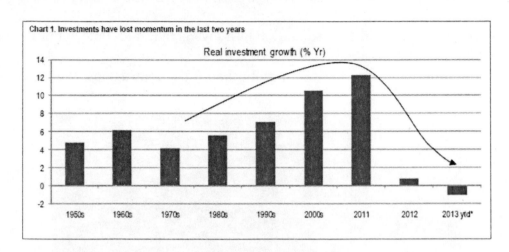

Chart 1. Investments have lost momentum in the last two years

Investments in hindsight

Investments grew more than 10% annually in 2000-11, despite the setback during the global financial crisis. However, investments have slowed down sharply since then (Chart 1).

This has led to a decline in the investment-to-GDP ratio from 32% of GDP in 2008 to 30% in 2012, a decline only matched by South Africa among peer countries (Chart 2). Brazil and Russia have also seen a decline, but it is has been relatively marginal. China and Indonesia, on the other hand, have gone through a more favourable investment cycle, although the investment cycle in China got overextended in the process.

A breakdown of investments by sectors shows that the decline in investments in India was led by the industry sector (Chart 3). Investments by service sector companies, on the other hand, inched up slightly and held broadly stable for the agricultural sector.

Within services, business services and real estate companies scaled back investments. However, trade-related services stepped up investments. This may partly be explained by the expansion of rural distribution networks by consumer goods companies tapping into the relatively solid rural growth story.

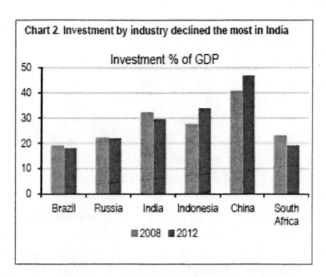

Chart 2. Investment by industry declined the most in India

Investment % of GDP

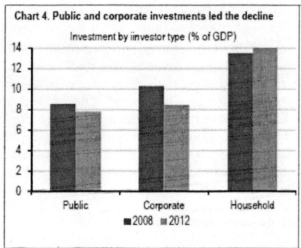

Chart 4. Public and corporate investments led the decline

Investment by iinvestor type (% of GDP)

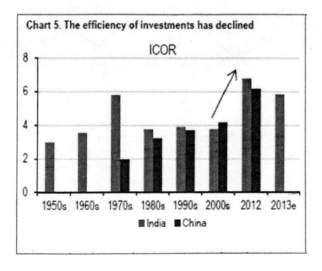

Chart 5. The efficiency of investments has declined

ICOR

Looking at investment by broad groups of investors (Chart 4), the data show that public and corporate investments led the decline. Household investments, however, rose by 1% of GDP between 2008 and 2012.

Disaggregation of this data reveals that public sector investments in both construction and 'machinery & equipment' fell as a share of GDP.

On the other hand, corporate construction-related investment rose, while investment in 'machinery & equipment' bore the brunt of the decline.

Meanwhile, households lowered investments in construction and ramped up investment in 'machinery & equipment.' The latter likely captured investments made by small businesses rolled into the household survey.

Investment is not just about quantity but also about quality, which we can write a thing or two about when it comes to China. In India's case there is, unfortunately, also evidence that the quality of investments has declined. This has been evident from the significant rise in recent years in the so called incremental capital-to-output ratio (ICOR) (Chart 5), which simply measures the investment ratio relative to the growth of the economy. Higher this ratio, the lower the productivity of investment.

What has been behind this decline in quality? For one, the shift from corporate to household investment has likely played a role, with household-led investments typically less productivity enhancing than public or corporate investments. Public investments have been held back by administrative delays and the need to squeeze capital outlays to make room for rising subsidies and compensate for weaker revenue collections. This has held back much needed investment in infrastructure, which has likely had adverse implications for productivity. Corporate investments suffered primarily when it came to investment in productivity-enhancing machinery, which also helps explain the rise in the ICOR.

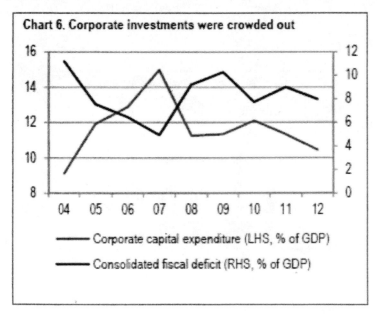

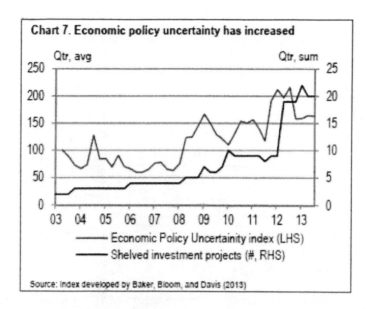

Chart 7. Economic policy uncertainty has increased

Source: Index developed by Baker, Bloom, and Davis (2013)

Why the drop in investment?

There are a lot of explanations for this, some complementary and some competing. Here are a handful of potential explanations:

Crowded out: The widening fiscal deficit since 2009 has crowded out private sector investment. Banks have essentially snatched up government bonds at the expenses of lending to the private sector, which has dampened private investment spending.

High inflation: High and volatile inflation increases uncertainty about returns from corporate investments, which typically make corporates hesitant to undertake investments. Moreover, high inflation may have weighed on funding conditions as a greater proportion of savings, as an inflation hedge, were channelled into gold rather than deposits and other financial savings instruments. Finally, it forced the RBI to raise policy rates.

Administrative and policy hurdles: Delays in obtaining project clearances, partly due to tighter environmental requirements, and rising policy uncertainty (Chart 7) soured the business climate. Moreover, economic reforms stalled in the years following the global financial crisis. These factors, in turn, led to a scaling back in new project announcements and the abandonment of existing projects (Chart 8).

Corporate investments were crowded out Chart 7. Economic policy uncertainty has increased

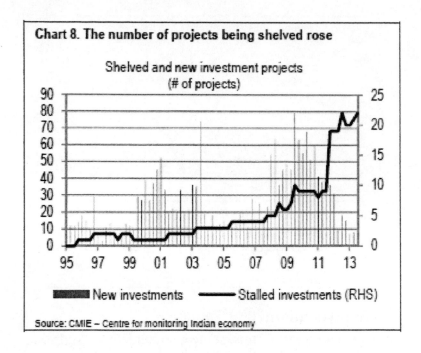

Chart 8. The number of projects being shelved rose

Shelved and new investment projects
(# of projects)

New investments ▬▬▬   Stalled investments (RHS) ▬▬▬

Source: CMIE – Centre for monitoring Indian economy

Chart 9. Weak global growth hurt expansion in the export sector

World GDP % y-o-y
Real investments % y-o-y (RHS)

A weaker global economy: Investments in the past decade have moved closely with the global business cycle (Chart 9). The decline in global growth since the global financial crisis has, therefore, likely explained at least part of the scale back in domestic investments, especially by the more externally oriented manufacturing and services companies.

Quantifying the drivers

To test these potential explanations, we have put together investment models to quantify their explanatory powers. The models use a combination of the following key explanatory variables that capture some of the potential explanations discussed above:

Real interest rates: Higher real financing costs will lower investment and could be a result of a monetary policy response to high inflation, spill-over from a tightening in global financial conditions, etc. The real interest rate used here is calculated as the prime lending rate minus the 12-month forward WPI consensus forecast to get a forward-looking measure of real funding costs.

Future returns: Investment demand, of course, depends importantly on the potential return. As long as this is high relative to funding costs, investment demand will remain high. We proxy potential returns by expected real GDP growth measured as the one-yearahead consensus real GDP growth forecast.

Lack of progress on structural reforms and administrative obstacles can do serious damage to the future returns on investment, whether real or perceived.

1 The model is based on quarterly data, and the variable we are trying to explain is the quarterly seasonally adjusted growth rate in real gross fixed capital formation.

2 For other recent investment models for India, see also a) Tokuoka, K., 2012, "Does the Business Environment Affect Corporate Investment in India?," IMF Working Paper 12/70, and b) Anand R. and V. Tulin, 2014, "India's investment slowdown: The role of confidence and uncertainty, IMF Country Report No. 14/58

Economic policy uncertainty: To capture this we have used an Economic Policy Uncertainty index3, which captures inflation and fiscal deficit uncertainty, and negative news about economic policies. The idea is that this index will pick up on policy-induced macroeconomic uncertainty, which would make businesses more cautious about investing. We also included a simple measure of inflation volatility to capture the same.

Global business cycle: We here use a measure of global industrial production. The model results confirm that these are important explanatory variables, although they cannot explain all the variation in the quarterly investment growth rate (Table 1). Moreover, they all have the expected sign.

High real interest rates have a negative impact on investment growth, which may compel some to blame the RBI for the struggling investment story. However, it is worth keeping in mind that real interest rates now are lower than they were before the global financial crisis. In fact, the drop in the real interest rate in 2007-13 would, on average, have added 0.5 percentage points to quarterly investment growth, around two percentage points in annualised terms.

3. This index is a weighted average of a) the dispersion of consensus inflation and fiscal deficit forecasts and b) negative news coverage of economic policies. For more detail, Baker, S.R., N. Bloom, and S.J. Davis, 2013, "Measuring Economic Policy Uncertainty", **Chicago Booth, Research Paper No. 13-02**.

Table 1. Regression results

Dependent variable = Quarterly investment growth, seasonally adjusted

	Model 1	Model 2	Model 3
Constant	5.79	4.54*	4.15**
World IP	0.96*	0.77**	0.56***
Real interest rate (R)	-1.34*		
Growth expectation (G)	1.17**		
G-R		1.68*	0.93**
CPI volatility	-0.44**	-0.48**	
EPU index			-0.03**
R-squared	32%	40%	37%

Note: *indicates it is significant at 1%, ** at 5%, *** at 10%

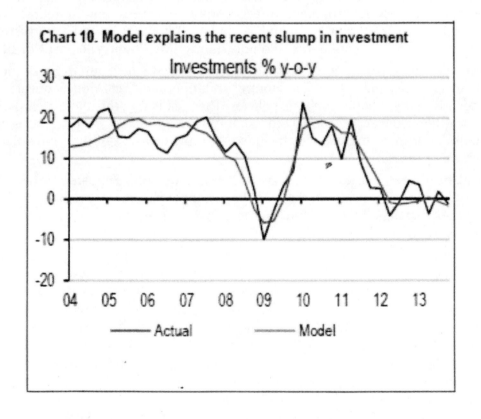

Chart 10. Model explains the recent slump in investment

Moreover, real interest rates should be held up against future expectations for growth. We have done this in model 2 and 3, where we, as the explanatory variable, use the difference between expectations for growth and real interest rates. The results show that as long as growth expectations remain relatively high, real interest rates are not a deterrent for investment; we saw this before the global financial crisis. For example, a one percentage point increase in the excess of expected real GDP growth over the real interest rate will increase quarterly investment growth by between 0.9-1.7 percentage points, which translates into 3.6-7.0 percentage points if annualised.

The positive role for growth expectations underscores the negative role that the lack of structural reform has likely played in lowering investment demand. The neglect on this front, coupled with the administrative hurdles holding back investment projects, has lowered growth expectations and held back investments more than any policy rate hikes by the RBI would have done.

Moreover, monetary policy is currently in neutral gear and is by no means tight; the real policy rate is still negative. Monetary policy can, therefore, not be blamed for the less upbeat growth expectations. If anything, the model suggests that more needs to be done to bring inflation under control. High volatility in inflation, as captured by the standard deviation of inflation, is clearly a negative for investment.

Moreover, the rise in economic policy uncertainty taking place in 2005-07 and 2012-13, as reflected in the EPU index, has shaved around 2.5 percentage points of the average quarterly investment rate, *around 10 percentage points in annualized terms*. The rise in the EPU index over this period does not just reflect higher uncertainty about inflation and monetary policy. Fiscal policy uncertainty has also increased during this period of time. On the back of this, there has been more negative news coverage of economic policies. All of this, in turn, has hurt business sentiment and, thereby, investment.

WHY HITACHI IS MAKING LONDON ITS GLOBAL RAIL HQ?

Hitachi is to make London the headquarters of its global rail business, underlining its aim to expand in the UK and to make Europe its biggest market.

It plans to increase its UK staff from 200 currently to about 1,800 within two to three years, as it takes aim at projects such as the HS2 high speed rail line and the retendering of rail franchises.

The Japanese conglomerate, which made the high-speed Javelin trains that run through Kent into London St Pancras, said it would bid for contracts on HS2, which it expected would open to tender within a decade.

Hitachi believes it would be a great idea to build high speed trains in the southeast. We've been working with HS2 for a couple of years now, advising them on the key interfaces between the train systems and what the infrastructure systems should be.

The move means key decisions will be made in London, and represents a shift from Japan, presently its biggest rail market by turnover, to a more international focus.

Next year it will open a new factory in the northeast at Newton Aycliffe, to build trains to run on the Great Western line and the East Coast main line. It also plans to open maintenance depots.

Hitachis sees it as a major operation in the UK and we want to build in the UK for the rest of Europe--The company had so far invested about half a billion pounds into the UK.

There's no reason why we can't expand to win business in other markets and create additional manufacturing capacity and challenge the traditional big three players of Alstom, Siemens and Bombardier.

Japan is Hitachi's biggest rail market by revenue, followed by Taiwan and then the UK, although the UK will soon move up to second place because of the Intercity Express Programme. Hitachi's contract, worth £1.2bn, will be built at its new factory.

Another unit of Hitachi secured a £700m deal to build Britain's new nuclear plants in 2012, taking over the two Horizon nuclear sites from its former German owners.

However, the debate over Britain's membership of the European Union was a concern, Mr Dormer said, and the company would prefer the UK to remain in the EU.

Hitachi had failed in a previous bid to enter the German market but has now pre-qualified for two contracts in Germany, to provide rolling stock for Berlin's S-Bahn line and a signalling contract for Deutsche Bahn.

It will find out later this year whether it has been successful on a bid to provide train traffic control system to Sweden's rail network.

Hitachi's rivals Bombardier and Siemens had lobbied against Hitachi being allowed access to the German market, arguing that the Japanese market was closed to foreign bidders.

Hitachi is bidding in Doha and planning to bid in Jeddah. It also plans to expand in eastern Europe, India, Turkey, Russia, and southeast Asia.

This is an incredible vote of confidence in a growing Britain that is exporting more and making great things once again.

Nothing says that better than the company that built the first bullet train putting its HQ here to sell abroad, alongside a new factory and new jobs in northern England. This is just the sort of growth we want to see more of as we invest in rail and build HS2.

Even as London steals New York's crown for best financial hub..

London has been named as the best city for "economic clout" by a new industry survey.

This means the U.K. capital steals New York's top spot, according to the survey conducted by multinational professional services network, PwC. London was named as the best city overall, with the report also heaping a wealth of other titles on the financial hub, naming it as the best for international travel and tourism and adding it was "technologically on top of its game."

The study called The Cities of Opportunity Index is an annual index of 30 major cities and is based on publicly available data from the World Bank, the International Monetary Fund and other national statistics organizations. London took the overall top spot with New York and Singapore in second and third respectively. Toronto, San Francisco, Paris, Stockholm, Hong Kong, Sydney and Chicago made up the rest of the top ten.

London's reputation as an economic powerhouse is well established, and reinforced when you consider it is the second most successful city in the index for attracting foreign direct investment.

High-performing cities in the index have to find the right balance between social and economic strengths. Like many big international cities, there's a price to pay for success. For London, while it has moved up the rankings on cost and environmental challenges, there are still lessons to be learned from international competitors on these issues.

HOW STARBUCKS SEEKS TO DOUBLE MARKET CAP TO $100BN

Starbucks wants to almost double its market capitalisation to $100bn, chief executive Howard Schultz said recently, even as the US coffee chain underscored the changing landscape facing retailers as more consumers shop online and by mobile phone.

Mr Schultz gave no date by which he expected to hit his ambitious target, which comes as the company is expanding its digital business and looking to dominate the $90bn global tea market with the growth of Teavana, the brand it bought in 2012.

With 20,000 stores in 64 countries, Starbucks has grown into one of the world's most visible brands, but it wants to expand its reach in emerging markets such as India and China as US sales growth has slowed.

Starbucks says that it wants to dominate the $ 90 Billion tea market the same way it conquered the global coffee market. The company is moving well past its latte-and-espresso roots—it plans to offer handcrafted sodas at 3000 stores this summer in addition to tea and alcohol. Starbucks bought Teavana in 2012 and it recently partnered with Oprah Winfrey for a collaboration on a tea flavor and merchandise.

It is also devoting more resources to mobile apps and customer loyalty cards, in an attempt to get more customers to buy its products at Starbucks stores, grocery stores and elsewhere.

Mobile transactions now account for 14 % of US store sales, the company said, with 5m mobile payments made every week. In response to customer demand, Starbucks will begin testing ordering ahead by mobile app, said Adam Brotman, chief digital officer.

The growth of mobile payments in Starbucks' stores is significantly bigger than the core growth of our business.

More than a quarter of US store purchases are made with Starbucks cards, which function as gift cards and loyalty cards that allow customers to rack up points toward free food or drinks. During the 2013 holiday season, when fewer US consumers did their shopping in physical stores, Starbucks estimated that one in eight adult Americans received a Starbucks cards as a gift.

You'd be hard pressed to find any retailer today who has a business of this scale, in relation to the fact that our average ticket value is $5.

- Howard Schultz, Starbucks chief executive

Mr Schultz has emphasised the "seismic shift" in retail towards ecommerce, and sees the cards as a way of driving customers back to Starbucks stores even as foot traffic at shopping centres – a traditional source of business from tired shoppers in search of a pick-me-up – has declined.

Customers can now earn points when buying Starbucks products outside its coffee shops, which the company hopes will encourage them to, in turn, visit the stores to redeem points.

Tea is another area Starbucks is eyeing for growth. Mr Schultz says he wants to "reinvent" the market for tea, which he described as "ripe for innovation". Since buying Teavana at the end of 2012, the company has opened about 40 stores in US malls and plans to open another 20 this year.

Recenty, Starbucks announced a collaboration with Oprah Winfrey, the US talk show host, to sell an Oprah-branded chai blend at Starbucks and Teavana stores in the US and Canada.

Since November 2008, Starbucks' market capitalisation has risen from $5bn to $57bn as its stock has climbed 948 per cent.

You'd be hard pressed to find any retailer today who has a business of this scale, in relation to the fact that our average ticket value is $5.

Starbucks: Grande standing

US coffee chain needs to keep the quality of its growth high

It's hard to think of a number much nicer or rounder: $100bn. That's the market capitalisation that Howard Schultz, Starbucks' boss, wants for his company. It is now a dreary and asymmetrical $57bn. Should it be so hard to get there? Starbucks has doubled its market cap in three years. And Mr Schultz doesn't need to rush. Having, apparently, taken forecasting lessons with an economist, he has set a target with no date attached.

The increase in Starbucks' market price has, unusually, not come from a ballooning valuation. While its price to earnings ratio is high at 27 it was already high, at 24, three years ago. It's the earnings: in the fiscal year ending in October 2010, they were $1.23 a share. This October, they should be double that.

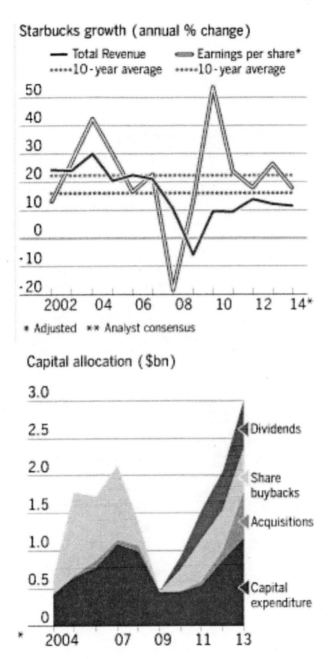

Starbucks growth (annual % change)

— Total Revenue ••••• Earnings per share*
•••••10-year average •••••10-year average

* Adjusted ** Analyst consensus

Capital allocation ($bn)

Growth at Starbucks

Capital allocation

How did it happen? Two drivers.

First, productivity of the US company-owned (as opposed to franchisee) stores. Even as the number of US stores has risen, revenue per store has grown at 6 per cent a year over three years; operating expenses per store have grown less than half as fast. Second, revenue from outside the shops – in grocery stores, restaurants and so on – has quadrupled, and now makes up 12 per cent of sales.

The strategy for sustaining growth has four pillars: more sales outside of the shops; in US stores, sell more stuff that isn't coffee (food, tea, booze); grow stores outside the US, especially in China; and do all the loyalty card/mobile payment stuff which all retailers are planning to do. All very sensible, but execution is all, especially in food and abroad, where Starbucks has consistently fumbled in the past.

While management grinds it out, watch whether growth continues to come largely from productivity at the store level, rather than only from growth in the store count or, worse, from acquisitions. And watch how Starbucks invests. A company that has lots of room to grow puts its cash flow to work internally, rather than by growing dividends or buying back shares. Big targets are fine. Quality is what gets you there.

IS THE U.S. UNEMPLOYMENT RATE SIGNALING A RECESSION:

A reliable source for recession forecasting is the unemployment rate, which can provide signals for the beginnings and ends of recessions. The unemployment rate model updated with the January figure of 6.7%, does not signal a recession now.

The model relies on four indicators to signal recessions:

A short 12-period and a long 60-period exponential moving average (EMA) of the unemployment rate (UER),

The 8-month smoothed annualized growth rate of the UER (UERg).

The 19-week rate of change of the UER.

Referring to the chart below, and looking at the end portion of it, one can see that none of the conditions for a recession start are currently present.

The UER is not forming a trough and its short EMA is well below its long EMA - the blue and red graphs, respectively, the spread being -0.50%.

UERg is currently at a low level, minus 14.6% – the green graph.

Also the 19-week rate of change of the UER is now at about minus 8.0%, far below the critical level of plus 8% - the black graph.

For a recession signal, the short EMA of the UER would have to form a trough and then cross its long EMA to the upside. Alternatively, the UERg graph would have to turn upwards and rise above zero, or the 19-week rate of change of the UER would have to be above 8%. Currently the trajectories of the unemployment rate's short- and long EMA are still downwards - none having a positive slope, UERg is far below zero, and the 19-week rate of change of the UER is also way below the critical level.

Based on the historic patterns of the unemployment rate indicators prior to recessions one can reasonably conclude that the U.S. economy is not likely to go into recession anytime soon.

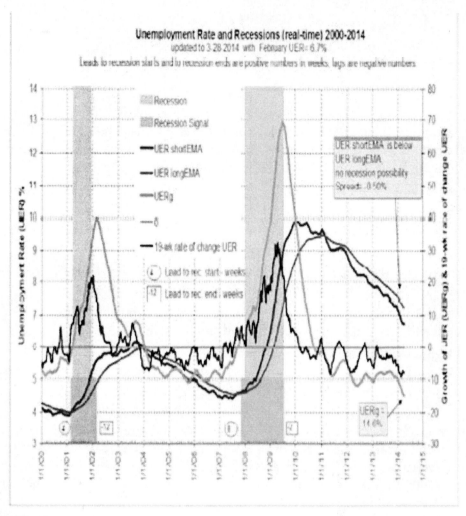

Appendix A

The model signals the start of a recession when any one of the following three conditions occurs:

- The short exponential moving average (EMA) of the unemployment rate (UER) rises and crosses the long EMA to the upside, and the difference between the two EMAs is at least 0.07.

- The unemployment rate growth rate (UERg) rises above zero, while the long EMA of the unemployment rate has a positive slope, and the difference between the long EMA at that time and the long EMA 10 weeks before is greater than 0.025.

- The 19-week rate of change of the UER is greater than 8.0%, while simultaneously the long EMA of the UER has a positive slope and the difference between the long EMA at the time and the long EMA 10 weeks earlier is greater than 0.015.

IS LOW GROWTH – THE NEW ECONOMIC REALITY

Until recently, the US was always the world's "consumer of last resort". Since the collapse of the Bretton Woods exchange rate system in the early-1970s and the subsequent huge increase in cross-border capital flows, the US easily absorbed more and more of the world's surplus savings. This was particularly so in recoveries after US recessions.

The US current account moved into modest deficit in the late-1970s and into much larger deficit in the 1980s. Thereafter, the deficits got even bigger, reaching a peak of almost 6 per cent of US gross domestic product before the onset of the global financial crisis.

The latest US recovery is, thus, unique. This time, the current account deficit has continued to shrink. Lots of explanations are offered, most obviously the decline in America's dependency on imported fossil fuels thanks to the shale energy revolution.

Yet, if that were true, Saudi Arabia and other oil producers should be running much smaller current account surpluses; mostly, they are not.

A more plausible explanation lies instead with the nature of the US's own economic recovery. It has been decidedly anaemic. In a dismal shift from the US experience in earlier economic cycles, domestic demand has risen at an average annual rate since the 2007 peak of only 0.6 per cent. That compares with average annual gains of more than 3 per cent during equivalent time periods from the 1970s onwards. The gains from the 2009 trough have been similarly insipid.

Domestic demand weakness reflects a whole host of factors: last year's sequestration courtesy of Washington; supply-side disappointment associated with abnormally low productivity growth; corporate conservatism; incredibly weak growth of real personal disposable income; and monetary stimulus that may have boosted the coffers of the low-spending wealthy but was not so helpful for the remaining 99 per cent of the income distribution.

Whatever the causes, however, it is clear that the US is not performing its traditional role as consumer of last resort. This has profound global implications. If the US current account deficit is not widening out in the usual way, it must follow that other countries are experiencing either smaller surpluses or bigger deficits. Put another way, the excess savings that used to flow into the US have gone elsewhere.

At first sight this might seem a good thing. After all, the widening of the US current account deficit in the years running up to the financial crisis was ultimately a reflection of excess inflows that drove down bond yields, encouraged a huge credit expansion, contributed to an unsustainable housing boom and, eventually, a partial meltdown of the global financial system. If excess savings are now going elsewhere, perhaps we should be cheering.

That assumes, however, that returns elsewhere are halfway decent. The evidence increasingly suggests they have not been. One offset to America's smaller current account deficit has been a much smaller Chinese current account surplus reflecting Beijing's attempt to boost domestic investment in response to flagging exports. Yet recent developments suggest that the marginal return on Chinese investment has plunged.

Another offset has been the rapid widening of current account deficits in parts of the emerging world; again, there is scant evidence to suggest that the associated capital inflows did anything other than create an unsustainable credit boom.

Now the UK finds itself in a similar position. Its current account deficit rose to more than 5 per cent of GDP in the third quarter of 2013 in only the first year of a recovery that is too heavily skewed towards housing and leverage.

Excess savings went elsewhere because the US no longer seemed to offer decent returns, a view reinforced by a Federal Reserve determined to keep monetary conditions as loose as possible.

Those savings, in turn, pushed returns lower elsewhere leading in some cases to economic disappointment and financial upheaval.

We have a global savings glut but, unlike the early years of the century, those savings have no place to go. Unless the US is able to reprise its role as consumer of last resort or other nations are able to pick up the baton, we may now be facing a world of persistently low growth and much lower returns – which, given weak productivity gains, may, unfortunately, be our new economic reality. That combination, in turn, might explain why, despite the best efforts of central banks, inflation in the developed world is mostly too low, not too high.

WILL RELEASING OIL FROM U.S. STRATEGIC RESERVES HURT RUSSIA?

World oil price could drop by $10-$12 per barrel

Russia's seizure of Crimea has prompted political leaders in Europe and North America to seek meaningful measures to convince Russia to pull back its troops.

In particular, they seek measures that would affect Russia immediately, putting internal pressure on the country's leaders to stop their aggression while leaving the rest of the world unharmed. Some propose accelerating natural gas exports from the US to Europe. However, this is no better than computer "vapourware" because the gas would not arrive for years.

A viable alternative to gas exports is releasing oil from the US Strategic Petroleum Reserve (SPR). These stocks are available today and could have a speedy impact on Russia. Given that the country depends on oil and natural gas exports for its survival, such an action would have a quick and significant effect if the release depresses oil prices.

The SPR now holds 694m barrels of crude. The federal government acquired the oil between 1977 and 2009 as a safeguard against severe disruptions of world oil markets. The original intention was to create a billion barrel reserve, to offset any prolonged interruption of US oil imports during some future conflict.

The US no longer needs such a large strategic reserve. The SPR cannot be entirely eliminated due to the International Energy Program commitment to hold reserves equal to 90 days of imports, but the US could easily sell 500,000 to 750,000 barrels per day for up to two years without breaching this obligation.

Kremlin pain

By my calculation, if the US did this and all else remained equal, the world oil price would drop by $10-$12 per barrel.

Although that would be only about a 10 per cent reduction in price, it would still inflict substantial pain on the Kremlin. A crude oil price decline of $10 per barrel would cut Russian export income by around $40bn, which amounts to roughly 10 per cent of the 2012 fuel export income Russia reported to the World Trade Organisation. Russia's GDP could fall as much as 4 per cent.

An SPR oil release could also exacerbate the rouble's decline and further increase the country's internal economic difficulties.

In addition, lower oil prices would offer significant benefits to European consumers who depend on natural gas from Russia, including those in Ukraine. That is because Russia links – or tries to link – the price of natural gas it exports to Europe to crude oil prices.

Thus, by liquidating the surplus SPR oil, the US would give Europe lower natural gas prices. In the US, lower crude oil prices would cut gasoline prices as much as 25 cents per gallon. And the profit generated from any sales of SPR oil – which costs, on average, $28 per barrel – could go to deficit reduction.

There are two big "ifs" to this scenario, however. The first is that Congress would probably have to authorise any SPR oil sales, especially if the oil was to be sold to foreign buyers. Approval could take weeks or months. However, Congress could surprise, especially if the step were seen as a way to impose sanctions on Russia.

Saudi reaction

The second "if" concerns the reaction of Saudi Arabia. The world's largest oil exporter would also see a reduction in income. It is likely, though, that the Saudis would acquiesce because they are locked in a struggle with Russia over Syria and Iran.

The Saudi Arabian leaders would probably welcome crude oil sales from the reserve as a clear effort to weaken Russia.

Saudi Arabia's economy, unlike Russia's, can tolerate lower oil prices because budgets are premised on lower oil prices, and because the country has accumulated large financial reserves that can be drawn when prices fall. Most likely the Saudis would say and do nothing as long as the US limited its price reduction goal to, say, 10 per cent rather than 50 per cent.

No doubt oil traders and producers in the US would agree. Some have argued that relaxing the US ban on crude exports would be preferable to an SPR release. However, increasing supply is the only way to have a real price impact on global markets.

Easing the export prohibition would not accomplish this but permitting the exports of oil now held in the SPR would.

Moreover, US strategic stocks are no longer strategic but rather surplus government property. Sooner or later the oil will re-enter the market, just as inventories of other commodities accumulated for crises have been sold when no longer needed.

In this case, strategic stocks may indeed serve a strategic purpose if the price declines curb Russia's belligerence.

HAS COPPER REALLY DECOUPLED?

I don't think so. What we are seeing is only a lagged effect of drop in copper markets reflecting in other financial markets of the world.

Copper decoupling

Decoupling effect as developed world markets ignore price fall

Decoupling. It is a simple word, into which much hope and fear has been distilled.

Recently, we have witnessed the dramatic decoupling of copper. Long a bellwether for the global economy, it dropped almost 10 per cent in just five trading days. It is now down about 14 per cent for the year, and 35 per cent from its all-time peak set in 2011.

Such things happen. Commodity markets are volatile, moving on sudden fluctuations in supply or demand. But there were no obvious disruptions to either supply or demand last week. Meanwhile, other base metals fared poorly, but nowhere near as badly as copper.

Chinese lenders, especially in the nonbank or "shadow" sector, often allow copper to be pledged as collateral. With expectations that the government is going to allow more bond defaults—the first happened last week—lenders are beginning to worry that copper's value will decline.

As financial conditions tighten, copper is liquidated when loans are either defaulted on or can't be rolled over, which can lead to worse financial conditions as companies' collateral loses value. This was the exact same effect that hit the entire U.S. household sector in 2008 when house prices fell, although it's important to note that a crisis that severe in China stemming from falling copper prices is hypothetically possible but not likely in our view."

The banking problems have more to do with copper's decline than fears over economic troubles.

It is however also possible that Dr.Copper is not sending a signal to the world of impending economic weakness but is instead sending a signal to the world that the banking system in China has very real problems....

I suspect that some banks have already called in their loans made in this manner, and that what we've seen in the past week is the first layer of that loan unwinding; however, there is no way to quantify that notion and we offer it up as it stands, without hard data. However, our fear is that the last banks in ... the smaller banks; the regional banks; the banks that are always last to the feeding trough ... are still holding copper collateralized loans that have gone from badly performing to horrid to now deeply under water in the matter of days. Panic liquidation has set in; the margin clerks are in charge and it is then that prices make their lows, but there is no way to tell when or where and at what prices those loans shall be finally liquidated.

Big picture, this market remains in trouble.

Technical analysts note a multiyear chart divergence between copper and the S&P 500 stock market index, which tend to run in tandem. Copper has the economic direction correct and stock market investors, rendered complacent by the Federal Reserve's $4 trillion in liquidity injections, could pay the price.

Irrespective of what copper's current flirtation with multiyear lows reflects, it is the long-term monthly chart of copper and the S&P that suggests some trouble—some very bearish trouble—may be ahead for both copper and the S&P. In turn, it seems likely that copper will turn out to be 'right' about whether 2013 was a false initial reaction in the S&P and one that many investors may come to wish they had ignored.

Demand for copper comes preeminently from China, which needs the metal as part of its boom in infrastructure building. So it is not unduly surprising that the Chinese stock market fell, along with stocks in several countries that have grown far wealthier supplying China with copper, such as Chile and Peru.

What is more surprising is the effect on stock markets in the developed world. There has barely been one. The MSCI World index, the most widely followed index of developed world equities, hit an all-time high on March 7, surpassing a high it set in late 2007 before the credit crisis, even as the copper sell-off was under way.

This is quite a decoupling. Commodity prices need not necessarily have much effect on share prices. They are revenue for some companies, but expenses for others. In the very long term, share prices do better in periods when commodity prices are trending downwards.

But in recent history, equity investors have bet the house on the notion that metals in general and copper in particular are a guide for equity prices. For a prolonged period from 2005 to 2011, the MSCI World moved almost perfectly in sync with the Dow Jones-UBS industrial metals index. This pattern broke down about two years ago, and the disjunction has become most dramatic recently.

Driving the period of extreme correlation was a thesis known as "decoupling". Emerging markets, led by China, had reached a stage in their growth where they could continue growing irrespective of any recession in the west. China would expand its middle class, buying raw materials from many other emerging markets to do so, and a recession in the west would not hurt.

But this version of "decoupling" was accompanied by an extreme coupling in markets. US and European companies would also be helped by booming copper prices and the growth in emerging markets. So as developed markets grew in the mid-2000s, copper, and emerging market stocks, grew even more.

The fallacy on which all this rested was revealed once the crisis hit. Emerging equities, along with commodities and currencies, all fell even more than the developed world, as investors rushed to liquidate holdings wherever they could. Copper dropped 69 per cent in barely six months. Then the rebound after the crisis was led by metals prices (copper gained 270 per cent in little over two years), and by Chinese stocks, as China embarked on a stimulus programme. The belief was that China had saved the world by spending so much.

Copper's steep fall might be a blunt instrument to help the Chinese authorities in their attempt to restore some balance to their economy

But did they take it too far? Total Chinese credit outstanding (including government debt) is now at about 230 per cent of GDP. It was only 80 per cent of GDP in 2002.

Many now fret about obvious signs of overcapacity – such as the copper sitting idle in Chinese warehouses – and about the risk of a Chinese credit crisis.

Is this China's Lehman moment? In a repeat of the dilemma that hit US authorities in 2008, China is trying to manage a series of defaults. It wants to inflict enough pain on banks to show that they must behave more prudently in future – but not so much that they lead to a crash.

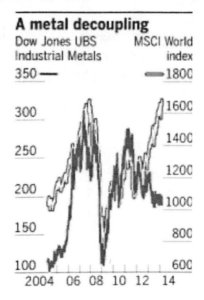

A metal decoupling

Dow Jones UBS Industrial Metals / MSCI World index

2004 06 08 10 12 14

Source: Thomson Reuters Datastream

Copper is used as collateral in many Chinese financial transactions. As a debt goes bad, creditors take the collateral, and sell it for what they can get, which means that its price falls. So the credit boom in China that pushed copper up in the first place is now pushing it down.

There is no need for this episode to end in the same way as the last Great Decoupling. Many emerging markets are involved in what could be a healthy rebalancing. And copper's steep fall might be a blunt instrument to help the Chinese authorities in their attempt to restore some balance to their economy.

London Metal Exchange copper for three-month delivery was $7,000 a tonne on March 6. By March 12, it was barely $6,500. It is ironic. This amounts, in part, to blowback from copper's convenient properties as a financing medium. That is how the metal has been used in China after normal credit became expensive for corporate borrowers.

Shanghai copper futures fell even harder than LME prices this week. In ports such as Shanghai's Yangshan, 700,000-750,000 tonnes of copper lie in duty-free bonded warehouses – a year's production at Antofagasta, a Chilean miner that is among the world's top producers. Most of this is probably pledged for loans, often in US dollars, and the funds may be lent on for yield elsewhere. So the trade is sensitive to a falling renminbi and credit generally – as it transpires Chinese companies can default, after all.

The financing trade may get more painful for prices, should this inventory be dumped in a market trying to absorb new low-cost production anyway. That makes guessing earnings for Antofagasta this year a crapshoot, for example, given its exposure to prices. But copper oversupply can be worked through with time, given that it is relatively easy to move.

So, what is the reality?

Oil can blow up, or leak. Iron ore is bulky. So much so that it endangers cargo ships if it gets too wet. Which is why puny humans might prefer to use copper when seeking collateral to borrow money against.

Metallurgically, copper is safe. Easy to store (a shed will do), the metal is usefully liquid in another sense. Once refined, one lot of it is much the same as another. Iron ore varies by quality (and moisture).

With copper flashing red, investors have reasons to worry, particularly as it heightens the prospect that China will fail to meet its economic growth target of 7.5 per cent, its lowest such projection since 1990.

For US equity investors sitting on large gains from a five-year bull market, the prospect of Chinese financial flu and weaker global growth should merit an appraisal of their portfolios.

Copper imports are used as loan collaterals, so when credit markets are tightening up, things could be very choppy; however supply tightness continues, so even if the electricity generation target falters (which is slated with a yoy increase of 14%), prices eventually would hold.

Let us try to evalutate what is the reality?

Copper financing in China is big.

How big? Try a tenth of all short-term FX loans — and 750,000 or so tonnes of metal in Shanghai bonded warehouses alone — big.

But then, they think it will mostly stay profitable...

This is despite the trade's apparent exposure to a fall in the renminbi against the dollar, and how copper futures are pricing in an unwind of this inventory at some point.

While some metals merchants could be subject to mark to market margin calls due to RMB depreciation, they might opt to do more transit trades to meet cash requirements rather than selling copper outright, although this may only last for a short period of time.

We believe that the recent sell-off is a combination of speculators trying to anticipate the unwinding of financing deals and a lack of buying in China due to sluggish real demand.

With the SHFE/LME arb moving deeper into negative territory (Figure 7) and higher costs associated with RMB, such trades could become less attractive. However, as long as the returns on the unsecured loan in CNY are sufficiently high, such trades could remain profitable.

Copper is hedged in financing deals and is 100% cash backed. (It is rare to get financing deals with copper prices un-hedged these days.) **As a result, falling copper prices do not trigger financing deal unwind...**

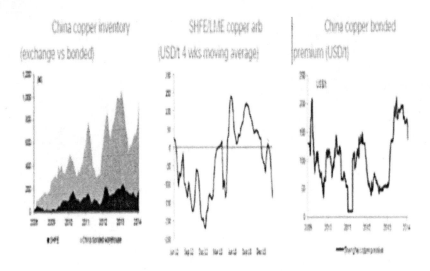

Yet more copper might leave China in the coming months, as metal leaves bonded warehouses and heads back into the LME system.

This is where we might make the (perhaps obvious) point that copper is as relatively easy to move around as it is to store, at least when it comes to finding a market-clearing price. This is handy when it looks like the world outside China has plenty of refined copper supply to get through anyway.

There is one commodity that isn't so fungible or well-behaved on boats, though:

Although a less attractive financing vehicle, the use of iron ore in import financing · has gathered pace since the end of last year. This has been a function of elevated liquidity pressure at steel mills. In contrast to copper, I believe iron ore financing is more vulnerable to unwind risks as iron ore positions are typically un-hedged thus subject to high volatility. **Furthermore, as a low value product with greater difficulty for storage, iron ore financing is not sustainable,**

Iron ore, which is harder to use as collateral, harder to move and harder to store – and for which Chinese demand is falling.

No wonder big iron ore-heavy miners like BHP and Rio seem keen to play down this financing trade.

It is not long since investors made a huge bet that emerging markets could pull the rest of the world through. It failed. The current bet, almost as emphatic, is that China and the complex of countries that rely on it can slow down without denting the prospects for corporate and economic growth elsewhere.

This second bet sounds barely any more promising than the first.

THE ROAD AHEAD FOR MISS JANET YELLEN

The Federal Reserve has changed its economic goalposts even as it continues winding down its stimulus program. The following is the road ahead as laid down by Miss Janet Yellen at her first press conference:

1) Tapering will continue: The central bank has been buying trillions in bonds since late 2008 in an effort to lower long-term interest rates. The goal: Stimulate the economy by making it cheaper to take out loans.

But the Fed has determined it's time to start winding down that stimulus program. Since December, the central bank has been slowly reducing its bond purchases at each meeting, in a process Wall Street has dubbed "tapering." The Fed was previously buying $85 billion in bonds each month, then reduced the amount to $75 billion in January, and then $65 billion in February. The same has been reduced to $ 55 billion beginning March of 2014.

2) The goalposts will change: The Fed has kept its key short-term interest rate near zero since 2008, also as a way to stimulate more spending.

Investors have become accustomed to low interest rates but are looking for signals about when the Fed might eventually raise rates as the economy strengthens.

So far, the Fed has said it wants to see the unemployment rate fall to around 6.5%, or inflation rise as high as 2.5%, before it will be ready to raise rates. But here's the problem: The unemployment rate, at 6.7% in February, is already nearing that point, and Yellen still thinks the economy is too weak.

She wants to abandon the numerical targets altogether and focus on qualitative information instead.

3) Weather put the Fed in wait-and-see mode: Severe winter storms throughout much of the country weighed on economic data over the last few months, making it hard to get a clean reading on the recovery. Retail sales, job growth, housing and manufacturing all seem to have been impacted, but it's unclear whether the slowdown was temporary.

The question is how much of this activity comes back in the spring, how much is simply lost, and how much the slowdown reflects other factors.

4) Yellen is still focused on jobs, jobs, jobs: Miss Yellen has emphasized that she remains deeply concerned about ongoing weakness in the labor market.

As of February, 3.8 million Americans were unemployed for at least six months, and 7.2 million workers were stuck in part-time jobs, even though they would prefer full-time hours. Yellen looks closely at both measures, and neither has improved much lately.

Meanwhile, inflation remains well under the Fed's goal for 2% over the long-run, so Yellen is unlikely to view rising prices as a major concern.

THE ALIBABA RIPPLE EFFECT—WHO'S NEXT?

With Alibaba's IPO on the near horizon, there is already a class of public Internet Asian stocks whose products have the flavor to me of Whatsapp prior to the Facebook acquisition — products that are massive in usage but somewhat off the radar of many US investors.

On the conference call announcing the Whatsapp acquisition, Mark Zuckerberg explained, "[Whatsapp] doesn't get as much attention in the U.S. as it deserves, because its community started off growing in Europe, India and Latin America. But WhatsApp is a very important and valuable worldwide communication network."

I call this the Whatsapp Scenario.

While many investors know these names and products backwards and forwards, many smart investors have not yet dug into the leading social media stocks and platforms in Asia. Here's a basic primer to a few:

The one that I find most exciting from a product standpoint is Tencent's (700 HK) **Wechat**. A Chinese hybrid of both Twitter and Whatsapp, Wechat allows for personal messaging, the following of news and brand accounts, and several other fun communications features. The "drift bottle," is my personal favorite — you can throw messages in bottles into a virtual sea that other users can pick up.

The Wechat app already has 300 million users and is available in English for just about every platform. If you're into tech and media investing and haven't played with Wechat, give it a quick download.

If Wechat were to roll out a game (think Candy Crush) on it's platform, onboarded U.S. celebrities and media properties, or make some other tweak, there's no reason to think it couldn't go viral in the US and hit investors' radars. I'm simply saying it's a possibility.

On 2014 Bloomberg consensus estimates, Tencent trades at roughly 10.4 times enterprise value-to-sales compared to Twitter at 22.82 and Facebook at 14.45.

Similarly, **Line** (which is very similar to Whatsapp but has a heavy emphasis on "stickers" users can send) is owned by Korean Internet search firm Naver. Line has 370 million users and is No. 1 in Japan, Thailand, and Taiwan. It may be spun out with an IPO this year at a value of $10 billion.

Another social app to watch, that is similarly sitting inside a larger stock is **Weibo**, which is owned by China's Sina Corp. Weibo is similar to Twitter but only has around 129 million monthly users. Alibaba owns an interest in Weibo, and Sina plans to take it public in the U.S. in the second quarter. Sina's 2014 enterprise value-to-sales multiple is just 4.49.

The final company worth mentioning is Youku Tudou, the "Youtube of China." The company just put up a 42-percent jump in revenue from a year earlier; 10 percent of revenue comes from mobile. It's one of the top five mobile apps in China, with the other four being messaging and web-browser apps. On the earnings calls, management lists Chevrolet, Lenovo, Nestle, DHL, and Ford as advertisers.

WHY AGRICULTURAL COMMODITIES ARE ON THE UPSWING AGAIN IN 2014?

Brazil's worst drought in decades is decimating crops but breathing new life into battered commodity markets.

It hardly has rained in some of the South American country's top farming regions since the start of the year, a period when precipitation is usually the heaviest. Traders, analysts and government forecasters who were calling for record harvests in coffee, sugar and soybeans as recently as December are cutting production estimates, triggering a spike in futures prices that may translate into higher costs for consumers later in the year.

Futures prices for the arabica coffee variety are up 67% since the start of the year. Raw-sugar prices have risen 8%. Soybeans, which have been affected by drought in some areas and too much rain in others, also are up 8%.

The withered coffee trees and parched sugar-cane fields stand in contrast to the bumper crops that have weighed on commodities in recent years. Soaring prices in markets in which Brazil is a key supplier show how quickly global commodity markets can swing from concerns about oversupply to fears of a shortage. The situation in Brazil also could presage a period of price volatility following an era of relatively low and stable prices on many raw materials that benefited companies and individual consumers, analysts say.

Brazil is the world's biggest grower and exporter of coffee and sugar. For soybeans, it was expected this year to surpass the U.S. as the top producer for the first time, though that is now unlikely because of the weather, analysts say.

So far this year, the weather in Brazil has been the largest surprise for commodity markets across the world.

When you have a major external effect, especially a drought that you can't quantify, that throws the entire supply-and-demand equation" out of whack.

The big gains in coffee, sugar and soybeans have helped propel the S&P GSCI commodity index 3.8% this year. The S&P 500 stock index is up 1.4%.

The weather is creating a lot of interest in some of these markets, and it's creating a lot of opportunities for investors.

Supply concerns in commodity markets haven't been isolated to Brazil's agricultural sector. U.S. supplies of natural gas, which is used to heat and generate electricity, have been stretched by a harsh winter and gas prices are up 10% this year.

Investors pulled $24 million from agricultural-commodity funds in February, though that was down from an average monthly outflow of $97 million last year, according to EPFR Global.

Even after this year's gains, prices for most commodities are well off the peaks hit in recent years. Sugar prices were twice as high three years ago, while soybean prices would need to rise another 25% to match their summer 2012 levels. Growers outside Brazil are predicting healthy crops in both markets, which could offset reduced production from the drought.

Some analysts say prices have risen too much and that it is too soon to know the drought's effect on Brazil's crops.

Still, Brazil's bad weather has put an end to forecasts of several more years of record output and global surpluses in the coffee and sugar markets. Brazil is the source of about one-third of the world's annual coffee crop, more than one-fifth of the sugar output, and about one-third of soybean output.

Now, some analysts are lowering their expectations. Copersucar SA, Brazil's biggest sugar exporter, said last month that Brazil's main sugar-cane-growing region will produce 32 million metric tons of the sweetener, 8.6% less than it previously expected.

Also in February, agricultural consulting firm Safras & Mercado cut its estimate of Brazil's soybean production to 86.1 million metric tons, down 6.2% from a month earlier.

Some experts say the drought in Brazil is likely to have ripple effects beyond the commodity markets directly affected. Ethanol refiners, which turn sugar cane into fuel, are predicting higher prices later this year, while chicken farmers say they will need to pass along rising grain costs to consumers.

The drought isn't a direct threat to chickens. The main issue for us is the cost of feed. Higher costs means higher prices.

Rising cost of breakfast leaves bitter taste

Your breakfast platter looks set to become more expensive. Drought, disease and rising demand have led to prices of eight key breakfast commodities rising on average almost 25 % this year, fuelling consumer fears of food inflation.

Everything we have for breakfast is up--the increases of coffee, orange juice, wheat, sugar, milk, butter, cocoa and pork. This has all happened unexpectedly but shows how quickly things can change.

Coffee has soared more than 70 per cent because of unseasonably dry weather in Brazil, while US pigs have been hit by a virus epidemic, leading to a more than 40 per cent rally in Chicago pork prices.

Wheat prices have been hit by political uncertainties. After edging higher because of the extreme cold winter in the US, they have been pushed further by the crisis in Ukraine, a key grain producer.

Dairy prices have been bolstered by high demand in emerging markets such as China and Russia where rising incomes have driven increased consumption of milk, butter and milk powder for infants.

Weather and political risk has entered the markets, while demand has grown.

Compared with the lacklustre performance of industrial commodities such as oil and copper since January, the strength in food commodities has attracted hedge funds and other investors, fuelling the price increases.

Financial speculators have started to pile into agricultural commodities, pushing net "long" or bullish positions to the highest level in four-and-a-half years.

Blistering food rally plays havoc with breakfast

A visit to a New York diner for an all-American breakfast, or to one of London's "greasy spoons" for a full English, will soon leave you short of change.

Unusual weather patterns, the crisis in Ukraine and disease are among the reasons why prices for commodities ranging from coffee to pork and wheat have soared. And there is a little sign of let-up.

There are further risks for breakfast commodities over the next few months against the backdrop of concerns that the El Niño weather phenomenon will prompt extreme weather in many parts of the world.

El Niño is the warming of Pacific sea surface temperatures that occurs naturally every few years. Depending on its strength it can trigger droughts in some parts of the world and heavy rains in others.

The price of toast could rise further if drought hits India, south-east Asia and Australia, driving up wheat prices. Hot chocolate drinkers may face higher prices as El Niño tends to mean hotter, drier weather in west Africa, the key region for cocoa.

There is a greater threat for producers of 'breakfast commodities' over the next few months.

Even smoked salmon lovers should fret about El Niño. The warming of sea temperatures around South America could affect anchovy harvests, adding pressure to the already high fishmeal prices, used to feed farmed salmon.

ON HOW CLIMATE CHANGE AFFECTS GUACAMOLE

Restaurant-chain Chipotle (CMG) issued an ominous warning about the effects of climate change on some of its menu items, including – brace yourselves – guacamole and salsa. In a regulatory filing with the Securities and Exchange Commission, Chipotle warned that increasing weather volatility, including global climate change could have a significant impact on the price or availability of some of its regular ingredients. "In the event of cost increases with respect to one or more of our raw ingredients, we may choose to temporarily suspend serving menu items, such as guacamole or one or more of our salsas, rather than paying the increased cost for the ingredients," the company stated in its most recent 10-k filing.

It would be an interesting corporate decision if Chipotle chooses to remove salsa or guacamole, rather than give customers the choice to pay a little more for those items. "Do you want to pay $2 extra for guacamole or $0.50 for salsa which you used to get for free?"

Part of Chipotle's appeal is that the company tries to buy from local farmers and also from organic farmers more than most other food chains. But will that make up for a dry burrito? I wonder how those consumers are going to feel if they're not going to have the choice to have guacamole or salsa with their Chipotle.

-----If you have anything to do with Mexican food, you need a salsa.

------Or if you have anything to do with Mexican entertainment, you need to have something to do with the salsa dance.

DOES FALL IN RENMINBI INDICATE
CHANGE IN CHINA POLICY?

There has been a significant weakening in China's exchange rate in recent days. Although the spot rate against the dollar has moved by only about 1.3 per cent, this is actually a large move by the standards of this managed exchange rate. Furthermore, the move is in the opposite direction to the strengthening trend seen in the exchange rate over the past three years.

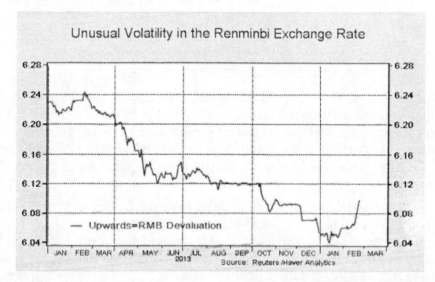

This has triggered some pain among investors holding long renminbi "carry" trades, along with much debate in the foreign exchange market about what the Chinese authorities are planning to do next. Since China does not explain its internal or external monetary policy in a transparent manner that is intelligible to outsiders, there is much scope for misunderstanding its true intentions. The key question is whether the Chinese authorities are changing their commitment to a strong exchange rate and, if so, why?

The rise in China's real exchange rate, amounting to more than 40 per cent since 2005, has been one of the forces which has helped the global economy to rebalance in recent years, encouraging a narrowing in the US trade deficit against China, and also allowing other emerging economies to absorb the effects of the devaluation in the Japanese yen without feeling too much pain.

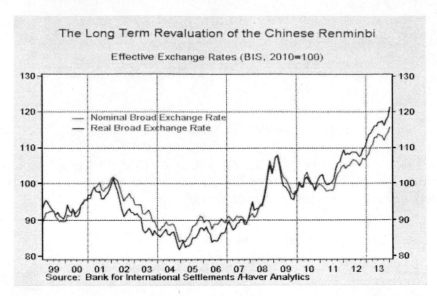

It has also helped China to hold down inflation, and boost consumption, which is a key requirement in its own internal rebalancing. And it has reduced the danger of a severe policy confrontation between China and the US, with the latter having largely dropped its complaints about "manipulation" of China's exchange rate. Overall, it is one of the things that has clearly gone right in the global economy in recent times.

The benign interpretation of the sudden reversal in the spot rate since mid-January is that it is all part of China's plan to introduce greater market forces into its economic system in the years ahead. This would include more scope for the exchange rate to be determined by the market, to which end Beijing has said that it will increase the width of the daily fluctuation band from the present plus or minus 1 per cent to plus or minus 2 per cent as soon as possible.

Until the recent reversal, the spot rate had been hugging the bottom end (ie, the strong end) of the band, and some investors had become convinced that long renminbi represented a safe, low volume trade. Capital inflows therefore increased, forcing the People's Bank of China to intervene in the markets by $500bn in 2013 (an act of quantitative easing similar in scale to the US Federal Reserve's QE3 programme last year).

Increasing the width of the band could have caused more inflows and a more rapid strengthening in the real exchange rate. To avoid the perception that this is a one-way trade, the Chinese central bank may have decided to mount a sharp but temporary squeeze on the carry traders.

A slightly less benign interpretation is that the PBOC has decided to call a halt to the trend appreciation in the real exchange rate for the time being. This is what the bank did when it was using all available instruments to boost gross domestic product growth in 2008-10, the only prolonged period of stability in the nominal exchange rate since 2005. The reason that this interpretation seems possible is that there has been a clear shift in interest rate policy since start of this year, with interbank rates being guided much lower than in the second half of 2013.

If the authorities have decided to take their foot off the monetary brakes for the time being, because the deflating of the credit bubble is damaging GDP growth and financial stability, it would make sense to allow the exchange rate to fall, alongside domestic interest rates.

But this would suggest that the authorities have blinked in the face of the January bailout of a high-profile trust product marketed by ICBC. It would also indicate that the process of deleveraging in the shadow banking sector is not going according to plan. Concerns from the rating agencies that China is encouraging yet more moral hazard in the financial system, making the eventual exit from the bubble even more difficult, would then look valid.

A nightmare interpretation, which seems highly improbable, is that China has decided to drive its exchange rate considerably lower, in order deliberately to increase its share of global export markets.

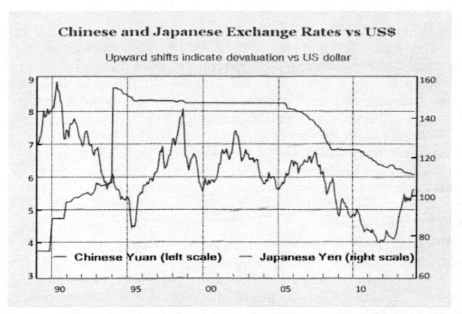

That was what happened when China devalued its official exchange rate in 1994, sending shockwaves through the emerging markets which (along with the decline in the yen) culminated in the Asian financial crisis of 1997.

In a hard landing scenario for the economy, China could become more attracted to a significant depreciation in its exchange rate, and that would clearly represent a profound shock to the rest of Asia and to the world. But the Chinese economy is not in a hard landing yet. GDP growth this year is officially expected to be about 7.5 per cent. Nor would China want to absorb the inflationary consequences of a major devaluation.

The nightmare scenario can therefore be safely ignored for now. But that still leaves a lot of questions to be answered. In my view, China has temporarily relaxed the monetary squeeze because of worries about financial stability, but has not reversed its medium-term exchange rate strategy yet.

GLOBAL STOCKS WILL REBOUND AFTER AUGUST 26, 2014–THE END IS NOT NIGH

Are investors too optimistic? Is this bull about to die in the throes of euphoria? Lately, it seems ever-more pundits say it is—there is too much cheer, and a big fall is ahead. With markets hitting all-time highs, extreme bearish views largely absent, optimism on the rise, and equity mutual funds finally seeing regularly positive net inflows, this theme isn't surprising. However, in my view, it doesn't pass the smell test.

First, I see precious little evidence investor sentiment has become euphoric. Sure, optimism is emerging after years of investors fearing a double-dip recession, a potential euro collapse, a US default not once but twice, a debt downgrade, the so called "fiscal cliff" and many others. But budding optimism isn't unbridled confidence and soaring expectations. Current sentiment doesn't appear consistent with the latter. If it were, investors would likely be bidding stocks sky-high without regard to earnings and revenue growth—not continually hand-wringing over whether sales will keep pace with earnings, as folks are today. Also, euphoria often brings widespread "it's different this time" claims, that some newly developed technology—railroads, radio or the Internet—has fundamentally changed the economic landscape to ensure perma-growth and end boom and bust. Today, we have the opposite, with most assuming we've reached the end of technology's power and failing to grasp the implications of developments like the shale boom and 3D-printing.

Additionally, even if sentiment were exceptionally strong, it still wouldn't necessarily mean the bull market is on the verge of ending. Absent an unexpected negative development ending a bull prematurely (like the advent of FASB 157—mark-to-market accounting—truncated the 2002-2007 bull before euphoria took hold), the recipe for a peak isn't just high expectations, but deteriorating fundamentals as well. A bull market peak is imminent not just when everyone is dancing, but when the music has already stopped—investors gradually notice and scurry for a safe haven from the impending downturn. This divergence between reality and expectations has characterized many more major market tops than not in modern history, and it's likely the next market peak will rhyme with previous ones, to borrow from a popular expression.

To demonstrate this point from recent history, let's go back to late 1999/early 2000, the final stages of the tech bubble. Many know investor sentiment rose to stratospheric heights during this period, but some may not know there were signs the music stopped before the ultimate market peak in 2000. First, the onslaught of tech IPOs, which mushroomed in the preceding years, had created a stock supply glut—an ominous sign, given supply and demand determine prices. But the market kept climbing anyway, thanks to outrageously high expectations for the future—demand later proven unwarranted. The yield curve had been flattening and finally inverted by 2000. Few noticed this classic sign of tough times in capital markets. Leading economic indicators, too, were in a little-noticed swoon. By December 31, 1999, Technology had swollen to comprise 29% of the S&P 500—the US's largest sector by 16 percentage points over Financials.[i] Yet many of the firms whose surging IPOs fueled the rise were burning cash. Many had no history or expectation for profits and a company history spanning only a few months or years—a shaky history of sales. Without solid cash flow—never mind profits—markets realized these firms would go under or have to raise more cash through secondary stock offerings, further diluting stock supply. The dot-com boom went bust. By the bottom in October 2002, Tech represented less than 13% of S&P 500 market capitalization. [ii]

Today's environment is virtually a mirror image—fundamentals are quite strong. Despite some popular social media IPOs over the last few years, total IPO activity has been quite modest, with early trades nowhere near the irrational frenzy for dot-com offerings. Most recent IPOs experienced low double-digit returns in their first few trading days—far lower than the triple-digit norms of the dot-com era. Offerings are also dwarfed by stock buybacks, cash acquisitions, and some private equity deals—overall stock supply is shrinking. Far from social media taking over Tech or the S&P 500's market cap, most social media firms aren't even included in this major US stock index. The yield curve is positively sloped and steepening as the Fed continues to reduce quantitative easing bond purchases.

The dollar's fate – tied to the yield curve?

A recent sharp flattening in the U.S. government bond yield curve could be a bearish sign for the dollar.

Yields on five-year Treasurys have shot up since last week's Federal Reserve meeting raised the prospect of interest rates rising sooner rather than later, narrowing the gap with 30-year bond yields to their tightest spread since 2009.

Although a rise in yields at the short-end of the yield curve usually boosts the appeal of the dollar, a fall in yields at the long-end reflects concerns about the economic outlook and this is weighing on the currency.

The dollar has touched 101.71 yen and is down more than three percent since the start of the year.

Part of the currency pair's weakness can be attributed to one of biggest stories in the financial market this week which is that the U.S. yield curve is flattening at an alarmingly rapid pace.

Typically yield curves flatten when inflation expectations are falling or investors are worried about slower growth but in this case, short-term rates are rising even as long-term rates are falling.

Recently, some of the flattening in the yield curve was unwound, with five-year yields falling after a strong auction of five-year Treasury notes.

The charts show a clear correlation between dollar/yen and the yield curve, suggesting the dollar could head lower against the yen if the yield curve flattens some more.

Recent comments by new Fed chief Janet Yellen suggesting interest rates could start to rise six months after the scaling back of monetary stimulus ends took markets by surprise, sparking a sharp rise in short-dated Treasury yields. U.S. dollar will need better-than-expected economic data to sustain its rally.

The attraction with [long-dated] U.S. Treasuries also has to do with the risk-on, risk-off dynamic and when you have geopolitical tensions in Eastern Europe or concerns about growth because we've had disappointing data in China.

It is the way in which the U.S. yield curve has flattened that was impacting dollar/yen.

The underlying message in the data is that the economy is still not gaining momentum, so it may be a case that this is reflected at the long-end of the curve.

Recent data shows orders for U.S. durable goods rose 2.2 percent from a month earlier after two straight months of falls. But the data also showed a surprise drop in core capital goods, a gauge of planned spending on capital goods.

For the uninitiated, let us understand what a yield curve is:

The shape of the yield curve and what does it signify

Follow the Curve

When it comes to predicting recessions or major downturns in the stock market, the yield curve is an important one to watch. It is so good in its predictive analysis that NBER declared it as having predicted every recession in the US since 1970. That sounds like an indicator one should probably reference every once in a while, especially when we start hearing the word "bubble" being tossed around.

So what is it exactly? The yield curve shows the amount of interest charged (or yield earned) as you move from short to long-term debt. The most followed yield curve is for US Treasuries, showing 3-month T-Bill yields all the way up to 30-year T-Notes.

So just how does the yield curve predict recessions? When it inverts. A normal yield curve exists when short-term interest rates are low and long-term interest rates are high due to a premium for holding long-term bonds. This is called a positive sloping curve. In a normal economic environment where the economy is growing and there are low inflation expectations, banks make money by lending money long-term at higher rates while paying depositors low rates tied to short-maturities. When interest rates invert, banks are paying higher rates of interest on deposits than they are making in loans. This squashes the credit machine, banks pull back on lending, the stock market heads lower, and the economy contracts.

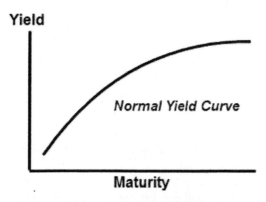

Here are two examples of the yield curve inverting at or prior to the 2000 and 2007 crashes:

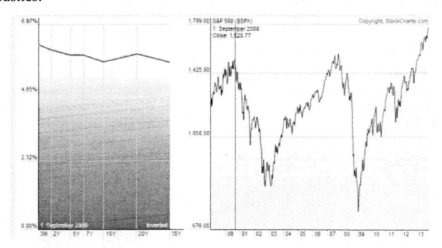

Source: StockCharts.com

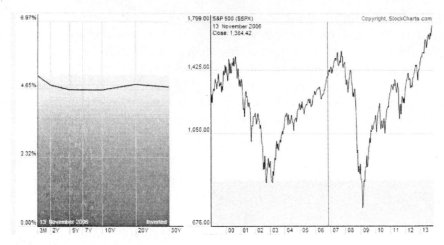

Source: StockCharts.com

Before there's a credit collapse, usually there's a credit bubble. This is caused by hugely profitable loans when the interest rate spread is wide between short and long-term maturities. Interest rate spreads are wide when we have a steeply sloping yield curve. Credit standards are lowered because the banks get overzealous at high levels of profit. But, with loans out to unworthy borrowers, who's left to borrow? The Federal Reserve Bank sees the credit bubble and begins raising rates it charges banks on short-term loans – usually until something breaks.

Lending Standards

The chart below shows lending standards coupled with the yield spread between 10-year and 2-year notes. As you can see, it's when the yield spread is low that banks begin to tighten lending standards, which typically leads to a recession down the road. And yield spreads are low when? When the yield curve is flat or inverted.

Source: Bloomberg

Keep in mind, the stock market's downtrend or uptrend can last a while despite the yield curve changing. That's to say that it's not a perfect timing indicator, but it's not something one should ignore either. It takes time for market sentiment to change. Housing prices topped mid-2006 but the housing and credit bubble didn't affect the stock market until the end of 2007.

The final chart I wanted to show is a table from Wikipedia on the yield Curve. It shows how all of the recessions in the US since 1970 have been preceded by an inverted yield curve. The chart shows the data of the inversion, the date of the start of the recession, the time it took until the recession started, how long the curve stayed inverted, and the duration of the recession. At the bottom, it shows the averages as well as standard deviation since 1969. On average, recessions start 12 months after the yield curve inverts.

Event	Date of Inversion Start	Date of the Recession Start	Time from Inversion to Recession Start	Duration of Inversion	Time from Disinversion to Recession End	Duration of Recession	Max Inversion
⬍	⬍	⬍	Months ⬍	Months ⬍	Months ⬍	Months ⬍	Basis Points ⬍
1970 Recession	Dec-68	Jan-70	13	15	8	11	-52
1974 Recession	Jun-73	Dec-73	6	18	3	16	-159
1980 Recession	Nov-78	Feb-80	15	18	2	6	-328
1981-1982 Recession	Oct-80	Aug-81	10	12	13	16	-351
1990 Recession	Jun-89	Aug-90	14	7	14	8	-16
2001 Recession	Jul-00	Apr-01	9	7	9	8	-70
2008-2009 Recession	Aug-06	Jan-08	17	10	24	18	-51
Average since 1969			12	12	10	12	-147
Std Dev since 1969			3.63	4.72	7.50	4.78	138.96

Source: Wikipedia

Dynamic Yield Curve

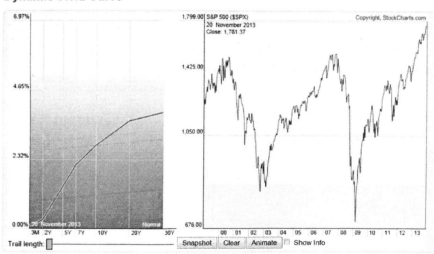

Are we in a credit Bubble? Lending standards are low. That's part of the criteria, but so is a flat or inverted yield curve. The yield spread between long-term rates and short-term rates is only widening as shown in the Bloomberg chart above. We won't see lending standards begin to rise until that spread narrows. It's only when that happens that credit is crunched and a bubble can pop. Mind you, even if the yield curve was inverted, it takes time for sentiment and the economy to change as well. On average, since 1970, it takes twelve months after the yield curve inverts for a recession to begin. We can have 10-15% corrections in the stock market as in 2010 and 2011, but these weren't the beginnings of a recession - merely corrections in an ongoing bull market. For two years, I've been bullish on the financials and four years bullish on the market. I still am, despite the bubble calls. Based on lending standards, the yield curve, and the yield spread, there's no credit bubble here. The business cycle looks healthy to me.

Corporate balance sheets are flush with cash, and strong revenue and profit growth enables firms to invest without spending down these buffers. Where an oversupply of tech equipment existed in 1999/2000, today we have pent up corporate demand after several years of underinvestment.

To be sure, investor sentiment is improving, but we're a long way from a euphoric top. Contrary to what some are suggesting, there is plenty of room for sentiment to improve—and lift markets higher—before this bull ends.

ARE FRONTIER MARKETS OVERVALUED?

The fondness felt by investors towards frontier markets has not dissipated since turmoil struck their emerging market cousins in October last year. In fact, feelings have climbed to a new pitch of devotion.

But the chart below raises an obvious question – has the ardour been overdone? Only rarely in the recent past have FM equity valuations traded at such a generous premium to EM counterparts.

FM equities are trading at an average price earnings ratio of 13.6 times and a price to book ratio of 1.8 times, representing a premium of 18 per cent and 28 per cent respectively to valuations on EM markets, according to MSCI. All ratios are calculated on a trailing basis, using company earnings over the latest available 12 month period.

Chart 2: Trailing PE, MSCI indices

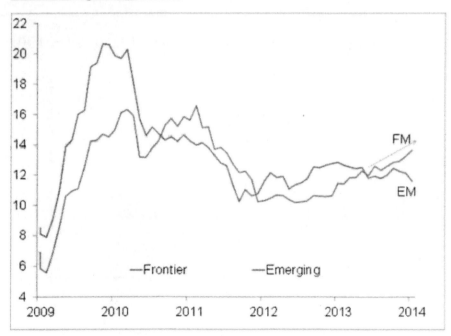

Source: MSCI

The 26 markets in the MSCI frontier index have often traded at a discount to those in the MSCI emerging index, reflecting the view that economies at the extremities of global capitalism are likely to be more risky and more vulnerable to sudden reversals than the more established EM asset class.

However, during the EM turmoil since October last year, the outlier status of FM markets was parlayed into a virtue. Sequestered by their remoteness from the tides of international liquidity, FM economies are also seen as less vulnerable to the withdrawal of liquidity as central banks around the world unwind their monetary stimulus programmes.

However, if a sharp FM correction was to occur, investors could face difficulty selling their holdings.

If I look through the ranks of widely-held stocks by FM funds — the likes of Bank of Georgia, or Nostrum Oil & Gas, or Nigerian Breweries — I am struck at how illiquid they still are.

To illustrate my point: those three stocks combined trade less in a day than Sberbank's GDR trades in 10 minutes. That's not a major problem now, with flows still trickling in… but if there is a move to the exit, that door will suddenly feel very small.

There are grounds, however, to think that the FM rally may not have run its course. For one thing, countries in the Gulf Co-operation Council (GCC), especially the UAE and Qatar – which are due to graduate from the FM to the EM index later this year – are performing strongly, driving up the aggregate valuation of FM equities (see chart).

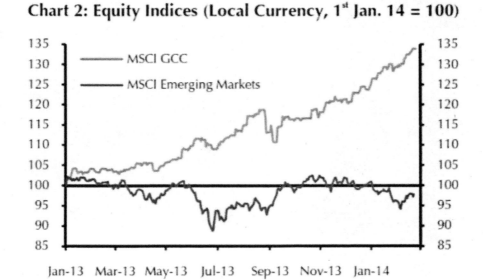

Chart 2: Equity Indices (Local Currency, 1ˢᵗ Jan. 14 = 100)

Source: Capital Economics

The Qatari government spending is set to increase 11.6 per cent in 2014 as the government boosts infrastructure upgrades ahead of the 2022 Fifa World Cup. He says this helps make Qatar attractive relative to Kuwait and Saudi Arabia, partly because Qatar's stock market is trading at 11.6 times prospective earnings compared to 16 times for Kuwait and 14.5 for Saudi Arabia.

Vietnam and Bangladesh are other frontier markets which have seen significant stock price surges backed by generally improving economic prospects.

On the other hand, the news from several key frontier markets has been turning steadily more negative. Nigerian president Goodluck Jonathan last week suspended the internationally respected central bank governor Lamido Sanusi, creating grave concerns among investors over the trajectory of governance.

Ukraine is poised in the uncertain aftermath of a revolution. Argentina's peso is down 22 per cent this year on the back of capital flight, rampant inflation and adverse reactions to the country's economic fragility. Kazakhstan devalued its currency by 18 per cent this year and the Ghanaian cedi is also sharply lower. Venezuela appears to be slipping deeper into financial distress as its currency, the bolívar, trades at 87.7 on the black market, nearly 14 times the official rate.

'NEW PARANORMAL' AND WHY BLACK SWANS ARE CIRCLING

With the market rebounding off the January selloff despite weakening economic signals and geopolitical turmoil, traders have been taking precautions against a return of the dreaded black swan.

The **CBOE SKEW Index**, which uses out-of-the-money—lower than the market price—options to discern fear of an unusual event hitting the market, has been pushed to levels indicative that something may be at hand.

Over the past few months, the black swan index, as it is nicknamed, has been trading above its normal area and is drawing attention on trading floors.

People are buying cheap protection. There are some people that think with the market sitting here we're ignoring too many risks, either from (Federal Reserve) tapering or emerging market instability from geopolitics. But that's trying to guess what a black swan event is, which by definition you can't do.

The index most recently traded around 132, which is above its 50-day moving average and well above the 200-day moving average.

Anything above 100 is considered a sign that traders are nervous, though it usually takes until about the 130 range before anyone starts noticing. The measure spent most of January below that level but recently breached it.

Even market bulls believe there are considerable signs that fear is creeping back into the market after a strong February that has seen the **S&P 500** gain nearly 3.5 percent in price and come just shy of breakeven for the year.

My short-term internal energy indicators are totally out of energy, the equity markets are pretty fatigued, the CBOE Skew Index has registered a reading whereby the option traders are expecting a downside 'black swan' event over the next 30 days, optimism is very tilted to the upside, and every overbought indicator I monitor is WAY overbought. As for me, I am confused awaiting the equity markets' trading resolution as to their near-term direction.

I rmemain convinced that this is a "new secular bull market" but is concerned over the turmoil in Ukraine as well as a general climate of European deflation.

In other words, I am long-term bullish but see ramifications of what I call the "New Paranormal" possibly exacting some damage in areas of the market.

As noted last year...2014 could be a year of speculative excess rather than one of macro, rate and asset allocation normalization. It remains hard to believe that an era of unprecedented intervention in financial markets by central banks will not threaten a parabolic overshoot in some asset prices.

Potential candidates: US biotech, internet stocks, floating rate debt.

However, the long-term picture is supported by easy monetary policy that will keep interest rates low as well as a belief that the soft patch in economic data that has greeted 2014 will be reversed:

Today rates are zero and likely to stay that way for the foreseeable future. And capital flight from emerging markets will add fuel to the fire as well as feed the strong bull markets in prime real estate in the West as well as high quality, high growth Best of Breed stocks.

'MARK TO MARKET' OR 'NOT TO MARKET'

According to Andrew Smithers, founder of the consultancy firm Smithers & Co, the financial information published by companies has become increasingly bogus in recent years, because of the huge incentive for modern management to produce highly volatile profits. This has been helped by the increased flexibility allowed with the change from "mark to cost" to "mark to market".

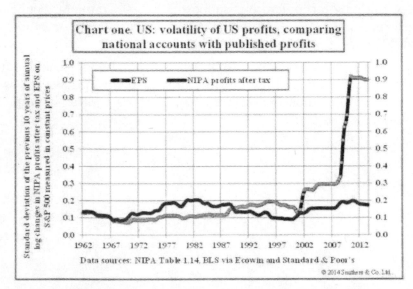

Chart one demonstrates the huge increase that has occurred in the volatility of the profits that US companies publish at a time when there has been no significant change in the volatility of profits shown in the national accounts. From 1952 to 2002 the two series had very similar volatilities but, since then, the earnings per share shown in the S&P 500 has become five times more volatile.

Why has this happened? The answer is because it pays management to have volatile profits and they can do it more easily than before with the change in accounting rules.

There has been a dramatic change in the amount and way that senior management is paid. Chart two shows that chief executive "bonuses", which include stock options, have risen by almost four times since 1992 and, in 2008, were 83 per cent of total remuneration.

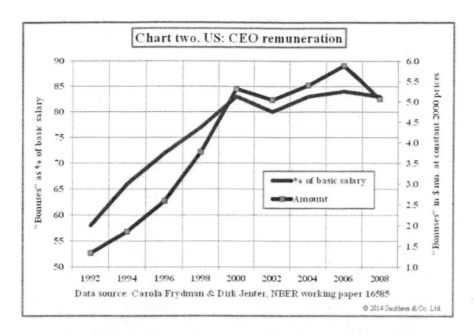

Chart two. US: CEO remuneration

Data source: Carola Frydman & Dirk Jenter, NBER working paper 16585

© 2014 Smithers & Co Ltd

There has been a huge change in incentives and, of course, behaviour has changed with it – that is the purpose of incentives. When new chief executives are appointed, they seek to depress the level of profits on their arrival. In downturns managements that survive will do the same, arguing that profit targets which are out of reach provide no incentive. This is usually accepted, so the target is "rebased".

Write-offs reduce companies' equity and increase future profits. A write-off is not just an admission that profits have been overstated, it is a promise to try and overstate them in the future. Return on equity rises because equity is reduced and future profits are increased. Companies with high RoE are praised by analysts and this is reflected in the reputation of their management and directly or indirectly in their pay.

This encourages bad practice and poor outcomes. RoE in anglophone economies has begun to resemble tractors in communist Russia. Just as targets for production encouraged the output of vast numbers of tractors which broke down, so targets for RoE serve to improve the published figures at the expense of a decline in the information they convey.

WHICH CENTRAL BANK WILL BE NEXT TO RAISE INTEREST RATES?

New Zealand's central bank has raised borrowing costs to 2.75 percent, making it the first developed world central bank to hike rates since the credit crisis began in 2007.

However, Thursday's move by the Reserve Bank of New Zealand is unlikely to trigger a race to raise rates elsewhere -- many western countries are still struggling with the after-effects of the global recession and credit crisis.

The ending of low interest rates would mark a turning point in the developed world's recovery from the global credit crisis – and ordinary people may not believe in the recovery until their savings rates start to rise once more.

However this is unlikely to happen any time soon. The crisis countries, including the U.S., Europe and U.K., aren't going to be in any position to raise rates any time soon.

One of the main reasons for the reluctance to raise is the fear of deflation, where prices shrink in real terms. While prices falling may initially seem like a good thing for consumers, this can also lead to jobs being lost and lower profits for businesses. And while central banks can deal with inflation by raising interest rates, it is more difficult to tackle deflation when interest rates are already at historic lows, as they are in the U.S., U.K., Japan and the euro zone.

The risk of deflation, especially in the euro zone, definitely exists.

If you look at European figures as measured by the Eurostat HICP index "at constant taxes," the vast majority of EU countries have seen a fall in real prices in the past seven months. This puts the ECB out of the rate-rising picture in the short term.

Meanwhile, the U.S. Federal Reserve is trying to unwind its massive asset purchasing program before hiking rates again, most analysts believe.

So that rules out the developed world's two most powerful central banks.

But the Bank of England, one of the Scandinavian central banks or the Bank of Canada, look most likely to hike rates soon.

The U.K.'s central bank is forecast to start raising rates around this time in 2015, and they could go up to 3 percent by 2017, according to Mark Carney, Governor of the Bank.

Yet the Bank may not in fact be able to raise rates until late 2015.

Bank of Canada will be next to raise rates, with a 0.25 basis point rise in the third quarter of 2014. Better than expected economic data would drive the rise.

Norway, which is one of the few developed countries not struggling with deflation after the fall in value of its currency last year, is another name which has been mentioned, along with the Swedish Riksbank.

The Danish central bank, which is currently running a negative deposit rate, might have to make a small rise of around 10 basis points, because of selling pressure around its currency.

Interest rates:

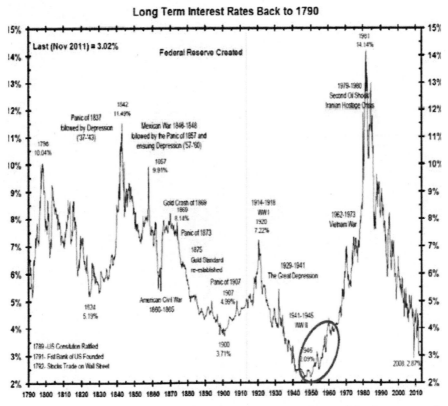

Long Term Interest Rates Back to 1790

While the chart clearly shows that interest rates have hit the same levels as last seen in 1946, the view that rates will rise strongly from current levels assumes that the same economic drivers exist today. In 1946, the United States had just exited WWII which left Europe and Japan in ruins. The United States became the manufacturing center of the industrialized world as we assisted in the rebuilding of Germany, Britain, France and Japan. That is no longer the case today as much of our industrial manufacturing has been outsourced to other countries for lower costs. The chart below shows interest rates overlaid against the annual changes in economic growth.

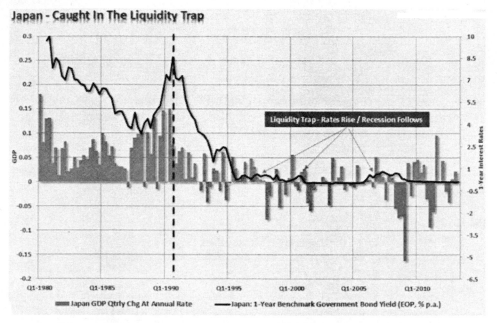

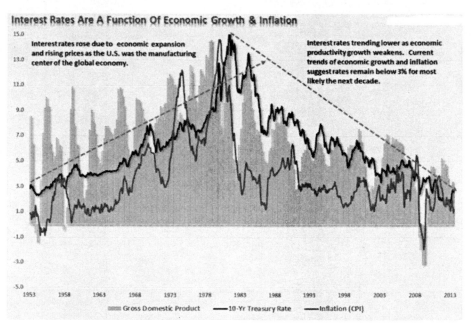

There could be serious financial turmoil when the Fed eventually raises interest rates, even without a lot of leverage in the financial system, according to this year's paper at the US Monetary Policy Forum in New York. If the analysis is correct then it is an argument against very easy monetary policy – but the paper is quite limited.

(The USMPF, organised by the Chicago Booth business school, is a once-a-year event where a group of market economists present a paper to a gathering of Fed pooh-bahs. The authors this year are Michael Feroli of JP Morgan, Anil Kashyap of Chicago Booth, Kermit Schoenholtz of NYU Stern and Hyun Song Shin of Princeton.)

The meat of this year's paper is a model of how the market can throw a wobbly when it realises the Fed may raise interest rates, as happened in the summer of 2013, with the infamous taper tantrum. The basic idea is that mutual funds worry about their performance relative to rivals, so they crowd into trades when the Fed lowers rates, but all rush for the exits when they suspect a rate rise is on its way.

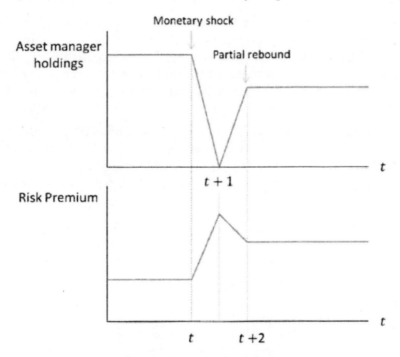

Figure 1.4 *Time paths for delegated agent positions and risk premiums following monetary tightening*

The authors draw some strong conclusions. "When investors infer that monetary policy will tighten," they say, "the instability seen in the summer of 2013 is likely to reappear." They argue that the Fed must not only weigh up the merits of more or less stimulus today, but a trade-off between "more stimulus today at the expense of a more challenging and disruptive policy exit in the future".

The paper is fine as far as it goes, but to be honest, that is not very far. The idea markets can have tantrums, and rate rises can trigger them, is not new to economics and blindingly obvious to those in the markets. The crucial questions are:

(1) How much economic damage do these tantrums cause and when do they outweigh the benefits of monetary stimulus? Last summer's taper tantrum

raised mortgage rates but does that outweigh the previous effects of QE3 in reducing them?

(2) Are such tantrums mainly the product of the market misunderstanding the Fed's intentions and thus avoidable with clearer forward guidance? In the paper's model, you can get instability even if the Fed's intentions are well understood, but it is not clear how often and to what degree.

(3) Can these no-leverage tantrums generate the kind of dynamics that lead to a bigger financial crisis?

The paper does not really try to answer these questions. Thus you are left with the result that Fed rate rises can upset the markets and thus easing now may have some later cost.

The main value of the paper is to show a mechanism where (a) a Fed move towards tightening can trigger market turmoil even when one might expect it to be priced in; and (b) stronger forward guidance can increase the chance of these reversals. Thus the Fed should prepare for turmoil when the time does come to raise rates, but without an argument about costs and benefits, it will be hard for the Fed to act on.

UPDATE: Fed governor Jeremy Stein and Minneapolis Fed president Narayana Kocherlakota discuss the paper – they like the model, and clearly think there is a need to think about instability triggered by unleveraged fixed income funds – although Mr Kocherlakota makes a similar point to mine about costs and benefits.

THE POSITIVE SIDE OF RISING
INTEREST RATES

When the Fed first hinted at winding down its quantitative easing (QE) program last May, headlines were convinced it signaled the death knell for the recovery—long-term interest rates would rise, loans would be more expensive, consumers would stop borrowing, and growth would stall. But here we are, nine months later, with the latest Fed data showing consumer borrowing rose for the second straight quarter in Q4 2013—and for the second quarter since before the financial crisis. The $241 billion rise was the biggest since Q3 2007, despite long-term interest rates finishing 2013 at their highest level since mid-2011. Rising rates, it would seem, are not economic kryptonite (Exhibit 1).

Exhibit 1: Household Debt and Long-Term Interest Rates

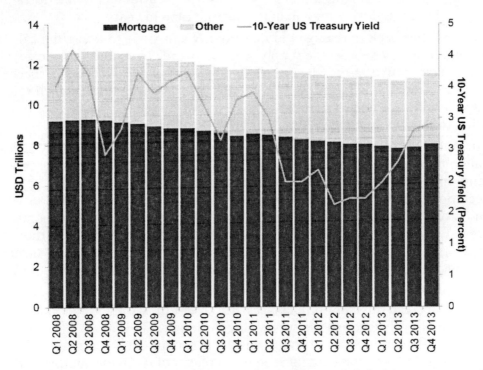

Source: Federal Reserve Bank of New York, Equifax and Federal Reserve Bank of St. Louis, as of 2/18/2014.

How did lending rise even though it became more expensive? Headlines credited "confidence" and resurgent demand. "Consumers are borrowing again," went the common media meme. Yet, according to the Fed's Senior Loan Officer Opinion Survey, this doesn't square with reality. On balance, loan officers have reported rising demand since 2012's outset. Folks have been plenty willing to borrow. Prime mortgage demand growth, too, has been strong—until Q3 and Q4 2013, when it leveled off some. It seems exceedingly difficult to argue the mythical animal spirits magically reappeared in Q3 and Q4.

What did change: Banks became more willing to lend. According to the same Fed survey, the number of banks tightening credit standards for consumer and mortgage lending fell over the same period.

It's always dangerous to pin changes in supply or demand for a product on any one variable—and a variety of factors likely made banks more willing to lend in the second half of 2013, like banks' own confidence in the sustainability of this expansion and, by extension borrowers' ability to repay. But in our view, the rise in long-term interest rates likely played a sizeable role. As we've written before, long-term rates represent banks' lending revenues. Falling rates means falling revenues—and when short-term rates (a proxy for banks' costs) are pegged near zero, falling long-term rates also means falling profits. That's a big incentive for banks to sit tight and lend to only the most creditworthy borrowers—and a big reason why lending fell while interest rates were ultra-low. Now that rates are higher, the higher potential profits encourage banks to lend to a much wider swath of customers. Some folks might find themselves qualifying for a loan for the first time in years.

This all ties back to the age old question: If you want to boost the sales of a product, do you try to boost the supply or the demand? In its quest to boost lending through quantitative easing, the Fed tried to boost demand. It probably succeeded. But higher demand didn't translate to higher household lending, which tells you the supply side mattered more. Now that lending is more profitable, we're finally starting to see supply increase, and household lending is finally rising.

In our view, this illustrates why QE was so misguided—and why investors should embrace, not fear, its end. Even if rates don't rise much after the Fed stops buying bonds—and they may not, considering how efficiently markets priced in expectations for the end of QE last year—we should see further gains in lending from here. It takes time for monetary policy changes to show up in economic data. We're only just now seeing an uptick in banks' net interest margins, even though 10-year US Treasury rates—the reference rate for most long-term lending—have risen for about 18 months. This lag suggests net interest margins have plenty of room to rise just to catch up with the rise in Treasury yields.

You won't read this many other places, however—most outlets continue focusing on demand, largely ignoring the supply side. As long as they do so, fear will persist, and the brightening reality of improving loan supply likely goes unnoticed. For stocks, this is bullish—it means there remains plenty of room for improving lending in a post-QE US to catch investors by surprise, pushing markets higher.

Therefore, As QE ends November 2014, the world will be a better place to live in.

My biggest 2014 positive surprise? How well the world will work when quantitative easing finally dies. As I've detailed multiple times, virtually everyone gets this wrong and backward. QE isn't expansive or bullish—just the reverse.

When it ends the party finally gets going good, as yield spreads widen and bank lending, money supply and economic growth finally take off—the exact U.K. experience after they ended their dismal version of this idiocy.

America's broad money supply has grown slower in this expansion than any you've lived through. That loosens soon. Enjoy the ride beginning December 2014.

ASIAN CURRENCY DEPRECIATION: AND THE WINNER IS?.. TOURISM!

The weak yen fuelled a rise in inbound tourism, with Tokyo Disneyland posting record year for both revenues and foreign visitors

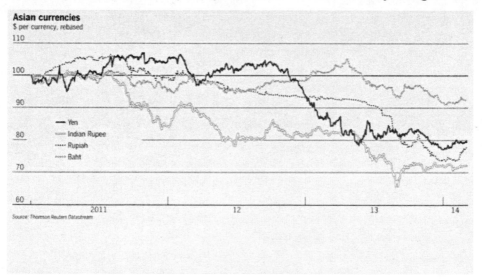

Mickey Mouse has emerged as one of the big beneficiaries of Abenomics but South Korean cabbage farmers who rely on sales of the spicy delicacy kimchi are missing out.

Radical central bank policies in the US and Japan have buffeted Asian currencies in the past 12 months, wiping 15 per cent off the Indian rupee, 10 per cent off the yen and a fifth off the Indonesian rupiah. But they have also created some unlikely winners and losers, from Indonesian cattle farmers to Japanese bath house owners.

The widening of South Korea's kimchi deficit – which sees the country import more of its national dish than it sells abroad – and the growing queues at Japanese theme parks are both manifestations of Abenomics, the pro-growth policies championed by Shinzo Abe, Japan's prime minister, that began with easy money and a devaluation in the yen.

The weaker currency has made holidaying abroad more expensive, fuelling a rise in inbound tourism and the number of Japanese taking "staycations". Last year Disneyland Tokyo posted a record year for revenue and visitor numbers. Tourist arrivals to Japan topped 10m for the first time in 2013, comfortably trumping the previous record of 8.6m, while outbound trips dropped by 5.5 per cent year-on-year.

The slide in Asian currencies, prompted by the global "taper tantrum" in May last year that hit many emerging markets, has also given some a surprise boost. The 20 per cent fall in the rupiah and the 9 per cent drop in the baht in the past year has helped Javanese and Thai cattle herders funnel their fresh milk into the cappuccinos of dollar-based Hong Kong and Singapore.

Although fuel bills and wage pressures are pushing up production costs, Thai milk is still about 20 per cent cheaper than the Australian equivalent in Hong Kong, while Indonesian milk is 30 per cent less expensive. Thus both are expanding their market share in the city's fridges and flat whites.

That news will be particularly welcome for the Indonesian authorities, who have been battling to close a damaging current account deficit. Rising exports – predominantly of commodities – are a key part of that effort, and were the main driver of Indonesia's better than expected fourth quarter economic performance. Deficit countries were hit hardest in last year's sell-off due to their reliance of external sources of funding.

But the latest round of the currency wars has also created plenty of losers. More tourism has not been enough to ease Japan's growing trade deficit, which is at a record this year. With most natural resources priced in dollars, the country has been forced to import more expensive fuel to keep the lights on during its nuclear shutdown.

Energy-dependent businesses, such as the famous Japanese bath houses, have felt the chill of rising costs. Data released last month showed that commodity imports have been a drag on growth, while domestic consumption is failing to pick up the slack.

Then there are the ailing South Korean cabbage patch owners. Japan is Korea's biggest export market for kimchi – the fiery pickled cabbage served with almost every Korean meal. The slide in the yen has sapped Japanese demand for increasingly expensive kimchi, while cheap Chinese imports into Korea are on the rise. South Korea posted a kimchi trade deficit last year of $28m, a sevenfold increase on the previous year's $4m.

The weaker rupiah also drained plush swimming pools in Jakarta apartment blocks as expats paid in rupiah downsized to smaller, cheaper homes following last year's slide in the local currency. While everyday items are priced in rupiah, many landlords and international schools charge expats in dollars.

In India, another country hit hard by capital outflows last year, local shampoo producers that price their sachets at Rs1 a pop have problems, too. Faced with the rising costs of imported chemicals, some companies are considering the unattractive option of a 100 per cent price increase.

WHY GETTY IMAGES IS GIVING AWAY 30M PHOTOS FOR FREE

Big media companies owned by profit-hungry private equity groups don't normally give their core products away for free.

But Getty Images, which was acquired for $3.3bn by Carlyle in 2012, is doing just that. The world's largest supplier of stock photos has made more than 30m images available to people to share for free on their blogs and social media sites, including tumblr, WordPress and Twitter.

This is not charity, however. Behind the move lies cold commercial logic. It's all about data, control and advertising.

In Getty's words, "the company is shifting its business model to become much more of a consumer tech company". The Seattle-based company says it "recognizes that in today's image-rich, digital world there are many situations where traditional licensing models are not appropriate or where they simply don't work."

In other words, Getty hasn't been able to stop people using its images without permission through force, so it is adopting a more pragmatic approach to the question of how to make money from its images.

Rather than giving away the raw image files for free, Getty is offering people a way to embed its images in their websites using a piece of web technology that links back to Getty's computer servers.

This has several benefits for Getty. The first is that the company and its photographers are credited for the use of the image. That makes the Getty brand more visible across the web, and is designed to attract people to its website where they can buy photos for commercial uses.

The second big attraction for Getty is that the technology gives it accurate data about how its photos are being used. This should enhance the company's ability to track consumer behaviour and react quickly to trends.

But perhaps the most tantalising part of the new technology is that it allows Getty to serve advertising within the images. The company has not started this yet but says it is thinking about doing so in future.

Getty started experimenting with advertising in its images last year. It has been working with startups such as Kiosked, whose technology is able to turn Getty photos on certain websites into interactive shops. When readers move their mouse over a "Kiosked" image, a pop-up window appears with a link to buy a particular product. For example, a photo of Rihanna would contain a link to buy her latest album or the dress she is wearing.

The potential is vast. The only question now is how many web users will start using Getty's new widget and how many will stick with their tried and tested method of "right-click, download and share".

WHEN LIFE GIVES YOU LEMONS, MAKE LEMONADE

A cartoon in a Mexican newspaper last week said it all: there are Adam and Eve, in the Garden of Eden, gazing wistfully at the forbidden fruit. But it's not an apple. It's a lime.

Just about everything to eat in Mexico gets served with a wedge of lime, but buying them lately has been tricky. At one recent Sunday market in Mexico City, stallholders rolled their eyes when asked for what is normally the most ubiquitous of fruit. "No, too expensive," was the answer rolled out at stall after stall.

The price of limes – confusingly called *"limón"* and which you need to go with your beer, in your margarita, on your taco or in your guacamole – has soared in recent weeks, fueling inflation which has struggled to remain within the central bank target.

The price of limes went up 21.55 per cent in the first fortnight of March alone. The rise is a whopping 222 per cent since December, according to this report. The government has warned that prices will not drop until late April.

How expensive are we talking here? As much as a lip-puckering 70 pesos ($5.30) at times in recent weeks making the cost of limes in the world's biggest producer of the fruit more expensive than a host of international cities.

Various factors have been blamed for the lime price climb, including extortion by crime bosses in the major lime-producing state of Michoacán and a blight in the nearby state of Colima.

But state consumer defence agency, Profeco, is not satisfied. It has now announced it will file a criminal complaint this week with the attorney general's office against whoever is found to be hoarding supplies to boost prices.

Producers blame distributors for the price spike and Bloomberg reports that lime growers have reportedly started fixing prices – potentially falling foul of anti-trust laws.

Mexico has flirted with the idea of importing more limes to steady supplies and bring down the prices, but has not done so yet. Meanwhile shoppers are cutting back.

To make matters worse, sunny spring temperatures are perfect for the thirst-quenching fruit that is temporarily out of reach.

When life gives you lemons, make lemonade, goes the old saying. *If only Mexicans could afford to.*

BONDS ARE NOT IN BUBBLE TERRITORY

Throughout the economic recovery, there have been a number of economists and policy types worried about a "bond bubble" – the idea that bonds are overpriced and could take a sudden tumble, giving financial markets and the economy the same sort of hits we saw from the collapse of the housing and stock bubbles.

This is seriously misguided thinking from any conceivable perspective. At the most basic level, such concerns are misplaced because there is nowhere near as much money at stake. Former U.S. Federal Reserve economist Andrew Flowers put the amount of money at stake in the bond market at $40 trillion in a recent **FiveThirtyEight column.** This compares to a stock market valued at around $28 trillion and the housing market at a bit over $20 trillion.

While that may make the bond market seem more important, the $40 trillion number is hugely misleading. The figure refers to total debt, much of which is short-term. This is important because short-term debt doesn't lose much value when interest rates rise. If we restrict our focus to debt that stands to lose substantial value when interest rates rise – remaining duration of five years or more – the volume of debt would be well under $20 trillion.

Even here, the room for losses in this market is not nearly as large as it was in the case of either the stock or housing bubbles. The stock market lost more than half of its value from its 2000 peak to its 2002 bottom. House prices lost more than one-third of their real value from the 2006 peak to the 2011 trough.

Just under a decade ago, when Alan Greenspan was Federal Reserve chairman, he described the then low level of a 10-year Treasury yielding 4.15 per cent against the backdrop of tightening monetary policy as a conundrum.

Today, many in the bond market are once more shaking their heads when they see the 10-year note yielding 2.68 per cent, down from 3 per cent at the start of January. Given that bond prices move inversely to yields, sections of the US Treasury market have performed strongly since the year began.

Long-term Treasury bonds or those with a maturity beyond 25 years have delivered a total return of 10 per cent in 2014, according to Barclays Indices.

The pressing question is why are long-dated government bonds doing so well and handily eclipsing this year's returns for lower rated company paper and equities? Moreover, what does this mean for the economy and to investors betting on stronger growth and better returns from riskier assets in the coming months?

Unlike 2005, when Mr Greenspan talked of a bond conundrum, the Fed is not raising its key borrowing rate.

However, the recent decline in long-term Treasury yields has occurred while the central bank has stepped back from buying long-term Treasuries via its taper of quantitative easing. A further cut of $10bn in the Fed's monthly bond purchases to $45bn is expected at the next Fed policy meeting.

To the extent QE benefited risk assets, the unwind of QE removes that as a prop. The interplay between equities and long-dated Treasury bonds has also been driven by pension funds and insurers cashing in on last year's 30 % rally in the S&P 500 and switching back into government bonds which back then in January had experienced a hefty rise during the preceding seven months.

It appears clear that the bond market has priced in the removal of QE, given last summer's rise in yields, and attention is now focused on when the Fed will finally start tightening policy.

While long-term yields have fallen, those for shorter dated maturities, which are more sensitive to monetary policy expectations, have risen since January. This has resulted in the shape of the yield curve – or the relationship between short- and long-term yields – flattening in the vernacular of the market. It's the kind of behaviour we see ahead of central banks shifting policy.

The yield curve quite naturally starts flattening well in advance of a hiking cycle and, indeed, by the start of the hiking cycle, much of the flattening has taken place.

It appears likely that, while a stronger economy stands to push bond yields higher, such a move will be led by shorter maturity Treasuries and not by those at the longer end.

Moribund inflation also supports the case for holding long-dated bonds and one message from the Treasury market stands at odds with the consensus call of a sharp rebound in the economy over the coming months. Low bond yields and inflation suggests an economy still deleveraging after the bursting of the housing and credit bubble.

The low level of long-term US bond yields is a function of the economy's hangover in the aftermath of the housing price bubble bursting. The structural forces resulting in low long-term bond yields are very strong and it could be another three years before the Fed's current policy pushes up inflation expectations and ultimately inflation itself.

So while many traders and investors shun long-term bonds and have duly missed the solid performance since January, their bearish stance may not be vindicated any time soon. When it comes to consensus about bond yields, the US Treasury market has long frustrated the wisdom of market mavens.

In any event, it is difficult to envision a scenario where the bond market loses even 10% of its value. Let's consider an extreme case: Suppose the interest rate on 30-year mortgages, which is currently around 4.15 %, rose to 5.5 % in a short period of time. This would be an extraordinary, albeit not impossible, increase. This would imply a drop in the price of a newly issued 30-year mortgage of roughly 19% -- a much smaller percentage decline than we saw with the collapse of either the stock or housing bubbles.

Furthermore, the overwhelming majority of outstanding debt has much less than 30 years until maturity. This means the potential loss in value would be far less than this 19% figure even in the wake of a sharp jump in interest rates.

While low interest rates are certainly providing a lift to the economy, it is not possible to tell a story of a comparable collapse in demand if bond prices were to tumble. In other words, there is no horrifying event that we need fear if the bond "bubble" were to burst.

MY STOCK RECOMMENDATIONS

The stock I highly recommend is **State Bank of India (SBIN, Rs 2260).** Available at P/E of 13 and Price/Book of just 1.56, it is India's largest public sector bank with the maximum number of outlets and reaches every nook and corner of the country.

Although there are fears of NPAs (Non Performing Assets), the fears are largely overblown. This stock is expected to rise significantly and could give 30 to 40 % return in a year. It has risen dramatically from 1500 to 2260 levels, wait for a correction. Buy at around 1700-1750 levels.

Various projects are completing at the same time and could lead to re-rating of **Reliance Industries (Ticker symbol: RIL) (India)** (Rs. 1050). In addition to an anticipated doubling of gas prices, some fundamental factors also could lead to Reliance re-rating. The firm's multi-year Rs 1 lakh-crore capex will expand its petrochemical capabilities by two-thirds by end of FY 16. Similarly, a coal gasification unit that will expand its refining margins and add nearly $ 1.5 Billion to its operating profits will come up by FY 16.

Dwindling natural gas production from KG-D6 has started inching up, and a likely revision in domestic gas prices will make more production viable. Subsidiaries such as retail have started contributing to earnings in FY 14. Its retail business has turned profitable, while shale gas business in the US is growing steadily. From $ 659 million f EBITDA the shale gas business is expected to post $ 1.2 Billion of EBITDA in FY 16. Its telecom venture is expected to launch in the second half of FY 15, where the pace of subscriber additions will determine its break-even.

Having risen 35% in the past three months, wait for a breather before buying RIL. A price of Rs 850 could be a good entry point. Expect the stock to triple in five years.

Seeing the coffee shortfall in Brazil, I rccommend iPath Pure Beta Coffee ETN, CAFE an investment product that tracks coffee prices.

Today's doggiest stock—high up most lists like "best brand," "most respected," "most innovative," "most new patents," etc.—is **International Business Machines** (IBM, 191). Now it only needs boredom to beat expectations. IBM has too much that can surprise positively (like cybersecurity consulting) versus ugllly for a quality stock in today's market at 13 times my 2014 earnings estimate with a 2% dividend yield.

Larsen and Toubro (Rs 1320) is a leading Indian construction and engineering stock available at a forward P/E multiple of 22. The company has been letdown by slowdown in infrastructure construction and spending by the incumbent government. Buy at around Rs 1000-1050 levels and enjoy a ride of upto 30% within a year.

Coca-Cola (KO)($40) : Berkshire Hatahway is a major shareholder in Coca-Cola Co. It's protagonist Warren Buffett says he drinks five Cokes in a day. Coca-Cola has wonderful brands that account for roughly 3% of all liquids consumed globally. Coca-Cola has been under a lot more pressure than it was 10 or 15 tears ago, particularly in the United States. But their sales went up last year as they have gone up every year.

Starbucks (SBUX) ($70.15) has a portfolio of assets that include 19,000 stores serving 70 million customers per week. It has the most effective social media initiatives of any company I follow—40 million Facebook followers, 5 million Twitter followers. While Starbucks has high labor costs; its throughput efficiency, augmented by mobile payment and advance ordering technology has allowed for earnings leverage as the same labor costs are amortized over many more clients per hour.

COSTCO (COST) ($113.50) is immensely popular because of its unique club model. More than 70 million members have a loyalty card to Costco and are responsible for about 75 % of its earnings before taxes. It has incredible shopper loyalty.

PFIZER (PFE) ($ 30.25) From big brand names like Advil and Viagra to post-patent-protected blockbusters like Lipitor, Diflucan and Zoloft, to its new leukemia drug, Bosulif, Pfizer's A-to-Z product line will generate moderate growth from aging baby boomers (and emerging markets). It sells at 18 times my 2014 EPS estimate with a 3.45% dividend yield.

U.K.-based **GlaxoSmithKline (GSK-GB) (1559 GBp)** is a similar A-to-Z druggie, which should have a similarly good 2014 but with shorter average patent lives and more nondrug consumer items (like Aquafresh and Sensodyne). It's trading at 16 times my 2014 earnings estimate with a 5% dividend yield.

In a major restructuring move, GSK will sell its oncology products business to Novartis for $ 14.5 Billion plus an additional $ 1.5 Billion contingent on a development milestone. GSK meanwhile will pay $ 7.1 Billion plus royalties for Novartis' vaccines business, excluding its flu business.The proposed transaction will boost Glaxo's plan to generate sustainable, broadly-sourced sales growth and will improve long-term earnings. It will generate $ 10.9 Billion in annual sales.

Fast Retailing (9883.T-JP: TOKYO STOCK EXCHANGE) (33700 JPY) 4 Mar 2014 | 8:36 PM ET

Fast Retailing is making a global expansion push, targeting the U.S. and China and potentially even acquiring U.S.-based J.Crew, but is the owner of the popular Uniqlo clothing brand moving too quickly?

Investors outside Japan might have some doubts about the Japanese retailer's plans.

The Japan-listed shares may be pricey, trading at more than 34 times earnings, compared with **Hennes & Mauritz** at around 23 times and **Inditex**, the owner of the Zara brand, at around 25 times, according to data from Thomson Reuters.

But some analysts appear unfazed.

The valuations are high--but it's a fantastically well-managed business. People are willing to pay that kind of premium for the aggressive expansion plans--the company has no debt on its balance sheet.

The expansion plans are ambitious. The Japanese retailer currently has 260 locations in China and it plans to open around 100 stores a year – or one every three to four days – for the next few years. It's also making its first foray into the U.S. market since its failed attempt in the 1990s.

At the same time, media have reported the company is interested in acquiring JCrew for around $5 billion. Fast Retailing has an acquisitive history, with previous purchases including the Theory brand, Comptoir Des Cotonniers, lingerie maker Princesse Tam.Tam and J Brand.

They're expanding fast, yes, but actually they can fund it easily through their own operating cash flow.

There are some concerns about the fast expansion, including the possibility the China market may become saturated.

The Chinese market is changing; it may be maturing. So that the luxury goods are now a downside risk, but the middle classes are still pointing to having spending power. That can be a very important building platform for the growth in greater China. The Uniqlo brand typically positions itself as affordable casual clothing.

Although the company failed at its initial attempt to enter the U.S. market, it is wading in again, with around 17 Uniqlo stores opened there so far. It is targeting $10 billion in sales there by 2020.

Based on the failure in the past, they've been fairly conservatively observing the U.S. market in the past two years intensively-- the company's plans to open 10-20 stores a year there.

This will be a big experiment and this will be a critical turning point for Uniqlo. If they do succeed this time in the U.S., I think they will become a true global SPA (specialty-retailer of private-label apparel.

Yamato also isn't very concerned about the potential J.Crew acquisition, believing the company won't overpay. Fast Retailing has walked away from acquisitions over price in the past, including an attempt to acquire Barneys.

While Yamato notes the $5 billion potential price tag for J.Crew might be expensive, probably Fast Retailing may want to acquire the CEO, the management of J.Crew, who have a good reputation within the U.S. apparel industry.

Five large stocks I like with fat gross margins overall and relative to peers.

a) Swiss-based **NOVARTIS (NVSEF, 84)** is the world's third-largest drug firm by most measures—a very diverse line. Its blockbusters include Diovan, a blood-pressure medication, and Gleevec, a cancer drug.

   As a result of a strategic review, Novartis has agreed to acquire GSK's oncology products for USD 14.5 Billion. It will also divest its vaccines business exckuding flu to GSK for USD 7.1 Billion plus royalties. In a separate transaction, it has agreed to divest its animal health business to Eli Lilly for USD 5.4 Billion.

   Novartis is well-run, and among the druggies it sports fatter gross margins (66%). Yet it's cheap versus peers at 22 times my 2014 earnings estimate. Dividend yield? 3.27%!

b) Another Swiss-based multiyear laggard is **Nestle** (NSRGY, 76). Investors yawn: 17 times 2014 earnings seems high for food firms. Dividend yield of 3.17%. So what's adding the color? A foodie with 50%-plus gross margins boggles the mind. How does it do that? Super brands plus super management leads to super-reliable profitability—again, something later-stage bull markets love as the later entrants digest their first stock-bites in years.

c) **Intel (INTC, 27)** lagged for years, too. I like that investors are used to being repulsed. Folks forget the obvious: 1) It's the prime generator of Moore's Law (our era's second most powerful force after raw capitalism), and 2) New CEOs, like Brian Krzanich, always clean house, depressing current earnings to boost future results (which markets love later). And 3) For such a competitive field its 58% gross margin astounds. Now it's time— at 15 times my 2014 earnings estimate with a 3.33% dividend yield.

d) Well run fat gross margin (58%) IT firm, of a different style, is **MasterCard** (MA, 74). Most think it's a credit card company. But it's also a payments-processing IT firm, albeit growing at a slower, safer rate than Apple or Facebook. It sells at 25 times my 2014 earnings estimate.

e) **Royal Dutch Shell (RDSB-GB: 2393 GBp).** At $215 billion in market cap it's neck and neck with PetroChina as the third-biggest energy firm. It's also well run and compellingly cheap–the cheapest of the biggies–at 40% of annual revenue, ten times my 2014 earnings estimate, with a 5% dividend yield.

No one does infectious disease better than **Gilead Sciences**, based in Foster City, Calif. Its blockbusters are for HIV. But nine other basic products span cardio, flu, liver and respiratory ailments and should help sustain enough growth to push the stock up despite being 22 times my 2014 earnings estimate.

Another favorite: Chicago's **ABBVIE ABBV** ($48) Abbott Labs' former biotech arm. There are few overlaps with Gilead; AbbVie aims at cancer, hepatitis, neuroscience, immunology, kidney and women's health. Moderate growth is pretty secure, yet it sells at only 18 times my 2014 earnings estimate, with a fat 3.46% dividend yield.

McDonald's (MCD, 99) has become incredibly tasty now. While suffering endless U.S. elitist condescension, note: America accounts for less than a third of its revenue.

Overseas potential is nearly endless for the world's most diverse global menu. For Singapore, it created the Shaka Shaka Chicken. In India,the McVeggie. And in Mexico,the McTrio. You won't get sick.

The 4% annual growth in the number of locations, plus increased same-store sales, is a happy meal when served with a 3.25% dividend yield and a P/E of 18.

Compare Aussie mining giant **BHP Billiton** (BHPLF, 35) and its gloriously bloated 66% gross margin with those of its peers. And that with in-the-dumps commodity prices! Simply better properties!

You may think those would be in the stock price already. I think not. BHP has barely budged in this bull market. It's down 25% from three years ago, now at 12 times my 2014 earnings estimate with a 4.68% dividend yield. Perfect for the back half of any bull market. –

I love revering oligopolies in general and have cited Australia's four-bank oligopoly as great but too expensive–preferring Canada's cheaper alternatives. **Australia & New Zealand Banking Group** (ANZBY, 31) -- number three in my pure oligopoly list is available for merely 15 times my estimate of September 2014 earnings. It has a 4.7% dividend yield.

Germany's **Bayer (BAYRY: 130)** is celebrating its 150th anniversary, and the stock is primed for partying. It's a moderate-growth technology firm divided into four similar-size businesses. One of its businesses has a wide array of proprietary drugs, another is big in general consumer health, and another is a global crop-science leader, including plant biotech, seeds and pesticides. The fourth leg of Bayer is materials, including plastics, coatings and adhesives.

To me the health care half is worth Bayer's price and you essentially get the rest for free–all at 22 times my 2014 earnings estimate, with a 2.21% dividend yield.

Air traffic is setting records globally. In the long term it's always been true that airlines don't make money. Chicago's **Boeing BA** ($ 128) is one exception. Forget my love of oligopolies. Boeing is part of a duopoly–with Airbus. Folks always fear that others will enter this market. But again, this is an unsubstantiated worry. Boeing will dominate for a long, long time. It will grow respectably, and at 0.9 times sales shares trade at a discount to the market. Boeing is 22 times my 2014 earnings estimate. Its stock has a 2.28% dividend yield.

Chevron CVX ($123) is simply the best giant energy firm out there. Currently you can buy its shares for almost no valuation premium. It sells for 11 times 2014 earnings and has a 3.24% dividend yield.

Thanks to the carnage and bailout of 2008, one investment bank remains dominant globally—the 800-pound gorilla, **Goldman Sachs Group GS** ($ 156). For Goldman's dominance you pay only 10 times my 2014 EPS estimate. Dividend yield is 1.40%.

As regards stock picking, both cheap value stocks and more glamorous growth stocks can work well in a portfolio—if done right.

So, do not pigeonhole themselves into one style. They often pick a strategy simply because it feels right in their gut. Value often smells better to a different breed of investor than growth does. But having different types of stocks in your portfolio can enhance returns.

Cisco Systems CSCO (USD 23) is an overblown, 1990s-highflier, takeover-crazy tech wreck that is now a big, cheap value stock—growing moderately with technology solutions spanning virtually everything we do in communications. Without it we don't grow. With a $116 billion ?market cap, 72,000 employees and $48 billion in revenue it sells at a mere 15 times my July 2014 earnings—with a 3.28% dividend yield.

Thousands of customers gripe about Comcast **CMCSA** (USAD 49) but can't resist paying monthly for its cable TV, home Internet and phone services. It's at the rotten core of our culture, like heroin to a junkie. If you can stomach owning NBC and are okay with peddling brain-wasting diversions to mid-America, it's a great money machine. It sells at 1.8 times revenue, 7 times cash flow and 19 times my 2014 earnings estimate, and sports a 1.82% dividend yield.

Britain's beverage giant SABMiller (SAB-GB) (3069 GBp) is an easy entry point for any of those fretters still tiptoeing into the back half of this bull market. It sells more than 200 beer brands globally, including Miller Lite, Blue Moon and Grolsch, and shares a duopoly with Anheuser-Busch InBev. It's a great emerging-world growth story, but it isn't cheap at 18 times my estimated March 2014 earnings. Huge staples like SABMiller rarely get cheaper late in bull markets, but here is an exception.

France's **L'Oreal Group** (LRLCY, 33), selling at a pricey 33 times earnings (1.77% Dividend Yield). It's a true glamour stock, but it's also the best in the business at selling glamour to women. L'Oréal just keeps growing, spanning cosmetics, perfumes and skin care, and it's even tops in nanotechnology.

The likes of Penélope Cruz, Beyoncé Knowles and Eva Longoria hawk its products. Its glamorous image will grow along with its stock price as this bull market evolves.

If you were to concentrate on stocks larger than the global markets' $80 billion average market capitalization. There are only 70 such megacaps.

The back half of almost every bull market has been led by this universe. Almost no one on Wall Street writes about this, but it works and has done so for decades. By sticking to these behemoths, you'll miss lots of excitement—but you'll also reduce the risk of underperforming. And if history repeats itself, this group will lead the market over the next few years.

Why does my late-bull megacap strategy work? Because skeptics who were originally resistant to owning stocks finally get up the courage to dip their toes in. They naturally find it easiest to buy what they know— giant, safe blue chips—stocks whose products are household names.

Small-cap cyclicals get all the attention early in every economic expansion because year-over-year earnings comparisons look great coming off a depressed base. However, as the expansions run, fewer firms are able to show improved earnings. The only ones that do are mature companies with years of experience managing real unit-volume growth. They are the standouts in an earnings growth deceleration phase.

It's also advisable to have a 60%/40% portfolio split between U.S. and foreign stocks.

Pfizer (PFE, 31) is the world's largest drug firm with a stunning A-Z array of big brand names like Advil and Viagra—and fits the high-consistency-of-earnings-growth theme perfectly. It continues to pump out new products. The latest: Bosulif, a daily pill to fight a rare form of blood and bone marrow cancer. It sells at 18 times my 2014 earnings estimate with a 3.41% dividend yield.

Truly, Cincinnati-based **Procter & Gamble (PG, 81)** is the mother of all brand names. Bounty. Iams. Charmin. Pampers, to name a few. It also has the world's best marketing capability—has for decades. That's why elite business schools like Harvard make case studies of the 'P&G way'.

Unfortunately, P&G has been a bit in the investor doghouse recently, which makes this a great time to buy—at 22 times my estimate of June 2014 earnings with a 3.16% dividend yield.

Google (GOOG, 537) is another buy, even at today's heady levels. In some markets, like search advertising and Web video, its competition doesn't even come close. Google drove nearly 70% of all Web searches last month. That means 11 billion searches were exposed to Google's ads. Uncle Sam should break it up but won't any time soon. Politicians, judges and lawyers are all too dependent on it. Buy huge, awe-inspiring monopoly power at 29 times 2014 earnings.

If the rich get richer and the poor poorer, the winner is France's $85 billion market cap **LVMH Moet Hennessy Louis Vuitton (LVMUY, 39).** It's the ultimate collection of luxury consumer discretionary brands spanning cosmetics, fashion, jewelry, spirits, watches, wine and much more. Think Christian Dior, Sephora, De Beers, TAG Heuer, Dom Pérignon. The list goes on. It sells at 21 times my estimate of 2014 earnings.

CNOOC (CEO, 166) is China's leading offshore oil and gas producer and its third-largest energy firm. It is responsible for almost a million barrels daily of oil-equivalent production (about 80% oil) and 3.2 billion barrels of reserves. Energy, emerging markets exposure and explicit backing of the Chinese government. Now that's a powerful combination, especially at 7 times my estimate of 2014 earnings and a 4.44% dividend yield.

Microsoft (MSFT, 40). Forget governments shutting down. If Windows magically imploded we would have the biggest recession ever. It's that basic. MSFT sports a 2.8% dividend yield and sells at 14.8 times my estimated 2014 earnings.

Microsoft's recent 5.44 billion euro acquisition of Nokia's devices business could give it the impetus to take a bigger slice of the smartphone pie.

Microsoft produces its own operating system (OS) for smartphones, but compared to other players, it is small in the market. The Windows smartphone OS had a 3.3% share of the total smartphone market, compared with Google Android's 78.6% and Apple's 15.2% in 2013, according to data from IDC.

Around 80% of the smartphones running a Windows operating system are already manufactured by Nokia, according to data provider HIS, making the telecommunications company an ideal partner for Microsoft. Control of Nokia's handset arm could help Microsoft bolster its smartphone offering.

Another good reason to buy is: Most folks have given up hope on Microsoft even with the new CEO Satya Nadella in driver's seat.

Schlumberger (SLB, 99) is the world's largest oilfield-services firm, in an arena globally ripe for rebound. It's the whole tool kit and is optimally postured to add business from large national oil firms. It sells at 18 times my 2014 earnings estimate, with a 1.6% dividend yield.

Also benefiting from the strength I foresee in energy is Dutch-based "supermajor" **Royal Dutch Shell** (RDS.B, 81). It's another supereasy buy for skeptics, especially those who fear inflation. It's the cheapest major oil at nine times my estimated 2014 earnings, 50% of annual sales, with a 4.46% dividend yield.

Housing's recent recovery has strengthened **Home Depot** (HD, 78). It has navigated well through the tough times. It's created huge efficiencies and scale, and it's gained market share. The stock sells at 1.3 times sales and 20 times my 2014 earnings estimate. It's an easy buy.

In the second half of nearly every bull market you need only own bigger-than-average stocks to beat the market. By that, I mean market value north of $78 billion, which is the average market capitalization of stocks in the MSCI All Country World Index.

Looking back to years like 1997 and 2005, smaller stocks tend not to work as well during times like these, when the bull market is midway through its long run. In a late-stage bull market, like we have now, keep it simple and stick with the biggest of the big.

Legendary investor Sir John Templeton said, "Bull markets are born on pessimism, grow on skepticism, mature on optimism and die on euphoria."

Skepticism remains thick, and we're far from seeing optimism or euphoria.

Hence, more bull ahead. And if I'm wrong and a bear lurks soon, mega-cap stocks will drop far less than more speculative smaller stocks.

Just as I advocated year after year here in the late 1990s, you should be able to beat the market simply by concentrating on the largest stocks. If you want to do some picking within that group of big names, here are five stocks I like now, all with market caps greater than $100 billion–three from the U.S. and two overseas. They pretty much make up their own globally diversified portfolio of five.

As a kid I learned that whenever a stock sells for a P/E at or below the firm's growth rate, buy it. That's **PepsiCo (PEP, 85)** now. It should earn over $70 billion in 2014 and grow long-term at 15% annually with a P/E of 19. Pepsi is half food, half drink. Its brands are all global leaders. It's vertically integrated in bottling, another growth business. PepsiCo trades at 1.7 times sales with a dividend yield of 2.27%.

Exxon Mobil (XOM, 100) has lagged the market all year on fears of limited upside with many of the world's untapped resources owned by rogue governments and downside with consensus calls for falling prices that will squeeze margins. This oil supermajor sells at 80% of annual revenues and 13 times 2014 earnings. As the world's dominant energy producer and marketer, Exxon should be just fine, and the stock should improve, too. While the dividend yield is only 2.6%, note that it pays out only about 20% of earnings and has room to give back more.

French pharmaceutical giant **Sanofi (SNY, 52)** has a better than average drug portfolio that's tilted heavily toward cancer and cardio. Yes, some patents expire soon, like those for Eloxatin, Plavix and Taxotere, but growth of existing and new products should more than make up for expirations. Fast growth out of the emerging markets helps, too. At 29 times estimated 2014 earnings, you get a reasonable valuation and a comfortably covered 3.4% dividend yield.

Australia's **BHP Billiton (BHP, 71)** the globe's biggest miner, is also one of this year's worst-performing global commodity stocks. The near-term concerns are that the slowdown in Chinese growth saps demand for BHP's metals. That's fair, but China's economy is still growing at a peppy pace of at least 7% a year. If you believe in the long-term rise of manufacturing and need for infrastructure in China and other emerging markets, you must believe in BHP. It's growing output at least enough to buy at 12 times my estimate of 2014 earnings with a 3.32% dividend yield. It should also prove to be a great hedge against commodity inflation.

Apple (AAPL, USD 525) (P/E: 13, Dividend Yield: 2.31%) by perception no longer represents the "shining example" of a hypergrowth company, and that means investors must stop treating it like one.

Yet, Apple dazzled investors with a big earnings beat on its Q1 2014 earnings. It also announced another big stock buyback and a dividend hike.

The acceleration of iPhone growth—about 44 million phones sold last quarter—also bodes well for the company, **especially as a blockbuster deal with China Mobile** opens up the world biggest wireless market to Apple.

Apple clearly proved it is still the industry leader and still has many products under its sleeves which are going to keep the earnings arena full with surprises.

The company's announcement for buying back $90 billion of shares was a smart move given the cash it has on its balance sheet, and a further announcement of stock split of seven-to-one, is going to bring a broad base of shareholders. The risk-reward on the trade right now is favorable.

When traders buy Apple shares two months before a major product launch, they see average outperformance of 10 to 15 %. In contrast, the two months following a product release translates to negative or zero percent outperformance.

Shareholders arrive at Apple headquarters for the 2013 annual meeting.

There are a lot things for investors to get excited about, and to potentially raise their numbers. And that's basically when the stock works.

Two immensely anticipated products for 2014—barring the new iPhone iteration—remain Apple television sets and the iWatch. The latter holds the most potential. Also, iWatch won't disappoint.

Soon, the i-phone will charge wirelessly, log users into websites by vouching for them, and make mobile payments by waving them them over sensors.

It's my view that the iWatch is coming and it will be transformative. They're opening up a new area. There are some people who want to be known as first in that area who are putting out little toys, but the iWatch will be the first serious attempt to really create a transformative product in that space. And nobody's going to block them.

Apply sold more than $1 billion worth of Apple TV set-top boxes in 2013. While the market for phones, tablets and computers dwarf the Apple TV sales, the number was positive news for Apple's television business.

With wearable tech, Apple still has the ability to create an entire market around its products, according to Leander Kahney.

For example, companies began producing tablet computers a decade ago, but it took Apple to revolutionize the tablet market in the past few years and force competitors to chase their products.

The same is true with wearables--they're not looking at something like the Fitbit. They're not looking at something like the [Samsung] Galaxy smartwatch. This is going to be a whole range of technology-enabled clothing or items that you put on.... I don't think we've seen anything like it yet.

Still, Apple's slow pace of growth concerns some investors.

Google made headlines by buying robotics companies, and **Facebook** recently agreed to pay up to $19 billion for instant messaging service WhatsApp. Why can't Apple buy wearable tech companies like Jawbone or Fitbit.

What's more, iPhones sell at a much higher premium than other smartphones—twice as much as the average price, about $650 versus $330, he said.

It's a fine strategy to have, but it's going to come at the expense of volume--Apple is going to be less effective in the emerging markets.

Has the iCar arrived? Apple launches in-car platform

Apple continues to innovate and iPhone, which changed the way we communicate with each other could enhance the way we drive for an enchanting experience

Apple

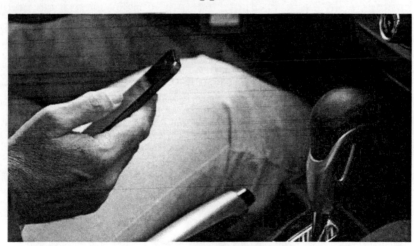

Speculation over the launch of an Apple iCar has excited the tech industry for some time, and now it looks as if the wait is finally over.

Recently, the tech giant unveiled a new platform that will enable drivers to integrate their iPhone and car entertainment system. The new product, called CarPlay, will be rolled out by Ferrari, Mercedes-Benz and Volvo.

iPhone users always want their content at their fingertips and CarPlay lets drivers use their iPhone in the car with minimized distraction.

Through use of the new platform, drivers will be able to make calls, use the Google Maps function, listen to music and access messages through use of voice or touch.

Users can control the program from the car's native interface or push and hold the voice control button on the steering wheel to activate Siri, the voice activation software.

According to **Apple**, once a driver's iPhone is connected to a vehicle with CarPlay integration, Siri will enable drivers to access their contacts, make calls, return missed calls or listen to voicemails without using their hands. Drivers will be able to dictate responses to messages, or simply make a call.

Apple said the product will also anticipate a driver's destination based on recent trips, via contacts, emails or texts and will provide routing instructions, traffic conditions and an estimated time of arrival.

Apple CarPlay is available as an update to iOS 7 and works with Lightning-enabled iPhones, including the iPhone 5s, iPhone 5c and iPhone 5.

BMW Group, Ford, General Motors, Honda, Hyundai Motor Company, Jaguar Land Rover, Kia Motors, Mitsubishi Motors, Nissan Motor Company, PSA Peugeot Citroën, Subaru, Suzuki and Toyota Motor Corp are also set to offer CarPlay in the future.

CarPlay will be available in select cars shipping in 2014.

Information on Apple's 'iOS in the Car' software was leaked by mobile app developer Steven Troughton-Smith in January.

A San Francisco Chronicle report of a meeting between electric car manufacturer Tesla and Apple back in October, reported last month, stoked expectations of a much-anticipated iCar.

Google, one of Apple's key competitors, is said to be close behind in this space. It has been using its Android operating system to develop partnerships with Honda, Hyundai and Vauxhaull, according to media reports.

Apple Ordering 90 Million iPhone 6 to Meet Huge Demand (Report)

Apple Ordering 90 Million iPhone 6 to Meet Huge Demand (Report)

It's no secret that the iPhone 6 is going be a big launch, as Apple will finally offer a bigger display to better challenge the likes of the Galaxy S5 and other flagship Android phones and phablets. In anticipation of huge demand, Apple has reportedly ordered 90 million iPhone 6 units from Foxconn.

To put Apple's reported order in perspective, the company sold 51 million iPhones during its fiscal first quarter that ended Dec. 28th, 2013. Is Apple really anticipating that large a leap in sales?

The iPhone 6 is expected to sport a super-strong sapphire crystal display, a more advanced camera and perhaps even wireless charging. In addition, there are rumors that this sequel will feature an even faster A8 chip with a quad-core CPU and graphics.

Apple's smartphone shipments are expected to rise a whopping 23 percent in 2014, compared to 13 percent last year.

Overall, analyst firm IDC predicts that smartphone growth will slow in 2014 to 19.3 percent, down from 39.2 percent in 2013. The reason: average prices keep dropping as demand shifts to China. In other words, the iPhone 6 will likely be a huge seller, helping it stay ahead of the industry average in terms of growth.

IMPORTANT LEGAL INFORMATION